praise for media and culture

[Chapter outlines] provide a quick reference for discussion preparation. I can be more certain that students are getting the significant content issues if they can address these highlights.

—Peter Croisant,
Geneva College

One of the strengths of *Media and Culture* has been its fresh look and up-to-date examples. These appear to continue with the fourth edition.

—Elizabeth M. Perse,
University of Delaware

I have read nearly every textbook out there, and I have found that none come close to the Campbell text in terms of insight, relevance, and clarity.

—Alison Rostankowski,
University of
Wisconsin–Milwaukee

I strongly believe that exploring the intersection between media and culture is one of the most effective ways to teach an introductory communication course to a generation that grew up on the media. Among the few textbooks that use the approach, Campbell's is the most comprehensive.

—Anthony A. Olorunnisola,
Pennsylvania State University

This is an excellent text. It's lively, thorough, and timely.

—Hazel Warlaumont,
California State
University–Fullerton

This book is an outstanding contribution to the field. It allows students to build upon their own experiences with various media they use, to see the ways in which those media are active constructors of culture.
— John Pantalone,
University of Rhode Island

The critical perspective has enlightened the perspective of all of us who study media, and Campbell has the power to infect students with his love of the subject.
— Roger Desmond,
University of Hartford

Campbell has created a wonderful book.
— Cynthia King,
American University

I will switch to Campbell because it is a tour de force of coverage and interpretation, it is the best survey text in the field hands down, and it challenges students. . . . Campbell's text is the most thorough and complete in the field . . . no other text is even close.
— Russell Barclay,
Quinnipiac University

media & culture

media & culture

an introduction to mass communication

FOURTH EDITION

RICHARD CAMPBELL

Middle Tennessee State University

Christopher R. Martin

University of Northern Iowa

Bettina Fabos

University of Northern Iowa

BEDFORD/ST. MARTIN'S

Boston • New York

"WE ARE NOT ALONE."

For my family—Chris, Caitlin, and Dianna

For Bedford/St. Martin's

Developmental Editors: Joshua Levy, Joanne Tinsley
Senior Production Editor: Harold Chester
Senior Production Supervisor: Joe Ford
Marketing Manager: Richard Cadman
Art Director: Lucy Krikorian
Text and Cover Design: Anna George
Copy Editor: Alice Vigliani
Indexer: Riofrancos & Co. Indexes
Photo Research: Anita Dickhuth
Composition: Monotype Composition Company, Inc.
Printing and Binding: R.R. Donnelley & Sons Company

President: Joan E. Feinberg
Editorial Director: Denise B. Wydra
Publisher for History and Communication: Patricia Rossi
Director of Marketing: Karen R. Melton
Director of Editing, Design, and Production: Marcia Cohen
Managing Editor: Erica T. Appel

Library of Congress Control Number: 2003100775

Manufactured in the United States of America.

9 8 7 6 5 4
f e d c b a

For information, write: Bedford/St. Martin's, 75 Arlington Street, Boston, MA 02116   (617-399-4000)

ISBN: 0-312-40462-X

Acknowledgments

Acknowledgments and copyrights appear at the back of the book on pages 595–597, which constitute an extension of the copyright page.

brief contents

preface

this new fourth edition of *Media and Culture* provides a special opportunity for me to reflect on this ongoing project and to say how grateful I am to all the teachers and students who have used and supported this book over the past six years. When I began writing the first edition of *Media and Culture* in the mid-1990s, I was motivated by a general dissatisfaction with the introductory texts in our field. I wanted to write a book with a critical edge that at the same time gave students a method for becoming better critics themselves. I also worked hard to place the facts about mass communication in a compelling narrative that would tell students the stories of mass media—how they came to be and how they affect our contemporary democracy. And finally, I tried to provide a larger context—one that grows from understanding media from the viewpoint of a former journalist and a current academic. Ultimately, the cultural context that I present in *Media and Culture* helps students see the media world and their part in that world as part of the larger ebb and flow of everyday life. With this context in place, I set out with two goals in mind: to enable students to become more knowledgeable as media consumers, and to help them be more fully engaged as citizens with a critical stake in the shape of their culture and our democracy.

Media and Culture, then, is both a personal and a global journey. As a textbook, it aims to provide maps for navigating the cultural terrain. It asks that we participate in the critical work of evaluating mass media and shaping their direction. In this journey, we have choices. We can watch the media as detached outsiders—as observers, we can praise them when they perform well and blame them for our social predicaments. Or we can become active participants—we can analyze the impact and investigate the consequences of the stories that media industries tell and sell. As involved citizens, we can challenge our media to perform at high levels and steer them to serve and preserve democratic ideals.

The journey through the media landscape is different for each of us and for each generation. As part of everyone's autobiography, the mass media are significant players. Newspapers, books, magazines, and radio shaped past generations. Along with these reconfigured older media forms, CDs, television, cable, and the Internet mark our contemporary time. But to understand our lives in the context of a larger world, we need some distance from our personal history with media forms. We need to stand back from our experience and view the media's impact on the world through a larger lens.

That's where this book comes in.

The Most Accessible Edition Yet

The fourth edition of *Media and Culture* is the most thorough revision since the second edition. New learning tools in every chapter help students understand the most important concepts, events, and people in the development of each medium and the democratic, ethical, and global implications of the mass media.

- **Chapter-opening outlines give students a road map to main points**. Each chapter outline previews the main ideas that students will learn in subsequent pages.

- **Innovative annotated timelines** are powerful visual study tools in each chapter that help students identify and understand the most important historical and cultural events. The timelines highlight key events, explain their significance, and refer students to more coverage in the text.

- **Expanded focus on the critical process**. New Applied Critical Process boxes in each chapter model the four-step process by applying it to fascinating media issues such as Internet spyware, paid placement for search engine results, and international television syndication. In addition, Critical Process exercises are now organized according to the four steps.

Still the Most Current Text Available

Because the mass media are always changing, so does *Media and Culture*. From Eminem to 3G wireless technology, from ClearChannel to Martha Stewart and the Osbournes, *Media and Culture* covers the most important developments in today's media, making this the most current text available and giving students the information they need to analyze today's hottest media trends.

- **More updated coverage** includes new and expanded information about current trends and events such as advertising and the Internet, the state of file sharing, the FCC's regulation of cable and the Internet, and developments in e-commerce.

- **Contains 25 percent new or fully revised feature boxes**. The four types of feature boxes — Case Study, Tracking Technology, Examining Ethics, Global Village — now cover pressing new issues such as the global proliferation of World Wide Web use, the rise and fall of the X-Games, and the influence of world music on the contemporary music scene.

- **Updated tables and figures** track the most recent economic, technological, and cultural developments in all media industries. Examples include new information on the leading media conglomerates such as Comcast, MSNBC, and AOL/Time Warner.

- **Revised design and art program** offers over 25 percent new images and uses color and design elements to help students better identify key concepts.

Still the Most Complete Coverage of the Mass Media

Along with these new additions, *Media and Culture,* Fourth Edition, retains the essential features that students and teachers alike have always praised. Throughout three editions and an update, *Media and Culture* has consistently been recognized for its unique critical approach, its rich cultural perspective, and its comprehensive coverage of every mass-media outlet.

- **A critical approach**. *Media and Culture* introduces students to four stages of the critical thinking and writing process — description, analysis, interpretation, and evaluation. The text uses these stages as a lens for examining the historical context and current processes that shape mass media as part of U.S. culture. This framework guides chapter content and informs the writing of each chapter as well as the new Applied Critical Process boxes in each chapter and the Critical Process exercises at the end of each chapter.

- **A cultural perspective**. *Media and Culture* uses a narrative approach to investigate media as part of the rituals of everyday culture. Most mass media—whether news, prime-time television, magazines, film, paperback novels, or advertising—make use of storytelling to tap into our shared beliefs and values, and so does this book. Each chapter presents the events and issues surrounding media culture as intriguing and informative narratives rather than as a series of unconnected facts and feats. *Media and Culture* presents the history of mass media as compelling and complicated stories that map the uneasy and parallel developments of consumer culture and democratic society.

- **A focus on media technology and convergence**. *Media and Culture* examines key technological developments that have changed the world, from the telegraph, our first binary communication system (with its electronic dots and dashes), to the Internet, our latest binary system (with its digital ones and zeros). The text studies our journey from the Industrial Age to the Information Age, featuring the phenomenon of *media convergence*: the confluence of home, school, and business computers, TV sets, telephones, radio, CD players, VCRs and DVDs, e-mail, video games, newspapers, fax machines, magazines, and communication satellites.

The organization of *Media and Culture* takes into account the dramatic influences of electronic and digital forms of communication on the social world. Because intersecting forms of mass communication integrate aspects of print, electronic, and digital culture in our daily lives, we begin with the stories of convergence. Rather than starting chronologically with the book, society's oldest mass medium, the industry chapters open with the media students know best: the Internet, music, radio, television, cable, and film. Placing past and present communication developments within contemporary contexts, *Media and Culture* looks at older media against the backdrop of new forms that have reshaped printed culture.

- **A concern for values and ethics**. To develop a critical perspective toward mass media, students must think about values and ethics as a routine and integrated part of the way they experience media in daily life. Media books often ghettoize the subject of ethics by treating it as a separate, isolated chapter near the end. *Media and Culture,* on the other hand, weaves into the media industry narratives rich discussions about the values depicted in mass communication and the ethical implications faced by media practitioners.

- **An exploration of media economics and democracy**. To become better citizens and discerning consumers, students must pay attention to the complex relationship between democracy and capitalism, between the marketplace of ideas and the global consumer market. To that end, *Media and Culture* addresses the significance of the dramatic rise in multinational media systems. It invites students to explore the implications of the 1996 Telecommunications Act and the vast control that a handful of mammoth international companies exercise over the production and distribution of commercial mass media. Ownership issues are an integral part of the individual media chapters. Additionally, Chapter 13 looks critically at the global picture and encourages students to participate in the debates over ownership. Each chapter ends with a discussion of the effects of various mass media on the nature of democratic life.

Supplements

Instructor's Resource Manual

Bettina Fabos, *University of Northern Iowa,* and Christopher R. Martin, *University of Northern Iowa;* ISBN 0-312-40992-3

The most comprehensive instructor's manual available for the introduction to mass communication course, this extensive resource provides a range of teaching approaches, tips for facilitating in-class discussions, suggestions for incorporating more writing assignments in the course, outlines, lecture topics, lecture spin-offs, critical process exercises, classroom media resources, and an annotated list of more than 200 video resources.

Companion Web site at bedfordstmartins.com/mediaculture

Along with the Online Study Guide, the site offers links to useful Web sites, Media Studies essays, and additional Critical Process questions. For instructors, the site offers PowerPoint presentations for each chapter. Available for both Macintosh and Windows formats, these PowerPoint slides highlight key information from the text, enabling instructors to make classroom presentations with greater visual impact. Instructors can customize the slides to fit their own needs. The site also offers instructors sample assignments and student quiz tracking.

Blackboard and WebCT e-packs

ISBN 0-312-40986-9
ISBN 0-312-40990-7

New e-packs offer instructors the power of online course management along with *Media and Culture*'s superior pedagogical content. Visit bedfordstmartins.com/mediaculture or www.WebCT.com for more information.

Media Presentations CD-ROM

ISBN 0-312-25045-2

CD-ROM technology and PowerPoint software let you build classroom presentations around three case studies: "Popular Music and Freedom of Expression" (Paul Fischer, Middle Tennessee State University), "Newspapers: From Print to the Web" (Craig Brandon, Keene State College), and "Photojournalism, Photography, and the Coverage of War" (Jim Kelley, Southern Illinois University). These presentations include visual and textual material that instructors can use as is for lectures or customize with additions from the Web or other sources.

Media Career Guide: Preparing for Jobs in the 21st Century, Fourth Edition

James Seguin, *Robert Morris College;* ISBN 0-312-40987-7

Practical and student-friendly, this revised guide includes a comprehensive directory of media jobs, practical tips, and career guidance for students considering a major in communication studies and mass media.

The Bedford/St. Martin's Video Resource Library

A wide selection of contemporary and historical media-related videos is organized around the issues explored in *Media and Culture*. Qualified instructors are eligible to select videos from the resource library upon adoption of the text.

Testing Program

Bettina Fabos, *University of Northern Iowa,* Christopher R. Martin, *University of Northern Iowa,* and Thomas Beell, *Iowa State University;* Computerized Test Bank ISBN 0-312-40994-X; Print Test Bank ISBN 0-312-40991-5

A complete testing program is available in print and as software formatted for Windows and Macintosh, with multiple choice, true/false, fill-in-the-blank, and short and long essay questions.

Acknowledgments

I am very grateful to everyone at Bedford/St. Martin's who supported this project through its many stages. I wish that every textbook author could have the kind of experience I had with these people: Chuck Christensen, Joan Feinberg, Patricia Rossi, Richard Cadman, Inge King, and Jessica Stockton. I also worked with many superb and supportive developmental editors: Joanne Tinsley, Joshua Levy, and Simon Glick, who edited the first three editions of *Media and Culture*, and editorial assistant Alice Mack. I particularly appreciate the tireless work of Erica Appel, managing editor, who oversaw the book's extremely tight schedule; Harold Chester, project editor, who kept the book on schedule while making sure I got the details right; Joe Ford, senior production supervisor; and Anna George, whose award-winning design keeps the book looking fresh from edition to edition.

I want to thank the many fine and thoughtful reviewers who contributed ideas to the fourth edition of *Media and Culture:* Fay Y. Akindes, University of Wisconsin–Parkside; Robert Arnett, Mississippi State University; Charles Aust, Kennesaw State University; Russell Barclay, Quinnipiac University; Bryan Brown, Southwest Missouri State; Peter W. Croisant, Geneva College; Mark Goodman, Mississippi State University; Donna Halper, Emerson College; Rebecca Self Hill, University of Colorado; John G. Hodgson, Oklahoma State University; Cynthia P. King, American University; Deborah L. Larson, Southwest Missouri State University; Charles Lewis, Minnesota State University–Mankato; Lila Lieberman, Rutgers University; Abbus Malek, Howard University; Anthony A. Olorunnisola, Pennsylvania State University; Norma Pecora, Ohio University, Athens; Elizabeth M. Perse, University of Delaware; Hoyt Purvis, University of Arkansas; Alison Rostankowski, University of Wisconsin–Milwaukee; Roger A. Soenksen, James Madison University; Hazel Warlaumont, California State University–Fullerton.

I would also like to thank the reviewers who contributed ideas to the previous editions of *Media and Culture.*

For the third edition: Gerald J. Baldasty, University of Washington; Steve M. Barkin, University of Maryland; Ernest L. Bereman, Truman State University; Daniel Bernadi, University of Arizona; Kimberly L. Bissell, Southern Illinois University; Audrey Boxmann, Merimack College; Todd Chatman, University of Illinois; Ray Chavez, University of Colorado; Vic Costello, Gardner-Webb University; Paul D'Angelo, Villanova; James Shanahan, Cornell University; Scott A. Webber, University of Colorado.

For the second edition: Susan B. Barnes, Fordham University; Margaret Bates, City College of New York; Steven Alan Carr, Indiana University/Purdue University, Fort Wayne; William G. Covington Jr., Bridgewater State College; Roger Desmond, University of Hartford; Jules d'Hemecourt, Louisiana State University; Cheryl Evans, Northwestern Oklahoma State University; Douglas Gomery, University of Maryland; Colin Gromatzky, New Mexico State University; John L. Hochheimer, Ithaca College; Sheena Malhotra, University of New Mexico; Sharon R. Mazzarella, Ithaca College; David Marc McCoy, Kent State University; Beverly Merrick, New Mexico State University; John Pantalone, University of Rhode Island; John Durham Peters, University of Iowa; Lisa Pieraccini, Oswego State College; Susana Powell, Borough of Manhattan Community College; Felicia Jones Ross, Ohio State University; Enid Sefcovic, Florida Atlantic University; Keith Semmel, Cumberland College; Augusta Simon, Embry-Riddle Aeronautical University; Clifford E. Wexler, Columbia-Greene Community College.

For the first edition: Paul Ashdown, University of Tennessee; Terry Bales, Rancho Santiago College; Russell Barclay, Quinnipiac University; Thomas Beell, Iowa State University; Fred Blevens, Southwest Texas State University; Stuart Bullion, University of Maine; William G. Covington Jr., Bridgewater State College; Robert Daves, *Minneapolis Star Tribune*; Charles Davis, Georgia Southern University; Thomas Donahue,

Virginia Commonwealth University; Ralph R. Donald, University of Tennessee–Martin; John P. Ferre, University of Louisville; Donald Fishman, Boston College; Elizabeth Atwood Gailey, University of Tennessee; Bob Gassaway, University of New Mexico; Anthony Giffard, University of Washington; Zhou He, San Jose State University; Barry Hollander, University of Georgia; Sharon Hollenbeck, Syracuse University; Anita Howard, Austin Community College; James Hoyt, University of Wisconsin–Madison; Joli Jensen, University of Tulsa; Frank Kaplan, University of Colorado; William Knowles, University of Montana; Michael Leslie, University of Florida; Janice Long, University of Cincinnati; Kathleen Maticheck, Normandale Community College; Maclyn McClary, Humboldt State University; Robert McGaughey, Murray State University; Joseph McKerns, Ohio State University; Debra Merskin, University of Oregon; David Morrissey, Colorado State University; Michael Murray, University of Missouri at St. Louis; Susan Dawson O'Brien, Rose State College; Patricia Bowie Orman, University of Southern Colorado; Jim Patton, University of Arizona; John Pauly, St. Louis University; Ted Pease, Utah State University; Janice Peck, University of Colorado; Tina Pieraccini, University of New Mexico; Peter Pringle, University of Tennessee; Sondra Rubenstein, Hofstra University; Jim St. Clair, Indiana University Southeast; Jim Seguin, Robert Morris College; Donald Shaw, University of North Carolina; Martin D. Sommernes, Northern Arizona State University; Linda Steiner, Rutgers University; Jill Diane Swensen, Ithaca College; Sharon Taylor, Delaware State University; Hazel Warlaumont, California State University–Fullerton; Richard Whitaker, Buffalo State College; Lynn Zoch, University of South Carolina.

There are many other people to thank. Along with a number of fine teachers at both the University of Wisconsin–Milwaukee and Northwestern University who helped shape the way I think about many of the issues raised in this book. I am especially grateful to my former students at Marquette University, the University of Wisconsin–Milwaukee, Mount Mary College, the University of Michigan, and my current students at MTSU. Some of my students have contributed directly to this text, and thousands have endured my courses over the years — and made them better. My all-time favorite former students, Chris Martin and Bettina Fabos, have now become essential co-authors. The following are their acknowledgments:

> As always, it has been a delight working with Richard Campbell on this project. We also appreciate the great energy, creativity, and talent that everyone at Bedford/St. Martin's brings to the book. From edition to edition, we also receive plenty of suggestions from *Media and Culture* users and reviewers, and from our own undergraduate and graduate students. We would like to thank them for their input and for creating a community of sorts around the theme of critical perspectives on the media. Most of all, we'd like to thank our daughters, Olivia and Sabine, who bring us joy and laughter every day, and a sense of mission to better understand the world of media and culture in which they live.

I am forever grateful for Chris and Bettina's fine writing, research savvy, and tireless work amid their own teaching schedules and writing careers, all while raising two spirited young daughters.

I remain most grateful, though, to the people I most love: my son, Chris (now a student at MTSU); my daughter, Caitlin (now a student at Tufts University); and, most of all, my wife, Dianna, whose daily conversations, shared interests, and ongoing support continue to be resources I draw on each day.

contents

Sounds and Images

3   **Sound Recording and Popular Music**   64

4 Popular Radio and the Origins of Broadcasting 104

5 Television and the Power of Visual Culture 142

6 Cable and the Specialization of Television   184

7 Movies and the Impact of Images   220

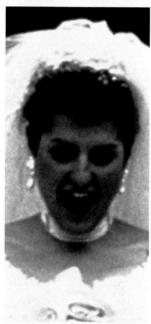

Words and Pictures

8 Newspapers and the Rise of Modern Journalism 262

9   Magazines in the Age of Specialization 298

10   Books and the Power of Print 338

The Business of Mass Media

11   Advertising and Commercial Culture   376

12 Public Relations and Framing the Message   418

13 Media Economics and the Global Marketplace   452

Democratic Expression and the Mass Media

16 Legal Controls and Freedom of Expression 536

media & culture

mass communication

a critical approach

CHAPTER 1

Culture and the Evolution of Mass Communication

Mass Media and the Process of Communication

Surveying the Cultural Landscape

Critiquing Media and Culture

On the morning of September 11, 2001, nineteen suicide terrorists commandeered four U.S. commercial airliners, flying two of them into the Twin Towers of New York's World Trade Center. Shortly thereafter, the 110-story towers collapsed. A total of 2,801 people from more than 75 countries died in the assault. Less than an hour after the towers were hit, a plane crashed into the Pentagon, killing another 189. Then an hour later, a fourth airliner—apparently headed to Washington, D.C.—crashed in a Pennsylvania field. On that flight, passengers—alerted to the earlier disasters through cell phone conversations with friends

and family who had seen TV reports—confronted the hijackers and managed to force the plane down, killing all 45 on board.

As on December 7, 1941, when Japan attacked Pearl Harbor, and again on November 22, 1963, when President John F. Kennedy was assassinated, the extraordinary events of 9/11 put the national media at the center of our lives. They gave us not only news but a place to go for assurance, helping make sense of tragedy. But as the U.S. military mounted a search for the suspected terrorist ringleaders in

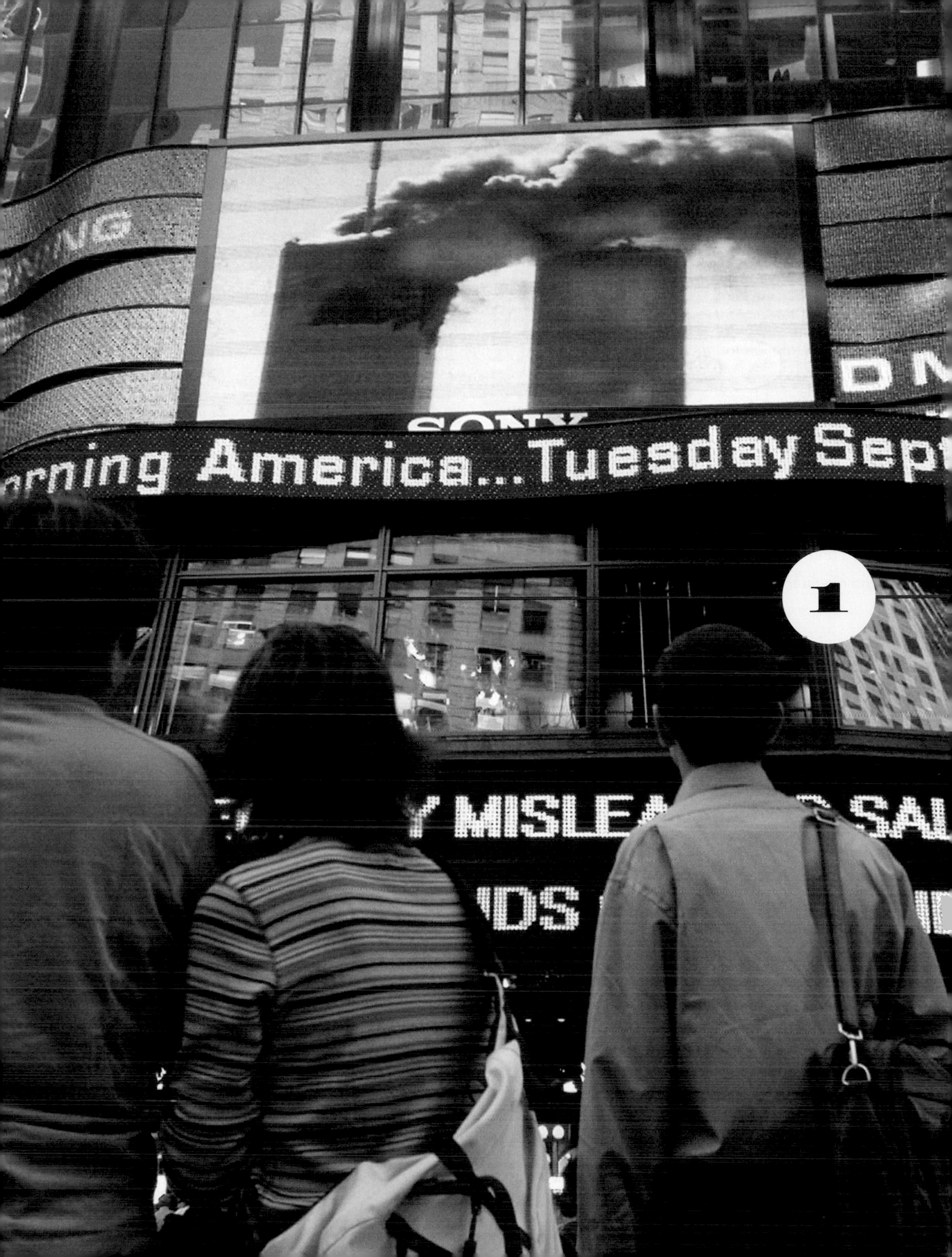

1

remote Afghanistan, a new round of assaults began, this time including an additional target: the media. Letters laced with deadly anthrax spores made their way into the mailrooms of U.S. newspapers and TV networks. The first reported casualty was a photojournalist from a Florida-based tabloid paper, and it was soon discovered that someone had tried to target national news anchors with infected letters. Whoever was behind the terror had calculated that another way to grab headlines and generate fear was to get the media to spread the panic.

Throughout our nation's history, we have looked to the national media for investigations and explanations. In the aftermath of 9/11, early polls praised the news media's response to the terror and the work of capable correspondents assigned to cover the new war. Still, we needed the larger picture, a broader historical context for understanding why U.S. institutions had become such symbolic targets: the Twin Towers—representing world commerce; the Pentagon—military power; and then the media—our society's channels of mass communication.

Throughout the twentieth century the United States had developed as a superpower in arms, commerce, and communication. This presented challenges. We were both admired and hated for our military prowess—imitated and despised for our pervasive popular culture. This ambivalence played out in 2003 when the Bush administration could not secure United Nations Security Council support for its eventual March invasion of Iraq. While covering 9/11 and the war in Iraq, our major media walked a fine line in serving as a national unifying force in a time of crisis and in investigating our nation's policies and politics. Critics questioned whether patriotic reporters and anchors could also ask the required tough questions: Why, for instance, did a nation spending $30 billion a year on foreign intelligence seem so clueless about the September 11 attacks? Or, how do we protect our civil liberties at the same time we grant the government—so seemingly unprepared for 9/11—broader latitude and even more money to protect citizens and wage war on terrorism?

While we may expect the media to ask hard questions—even in

the face of the patriotic fervor that swept the country after 9/11—what about the news media's own shortcomings? After the terrorist attacks, and with the 2003 invasion of Iraq, how well equipped were the media to help Americans understand the global context? Since the late 1980s, the major networks had been dismantling foreign bureaus and cutting overseas reporting staffs. They had to quickly rebuild these staffs to cover the wars in Afghanistan and Iraq. In addition, in many newsrooms and TV stations across America, investigative reporting units had been scrapped as media managers sought to maximize profits. With citizens in need of information and analysis about the world, our nation's major media had chosen to concentrate on filling 24-hour cable news cycles mostly with self-promoting "talking heads" who traffic in instant opinions—opinions that often lack the kind of detail and context that come from field correspondents' reporting news, verifying information, and telling stories.

given their pivotal place in our democracy, what exactly are the roles and responsibilities of the media in the wake of the 9/11 tragedies and the war in Iraq? In such times, how do we demand higher standards from our news media and popular culture? In this book, we take up such questions. Beyond the 2001 terrorist attacks or the 2003 invasion of Iraq, another event we can examine is the 1999 shootings at Columbine High School in Littleton, Colorado, where two teenage boys from this Denver suburb planted as many as fifty bombs and killed twelve fellow students and a respected teacher before taking their own lives. Clearly, the mayhem in Colorado resulted from a number of tangled forces—some explainable, some inexplicable. Mass media certainly played several roles—as manufacturers of youth culture, as reporters of tragic events, as intruders into families' private grief, and as definers of how we think about social issues. Even as the tragedy unfolded, local TV news anchors spoke on air to terrified students using their cell phones—students trapped in classrooms who could have accidentally given away their locations to the killers watching TV coverage on school monitors.

At its worst, the media's appetite for telling and selling stories leads them not only to document tragedy but also to exploit or misrepresent it. Many social critics are uneasy with the way our culture—particularly TV and cable—seems to hurtle from one media event to another. News saturates the airwaves with 24-hour coverage, accompanied by specially chosen theme music. The Columbine tragedy is titled "Terror in the Rockies" and the war in Iraq is packaged as "Operation Iraqi Freedom"—a Pentagon term. Rather than maintain a critical distance, most mainstream news media began using other government-inspired phrases as their own, such as "shock and awe" (i.e., the early bombing strikes on Baghdad) and "embedded" journalists (i.e., the five hundred reporters the Pentagon permitted to accompany the troops to document the war).

In this book, we examine media as a central force in shaping our culture and democracy. We investigate issues such as the media coverage of terrorism or teenage violence to see ways the mass media fail us as well as the ways they succeed. After all, they have an impact beyond reporting acts of terrorism or telling tragic stories. The media—in all their various forms, from mainstream newspapers to radio talk shows to Internet chat rooms—try to bring understanding to events that affect all of us. At their best, our media reflect and sustain the values and traditions of a vital democracy. Not only do the Harry Potter book series and TV shows like *Survivor* or *American Idol* engage and entertain diverse audiences, but our newspapers and Internet Web sites also watch over society's institutions, making sense of important events and chronicling the ebb and flow of daily life.

The growth of media industries, commercial culture, and new converging technologies—fiber-optic cable, computers, television, satellites—offers a challenge to all of us. If we can learn to examine and critique the powerful dynamics of the media, we will be better able to monitor the rapid changes going on around us.

66 Embed, n. A war correspondent tagging along with a combat unit, who is said to be 'embedded' (a Pentagon term) or 'in bed with the Pentagon' (the journalism-school definition). 99

—David Olive, *Toronto Star,* March 23, 2003

● An "embedded" journalist reports from Iraq at the start of the war in March 2003.

In this chapter, we will examine key concepts and introduce critical processes for investigating media industries and issues. In the chapters that follow, we will investigate the history and structure of media's major institutions. In the process, we will develop an informed and critical view of the multiple impacts these institutions have had on community and global life. Our goal is to become not only more critical as consumers of mass media but also more engaged as citizens who accept some responsibility for the shape and direction of media culture.

Culture and the Evolution of Mass Communication

One way to understand the role and impact of the media in our lives is to understand the cultural context in which the media operate. Often, culture is associated with art, the unique forms of representational expression that give pleasure and raise awareness about what is true, good, and beautiful. Culture, however, can be viewed as a broader category that identifies the ways in which people live and represent themselves at particular historical times. This idea of culture encompasses fashion, sports, architecture, education, religion, and science, as well as mass media. Although we can study permanent cultural forms, such as novels or songs from various historical periods, culture is always changing. It includes a society's art, beliefs, customs, games, technologies, traditions, and institutions. It also encompasses a society's modes of **communication**: the process of creating symbol systems that convey information and meaning (for example, language systems, Morse code, motion pictures, or computer codes).

Culture is made up of both the products that a society fashions and, perhaps more important, the processes that forge those products and reflect a culture's diverse values. Thus, **culture** may be defined as the symbols of expression that individuals, groups, and societies use to make sense of daily life and to articulate their values. According to this definition, when we listen to music, read a book, watch television, or scan the Internet, we are not asking "Is this art?" but are instead trying to identify or connect with something or someone. In other words, we are assigning meaning to the song, book, TV program, or Internet site. Culture, therefore, is a process that delivers the values of a society through products or other meaning-making forms. For instance, the American ideal of rugged individualism has been depicted for decades through a tradition of book, movie, and television western and detective stories.

Culture links individuals to their society, providing shared and contested values, and the mass media help distribute those values. The **mass media** are the cultural industries—the channels of communication—that produce and distribute songs, novels, newspapers, movies, Internet services, and other cultural products to large numbers of people. The historical development of media and communication can be traced through several overlapping eras in which newer forms of technology and knowledge disrupted and modified older forms. These eras, which all still operate to greater or lesser degrees, are oral, written, print, electronic, and digital. The first two eras refer to the communication of tribal or feudal communities and agricultural economies. The last three phases feature the development of **mass communication**: the process of designing and delivering cultural messages and stories to large and diverse audiences through media channels as old as the book and as new as the Internet. Hastened by the growth of industry and modern technology, mass communication accompanied the gradual shift of rural populations to urban settings and the rise of a consumer culture.

Oral and Written Communication Begin the Dialogue

In most early societies, information and knowledge first circulated slowly through oral traditions passed on by poets, teachers, and tribal storytellers. As alphabets and the written word developed, however, a manuscript culture began to complement and then overshadow oral communication. Documented and transcribed by philosophers, monks, and stenographers, the manuscript culture served the ruling classes. Working people were generally illiterate, and the gap between peasants and rulers was vast. These eras of oral and written communication developed slowly over many centuries. Although exact time frames are disputed, historians generally consider these eras as part of civilization's premodern period, spanning the epoch from 1000 B.C. to the mid-fifteenth century.

Early tensions between oral and written communication played out among ancient Greek philosophers and writers. Socrates (470–399 B.C.), for instance, made his arguments through public conversations and debates. This dialogue style of communication became known as the Socratic method, and it is still used in university law schools and college classrooms. Many philosophers who supported the superiority of the oral tradition feared that the written word would threaten public discussion by offering fewer opportunities for the give and take of conversation. In fact, Socrates' most famous student, Plato (427–347 B.C.), sought to banish poets, whom he saw as purveyors of thoughts less rigorous than those generated in oral, face-to-face, question-and-answer discussions. These debates foreshadowed similar discussions in the twentieth century regarding the dangers of television and the Internet. Do contemporary technologies, such as TV talk shows and anonymous cyberspace chat rooms, cheapen public discussions and prevent us from forming face-to-face associations and talking to one another more personally?

Printed Communication Spreads the Word

The invention of the printing press and movable metallic type in the fifteenth century provided the industrial seed that spawned modern mass communication. From the time of Johannes Gutenberg's invention, it took about four hundred years for the print era to evolve and to eclipse oral and written traditions.

The printing press, among its many contributions, introduced a method for mass production. Presses and publications spread rapidly across Europe in the late 1400s and early 1500s. Many early books were large, elaborate, and expensive, taking months to illustrate and publish. They were usually purchased by wealthy aristocrats, royal families, church leaders, and prominent merchants and politicians. Gradually, however, printers reduced the size and cost of books, making them available to more people.

With the print revolution, the book became the first mass-marketed product in history. The printing press combined three elements necessary for this innovation. First, duplication, or machine copying, replaced the tedious manuscript system in which scribes hand-copied a text several times to produce multiple copies. Second, duplication could be done rapidly, producing mass quantities of the same book. Third, the faster processing of multiple copies brought down the cost of each unit, making books more affordable to less affluent people. These three basic elements would provide the impetus for the Industrial Revolution, assembly-line production, modern capitalism, and the rise of consumer culture in the twentieth century.

The printing press also paved the way for major social and cultural changes by transmitting knowledge across national boundaries. Mass-produced printed materials spread information faster and farther than ever before, extending communication outside the realm of isolated community life. Such widespread information ushered in the concept of nationalism, prompting people to think of themselves not merely as

● Before the invention of the printing press, books were copied by hand in a labor-intensive process. This beautifully illuminated page is from an Italian Bible from the early 1300s.

members of families or tribes but as part of a country whose interests were broader than local or regional concerns.

With the revolution in industry came the rise of the middle class and an elite business class of owners and managers who gained the kind of clout once held only by the nobility or the clergy. Whereas oral and writing societies featured decentralized local governments, the print era marked the ascent of more centralized nation-states. As print media diminished the role of oral and manuscript communication, they also became key tools for commercial and political leaders to distribute information and maintain social order.

As with the Internet today, however, it was difficult for a single business leader or political party in democratic societies to gain total control over books and technology (although the king did control printing-press licenses in early-nineteenth-century England). Instead, the mass publication of pamphlets, magazines, and books helped spread and democratize knowledge. Literacy rates rose among the working and middle classes as publications of all sorts became affordable. Industrialization required a more educated workforce, but printed literature and textbooks also encouraged compulsory education, thus extending learning beyond the world of wealthy upper-class citizens.

Just as the printing press fostered nationalism, it also nourished the competing ideal of individualism, which would become a fundamental value in American society in the nineteenth and twentieth centuries. With all sorts of ideas and treatises available, people came to rely less on their local community and their commercial, religious, and political leaders for guidance. By challenging tribal life, the printing press "fostered the modern idea of individuality," disrupting "the medieval sense of community and integration." [1] In urban and industrial environments, many individuals became cut off from the traditions of rural life, which had encouraged community cooperation in premodern times.

By the mid-nineteenth century, the ideal of individualism affirmed the rise of commerce and increased resistance to government interference in the affairs of self-reliant entrepreneurs. The democratic impulse of individualism also undermined religious authority. Printers and writers circulated views counter to traditional doctrine. Ultimately, the printing press and the wide distribution of knowledge jumpstarted large social movements, including the Protestant Reformation and the Industrial Revolution.

Electronic and Digital Communication Bring Immediacy to the Message

In Europe and America, the impact of industry's rise was enormous: Factories replaced farms as the main centers of work and production. During the 1880s, roughly 80 percent of Americans lived on farms and in small towns; by the 1920s and 1930s, most of this population had shifted to urban areas, where new industries and economic opportunities beckoned. The city had overtaken the country as the focus of national life.

In America, the gradual transformation from an industrial, print-based society to an informational era began with the development of the telegraph in the 1840s. The telegraph made four key contributions to communication. First, it separated communication from transportation, making media messages instantaneous—unencumbered by stagecoaches, ships, or the pony express.[2] Second, the telegraph, in combination with the rise of mass-marketed newspapers, transformed "information into a commodity, a 'thing' that could be bought or sold irrespective of its uses or meaning."[3] By the time of the Civil War, news had become a valuable product, foreshadowing its contemporary role as a phenomenon that is both enormously profitable and overwhelmingly ubiquitous. Third, the telegraph made it easier for military, business, and political leaders to coordinate commercial and military operations, especially after the installation of the transatlantic cable in the late 1860s. Finally, the telegraph foreshadowed future technological developments, such as the fax machine and the cellular phone.

The rise of film at the turn of the twentieth century and the development of radio in the 1920s were early signposts, but the electronic phase of the Information Age really began in the 1950s and 1960s. The dramatic impact of television on daily life marked the arrival of a new visual and electronic era. With the coming of the latest communication gadgetry—ever smaller personal computers, cable television, DVDs, direct-broadcast satellites, cellular phones, beepers, faxes, and electronic mail (e-mail)—the Information Age passed into a digital phase. Electronic innovations, for instance, included hand-cranked and later rotary-dial telephones, whereas digital innovations brought Touch-Tone and voice recognition technology. In **digital communication**, images, texts, and sounds are converted (encoded) into electronic signals (represented as varied combinations of binary numbers—ones and zeros), which are then reassembled (decoded) as a precise reproduction of, say, a TV picture, a magazine article, a song, or a telephone voice. On the Internet's various World Wide Web pages, image, text, and sound are all digitally reproduced and transmitted globally.

New electronic and digital technologies, particularly cable television and the Internet, have developed so quickly that traditional leaders in communication have lost some of their control over information. For example, in the 1992 and 1996 presidential campaigns the network news began to lose its influence and audience to CNN's Larry King, the Comedy Channel, MTV, radio talk shows, and Internet newsgroups and chat lines. Moreover, the technology of e-mail, which has assumed some of the functions of the postal service, is outpacing attempts to control it within national borders. A professor sitting at her desk in Murfreesboro, Tennessee, can instantly send a message to a research scientist in Warsaw, Poland, who can now respond without fear of government agents opening his mail. As recently as 1990, written letters between the two might have taken months to reach their destinations.

Media Convergence Comes of Age

As the millennium turned, the electronic and digital eras fostered the age of **media convergence**, which refers to the appearance of older media forms on the newest media channels—for example, magazine articles or radio programs now accessible on the Internet. But this convergence is not particularly new. Back in the late 1920s, the Radio Corporation of America (RCA) purchased the Victor Talking Machine Company and ushered in machines that could play both radio and recorded music. And in the 1950s, the radio and the recording industries again united during the emergence of television. Media convergence is also much broader than the simple merging of older and newer forms along an information superhighway. In fact, the various eras of communication are themselves reinvented in the Age of the Internet. Oral communication, for example, finds itself reconfigured, in part, as e-mail and in Internet instant messaging. And print communication finds itself re-formed in the thousands of newspapers now available worldwide in digital formats. It is also important to keep in mind the wonderful irony of media convergence: That is, the first major digital retailer, Amazon.com, made its name by selling the world's oldest mass medium—the book—on the world's newest mass medium—the Internet.

> **"**We are in great haste to construct a magnetic telegraph from Maine to Texas; but Maine and Texas, it may be, have nothing important to communicate. . . . We are eager to tunnel under the Atlantic and bring the old world some weeks nearer to the new; but perchance the first news that will leak through into the broad flapping American ear will be that Princess Adelaide has the whooping cough.**"**
>
> —Henry David Thoreau, *Walden,* 1854

● Although it has not been as influential as the printing press, the palmtop—one achievement of our miniaturized, digital age—combines an address book, calendar, watch, alarm clock, and note pad with powerful mobile Internet and e-mail access.

Mass Media and the Process of Communication

Although often labeled and discussed disparagingly as "the media," mass communication institutions are not a single entity. The mass media constitute a wide variety of industries and merchandise, from documentary news programs about famines in Africa to infomercials about vegetable slicers, psychic therapists, or hair management. The word *media* is, after all, a Latin plural form for the singular noun *medium*. Television, newspapers, music, movies, magazines, books, billboards, direct mail, broadcast satellites, and the Internet are all part of the media; and they each remain quite capable of either producing worthy products or pandering to society's worst desires, prejudices, and stereotypes.

Considering the diversity of mass media, to paint it all with the same broad brush would be inaccurate. Yet that is often what we seem to do, which may instead reflect the distrust many of us hold toward prominent social institutions, from local governments to daily newspapers. Of course, when one recent president has an extramarital affair with a young White House intern and another has appointees linked to unethical corporate misbehavior, our distrust of both our institutions and the media is understandable. In this text, we will attempt to replace a sometimes misdirected and cynical perception of the media with an attitude of genuine criticism. To do so, we can begin by understanding competing models of mass communication.

A Linear Model of Mass Communication

To develop an interpretive or critical perspective toward the media, we need insight into how the mass-communication process works. One of the older and more influential ideas about the way media work is depicted in a linear model of communication. In this model, mass communication is conceptualized as the process of producing and delivering messages to large audiences. According to the linear model, mass communication is a component system, made up of **senders** (the authors, producers, and organizations) who transmit **messages** (the programs, texts, images, sounds, and ads). Through a **mass-media channel** (newspapers, books, magazines, radio, television, or the Internet), senders pitch their messages to large groups of **receivers** (readers, viewers, citizens, and consumers). In the process, **gatekeepers** (such as editors, producers, and other media managers) function as message filters. Media gatekeepers make decisions about what messages actually get produced for particular audiences. The process occasionally allows **feedback**, in which citizens and consumers return messages to senders or gatekeepers through letters to the editor, phone calls, e-mail, or Web-site postings, or as audience members of talk shows.

Although the linear model explains certain aspects of the communication process, media messages usually do not flow smoothly from a sender at point A to a receiver at point Z. Like fish in turbulent water, words and images are in flux, spilling into each other and crisscrossing in the flow of everyday life. Media messages are encoded and sent in written and visual forms, but senders often have very little control over how their intended messages are decoded or whether the messages are ignored or misread by readers and viewers.

A Cultural Approach to Mass Communication

Moving beyond a simple sender-message-receiver model, we offer a cultural component to the study of the media. Working under this model, it is important to recognize that individuals and societies bring diverse meanings to messages, given varying factors such as gender, age, educational level, ethnicity, and occupation. For instance, when the rapper Ice-T's heavy-metal group Body Count produced the song "Cop Killer" in the early 1990s, police organizations and urban teens interpreted the lyrics in dramatically different ways. Some police groups wanted to ban the song, arguing that it would lead to violence, whereas fans of the band asserted that the song accurately portrayed the power of police authority in urban America.

It is sometimes easy to assume that producers of media messages are the active creators of communication and that audiences are merely passive receptacles. This may describe some situations, but as the "Cop Killer" example illustrates, audiences also shape media messages to fit their own values and viewpoints. This phenomenon is known as *selective exposure:* Audiences seek messages and produce meanings that correspond to their own cultural beliefs and values. Thus in the process of mass communication, audiences are actively interpreting, refashioning, or rejecting the cultural messages that flow through various media channels.

At its most significant level, the mass-communication process can alter a society's perception of events and attitudes. Throughout the twentieth century and during the recent war in Afghanistan, for instance, courageous journalists covered armed conflicts, helping the public comprehend the magnitude and tragedy of such events. In the 1950s and 1960s, television news reports on the Civil Rights movement led to crucial legislation that transformed the way many white people viewed the problems and aspirations of African Americans. In the mid-1990s, the best media coverage in the aftermath of the first O.J. Simpson trial stirred public discussion regarding both legal reform and domestic abuse. In the late 1990s, the President Clinton–Monica Lewinsky affair sparked heated debates over private codes of behavior and public abuses of authority. And in 2001–2002, the *Boston Globe*'s coverage of the Catholic Church's cover-up of sexual abuse by some of its priests demonstrated that a story that had been viewed as an occasional isolated regional occurrence was truly a major national problem and a nightmare for the Church. In each of these instances, the mass media played a key role in changing individual awareness, cultural attitudes, and even public policy.

The Impact of Media in Everyday Life

The earliest debates about the impact of culture and media on daily life date from the ancient Greeks. Socrates, himself accused of corrupting youths, worried that children exposed to stories "without distinction" would "take into their souls teachings that are wholly opposite to those we wish them to be possessed of when they are grown up."[4] The playwright Euripides, on the other hand, believed that art should imitate life, that characters should be real, and that artistic works should reflect the actual world even when that reality was sordid.

In *The Republic,* Plato developed the classical view of art: It should aim to instruct and uplift. He worried that some staged performances glorified evil and that common folk watching might not be able to distinguish between art and reality. Aristotle,

Plato's student, occupied a middle ground in these debates, arguing that art should provide insight into the human condition but should entertain as well.

Since the time of the early Greeks, concerns about the impact of culture have continued. At the turn of the nineteenth century, for example, newly arrived immigrants who spoke little English gravitated toward cultural events (such as boxing, vaudeville, and the new medium of silent film) for which enjoyment did not depend solely on understanding the English language. Consequently, these popular events occasionally became a flash point for many groups, including the Daughters of the American Revolution, local politicians, religious leaders, and police vice squads, who not only resented the commercial success of immigrant culture but feared that these "low" cultural forms would undermine traditional American values.

In the United States in the 1950s, the emergence of television and rock and roll generated countless points of contention. For instance, the phenomenal popularity of Elvis Presley set the stage for many of today's debates over hip-hop lyrics and television's negative influence. In 1956 and 1957, Presley made three appearances on the *Ed Sullivan Show*. The public outcry against Presley's "lascivious" hip movements was so great that by the third show the camera operators were instructed to shoot the singer from the waist up. Thousands of protective parents refused to allow their children to watch Presley's performances. In some communities, objections to Presley were motivated by class bias and racism. Many white adults believed that this "poor white trash" singer from Mississippi was spreading rhythm and blues, a "dangerous" form of black popular culture.

Today, the stakes are even higher. Given the reach and spread of print, electronic, and digital communication, culture and its myriad mutations play an even more controversial role in society. People used to share their common interests in radio or TV characters and major news stories in backyard, barroom, and coffee-shop conversations, but the proliferation of specialized publications and personalized channels has fragmented the media audience. Many citizens have become critical of the lack of quality in so much contemporary culture and are concerned about the overwhelming amount of information now available. Even the computer, once heralded as the educational salvation of children, has created confusion. Today, when kids announce that they are "on the computer," parents may wonder whether they are writing a term paper, playing a video game, talking to cyberspace strangers, shopping for sneakers, or peeking at pornography.

By 2002, the mass media had given the public much to be concerned about. Talk shows exploited personal problems for commercial gain, and so-called reality shows glamourized outlandish and often dangerous stunts (see "Examining Ethics: Staging Stunts Takes TV to New Low" on page 14). Television research once again documented the connection between aggression in children and violent entertainment programs. Children watched nearly forty thousand TV commercials each year. Debates also raged about curbing kids' exposure to pornography and adult subject

● In the 1950s, television images of early civil rights struggles visually documented the inequalities faced by black citizens. In 1957, the governor of Arkansas refused to allow black students like Elizabeth Eckford (*foreground*) to enter Little Rock's Central High School, even though segregation had been outlawed by the Supreme Court in 1954. In response, President Dwight Eisenhower sent in the army to integrate the school and control angry white mobs.

Staging Stunts Takes TV to New Low

Premiering in October 2000, MTV's *Jackass* took television to a new low, according to some critics. Characters on the short-lived program were doused with pepper spray, tipped over in a portable outhouse, and set afire on a barbeque. After the latter episode, a thirteen-year-old boy—minus the fire-resistant suit—repeated the stunt and nearly died.[1]

Programs like *Jackass* have appeared primarily for two reasons. First, this kind of "reality-based" TV is cheap to produce; it doesn't require expensive scripts and sets or professional writers and actors. Second, reality shows are the next wave in stunt TV, descended directly from the 1990s daytime talk genre in which thousands of regular folks paraded their personal problems before an ever-growing number of talk hosts.

These new reality programs are the trashy descendents of the *Jenny Jones Show* and the *Jerry Springer Show,* two talk shows whose program stunts also aspired to new lows. For many, Springer—a former TV news anchor and once the mayor of Cincinnati—became a symbol of the worst aspects of American popular culture. Outtakes from his show—too racy or explicit for television—were later packaged as semi-pornographic videos. The *Springer* show, which debuted in 1991, has routinely encouraged fighting among family members and groups of former friends and lovers.

In May 2000, the *Springer* show hit a new low point when it was apparently involved in a real-life murder. Three months after airing "Secret Mistresses Confronted," the story of a man whose latest wife (wife number four) was allegedly being stalked by

the man's third wife, the man killed his former wife after
an argument. Early in 2002, the son of the murdered wife
filed suit against the *Springer* show, alleging it was the trigger
for the murder and had used deceptive means to lure his
mother on the show. She apparently was told that she would
be reconciled with her former husband, who would renounce
wife number four on the air. Instead, the husband and the
new wife accused the former wife of stalking and revealed to
her that they had indeed recently married. In May 2002,
the husband was sentenced to life for second-degree
murder.[2]

This *Springer* episode was the second TV talk show with
links to a murder. In March 1995, the *Jenny Jones Show* taped
a program in Chicago about secret admirers. One participant,
Scott Amedure, who identified himself as gay, revealed his af-
fections for another guest, Jonathan Schmitz. Humiliated by
the revelation, Schmitz returned to Michigan, bought a shot-
gun, and three days later killed Amedure. Although the program never aired, the story intensified public concern over talk
shows, which were already under attack for exploiting personal
problems and pathologies for commercial gain and public
spectacle.[3]

As a result, some local TV stations dropped the most offensive programs, and large advertisers such as Philip Morris
and Procter & Gamble reduced their advertising support.
Meanwhile, the *Jenny Jones Show* disavowed legal responsibility, claiming that guests had been told their admirers might
be of either sex. In 1996, after Schmitz's doctors and family
documented his precarious psychological history, he was convicted of second-degree murder. Amedure's family immediately
filed—and eventually won—a $25 million civil suit against
the *Jenny Jones Show,* arguing that the program's producers
had done a poor job of screening its guests.

Although these incidents were tragic and atypical, provocative talk-show topics and tactics became standard daytime
fare and spawned the new wave of cable shows such as *Jackass, Fear Factor* (on which contestants were coerced to eat a
pig's uterus), *Dog Eat Dog,* and *Harassment,* a show whose
MTV debut was suspended when the producers startled an unsuspecting couple by planting a fake mutilated corpse in the

bathroom of their Las Vegas hotel. The couple sued MTV,
which then put the show on hold pending the legal outcome.

Such programs and practices on TV shows raise serious
ethical questions. Complicating any discussion of ethics,
however, are the competing values that govern how talk and
reality shows handle topics and guests. Most media organizations have ethical codes that guide the way in which professionals should behave in different situations. But beyond
self-regulatory codes, how can consumers criticize and shape
the ethics of media institutions?

Arriving at ethical decisions is a particular kind of criticism
involving several steps. These include (1) laying out the case;
(2) pinpointing the key issues; (3) identifying the parties involved, their intent, and their competing values; (4) studying
ethical models and theories; (5) presenting strategies and options; and (6) formulating a decision or policy.[4] As a test case,
we will look at the topic of deception regarding TV show guests
and contestants. Our goal will be to make some ethical decisions and to lay the groundwork for a policy that programs
might implement regarding suitable treatment of guests. We
will follow the six steps just mentioned. (See Chapter 14, page
489, for details on confronting ethical problems.)

Examining Ethics Activity

As a class or in smaller groups, design a policy to guide shows
regarding staged stunts and what information needs to be
revealed to prospective guests or contestants. Start by researching the topic; find as much information as possible. For
example, you might want to examine the guidelines from other
talk and reality shows.

Do they provide appropriate preparation for guests, and
what form does this take? Do these programs deceive guests,
and is deception ever permissible? Indicate whether the ethics
policy should be government mandated or an industrywide
guideline. Finally, if time allows, send the policy to various
shows; ask for their evaluations and whether they would consider implementing it.

Figure 1.1
Culture as a Skyscraper

Culture is diverse and difficult to categorize. Yet throughout the twentieth century we tended to think of culture not as a social process but as a set of products sorted into high, low, or middle positions on a cultural skyscraper. Look at this highly arbitrary arrangement and see if you agree or disagree. Write in some of your own examples.

Why do so many people view culture this way? What are the strengths and limitations of thinking about culture in these terms?

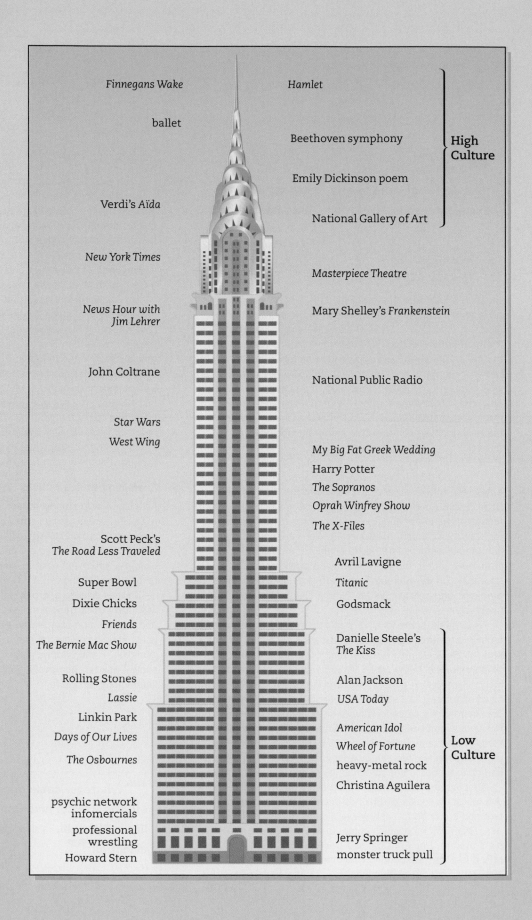

Finnegans Wake   Hamlet

ballet

Beethoven symphony   **High Culture**

Emily Dickinson poem

Verdi's Aïda

National Gallery of Art

New York Times

Masterpiece Theatre

News Hour with Jim Lehrer   Mary Shelley's Frankenstein

John Coltrane   National Public Radio

Star Wars
West Wing

My Big Fat Greek Wedding
Harry Potter
The Sopranos
Oprah Winfrey Show
The X-Files

Scott Peck's The Road Less Traveled

Avril Lavigne

Super Bowl   Titanic
Dixie Chicks   Godsmack
Friends
The Bernie Mac Show   Danielle Steele's The Kiss

Rolling Stones   Alan Jackson
Lassie   USA Today
Linkin Park
Days of Our Lives   American Idol
The Osbournes   Wheel of Fortune
    heavy-metal rock
    Christina Aguilera   **Low Culture**

psychic network infomercials
professional wrestling   Jerry Springer
Howard Stern   monster truck pull

matter on the Internet. Yet, although media depictions may worsen social problems, research has seldom demonstrated that the media directly cause our society's major afflictions. For instance, when a young middle-school student kills a fellow student over a pair of basketball shoes, should society blame the ads that glamourized the shoes and the network that carried the ad? Or are parents, teachers, and religious leaders failing to instill strong moral values? Or are economic and social issues involving gun legislation, consumerism, and income disparity at work as well? Even if the shoe manufacturer bears responsibility as a corporate citizen, did the ad itself cause the tragedy, or is the ad symptomatic of larger problems?

With American mass-media industries earning more than $200 billion annually, the economic stakes are high. Large portions of media resources now go toward studying audiences, capturing their attention, and taking their consumer dollars. This process involves trying to influence everything from how people vote to how they shop. Like the air we breathe, the fallout from the mass media surrounds us. But to monitor the media's "air quality"—to become media literate—a responsible citizenry must attend more thoughtfully to diverse media messages that are too often taken for granted.

Surveying the Cultural Landscape

Some cultural phenomena gain wide popular appeal, and others do not. Some appeal to certain age groups or social classes; some, such as rock and roll, jazz, and classical music, are popular worldwide. Other cultural forms, such as Tejano, salsa, or Cajun music, are popular only in certain regions or communities. Some aspects of culture are considered elite in one place (opera in the United States) and popular in another (opera in Italy). Throughout history, however, most societies have arranged culture into hierarchical categories.

Culture as a Skyscraper

Throughout twentieth-century America, critics and audiences took for granted a hierarchy of culture that exists to this day and can be visualized, in some respects, as a modern skyscraper. The top floors of the building house **high culture**, such as ballet, the symphony, art museums, and classical literature. The bottom floors—and even the basement—house popular or **low culture**, including such icons as soap operas, rock and rap music, talk radio, comic books, and monster truck pulls (see Figure 1.1). High culture, identified with "good taste" and often supported by wealthy patrons and corporate donors (the kind of folks who might favor sky-boxes and penthouses), is associated with "fine art," which is available primarily in libraries, theaters, or museums. In contrast, low or popular culture is aligned with the questionable tastes of the "masses," who enjoy the commercial "junk" circulated by the mass media. Whether or not we agree with this cultural skyscraper model, the high-low hierarchy has become so entrenched that it often determines or limits the ways in which we view culture today.[5]

Some critics are concerned that popular culture in the form of contemporary movies, television, and rock music distracts students from serious literature and philosophy, thus ruining their imagination and undermining their ability to recognize great art.[6] Discounting a person's ability to value Aristotle and Aerosmith concurrently, this critical view pits popular culture against the more traditional forms of high art and culture. The assumption is that because popular forms of culture are

● Mary Shelley, the author of *Frankenstein,* might not recognize our popular culture's mutations of her Gothic classic. First published in 1818, the novel has inspired numerous interpretations, everything from the scary—Boris Karloff in the classic 1931 movie—to the silly—the Munster family in the 1960s TV sitcom.

made for profit, they cannot be experienced with the same personal intensity as more elite art forms.

Another concern is that popular culture exploits classic works of literature and art. The best example may be Mary Wollstonecraft Shelley's dark Gothic novel *Frankenstein,* written in 1818 and ultimately transformed into multiple popular forms. Today, the tale is best remembered by virtue of a 1931 film version starring Boris Karloff as the towering monster. In addition to the movies, television turned the tale into *The Munsters,* a mid-1960s situation comedy. Eventually, the monster was resurrected as sugar-coated Frankenberry cereal. In the recycled forms of the original story, Shelley's powerful themes about abusing science and judging people on the basis of appearances are often lost or trivialized.

Unlike an Italian opera or a Shakespearean tragedy, many elements of popular culture have a short life span. The average newspaper circulates for about twelve hours, then lands in a recycle bin or at the bottom of a bird cage; the average magazine circulates for about five to seven days; a new Top 40 song on the radio lasts about one month; and the average TV series survives for less than ten weeks. Although endurance does not necessarily denote quality, in the view of many critics, better forms of culture have staying power. These critics argue that popular forms promote a culture that is unstable and fleeting, that they follow rather than lead public taste. In the television industry in the 1960s and 1970s, this was known as "least objectionable programming," or LOP: TV's network executives were often accused of pandering to mediocrity by airing bland, disposable programming that would not disturb or challenge a "normal" viewer.

A final concern is that popular culture not only undermines or exploits high culture but has inundated the cultural environment, driving out higher forms of culture and cheapening public life.[7] This concern is supported by data showing that TV sets are in use in the average American home for more than seven hours a day, exposing adults and children each year to thousands of hours of TV commercials and popular culture. According to critics, the prevalence of media products prevents the public from experiencing genuine art. Forty or more radio stations are available in most cities; cable systems with at least seventy-two channels are in place in 70 percent of all U.S. households; and CD players, Internet services, VCRs, and now DVD players are increasing in popularity. Thus the chance of more refined culture transforming the media environment or even finding a substantial audience seems small.

There is also concern that the impact of popular culture, especially its visual forms (such as TV advertising and daytime talk shows), has undermined democratic reasoning. According to this view, popular media may inhibit social progress by transforming audiences into cultural dupes, seduced by the promise of products. A few multinational conglomerates, which make large profits from media products, may be distracting citizens from examining economic disparity and implementing change. Seductive advertising images showcasing the buffed and polished bodies of professional models frequently contradict the actual lives of many people, who cannot hope to achieve a particular "look" or may not have the financial means to obtain all the cosmetic products offered in the marketplace. In this environment, art and commerce have become blurred, restricting the audience's ability to make cultural distinctions. Sometimes called the "Big Mac" theory, this view suggests that people are so addicted to mass-produced media menus that they have lost not only the will to challenge social inequities but also their discriminating taste for finer fare.

Culture as a Map

To depict culture as an ongoing process—rather than as a vertically organized hierarchy of products—and to account for our diverse and individual tastes, it might help to imagine culture as a map rather than as a skyscraper. Maps represent large, unwieldy spaces that spread out in all directions. Maps highlight main highways and familiar urban centers, but they also include scores of side roads and small towns, diverting our focus to unexplored areas.

Whereas the hierarchical skyscraper model of culture too easily presents culture on a simple high-to-low scale, a map model depicts culture in a more complex way. On the one hand, cultural phenomena—such as the stories we read in books or watch at the movies—offer places to go that are conventional, recognizable, stable, and comforting sites. But on the other hand, our culture's storehouse of stories may tend toward the innovative, unfamiliar, unstable, and challenging. Most forms of culture, however, demonstrate both tendencies. For example, we may buy the CDs of a favorite artist or watch our favorite TV programs for *both* their innovation *and* their familiarity. We may listen to a song or watch a program to complement a mood, to distance ourselves from problems, or to reflect critically on the song's lyrics or the TV show's meanings.

> **“ TV is a genre of reruns, a formulaic return to what we already know. Everything is familiar. Ads and old programs are constantly recycled. It's like mythology, like the Homeric epics, the oral tradition, in which the listener hears passages, formulae, and epithets repeated over and over again. There is a joy in repetition, as children know when they say, 'Mommy, tell me that story again.' ”**
>
> —Camille Paglia,
> *Harper's,* 1991

The appeal of culture is often its ring of familiar stories, pulling audiences toward the security of repetition and the common landmarks on the cultural map. Consider, for instance, television's *Lassie* series. More than five hundred episodes exist in syndication; many had a familiar and repetitive plot line: Timmy, who arguably possessed the poorest sense of direction and suffered more concussions than any TV character in history, gets lost or knocked unconscious. After finding Timmy and licking his face, Lassie goes for help and saves the day. Adult critics might mock this melodramatic formula, but many children find comfort in the predictability of the

● Mary Hart, co-host of *Entertainment Tonight*. *Entertainment Tonight* features gossipy stories and interviews with celebrities, "scoops" about the entertainment industry, and has the general appearance of a television news program, blurring the line between entertainment and news.

story. This quality is also illustrated when night after night children ask their parents to read Margaret Wise Brown's *Good Night, Moon* or Maurice Sendak's *Where the Wild Things Are*. Like children, adults also seek a kind of comfort, often returning to the same songs, the same plays, the same poems, and the same TV programs.

In our cultural adventures, however, we also seek new stories and new places to go—those aspects of culture that may demonstrate originality and complexity. For instance, James Joyce's *Finnegans Wake* (1939) created language anew and challenged readers, as the novel's poetic first sentence illustrates: "riverrun, past Eve and Adam's, from swerve of shore to bend of bay, brings us by a commodius vicus of recirculation back to Howth Castle and Environs." A revolutionary work, crammed with historical names and topical references to events, myths, songs, jokes, and daily conversation, Joyce's novel remains a challenge to understand and decode. His work demonstrated that part of what culture provides is that impulse to explore new places. In our everyday lives we return to our favorite TV programs and recording artists, but we may also tire of old shows and favorite singers. So we strike out in new directions, searching for something different.

We know that people have complex cultural tastes, needs, and interests based on their different backgrounds. It is not surprising, then, that our cultural forms and stories—from blues music and opera to comic books and classical literature—contain a variety of messages. Just as Shakespeare's plays were packed with both obscure and popular references, TV episodes of *The Simpsons* today include allusions to the Beatles, Kafka, the *Adventures of Ozzie & Harriet*, Tennessee Williams, talk shows, Aerosmith, *The X-Files*, and *Citizen Kane*. In other words, as part of an ongoing

● In the 1990s Internet cafés popped up in response to increasing demand for Internet service. In a twist on the traditional coffee shop, customers could now surf the Internet while sipping their lattes.

process, cultural products and their meanings are "all over the map." This suggests that in spite of many critics' tendencies to rank culture vertically, we should not think about our cultural environment merely as a product hierarchy but as a changing road map that spreads out in many directions.

Some critics of popular culture—often without presenting supportive evidence—assume that society was better off before the latest developments in mass media. They resist the idea of redrawing established cultural maps. The nostalgia for some imagined "better past" has often operated as a device for condemning new cultural phenomena. In the nineteenth century, in fact, a number of intellectuals and politicians worried that rising literacy rates among the working class might create havoc: How would the aristocracy and intellectuals maintain their authority and status if others could read? Throughout history, a call to return to familiar terrain, to "the good old days," has been a frequent response to new, "threatening" forms of popular culture, which over the years have included the waltz, silent movies, ragtime, jazz, comic books, rock and roll, soap operas, heavy-metal rock, hip-hop, tabloid newspapers, and "reality" television programs.

Shifting Values in Modern Culture

In contemporary life, cultural boundaries are being tested; the arbitrary lines between information and entertainment have become even more blurred. Consumers now read newspapers on their computer screens. Media corporations do business across vast geographic boundaries. We are witnessing *media convergence,* in which satellite dishes, TV screens, and cable or computer modems easily access new and old forms of mass communication. For a fee, everything from magazines to movies is channeled into homes through computer modems, TV cables, or satellite transmissions. To place these shifts and convergences in historical context, scholars have traced the meandering route of cultural values through the *modern* period (from the full-blown arrival of the Industrial Revolution in the nineteenth century) to one that is frequently labeled *postmodern,* or contemporary.

What it means to be modern is complicated. As we have seen, the process of modernization involved individuals and societies responding to changing economic circumstances. Captains of industry employed workforces and new technology, creating efficient manufacturing centers and inexpensive products aimed at making everyday life both better and more profitable. Printing presses and assembly lines made major contributions in this transformation, and modern advertising spread the word about new gadgets to American consumers.

Cultural responses to modernization often manifest themselves in the mass media. For example, Aldous Huxley, in *Brave New World* (1932), created a fictional world in which he cautioned readers that modern science and technology posed a threat to individual dignity. Charlie Chaplin's film *Modern Times* (1936), set in a futuristic manufacturing plant, also told the story of the dehumanizing impact of modernization and machinery. Writers and artists, in their criticisms of the modern world, often point to technology's ability to alienate people from one another, capitalism's tendency to foster greed, and government's inclination to create bureaucracies that oppress rather than help people.

Among the major values of the modern period, four typically manifest themselves in the cultural environment: celebrating the individual, believing in rational order, working efficiently, and rejecting tradition. These values of the modern period were originally embodied in the printing press and later in newspapers and magazines. The print media encouraged the vision of individual writers, publishers, and readers who circulated new ideas. Whereas the premodern period was guided by strong beliefs in a natural or divine order, becoming modern meant elevating individual self-expression to a central position. Along with democratic breakthroughs, however, individualism and the Industrial Revolution triggered modern forms of hierarchy, in which certain individuals and groups achieved higher standing in the social order. For example, those who managed commercial enterprises gained more control over the economic ladder, but an intellectual class of modern experts, who mastered specialized realms of knowledge, gained increasing power over the nation's social, political, and cultural agendas.

To be modern also meant to value the capacity of organized, scientific minds to solve problems efficiently. Progressive thinkers maintained that the printing press, the telegraph, and the railroad in combination with a scientific attitude would foster a new type of informed society. At the core of this society the printed mass media, particularly newspapers, would educate the citizenry, helping to build and maintain

NEW YORK SUN

VOLUME II.   NEW YORK, JULY 4, 1834   NUMBER 23.

POLICE OFFICE

Patrick Ludwick was sent up by his wife, who testified that she had supported him for several years in idleness and drunkenness. Abandoning all hopes of a reformation in her husband, she bought him a suit of clothes a fortnight ago and told him to go about his business, for she would not live with him any longer. Last night he came home in a state of intoxication, broke into his wife's bedroom, pulled her out of bed, pulled her hair, and stamped on her. She called a watchman and sent him up. Pat exerted all his powers of eloquence in endeavoring to excite his wife's sympathy, but to no purpose. As every sensible woman ought to do who is cursed with a drunken husband, she refused to have anything to do with him hereafter—and he was sent to the penitentiary.

ANN ARBOR NEWS POLICE BEAT

November 19, 1995

Ann Arbor police expect to arraign on Monday an Allen Park man who is accused of assaulting his female companion in a local hotel room early Friday morning after she refused to have sex with him.

The 48-year-old man was arrested Saturday in Allen Park by police there, Ann Arbor police said Saturday. The 33-year-old woman, who lives in Wyandotte, told investigators that the man struck her in the head with a bottle and punched her when she would not consent to sex.

Employees at the Ramada Inn Ann Arbor, 3750 Washtenaw Ave., said the man and woman checked in around 2 a.m. Friday.

Figure 1.2
Premodern vs. Modern News

These two stories, separated by 161 years, illustrate some differences between premodern and modern news. The 1834 story includes asides, humor, and opinion by the writer; the 1995 story seems objective, stripped of any direct evidence of the reporter's viewpoint. The 1834 story is more dramatic in its description of the crime; the 1995 story focuses on the facts—who, what, when, where—revealing that even specific ages and the exact address of the motel seem important. The 1834 story treats the crime irreverently; the 1995 story treats the crime seriously. What are the pros and cons of each style? What attitudes toward the victims are represented by the different styles of reporting?

an organized social framework.[8] Journalists strove for the modern ideal through a more objective and efficient approach to reporting. They discarded decorative writing and championed a lean look. Modern front-page news de-emphasized description, commentary, and historical context. The lead sentences that reported a presidential press conference began to look similar, whether they were on the front page in Biloxi, Mississippi, or Zap, North Dakota. Just as modern architecture made many American skylines look alike, the front pages of newspapers began to resemble one another (see Figure 1.2, above).

Finally, to be modern meant to throw off the rigid rules of the past, to break with tradition. Modern journalism became captivated by timely and immediate events. As a result, the more standardized forms of front-page journalism, on one hand, championed facts and current events while efficiently meeting deadlines. But on the other hand, modern newspapers often failed to analyze sufficiently the ideas underlying these events.

Shifting Values in Postmodern Culture

For many people, the changes occurring in contemporary, or postmodern, society are identified only by a confusing array of examples: music videos, remote controls, Nike ads, shopping malls, fax machines, David Letterman, *South Park, USA Today,* cell

	Premodern (roughly pre-1800s)	Modern (roughly post-1800s)	Postmodern (since 1950s)
Range of work hierarchies	peasants/ merchants/rulers	factory workers/ managers/ national CEOs	temp workers/ managers/ global CEOs
Major work sites	field/farm	factory/office	office/home/"virtual" or mobile office
Communication reach	local	national	global
Communication transmission	oral/manuscript	print/electronic	electronic/digital
Communication channels	storytellers/elders/ town criers	books/newspapers/ magazines/radios/ television	television/cable/ Internet/ multimedia
Communication at home	quill pen	typewriter/office computer	personal computer/ laptop computer/ Palm Pilot

*The examples in this table identify some of the significant trends in the premodern, modern, and postmodern periods of society.

Note: For a slightly different view, see Charles Jencks, "The Three Eras of Civilization," in *What Is Post-Modernism?* 3rd ed. (New York: St. Martin's Press, 1989), 47.

phones, *TRL*, hip-hop, and Eminem. Some critics argue that postmodern culture represents a way of seeing—a condition (or malady) of the human spirit. Chiefly a response to the modern world, controversial postmodern values are playing increasingly pivotal roles in our daily lives. Four values, in particular, are identified here as markers of the so-called postmodern period: opposing hierarchy, diversifying and recycling culture, questioning scientific reasoning, and embracing paradox (see Table 1.1, above).

One of the main values of contemporary culture is an opposition to hierarchy. Many artists are challenging the sometimes arbitrary line between high and low culture, and others are blurring the distinctions between fact and fiction or art and commerce. For example, a new television vocabulary now includes *docudrama* (NBC's 2000 miniseries *The 70s*), *infotainment* (*Entertainment Tonight, Access Hollywood*), and *infomercials* (fading celebrities selling everything from anti-wrinkle cream to psychic dating services). On cable, MTV's Tom Green produces a dark comedic documentary on his personal battle with testicular cancer. In magazines, arresting clothing or cigarette ads combine stark social commentaries with low-key sales pitches. At the movies, *Pulp Fiction* (1994), *Fargo* (1996), *Moulin Rouge* (2001), and *The Man Who Wasn't There* (2001) fuse the comic and the tragic in film tributes to postmodern style. And in music, Madonna champions oppressed groups at the same time that her songs make her wealthy and a global icon for consumer culture.

Another contemporary value (or vice) of the so-called postmodern period emphasizes diversity and fragmentation, including the wild juxtaposition of old and new cultural styles. In a suburban shopping mall, for instance, Waldenbooks and Gap clothes border a Vietnamese, Italian, and Mexican food court, while a Muzak version of the Beatles' "Revolution" plays in the background. Part of this stylistic diversity involves borrowing and then transforming earlier ideas from the modern period. In music, hip-hop deejays and performers sample old R&B, soul, and rock classics to reinvent songs. Borrowing in hip-hop is often so pronounced that the original artists and record companies have frequently filed for copyright infringement. Critics of postmodern style contend that such poaching devalues originality, emphasizing surface over depth and recycled ideas over new ones. Throughout the twentieth century, for example, films were adapted from books and short stories. Now, films often derive from popular TV series: *The Brady Bunch, The Fugitive, The Mask of Zorro, Mission Impossible,* and *Charlie's Angels,* to name just a few.

Another tendency of postmodern culture is to raise doubts about scientific reasoning. Rather than seeing science purely as enlightened thinking, postmodernists view it as laying the groundwork for modern bureaucratic problems. They reject rational thought as "the answer" to every social problem, lauding instead the premodern values of small communities. Internet users, for example, are seen as reclaiming in digital form lost conversational skills and letter-writing habits. Even the current popularity of radio and TV talk shows, according to this view, is partly an attempt to recover lost aspects of oral traditions. Given the feelings of powerlessness and alienation that mark the contemporary age, one attraction of the talk-show format has been the way it encourages ordinary people to participate in discussions with celebrities, experts, and each other.

Although some forms of contemporary culture raise questions about rational science, other postmodern cultural forms warmly embrace technology. Blockbuster films such as *Jurassic Park, Titanic,* and *The Matrix* do both, presenting stories that challenge modern science but depend on technological wizardry for their execution. During the modern period, art and literature frequently criticized the potential dangers of machines. Postmodern style, however, does not seem as critical of new technologies.

Many forms of contemporary culture generally accept technology. There is, however, a fundamental paradox in this uneasy postmodern alliance. As modern writers and artists have pointed out, new technologies often eliminate jobs and physically isolate us from one another. Conversely, new technologies can draw people together to discuss politics on radio talk shows, electronic town-hall meetings, or Internet newsgroups. Our lives today are full of such incongruities.

Critiquing Media and Culture

Just as communication is not always reducible to the linear sender-message-receiver model, many forms of media and culture are not easily represented by the high-low metaphor. We should, perhaps, strip culture of such adjectives as *high, low, popular,* and *mass.* These modifiers may artificially force media forms and products into predetermined categories. Rather than focusing on these labels, we might instead look at a wide range of issues generated by culture, from the role of storytelling in the mass media to the global influences of media industries on the consumer marketplace. We should also be moving toward a critical perspective that takes into account the intricacies of the cultural landscape.

A fair critique of any cultural form requires a working knowledge of the particular book, program, or music under scrutiny. For example, to understand W. E. B. Du Bois's essays, critics immerse themselves in his work and in the historical context in which he wrote. Similarly, if we want to develop a meaningful critique of *The Simpsons,* it is essential to understand the contemporary context in which the program is produced.

To begin this process of critical assessment, we must imagine culture as more complicated and richer than the high-low model allows. We must also assume a

Mixed Messages Bombard Teens on Sex and Violence

by Todd Purdum

America is obsessed with youth, awash in the largest generation of young people since the baby boomers themselves passed through. More than 70 million strong and growing, young people today constitute both an irresistible market and a powerful marketing tool. . . .

The Federal Trade Commission's finding that entertainment companies regularly market violent movies and video games to people too young to buy them legally is just a recent example.

"It's obviously very confusing to teen-agers," said the author Thomas Hine, whose sociological survey, *The Rise and Fall of the American Teen-ager* (Bard/Avon), was published in 1999.

"On the one hand, there's this long tradition of criticisms of youth culture by people who haven't the slightest idea about it. At the turn of the 20th century, ragtime was seen as a great evil. By the 1920s, *The Ladies Home Journal* was crusading against jazz. It went out of its way to say that ragtime was wonderful.

"There's always a new evil. But that's the funny thing, because we count on young people for that, to be the ones who are finding the new."

Pity the poor teen-ager, caught in the cultural cross-fire.

"We market to them, and then we stigmatize our teens as being so much involved in risky behavior," said Dr. Lynn Ponton, an adolescent psychiatrist at the University of California at San Francisco and the author of *The Sex Lives of Teen-agers* (Dutton 2000). . . .

There are two easy explanations for society's current glorification of youth: money and sex.

The money part is straightforward. "Teen-agers are going to spend $160 billion this year, a 60% increase over three years ago," Hine said. That's a lot of money, and everyone wants a share.

The sexual part is more complex. . . .

Today . . . baby boomers are loath to cede center stage to the coming generations—along with the status that comes with hipness and desirability. So adults have begun seduously aping teens.

"There's a trend we call generational blur, something that's been growing over the last 20 years," said Irma Zandl, a marketing expert in Manhattan whose Zandl Group tracks tastes and trends among the under-30 set.

"There used to be a certain set of behaviors and ways of dress that if you were an adult you left behind. But as society's become much more casual, those rules are really blurred. There isn't that much distinction between how teen-agers and adults dress; they're all wearing khakis and jeans and sneakers."

This year, for the first time, Zandl said, she has spotted even pregnant women in their 30s and 40s wearing low-waisted pants and baring their midriffs, as if they were Britney Spears onstage. Using teen-age sexuality to maintain desirability in this way is a dicey thing, all but putting parents in a disquieting sexual competition with their children.

And it points up how complicit adults are in encouraging some of the very ills they condemn.

The popular-culture industry has been aimed at teen-agers since the 1950s, when the movie and recording industries, threatened by the rise of television, began selling them angst and sex. Those were the subjects, whether in *Rebel Without a Cause,* or in pop hits like Nat King Cole's "They Try to Tell Us We're Too Young (Too Young to Really Be in Love)."

Since then, the concentration on youth has waxed and waned with the size of the adolescent population. Sean Daniel, who as a studio executive or producer has had a hand in movies including *Animal House, Fast Times at Ridgemont High, The Breakfast Club,* and *Dazed and Confused,* said simply, "I can tell you we are in yet another cycle where youth rules."

The corollary is not, however, that Hollywood can successfully sell teens anything.

Teen-agers will "unstoppably seek out the culture they want," Daniel said. They will sneak into theaters to see films they aren't supposed to (or sneak into music stores to buy CDs they aren't supposed to hear).

Cultural critics, however, usually look for a villain and make the easy assertion that kids seek out entertainment disapproved of by adults because of exploitative corporate marketing.

"Who's kidding who?" Daniel asks. "The reality of teen-age life is R-rated."

That said, like many of his colleagues in Hollywood, Daniel acknowledges concern about a "measurably greater intensity" in the images that bombard the culture, from the big screen to the Internet, and he draws a distinction between the widespread use of violence and sexual imagery and themes, which troubles him less.

"I suspect," he said, "that no good comes from America's essential prudishness," and he praises movies like *There's Something About Mary* for their "hilarious embrace of the awkwardness of life and the power of romance in it." Moreover, Daniel said that a culture in which teen-agers cannot find their lives portrayed on their own terms is not a healthy one.

Of course, many parents may take precisely the opposite view. And there is ample evidence that the gulf between parents and their teen-agers remains as large as ever.

A new survey sponsored by Students Against Drunk Driving and Liberty Mutual Insurance found that teen-agers were more concerned with problems like drinking and driving and teen-age suicide, while their parents were more worried about car accidents or casual sex. Only 5% of parents surveyed thought their children would drink and drive; 21% of teen-agers said they already had.

But Zandl, the marketing expert, notes that more young people than ever say their parents are their role models. So when adults express concern about the cultural influences affecting their children, the first place to look may not be Hollywood, but much closer to home.

Source: Todd Purdum, "Mixed Messages Bombard Teens on Sex and Violence," *The New York Times News Service,* September 17, 2000, Section 4, p. 1.

critical stance that enables us to get outside our own preferences. We may like or dislike Faith Hill's pop country, Ricky Martin's Latin rhythms, or Chuck D's political rap, but if we want to criticize these musical styles intelligently, we should understand what the various types of music have to say and why their messages have appeal for particular audiences. The same approach applies to other cultural forms. If we critique a newspaper article, we must account for the language that is chosen and what it means; if we analyze a film or TV program, we need to slow down the images in order to understand how they try to make sense.

Media Literacy and Steps in the Critical Process

It is easy to form a cynical view of the stream of TV advertising, talk shows, rock stars, and news tabloids that flood the cultural landscape. But cynicism is no substitute for solid criticism. To become literate about media involves striking a balance between taking a critical position (developing knowledgeable interpretations and judgments) and becoming tolerant of diverse forms of expression (appreciating the distinctive variety of cultural products and processes). A cynical view usually involves some form of intolerance and either too little or too much information. For example, after enduring the glut of news coverage devoted to the 2000 presidential election, we might easily have become cynical about our political system. However, *information* in the form of news facts and *knowledge* about a complex social process such as a national election are not the same thing. The critical process stresses the subtle distinctions between amassing information and becoming knowledgeable, or attaining **media literacy**.

Developing a media-literate critical perspective involves mastering four overlapping stages that build on each other:

- *Description:* paying close attention, taking notes, and researching the subject under study
- *Analysis:* discovering and focusing on significant patterns that emerge from the description stage
- *Interpretation:* asking and answering the "What does that mean?" and "So what?" questions about one's findings
- *Evaluation:* arriving at a judgment about whether something is good, bad, or mediocre, which involves subordinating one's personal taste to the critical assessment resulting from the first three stages

Let's look at each of these stages in greater detail.

Description

If we decide to focus on how well the news media serve democracy, we might critique the fairness of several programs or individual stories from *60 Minutes* or the *New York Times*. We start by describing the programs or articles, accounting for their reporting strategies, and noting what persons are featured as interview subjects. We might further identify central characters, conflicts, topics, and themes. From the notes taken at this stage, we can begin comparing what we have found to other stories on similar topics. We can also document what we think is missing from these accounts—the questions, viewpoints, and persons that were not included—and other ways to tell the story.

Analysis

In the second stage of the critical process, we isolate *patterns* that call for closer attention. At this point, we decide how to focus the critique. Because *60 Minutes* has produced thousands of hours of programs, our critique might spotlight just a few key patterns. For example, many of the program's reports are organized like detective stories, reporters are almost always visually represented at a medium distance, and interview subjects are generally shot in tight close-ups. In studying the *New York Times,* on the other hand, we might limit our analysis to countries that get covered more regularly than others, recurring topics chosen for front-page treatment, or the number of quotes from male and female experts.

Interpretation

In the interpretive stage, we try to determine the *meanings* of the patterns we have analyzed. The most difficult stage in criticism, interpretation demands an answer to the "So what?" question. For instance, the visual space granted to *60 Minutes* reporters—compared with the close-up shots used for interview subjects—might mean that the reporters appear to be in control. They are given more visual space in which to operate, whereas interview subjects have little room to maneuver within the visual frame. As a result, the subjects often look guilty and the reporters look heroic—or, at least, in charge. Likewise, if we look again at the *New York Times,* its attention to particular countries might mean that the paper tends to cover nations in which the United States has more vital political or economic interests, even though the *Times* might claim to be neutral and even-handed in its reporting of news from around the world.

Evaluation

The fourth stage of the critical process focuses on making an informed judgment. Building on description, analysis, and interpretation, we are better able to evaluate the fairness of a group of *60 Minutes* or *New York Times* reports. At this stage, we can grasp the strengths and weaknesses of the news media under study and make critical judgments measured against our own frames of reference—what we like and dislike as well as what seems good or bad about the stories and coverage we analyzed.

This fourth stage differentiates the reviewer (or *previewer*) from the critic. Most newspaper reviews, for example, are limited by daily time or space constraints. Although these reviews may give us important information about particular programs, they often begin and end with personal judgments—"This is a quality show" or "That was a piece of trash"—which should be the final stage in any substantial critical process. Regrettably, many reviews do not reflect such a process; they do not move much beyond the writer's own frame of reference.

Benefits of a Critical Perspective

Developing an informed critical perspective allows us to participate in a debate about media culture as a force for both democracy and consumerism (see, for example, "Case Study: Mixed Messages Bombard Teens on Sex and Violence" on page 26). On the one hand, the media can be a catalyst for democratic tendencies. Consider the role of television in documenting racism and injustice in the 1960s; the use of video technology to reveal oppressive conditions in China and Eastern Europe or to document crimes by urban police departments; and the appearance of political rap music as black-produced commerce drawing attention to social injustice. The media have also helped to renew interest in diverse cultures around the world (see "The Global Village: Bedouins, Camels, Transistors, and Coke" on page 30).

> **" A cynic is a man who, when he smells flowers, looks around for a coffin."**
>
> —H. L. Mencken

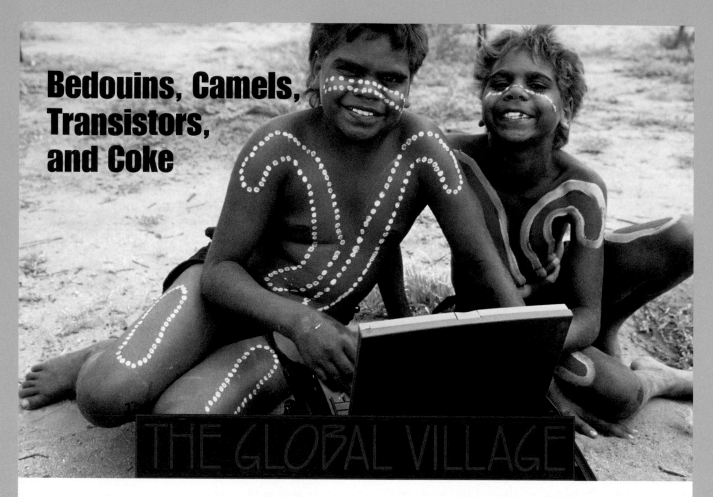

Bedouins, Camels, Transistors, and Coke

THE GLOBAL VILLAGE

Upon receiving the Philadelphia Liberty Medal in 1994, President Václav Havel of the Czech Republic described postmodernism as the fundamental condition of global culture, "when it seems that something is on the way out and something else is painfully being born." He described this "new world order" as a "multicultural era" or state in which consistent value systems break into mixed and blended cultures:

> For me, a symbol of that state is a Bedouin mounted on a camel and clad in traditional robes under which he is wearing jeans, with a transistor radio in his hands and an ad for Coca-Cola on the camel's back. . . . New meaning is gradually born from the . . . intersection of many different elements.[1]

Many critics, including Havel, think that there is a crucial tie between global politics and postmodern culture. They contend that the people who overthrew the former Yugoslavia and the Soviet Union were the same people who valued American popular culture—especially movies, rock music, and television—for its free expression and democratic possibilities.

As modern communist states were undermined by the growth and influence of transnational corporations, citizens in these nations capitalized on the developing global market, using portable video and audio technology to smuggle out tapes of atrocities perpetrated by totalitarian regimes. Thus it was difficult for political leaders to hide repressive acts from the rest of the world. In *Newsweek*, CBS news anchor Dan Rather wrote about the role of television in the 1989 student uprising in China:

Television brought Beijing's battle for democracy to Main Street. It made students who live on the other side of the planet just as human, just as vulnerable as the boy on the next block. The miracle of television is that the triumph and tragedy of Tiananmen Square would not have been any more vivid had it been Times Square.[2]

At the same time, we need to examine the impact on other nations of the influx of popular culture—the second-biggest American export (after military and airplane equipment). Has access to an American consumer lifestyle fundamentally altered Havel's Bedouin on the camel? What happens when CNN or MTV is transported to remote African villages that share a single community TV set? What happens when Westernized popular culture encroaches on the rituals of Islamic countries where the spread of American music, movies, and television is viewed as a danger to tradition? These questions still need answers. A global village, which through technology shares culture and communication, can also alter traditional rituals forever.

To try to grasp this phenomenon, we might imagine how we would feel if the culture from a country far away gradually eroded our own established habits. This, in fact, is happening all over the world as American culture becomes the world's global currency. Although newer forms of communication such as instant messaging have in some ways increased citizen participation in global life, in what ways have they muted the values of older cultures? Our current postmodern period is double-coded: It is an agent both for the renewed possibilities of democracy and for the worldwide spread of consumerism and American popular culture.

On the other hand, competing against these democratic tendencies is a powerful commercial culture that reinforces a world economic order controlled by fewer and fewer multinational corporations. For instance, when Poland threw off the shackles of the Soviet Union in the late 1980s, one of the first things its new leadership did was buy and dub the American soap operas *Santa Barbara* and *Dynasty*. For some Poles, these shows were a relief from sober Soviet political propaganda, but other Poles worried that their country had inherited another kind of indoctrination—one starring American consumer culture.

This example illustrates that contemporary culture cannot easily be characterized as one thing or another. Binary terms such as *liberal* and *conservative* or *high* and *low* have less meaning in an environment where so many boundaries have been blurred, so many media forms have converged, and so many diverse cultures co-exist. Modern distinctions between print and electronic culture have begun to break down largely because of the increasing number of individuals who have come of age in *both* a print *and* an electronic culture.[9] Either/or models of culture, such as the high-low perspective, are making room for more inclusive models, similar to the map metaphor for culture discussed earlier.

What are the social implications of the new, blended, and merging cultural phenomena? How do we deal with the fact that public debate and news about everyday life now seem as likely to come from Oprah, *The Simpsons*, or popular music as from the *New York Times*, *Nightline*, or *Newsweek*?[10] Clearly, such changes challenge us to reassess and rebuild the standards by which we judge our culture. The search for answers lies in recognizing the links between cultural expression and daily life. The search also involves monitoring how well the mass media serve democratic practices and involve a rich variety of people, not just as consumers but also as informed citizens.

Democracy requires the active participation of interested citizens. Part of this involvement means watching over the role and impact of the mass media, a job that belongs to each citizen, not just to paid media critics. In this textbook, we will begin the job by examining the historical contexts and current processes that shape media products. By probing various media industries, we can then develop a framework for tracking the ways in which media industries perform. By becoming more critical consumers and engaged citizens, we will be in a better position to influence the relationships among mass media, democratic participation, and the cultural landscape that we inhabit.

www.

To create an individualized study plan for Chapter 1, go to the interactive *Media and Culture* Online Study Guide at: bedfordstmartins.com/mediaculture

REVIEW QUESTIONS

Culture and the Evolution of Mass Communication

1. Define *culture, mass communication,* and *mass media,* and explain their interrelationships.

2. What are the key technological breakthroughs that accompanied the transition to the print and electronic eras? Why were these technologies significant?

Mass Media and the Process of Communication

3. Explain the linear model of mass communication and its limitations.

4. In looking at the history of popular culture, explain why newer forms of media seem to threaten status quo values.

Surveying the Cultural Landscape

5. Describe the skyscraper model of culture. What are its strengths and limitations?

6. Describe the map model of culture. What are its strengths and limitations?

7. What are the chief differences between modern and so-called postmodern values?

Critiquing Media and Culture

8. What are the four steps in the critical process? Which of these is the most difficult and why?

9. What is the difference between cynicism and criticism?

10. Why is the critical process important?

QUESTIONING MEDIA

1. Using music or television as an example, identify a performer or program you once liked but began to dislike as you grew older and your tastes changed. Why do you think this happened? Do you think your early interests in popular television or music have had an impact on shaping your identity? Explain.

2. From your own experience, cite examples in which you think the media have been treated unfairly. Draw on comments from parents, teachers, religious leaders, friends, news media, etc. Discuss whether these criticisms have been justified.

3. Pick an example of a popular media product that you think is harmful to children. How would you make your concerns known? Should the product be re-moved from circulation? Why or why not? If you think the product should be banned, how would you do it?

4. Make a critical case either defending or condemning Comedy Central's *South Park,* a TV talk show, professional wrestling, a hip-hop group, a soap opera, or TV news coverage of the 2001 terrorist attacks on the United States. Use the four-step critical process to develop your position.

5. Although in some ways postmodern forms of communication, such as e-mail, MTV, and CNN, have helped citizens participate in global life, in what ways might these forms harm more traditional or native cultures?

SEARCHING THE INTERNET

http://www.mediahistory.umn.edu

Hosted by the University of Minnesota, the Media History Project was founded to discover and understand trends in practices in various media. You'll find information about media research and theory, historical time lines, key terms and concepts, and links to related sites.

http://www.aml.ca

Canada's Association for Media Literacy offers a site designed to teach students and citizens about the significance of media education. Broadly international in flavor, this site tracks the worldwide media literacy movement, offering notes and summaries from a variety of conferences and panels.

http://www.mediaed.org

The Media Education Foundation site features a guide to critical video resources, study guides, current articles, free catalogue, and job/internship information.

http://www.media-awareness.ca

The Media Awareness Network is another cutting-edge Canadian site, offering an array of critical strategies for teaching children and students how to deal with media. Featuring news about media developments and issues, the site also has specific ideas for teachers, students, parents, and community leaders.

http://www.acmecoalition.org

ACME—the Action Coalition for Media Education—offers this site that links citizens in working groups around issues such as media curriculum ideas for schools; support for independent and alternative media initiatives; support for media reform and legislative campaigns; and training in media education for students, parents, and community groups.

THE CRITICAL PROCESS

In Brief

Develop a model or metaphor for categorizing culture, other than the skyscraper model offered on page 16. How would your model help us better understand the ways in which culture works? Discuss your model.

In Depth

In small groups, or as a class, write the headings *Quality* and *Trash* on the board or on a sheet of paper. As a group, agree on several television shows that serve as examples of trashy programs and quality programs. In another column, if necessary, place any programs that are in dispute—those that may divide group opinion. (Films, books, magazines, and advertisements could be used here as well.) Your column headings should look like this:

> Quality   Trash   In Dispute

1. For each set of programs, gather information and evidence. On a separate piece of paper, *describe* the programs by listing their narrative features: basic plots, central conflicts or tensions, typical subject matter, major themes, main characters, and how tensions are resolved.

2. Now return to your listing of programs. Under each category, name and *analyze* the attributes that led your group to classify the programs as you did. Identify as many characteristics as you

can, and then summarize which virtues are essential to a quality show, which vices make a show trashy, and which elements make a particular show hard to classify.

3. Examine the patterns among the characteristics you have chosen, and *interpret* what this means. Why did you pick the characteristics you did for each category? Why did you associate particular features with quality or with trash? What made your disputed programs a problem for different members of your group? Why do some viewers (or readers) gravitate toward trashy shows? What might the programs mean to those audiences? For the programs you could not easily categorize, what led to their disputed standing?

4. *Evaluate* the programs on your lists. Assess whether these shows are good or bad for society. Should restrictions be placed on some programs even if this means testing the First Amendment protection of the press and free speech?

   Discuss the differences that were evident in your group between individual tastes and the critical standards used to make judgments. Are more categories needed to evaluate programs adequately? If so, what categories should be added?

   What standards did your group use to judge merit? Is there such a thing as a "good" trashy program? Give an example. Why is it important to make critical judgments of this kind?

KEY TERMS

the internet and new technologies

media at the crossroads

While the United States was busy with efforts to put the country on the information superhighway, other parts of the world bypassed the land highway and took to the air. Japan, Norway, Sweden, and Finland have become leaders among nations that never had a wired Internet structure as sophisticated as that of the United States but instead leapfrogged into the post-PC era by developing wireless Internet networks.

Cell phones—not desktop or laptop computers—are the central user device of wireless Internet networks and have become everyday technology, especially in Scandinavia, home to major cell phone manufacturers Ericsson (headquartered in Sweden) and Nokia (located in Finland). In fact, Finland has the highest rate of mobile phone use in the world—involving more than 75 percent of the population, compared with about 45 percent in the United States. Mobile phones are nearly essential equipment to Finnish teens, who access the Internet to check sports scores, order train tickets, and—by typing quickly on the tiny built-in keyboard—send

2

short instant messages to their friends. In Finland and elsewhere in Europe, mobile phones are also beginning to double as credit cards, enabling mobile phone users to pay at cash registers by pushing a button on their phone instead of swiping a plastic credit card.

The development of mobile phone networks in Europe contrasts with the U.S. experience. In the United States, federal regulations have permitted several cell phone standards to be deployed, but with the effect of prohibiting roaming cell phone customers from being able to freely use their phones outside of the patchwork regions serviced by their company. Europe is united by a single mobile phone standard (GSM, which stands for Global System for Mobile Communications), meaning the phones work across all borders. Moreover, in Europe cell phones are often less expensive than those that rely on land telephone lines; this explains why by 2002, two out of three Europeans owned a mobile phone.

Although Europe's wireless networks are further along than those in the United States, they are still a few years away from the Internet-connected mobile communicators of the future. Considered to be the *third generation (3G)* of phone networks, the pocket-size mobile communicators—already introduced in Japan—enable users to download and play music, take and send digital snapshots, retrieve data from fixed computers, and still make old-fashioned voice phone calls. But to get to the proposed global wireless Internet network with an enormous array of 3G services, the world will have to give up first-generation analog telephones—still widely in use—and the comparatively primitive second-generation digital cell phones, which are still growing in popularity.

Meanwhile, the United States and Europe both lag behind South Korea in rates of adoption of high-speed, broadband Internet service, typically made through cable systems, DSL (digital subscriber line) telephone lines, or satellite connections. Broadband connections are the next generation of computer-based Internet service; they enable faster downloads, synchronous online multi-user games, and uninterrupted streaming media. Although about 10 percent of U.S. households have high-speed Internet access—better than the average of 3 percent of households in Europe—South Korea's national effort since 1998 to deploy broadband networks connected 57 percent of the country's households by 2002, making Korea the enviable global leader in broadband.

the **Internet**—the vast network of telephone and cable lines and satellite systems designed to link and carry computer information worldwide—has often been described as an *information highway*. Imagine the traditional media—books, newspapers, television, and radio—as an older interstate highway system now intersected by a sprawling, poorly planned major freeway system (the Internet), much of which is still under construction and is fed by thousands of new capillary roads, some paved, some dirt, some extending into remote locations around the globe. In addition, many side roads along the highway are virtually unregulated, open to all kinds of opportunities and mischief.

Unlike interstate highways built by federal and state governments, however, the information highway has been taken over and expanded by private enterprise, although it was initially established and subsidized by the government. What difference will this make? If we look to the history of another medium, we know that when private commercial managers took over radio broadcasting in the 1920s and 1930s, they helped build the United States into the world's foremost producer of communication technology and content. At the same time, though, they dramatically thwarted the growth of nonprofit and educational broadcasting.

The full impact of the Internet and the expanding information highway, like that of all emerging mass media, will evolve over time. Cable TV, for example, which operated in only 13 percent of American households in 1975, took nearly twenty years to reach 60 percent of U.S. homes. As a mass medium, the Internet has had a much more rapid ascent: More than 61 percent of U.S. households were connected to the Internet by 2002, just ten years after the introduction of the first World Wide Web browsers.

Unlike cable and earlier mass media, the Internet is also unique in that there is no limit on how large its databases of content can grow. Although it's difficult to fully assess how the Internet will change the world, it was very clear after the September 11, 2001, terrorist attacks on the United States how ingrained the Internet is in global economies, politics, and cultures. Millions around the world turned to the Internet that day to find information on the attacks and communicate with others. Later, it became clear that at the same time that Internet access has helped relief agencies in aiding victims of terror, it has also served as a covert message conduit for global terrorism.

The Internet remains a major medium for the global economy. But the slowing of the dot-com business world in 2000 and the September 11 attacks a year later have led to a new caution about the Internet. On October 26, 2001, the United States enacted a new antiterrorism law—called the USA Patriot Act—that granted sweeping new powers to law enforcement agencies for intercepting computer communications, including e-mail messages and Web browsing. Other nations were expected to follow the United States' lead on increasing Internet surveillance. Although some provisions of the law expire in four years, the debate over security measures versus civil liberties will continue to shape communication on the Internet and in the entire world for years to come.

In later chapters we will explore the impact of traditional media such as books, radio, and television—and how they evolved to their current state. But first we will analyze the ongoing Internet revolution, as we both witness and participate in the emergence of this dynamic medium. As governments, corporations, and public and private interests vie to shape the evolution of this new medium, answers to many questions remain ambiguous. Who will have access to the Internet, and who will be left behind? Who or what will manage the Internet, and what are the implications for the future and for democracy?

> **❝ This unfathomable tragedy [of September 11, 2001] reminds me of the original reason the Internet was invented in 1969—to serve as a decentralized network that couldn't be brought down by a military attack. ❞**
>
> —Rogers Cadenhead, creator of the "WTCattack" mailing list on Yahoo!, September 2001

The task for critical media consumers is to sort through competing predictions about the Internet and new technology, analyzing and determining how the "new and improved" Information Age can best serve the majority of citizens and communities.

Origins of the Internet

Although many branches of the Internet still resemble dirt roads on the information highway, the rapid technological advances that accompany the new routes pose a major challenge to cable TV and to the more traditional media. From its humble origins as an attack-proof military communications network in the 1960s, the Internet had become increasingly interactive by the 1990s, allowing immediate two-way communication (like telephones) and one-to-many communication (like radio and television) between senders and receivers of media messages. With its ability to transport both personal conversation and mass communication, the Internet has begun to break down conventional distinctions among various media and between private and public modes of communication.

The Evolution of a New Mass Medium

The term *Industrial Age* usually refers to the period spanning the development of the steam engine in the 1760s to mass assembly-line production in the 1900s, an era that transformed manufacturing and consumer culture. By a similar measuring stick, the *Information Age* has barely begun. It has passed through an early phase marked by broadcasting to a phase that features the convergence of personal computers, telephone lines, electronic mail, cable television, and communication satellites.

Most mass media evolve through various stages, which are initiated not only by the diligence of great inventors, such as Thomas Edison, but by social, cultural, political, and economic circumstances. For instance, both telegraph and radio developed as newly industrialized nations sought to expand military and economic control over colonies and to transmit information more rapidly. The phonograph, too,

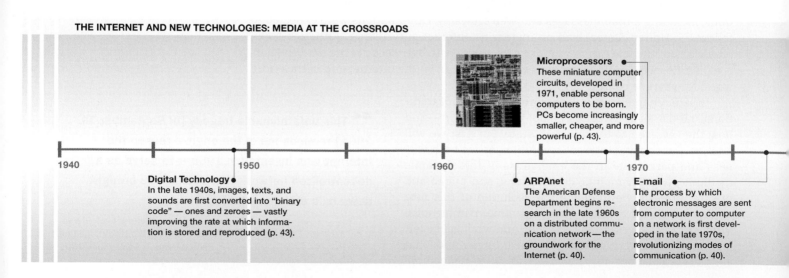

THE INTERNET AND NEW TECHNOLOGIES: MEDIA AT THE CROSSROADS

Microprocessors
These miniature computer circuits, developed in 1971, enable personal computers to be born. PCs become increasingly smaller, cheaper, and more powerful (p. 43).

1940   1950   1960   1970

Digital Technology
In the late 1940s, images, texts, and sounds are first converted into "binary code" — ones and zeroes — vastly improving the rate at which information is stored and reproduced (p. 43).

ARPAnet
The American Defense Department begins research in the late 1960s on a distributed communication network—the groundwork for the Internet (p. 40).

E-mail
The process by which electronic messages are sent from computer to computer on a network is first developed in the late 1970s, revolutionizing modes of communication (p. 40).

emerged because of the social and economic conditions of a growing middle class with more money and leisure time. Today, the information highway is a contemporary response to similar sets of concerns: transporting messages more rapidly while appealing to middle- and upper-middle-class consumers.

Typically, media innovations emerge in three stages. First is the *novelty* or *development stage* in which inventors and technicians try to solve a particular problem, such as making pictures move, transmitting voices through the air without wires, or sending mail electronically. Second is the *entrepreneurial stage* in which inventors and investors determine a practical and marketable use for the new device. For example, early radio or wireless technology relayed messages to and from places where telegraph wires and cables could not go, such as military ships at sea. Part of the information highway also had its roots in the ideas of military leaders who devised a communication system—now known as the Internet—that could survive nuclear wars or natural disasters.

The third phase in a new medium's development involves a breakthrough to the *mass-medium stage*. At this point, businesses figure out how to market the new device as an appealing product for home or office. Although the government and the navy played a central role in radio's early years, it was commercial entrepreneurs who eventually took radio into its broadcasting phase, where it began reaching millions of people. In the same way, Pentagon and government researchers developed the prototype for the Internet, but commercial interests began taking over, extending its reach nationally and globally. With the release of the World Wide Web in 1991, and the introduction of user-friendly graphic browsers like Mosaic in 1993 and Netscape in 1994, the Internet entered its mass-medium stage.

By the late 1980s and 1990s, online computer services and the Internet had begun featuring all sorts of mass-communication—and advertising—services and marketing them through computers, modems, and phone lines. Following this innovation, the Internet grew rapidly, becoming "the most wide-ranging interactive mass medium in history."[1] By 2002, about 460 million people worldwide (roughly 165 million of them in the United States) used the Internet regularly, with two new subscribers joining every second. Global Internet use is expected to rise to 850 million by 2004.[2]

> " The medium, or process, of our time—electric technology—is reshaping and restructuring patterns of social interdependence and every aspect of our personal life. "
>
> –Marshall McLuhan, 1967

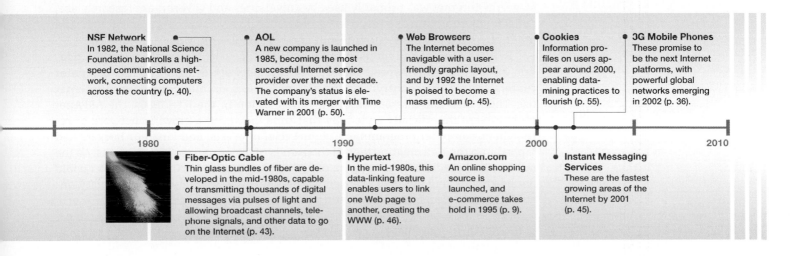

NSF Network
In 1982, the National Science Foundation bankrolls a high-speed communications network, connecting computers across the country (p. 40).

AOL
A new company is launched in 1985, becoming the most successful Internet service provider over the next decade. The company's status is elevated with its merger with Time Warner in 2001 (p. 50).

Web Browsers
The Internet becomes navigable with a user-friendly graphic layout, and by 1992 the Internet is poised to become a mass medium (p. 45).

Cookies
Information profiles on users appear around 2000, enabling data-mining practices to flourish (p. 55).

3G Mobile Phones
These promise to be the next Internet platforms, with powerful global networks emerging in 2002 (p. 36).

1980 1990 2000 2010

Fiber-Optic Cable
Thin glass bundles of fiber are developed in the mid-1980s, capable of transmitting thousands of digital messages via pulses of light and allowing broadcast channels, telephone signals, and other data to go on the Internet (p. 43).

Hypertext
In the mid-1980s, this data-linking feature enables users to link one Web page to another, creating the WWW (p. 46).

Amazon.com
An online shopping source is launched, and e-commerce takes hold in 1995 (p. 9).

Instant Messaging Services
These are the fastest growing areas of the Internet by 2001 (p. 45).

The Birth and Growth of the Internet

The real national highway system and the contemporary information highway have similar military origins. During the Eisenhower administration in the 1950s, military and government leaders originally planned an interstate highway grid to make transporting military vehicles across the country easier in the event of a national emergency. An interconnected network of freeways enabled a driver to take several different routes to get from point A to point B in the continental United States. Like the national highway system, the Internet originated with military-government planning and with national security as one of its goals. Begun in the late 1960s by the Defense Department's Advanced Research Projects Agency (ARPA), the original Internet—called **ARPAnet** and nicknamed the Net—enabled military and academic researchers to communicate on a distributed network system (see Figure 2.1). The network design of what would become the Internet differed from the centralized style of telephone communication at the time, whereby calls were routed through a central switcher. A distributed network system offered two advantages to the researchers and military units developing the Net. First, because multiple paths linked one computer site to another, communications "traffic" would be less likely to get clogged at a single point. This helped convince computer researchers in the 1960s to sign on to the network project—they could share research and data on the new network without their computers becoming overrun by the traffic of others' messages. Second, because the network was like an interconnected web, the Internet offered a communication system that was more impervious to technical screwups, natural disasters, or military attacks. If a "bridge" was out on one "road" of the highway, Net traffic could take another path.

In developing one of the Net prototypes for the military, the Rand Corporation, a Cold War think tank, conceptualized a communications network that had no central authority. Ironically, one of the most hierarchically structured and centrally organized institutions in our culture, the national defense industry, created the Internet, possibly the least hierarchical and most decentralized social network ever conceived. Each computer hub in the Internet has similar status and power, so nobody can own the system outright and nobody has the power to kick others off the network. There isn't even a master power switch, so authority figures cannot shut off the Internet during an emergency.

During its developmental stage, the military computer network permitted different people in separate locations to communicate with one another. By simply leasing existing telephone lines, they used the system to send *e-mail* and to post information on computer *bulletin boards,* sites that listed information about particular topics such as health issues, computer programs, or employment services. At this stage, the Internet was primarily used by universities and government research labs, and later by corporations—especially companies involved in computer software and other high-tech products—to transmit and receive text information.

By 1982, the Net had hit its entrepreneurial stage: The National Science Foundation invested in a high-speed communications network designed to link computer centers around the country. This innovation led to a dramatic increase in Internet use. Then, after the dissolution of the Soviet Union in the late 1980s, the ARPAnet military venture officially ended. By that time, however, a growing network of researchers, computer programmers, commercial interests, and amateur hackers had tapped into the Net, creating tens of thousands of decentralized intersections. As the military had predicted, the absence of a central authority meant that the Net could not be knocked out. By 1993, the Net had developed basic multimedia capability, enabling users to transmit pictures, sound, and video.

Just as most radio pioneers did not foresee the potential of radio, many pioneers of the Net did not predict how rapidly its mass appeal would spread beyond national

Figure 2.1 Distributed Networks

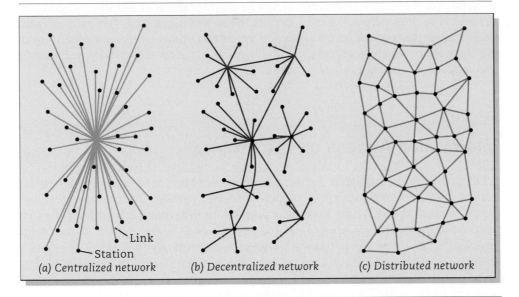

Link
Station
(a) Centralized network   (b) Decentralized network   (c) Distributed network

Source: Katie Hafner and Matthew Lyon, *Where Wizards Stay Up Late* (New York: Simon & Schuster, 1996).

Paul Baran, a young computer scientist at the Rand Corporation in the Cold War era, worked on developing a national communication system that could survive a nuclear attack. Centralized networks (a) are vulnerable because all the paths lead to a single nerve center. Decentralized networks (b) are less vulnerable because they contain several main nerve centers (our long-distance phone system today is mostly decentralized). But in a distributed network (c), which resembles a net, there are no nerve centers; if any connection is severed, information can be immediately rerouted and delivered to its destination.

and military interests. The Internet system comprises worldwide computer networks that communicate directly through Internet Protocol (IP), a computer language that allows any computer on any network to send data electronically to any other computer on an equal basis.[3] By 2002, the worldwide Internet consisted of more than 120 million hosts—computers also known as **servers**, which are run by individuals, universities, corporations, and government agencies. The hosts serve as entry points for Internet traffic and are interconnected by special high-speed data lines.

The Net allows users to find information on virtually any subject, to talk with computer pen pals all over the world, and to participate in discussions about favorite hobbies and social issues. Over the Net, users can also trade software, organize clubs, play games, arrange dates, find internships, and download articles, documents, and books. In the beginning, such connections took place in **newsgroups**, which now account for tens of thousands of loosely organized computer conferences that consist of bulletin boards and individual messages, or postings, which are circulated to subscribers twenty-four hours a day.

During the 1990s the number of Internet users doubled each year, and this growth drew the attention of commercial interests. Companies have found ways to profit from the increased traffic on the Internet, turning users into consumers by offering product information, selling products, providing services, and selling advertising space. With a computer and an Internet connection, users can go online to purchase a CD, search for hotels in Paris, sell a stock, or buy a car—all in the same afternoon.

Governments have established an Internet presence as well, providing information online, posting important documents, and distributing such items as tax forms. In the United States, the Internet has been heralded for embracing the public's right-to-know, with thousands of government documents posted for easy public access. However, after September 11, 2001, that effort was severely curtailed, as the U.S. government moved to restrict

> **"** The Internet . . . works like a nonprofit food co-op; it has no owner, is managed by volunteers, and derives operating costs from its members, who pay connection fees to large regional computer hubs that direct the system's traffic. **"**
>
> **–Steve Stecklow,**
> ***Wall Street Journal*, 1993**

seemingly benign public information such as Clean Air Act reports on industrial sites, for fear that such information would be used for terrorist purposes. Elsewhere, in nations such as China, the world's millions of Net users have generally circumvented attempts to block certain information. In fact, many users take advantage of the Net's ability to cross borders, circulating banned or controversial writing or art that may have been suppressed by authoritarian governments.

Information Access on the Internet

What generally distinguishes the Internet from older media is not only the revolutionary ways in which data are stored and retrieved but also the increasing convergence of mass media. Three innovations make the Internet a particularly distinct mass medium, offering unprecedented opportunities to communicate. First, it is interactive, enabling receivers to respond almost immediately to senders' messages. Prior to the digital age, traditional print media had few feedback avenues, relying mainly on letters to the editor, which might or might not be acknowledged. Now, however, online editors can respond more quickly to thousands of individual users. Whereas magazine and newspaper editors have traditionally restricted the number of letters they print due to space limitations, the information highway makes it possible to post most feedback letters.

The second way in which the Internet is innovative is that it enables many traditional media to appear on computer screens. Users can call up a magazine story, a music video, a banned book, or a radical newsletter. Previously, one mass-media company delivered a product—a newspaper or a TV program—to a mass audience. Now, however, the Internet multiplies the channels of delivery, thus transforming consumers' traditional interactions with the mass media. The Internet not only connects consumers to other media but also personalizes this experience by enabling them to call up mass media on demand.

Third, the Internet allows individuals to create and distribute their own messages. More easily than other media, the Internet enables people to become producers rather than just consumers of media content. For example, the cost of owning and operating a television station or newspaper is prohibitive for most people, but the cost of buying a computer, a modem, and Internet access is relatively modest. In addition, because the Internet is decentralized and unhierarchical, there are no gatekeepers to prevent individuals from creating and displaying their own messages. The Internet is inherently democratic and messy. Anyone can use it to express his or her ideas, and all ideas seem functionally equal: An individual's home page sits shoulder-to-shoulder with the home pages of billion-dollar corporations, research universities, and national governments.

Technological Breakthroughs and Converging Media

The information highway has blurred the boundary between point-to-point communication and mass communication. The highway has linked home, school, and business computers, TV sets, radios, CD and DVD recorders and players, VCRs, digital cameras, e-mail, video games, scanners, newspapers, fax machines, magazines, and communications satellites. This capability makes it possible for anyone to become a player on the information highway—from cable TV companies and regional telephone providers to computer-software firms and individual entrepreneurs. But the new convergences have had the greatest impact on two communications media—the telephone and the personal computer—that developed primarily as forms of

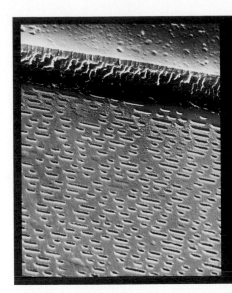

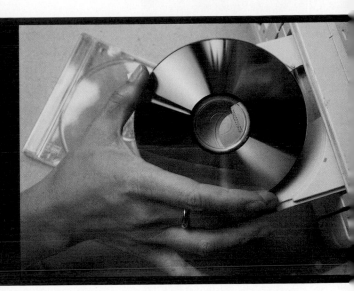

This microphoto of a common object, a compact disc, is magnified at 1,500 times its original size. CDs are made of plastic, pressed with a series of fine depressions (yellow/red dashes) representing a digitized musical signal that is read by a laser. To reflect the laser light, the music layer is coated with an invisible film of metal that follows the depressions.

point-to-point or personal communication, not as mass communication. Both, however, have become central players in the Information Age and mass-communication revolutions.

Three key technological developments have made possible today's intersection of mass media along the information highway. The first innovation involved **digital communication**, which was central to the development of the first computers in the 1940s. In digital technology an image, text, or sound is converted into electronic signals represented as a series of binary numbers—ones and zeros—which are then reassembled as a precise reproduction of an image, text, or sound. Digital signals operate as pieces, or bits (from BInary digiTS), of information representing two values, such as yes/no, on/off, or 0/1. For example, a typical compact-disc track uses a binary-code system in which zeros are microscopic pits in the surface of the disc and ones are represented on the unpitted surface. Used in various combinations, these digital codes can duplicate, store, and play back the most complex kinds of media content.

The second technological breakthrough occurred in 1971 with the introduction of **microprocessors**, miniature circuits that can process and store electronic signals. This innovation facilitated the integration of thousands of transistors and related circuitry into thin strands of silicon along which binary codes traveled. With this innovation, manufacturers were able to introduce the first personal computers (PCs), relatively inexpensive machines that consumers could purchase for home use. PCs were smaller, cheaper, and increasingly more powerful and were no longer just a tool for the office. According to Moore's Law (coined in 1965 by Gordon Moore, a former chairman of Intel, which is a leading builder of microprocessors), computer-chip power doubles about every eighteen months. Because of microtechnology, a single PC that now fits on an individual's lap is more than 400,000 times more powerful than the bulky computer systems that occupied entire floors of office buildings during the 1960s.[4] In addition, even as computing power has increased, the cost of personal computers has dropped dramatically in the last fifteen years, allowing more consumers to purchase them for home use.

In the mid-1980s, the third technological development, **fiber-optic cable**, featured thin glass bundles of fiber capable of transmitting thousands of messages that had been digitally converted into shooting pulses of light. Fiber-optic technology has allowed information to be transported via lasers. With their ability to carry broadcast channels, telephone signals, and all sorts of digital codes, thin fiber-optic cables

> **❝ You can never be too rich, too thin, or have too much bandwidth. ❞**
>
> *– Wall Street Journal headline, 2000*

● Fiber-optic laser beams carry more than 150,000 times as much information as do older copper phone wire and coaxial TV cables. About forty fiber-optic strands together can carry more than a million digitally compressed telephone conversations, or two thousand cable TV channels.

began replacing the older, bulkier copper wire used by phone and cable companies. Nicholas Negroponte, the founding director of MIT's Media Lab, points out that "a fiber the size of a human hair can deliver every issue ever made of the *Wall Street Journal* in less than one second."[5] With the increased speeds of the new media technology, few limits exist with regard to the amount of information that digital technology can transport. The chief problems now center around what to put on the information highway, who will run it, and who will have access.

Media Convergence and Content Accessibility

Digital technology now permits multiple and immediate computer access to traditional media such as newspapers, magazines, television programs, movies, and sound recordings. As noted in Chapter 1, this phenomenon is called *media convergence*, whereby old and new media are available via the integration of personal computers, high-speed data links, and digital storage formats. For example, multimedia content—mixing audio, video, and data—can be delivered in a number of forms, including through telephone lines, high-bandwidth cable, and digital satellite services.

The multimedia format brings an unprecedented number of content choices and styles to the user, all at once. For example, an Internet site like ESPN.com carries the latest sports scores and full-length text reports on games, streams live audio from sources like ESPN Radio, and offers downloadable video highlights of sporting events. It's also the place to purchase ESPN sportswear and participate in scheduled live chats with sports personalities. Similarly, a multimedia CD-ROM like the *Encyclopaedia Britannica* offers more than seventy-eight thousand articles, three hours of video and two hours of sound samples, a full built-in dictionary, and thousands of hypertext links to Internet sources, including *Encyclopaedia Britannica*'s own continuously updated Web site. Thus an entry on rock and roll's 1964 "British invasion" is able to present text-based articles on groups like the Beatles, the Kinks, the Who, and the Rolling Stones, samples of songs, sound effects of screaming crowds, picture albums of mod 1960s clothing, and interactive flow charts delineating several groups' musical influences.

Once created or received, the digital content can be stored in a number of formats that are widely available. A word-processed school paper can easily be stored on a traditional 3.5-inch high-density disk. A whole semester's worth of papers can be stored on a Zip disk, which holds about seventy times more information than a high-density disk. A Zip disk can also hold audio samples, or even a short video clip. For other multimedia content, a **CD-ROM** holds as much information as seven hundred conventional disks. However, CD-ROM stands for compact-disc read-only memory, and users cannot enter or store new data. Although CD-ROMs are the preferred format for stored data such as encyclopedias, music recordings, video games, and software programs, a new generation of CDs released in the 1990s—called **CD-Rs** (recordable) and **CD-RWs** (rewriteable)—allows users to put their own content on CDs.

The greatest leap in digital storage comes with the **DVD** (digital versatile disc), which made its retail debut in 1997. The DVD uses digital compression to store a great deal of information—enough space for a two-hour Hollywood movie—on a disk that looks similar to a standard CD. The DVD is the successor to the home VCR for playing movie rentals, because it offers higher resolution and never needs to be rewound. Like the CD, the DVD has become recordable and rewriteable, which allows it to branch out from home-entertainment uses to include business and computer storage. Because of its greater storage capabilities—from twelve to twenty-six times the space of compact discs—the DVD is expected to eventually surpass CDs as the medium for video and music releases, home recording, and file storage.

Add to this mix digital audiotapes (DATs) and CD mini-discs for audio projects, digital still and video cameras, scanners, and free media players that can be downloaded from the Web, and it becomes clear that people have a formidable array of tools for experiencing and creating media convergence. Equipment and functionality that were once available only to media professionals are now available to the general public at much more affordable prices.

Mapping the Internet

One of the major problems of the information highway, especially Internet intersections, has been its complexity and disorganization. Originally lacking any basic directory services, the networks were like an enormous free-floating library without a Dewey decimal system. This situation has changed. Five major mapping systems currently exist for negotiating the Internet's sprawling terrain. We will consider each in turn. The first map is implemented by commercial **Internet service providers**, such as America Online (AOL), EarthLink, Prodigy, and the Microsoft Network, which bring the Internet into people's homes, schools, and offices. A second mapping system features the **World Wide Web**, initially a free and open system for organizing and standardizing communication on the Internet. The Web moved the Internet from a message-delivery system to an easy-to-navigate mass medium. At the third mapping level are Web **browsers**, software environments that help users navigate the Web. A fourth mapping system developed with Web **search engines** and **directories**, which help users to find the right Web sites among the millions available. The most recent mapping system—**instant messaging services**—links friends in a real-time social environment by creating a personal network of "buddies" on the Internet.

Internet Service Providers

Although many individuals access the Internet through their university or business accounts, home users often purchase a commercial online service, also called an Internet service provider (ISP). The largest by far is America Online (AOL), which began in the 1980s and struck a merger with the world's largest media company, Time Warner, in 2000, making an even more dominant media corporation. By 2003,

● Sports sites are among the most popular on the World Wide Web. This site, the Duke Basketball Report, covers the Duke University men's basketball team and is one of the most visited college fan sites.

DUKE *BASKETBALL REPORT*

HEADLINES FEATURES FUN STUFF SCHEDULES LINKS ARCHIVES **MY** DBR

Wake Scores 81 - In The First Half 11/08/01 02:05

Feinstein, The Baltimore Sun, Preview Season 11/08/01 02:03

Let The Season Begin! 11/08/01 02:02

Clint & Co. On Nasty Boys & Team Swish 11/08/01 00:34

ACC Preview # 6 - Maryland 11/08/01 00:18

Sunday Is Big Time For Women's Hoops

Let The Season Begin!
November 08, 2001

Here's the first article we've seen - that we haven't written anyway - professing some skepticism about Maryland this season.   It focuses more on Duke-Maryland than Maryland in general, but nonetheless, it does touch on what we think are the key questions - how does Maryland replace Terence Morris and Danny Miller, and will Byron Mouton be able to step up to that challenge?

FULL STORY

> **"** In less than three years, the Internet's World Wide Web has spawned some 10 million electronic documents at a quarter million Web sites. By contrast, the Library of Congress has taken 195 years to collect 14 million books. **"**
>
> –Tim Miller, New Media Resources, 1995

AOL had more than 37 million subscribers, more than five times the number of its nearest competitors. In addition to providing access to the Internet, AOL offers its own search engine, an AOL instant messenger service, and an online shopping mall. Other major online services include EarthLink, which was established in 1994; CompuServe, purchased in the late 1970s by the tax firm H&R Block and acquired by AOL in 1997; and Prodigy, originated by IBM and Sears in the late 1980s and bought by the giant regional telephone company SBC Communications in 2000. The computer-software giant Microsoft entered the ISP business in 1995, with the Microsoft Network (MSN). Alongside the national online services, hundreds of local services, many of them operated by regional telephone companies, compete to offer consumers access to the Internet. Free ISPs, such as Juno and NetZero, have also gained popularity in recent years and derive revenue from targeting advertising at registered users.

The World Wide Web

By the early 1990s, the World Wide Web had become the most frequently visited region of the Internet (other regions of the Net include e-mail service and Usenet discussion groups, such as alt.tv.talkshows). Developed in the 1980s by software engineer Tim Berners-Lee, the Web was initially a text-only data-linking system that allowed computer-accessed information to associate with, or link to, other information no matter where it was on the Internet. Known as *hypertext*, this data-linking feature of the Web was a breakthrough for those attempting to use the Internet. Hypertext is a nonlinear way of organizing information, enabling a user to click on a highlighted word, phrase, picture, or icon and skip directly to other files related to that subject in other computer systems.

By using standardized software, today users can navigate through most features of the Internet, including text data such as e-mail, photo-image files, and video and audio clips. **HTML (HyperText Markup Language)**, the written code that creates Web pages and links, is a language that all computers can read, so computers with varying operating systems, such as Windows and Macintosh, can communicate easily. *Java*, an HTML-compatible language developed by Sun Microsystems in the mid-1990s, is also universally readable by computers and allows small interactive programs to run on Web pages, creating moving graphic elements such as three-dimensional animations and menus that pop up as a mouse pointer passes over them. XHTML, a new form of HTML first released in 2000, is designed to bring graphically rich Web pages to small-device platforms such as cell phones, palm-top computers, and cars.

The millions of "pages," or sites, on the Web communicate everything from a point of view to a job résumé to a wide variety of consumer products. A Web page can be designed on an ordinary word-processing program that has a feature for writing hypertext commands. Almost all national TV commercials now include the product's Web-site address, where more information about a company or its product can be found. The number of sites on the Web jumped from just 130 in 1993 to more than 38 million in 2002.[6]

Web Browsers

The software packages that help users navigate the Web are called Web browsers. The most popular browsers, Netscape's Communicator and Microsoft's Internet Explorer (which displaced Netscape as the most popular browser in 1998, leading to further criticisms about Microsoft's industry dominance), handle Web files and links, and translate them into a more user-friendly graphic layout. Popular commercial ISPs such as America Online and MSN TV (formerly WebTV) offer their own built-in browser environments. There are also a number of lesser-known free Web-browser alternatives, including Opera, Mozilla, and NeoPlanet.

Search Engines and Directories

Browsers display the Web on your computer screen, but how do you find the appropriate pages to visit? Directories are one of the original methods to find your way around the Web; they rely on people to review and catalogue Web sites, creating categories with hierarchical topic structures that can be browsed. Search engines and directories such as Yahoo!, LookSmart, and Ask Jeeves maintain staffs of paid editors to review the sites, whereas open directory projects at Netscape and Lycos depend on volunteer Net citizens from around the world to maintain certain topic areas. Search engines offer a different route to finding content by allowing users to enter key words or queries to locate related Web pages.

Search engines work in three different ways. Some, such as Lycos and Yahoo!, return search information from their directory catalogues. Although cataloguing engines may not return as many Web sites for each search request, chances are that the sites provided will be more relevant to the search terms. Others, such as AltaVista or HotBot, send out computer "spider" programs that automatically visit and record site data, creating huge but somewhat unfiltered lists for searches. Google provides a more precise automated search engine that mathematically ranks Web pages' "popularity" based on how many other pages are linked to them. Finally, metasearch engines, such as DogPile or Metacrawler, search across multiple search engines, often ending up with the widest range of results.

Because search engines are popular entry points, or *portals*, to the Web, the home pages of search engines now offer not only a search button but also several "channels" that provide shortcuts to the day's news stories, up-to-the-minute sports scores, and links to advertisers' Web sites. The idea behind these channels is to keep users connected to the search engine site for as long as possible and thus be able to offer an attentive audience to Web advertisers.[7] The channel locations on the search engines' Web pages are also typically paid for by the content providers, creating

> **"** We want to be the only place someone has to go to find anything or get connected to anyone. **"**
>
> **– Jeff Mallett,**
> **Yahoo!'s president**
> **and CEO, 1999**

another revenue stream for search engine sites. In the pursuit of greater revenue, most search engines have compromised their usefulness as locators of Web content. By accepting payment for listing certain Web sites at the top of a result list—and not notifying users of this practice—search engines are increasingly ensuring that the best-financed sites on the Web get the most visitors, whereas non-profit Web sites that can't afford priority placement become increasingly marginalized. Although this practice generates funds for commercial search engines, it does not bode well for search engines as research tools for the Web (see "Applied Critical Process: The Search Engine Sell-Out" on page 49). At present, there are no search engines that operate in the nonprofit sphere.

Instant Messaging Services

The Internet's trendiest and fastest-growing feature since the late 1990s is instant messaging, or IM. Users assemble personalized buddy lists of sometimes more than one hundred people, and depending on who is also online at a certain moment, they can chat with their buddies in real time. Messages tend to be short and conversational, with one small window assigned to each buddy and with users often negotiating up to twenty conversations at a time. Although instant messaging can organize immediate Web conversations among co-workers or family members, its most popular use is as an extended social scene among twelve- to nineteen-year-olds, who log on after school and chat for hours with their friends. By far the most dominant instant message service is AOL Instant Messenger (AIM), which in 2002 had more than twice as many subscribers as its nearest rival, MSN. AOL purchased instant messenger service ICQ, which became the model for AIM, in 1998. Together with ICQ, which continues to dominate instant messaging in Europe, AOL boasts more than 180 million worldwide IM subscribers. Because AOL and ICQ prohibit their users from exchanging messages with competing IM systems, such as Microsoft's MSN Messenger Service and Yahoo!'s Messenger, AOL has been under considerable

The Search Engine Sell-Out

Given that search engines are becoming increasingly commercialized and are using covert and not-so-covert methods to promote sponsored Web sites, we want to know if commercialization affects Web search engine results.

Description. We've chosen Google and Overture for our research on the "University of Michigan" (our search term). Our aim is to find Web sites that take us to the University's main page and/or tell us something about the institution. In examining the first ten results of Google versus the first ten results of Overture, we found that Google listed "The University of Michigan" <www.umich.edu> first, followed by other Web sites connected to the institution, including its weather service, the library, a number of departments, and the school newspaper. Overture's first ten results all featured e-commerce sites, including U of M Neon Signs, SportsFan products, U of M jewelry, U of M car tags, U of M blankets, a commercial graduate school service, and an alumni registry.

Analysis. What sort of patterns emerge here? The first page (first ten results) of Google reflects the topic we're looking for. The first page of Overture reflects commercial priorities, but doesn't lead us to any actual University of Michigan sites.

Interpretation. The two search engines have different searching methods. Google prioritizes sites based on the number of links to that site from other pages. Overture prioritizes Web sites according to the highest bidder. Overture is open about its highest-bidder practices, detailing its paid placement strategies on its home page. Since research has indicated that most people don't go beyond the first two or three pages of a search engine list (with many not going past the first page), this has ramifications about the availability of nonprofit Web sites to those using most search engines.

Evaluation. Are the results of search engines with paid placement of listings acceptable or unacceptable? Overture is up front about its commercial priorities, but an increasing number of search engines (e.g., Lycos, AltaVista, MSN, Yahoo!) are using Overture to power their searches without acknowledging its paid placement practices. Is it ethical for search engines to use paid placement in their search results without clear disclosure?

attack for exhibiting monopolistic tendencies. The fight, from Microsoft's and Yahoo!'s perspective, is worth fighting: Instant messaging is one of the Internet's "stickiest" portal services, with users tending to remain on the same advertising-strewn screen for hours. IM message windows also operate as full-service portals, providing buttons linking users to their e-mail, news briefs, and Web search engines. In addition, IM users fill out detailed profiles when signing up for the service, providing advertisers with multiple ways to target them as they chat with their friends.

Ownership Issues on the Internet

The contemporary era is distinguished not only by the revolutionary ways in which data are transmitted but also by the increasing convergence of owners and players in mass-media industries. Large media firms, such as Disney, AOL Time Warner, and Microsoft, are buying up or investing in smaller companies and spreading their economic interests among books, magazines, music, movies, radio, television, cable, and Internet channels.

As with the automobile or film industries of an earlier era, many players and companies are jockeying for position. With the passage of the sweeping overhaul of the nation's communication regulations in the **Telecommunications Act of 1996**, most regional and long-distance phone companies now participate in both cable and Internet-access businesses. The phone companies, like cable TV firms, have the added advantage of controlling the wires into most American homes and businesses. As cable and phone companies gradually convert older wiring into high-speed fiber-optic lines, they are wrestling for control of Internet circuitry and intensifying the battle over mass-communication delivery systems.

Given the paucity of regulations governing the Internet industry, and the industry's rapid growth, it is not surprising to see a recent spate of mergers, joint ventures, consolidations, and power grabs. Although all of these mergers were an attempt to find a dominant position in the Information Age, some companies have loomed larger than others. Microsoft, for example, built a near-monopoly dominance of its Windows operating systems and Web-browser software throughout the 1990s. The U.S Department of Justice brought an antitrust lawsuit against Microsoft in 1997, arguing that it used its computer operating system dominance to sabotage its competitors. But Microsoft prevailed in 2001, when the Department of Justice dropped its efforts to break Microsoft into two independent companies.

Another powerful conglomerate, telephone giant AT&T, began to position itself as a one-stop communications company in the late 1990s, bringing telephone, Internet, cable service, and entertainment content to its customers across the country. First, AT&T acquired TCI, Inc., the largest cable-television system operator, in 1998, giving AT&T a direct cable link into millions of households. A few months later AT&T bought Excite, a leading Internet search engine and portal, and created a high-speed cable-based Internet service called Excite@Home. Then AT&T made a deal with Time Warner in 1999 to offer telephone service in thirty-three states over Time Warner's cable systems. The acquisition of MediaOne, another major cable company, in 2000 enabled AT&T to surpass its rival, Time Warner, in providing cable (and Internet) service to homes. However, by late 2000, AT&T's ambitious strategy of corporate convergence faltered under a crushing debt. It ultimately broke up the company into independent cable, wireless, business services, and long-distance companies, each one still bearing the AT&T brand.

Time Warner, too, expanded its cable television service to include a high-speed Internet service called Road Runner (after the familiar Warner Brothers cartoon character). But the huge company had limited success in developing an Internet presence through its now-defunct pathfinder.com site. Then, in 2000, the media conglomerate announced plans to become part of the Internet empire of America Online. As the world's largest Internet service provider, AOL had already expanded its operations by acquiring the Web-browser company Netscape in 1998. It also purchased the instant message service ICQ and emerged as the leading IM platform. AOL made other strategic investments in wireless, interactive television (including AOLTV), and marketing technologies.

The desire of corporations to tap into the Internet economy is clear. The increasing dominance of commercial interests on the Internet is affecting the way in which the information highway—once a nonprofit, government-subsidized medium known for freely accessible information—is evolving. Indeed, the phenomenon of a fifteen-year-old Internet start-up like AOL acquiring Time Warner, the world's largest media conglomerate, in 2000 certainly speaks to the power of the Internet in the twenty-first century. But, as the investors grew increasingly disappointed with AOL Time Warner's poor financial performance in the following years, it became clear that not all ambitious corporate strategies to cash in on the information highway would be successful.

The Privatization of the Internet

With many pathways along the information highway now dictated by corporate and commercial interests, critics predict that Internet programs in particular will increasingly favor those who have the money to develop content or technology. The favored ones are likely to be business firms and university research institutes, which depend on large corporations for funding. By 1994, several noncommercial university consortiums, which had been running regional computer hubs and Internet services, were selling the rights to manage their services to private corporations. Businesses maintain that they can provide improved services at affordable costs. Critics, however, warn that the increasing privatization of Internet services could threaten their continued development as a democratic network of relatively equal individuals and institutions.

The U.S. government has already privatized the assignment of **domain names**, which are the basic element of a Web site's address. From 1993 to 1998—the first five years of the Web's phenomenal growth—the United States' National Science Foundation supervised the assignment of World Wide Web domain names through a private contractor and gave rise to the now-familiar Web-name extensions (e.g., ".com," ".net," ".org," and ".edu"). In 1998, the U.S. government established a new international authority to administer and expand Net domain names—the Internet Corporation for Assigned Names and Numbers (ICANN)—which internationalized the assignment of domain names but also put this task in the hands of a private bureaucracy. In its first major act, ICANN created seven new top-level domain-name extensions in 2000: ".name" for personal Web sites, ".biz" for businesses, ".pro" for professionals such as doctors and lawyers, ".museum" for museums, ".aero" for airlines, ".coop" for business cooperatives, and ".info" for general use.

Further privatization is ensured for what is called **Internet2 (I2)**, the more advanced, second generation of the Internet, first deployed on an experimental basis in 1999 by a consortium of research universities and technology companies. Because it will support two-way interactive video, I2 will be coveted by businesses, which, among other benefits, will be able to use the technology to cut down on costly business travel through increased use of online meetings. I2 will also promote advanced interactive television technologies, steering future Internet use more toward a television model. Once again, the U.S. government is providing the seed money to start I2, but it will be controlled by commercial interests.

A Clash of Values

Discussing the economic implications of the information highway, critics Daniel Burstein and David Kline associate the Internet with a series of personality traits: "Free. Egalitarian. Decentralized. Ad hoc. Open and peer-to-peer. Experimental. Autonomous. Anarchic." They contrast these traits with the personality of modern business organizations: "For profit. Hierarchical. Systematized. Planned. Proprietary. Pragmatic. Accountable. Organized and reliable."[8] Given this clash of values, the development of the Internet should remain unstable and dynamic over the next several years, despite the attempts to commercialize access to the Net's vast regions. Unlike phone, movie, broadcast-network, and cable TV businesses, where ownership has become increasingly consolidated in the hands of a few powerful firms, many parts of the Internet have so far eluded centralization. In fact, the Internet is less likely to suffer from the same economic limitations of other mass media because it was not designed to be an efficiently managed, tightly controlled, and secure system.

An antiauthoritarian spirit resides in the Net, from the easily downloadable shareware and freeware to the work of self-described "hacktivists," who use their

● Linus Torvalds, the Finnish software developer, holds a license plate bearing the name of his invention, the Linux computer operating system. Since Torvalds's first version of Linux in 1991, hundreds of other developers around the world have contributed improvements to this open-source software rival of Microsoft's Windows. The penguin, below, is the Linux software icon.

hacker skills to bring political protest to the Internet.[9] Even though a 1999 study found that more than 83 percent of the Internet serves commercial purposes,[10] not all efforts to commercialize the Internet have been effective, and to a large extent the Internet ethos of free information is alive and well. The terrorism attacks of September 11, 2001, changed this to some extent, as subsequent antiterrorism laws included greater government surveillance of the Internet. Nevertheless, the free trade of information on the Internet continues.

Alternative Voices

As the information highway becomes increasingly jammed with commercial traffic and interests, the pioneering spirit of its early days endures. Microsoft has become the predominant corporation of the Information Age, but independent software creators persist in developing alternate visions of the information highway. One of the best examples of this is the development of **open-source software**. In the early days of computer code writing, amateur hackers collectively developed software on an open-source ethic, freely sharing the program source code and ideas to upgrade and improve programs. Beginning in the 1970s, Microsoft put an end to much of this activity by making software development a business in which programs were developed privately and users were required to pay for them—and all the necessary upgrades.

Some hackers are still developing noncommercial, open-source software. As Microsoft fought an antitrust lawsuit by the U.S. Justice Department between 1999 and 2001, some experts argued that Linux (pronounced linn-ucks), a free, open-source software operating system, might be a significant challenger to Windows.[11] Linux was established in 1991 by Linus Torvalds, a twenty-one-year-old student at the University of Helsinki. Since then, professional computer programmers and hobbyists around the world have e-mailed improvements back and forth, creating a sophisticated software system that even Microsoft has acknowledged is a credible alternative to expensive commercial programs. Because Linux can operate across disparate platforms, it is increasingly being seen as the Internet's future operating system. Companies like IBM, Dell, and Sun Microsystems have embraced Linux, and many major companies run their computer systems on Linux. Still, by 2002 the greatest impact of Linux was not on the PC desktops of everyday computer users, but instead on the operation of behind-the-scenes computer servers.

Another open-source movement involves software for **portals**, which creates a highly organized point-of-entry to the Web for a major site, such as that of a university. Not wanting to rely on commercial portal software that is supported, in part, by on-screen advertising banners, a number of colleges and universities joined forces in 2000 to develop an open-source and advertising-free equivalent, called uPortal. "We don't want the campus Web to look like a NASCAR race car," said an administrator from the University of Delaware, one of the schools involved in the project.[12]

The Linux and uPortal developers illustrate that although the information highway has become a mass medium, it is evolving in such an open way that a small number of individuals can still make an enormous impact and compete with even the largest of corporations.

Free Expression, Security, and Access

In recent years, three issues about the Internet have commanded the most attention: the suitability of online material, the security of personal and private information, and the accessibility of the Internet. With each of the issues there have been heated debates, with many questions but no easy answers: Should the Internet be a completely open forum, or should certain types of communications be limited or prohibited? Should personal or sensitive government information be private, or should the Internet be an enormous public record? Should all people have equal access to the Internet, or should it be available to only those who can afford it?

The Battle over Inappropriate Material

The question of what constitutes appropriate content has been part of the story of most mass media, from debates over lurid pulp fiction in the nineteenth century to opposition to sexually explicit themes and images during film's early years. The demand for X-rated movies also helped drive the VCR–video store boom of the 1980s, and today eliminating some forms of sexual content from television remains a top priority for many politicians and public interest groups. It is not surprising that public objection to indecent and obscene Internet material has led to various legislative efforts to tame the Web, including the Communications Decency Act in 1996 and the Children's Online Protection Act in 1998. Both efforts were judged unconstitutional, however, and sexual content on the Internet continues to flourish.

In an effort to promote self-regulation, many commercial online services and some informal newsgroups have instituted rules aimed at curbing inappropriate language and material at sites that children might visit. Filtering software that screens out many indecent or inappropriate sites has also become popular in some schools and among concerned parents. Although some studies indicate that only 1.5 percent of all communication on the Internet is pornographic, others suggest that topics related to sex are still among the most widely used search terms on the World Wide Web.[13]

Although the "back alleys of sex chat" of the Internet have caused considerable public concern, Internet sites that carry potentially dangerous information (e.g., bomb-building instructions, hate speech) have also incited calls for Internet censorship, particularly after the 1999 high school shootings in Littleton, Colorado, and the terrorism of September 11, 2001.

■ SCIENCE & SOCIETY

Hatemongering on the data highway

Bigotry carves out a niche in cyberspace

Chicago computer buff Bob Arbetman was happily surfing through cyberspace one night when his attention was drawn to a bulletin board offering titled HOLOHOAX.TXT. Tapping in, Arbetman found himself in touch with a professional Holocaust denier whose message, he says, was rabidly antisemitic. "It was straight neo-Nazi propaganda," recalls the 37-year-old electrical engineer.

Outraged by what he was downloading, Arbetman alerted the Simon Wiesenthal Center, the Los Angeles-based institute that exposes neo-Nazis and other bigots. His tip and calls from others who had encountered similar online, often violent, antiblack, antigay, antisemitic hate messages triggered an extensive three-year investigation by Wiesenthal researcher Rick Eaton. The result, *U.S. News* has learned, is a massive dossier of cyberspace hatemongering that the Wiesenthal Center has just submitted to FCC Chairman Reed Hundt. "It may be time for the FCC to place a cop on the superhighway of information," says Rabbi Abraham Cooper, Wiesenthal Center associate dean.

A right to hate. But any attempt to police cyberspace is fraught with practical and legal issues.

television or radio, and so subject to control, or more like the telephone system or the mail, which have greater freedoms over the content of the messages. Unless hate mail directly interferes with civil liberties, insists Godwin, "I can't conceive

invitations to violence and hate. A file called HOMOBASH describes shooting a gay person in the face with a handgun. A graphic titled MONKEY pictures blacks copulating with animals and suggests this was the start of the AIDS epidemic. Another shows a bare-chested, hooknosed Jew holding a bloody knife and standing in a sea of gentile blood.

Some commercial networks, such as Prodigy, say they have taken steps to ban the use of their systems by propagandists of bias. Vinton Cerf, president of the Internet Society, a user organization, says he and his colleagues are preparing a set of voluntary norms they hope will put restraints on racists and other objectionable E-mailers. But guidelines may have little effect in a freewheeling venue such

The Challenge to Keep Personal Information Private

As personal computers increasingly become gateways into our private lives, government and commercial surveillance, online fraud, and unethical data-gathering methods have made the Internet treacherous at times. Government agencies around the world have obtained communication logs, Web browser histories and private online records of individual users who thought their online activities were private. In the United States, for example, the USA Patriot Act became law about a month after the September 11 attacks, granting sweeping powers to law enforcement agencies to intercept computer communications, including e-mail messages and Web browsing.

Besides surveillance, the Internet is also increasingly a conduit for online robbery and identity theft—illegally obtaining personal credit and identity information. Computer hackers have infiltrated Internet databases from banks and hospitals to the Pentagon, stolen credit card numbers from online retailers, and shut down entire companies for days. Identity theft victimizes hundreds of thousands of people a year and clearing one's name can take countless hours and hundreds of dollars. More than $12 billion worldwide is lost to online fraud artists every year.

Another privacy problem concerns undisclosed data-collection practices. Despite justifiable concerns about transmitting personal information online, people are increasingly warming to the idea of **e-commerce**, selling and purchasing products and services on the Internet, especially as more companies offer products online and assure customers of online security with more rigorous data-encryption standards. With the growth in e-commerce, however, comes the growth of online marketing strategies and attempts to collect information on Web users for commercial purposes. One increasingly common method of gathering information on users is through **cookies**, information profiles about a user that are usually automatically accepted by the Web browser and stored on the user's own computer hard drive. Cookies work as "spies," sending back information to track the user's subsequent visits within that Web site. In a relatively benign situation, cookies can tell a Web site that the user is cleared for access to an authorized site, such as a library database that is open only to university faculty and students. More intrusive are Web sites that use cookies to record the user's Internet account, the last several Web pages visited, and other information stored in that person's Web-browser directory. In these cases, the Web sites create a marketing profile of users and can target them for certain advertisements. Cookies are automatically accepted by most browsers, although preference commands can be set to reject cookies or provide warnings when a Web site is trying to set such a system. Nevertheless, many Web sites require the user to accept cookies in order to gain access to the site. Even more intrusive is **spyware**, which is often secretly bundled with free downloaded software, such as peer-to-peer file-sharing programs Limewire, KaZaA, and Morpheus, and permits a third party to retrieve personal information on computer users and send pop-up ads to users' computer screens. (See "Tracking Technology: Freeware's Dirty Secret: Spyware" on page 56.)

In 1998, the U.S. Federal Trade Commission (FTC) developed fair information practice principles for online privacy to address the issues of notice, choice, access, and security. These principles require Web sites to (1) disclose their data-collection practices, (2) give consumers options for choosing whether and how personal data may be collected, (3) permit individuals access to their records to ensure data accuracy, and (4) secure personal data from unauthorized use. Unfortunately, the FTC has no power to enforce fair information practices on the Internet, and most Web sites' own self-enforcement has been dismal. According to a 2000 FTC study, 97 percent of Web sites collect personal identifying information, but only 20 percent implement, at least in part, the four fair information practice principles.[14]

One of the most important elements in the online data-collection debate is whether Web sites should be required to use **opt-in** or **opt-out policies.** Opt-in data policies, favored by consumer and privacy advocates, require that the Web site gain explicit permission from online consumers before the site can collect their personal data. Opt-out data policies, favored by data-mining corporations, involve the automatic collection of personal data unless the consumer goes to the trouble of filling out a specific form to "opt out" of the practice. According to the FTC, most Web sites follow opt-out policies, and the opt-out consent is often buried at the end of long pages in prechecked click boxes that the consumer has to take the time to uncheck.[15]

The Economics of Access and the Digital Divide

A key economic issue of our times is whether the cost of getting on the information highway will undermine equal access. Mimicking the economic disparity between rich and poor that grew more pronounced during the 1980s and 1990s, the term **digital divide** refers to the growing contrast between "information haves," or digital highway users who can afford to acquire multiple media services, and "information have-nots," or people who may not be able to afford a computer or the monthly bills for Internet service connections, much less the many options now available on the highway. For example, a recent study found that 95 percent of children in households in the United States with an annual income of $75,000 or more have a computer in the home, whereas only 33 percent of children in households earning less than $15,000 a year have a home computer. Similarly, the higher-income children

Freeware's Dirty Secret: Spyware

Just say no.

That's what we tell our kids to do when someone offers them drugs. But perhaps we should consider saying it ourselves when someone offers us the computer drug of the new millennium—free software.

Over the past year we've learned that the free software that the kids use to swap MP3 music files over the Internet comes at a price— spyware that tracks our movements across the Web, even when the programs aren't being used, and sometimes after they've been uninstalled. But those programs are just the tip of the iceberg. Somebody has to pay for all that "free" content out there. Usually it's an advertiser who wants our eyeballs, or a marketer who wants information about us that we'd just as soon keep private. They'll do anything they can to get our attention or learn who we are and what we do. That includes spying on us and sneaking software onto our computers. . . .

Yes, it's time to consider saying no. Here are some reasons why: If you're among the millions who have downloaded the free Kazaa file-trading program since February, you've also unknowingly downloaded bits and pieces of software designed to make your computer a cog in an entirely new, but unannounced, peer-to-peer network for the distribution of copy-protected music.

The same software can even take over your PC for use as a number cruncher in third-party projects that require massive computing power.

Brilliant Digital Entertainment, the company that invented the scheme, plans to activate the dormant software in the next few months. It came to light when a reporter for CNet's News.com discovered it in a regular SEC filing.

Company officials say they won't take over any PC without the consent of the owner.

However, many users may already have given their "consent" by checking "Yes" boxes that appeared on their screens when they downloaded Kazaa. Many more will undoubtedly click "Yes" out of habit when Brilliant gets around to turning on the sleeping programs.

If you get the chance, maybe you should just say no. Or just get rid of the software entirely. . . .

Do you hate those little animated ads that jump up and down on your screen—obscuring whatever's behind them— when you're unfortunate to hit a Web site that's desperate for advertising revenue?

They're known as "Shoshkeles," named for the daughter of a founder of United Virtualities, the company that created these creatures to make you a captive of the advertiser for a few seconds, at least.

But if Shoshkeles are annoying, they're nothing compared to what the company plans next.

Its newest technology, known as Ooqa Ooqa, will take over the toolbar of your Web browser and turn it into a billboard for whoever's willing to pay for it. It can replace your Forward and Back buttons with buttons that take you to the advertiser's Web site and otherwise change the way your browser works.

Of course, you'll be able to opt out of the hijacking, according to the company. If you get asked, just say no. . . .

Do you have the e-mail preview window of Outlook or Outlook Express turned on? Turn it off. Now.

I know it's convenient, and the fancy formatting and graphics that appear in the e-mail may be attractive. But the Outlooks (and Netscape's e-mail client) use Web browser functions to display those fancy messages. That means the cookies, Web bugs, and other tricks that Web sites and advertisers use to track your comings and goings all go to work when that e-mail appears on your screen.

A new trick is the inclusion of a tracking number in the subject line—a favorite device of spammers, who now know exactly who read their message.

You don't have to open an e-mail to activate these spy features—displaying it in the preview window is enough.

I've turned mine off, as much as I liked it, and you should too.

If a message is obviously spam, you can delete it without reading it—or tipping off the spammer that he's made a hit. It's another way to just say no.

Source: Mike Himowitz, "Beware of Freeware Set to Bug Your PC and You," *Baltimore Sun,* April 11, 2002 p. 1C.

are four times more likely to have Internet access from their home than the lower income children. The digital divide is also apparent in terms of race, despite improvements in recent years. By 2001, in the United States, 50 percent of non-Hispanic white children had home Internet access, compared to 25 percent of black children and 20 percent of Hispanic children. The digital divide is even evident in geographic terms, with suburban children being more likely to have home computer and Internet access than rural or urban children. At the state level, children from the northern states have much higher rates of home Internet access than do children from the southern and southwestern states.[16]

Some communities and organizations have addressed the access problem by installing computers equipped with Internet connections in libraries, banks, schools, and other public locations; this gives most community members entry to the Internet. Other cities are offering free Internet access to their entire citizenry. For example, in 2001 the city of Houston launched a multimillion-dollar program to bring Internet access to its three million area residents. "We are at a point in society where equal access to the Internet must be guaranteed. It must be a right and not a privilege," said Houston mayor Lee Brown.[17]

Globally, though, the have-nots face an even greater obstacle in connecting to the Internet. Although the Web claims to be worldwide, countries like the United States, Norway, Sweden, Finland, Japan, Israel, Australia, Britain, and Germany account for most of its international flavor. In nations such as Jordan, Saudi Arabia, Syria, Iraq, China, and Myanmar, the governments permit limited or no access to the Web. (See "The Global Village: The Internet's Iranian Frontier" on page 59.) In countries like Argentina, Colombia, Brazil, and Mexico, an inadequate telecommunications infrastructure means that consumers must endure painfully long waits in order to participate. In other countries, phone lines and computers are almost nonexistent. For example, Haiti, a country of about eight million people, has just sixty thousand phone lines and no electricity in most households. Internet service arrived in limited locations in Haiti in 2000, but with an annual per capita income of less than $400, the $37.50 it takes to buy a twenty-hour block of time at an Internet café is a princely sum for all but the economic elite in the island nation.[18]

● Today, virtually every U.S. public school is wired to the Internet, although access speeds and the amount of equipment per student vary widely. An estimated $8 billion was spent on technology in the 2000–2001 school year, with most of the money going toward hardware and software; only a small percentage went to teacher training.

Media critic Marc Gunther offers an analogy for access to virtual and real highways: "If the information highway becomes a vital communications link in the 21st Century, who will be able to ride? . . . The interstates of the 1950s helped relocate jobs to the suburbs and beyond, leaving city folks stranded unless they owned cars."[19] Whereas traditional media made the same information available to everyone who owned a radio or a TV set, the information highway could create economic tiers and classes of service. It could become a toll road rather than a freeway, with wealthy users buying different levels of privacy, specialty access, and Internet capabilities. Policy groups, media critics, and concerned citizens continue to debate the implications of media access for democratic societies, which have traditionally valued the equal opportunity to acquire knowledge.

★ Citizens, Cyberspace, and Democracy

Throughout the twentieth century, Americans closely examined emerging mass media for their potential contributions to democracy and culture. As radio became more affordable in the 1920s and 1930s, we hailed the medium for its ability to reach and entertain even the poorest Americans caught in the Great Depression. When television developed in the 1950s and 1960s, it also held promise as a medium that could reach everyone, even those who were illiterate or cut off from printed information. Despite the criticisms of the Internet's accessibility and continuing national and international digital divides, many have praised the Internet for its democratic possibilities and for its accessibility. Some advocates even tout it as the most decentralized social network ever conceived.

Unlike many media industries, the Internet has developed largely from the bottom up. Just as amateur radio operators influenced the growth of wireless communication in the early twentieth century, the development of the Internet owes a large debt to amateurs — students, engineers, and computer buffs. There are several disadvantages, however, to the decentralized nature of the Internet. One drawback has been the increased circulation of **spam** and spurious "news" — the Internet equivalent of unwanted junk mail and backroom gossip. Unlike traditional media, which routinely employ editors as information gatekeepers, many individuals and newsgroups on the Internet send out data that are not checked by anyone. Most media screen material for accuracy, fairness, appropriateness, and decency, but such screening is more difficult to accomplish on the Internet.

Hoaxes have also spread like wildfire as pranks and fraudulent e-mails go unchecked and are naively forwarded around the globe. For example, one e-mail hoax, widely circulated during the aftermath of the September 11, 2001, terrorist attacks in New York City and Washington, D.C., asked people across the United States to step outside with a lighted candle at 7:00 EST on the Friday night following the attacks. The e-mail explained that candle holders would be photographed by a NASA satellite and that the photo would serve as a memorial to attack victims. Thousands of people forwarded the message to friends and family and dutifully stood outside at the specified time, holding candles, despite the fact that NASA had had no part in creating the plan.

Although the Internet is subject to misinformation, it is also a source of unique and valuable information — for example, Web sites that disclose financial contributions to candidates for public office.[20] As such, the Internet offers a diverse array of communication models. In such a decentralized system, millions of message groups send out bits of information, allowing millions of other interested users to receive and respond. Instead of the few-to-many model of traditional media, the Internet

> **"** [The Internet] is a way for . . . the struggle in our country, and the many other countries where there are a lot of human rights abuses, to be brought out into the open. **"**
>
> – Janai Robert Orina, Kenyan human rights worker, 1998

> **"** Local [Saudi] newspapers report that girls devote much of their surf time to chatting. The question that troubles Saudi society is: 'With whom?' **"**
>
> – David Hirst, *The Guardian*, 1999

THE GLOBAL VILLAGE

The Internet's Iranian Frontier

SHAHKOOH, Iran (AP) — At first glance, this could be any sleepy Iranian hamlet. Women weave carpets on traditional looms. Tea brews over open fires. Donkeys outnumber cars. But listen closely: That clacking is fingers on keyboards and that crackling is modems connecting to the Internet.

Welcome to the mountain village that lacks an elementary school, possesses just one central outhouse — but has gone global. No other Iranian village has progressed as far as Shahkooh, 240 miles northeast of Tehran, in tapping the Internet's potential to widen its horizons. Villagers credit a native son, Ali Akbar Jalali, who left to study in the provincial capital and went on to earn an electrical engineering degree in the United States, raised the idea during a 1999 visit.

The first computer was purchased with money raised by villagers. A government grant paid for a second, and several more came courtesy of a charity formed by Iranians in London. Villagers who know something about computers volunteer as teachers in the computer center set up in Shahkooh's mosque. Classes are free. The village even has its own Farsi-language Web site, Shahkooh.com. The goal is to teach computer skills to anyone interested among its 6,000 residents — from chador-clad girls to sunburned farmers.

The hardware alone makes Shahkooh unique among villages. Even in cities, a minority of Iranians are wired. Only 2 million out of Iran's 70 million people — about 3 percent — have Internet access.

Yet Iran could now be ripe for a high-tech surge a generation after the conservative clerics behind the 1979 Islamic Revolution tried — and failed — to insulate the nation from modern influences.

Nearly half Iran's population is under age 25, and it's eager to get online.

After the 1997 election of reformist President Mohammad Khatami, Internet cafés have sprouted in Iranian cities and Internet providers offer unrestricted access — even to adult and anti-government sites.

That may be due to the relative scarcity of Internet access among clerics in Qom, the country's religious center. In fact, Iran's clerics have pushed for restrictions on access. Last year, the Supreme Cultural Revolution Council, a conservative-dominated body, ordered all private Internet access companies under state control.

The order was never implemented, but parliament, according to lawmaker Kazem Jalali, is considering legislation that would require Internet providers to block access to adult sites and others. Hard-liners are also becoming increasingly concerned about Iranians' access to information, fearing it is stirring pro-reform sentiment.

In Shahkooh, the Web is not controversial. It is seen as an essential tool to promote knowledge and prepare for jobs in a country choking from unemployment, which some analysts place at more than 30 percent. Since Shahkooh.com was launched, more than two dozen villagers have become entrepreneurs. . . . The dot-com businessmen also perform Internet searches and sell the information they glean. And Shahkooh.com promotes local handicrafts such as carpets. . . . It's far easier to reach this village 6,600 feet above sea level by e-mail than road. . . . Each year, at least 400 villagers learn computer basics. . . . Besides giving Shahkooh's people e-mail and Web access, the Internet also offers familiarity with English, which is almost unknown in Iran outside the country's main cities. Villagers most like study- or job-related Web sites as well as those offering health and sports content.

Source: Associated Press, "Internet reaches another technological outpost . . . the Iranian village," SiliconValley.com, July 4, 2002 <http://www.siliconvalley.com/mld/siliconvalley/news/3601630.htm>.

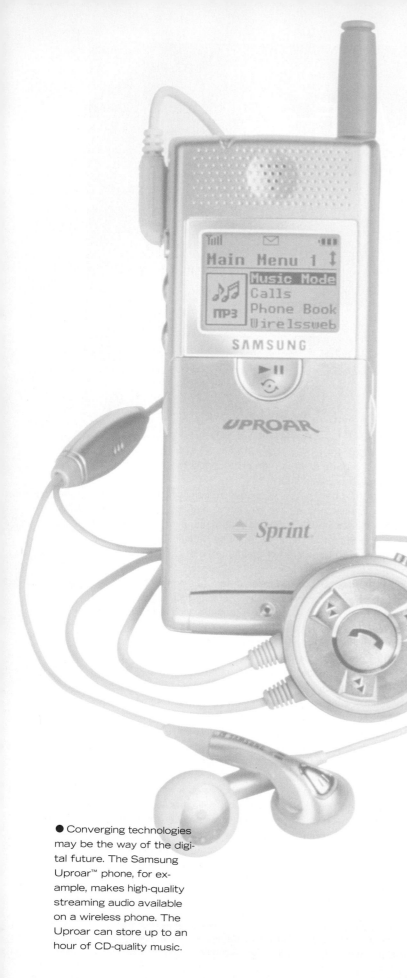

offers more opportunities for both one-to-one and many-to-many communication encounters.

The biggest threat to the Internet's democratic potential may well be its increasing commercialization. Similar to what happened with the radio and television media, the growth of commercial "channels" on the Internet has far outpaced the emergence of viable nonprofit channels, as fewer and fewer corporations have gained more and more control. The passage of the 1996 Telecommunications Act cleared the way for cable TV systems, computer firms, and telephone companies to merge their interests in advancing communication technology. Although there was a great deal of buzz about lucrative Internet start-ups in the 1990s, it has been large corporations such as Microsoft and AOL Time Warner that have weathered the low points of the dot-com economy and maintained a controlling hand in the new information systems.

It is estimated that 75 percent of households in the United States and Canada will be linked to the Internet by 2005—up from 50 percent in 2000—thus greatly increasing its democratic possibilities, but also tempting commercial interests to gain even greater control over it and intensifying problems for agencies that are trying to regulate it. If the past is any predictor, it seems realistic to expect that the Internet's potential for widespread democratic use could be partially preempted by narrower commercial interests. As media economist Douglas Gomery warns, "Technology alone does not a communication revolution make. Economics trumps technology every time."[21]

On the more positive side of the ledger, the new technologies may be so uniquely accessible that they offer at least the potential for enriching democratic processes. Books, newspapers, magazines, radio, film, and television widened and expanded the reach of media, but they did not generate equivalent avenues for response and debate. Defenders of the digital age argue that newer media forms—from the MP3 music of emerging musicians to online streaming of independent short films to an enormous variety of Internet newsgroups—allow greater participation. Individuals can create their own Web sites and seek the Web sites of others, joining and encouraging conversations about such things as movies, politics, or the the best way to baste a turkey. In response to these new media forms, older media are using Internet technology to increase their access to and feedback from varied audiences, soliciting e-mail from users and fostering discussions in chat rooms.

Despite the potential of new media forms, skeptics raise doubts about the participatory nature of discussions on the Internet. For instance, critics warn that Internet users may be searching out only those people whose beliefs and values are similar to their own. Al-

● Converging technologies may be the way of the digital future. The Samsung Uproar™ phone, for example, makes high-quality streaming audio available on a wireless phone. The Uproar can store up to an hour of CD-quality music.

though it is important to be able to communicate across vast distances with people who have similar viewpoints, these kinds of cyberspace discussions may not serve to extend the diversity and tolerance that are central to democratic ideals.

To take a critical position on the information-highway debates, we must analyze and judge its possibilities and limitations. Such a position should be grounded in the knowledge that the media are converging nationally and globally, changing the nature of mass communication. One of these changes is *mass customization*, whereby product companies and content providers can customize a Web page or media form for an individual consumer. For example, Internet portals such as Yahoo! allow users to personalize their front-page services by choosing their own channels of information—their favorite newspapers or sports teams, local movie listings and weather broadcasts, and many other categories—within the Yahoo! interface. Users of My Yahoo! and similar services have the benefits of a personal home page without going through the steps of creating a home page of their own. They are, however, subject to the banner ads of Yahoo!, which are also customized for the user on the basis of his or her shopping and surfing habits. Such mass customization services blur the boundary between one-to-one communication, which we generally associate with an office conversation or a telephone call, and mass communication, which we associate with daily newspapers or TV programs.

It is also no longer very useful to discuss print media and electronic or digital media as if they were completely segregated forms. We live in a world in which a ten-year-old can simultaneously watch an old TV rerun on cable and read the latest Harry Potter book; in which a twenty-year-old can make sense of a nineteenth-century poem while wearing a portable MP3 player blasting out recently downloaded techno music. Moreover, it is now possible to access old TV reruns, horror thrillers, classic literary texts, and alternative music—all through a home computer and Internet connection. Today, developments in word processing, e-mail, books on tape, cable-access channels, DVDs, children's pictorial literature, magazine advertising, and Internet newsgroups are integrating aspects of both print and electronic culture at the crossroads of everyday life.

> ❝ Unfortunately, there has been far too little discussion of the deeper citizenship issues that stir like fault pressures beneath the bedrock surface of the emerging Information Highway. ❞
>
> —Mitch Kapor, founder, Lotus Software, 1993

> ❝ The Internet will soon be so pervasive that not having access to the technology or not knowing how to use it will be the equivalent of not knowing how to read or write. ❞
>
> —Michael Fleisher, chief executive of Gartner Group, a technology consulting firm, 2000

www.

To create an individualized study plan for Chapter 2, go to the interactive *Media and Culture* Online Study Guide at: bedfordstmartins.com/ mediaculture

REVIEW QUESTIONS

Origins of the Internet

1. What are the three stages in the development of a mass medium?

2. How did the Internet originate? What does its development have in common with earlier mass media?

Information Access on the Internet

3. How does media convergence distinguish a different phase in mass-media history?

4. What three key technological developments have made possible today's intersection of mass media along the information highway?

5. What are the five major mapping systems of the Internet? How do they make the Internet more organized for the user?

6. How does the World Wide Web work? Why is it significant in the development of the Internet?

Ownership Issues on the Internet

7. What are the key issues involving ownership of the Internet? How do these issues differ from earlier ownership issues in other mass media?

8. Who are the major players vying for control of the Internet?

Free Expression, Security, and Access

9. What are the central concerns about the Internet regarding freedom of expression, security, and access?

10. What is the digital divide, and what does it have to do with the information highway?

Citizens, Cyberspace, and Democracy

11. What are the key problems involving the expansion of the information highway? How can the information highway make democracy work better?

QUESTIONING THE MEDIA

1. What was your first encounter with the Internet like? How did it compare with your first encounters with other mass media?

2. What features of the information highway are you most excited about? Why? What features are most troubling? Why?

3. What are the advantages of an electronic-digital highway that links televisions, computers, phones, audio equipment, homes, schools, and offices?

4. Do you think virtual communities are genuine communities? Why or why not?

5. As we move from a print-oriented Industrial Age to a digitally based Information Age, how do you think individuals, communities, and nations will be affected?

SEARCHING THE INTERNET

http://www.cdt.org

The Center for Democracy and Technology, a nonprofit group, works to promote "democratic values and constitutional liberties in the digital age" by tracking industry and legislative actions that affect such issues as privacy, bandwidth, domain names, and free expression.

http://www.eff.org

The Electronic Frontier Foundation was formed to protect civil liberties on the Internet and "to help civilize the electronic frontier; to make it truly useful and beneficial not just to a technical elite, but to everyone."

http://www.internet2.edu

Detailing the latest developments of Internet2, this site offers information on the private consortium of more

than 180 universities and corporations that are building and testing the Internet's multimedia-friendly second generation.

http://www.zdnet.com

ZDNet.com is a comprehensive site for computer and Internet news.

http://urbanlegends.about.com

About.com's extensive directory of urban myths, legends, Internet hoaxes, and Netlore.

http://www.isoc.org/internet/

The Internet Society is an international organization concerned with the future of the Internet. Its site contains excellent links to several Internet histories.

THE CRITICAL PROCESS

In Brief

This "think-pair-share" exercise focuses on the Internet and its content.

Think: On your own, spend two to three minutes writing down what kind of content—if any—you think should not be on the World Wide Web. Be sure to consider pornography, hate speech, and potentially violent information, such as how to make bombs.

Pair: Turn to your neighbor and compare notes. Do your concerns about certain kinds of Internet content matter only if children might see it? Did either of you list excessive commercialism as a problem? What are the most valuable things about the Internet?

Share: As a class, consider the content of the Internet. Should anything on the Internet be censored? What is the value of the Internet to our society? The Internet is fairly new—does it seem to be developing in a positive direction? If you could rethink the direction and uses of the Internet, what would they be?

In Depth

Description. Interview a sample of people about their online privacy. In what kinds of ways has their privacy been violated through their Internet use? Do they regularly have to divulge personal information

to gain access to certain Web sites? Do they enter contests or play games that require them to enter their e-mail address or disclose specific interests? What types of Web sites try to gather the most personal information from them? Have they noticed any Internet advertising targeting their personal tastes? Do they contend with increasing amounts of spam e-mail? Do they feel comfortable purchasing things online? What is their biggest complaint about being online? Does it have anything to do with privacy?

Analysis. What sort of patterns emerge from your interviews? Are there common ways that online privacy seems to be consistently violated? Are there certain strategies for maintaining privacy on the Internet? Do these work pretty well? Do the interviewees generally seem to be concerned, or unconcerned, about their online privacy? Do your questions make them consider their online privacy for the first time?

Interpretation. Are current marketing practices merely inconvenient, or is there something more insidious going on? Do Internet privacy incursions undercut the usefulness of the medium?

Evaluation. Are data mining, spam, and other invasions of privacy tolerable "costs" for the benefits of the Internet? What should be the standards of privacy for the Internet? How should they be enforced?

KEY TERMS

sound recording

and popular music

No one expected Mariah Carey's career could unravel so quickly.

In early 2001, Carey reigned as the top pop diva of the past decade, with more than 140 million albums sold and more No. 1 songs than any musical artist except Elvis and the Beatles. Her professional career began when she was nineteen years old, on one fortunate evening in 1988, when she met then–Columbia Records head Tommy Mottola at a New York party and handed him her demo tape. Mottola heard her multi-octave voice and signed her the very next day. He soon divorced his wife and married Carey (twenty years his junior) and personally managed her career. Carey's hits—including "Vision of Love," "Emotions," and "Hero"—dominated the 1990s, a decade when she scored at least one No. 1 hit each year. When Carey and Mottola divorced in 1998, the music industry anticipated she would move to a new label as soon as her Columbia contract expired.

That time came in April 2001, when the hotly pursued Carey signed an $80 million four-album deal with EMI's Virgin Records.

For EMI, having Carey on board seemed like money in the bank. But shortly thereafter, the first frayed threads of Carey's tightly managed image began to appear. First, there were strange rambling messages that she posted on her Web site. Then, an equally strange unscheduled appearance on MTV's *Total Request Live,* where she again rambled incoherently and stripped down to her sports bra. In the following days, she was admitted to a New York hospital with cuts and was later rehabilitated at a psychiatric hospital. Her publicist denied Carey had attempted suicide, saying she had suffered "an emotional and physical breakdown." At about the same time, her three-year relationship with Spanish singer Luis Miguel was ending.

Carey's meltdown couldn't have come at a worse time. She dropped out of a headlining appearance for MTV's twentieth anniversary special and canceled promotional appearances for her upcoming soundtrack and semi-autobiographical movie, *Glitter.* But things got worse. The film

and soundtrack had the misfortune of opening on September 11, 2001, and the film got lost in the tragedy of the times, but not before critics panned it. The soundtrack, her first recording for Virgin Records, sold only about 500,000 copies, nowhere near the millions in sales that everyone had expected.

Only time will tell if what happened next was one of the best or worst decisions ever made in the music industry. In January 2002, EMI's Virgin Records terminated its contract with pop diva Mariah Carey, paying her nearly $50 million for *not* making any more recordings for Virgin Records. EMI, the smallest of the five corporations that dominate the music industry, called the buyout "the most prudent course of action for EMI," which was reeling from a huge slump in profits. EMI's stable of stars on its main labels, Capitol and Virgin, were either retired (Pink Floyd, Queen) or likely past their best-selling days (Garth Brooks, Janet Jackson, the Rolling Stones). EMI had already failed to renew the expensive contracts of aging stars Rod Stewart and David Bowie. So, in the case of Mariah Carey, the

record company was attempting to cut its losses, anticipating that it would be more expensive to record and promote three more albums (with such contractual requirements as hairdressers, masseurs, first-class hotels, and lavish videos) than it would be to cultivate less expensive talent. Still, a big star, even one who might be on the slide, is hard for the industry to ignore. After a few months' rest, Carey rebounded with a new contract worth more than $20 million for a minimum of three records with Island/Def Jam, a division of Universal, the largest recording corporation.

The story of Mariah Carey and her recording contracts illustrates the fine balance of the recording industry's success and excess. In an industry where the vast majority of recordings don't break even, Carey's career so far has been extraordinary. But as she reached age thirty-two, was her career near an end, or was Mariah Carey simply a mismanaged pop commodity who could be revived with another label and new handlers?

t he medium of sound recording has had an immense impact on our culture. The music that helps to shape our identities and comfort us during the transition from childhood to adulthood resonates throughout our lives. It stirs debate among parents and teenagers, teachers and students, politicians and performers.

Throughout its history, popular music has been banned by parents, business outlets, radio stations, school officials, and even governments seeking to protect young people from the raw language and corrupting excesses of the music world. At a time when various forms of rock music have become an ever-present annoyance to many, it is easy to forget that in the late 1700s authorities in Europe, thinking that it was immoral for young people to dance close together, outlawed the waltz as "savagery." A hundred years later, the Argentinean upper class tried to suppress the tango, the urban roots of which could be traced to the bars and bordellos of Buenos Aires. The first Latin music and dance to gain international popularity, the tango migrated to Paris in the early twentieth century and was condemned by the clergy for its impact on French youth. During the 1920s, some adults criticized the Charleston, a dance that featured cheek-to-cheek contact by partners. Rock and roll in the 1950s and hip-hop in the 1980s and 1990s added their chapters to the age-old battle between generations.

To place the impact of popular music in context, in this book we will begin by investigating the origins of recording's technological "hardware." We will review Thomas Edison's early phonograph, Emile Berliner's invention of the flat disk record, and the development of audiotape and compact discs. We will study radio's early threat to sound recording and the subsequent alliance between the two media when television arrived in the 1950s.

In this chapter we will also examine the content and culture of the music industry. The predominant role of rock music is a key point of reference. Many important forms of music have become popular—including classical, tango, jazz, salsa, country, blues, gospel, hip-hop, and folk—but no other musical expression has had such an extraordinary impact on other mass-media forms. With the introduction of music videos in the early 1980s, rock music dramatically changed the cable and TV landscapes. More significant, rock music simultaneously linked and transformed the fundamental structure of two mass-media industries: sound recording and radio. Beginning in the 1950s, rock music created an enormous and enduring consumer youth market for sound recordings, and it provided much-needed content for radio at a time when television had "borrowed" most of radio's longtime programming. Rock music has influenced a diverse array of international cultures, operating as a kind of common ground for fans worldwide. In this chapter we will look at rock and other contemporary forms of popular music as we survey the growth of sound recording as a mass medium. Finally, we will examine economic and democratic issues facing the recording industry.

> **❝ If people knew what this stuff was about, we'd probably all get arrested. ❞**
> —Bob Dylan, 1966

Technology and the Development of Sound Recording

New mass media have often been defined in terms of the communication technology that preceded them. For example, movies were initially called *motion pictures,* a term that derived from photography; radio was referred to as *wireless telegraphy;* and television was often called *picture radio.* Sound recording instruments were initially labeled "talking machines" and later called *phonographs,* when Thomas Edison made a recording device in 1877 that played back voices. Edison's invention was the result

● An Edison Standard Phonograph, circa 1900, for playing wax cylinders.

of tinkering with existing innovations, the tele*phone* and the tele*graph*. The origin of *tele-* is the Greek word for "far off"; *phono-* and *-graph* come from the Greek words for "sound" and "writing." This early blending of technology foreshadowed our contemporary era, in which media as diverse as newspapers and movies are converging on the information highway. Before the Internet, however, the first major media convergence involved the relationship between the sound recording and radio industries.

From Wax Cylinders to Flat Disks: Sound Recording Becomes a Mass Medium

In the 1850s, the French printer Leon Scott de Martinville conducted the first experiments with sound recording. Using a hog's hair bristle as a needle, he tied one end to a thin membrane stretched over the narrow part of a funnel. When the inventor spoke into the funnel, the membrane vibrated and the free end of the bristle made grooves on a revolving cylinder coated with a thick liquid called *lamp black*. Different sounds made different trails in the lamp black. However, de Martinville could not figure out how to play back the sound. That is what Thomas Edison did in 1877. He recorded his own voice by using a needle to press his voice's sound waves onto tinfoil wrapped around a metal cylinder about the size of a cardboard toilet-paper roll. After recording his voice, Edison played it back by repositioning the needle to retrace the grooves in the foil, a material he later replaced with wax.

As we discussed in Chapter 2, most new media pass through three developmental stages. The first is the novelty stage, in which inventors experiment to solve a particular problem, such as how to play back recorded music. In the second, or entrepreneurial, stage, inventors and investors work out a practical and marketable use for the new device. Edison, for example, initially thought of his phonograph as a kind of answering machine; he envisioned a "telephone repeater" that would "provide invaluable records, instead of being the recipient of momentary and fleeting communication."[1]

In the third stage, entrepreneurs figure out how to market the new device as a consumer product. For sound recording, a key breakthrough at this stage came from Emile Berliner, a German engineer who had immigrated to America. In the late 1880s, he began using a flat spinning five-inch disk to trace voices. Through a photoengraving process, he recorded the sounds onto disks made of metal and shellac. These disks became the first records. Using Edison's ideas, Berliner developed a machine for playing his disks on the first turntable, which he called a *gramophone*.

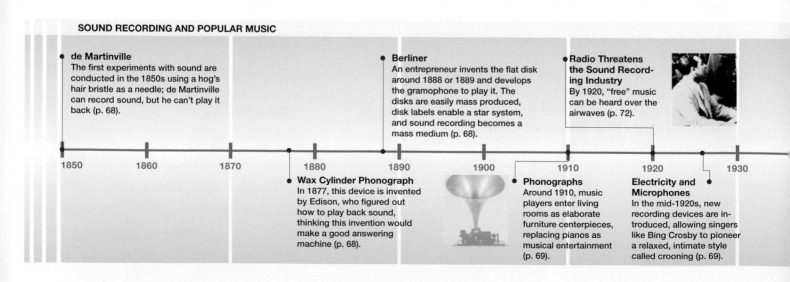

SOUND RECORDING AND POPULAR MUSIC

de Martinville
The first experiments with sound are conducted in the 1850s using a hog's hair bristle as a needle; de Martinville can record sound, but he can't play it back (p. 68).

Berliner
An entrepreneur invents the flat disk around 1888 or 1889 and develops the gramophone to play it. The disks are easily mass produced, disk labels enable a star system, and sound recording becomes a mass medium (p. 68).

Radio Threatens the Sound Recording Industry
By 1920, "free" music can be heard over the airwaves (p. 72).

1850   1860   1870   1880   1890   1900   1910   1920   1930

Wax Cylinder Phonograph
In 1877, this device is invented by Edison, who figured out how to play back sound, thinking this invention would make a good answering machine (p. 68).

Phonographs
Around 1910, music players enter living rooms as elaborate furniture centerpieces, replacing pianos as musical entertainment (p. 69).

Electricity and Microphones
In the mid-1920s, new recording devices are introduced, allowing singers like Bing Crosby to pioneer a relaxed, intimate style called crooning (p. 69).

Berliner also developed a technique that enabled him to stamp and mass-produce his round records. Previously, using Edison's cylinder, performers had to play or sing into the speaker for each separate recording. Berliner's technique featured a master recording from which copies could be easily duplicated in mass quantities. In addition, the industry realized that disks needed to have places for labels, so that the music could be differentiated by title, performer, and songwriter. This led to the development of a "star system," because fans could identify and choose their favorite sounds and artists.

Another breakthrough occurred in the early twentieth century when the Victor Talking Machine Company placed the hardware, or "guts," of the record player inside a piece of furniture. These early record players, known as Victrolas, were mechanical and had to be primed with a crank handle. Electric record players, first available in 1925, gradually replaced Victrolas in the late 1920s as more homes were wired for electricity.

In the 1940s, because shellac was needed for World War II munitions production, the record industry turned to a polyvinyl plastic record. The vinyl recordings turned out to be more durable than shellac records, which broke easily. In 1948, CBS Records introduced the 33⅓-revolutions-per-minute (rpm) *long-playing record* (LP), with about ten minutes of music on each side. This was an improvement over the three to four minutes of music contained on the existing 78-rpm records. The next year, RCA developed a competing 45-rpm record, featuring a quarter-size hole (best suited for jukebox use). The two new standards were technically incompatible, meaning they could not be played on each other's machines. A five-year marketing battle ensued, similar to the VHS vs. Beta war over consumer video standards in the 1980s, or the Macintosh vs. Windows battle over computer-operating-system standards in the 1980s and 1990s. In 1953, CBS and RCA compromised. The 33⅓ record became the standard for long-playing albums and collections of music, and 45s became the format for two-sided singles. Record players were designed to accommodate 45s, 33⅓ LPs, and, for a while, 78s. The 78-rpm record, however, eventually became obsolete, doomed to antique collections along with Edison's wax cylinders.

From Audiotape to CDs, DVDs, and MP3s: Analog Goes Digital

Berliner's flat disk would be the key recording advancement until the advent of **audiotape** in the 1940s, when German engineers developed the technology for making plastic magnetic tape (which U.S. soldiers then confiscated at the end of the war).

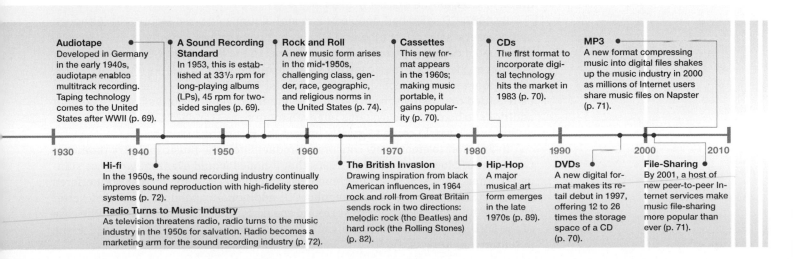

Audiotape ●
Developed in Germany in the early 1940s, audiotape enables multitrack recording. Taping technology comes to the United States after WWII (p. 69).

A Sound Recording Standard ●
In 1953, this is established at 33⅓ rpm for long-playing albums (LPs), 45 rpm for two-sided singles (p. 69).

Rock and Roll ●
A new music form arises in the mid-1950s, challenging class, gender, race, geographic, and religious norms in the United States (p. 74).

Cassettes ●
This new format appears in the 1960s; making music portable, it gains popularity (p. 70).

CDs ●
The first format to incorporate digital technology hits the market in 1983 (p. 70).

MP3 ●
A new format compressing music into digital files shakes up the music industry in 2000 as millions of Internet users share music files on Napster (p. 71).

1930   1940   1950   1960   1970   1980   1990   2000   2010

Hi-fi ●
In the 1950s, the sound recording industry continually improves sound reproduction with high-fidelity stereo systems (p. 72).

Radio Turns to Music Industry
As television threatens radio, radio turns to the music industry in the 1950s for salvation. Radio becomes a marketing arm for the sound recording industry (p. 72).

The British Invasion ●
Drawing inspiration from black American influences, in 1964 rock and roll from Great Britain sends rock in two directions: melodic rock (the Beatles) and hard rock (the Rolling Stones) (p. 82).

Hip-Hop ●
A major musical art form emerges in the late 1970s (p. 89).

DVDs ●
A new digital format makes its retail debut in 1997, offering 12 to 26 times the storage space of a CD (p. 70).

File-Sharing ●
By 2001, a host of new peer-to-peer Internet services make music file-sharing more popular than ever (p. 71).

Audiotape's lightweight magnetized strands of plastic finally made possible sound editing and multiple-track mixing, in which instrumentals or vocals could be recorded at one location and later mixed onto a master recording in another studio.

The first machines developed to play magnetized audiotape were bulky reel-to-reel devices. But by the mid-1960s, engineers had placed reel-to-reel audiotapes inside small plastic cassettes. Audiotape also permitted "home dubbing": Consumers could copy their favorite records onto tape or record songs from the radio. This practice denied sales to the recording industry; during the period from the mid to late 1970s, record sales dropped by 20 percent. Meanwhile, blank audiotape sales doubled. Some thought audiotape would mean the demise of record albums because of its superior sound and editing capability, but commercial sales of albums did not plummet until the compact disc came along in the 1980s.

In 1958, engineers developed stereophonic sound, or **stereo**, which eventually made monophonic (one-track) records obsolete. Stereo permitted the recording of two separate channels, or tracks, of sound. Recording-studio engineers, using audiotape, could now record many instrumental or vocal tracks, which they "mixed down" to the two stereo tracks. Playing the channels back through two loudspeakers creates a more natural sound distribution that fills a room.

The biggest recording advancement came in the 1970s, when electrical engineer Thomas Stockham developed **digital recording**, in which music is played back by laser beam rather than by needle or magnetic tape. Digital recorders translate sound waves into computer-like on/off impulses and store the impulses on disks in binary code. When these are played back, the laser decodes, or "reads," the stored impulses; a microprocessor translates these numerical codes into sound and sends them through the loudspeakers. This technique began replacing Edison's **analog recording** technique, which merely captured the fluctuations of the original sound waves and stored those signals on records or cassettes as a continuous stream of magnetization—analogous to the actual sound. Incorporating purer, more precise digital techniques (which do not add noise during recording and editing sessions), **compact discs**, or **CDs**, hit the market in 1983.

By 1987, CD sales had doubled LP record album sales (see Figure 3.1). Although audiocassette sales outnumbered CD sales by two to one as recently as 1988, by 2000 CDs outsold cassettes by more than ten to one. In the late 1990s, CDs solidified their position as the leading music format with the introduction of CD-Rs (recordable CDs, which consumers can record on only once) and CD-RWs (rewriteable CDs, which can be recorded over many times). Recordable and rewriteable CD units became popular additions to home stereo systems but even more so as standard equipment on computers, which would come to greatly impact the recording industry.

In an effort to create new consumer product lines, the music industry promoted two advanced formats in the late 1990s that it hoped would eventually replace standard compact discs. Sony's Super Audio CD and the DVD-Audio format both offered greater storage capacity than a regular CD; additional capabilities included better fidelity, multichannel music (for surround speakers and subwoofers), and in the case of the **DVD**, graphics, music lyrics, music videos, and artist interviews, as well as the potential for interactivity.

Figure 3.1
Annual Record, Tape, CD, and DVD Sales

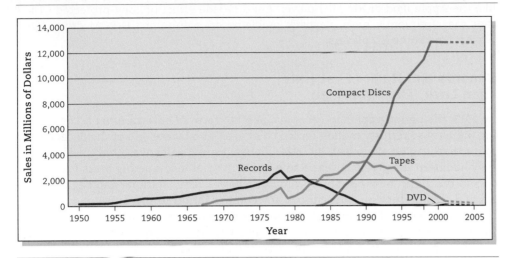

Source: Recording Industry Association of America.

But the introductions of the Super Audio CD and DVD-Audio were ill-timed for the industry, because the biggest development in music formats in the late 1990s was one popularized by music enthusiasts—the **MP3**. The MP3 file format, developed in 1992 as part of a video compression standard, enables music to be compressed into smaller, more manageable files. With the increasing popularity of the Internet in the mid-1990s, computer users began adapting the MP3 format to swap music online, because a song encoded in the MP3 format could be uploaded or downloaded on the Internet in a fraction of the time it took to send or receive non-compressed music.

By the end of 1999, the year the Internet's Napster file-sharing service brought the MP3 format to popular attention, music files were widely available on the Internet—some for sale, some of them legally available for free downloading, and many traded in violation of copyright rules—and music fans typically downloaded MP3 files and "burned" the songs to CDs, even when industry-manufactured CDs and DVDs had higher quality. Some music fans skipped CDs altogether, keeping their music on computer hard drives and essentially using their computer as a stereo system. The music industry fought the proliferation of the MP3 format with an array of lawsuits, but the format's popularity continued to increase, as other Internet file-sharing systems such as KaZaA, Morpheus, and iMesh have succeeded Napster. New styles of MP3 players have spread the format to home-stereo component systems, cars, Walkman-like devices, and even cell phones, making computer audio files an increasingly viable music format, and leading the music industry to begrudgingly realize that it needed to somehow adapt its business to the format. But the recording industry also fought back in 2002 with increasing distribution of releases on copy-protected CDs. The discs are supposed to prevent digital copies of the CDs being burned to CD for illegal resale, or uploaded for illegal distribution on the Internet. But the copy-protected CDs created controversy because they also prevent

● As computers evolve into sound and multimedia systems, they are increasingly outfitted with sound reinforcement accessories, such as speaker towers and subwoofers.

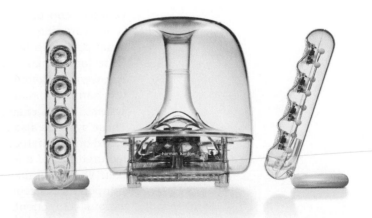

consumers from legally copying CDs for their own personal use (similar to copying LPs to cassette tapes) or making MP3 files out of tracks for their own digital players, like the Apple iPod or Rio MP3 player. Another side effect of copy-protected CDs is that they frequently have playback problems on computer CD-ROM drives, DVD players, and some CD players.

Records and Radio: First Hate, Then Love, Then Marriage

By 1915, the phonograph had become a popular form of entertainment. The recording industry sold thirty million records that year, and by the end of the decade sales more than tripled each year. By 1924, though, record sales were only half of what they had been the previous year. Radio had arrived as a competing mass medium.

To the alarm of the sound recording industry, radio stations had begun broadcasting recorded music, but without any compensation to the music industry. The American Society of Composers, Authors, and Publishers (ASCAP), founded in 1914 to collect copyright fees for publishers and writers, charged that radio was contributing to plummeting sales of records and sheet music. So, by 1925, music rights fees were established, charging stations between $250 and $2,500 a week, and causing many stations to leave the air. But other stations started their own live, in-house orchestras, disseminating "free" music to listeners, and giving radio an edge over the recording industry.

Throughout the late 1920s and the onset of the Depression, record and phonograph sales continued to fall. The industry got a boost when Prohibition ended in 1933 and record-playing jukeboxes became the standard musical entertainment in neighborhood taverns. The music industry's biggest boost came in the 1950s. Television had arrived, pilfering radio's variety shows, crime dramas, and comedy programs, as well as its advertising revenue. Radio turned to the record industry for a cheap source of content. This time, when songs were played on the air, record sales rose. Once the threatened medium in the 1930s, the music industry saved radio in the 1950s. The marriage of the two media would eventually enable both to prosper economically at record levels.

Just as radio would later seek improved sound quality (through FM and stereo) to retain an edge over television, the recording industry survived during radio's golden age by continually improving sound reproduction. With RCA's acquisition of the Victrola company in 1929 came the development of radio-phonograph players. Then, in the 1930s, RCA began experimenting with *high-fidelity systems,* which improved phonographic sound dramatically. In the 1950s, these "hi-fi" systems were introduced to the consumer market. Designed to produce the best fidelity (that is, faithfulness to the music or voice without noise or distortion), the systems came in two varieties: console and component.

A variation on the Victrola, *console systems* combined several elements—radio tuner, turntable, speakers, and amplifier—all hardwired inside a piece of furniture. Hi-fis looked like dining-room sideboards and, based on the market research of the day, were marketed primarily to women. By the 1950s, when this consumer market was saturated, manufacturers "unpacked" the furniture and introduced *component systems,* which enabled consumers to mix and match different models and parts. These systems also permitted easier replacement of various elements. Once again, based on research that tapped into existing gender stereotypes, component systems featured lots of dials, chrome, and control panels—new marketing ploys aimed at men. Today, companies have created another market by melding the console and component concepts into *entertainment systems.* These systems allow users to stack various components, including a CD and a tape player, a television, a radio, and a DVD player, within a large piece of furniture.

U.S. Popular Music and the Formation of Rock

In general, **pop music** appeals either to a wide cross section of the public or to sizable subdivisions within the larger public based on age, region, or ethnic background (for example, teenagers, southerners, Mexican Americans). U.S. popular music today encompasses styles as diverse as blues, country, Tejano, salsa, jazz, rock, reggae, punk, hip-hop, and electronica. The word *pop* has also been used to distinguish popular music from classical music, which is written primarily for ballet, opera, ensemble, or symphony. As various subcultures have intersected, U.S. popular music has developed organically, constantly creating new forms and reinvigorating older musical styles.

The Rise of Pop Music

Although we sometimes assume that popular music depended on the phonograph and the radio for success, it actually existed prior to the development of these media. In the late nineteenth century, the sale of sheet music for piano and other instruments spread rapidly in an area of Manhattan along Broadway known as Tin Pan Alley. During the popular ragtime era in the early 1900s, *tin pan* was a derisive term used to describe the way that quickly produced tunes supposedly sounded like cheap pans clanging together. The tradition of song publishing that began in Tin Pan Alley in the late 1800s continued through the 1950s, with such rock-and-roll writing teams as Jerry Lieber–Mike Stoller and Carole King–Gerry Goffin. Major influences during the earlier period included the marches of John Philip Sousa, the ragtime piano pieces of Scott Joplin, and the show tunes and vocal ballads of Irving Berlin, Hoagy Carmichael, George Gershwin, and Cole Porter.

At the turn of the century, with the newfound ability of song publishers to mass-produce sheet music for a growing middle class captivated by a piano craze, popular songs moved from novelty stage to business enterprise. With the emergence of the phonograph, song publishers also discovered that recorded tunes boosted interest in and sales of sheet music. Although the popularity of sheet music would decline rapidly with the development of the radio in the 1920s, songwriting along Tin Pan Alley played a key role in transforming popular music into a mass medium.

As sheet music grew in popularity, **jazz** developed in New Orleans. An improvisational and mostly instrumental musical form, jazz absorbed and integrated a diverse body of musical styles, including African rhythms, blues, and gospel. Jazz influenced many bandleaders throughout the 1930s and 1940s. Groups led by Louis Armstrong, Count Basie, Tommy Dorsey, Duke Ellington, Benny Goodman, and Glenn Miller were among the most popular of the jazz, or "swing," bands, whose music also dominated radio and recording in their day.

The first vocal stars of popular music in the twentieth century were products of the vaudeville circuit (which radio, movies, and the Depression would bring an end to in the 1930s). In 1929, Rudy Vallee wrapped himself in a raccoon coat and sang popular songs into a megaphone. In the 1930s, the bluesy harmonies of a New Orleans vocal trio, the Boswell Sisters, influenced the Andrews Sisters, whose boogie-woogie style helped them sell more than sixty million records in the late 1930s and 1940s. Also in the 1930s, Bing Crosby pioneered a relaxed, intimate style called *crooning;* he popularized Irving Berlin's "White Christmas," one of the most *covered* songs in recording history. (A song recorded or performed by another artist is known as **cover music.**) In one of the first mutually beneficial alliances between sound recording and radio, many early pop vocalists had network or regional radio programs, which vastly increased their exposure. Ironically, their record sales, promoted on

> **❝ Music should never be harmless. ❞**
> —Robbie Robertson, The Band

> **❝ Frank Sinatra was categorized in 1943 as 'the glorification of ignorance and musical illiteracy.'❞**
> —Dick Clark, *The First 25 Years of Rock & Roll*

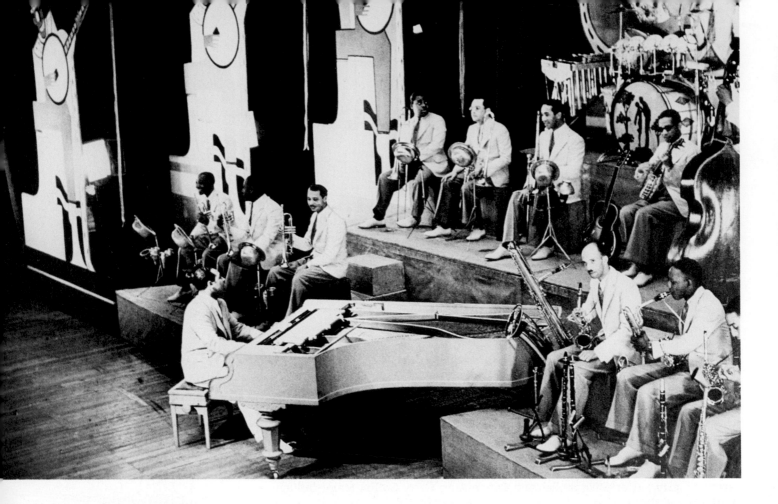

● Duke Ellington (1899–1974), writer of more than 1,500 compositions, from pop songs (including the catchy "It Don't Mean a Thing [If It Ain't Got That Swing]") to symphonies and ballets. Most of his work, though, was composed for his sixteen-member dance band, which over fifty years featured many of the greatest talents of jazz.

radio, boosted sound recording at a time when the record industry was threatened by the growing popularity of radio.

Frank Sinatra arrived in the 1940s. His romantic ballads foreshadowed the teen love songs of rock and roll's early years. Nicknamed "The Voice" early in his career, Sinatra, like Crosby, parlayed his music and radio exposure into movie stardom. (Both singers made more than fifty films apiece.) Helped by radio, Vallee, the Andrews Sisters, Crosby, and Sinatra were among the first vocalists to become popular with a large national teen audience. Their record sales helped stabilize the industry, and in the early 1940s, Sinatra's concerts alone caused the kind of audience riots that would later characterize rock-and-roll performances.

Rock and Roll Is Here to Stay

The cultural storm called **rock and roll** hit in the 1950s. (Like the early meaning of *jazz, rock and roll* was a blues slang term that sometimes meant "sex.") It combined the vocal and instrumental traditions of popular music with the rhythm-and-blues sounds of Memphis and the country beat of Nashville. Early rock and roll was therefore considered the first "integrationist music," merging the black sounds of rhythm and blues, gospel, and Robert Johnson's screeching blues guitar with the white influences of country, folk, and pop vocals.[2] Only a few musical forms have ever sprung from such a diverse set of influences, and no new style of music has ever had such a widespread impact on so many different cultures. From an economic perspective, no single musical form prior to rock and roll had ever simultaneously transformed the structure of two mass-media industries: sound recording and radio.

Many social, cultural, economic, and political factors contributed to the growth of rock and roll around the 1940s and 1950s. Radio, which saw its network programs converting to television, was seeking inexpensive forms of content. Radio deejays, particularly Alan Freed in Cleveland (and later on WINS in New York), began exposing more white people to black music. Some white teens cruising the radio dial had already discovered black-oriented stations, however, and had adopted the different rhythms as dance music.

The migration of southern blacks to northern cities in search of better jobs during the first half of the twentieth century had helped spread different popular music styles. In particular, **blues** music came to the North, influenced by African American spiritu-als, ballads, and work songs from the rural South, and exemplified in the music of Robert Johnson, Son House, and Charley Patton. Starting in the late 1930s, the electric guitar — a major contribution to rock music — made it easier for musicians "to cut through the noise in ghetto taverns" and gave southern blues its urban style, popularized in the work of Muddy Wa-ters, Howlin' Wolf, B.B. King, and Buddy Guy.

During this time, **rhythm and blues**, or **R&B**, de-veloped in various cities. Featuring "huge rhythm units smashing away behind screaming blues singers," R&B merged urban blues and big-band sounds.[3] As with hip-hop today, young listeners were fascinated by the explicit (and forbidden) sexual lyrics in songs like "Annie Had a Baby," "Sexy Ways," and "Wild Wild Young Men." Although it was banned on some sta-tions, by 1953 R&B aired on 25 percent of all radio stations for at least a few hours each week. In those days, black and white musical forms were segregated: Trade magazines tracked R&B record sales on "race" charts, which were kept separate from white record sales tracked on "pop" charts.

● Among the most influential and innovative American guitarists, Robert Johnson (1911–1938) played the Mississippi delta blues and was a major influ-ence on early rock and rollers, especially the Rolling Stones and Eric Clapton. His intense slide-guitar and finger-style playing also inspired generations of blues artists, including Muddy Waters, Howlin' Wolf, Bonnie Raitt, and Stevie Ray Vaughan.

Another reason for the growth of rock and roll can be found in the repressive and uneasy atmosphere of the 1950s. With the constant concern over the atomic bomb, the Cold War, and communist witch-hunts, young people were seeking forms of escape from the menacing world created by adults. Teens have traditionally sought out music that has a beat — music they can dance to. In Europe in the late 1700s they popularized the waltz, and in America during the 1890s they took up a dance called the cakewalk. The trend continued during the 1920s with the Charleston, in the 1930s and 1940s with the jazz swing bands and the jitterbug, in the 1970s with disco, and in the 1980s and 1990s with hip-hop. Each of these twentieth-century musical forms began as dance and party music before its growing popularity eventually energized both record sales and radio formats.

Perhaps most significant to the growth of rock and roll, the border that had separated white and black cultures began to break down. This process started with music and among the young, but it got a boost during the Korean War in the early 1950s when President Truman signed an executive order integrating the armed forces. Young men drafted into the service were thrown together with others from very different ethnic and economic backgrounds. The biggest legal change, though, came with the *Brown v. Board of Education* decision in 1954. With this ruling the Supreme Court ruled unconstitutional "separate but equal" laws, which had kept white and black schools, hotels, restaurants, rest rooms, and drinking fountains seg-regated for decades. Thus mainstream America began to wrestle seriously with the legacy of slavery and the unequal treatment of African American citizens. A cultural reflection of the times, rock and roll would burst from the midst of these social and political tensions.

● Richard Wayne Penniman (Little Richard) was inducted into the Rock and Roll Hall of Fame in 1986. Little Richard played a key role in getting black music played on white radio stations and sold in mainstream record stores. His flamboyant, gender-tweaking style has been a major influence on many performers—notably Elton John and David Bowie in the 1970s, Culture Club and Prince in the 1980s, and Marilyn Manson and Dennis Rodman in the 1990s.

Rock Muddies the Waters

In the 1950s, legal integration accompanied a cultural shift, and the industry's race and pop charts blurred. White deejay Alan Freed had been playing black music for his young audiences since the early 1950s, and such white performers as Johnnie Ray and Bill Haley had crossed over to the race charts to score R&B hits. Black artists like Chuck Berry were performing country songs, and for a time Ray Charles even played in an otherwise all-white country band. Revitalizing record sales and changing the sound of radio, rock and roll exploded old distinctions and tested traditional boundaries in five critical ways.

High and Low Culture

In 1956, Chuck Berry's song "Roll Over Beethoven" introduced rock and roll to high culture: "You know my temperature's risin' / the jukebox is blowin' a fuse . . . Roll over Beethoven / and tell Tchaikovsky the news." Although such early rock-and-roll lyrics seem tame by today's standards, at the time these lyrics were written, rock and rollers were challenging music decorum and the rules governing how musicians should behave (or misbehave): Berry's "duck walk" across the stage; Elvis Presley's pegged pants and gyrating hips, influenced by blues performers he admired; and Bo Diddley's use of the guitar as a phallic symbol, another old blues tradition. An affront to well-behaved audiences of classical music, such acts and antics would be imitated endlessly throughout rock's history. In fact, rock and roll's live exhibitions and the legends about them became key ingredients in promoting record sales.

Masculine and Feminine

Rock and roll was also the first popular music that overtly confused issues of sexuality. Although early rock largely attracted males as performers, the most fascinating feature of Elvis Presley, according to the Rolling Stones' Mick Jagger, was his androgynous appearance.[4] During this early period, though, the most sexually outrageous rock-and-roll performer was Little Richard (Penniman), who influenced a generation of extravagant rock stars.

Wearing a pompadour hairdo and assaulting his Steinway piano, Little Richard was considered rock's first drag queen, blurring the boundary between masculinity and femininity (although his act had been influenced by a flamboyant six-and-a-half-foot-tall gay piano player named Esquerita who hosted drag-queen shows in New Orleans in the 1940s).[5] Little Richard has said that given the reality of American racism, he feared the consequences of becoming a sex symbol for white girls: "I decided that my image should be crazy and way out so that adults would think I was harmless. I'd appear in one show dressed as the Queen of England and in the next as the pope."[6] By the end of the 1950s, although white parents may not have been overly concerned about their daughters falling for Little Richard, most adults did not view rock and roll as harmless.

Black and White

Rock and roll also blurred geographic borders between country and city, between black urban rhythms from Memphis and white country & western music from Nashville. (See "Case Study: A Cultural Icon: Patsy Cline," page 79.) Early white rockers such as Buddy Holly and Carl Perkins combined country or hillbilly music, southern gospel, and Mississippi delta blues to create a sound called **rockabilly**. Raised on bluegrass music and radio's Grand Old Opry, Perkins (a sharecropper's son from Tennessee) mixed these influences with music he heard from black cotton-field workers and blues singers like Muddy Waters and John Lee Hooker, both of whom used electric guitars in their performances. In 1956, Perkins recorded "Blue Suede Shoes"; a Presley cover version made the song famous.

Conversely, rhythm and blues spilled into rock and roll. The urban R&B influences on early rock came from Fats Domino ("Blueberry Hill"), Willie Mae "Big Mama" Thornton ("Hound Dog"), and Big Joe Turner ("Shake, Rattle, and Roll"). Many of these songs, first popular on R&B labels, crossed over to the pop charts during the mid to late 1950s (although many were performed by more widely known white artists). Chuck Berry, who originally played country music to supplement his day jobs as a beautician and carpenter, tore down these boundaries. His first hit was "Maybellene," modeled on an old country song called "Ida Red." To earn royalties, since the country version was too old for copyright, Chess Records asked Berry to make some changes, and he renamed the song after a popular cosmetic product. Chess gave the record to Alan Freed, who attached his name to the credits in exchange for radio play. "Maybellene" became a No. 1 R&B hit in July 1955 and crossed over to the pop charts the next month, where it climbed to No. 5.

Although rock lyrics in the 1950s may not have been especially provocative or overtly political, soaring record sales and the crossover appeal of the music itself represented an enormous threat to long-standing racial and class boundaries. In 1956, the secretary of the North Alabama White Citizens Council bluntly spelled out the racism and white fear concerning the new prominence of African American culture: "Rock and roll is a means of pulling the white man down to the level of the Negro. It is part of a plot to undermine the morals of the youth of our nation."[7]

North and South

Not only did rock and roll muddy the urban and rural terrain, but in doing so it combined northern and southern influences as well. In fact, with so much blues, R&B, and rock and roll rising from the South, this region regained some of the cultural standing that it had lost after the Civil War. With many northern middle-class teens

● Although his unofficial title, "King of Rock and Roll," has been challenged by Little Richard and Chuck Berry, Elvis Presley remains the most popular solo artist of all time. From 1956 to 1962, he recorded seventeen No. 1 hits, from "Heartbreak Hotel" to "Good Luck Charm." According to Little Richard, Presley's main legacy was that he opened doors for many young performers and made black music popular in mainstream America.

influenced by southern "lower-class" music, rock and roll challenged stereotypes regarding class as well as race. Like the many white male teens today who are fascinated by hip-hop (buying the majority of hip-hop CDs on the commercial market), Carl Perkins, Elvis Presley, and Buddy Holly—all from the rural South—were fascinated with and influenced by the black urban styles they had heard on the radio or seen in nightclubs.

But the key to record sales and the spread of rock and roll, according to famed record producer Sam Phillips of Sun Records, was to find a white man who sounded black. Phillips found that man in Elvis Presley. Commenting on Presley's cultural importance, one critic wrote: "White rockabillies like Elvis took poor white southern mannerisms of speech and behavior deeper into mainstream culture than they had ever been taken, at the same time he was being reviled for seducing white youth with black music." [8]

The Sacred and the Secular

Just as the new music confronted racial, sexual, regional, and class taboos, for many mainstream adults it also constituted an offense against God. In fact, many early rock figures had close ties to religion. As a boy, Elvis Presley had dreamed of joining the Blackwoods, one of country-gospel's most influential groups. As a teen, Jerry Lee Lewis was thrown out of a Bible institute in Texas. Also influenced by church gospel music, Ray Charles changed the lyrics of an old gospel tune: "I've got a Savior / way over Jordan / he's saved my soul, oh yeah!" became "I got a woman / way over town / she's good to me." A top R&B hit in 1955, "I Got a Woman" became one of Charles's signature songs. The recording drew criticism from many African American church leaders and members, who worried about the impact of such worldly music on black youths.

Many people in the 1950s thought that rock and roll violated the boundary between the sacred and the secular. In the late 1950s, public outrage was so great that even Little Richard and Jerry Lee Lewis, both sons of southern preachers, became convinced that they were playing the "devil's music." By 1959, Little Richard had left rock and roll to become a minister. Lewis, too, feared that rock was no way to salvation. He had to be coerced into recording "Great Balls of Fire," a song by Otis Blackwell that turned an apocalyptic biblical phrase into a highly charged sexual teen love song. The tune, banned by many radio stations, nevertheless climbed to No. 2 on the pop charts late in 1957.

Battles in Rock and Roll

With the blurring of racial lines, performers and producers played a tricky game as they tried to get R&B music accepted in the 1950s. Two prominent white disc jockeys used different methods. Alan Freed, credited with popularizing the term *rock and roll,* played original R&B songs from the race charts and the black versions of early rock and roll. In contrast, Philadelphia deejay Dick Clark believed that making black music acceptable to white audiences required cover versions by white artists.

Some music historians point to Jackie Brenston's "Rocket 88" and other R&B songs from the early 1950s as examples of the first rock and roll. But Bill Haley and the Comets, a former country group, scored the first No. 1 rock-and-roll hit on the Billboard pop chart in May 1955 with "Rock Around the Clock." The record had been an R&B hit in 1954, but it gained popularity and notoriety in the 1955 teen rebellion movie *Blackboard Jungle.* For many parents, the song became a symbol of juvenile delinquency and raised concerns about negative influences in the changing recording industry.

A Cultural Icon: Patsy Cline

by Douglas Gomery

In March 1963 Patsy Cline's life was cut short at age thirty in an airplane accident caused by a tornado-like thunderstorm. Forty years later, she can still sell nearly one million "units"—CDs, audio- and videocassettes, and DVDs—around the world each year. These numbers place her in a category with icons like the Beatles, Elvis, Michael Jackson, and Madonna.

On the surface Patsy Cline led a rags-to-riches life that was tragically cut short. She grew up poor in the Shenandoah Valley of Virginia listening to Nashville's Grand Ole Opry, singing in church, and winning amateur talent contests. Before she turned twenty, she was singing professionally in and around Washington, D.C., which led to local TV shows, which led to national TV exposure in January 1957 as the winner of Arthur Godfrey's Talent Scouts, then a CBS fixture on Monday nights.

Late in 1959, Patsy, her husband, and their infant daughter moved to Nashville. By 1960 she was a regular on the Grand Ole Opry and had signed with Decca, a major label. A year later, producer Owen Bradley added violins to his studio unit (replacing fiddles) and pushed Patsy toward a pop sound. Background singers The Jordanaires smoothed her sound as they did with Elvis. By July 1961, "I Fall to Pieces" became a major hit. In the process Bradley and Cline helped invent what today is known as the "Nashville Sound" and firmly established that city's place in popular music.

Patsy Cline made a national name for herself between Buddy Holly's death in 1959 and the Beatles' first

appearance on TV's *Ed Sullivan Show* in 1964. Her career was brief, but her 100-plus recordings—and changing technology—ensure her enduring influence. Her *Greatest Hits* album—released in March 1967, four years after her death—has remained in print through 45-rpm singles, 33⅓ long-playing albums, audiocassettes, and CDs. The top-selling country album throughout the 1990s, the album had sold more than 10 million units by 2000.

Why? Even if she has been categorized as a "country singer," far more pop fans own Patsy Cline music than do hard-core country devotees. Patsy's voice "crosses over"; her aching ballads and pop rhythms seem as relevant and universally appealing today as when she died. In her own way she surprised the world by having a hit, as one announcer on the Grand Ole Opry put it, "way up there" on both the country and pop charts. If Elvis was the "hillbilly cat" who merged blues with country and created millions of fans around the world, Patsy merged pop with traditional country ballad singing and became a cultural icon.

Cline rarely wrote or composed, but because of her recognizable, singular voice she made all songs her own. "Crazy" is a Patsy Cline original even if it was written and composed by Willie Nelson. Her signature song, "Crazy" ranked as the most-played song in jukebox history as of 2000.

Two generations around the world have now discovered and embraced her. Moreover, her unique and compelling crossover appeal continues to lure new fans and admirers. Since Cline's recordings transcend musical categories and tastes, she is what the industry calls an "evergreen"—like Elvis and the Beatles—who has become part of the rich and varied texture that is our recorded musical heritage.

Douglas Gomery teaches media history at the University of Maryland.

Cover Music Undermines Black Artists

Since the integration of popular music in the 1960s, black and white artists have recorded and performed each other's original tunes. For example, Otis Redding, an established R&B songwriter, covered the Rolling Stones' "Satisfaction" in 1966. Both the Rolling Stones and Eric Clapton covered Robert Johnson's 1930s blues songs, and Clapton had a No. 1 hit in 1974 with Bob Marley's reggae tune "I Shot the Sheriff." More recently, in 2001, Destiny's Child scored a Top 10 hit with their cover of Samantha Sang's 1978 disco-era ballad "Emotion."

Although today we take such rerecordings for granted, in the 1950s cover music was racially coded. Almost all popular covers were attempts by white producers and artists to capitalize on popular songs from the R&B charts and transform them into hits on the pop charts. Occasionally, white producers would list white performers like Elvis Presley, who never wrote songs himself, as co-writers for the tunes they covered. More often, dishonest producers would buy the rights to potential hits from naive songwriters, who seldom saw a penny in royalties or received credit as the writers.

During this period, black R&B artists, working for small record labels, saw many of their popular songs covered by white artists working for major labels. These cover records, boosted by better marketing and ties to white deejays, usually outsold the original black versions. Covers also slowed sales of the original releases and hampered smaller labels. For instance, the 1954 R&B song "Sh-Boom," by the Chords on Atlantic's Cat label, was immediately covered by a white group, the Crew Cuts, for the major Mercury label. Record sales declined for the Chords, although jukebox and R&B radio play remained strong for their original version. As rock critic Ed Ward suggested: "With 'Sh-Boom,' the pop establishment had found itself a potent weapon to use against R&B records—whiten them up and use the corporate might of a major label to get them to places a hapless [small label] caught with a hit on its hands could never reach."[9]

By 1955, R&B hits regularly crossed over to the pop charts, but inevitably the cover music versions were more successful. LaVern Baker's 1955 hit "Tweedlee Dee" for Atlantic was quickly covered by Georgia Gibbs for Mercury. Baker's version went to No. 14; two weeks later, Gibbs's cover reached No. 2 and stayed in the Top 40 for nineteen weeks. Pat Boone's cover of Fats Domino's "Ain't That a Shame" went to No. 1 and stayed on the Top 40's pop chart for twenty weeks, whereas Domino's original made it only to No. 10.

During this time, Pat Boone ranked as the king of cover music, with thirty-eight Top 40 songs between 1955 and 1962. His records were second in sales only to Presley's. Slowly, however, the cover situation changed. After watching Boone outsell his song "Tutti-Frutti" in 1956, Little Richard wrote "Long Tall Sally," which included lyrics written and delivered in such a way that he believed Boone would not be able to adequately replicate them. "Long Tall Sally" went to No. 6 for Little Richard and charted for twelve weeks; Boone's version got to No. 8 and stayed there for nine weeks.

Overt racism lingered in the music business well into the 1960s. When the Marvelettes scored a No. 1 hit with "Please Mr. Postman" in 1961, their Tamla/Motown label had to substitute a cartoon album cover because many record-store owners feared customers would not buy a recording that pictured four black women. A turning point, however, came in 1962, the last year that Pat Boone, then age twenty-eight, ever had a Top 40 rock-and-roll hit. That year Ray Charles covered "I Can't Stop Loving You," a 1958 country song by the Grand Old Opry's Don Gibson. This marked the first time that a black artist, covering a white artist's song, had notched a No. 1 pop hit. With Charles's cover, the rock-and-roll merger between gospel and R&B, on one hand, and white country and pop, on the other, became complete. In fact, the relative acceptance of black crossover music provided a more favorable cultural context for the political activism that spurred important civil rights legislation in the mid-1960s.

Payola Creates the Hits

Besides the overt racism evident in the business of rock and roll, in the 1950s, the recording and radio industries generated the payola scandals. In the music industry, **payola** is the practice of record promoters paying deejays or radio programmers to play particular songs. (The term originated as slang, combining the bribery term *pay-off* with the generic ending of *Victrola*.) As recorded rock and roll became central to commercial radio in the 1950s, independent promoters hired by record labels used payola to pressure deejays to play songs by the artists whom they represented. In the 1950s, as today, fewer than 10 percent of new releases became hits or sold more than the fifty thousand copies needed for a major label to make money on them. With the industry releasing a hundred new singles per week by the end of the 1950s, the demand for airplay—essential to establishing hit-record sales—was enormous. Although payola was considered unethical and a form of bribery, no laws prohibited its practice.

Following closely on the heels of television's quiz-show scandals, congressional hearings on radio payola began in December 1959. After a November announcement of the upcoming hearings, stations across the country fired deejays, and many others resigned. The hearings were partly a response to generally fraudulent business practices and partly an opportunity to blame deejays and radio for rock and roll's negative impact on teens.

In 1959, shortly before the hearings, a Chicago deejay decided to clear the air. He broadcast secretly taped discussions in which a representative of a small independent record label acknowledged that it had paid $22,000 to ensure that a record would get airplay. The deejay, Phil Lind of WAIT, got calls threatening his life and had to have police protection. At the hearings in 1960, Alan Freed admitted to participating in payola, although he said he did not believe there was anything illegal about such deals. His career soon ended. Dick Clark, then an influential twenty-nine-year-old deejay and the host of TV's *American Bandstand*, would not admit to practicing payola. But the hearings committee chastised Clark and alleged that some of his complicated business deals were ethically questionable. Congress eventually added a law concerning payola to the Federal Communications Act, prescribing a $10,000 fine and/or a year in jail for each violation. But given both the interdependence between radio and recording and the high stakes involved in creating a hit, the practice of payola undoubtedly persists. Along with MTV, radio still has enormous influence in making or breaking songs, careers, and a record label's investment.

Taming Rock and Roll's Rebels

By late 1959, many key figures in rock and roll had been tamed, partly by mounting social pressure against the music so often accused of undermining the morals of U.S. youths. Jerry Lee Lewis was exiled from the industry, labeled southern "white trash" for marrying his thirteen-year-old third cousin; Elvis Presley was drafted into the army; Chuck Berry was run out of Mississippi and eventually jailed for gun possession and transporting a minor (with a prostitution record) across state lines; and Little Richard left rock and roll to sing gospel music. Then, in February 1959, in a plane crash in Iowa, Buddy Holly ("Peggy Sue"), Richie Valens ("La Bamba"), and the Big Bopper ("Chantilly Lace") all died—a tragedy mourned in Don McLean's 1971 hit "American Pie" as "the day the music died."

Although rock and roll did not die in the late 1950s, the U.S. recording industry decided that it needed a makeover. To protect the enormous profits the new music had been generating, record companies began to discipline some of rock's rebellious impulses. In the early 1960s, the industry tried to clone Pat Boone by featuring a new generation of clean-cut white singers, including Frankie Avalon, who made

● The Beatles led the British invasion of America's pop charts in 1964 and made several appearances on the *Ed Sullivan Show*. They championed innovations that are still found in music today, such as thematic albums, multitrack recording, and looping (a forerunner to sampling).

beach-movie musicals, and Ricky Nelson, from TV's popular series *Adventures of Ozzie & Harriet*. Rock and roll's explosive violations of class and racial boundaries were transformed into simpler generation-gap problems. By the early 1960s, the music had developed a milder reputation for merely fostering disagreements among parents and teens.

A Changing Industry: Reformations in Popular Music

As the 1960s began, rock and roll may have been tamer and "safer," as reflected in the surf and road music of the Beach Boys and Jan & Dean, but it was beginning to branch out in several directions. For instance, the success of producer Phil Spector's so-called all-girl groups, such as the Crystals ("He's a Rebel") and the Ronettes ("Be My Baby"), and other groups, such as the Shangri-Las ("Leader of the Pack"), challenged the male-dominated world of early rock. In addition, rock music and other popular styles went through cultural reformations that significantly changed the industry. We will consider them in this section, including the internationalization of sound recording during the "British invasion," the development of soul and Motown, the political impact of folk-rock, the rejection of music's mainstream by punk and grunge performers, the reassertion of black urban style in the phenomenon of hip-hop, and the underground pulse of electronica.

The British Are Coming!

Rock recordings today remain among America's largest economic exports, bringing in billions of dollars a year from abroad. In cultural terms, the global trade of rock and roll is even more evident in exchanges of rhythms, beats, vocal styles, and musical instruments to and from the United States, Latin America, Europe, Africa, and Asia. The origin of rock's global impact can be traced to England in the late 1950s,

● Following on the heels of the Beatles came the Rolling Stones, whose name was inspired by a Muddy Waters song. The blatant sexuality of strutting lead vocalist Mick Jagger helped ensure the "bad boy" reputation of the group, which charted its first No. 1 hit in the summer of 1965 with "(I Can't Get No) Satisfaction."

when the young Rolling Stones listened to the urban blues of Robert Johnson and Muddy Waters and the young Beatles tried to imitate Chuck Berry and Little Richard.

Until 1964, rock-and-roll recordings had traveled on a one-way ticket to Europe. Even though American artists regularly reached the top of the charts overseas, no British performers had yet appeared on any Top 10 pop lists in the States. This changed almost overnight. In 1964, the Beatles invaded with their mop haircuts and pop reinterpretations of American blues and rock and roll. By the end of the year, more than thirty British hits had landed on American Top 10 lists.

Ed Sullivan, who booked the Beatles several times on his TV variety show in 1964, helped promote their early success. Sullivan, though, reacted differently to the Rolling Stones, who had initially been rejected by British television because lead singer Mick Jagger sounded "too black." Before the Stones performed on Sullivan's program in 1964, he made them change a lyric from "let's spend the night together" to "let's spend some time together"; then he issued an apology to viewers following the Stones' performance. The Stones were not invited back. Performing black-influenced music and struggling for acceptance, the band was cast as the "bad boys" of rock in contrast to the "good" Beatles. Despite Sullivan's lack of support, the Stones would go on to inspire harder versions of rock music in the 1970s—what one conservative critic called "a relentless percussive assault on the human ear." [10]

With the British invasion, rock and roll unofficially became *rock,* sending popular music and the industry in two directions. On the one hand, the Stones, influenced by both blues and 1950s rock and roll, emphasized hard rhythms and vocals in their performances. Their music would influence a generation of hard-rock and heavy-metal performers, two of the many subgenres of rock that developed in the 1970s. The Beatles, on the other hand, influenced by Frank Sinatra as well as by rock and roll, more often stressed melody. Their music inspired rock's softer digressions. With the Beatles arriving shortly after the assassination of John F. Kennedy, America welcomed their more melodic and innocent recordings.

In the end, the British invasion verified what Chuck Berry and Little Richard had already demonstrated—that rock-and-roll performers could write and produce popular songs as well as Tin Pan Alley had. The success of British groups helped change an industry arrangement in which most pop music was produced by songwriting teams hired by major labels and matched with selected performers. Even more important, however, the British invasion showed the recording industry how older American musical forms, especially blues and R&B, could be repackaged as rock and exported around the world.

Motor City Music: Detroit Gives America Soul

Ironically, the British invasion, which drew much of its inspiration from black influences, siphoned off many white listeners from a new generation of black performers. Gradually, however, throughout the 1960s, black singers like James Brown, Sam Cooke, Aretha Franklin, Ben E. King, and Wilson Pickett found large and diverse audiences. Transforming the rhythms and melodies of older R&B, pop vocals, and early rock and roll into what became labeled as **soul**, they countered the British invaders with powerful vocal performances. It is hard to define soul music, which mixes gospel, blues, and urban and southern black styles, with slower, more emotional and melancholic lyrics. Soul contrasted sharply with the emphasis on loud, fast instrumentals that had become so important to rock music.[11]

The main independent label that nourished soul and black popular music was Motown, started by former Detroit autoworker and songwriter Berry Gordy with a $700 investment in 1960. "Motown" is a nickname for Detroit—the Motor City—the capital of auto production in the United States. Beginning with Smokey Robinson and the Miracles, whose "Shop Around" hit No. 2 late in 1960, Motown groups rivaled the pop success of British bands throughout the decade. Robinson, who later became a vice president of Motown, also wrote "My Girl" for the Temptations and "My Guy" for Mary Wells—both No. 1 hits in the mid-1960s. In the 1960s and 1970s, Motown produced the Four Tops, Martha and the Vandellas, and the Jackson 5. But the label's most successful group was the Supremes, featuring Diana Ross. Between 1964 and 1969, this group scored twelve No. 1 singles. These Motown groups had a more stylized, softer sound than the grittier southern soul (or funk) of Brown and Pickett. Motown producers realized at the outset that by cultivating romance and dance over rebellion and politics, black music could attract a young, white audience.

Popular Music Reflects the Times

Popular music has always been part of its time. So, in the social upheavals that the Civil Rights movement, the women's movement, the environmental movement, and the Vietnam War brought to the 1960s and early 1970s, music did not remain politically quiet. Even Motown acts sounded edgy, with hits like Edwin Starr's "War" (1970)

● Known worldwide as "The Queen of Soul," Aretha Franklin first started singing gospel music at a Baptist church in Detroit, where her father was a pastor. She was only fourteen when she made her first recordings, but became a star in 1967 with Top 10 hits like "Respect," "(You Make Me Feel Like) A Natural Woman," and "Chain of Fools."

and Marvin Gaye's "What's Goin' On" (1971). But the music genre that most clearly responded to the political happenings was folk music, which had long been the sound of social activism. In the 1960s, folk blended with rock and roll to create a new sound for the era. Later, rock became entwined with the drug counterculture, but by the 1970s it was increasingly part of mainstream consumer culture.

Folk Inspires Protest

In its broadest sense, **folk music** in any culture refers to songs performed by untrained musicians and passed down mainly through oral traditions. Folk encompasses old-time music from the banjo and fiddle tunes of Appalachia to the accordion-led zydeco of Louisiana and the folk-blues of the legendary Leadbelly (Huddie Ledbetter). Given its rough edges and amateur quality, folk is considered a more democratic and participatory musical form. Folk, in fact, inspired many writers and performers of popular music to become more socially aware.

During the 1930s, folk became defined by a white musician named Woody Guthrie ("This Land Is Your Land"). Like many blues singers, Guthrie also brought folk music from the country to the city. He wrote his own songs, promoted social reforms, and played acoustic guitar. Groups such as the Weavers, featuring labor activist and songwriter Pete Seeger, carried on Guthrie's legacy. In 1950, before rock and roll, the Weavers' cover of Leadbelly's "Good Night, Irene" stayed at the top of the pop charts for thirteen weeks. Although the group was regularly blacklisted for political activism, the Weavers' comeback concert at Carnegie Hall in 1955 reenergized folk and inspired a new generation of singer-songwriters, including Joan Baez, Bob Dylan, Simon & Garfunkel, James Taylor, Carly Simon, and Joni Mitchell.

Significantly influenced by the blues, Bob Dylan identified folk as "finger pointin' " music that addressed current social circumstances, such as the growing Civil Rights movement and the Vietnam War. For many folk followers who had grown up on less overtly political rock and roll, acoustic folk music represented both a maturing process and a return to traditional, de-amplified values.

Folk Gets Electrified

When the Byrds electrified folk recordings in the 1960s, they invented **folk-rock**, a sound that went on to influence a long list of performers, from the Grateful Dead to R.E.M. Partly a response to the British invasion, amplified folk-rock earned the Byrds a No. 1 hit in 1965 with a cover of Dylan's folk song "Mr. Tambourine Man." The Byrds had grabbed the attention of Dylan, who had also been influenced by a British group, the Animals, and their 1964 hit "The House of the Rising Sun."

Dylan's career as a folk artist had begun with his performances in New York's Greenwich Village in 1961. His notoriety as a songwriter was spurred by his measured nonchalance and his unique nasal voice. Then, at a key moment in popular music's history, Dylan walked onstage at the 1965 Newport Folk Festival fronting a full, electric rock band. He was booed and

> **❝ The pump don't work 'cause the vandals took the handles. ❞**
>
> –Bob Dylan, "Subterranean Homesick Blues," 1965

● Born Robert Allen Zimmerman in Minnesota, Bob Dylan took his stage name from Welsh poet Dylan Thomas. He led a folk music movement in the early 1960s and continues to tour extensively today.

cursed by traditional "folkies," who saw amplified music as a sellout to the commercial recording industry. For many critics, however, Dylan's move to rock was aimed at reaching a broader and younger constituency. For Dylan, who would later experiment with country and gospel music before returning to the blues, it was a matter of changing with the times and finding sounds that matched his interests. By 1965, Dylan had his first major hit, "Like a Rolling Stone," a six-minute blues-rock tune boosted by new "progressive rock" radio stations that played longer cuts.

Rock Turns Psychedelic

Alcohol and drugs have long been associated with the private lives of blues, jazz, country, and rock musicians. These links, however, became much more public in the late 1960s and early 1970s, when authorities busted members of the Rolling Stones and the Beatles. With the increasing role of drugs in youth culture and the availability of LSD (not made illegal until the mid-1960s), more and more rock musicians experimented with and sang about drugs in what were frequently labeled rock's psychedelic years. A number of performers believed, as did various writers and artists from other eras, that artistic expression could be enhanced by mind-altering drugs. The music of this period fed on liberal drug laws and a large college-student population, the targeted consumers for much of this music. In the past, musicians had not publicized their drug and alcohol habits. The 1960s drug explorations, however, coincided with the free-speech movement, in which taking drugs was seen by some artists as a form of personal expression and a public challenge to traditional values.

The rock-drug connection was also a cultural response to the perceived failure of traditional institutions to deal with social problems such as racism and political issues such as America's involvement in the Vietnam War. Students and musicians used drugs not only to experiment or get high, or out of boredom or addiction, but to drop out of conventional society. Some dropped all the way out. During this time, incidents involving drugs or alcohol claimed the lives of several artists, including Janis Joplin, Jimi Hendrix, and the Doors' Jim Morrison.

At the time, the recording industry generally did little to confront the problem of drug dependency and alcoholism among musicians. As long as artists produced hits, record companies either ignored the problem or, in a few cases, made sure that musicians were supplied with drugs to sustain their routines and energy levels. With the rise in cocaine and heroin addiction among musicians in the 1980s and 1990s, the industry faced a new set of challenges. Critics and scholars alike linked the 80 percent rise in drug use among twelve- to seventeen-year-olds between 1992 and 1997 to increased drug use among their rock-group role models.[12] In this case, though, the National Academy of Recording Arts and Sciences, which sponsors the Grammy Awards, brought together hundreds of industry managers and agents to discuss drug issues. Many critics contend, however, that until record companies are willing to terminate contracts and drop their support of artists unwilling to take responsibility for their addictions, problems and tragedies will persist.

Rock Becomes Mainstream

Following the historic Woodstock concert in August 1969, which drew more than 400,000 fans to a New York farm, the deaths of Joplin and Hendrix in 1970, and the announcement late in 1970 that the Beatles had officially disbanded, rock music reached a crossroads. Considered a major part of the rebel counterculture in the 1960s (despite its profits), rock music in the 1970s was increasingly viewed as the centerpiece of mainstream consumer culture. With major music acts earning huge profits, rock soon became another product line for manufacturers and retailers to promote, package, and sell.

● Janis Joplin, performing in 1968 at the Newport Folk Festival with her band, Big Brother and the Holding Company. Her brief but brilliant career as a blues-rock singer ended with a heroin overdose in 1970. Her only top single, "Me and Bobby McGee," was released posthumously in 1971.

Nevertheless, some rock musicians continued the traditions of early rock. In the 1970s, stars like Bruce Springsteen emerged to carry on rock's integrationist legacy, combining the influences of Chuck Berry and Elvis Presley with the folk-rock poetry of Bob Dylan. Britain's Elton John drew upon the outrageous stage performances of Little Richard and the melodic influences of the Beatles. Generally, though, in the 1970s business concerns steered rock and its stars toward a new form of segregation, one that divided popular music along lines of class and race. Both the recording industry and album-oriented rock formats on radio began to aggressively market and program harder rock music and to aim it primarily toward middle-class white male teens.

Another sign that rock and roll had become synonymous with mainstream culture was the continued blurring of the distinction between the sacred and the secular. By the 1970s, rock and roll's earliest foes—religious institutions—had begun to embrace forms of rock as a means of retaining and attracting young churchgoers. In some Catholic churches, rock infiltrated via special church services that featured folk guitar versions of hymns. In many Protestant churches, where gospel music was already a familiar style, contemporary Christian gospel and Christian rock emerged, melding Bible-based lyrics with music that mimicked R&B, Top 40 pop, and even heavy metal. By the mid-1990s, Christian rock boasted a number of acts that featured newly minted contracts with major labels, and by 2000, it was one of the fastest-growing segments of the music industry. Bands like Jars of Clay, Audio Adrenaline, and dc Talk crossed over into mainstream radio and MTV, charting million selling CDs.

● Rising from the streets of late-1960s New York City, the pre-punk sounds of the Velvet Underground helped set the stage for punk groups like the Ramones and the Sex Pistols. While much of the U.S. focused on psychedelic music and the hippie movement, the Velvet Underground played as the house band for Andy Warhol's Factory and became synonymous with downtown bohemian chic. Although the group never became commercially successful, its sonic experimentation and gritty realism influenced generations of performers, including Joy Division, R.E.M., and Nirvana.

Alternative Sounds of Punk and Grunge

In the United States and Britain in the mid-1970s, **punk rock** challenged the orthodoxy and commercialism of the record business. Punk has generally been characterized by loud, unpolished distortions, a jackhammer beat, primal vocal screams, crude aggression, and defiant or comic lyrics. By this time, the glory days of rock's competitive independent labels had ended, and rock music was controlled by six major companies: CBS, Warner, Polygram, RCA, Capitol-EMI, and MCA. According to critic Ken Tucker, this situation gave rise to "faceless rock—crisply recorded, eminently catchy," featuring anonymous hits by bands with "no established individual personalities outside their own large but essentially discrete audiences" of young white males.[13]

In avoiding rock's consumer popularity, punk attempted to recover the early amateurish and offensive energies of rock and roll. Essentially, any teenager with a few weeks of guitar practice could learn the sound, making music that was both more democratic and more discordant than rock. In the early 1970s, pre-punk groups like the Velvet Underground set the stage for the Ramones and the Dead Kennedys. In England, the music of the Sex Pistols ("Anarchy in the U.K."), one of the most controversial groups in rock history, was eventually banned for offending British decorum.

Punk, of course, was not a commercial success in the United States in the 1970s, lack of widespread popularity being one of punk's goals. Nevertheless, punk made contributions, especially by "defining the big business of the rock industry and then

condemning it." Punk also offered women the opportunity "to participate fully in the rock world for the first time in the history of the music."[14] In the United States, for instance, poet and rocker Patti Smith helped pioneer punk in the mid-1970s, and in Britain, Siouxsie & the Banshees assaulted commercial rock's fixation on all-male groups.

Taking the spirit of punk and infusing it with attention to melody, **grunge** represented a significant development in rock in the 1990s. Grunge's commercial breakthrough can be traced to the "Smells Like Teen Spirit" cut on the album *Nevermind* by Nirvana, led by songwriter and vocalist Kurt Cobain. In 1992, *Nevermind* was the top-selling album in America, its popular success ironically built on satirizing some of the rock music of the 1970s and 1980s. One critic described a Cobain song as "stunning, concise bursts of melody and rage that occasionally spilled over into haunting, folk-styled acoustic ballad."[15] Suffering from stomach problems, drug addiction, and severe depression, Cobain committed suicide in 1994.

Influenced by punk, grunge groups adopted an alienated performing style that was in direct contrast to the slick theatrics of 1970s and 1980s rock. Taking a cue from low-key folk singers and 1960s rock bands like the Grateful Dead, grunge spoke the low-maintenance language of the garage: torn jeans, T-shirts, long underwear, worn sneakers, and old flannel shirts. But with the music's success, grunge's antistyle became commercially viable as hundreds of new garage bands emulated it.

Nirvana's influences paved the way for a variety of punk and alternative groups in the 1990s, including Nine Inch Nails, Smashing Pumpkins, Soundgarden, Stone Temple Pilots, and Pearl Jam.

In some critical circles, both punk and grunge are considered subcategories or fringe movements of **alternative rock**. This vague label describes many types of

● Nirvana's lead singer, Kurt Cobain, during his brief career in the early 1990s. The release of Nirvana's *Nevermind* in September 1991 bumped Michael Jackson's *Dangerous* from the top of the charts and signaled a new direction in popular music. Other grunge bands soon followed Nirvana onto the charts, including Pearl Jam, Alice in Chains, Stone Temple Pilots, and Soundgarden.

experimental rock music that offered a departure from the theatrics and staged extravaganzas of 1970s glam rock, which showcased such performers as David Bowie and Kiss. Appealing chiefly to college students, alternative rock has traditionally opposed the sounds of Top 40 and commercial FM radio. In the 1980s and 1990s, U2 and R.E.M. emerged as successful groups often associated with alternative rock. A key dilemma for successful alternative performers, however, is that their popularity results in commercial success, ironically a situation that their music often criticizes. Caught in this very predicament, Pearl Jam in 1993 tried to play down its commercial success by refusing to release any music-video singles from its No. 1 album, Vs., which had sold more than five million copies. Pearl Jam has continued to withdraw from the MTV spotlight and has since released only one music video, an all-animation piece for "Do the Evolution." It also chose to perform in smaller arenas and on college campuses rather than in the gigantic, impersonal sports stadiums preferred by established rock bands.

Hip-Hop Redraws Musical Lines

With the growing segregation of radio formats and the dominance of mainstream rock by white male performers, the place of black artists in the rock world diminished. By the late 1980s, no major popular black successor to Chuck Berry or Jimi Hendrix had emerged in rock. These trends, combined with the rise of "safe" dance disco by white bands (the Bee Gees), black artists (Donna Summer), and integrated groups (the Village People), created a space for the culture that produced hip-hop music.

In some ways a black counterpart to the spirit of white punk, **hip-hop music** also stood in direct opposition to the polished, professional, and less political world of soul. Hip-hop's combination of social politics, male swagger, and comic lyrics carried forward long-standing traditions in blues, R&B, soul, and rock and roll. Like punk, hip-hop was driven by a democratic, nonprofessional spirit—accessible to anyone who could talk (or "rap") to a funky beat in street dialect. But rap is just one part of the hip-hop sound, which can also include cutting (or "sampling") records on a turntable. Hip-hop deejays emerged in Jamaica and New York, scratching and recueing old reggae, disco, soul, and rock albums. As dance music, hip-hop developed MCs (masters of ceremony) who used humor, boasts, and "trash talking" to entertain and keep the peace at parties.

When the Sugarhill Gang released "Rapper's Delight" in 1979, the music industry viewed it as a novelty song, even though the music was rooted in a long tradition of party deejays playing soul and funk music through powerful sound systems. Then, in 1982, Grandmaster Flash and the Furious Five released "The Message" and infused rap with a political take on ghetto life. Rap also continued the black musical tradition of elevating the spoken word over conventional instruments, which were displaced by turntables. Although hip-hop was at first considered party music, its early political voices, including Public Enemy and Ice-T, addressed civil rights issues and the worsening economic conditions facing urban America.

Hip-hop exploded as a popular genre in 1984 with the commercial successes of groups like Run-DMC, the Fat Boys, and LL Cool J. That year, Run-DMC's album Raising Hell became a major crossover hit, the first No. 1 hip-hop album on the popular charts (thanks in part to a collaboration with Aerosmith on a rap version of the group's 1976 hit "Walk This Way"). Like punk and early rock and roll, hip-hop was cheap to produce, requiring only a few mikes, speakers, amps, turntables, and vinyl record albums. With

> " We're like reporters. We give them [our listeners] the truth. People where we come from hear so many lies the truth stands out like a sore thumb. "
> —Eazy-E, N.W.A., 1989

> " The creative and commercial emergence of women has been rivaled only by the growth of hip-hop as the most vital development in pop music in the '90s. "
> —Robert Hilburn, New York Times, 1999

CDs displacing LPs as the main recording format in the 1980s, partially obsolete hardware was "reemployed" for use by hip-hop artists, many of whom had trained in vocational colleges for industrial jobs that evaporated in the 1970s and 1980s.

Because most major labels and many black radio stations rejected the rawness of hip-hop, the music spawned hundreds of new independent labels. Although initially dominated by male performers, hip-hop was open to women, and some—Salt-N-Pepa and Queen Latifah (Dana Owens) among them—quickly became major players. Soon white groups like the Beastie Boys and 3rd Bass, and more recently Limp Bizkit and Kid Rock, were also combining hip-hop and punk influences in commercially successful music.

Hip-hop, like punk, defies mainstream culture. Some rap has drawn criticism from both the white and black communities for lyrics that degrade women or applaud violence. Rappers respond that punk has often been more explicit and offensive but that punk's lyrics are less discernible under the guitar distortion. The conversational style of rap, however, makes it a forum in which performers can debate such issues as gender, class, and drugs. A few hip-hop artists have also fought extended battles over copyright infringement, since their music continues to sample rock, soul, funk, and disco records. The 1998 hit "Hard Rock Life" by Jay-Z, for instance, samples a loop from the Broadway musical *Annie* (1982).

Although hip-hop encompasses many different styles, including various Latin offshoots, its most controversial subgenre is probably **gangsta rap**. This style developed in Los Angeles in 1987, partly in response to drug-related news stories that represented, at least for many African American communities, a one-sided portrait of life in urban America. This offshoot of rap drew major national attention in 1996 with the shooting death of Tupac Shakur, a performer, actor, and ex-con who lived the violent life he sang about on albums like *Thug Life*. But although Shakur was criticized for his criminal lifestyle, he was revered by many fans for telling hard truths about urban problems and street life. In 1997, Notorious B.I.G. (Christopher Wallace, a.k.a. Biggie Smalls), whose followers were prominent suspects in Shakur's death, was shot to death in Hollywood. He was considered Shakur's main gangsta-rap rival.[16]

In the wake of Shakur's and B.I.G.'s deaths, the business and sound of hip-hop changed with the rise of Sean "Puffy" Combs (now known as P. Diddy). He led Bad Boy Entertainment (former home of Notorious B.I.G.) away from gangsta rap to a more danceable hip-hop that combined singing and rapping with musical elements of rock and soul. In the late 1990s, Bad Boy was New York's hottest label. But Combs's increasingly commercialized, sample-heavy style angered many in the hard-line hip-hop community, who blamed him for diluting a purist urban art form. Meanwhile, gangsta rap continued to revisit the same themes established in the late 1980s but, for some, had lost much of its freshness.

Throughout hip-hop's history, artists have occasionally characterized themselves as street reporters who tell alternative stories of city life. Chuck D of Public Enemy has maintained that most hip-hop music offers interpretations of urban experience and the war on drugs that are very different from network-news portrayals. Despite the conflicts generated around hip-hop, it remains a major development in popular music. Like early rock and roll, hip-hop's crossover appeal, particularly to white male adolescents, seems rooted in a cultural style that questions class and racial boundaries and challenges status quo values.

Electronica Reinvents Popular Music

By the late 1990s, interest in hip-hop remained steady, but rock's influence as a genre waned, dropping from 32.5 percent of music sales in 1997 to 24.4 percent in 2001. In ascendancy were well-promoted pop acts, including the Backstreet Boys, Britney

Spears, Christina Aguilera, and 'N Sync. Outside of the spotlight, though, another form of music, called techno or **electronica**, was emerging from its underground origins. With beginnings in Britain in the 1980s and Detroit house music in the 1990s, electronica featured keyboards, drum machine beats, and music samples often sequenced with computers. Dozens of subgenres have developed as well, including minimal techno, drum 'n' bass, jungle, trip-hop, and trance. The development of electronica's various sounds is similar to the hybrid styles of rock and roll fifty years earlier. For example, *Goa trance* is a type of Asian electronica that combines a heavy beat with meandering keyboard tunes and the sounds of traditional Indian instruments.

The central elements of electronica culture are *raves*— late-night underground parties often held in urban warehouses or outdoors—characterized by an atmosphere of dancing, group vibes, and often designer drugs such as ecstasy. As in the case of rock and roll, some observers— including a 1998 television report on 20/20 titled "Stop the Raves"—have criticized electronica for fostering a drug culture. The creators of electronica are largely anonymous, so, as in hip-hop, the deejay who spins the music at clubs and parties is often the "star" of the music. Still, with electronica's increasing popularity in dance clubs, artists like Moby, Fatboy Slim, the Chemical Brothers, and Groove Armada have become familiar in sound, if not in name. In fact, because electronica's sound is contemporary and usually instrumental, it has become a frequently used background music for television commercials. For example, all eighteen tracks on Moby's 1999 recording *Play* were licensed for commercial use and have appeared in ads promoting everything from cars to computer software.

● Partygoers dance to the electronica sounds at a rave. Often criticized for their drug-friendly atmosphere, raves introduced a subculture of music that has now become mainstream.

The Business of Sound Recording

For many artists in the recording industry the relationship between music's business and artistic elements is an uneasy one. The lyrics of hip-hop or alternative rock, for example, often question the commercial values of popular music. Both hip-hop and rock are built on the assumption that musical integrity requires a separation between business and art. But, in fact, the line between commercial success and artistic expression grows hazier each day. When the questioning of commercialism resonates with enough fans, popular artists often stand to make a lot of money. In order to understand this situation, we will examine the business of sound recording.

By 2002, after several years of slow but steady growth, the global music market had reached about $40 billion in value. Although the United States accounted for a 37 percent share of the world's music sales, other nations such as Japan (16.7 percent), the United Kingdom (7.6 percent), Germany (7.4 percent), and France (5.2 percent) continued to be significant markets in the music industry. In economic terms, the music business generates more revenue in the United States than all other media except television. It also constitutes a global **oligopoly**: a business situation in which a few firms control most of an industry's production and distribution resources. Such global reach gives these firms enormous influence over what types of music gain worldwide distribution and popular acceptance.

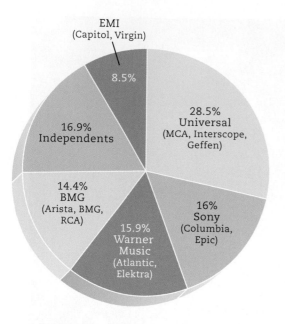

EMI
(Capitol, Virgin)

8.5%

28.5%
Universal
(MCA, Interscope,
Geffen)

16.9%
Independents

14.4%
BMG
(Arista, BMG,
RCA)

15.9%
Warner
Music
(Atlantic,
Elektra)

16%
Sony
(Columbia,
Epic)

Figure 3.2
U.S. Market Share of the Major Labels in the Recording Industry, 2001

Source: SoundScan.

> **❝** It's so fun to watch major labels get scared. They were so arrogant about being the only game in town for so many years. Now they've got to compete with people who are actually smart. **❞**
>
> – Jenny Toomey, musician and independent label owner, 2000

Five Major Labels Control Most of the World's Popular Music

From the 1970s to the late 1990s, six companies controlled popular music. Then, in 1998, Universal acquired Polygram, leaving five corporations that produce about 85 percent of all American CDs and cassettes and control 80 percent of the global market. The largest music corporation by far is Universal, part of the gigantic French conglomerate Vivendi Universal. Between 1995 and 2000, Universal was owned by the Canadian company Seagram, which was shifting its core business from distilled beverages (including brands such as Chivas Regal and Absolut vodka) to entertainment media with the 1995 purchase of MCA, better known as Universal Studios. In 2000, however, Seagram itself was swallowed up in a $33.7 billion takeover. The new company, Vivendi Universal, also has holdings in the film, television, cable, Internet, telecommunication, theme park, railway, energy, waste management, and water industries. About one in four recordings sold worldwide is a Universal product .

Whereas virtually all major labels were once American-owned, by 2002, only one major company, Warner Music (a subsidiary of AOL Time Warner), claimed the United States as its home base. In addition to Universal and Warner, the other global players are Sony, the Japanese company that bought CBS Records in the 1980s; BMG, owned by Bertelsmann in Germany, which bought RCA Records in the 1980s; and EMI, owned by Britain's EMI Group—the only company of the big five not controlled by a major multinational media conglomerate (see Figure 3.2). Each "major" owns and operates several labels, most of them formerly independent companies. The music industry as a whole—the five majors and the independents—produces more than 38,000 new full-length audio releases each year.

The Indies Spot the Trends

The rise of rock and roll in the 1950s and early 1960s showcased a rich diversity of independent labels, all vying for a share of the new music. These labels included Sun, Stax, Chess, Motown, and Atlantic. Today, most of these independents have folded or have been absorbed by majors. However, in contrast to the five global players, some five thousand large and small production houses—sometimes called **indies**—record less commercially viable music, or music they hope will become commercially viable. Often struggling enterprises, indies require only a handful of people to operate them. They identify forgotten older artists and record new innovative performers. To keep costs down, indies usually depend on wholesale distributors to promote and sell their music. Producing about 15 percent of America's music by 2003, indies often enter into deals with majors to gain the widest distribution for their artists. They may also entrust their own recordings or contracts to independent distributors, who ship new recordings to various retail outlets and radio stations. The Internet has also become a low-cost distribution and promotion outlet for independent labels, which often use Web sites for recording and merchandise sales, fan discussion groups, and regular e-mail updates of tour schedules and new releases.

In the music business, the majors frequently rely on indies to discover and initiate distinctive musical trends that first appear on a local level. For instance, although hip-hop was and still is rejected by many radio stations and major labels, indies such as Sugarhill, Tommy Boy, and Uptown emerged in the 1980s to produce this music for regional markets. In the early 1990s, punk faced similar problems and relied on labels such as Kill Rock Stars, Dischord, and Aargh! Records. Another independent label, Crammed (based in Brussels, Belgium), specializes in eclectic world music from new electronica to mutant pop. Indies play a major role as the music industry's risk-takers, since major labels are reluctant to invest in lost or commercially unproven artists.

Once indies become successful, the financial inducement to sell out to a major label is enormous. Seattle indie Sub Pop (Nirvana's initial recording label), faced with the commercial success of alternative rock, sold 49 percent of its stock to Time Warner for $20 million in 1994. Throughout the 1990s, Polygram, Sony, and EMI aggressively pursued the punk label Epitaph, which rejected takeover offers as high as $50 million and remains independent. In 2000, British independent London Records—home to acts such as All Saints and the Brand New Heavies—sold out to Warner Music. All five majors remain busy looking for and swallowing up independent labels that have successfully developed artists with national or global appeal.

Making, Distributing, and Profiting from a Recording

Like most mass media, the music business is divided into several areas, including artist development, technical facilities, sales and distribution, advertising and promotion, and administrative operations. Recording companies, whether major or minor, are generally driven by **A&R (artist & repertoire) agents**: the talent scouts of the music business who discover, develop, and sometimes manage artists. A&R executives listen to demonstration tapes, or *demos,* from new artists; and they decide whom to hire and which songs to record. Before Chuck Berry, Little Richard, and rock's British invasion, few commercially successful performers wrote their own music, so A&R agents had to match them with songs and writers—a practice still prevalent in country music.

The technical group at a recording label oversees the entire production process. A typical recording session is a complex process that involves musicians and audio technicians and is directed by a session engineer and a producer. George Martin, for example, served as both chief engineer and producer for the Beatles' sessions in the 1960s. He is credited with introducing orchestral sounds to rock music, a trend that many rock groups copied in the 1970s.

Today, the engineer and producer roles usually fall to different people. A chief engineer oversees the technical aspects of the recording session, everything from choosing recording equipment to arranging microphone placement. In charge of the overall recording process, the producer handles most nontechnical elements of the session, including reserving studio space and hiring musicians. During recording, the producer takes command and in most cases decides whether certain vocal or instrumental parts work well or need to be rerecorded.

Most popular CDs and tapes are now produced part by part. Using separate microphones, the vocalists, guitarists, drummers, and other musical sections are digitally recorded onto audio tracks. To produce one song, as many as two or three dozen tracks might be recorded, often at different times and in different studios. Controlling the overall sound quality, the chief engineer mixes the parts onto a two-track stereo master tape. Mixing engineers specialize in other postproduction editing; they mix the multiple tracks after the recording sessions. Mastering engineers prepare the song for transfer to a final version on audiotape and CD. Remix engineers work with tapes that are already mastered, removing flaws or adding new instrumental or vocal parts. Because digital keyboard synthesizers are able to reproduce most instrumental sounds, engineers can now duplicate many instrumental parts without recalling studio musicians.

Throughout the recording and postproduction process, the marketing department plans strategies for packaging, promoting, and selling a recording. In addition to arranging advertising in various media, this department might design point-of-purchase displays that use signs, posters, and other eye-catching gimmicks to encourage in-store impulse buying, which accounts for nearly 15 percent of all CD and audiotape sales.

> **66** Teenagers listen to $5^{1}/_{2}$ hours of music daily but only listen to their parents five minutes a day. **99**
> —CNN survey, 2000

Selling the Music

Distributing and selling CDs and tapes is a tricky part of the business. Most recordings are sold at direct retail record stores, which offer variety and account for about 42 percent of all record sales—down from a 70 percent share of record sales in 1990. The record store business is led by large but struggling chains such as Sam Goody (now a subsidiary of Best Buy) and Tower Records, each of which operates hundreds of stores nationally, mostly in high-rent shopping malls, in urban centers, and near college campuses. Direct retailers specialize in music, carefully monitoring new releases by major labels and independents. Like chain bookstores, direct music retailers keep a large inventory. Their staffs can also track down and order obscure recordings that the store may not have on hand. In addition, used-CD stores and inventories have developed as a by-product of the durability of digital recordings. Book chains such as Barnes & Noble and Borders are also direct retailers of recordings as part of their "superstore" books and media product mix.

Gaining on direct retail record stores are general retail outlets, like Wal-Mart, which have also captured about 42 percent of CD and tape sales. Because music is not the main focus of these stores, general retail outlets contract with *rack jobbers* to stock their stores' music racks or shelves with the latest CDs, audiocassettes, and music videos. Rack jobbers either lease shelf space from the stores or sell recordings directly to them. By managing inventories and orders, rack jobbers perform record-keeping tasks that many retailers prefer to avoid. To earn the highest profits, rack jobbers generally stock the most popular music, screen controversial titles for some of their clients, and ignore obscure musical forms.

Another 6 percent of recording sales each year come from *music clubs* such as BMG and Columbia. Like book clubs, music clubs use direct mail and inserts in Sunday newspapers to promote or advertise new and old releases. They might offer prospective members ten CDs for the price of one as an incentive to join. In exchange, for example, consumers may agree to buy at least three or four CDs at the regular price (about $15 to $17, plus a typical $2 shipping charge) over the next three or four years. Like major book clubs, music clubs sort through many possible new releases, identifying the commercial hits or "hot" groups. Through clubs, consumers are generally offered music by only the most popular and profitable performers.

Internet Distribution Outlets

In 1997, the recording industry began to track Internet sales of music for the first time. Although Net-based sales accounted for only 0.3 percent of music purchases that year, sales have climbed to nearly 3 percent of the U.S. market. Internet music purchases are made via Web-page order forms on independent music sites or through such retailers as CDNOW (acquired by Bertelsmann in 2000) and Amazon.com. Music sites typically allow computer users to download and listen to short segments of songs for free as they browse among possible purchases.

By the late 1990s, though, getting music from the Internet had taken on another meaning. Music fans engaged in digital music file-sharing, popularized by the easy-to-use Napster Web-site service. Napster and other file-sharing services had put millions of songs on the Internet that could be downloaded directly to computer hard drives for free. By late 2002, approximately three million people were connected to KaZaA.com, which had become the most popular file-swapping service, and shared more than 500 million files daily.[17]

The enormous popularity of online digital swapping services, despite the legal suspension of Napster's service in 2001 and Audiogalaxy's in 2002, called attention to the fact that the industry had failed to quickly adapt to the Internet as a new for-profit distribution outlet. The recording industry began to play catch-up, and by 2002, the five major recording corporations teamed up to develop two for-profit Internet sites to sell music online. AOL Time Warner, BMG, and EMI created MusicNet (along with online partner RealNetworks), while Sony and Universal invented Pressplay. (EMI, along with several independent labels, also licensed its music to Pressplay.) The Web services ranged in price from $9.95 to $24.95 per month, depending on the subscription plan. But critics assailed the two services for their inflexibility, as they confined listening to the computer only, via streaming or downloads, and limited or prohibited burning songs to CDs.

MTV Influences the Music Business

Virtually every artist today who introduces a new CD or cassette also makes an accompanying video for distribution on cable channels such as MTV, Country Music Television (CMT), Black Entertainment Television (BET), or VH1. By 2002, a typical music video cost a recording company and its artists between $150,000 and $500,000 to produce. However, some major stars and their labels spend in excess of a million dollars for a single video; the record amount is $7 million for Michael Jackson's 1995 video "Scream," laden with special effects and featuring Michael and Janet Jackson in an austere, weightless spaceship environment. Initially, MTV was important to recording companies and new artists. If artists had difficulty getting radio play, the cable channel became another venue for launching performers. MTV has become so influential today, however, that videos are often a must: Radio stations may choose not to play a particular rock artist until a demand has been created by MTV airings.

Dividing the Profits

A look at the various costs and profits from a typical CD reveals how money circulates in the recording industry. For a CD that retails at Tower Records for $16.98, the wholesale price is about $10.70, leaving the remainder as retailer profit. The more heavily discounted the CD, the less retail profit there is. The wholesale price represents the actual cost of producing and promoting the recording, plus the recording label's profits. The record company reaps the highest profit (close to $5.50 on a typical CD) but, along with the artist, bears the bulk of the expenses: manufacturing costs, packaging and CD design, advertising and promotion, and artists' royalties (see Figure 3.3 for proportional breakdown of costs). The physical product of the CD itself costs less than 25 cents to manufacture.

> **"** We're on the threshold of a whole new system. The time where accountants decide what music people hear is coming to an end. Accountants may be good at numbers, but they have terrible taste in music. **"**
>
> —Rolling Stones guitarist Keith Richards

Figure 3.3
Where Money Goes on a $16.98 CD

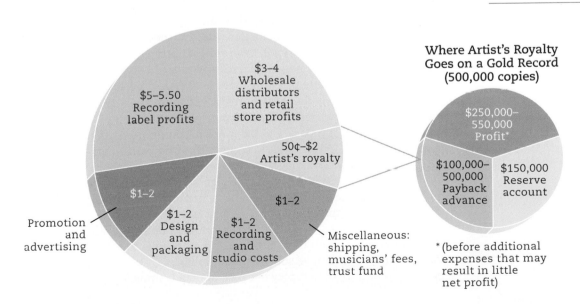

$5–5.50
Recording
label profits

$3–4
Wholesale
distributors
and retail
store profits

50¢–$2
Artist's royalty

$1–2

Promotion
and
advertising

$1–2
Design
and
packaging

$1–2
Recording
and
studio costs

Miscellaneous:
shipping,
musicians' fees,
trust fund

Where Artist's Royalty
Goes on a Gold Record
(500,000 copies)

$250,000–
550,000
Profit*

$100,000–
500,000
Payback
advance

$150,000
Reserve
account

*(before additional
expenses that may
result in little
net profit)

The punk band Fugazi is one of the leading acts of the independent Dischord Records label. Ian MacKaye, lead singer of Fugazi, began Dischord Records in 1980 to document the Washington, D.C.-area punk scene. Dischord sells CDs for only $10-12, but remains profitable and pays royalties to its bands.

An artist who has negotiated a typical 11 percent royalty rate would earn about $1.80 for a CD whose suggested list retail price is $16.98. So, a CD that "goes gold"— that is, sells 500,000 units—would net the artist around $900,000. But out of this amount, the artist repays the record company the money it has advanced him or her—from $100,000 to $500,000—for recording and music video costs, travel expenses, and promotional efforts. Another $150,000 might have to be set aside in a reserve account to cover any unsold recordings returned by record stores. After the artist pays band members, managers, and attorneys with the remaining money, it's quite possible that the artist will have almost nothing—even after a certified gold CD.

New artists usually negotiate a royalty rate of between 8 and 12 percent on the retail price of a cassette or CD. A more established performer might negotiate a 15 percent rate, and popular artists might get more than 15 percent. However, most lesser-known songwriters and performers remain in debt. For every Britney Spears, whose second album, *Oops . . . I Did It Again,* sold more than 1.3 million copies in its first week, there are thousands of songwriters and performers who cannot overcome their debts to various managers, producers, and record labels.

Independent producers or labels sign songwriters, singers, or groups and then advance them money to cover expenses, hoping for a hit song or album. More than 95 percent of all musicians who receive advances, however, do not recoup them through recording sales. Indeed, large numbers of artists fall gravely in debt or declare bankruptcy when their cut of record sales fails to cover their costs. Toni Braxton and TLC, for example, sold eighteen million CDs between them in the late 1990s but had to declare bankruptcy because of disadvantageous recording contracts: TLC received less than 2 percent of the gross, and Braxton received only 35 cents per album, far lower than the typical royalty rate.

In addition to sales royalties received by artists from their publishing companies, two other kinds of royalty payments exist: mechanical and performance royalties. Songwriters protect their work by obtaining an exclusive copyright on each song, ensuring that it will not be copied or performed without permission. To protect their copyrights, songwriters assign their creations to a publisher, who represents the songs by trying to sell them in printed form or by having them recorded by a major label or indie. Songwriters and publishers receive a *mechanical royalty* when they allow a song to be recorded. They are paid at a rate of about 7.55 cents per song, or about $0.75 for each CD or audiotape sold.

The owner of a song's copyright, which is not always the songwriter, also receives a *performance royalty* whenever the music is used on radio or television. Because songwriters are seldom wealthy enough to underwrite the original costs of producing a CD or tape, they often sell their copyrights to music publishers. On behalf of songwriters and publishers, performance royalties are collected by several national licensing associations, the largest of which are ASCAP and Broadcast Music, Inc. (BMI). These groups keep track of recording rights, collect copyright fees, and license music for use in TV commercials or films. Radio stations annually pay licensing fees of between 1.5 and 2 percent of their gross annual revenues, and they generally play only licensed music.

Pirates, Counterfeits, and Bootlegs

In the late 1980s, the collapse of the communist governments throughout Eastern Europe and the growth of wide-open economies worldwide led to a flourishing illegal market in the music industry. In the absence of international policing of copyright laws, manufacturing plants were set up, especially throughout China and other parts of Asia, to copy unauthorized CDs and cassettes. These illegal firms sold recordings at cut-rate prices, with no profits going to the original recording companies or to the artists themselves.

Unauthorized recordings were a part of the music industry for much of the twentieth century, and the recent popularity of digital technologies has made the illegal copies both better in quality and easier to make. The recording industry identifies four forms of illicit copying. First, as just described, are *counterfeits,* which duplicate the audio content of a recording as well as the original artwork, label, trademark, and packaging. Second are *pirates,* which copy only the audio portion of an original recording, often illegally reissuing out-of-print material or compilations such as "greatest hits" albums without official permission from the songwriter or copyright holder. A third form of unauthorized recordings involves *online piracy,* that is, the illegal uploading, downloading, or streaming of copyrighted material. Finally, *bootlegging* occurs from unauthorized or stolen tape recordings of live concerts, informal studio sessions, or live radio or TV appearances. Individuals duplicate these recordings and then sell them for profit without paying fees to the artists.

Although bootlegging has been a part of musical lore ever since tape recorders appeared in the 1930s, it reached its heyday in the 1960s. With informal folk and rock

● Rap artist Marshall Mathers (better known as Eminem) burst onto the music scene with an original style and highly controversial and explicit lyrics. In fact, after the release of his second album *The Marshall Mathers LP,* parents and politicians alike began speaking out against both Eminem for writing the songs and Interscope Records (his parent company) for allowing the album to be recorded. Despite the bad publicity, the record has sold over seven million copies.

Music's Mooks and Midriffs: Does the music industry sell music or sexual stereotypes?

Description. Consider the top 20 popular recording artists of any given week. What is their appearance and behavior? Is their image featured on the recording packaging? How are they portrayed in music videos?

Analysis. Note the similarities in representations of artists of the same sex, and the way the artists depicted in videos or photos interact with others. We can observe, for example, that the top female pop performers such as Mandy Moore and Britney Spears, who are marketed to girls age eight to fourteen, act slinky and provocative beyond their teenage years. Rachel Dretzin and Barak Goodman, the producers of the documentary *Merchants of Cool,* support this analysis. They charge that the entertainment industry, including MTV and the music recording industry, have created stereotypical "midriffs," a highly sexualized, world-weary sophisticate who is most valued for her body. For boys, the stereotype is the "mook," who is noted for being infantile, boorish, crude, misogynistic, and very, very, angry.

Interpretation. What do the patterns mean? One might suggest that such stereotypical images set an unfair standard for female and male behavior and appearance. Musical performer Sheryl Crow, for example, commented that the two stereotypes began with women's representations in rap video and MTV's emphasis on bikinis and sexiness. In her words, men were allowed to be "overweight and slobbish," and the women had to be "buff and perfect."[1]

Evaluation. Consider how the dominance of these stereotypical images affects the audience (by celebrating these images). We might consider that these stereotypes are marketing tools. But do they sell sexual images and activity to increasingly younger girls and boys? As the producers of *Merchants of Cool* argue, the entertainment industry creates a feedback loop of the mook and midriff stereotypes, in which the audience mimics the representations they see and hear every day.[2] For example, the fashion industry is now targeting six-year-old girls with provocative Britney Spears–like clothing.

Do such commercialized stereotypes ultimately go against the spirit of nonconformity and innovation in popular music? What performers and videos buck the trend?

---

concerts increasing, many musicians paid scant attention to those who recorded their performances. The most famous bootleg album from this period was a Bob Dylan collection, *The Great White Wonder,* a set of demo tapes and informal sessions that surfaced during the late 1960s while Dylan was recovering from a motorcycle accident. The Grateful Dead, arguably the most-taped artists in music history, were unable to stop the illegal recording of their lengthy concerts and eventually urged fans to tape their performances. Contemporary bands, such as Phish and the Dave Matthews Band, encourage fans to audiotape their concerts for personal use or trading, but ask them to not sell bootleg copies, which undermines their livelihood.

With the advent of recordable and rewriteable CDs and Internet sites offering illegal downloads of copyrighted music in the MP3 format, the recording industry's battle against unauthorized recordings has become even more complicated. By 2002, one in two CDs sold worldwide was an unauthorized recording.[18]

Alternative Voices

A few artists, concerned that they would lose complete creative control if they signed with a major label, have demonstrated an alternative path to success in the music industry. The Washington, D.C., punk band Fugazi has become nationally prominent while shunning offers from the majors and running its own label. Likewise, Canadian artist Loreena McKennitt has slowly built audiences for her blend of Celtic style and world music through touring, airplay on public radio, and word of mouth. She now has a string of recordings that have gone gold on her own Quinlan Road label. (See "The Global Village: The International Beat of World Music," page 100.)

Perhaps the artist to push the boundaries of economic independence the furthest is folk-rocker Ani DiFranco, who has sold more than 2.5 million recordings on her Righteous Babe label, and whose live-show ticket sales have put her in the fifty top-grossing music tours since 1996. DiFranco established her small record label in her native Buffalo, New York, in 1990 and created a thriving mini-industry in a city sometimes known for its bleak economy. She makes it a point to contract with local businesses to manufacture her CDs, posters, newsletters, and T-shirts, even when those items could be produced less expensively elsewhere. DiFranco has now attained such a level of success and self-sufficiency that she doesn't need the help of a major label.

Although the Internet and MP3 music files have received notoriety for the unauthorized trading of songs, the Net has also been a distribution site for musical artists resisting the major labels or seeking an audience. Rapper Chuck D, who broke away from Universal's Def Jam label to form his own Web sites, including <www.rapstation.com>, is using the Internet to develop cohesive online fan communities, while others use it to generate revenue by marketing CDs, T-shirts, and other merchandise. Artists may eventually use the Web to collect annual fan subscriptions, charge for early access to new music, offer special deals on collector's items, and boost attendance at shows. Thousands of aspiring artists have used the Internet like a sort of minor-league system, putting their work on Web sites for free in order to build interest, and using e-mail lists to stay in contact with fans. Some Web sites that feature unsigned bands, such as MP3.com and the Internet Underground Music Archive <www.iuma.com>, even pay a small fee to the band each time someone downloads their music, generating up to $100,000 for the most successful unsigned artists.[19]

Recordings, Free Expression, and Democracy

From sound recording's earliest stages as a mass medium, when the music industry began stamping out flat records with labels—which identified artists and turned them into stars—to the breakthrough of MP3s and Internet-based music services, fans have been sharing music and pushing culture in unpredictable directions. Sound recordings allowed for the formation of rock and roll, a genre drawing from such a diverse range of musical styles that its impact on culture is unprecedented: Low culture challenged high-brow propriety; black culture spilled into white; southern culture infused the North; masculine and feminine stereotypes broke down; and artists reconfigured sacred songs into sexually charged (and deeply threatening) lyrics and rhythms. Attempts to tame the music were met by new affronts, including those from Britain, Detroit, and the political and psychedelic fringe. The gradual mainstreaming of rock led to the establishment of other culture-shaking genres, including punk and grunge, hip-hop, and electronica.

The battle over popular music's controversial lyrics and visual styles speaks to the heart of democratic expression. Indeed, popular recordings have a history of confronting stereotypes and questioning conventions. Nevertheless, popular recordings—like other art forms—also have a history of reproducing old stereotypes: limiting women's access as performers, fostering racist or homophobic attitudes, and celebrating violence and misogyny.

The International Beat of World Music

In 1987, nineteen people met in a room above a pub in Islington, England, with a mission to define a new genre of music. After much discussion, we settled on the term *world music*. But although it has become widely accepted, somehow the phrase has never sounded as enticing as the music it describes. The best generic definitions of a musical style convey its sound or rhythm, preferably with an extra spice of mystery or daring: *Jazz* and *rock'n'roll* were euphemisms for making love; funk conjured the sounds and smells of sex; and reggae was a made-up word that had emphasis at the front and fell away at the end, just like the music itself.

Each word could be part of a song lyric and all were spontaneous inventions, a chance remark made by one person, picked up by another and settled upon by everyone else. By contrast, *world music* feels like a marketing term. Radio Nova in Paris describes its output as "sonar mondial," which has the euphony that we missed. But it's too late to turn back now. *World music* is a dictionary definition, an ever-expanding section in record shops, and a category at the Mobo awards. There are dozens of world music festivals held all around the world and an annual trade fair.

In Britain and the USA, world music has tended to imply music outside the mainstream, apparently disconnected with any music that is commercially successful. But it never had that interpretation in France, where a succession of performers have had hits sung in languages other than French or English, including the Gipsy Kings (who are French but mostly sing in Spanish), Alpha Blondy (the reggae singer from Côte d'Ivoire), Mory Kante (Guinea), Khaled (Algeria), and Cesaria Evora (Cape Verde). Significantly, most of them have sold far more records in the rest of the world than conventional pop and rock acts from France.

In the late 1980s, Les Négresses Vertes and Mano Negra redefined what French rock music could sound like, bringing together reggae and rai, punk, flamenco, and ska into an infec-

In the mid-1990s Manu Chao spent over a year in Latin America and Africa, recording fragments of songs, conversations, and radio shows. He stitched the results together for the album *Clandestino,* singing in French, Spanish, and English and strumming an acoustic guitar. Following the same blueprint, *Estación Próxima: Esperanza* was the best-selling album of 2002 in Europe.

tious brew that worked particularly well in live shows. In many ways, it had been the Jamaican and African influences in the music of British bands like the Specials, the Beat, and the Clash that opened the doors to such hybrids in the first place, but while the rest of the world took these multicultural visions seriously, later generations of British musicians have mostly closed down the range of their sources and resources.

Meanwhile, world music mostly matches the production methods of the rest of pop, with producers in control. Among the best albums this year were two made by trios of musicians who acted as their own producers, recruiting additional musicians for particular songs. *La Revancha del Tango* is the debut album by the Gotan Project (from France), and *El Cruzando del Río* is the third from Radio Tarifa (Spain); both feature accordion and Spanish-language vocals but are otherwise dissimilar in just about every way.

There's one more twist to the tale of world music. The soundtrack of *O Brother, Where Art Thou?* was released in 2000. Its songs, by Emmylou Harris, Alison Krauss, and Gillian Welch, sounded particularly effective when juxtaposed with tracks from both east Europe and west Africa, particularly those by the Romanian Gypsy group Taraf De Haidouks, and the Malian singer Rokia Traore.

Meanwhile, *O Brother* has become a grapevine phenomenon, selling several million copies and becoming the best-selling country music album in the USA for five months, despite being ignored by country radio stations. So world music radio programmers stretched out a welcoming arm to embrace yet another set of sounds into its ever-expanding range, making room for the lonesome fiddles and mandolins of Bill Monroe and Hank Williams.

Source: Adapted from Charlie Gillett, "Go global: The idea of world music was invented here. So how come Britain is missing out on so much of it, asks Charlie Gillett," *The Guardian* (London). November 1, 2001, p. 11.

Popular musical forms that test cultural boundaries face a dilemma: how to uphold a legacy of free expression while resisting co-optation by giant companies bent on consolidating independents and maximizing profits. For example, since the 1950s forms of rock music have been teetering at the edge of what's acceptable—becoming commercial, pulling back, reemerging as rebellious, and then repeating the pattern. The congressional payola hearings of 1959 and the Senate hearings of the mid-1980s triggered by Tipper Gore's Parents Music Resource Center (which led to music advisory labels) are a few of the many attempts to rein in popular music, whereas the infamous antics of heavy metal's Ozzy Osbourne, the blunt rap lyrics of Public Enemy, and the independent path of Ani DiFranco are among those actions that pushed popular music's boundaries.

Still, this dynamic between popular music's clever innovations and capitalism's voracious appetite is crucial to sound recording's constant innovation and mass appeal. The major labels need resourceful independents to develop new talent. So, ironically, successful commerce requires periodic infusions of the diverse sounds that come from ethnic communities, backyard garages, dance parties, and neighborhood clubs. At the same time, nearly all musicians need the major labels if they want wide distribution or national popularity. Such an interdependent pattern is common in contemporary media economics.

No matter how it is produced and distributed, popular music endures because it speaks to both individual and universal themes, from a teenager's first romantic adventure to a nation's outrage over social injustice. Music often reflects the personal or political anxieties of a society. It also breaks down artificial or hurtful barriers better than many government programs do. Despite its tribulations, music at its best continues to champion a democratic spirit. Writer and free-speech advocate Nat Hentoff addressed this issue in the 1970s when he wrote: "Popular music always speaks, among other things, of dreams—which change with the times."[20] The recording industry continues to capitalize on and spread those dreams globally, but in each generation musicians and their fans keep imagining new ones.

www.

To create an individualized study plan for Chapter 3, go to the interactive *Media and Culture* **Online Study Guide at: bedfordstmartins.com/ mediaculture**

REVIEW QUESTIONS

Technology and the Development of Sound Recording

1. The technological configuration of a particular medium sometimes elevates it to mass-market status. Why did Emile Berliner's flat disk replace Edison's wax cylinder, and why did this reconfiguration of records matter in the history of the mass media? Can you think of other mass-media examples in which the size and shape of the technology have made a difference?

2. How did sound recording survive the advent of radio?

U.S. Popular Music and the Formation of Rock

3. How did rock and roll significantly influence two mass-media industries?

4. Although many rock-and-roll lyrics from the 1950s are tame by today's standards, this new musical development represented a threat to many parents and adults at that time. Why?

5. What moral and cultural boundaries were blurred by rock and roll in the 1950s?

6. Why did cover music figure so prominently in the development of rock and roll and the record industry in the 1950s?

A Changing Industry: Reformations in Popular Music

7. Explain the British invasion. What was its impact on the recording industry?

8. How did soul music manage to survive the British invasion in the 1960s?

9. What were the major influences of folk music on the recording industry?

10. Why did hip-hop and punk rock emerge as significant musical forms in the late 1970s and 1980s? What do their developments have in common, and how are they different?

The Business of Sound Recording

11. What companies control the bulk of worldwide music production and distribution?

12. Why are independent labels so important to the music industry?

13. What accounts for the cost of a typical CD recording? Where do the profits go?

14. What are the four types of unauthorized recordings that plague the recording business?

Recordings, Free Expression, and Democracy

15. Why is it ironic that so many forms of alternative music become commercially successful?

QUESTIONING MEDIA

1. Who was your first favorite group or singer? How old were you at the time? What was important to you about this music?

2. If you ran a noncommercial campus radio station, what kind of music would you play and why?

3. Think about the role of the 1960s drug culture in rock's history. How are drugs and alcohol treated in contemporary and alternative forms of rock and hip-hop today?

4. Is it healthy for or detrimental to the music business that so much of the recording industry is controlled by five large international companies? Explain.

5. Do you think the Internet as a technology helps or hurts musical artists? Why do so many contemporary musical performers differ in their opinions about the Internet?

6. Do you think the global popularity of rock music is mainly a positive or a negative cultural influence? What are the pros and cons of rock's influence?

Visit <www.mediaculture.com> for related Internet links.

SEARCHING THE INTERNET

http://www.riaa.com

Web site of the Recording Industry Association of America, a trade group that promotes U.S. recording companies; loaded with updated statistics and industry legislation.

http://www.allmusic.com

With more than a half-million album recordings listed in its database, plus over 200,000 album reviews, the All Music Guide is an excellent resource for researching recorded music of all genres.

http://www.mp3.com

The major site on the Internet for information on the MP3 music format, including downloadable MP3 players and a huge variety of free MP3 music files. MP3.com is now part of Vivendi Universal.

http://www.billboard.com

The online site for *Billboard* magazine, which charts music recordings according to weekly sales.

http://www.rapstation.com

A site developed by seminal hip-hop figure Chuck D (Public Enemy), rapstation.com features independent hip-hop news, lyrics, and free downloads. The site is also affiliated with bringthenoise.com, an Internet hip-hop radio network; slamjamz.com, an interactive record label; and publicenemy.com, Chuck D's group.

http://www.rockhall.com

The site includes a virtual tour of Cleveland's Rock and Roll Hall of Fame museum, audio files and biographies of inductees, and an interactive timeline.

http://arts.endow.gov/endownews/news01/songlist.html

This site includes the list of the top 365 music recordings of all time, voted on by music lovers across the country and compiled for the "Songs of the Century" project—a nationwide education curriculum intended to promote a better understanding of the cultural influence of popular music.

In Brief

Survey the class to discover how many individuals download copyrighted digital audio files from the Internet.

1. Because the unauthorized downloading of copyrighted music is inherently unethical, why are so many people doing it?

2. Considering how the profits on a typical CD sale are divided, who is getting hurt by online piracy?

3. If most music becomes distributed on the Internet, how much would you pay per month for a service allowing unlimited downloads of music?

In Depth

In small groups, take on the investigation of a small independent recording company (of which there are tens of thousands throughout the United States and the world). Visit their Web site, and/or e-mail them or call them on the telephone. In your investigation, try to proceed through the four steps of the critical process:

Description. What kind of music does this label specialize in? Is the label limited to only one genre? What are some of the groups the label produces? Where and how does the label identify its musical artists? How does the label describe itself? How does the label distribute its recordings to consumers?

Analysis. Looking at the variety of groups the label produces, is there a kind of fan the label is trying to target? How does this label go about promoting its artists and getting a recording to the consumer? Does the label face any obstacles in popularizing its artists? Is the label fiercely independent, or is its goal to eventually sell to a major label? Is the label struggling, or is it financially viable?

Interpretation. From what you've gathered so far from your research, what are the major problems facing independent labels in the recording industry? Do you see independent labels overcoming these problems? How?

Evaluation. What is the value of small independent recording companies to the entire recording industry? What would be different about the recording industry as a whole if small independent labels didn't exist?

Add other questions and information as you go along. Meet with the members of your group to discuss your findings. Your group might want to prepare a chart or provide information on your label that can be shared with the rest of the class.

(Note: This assignment can be adapted to other media industries covered in this text.)

KEY TERMS

audiotape, 69
stereo, 70
digital recording, 70
analog recording, 70
compact discs (or CDs), 70
DVD, 70
MP3, 71
pop music, 73
jazz, 73

cover music, 73
rock and roll, 74
blues, 75
rhythm and blues (or R&B), 75
rockabilly, 77
payola, 81
soul, 84
folk music, 85
folk-rock, 85

punk rock, 87
grunge, 88
alternative rock, 88
hip-hop music, 89
gangsta rap, 90
electronica, 91
oligopoly, 91
indies, 92
A&R (artist & repertoire) agents, 93

popular radio

and the origins of broadcasting

Let's say you live in the Detroit area, the seventh largest radio market in the United States. It's summer, and you're spending a lot of time in your car, and outside, listening to the radio. You tune in to one of the market's top stations, WNIC-FM, an adult contemporary format. You're a chronic channel switcher, so you also try urban formats WJLB-FM and WMXD-FM, and then the contemporary hit sounds of WKQI-FM. Later in the day you are back in your car, cruising to a classic hits station, a sports talk station (because you saw a billboard for it), and yet another

sports station. All summer you heard plenty of concert promotions and attended a lot of shows: Madonna at the Palace at Auburn Hills, Maxwell and Alicia Keys at the Fox Theater downtown, Weezer at Cobo Arena, and Destiny's Child, Nelly, Eve, and Dream at the DTE Energy Music Theater north of the city.

What you didn't know about your summer is that nearly every public popular music experience you had was brought to you by one company, Clear Channel Communications. Clear Channel, the largest radio station chain in the

country, owns seven stations in Detroit, capturing about one-quarter of the metro area's radio audience. Nationally, Clear Channel owns more than 1,200 radio stations in the United States—more than 10 percent of all stations—and has up to eight stations in nearly every top 50 market. In the rock music radio format, Clear Channel controls the musical diet of more than 60 percent of the nation's listeners. Clear Channel also runs one of the country's largest billboard and outdoor sign businesses, which often advertises their radio stations.

But radio is just one part of the Clear Channel empire. In August 2000, a merger united Clear Channel and SFX, the largest live event promoter/producer in the world. The various divisions of SFX (now known as Clear Channel Entertainment) manage sports figures like Andre Agassi and Kobe Bryant; produce shows ranging from Broadway plays and Riverdance to Monster Truck Shows; and stage concert tours including the Backstreet Boys, U2, Janet Jackson, and Madonna. Clear Channel Entertainment claims that 66 million

people attend more than 26,000 events that it promotes and/or produces each year. Moreover, the conglomerate owns or has exclusive operating agreements to about 135 live venues, including the Detroit venues mentioned above.

With the acquisition of SFX, Clear Channel gained more of a lock on popular music in the United States, creating unprecedented synergies between radio and live music events. But some competitors are calling the "natural synergy" an illegal monopoly. For example, in an antitrust lawsuit filed against Clear Channel in a Denver federal court, concert promoter Nobody in Particular Presents (which has handled concerts for Pearl Jam, Sarah McLachlan, and others) charged that "Clear Channel repeatedly has used its size and clout to coerce artists to use Clear Channel to promote their concerts or else risk losing air play and other on-air promotional support."[1] Because touring bands need the promotional support and airplay of local radio stations, Clear Channel has great leverage over all other concert promoters.

Clear Channel is part of a larger trend in radio fueled by the unprecedented consolidation in radio-station ownership since the 1996 Telecommunications Act. Under the new, relaxed ownership rules—where consolidation reigns—it is much less expensive for a large corporate radio group to carry a syndicated program on all its stations than to locally program each individual station. Proponents of this system argue that nationally syndicated programs link the country together, creating deejay and talk-radio stars like Tom Joyner, Howard Stern, and Bob Kevoian and Tom Griswold (*The Bob & Tom Show*), all of whom reach large, nationwide audiences. But when radio segments are filled by national programming, the local deejays and talk anchors who emphasize regional ideas and interests are displaced. While this increasing reliance on syndicated programming may be cost-effective for owners, in many ways the radio industry is beginning to resemble the fast-food industry: less local flavor, fewer choices, and more national chains offering the same fare to popular demographic groups that advertisers target throughout the country.

he impact of radio in the twentieth century was immense, and from all indications its influence has not faded. From the early days of network radio, which gave us "a national identity" and "a chance to share in a common experience,"[2] to the more customized, demographically segmented medium today, radio's influence continues to reverberate throughout the airwaves. Though television has displaced radio as our most common media experience, radio has specialized and survived. The daily music and persistent talk that resonate from radios all over the world continue to play a key role in contemporary culture.

The story of radio from its invention at the turn of the last century to its survival in the age of television is one of the most remarkable in media history, and it will be the focus of this chapter. We will examine the cultural, political, and economic factors surrounding radio's development and perseverance. We will explore the origins of broadcasting, from the early theories about mysterious radio waves to the critical formation of RCA as a national radio monopoly. We will then probe the evolution of commercial radio, including the rise of NBC as the first network, the development of CBS, and the establishment of the first federal radio acts. Reviewing the fascinating ways in which radio reinvented itself in the 1950s, we will also examine television's impact on radio programming and its advertising base, focusing on the invention of FM radio, radio's convergence with sound recording, and the influence of various formats. Finally, we will survey the economic health, increasing conglomeration, and cultural impact of commercial and noncommercial radio today, including the emergence of a new noncommercial low-power FM service in 2000.

> **"** The telegraph and the telephone were instruments for private communication between two individuals. The radio was democratic; it directed its message to the masses and allowed one person to communicate with many.
>
> The new medium of radio was to the printing press what the telephone had been to the letter: it allowed immediacy. It enabled listeners to experience an event as it happened.**"**
>
> —Tom Lewis, *Empire of the Air,* 1991

Early Technology and the Development of Broadcasting

The wired and electronic transmissions of media messages have always required three ingredients: power (electricity); symbols (Morse code, music, or language); and a transmission-reception system (such as radio and TV stations and sets). Because of these requirements, radio did not emerge as a full-blown mass medium until the 1920s, though it had been evolving for a number of years.

Inventions Leading to the Modern Age of Mass Media

The **telegraph**—the precursor of radio technology—was invented in the 1840s. American artist-inventor Samuel Morse developed the first practical system, sending electrical impulses from a transmitter through a cable to a reception point. Using a symbol system that became known as **Morse code**—a series of dots and dashes that stood for letters in the alphabet—telegraph operators transmitted news and messages simply by interrupting the electrical current along a wire cable. By 1844, Morse had set up the first telegraph line between Washington, D.C., and Baltimore, Maryland. By 1861, lines ran coast to coast. By 1866, the first transatlantic cable ran between Newfoundland and Ireland along the ocean floor. Although it transmitted only about six words per minute, this cable was the forerunner of today's global communication technologies, including the Internet, faxes, and satellite transmissions.

Along with this revolution came a recognition of the telegraph's limitations. For instance, the telegraph dispatched complicated language codes, but it was unable to transmit the human voice. Armies benefited from telegraphed information, but ships still had no contact with the rest of the world. As a result, navies could not find out that wars had ceased on land and often continued fighting for months. Commercial shipping interests also lacked an efficient way to coordinate and relay information from land and between ships. What was needed was a telegraph without the wires.

The key development in wireless transmissions came from James Maxwell, a Scottish physicist who in the mid-1860s elaborated on some earlier ideas about electricity and magnetism. Maxwell theorized that there existed **electromagnetic waves**: invisible electronic impulses similar to visible light. Maxwell's equations showed that electricity, magnetism, light, and heat are part of the same electromagnetic spectrum and radiate in space at the speed of light, about 186,000 miles per second (see Figure 4.1). Maxwell further theorized that a portion of these phenomena, later known as **radio waves**, could be harnessed so that signals could be sent from a transmission point and obtained at a reception point. As one historian commented on the significance of Maxwell's ideas: "Every appliance we have today, from an electric generator to the microwave oven in the kitchen—and, of course, the radio—operates according to his fundamental equations. As Newton revolutionized mechanical science in the seventeenth century, so Maxwell revolutionized electrical science in the nineteenth."[3]

It was German physicist Heinrich Hertz, however, who in the 1880s proved Maxwell's theories. Hertz created a crude device that permitted an electrical spark to leap across a small gap between two steel balls. As the electricity jumped the gap, it emitted electromagnetic waves and marked the first recorded transmission and reception of a radio wave. Hertz's experiments profoundly influenced two inventor-entrepreneurs, Guglielmo Marconi and Lee De Forest, who at the turn of the last century began marketing wireless communication systems for businesses.

Marconi Invents Wireless Telegraphy

In 1894, Guglielmo Marconi, a twenty-year-old, self-educated Italian engineer, read Hertz's work and set about trying to make wireless technology practical. Marconi understood that developing a way to send high-speed messages over great distances

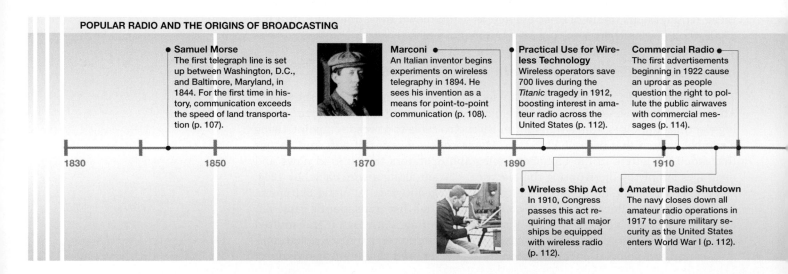

POPULAR RADIO AND THE ORIGINS OF BROADCASTING

Samuel Morse
The first telegraph line is set up between Washington, D.C., and Baltimore, Maryland, in 1844. For the first time in history, communication exceeds the speed of land transportation (p. 107).

Marconi
An Italian inventor begins experiments on wireless telegraphy in 1894. He sees his invention as a means for point-to-point communication (p. 108).

Practical Use for Wireless Technology
Wireless operators save 700 lives during the *Titanic* tragedy in 1912, boosting interest in amateur radio across the United States (p. 112).

Commercial Radio
The first advertisements beginning in 1922 cause an uproar as people question the right to pollute the public airwaves with commercial messages (p. 114).

1830 — 1850 — 1870 — 1890 — 1910

Wireless Ship Act
In 1910, Congress passes this act requiring that all major ships be equipped with wireless radio (p. 112).

Amateur Radio Shutdown
The navy closes down all amateur radio operations in 1917 to ensure military security as the United States enters World War I (p. 112).

Figure 4.1 The Electromagnetic Spectrum

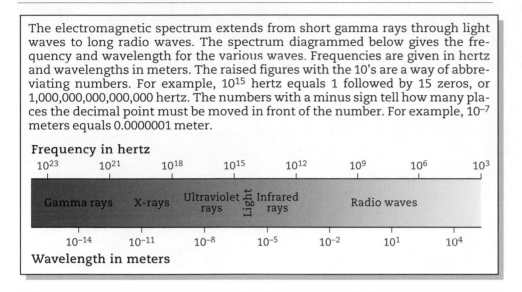

The electromagnetic spectrum extends from short gamma rays through light waves to long radio waves. The spectrum diagrammed below gives the frequency and wavelength for the various waves. Frequencies are given in hertz and wavelengths in meters. The raised figures with the 10's are a way of abbreviating numbers. For example, 10^{15} hertz equals 1 followed by 15 zeros, or 1,000,000,000,000,000 hertz. The numbers with a minus sign tell how many places the decimal point must be moved in front of the number. For example, 10^{-7} meters equals 0.0000001 meter.

Frequency in hertz

10^{23}	10^{21}	10^{18}	10^{15}	10^{12}	10^{9}	10^{6}	10^{3}

Gamma rays　X-rays　Ultraviolet rays　Light　Infrared rays　Radio waves

10^{-14}	10^{-11}	10^{-8}	10^{-5}	10^{-2}	10^{1}	10^{4}

Wavelength in meters

Source: *The World Book Encyclopedia*, Chicago, 1988.

would transform communication, the military, and commercial shipping. Although revolutionary, the telephone and the telegraph were limited by their dependence on wires.

Marconi improved on Hertz's experiments in a number of important ways. First, to the spark-gap transmitter he attached a Morse telegraph key, which could send out dot-dash signals. The electrical impulses traveled into a Morse inker, the machine that telegraph operators used to record the dots and dashes onto narrow strips of paper. Second, Marconi discovered that grounding—connecting the transmitter and receiver to the earth—greatly increased the distance over which he could send signals.

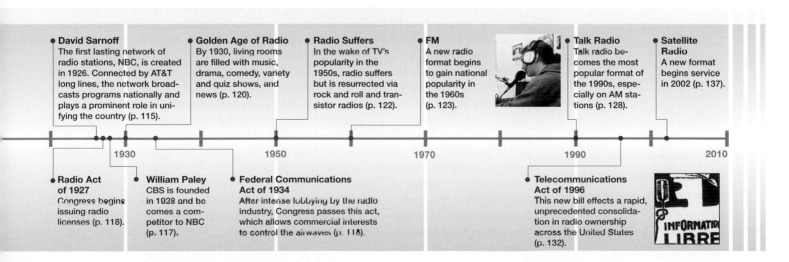

David Sarnoff
The first lasting network of radio stations, NBC, is created in 1926. Connected by AT&T long lines, the network broadcasts programs nationally and plays a prominent role in unifying the country (p. 115).

Golden Age of Radio
By 1930, living rooms are filled with music, drama, comedy, variety and quiz shows, and news (p. 120).

Radio Suffers
In the wake of TV's popularity in the 1950s, radio suffers but is resurrected via rock and roll and transistor radios (p. 122).

FM
A new radio format begins to gain national popularity in the 1960s (p. 123).

Talk Radio
Talk radio becomes the most popular format of the 1990s, especially on AM stations (p. 128).

Satellite Radio
A new format begins service in 2002 (p. 137).

1930　1950　1970　1990　2010

Radio Act of 1927
Congress begins issuing radio licenses (p. 118).

William Paley
CBS is founded in 1928 and becomes a competitor to NBC (p. 117).

Federal Communications Act of 1934
After intense lobbying by the radio industry, Congress passes this act, which allows commercial interests to control the airwaves (p. 118).

Telecommunications Act of 1996
This new bill effects a rapid, unprecedented consolidation in radio ownership across the United States (p. 132).

INFORMATION LIBRE

● Guglielmo Marconi (left) in a receiving station in Glace Bay, Nova Scotia, in 1907, communicating with a parallel station off the coast of Ireland.

The Italian government, not understanding what Marconi had accomplished, refused to patent his invention. Thus in 1896 he left for England, where he finally received a patent on **wireless telegraphy**, a form of voiceless point-to-point communication. In London, in 1897, he formed the Marconi Wireless Telegraph Company, later known as British Marconi, and began installing wireless technology on British naval and private commercial ships. In 1899, he opened a branch in the United States, establishing a company nicknamed American Marconi. That same year, he sent the first wireless Morse code signal across the English Channel to France, and in 1901 he relayed the first wireless signal across the Atlantic Ocean.

Although Marconi was a successful innovator and entrepreneur, his vision was limited. He saw wireless telegraphy only as point-to-point communication, much like the telegraph and the telephone, and not as a one-to-many mass medium. He also confined his applications to military and commercial ships. In limiting his patents to Morse-code transmission, Marconi left it to others to explore the transmission of voice and music via the wireless.

De Forest Invents Wireless Telephony

In 1899, inventor Lee De Forest (who subsequently liked to call himself "the father of radio") wrote the first Ph.D. dissertation on wireless technology. Understanding the extent and influence of Marconi's innovations, De Forest decided that he could ensure his future livelihood and place in history by going beyond Marconi. In 1901, De Forest challenged the Italian inventor, who had contracted with the Associated Press to cover New York's International Yacht Races. De Forest signed up to report the races for a rival news service. The two rivals' transmitters jammed each other's signals so badly, however, that officials ended up relaying information on the races the premodern way—with flags and hand signals. The event symbolized a problem that would persist throughout radio's early development: noise and interference from too much competition for a finite supply of radio waves.

In 1902, De Forest set up the Wireless Telephone Company to compete head-on with American Marconi, by then the leader in the field of wireless communication. A major difference between Marconi and De Forest was the latter's interest in wireless voice and music transmissions, which became known as **wireless telephony** and, later, as radio. Although occasionally accused of stealing others' ideas, De Forest

❝ I discovered an Invisible Empire of the Air, intangible, yet solid as granite. ❞

–Lee De Forest, inventor

went on to patent more than three hundred inventions. De Forest's biggest breakthrough was the development of the Audion, or triode, vacuum tube. Until the arrival of transistors and solid-state circuits, the Audion powered radios by detecting signals and then amplifying them. De Forest's improvements in detection, conduction, and amplification greatly increased listeners' ability to hear dots and dashes and, later, speech and music on a receiver set. His modifications were essential to the development of voice transmission, long-distance radio, and eventually television. In fact, many historians consider De Forest's improvements to the vacuum tube the beginning of modern electronics.

The credit for the first voice broadcast belongs to Canadian engineer Reginald Fessenden, formerly a chief chemist for Thomas Edison. Fessenden went to work for the U.S. Navy and eventually for General Electric (GE), where he played a central role in improving wireless signals. Both the navy and GE, however, were interested in the potential for simple voice transmissions that did not require Morse code. On Christmas Eve in 1906, after GE had built Fessenden a powerful transmitter, he gave his first public demonstration, sending a voice through the airwaves from his station at Brant Rock, Massachusetts. A radio historian describes what happened:

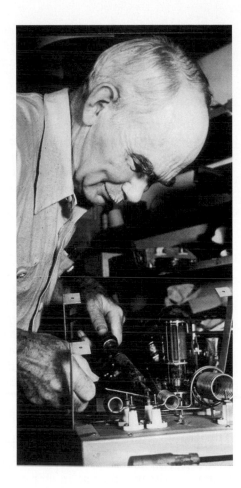

● Inventor Lee De Forest (1873–1961) continued working in his Los Angeles workshop well into the 1950s. His lengthy radio career was marked by incredible innovations, missed opportunities, and poor business practices. In the end, De Forest was upset that radio content had stooped, in his opinion, to such low standards. With a passion for opera, he had hoped radio would be a tool for elite culture.

> That night, ship operators and amateurs around Brant Rock heard the results: "someone speaking! . . . a woman's voice rose in song. . . . Next someone was heard reading a poem." Fessenden himself played "O Holy Night" on his violin. Though the fidelity was not all that it might be, listeners were captivated by the voices and notes they heard. No more would sounds be restricted to mere dots and dashes of the Morse code.[4]

Ship operators, who had not seen the publicity announcing Fessenden's broadcast, were astonished to hear voices rather than the familiar Morse code. (Some operators actually thought they were having a supernatural encounter.) The wireless medium was quickly moving from its use as a point-to-point communication tool (wireless operator to wireless operator) toward a one-to-many communication tool. As a medium for mass communication, radio broadcasts offered the possibility of sending voice and music to thousands of people. **Broadcasting**, once an agricultural term that referred to the process of casting seeds over a large area, would come to mean the transmission of radio waves (and, later, TV signals) to a broad public audience. Prior to radio broadcasting, the wireless was considered only a form of **narrowcasting**, the kind of person-to-person communication that was possible via the telegraph and telephone.

In 1907, De Forest followed Fessenden's first broadcast by sending radio voices and music—actually, a performance by Metropolitan Opera tenor Enrico Caruso—to his friends in New York. The next year, De Forest and his wife, Nora, played records into a microphone from atop the Eiffel Tower in Paris. The signals were picked up four hundred miles away. Radio had passed from an inventor's toy to a business venture; it was now poised to explode as a mass medium.

Regulating a New Medium

The two most important international issues affecting radio in the 1900s were ship radio requirements and signal interference. Congress passed the Wireless Ship Act in 1910, which required that all major U.S. seagoing ships carrying more than fifty passengers and traveling more than two hundred miles off the coast be equipped with wireless equipment with a one-hundred-mile range. The importance of this act was underscored by the *Titanic* disaster two years later. A brand-new British luxury steamer, the *Titanic* sank in 1912. Although fifteen hundred people died in the tragedy, wireless reports played a critical role in pinpointing the *Titanic*'s location, enabling rescue ships to save seven hundred lives.

In the wake of the *Titanic* tragedy, Congress also passed the **Radio Act of 1912**, which addressed the problem of amateur radio operators increasingly cramming the airwaves. A short policy guide, this first Radio Act required all wireless stations to obtain radio licenses from the Commerce Department. Because radio waves crossed state and national borders, legislators determined that broadcasting constituted a "natural resource"—a kind of interstate commerce. With this act, America also formally adopted the SOS Morse-code distress signal that other countries had been using for several years. The Radio Act of 1912 governed radio's development and regulated the new medium until 1927.

The Deals That Made Radio an American Medium

By 1915, more than twenty American companies sold point-to-point communication systems, primarily for use in ship-to-shore communication. Having established a reputation for efficiency and honesty, American Marconi, the U.S. subsidiary of British Marconi, was the biggest and best of these companies. But in 1914, with World War I beginning in Europe and with America warily watching the conflict, the U.S. Navy questioned the wisdom of allowing a foreign-controlled company to wield so much power. American corporations in competition with Marconi, especially General Electric and AT&T, capitalized on the navy's xenophobia and succeeded in undercutting Marconi's influence.

Wireless telegraphy played an increasingly large role in military operations as the navy sought tight controls on information. When the United States entered the war in 1917, the navy closed down all amateur radio operations and took control of key radio transmitters to ensure military security. As the war was nearing its end in 1919, British Marconi placed an order with GE for twenty-four potent new alternators, which were strong enough to power a transoceanic system of radio stations that could connect the world. But the U.S. Navy, influenced by Franklin Roosevelt, at that time the navy's assistant secretary, grew concerned and moved to ensure that such powerful new radio technology would not fall under foreign control. Roosevelt was guided by President Woodrow Wilson's goal of developing the United States as an international power, a position greatly enhanced by American military successes during the war. Wilson and the navy saw an opportunity to slow Britain's influence over communication and to promote a U.S. plan for the control of the emerging wireless operations. Thus corporate heads and government leaders conspired to make sure radio communication would serve American interests.

Some members of Congress and the corporate community opposed federal legislation that would grant the government or the navy a radio monopoly. Consequently, General Electric developed a compromise plan that would create a

private-sector monopoly. First, GE broke off negotiations to sell key radio technologies to European-owned companies like British Marconi, thereby limiting those companies' global reach. Second, GE took the lead in founding a new company, **Radio Corporation of American (RCA)**, which soon acquired the holdings of American Marconi and radio patents of other U.S. companies. By the end of 1919, RCA had pooled the necessary technology and patents to monopolize the wireless industry and expand American communication technology throughout the world.[5]

Under RCA's patents pool arrangement, wireless patents from the navy, AT&T, GE, the former American Marconi, and other companies were combined to ensure U.S. control over the manufacture of transmitters and receivers. Initially AT&T manufactured most transmitters, while GE (and later Westinghouse) made radio receivers. RCA administered the pool, collecting and distributing patent royalties to pool members. To protect individual profits from existing patents, the government did not permit RCA to manufacture equipment or to operate radio stations under its own name for several years. Instead, RCA's initial function was to ensure that radio parts were standardized by manufacturers and to control frequency interference by amateur radio operators, which became an increasing problem after the war.

At this time, the control of patents, amateur radio operators, and foreign radio competitors was among RCA's major concerns. A government restriction mandated that no more than 20 percent of RCA—and eventually any U.S. broadcasting facility—could be owned by foreigners. This restriction, later raised to 25 percent, became law in 1934 and applied to all U.S. broadcasting stocks and facilities. Because of this rule, in 1985 Rupert Murdoch, the head of Australia's giant News Corp., became a U.S. citizen so that he could buy a number of TV stations as well as form the Fox television network.

RCA's most significant impact was that it gave the United States almost total control over the emerging mass medium of broadcasting, which had not been anticipated by most wireless companies. At the time, the United States was the only

● French engineers transmitted an early wireless signal from the Eiffel Tower in 1898. Their Morse code transmission was picked up almost three miles away. Two years earlier, twenty-two-year-old Guglielmo Marconi had sent a signal two miles across his parents' estate in Bologna, Italy.

country that placed broadcasting under the care of commercial, rather than military or government, interests. By pooling more than two thousand patents and sharing research developments, RCA ensured the global dominance of the United States in mass communication, a position it maintained in electronic hardware into the 1960s and maintains in program content today.

The Evolution of Commercial Radio

When Westinghouse engineer Frank Conrad set up a crude radio studio above his Pittsburgh garage in 1916, placing a microphone in front of a phonograph to broadcast music and news to his friends (whom Conrad supplied with receivers) two evenings a week on experimental station 8XK, he unofficially became one of the medium's first disc jockeys. In 1920, a Westinghouse executive who had become intrigued by Conrad's curious hobby realized the potential of radio as a mass medium, and a new opportunity to sell radio receivers to the general public. Westinghouse then established station KDKA, which is generally regarded as the first commercial broadcast station. KDKA is most noted for airing national returns from the Cox-Harding presidential election on November 2, 1920, an event most historians consider the first professional broadcast. Other amateur broadcasters could also lay claim to being first. One of the earliest stations, operated by Charles "Doc" Herrold in San Jose, California, began in 1909 and later became KCBS. Additional experimental stations—in places like New York; Detroit; Medford, Massachusetts; and Pierre, South Dakota—broadcast voice and music prior to the establishment of KDKA. But KDKA's success, with the financial backing of Westinghouse, signaled the transformation of the age of point-to-point wireless into the age of broadcast radio.

> **"**I believe the quickest way to kill broadcasting would be to use it for direct advertising.**"**
>
> —Herbert Hoover, Secretary of Commerce, 1924

In 1921, the U.S. Commerce Department officially licensed five radio stations for operation; by early 1923, more than six hundred commercial and noncommercial stations were operating. Some stations were owned by AT&T, GE, and Westinghouse, but many were run by amateurs or were independently owned by universities or businesses. Later, the government permitted RCA to acquire its own stations. By the end of 1923, as many as 550,000 radio receivers, most manufactured by GE and Westinghouse, had been sold for about $55 each. Just as the "guts" of the phonograph had been put inside a piece of furniture to create a consumer product, the vacuum tubes, electrical posts, and bulky batteries that made up the radio receiver were placed inside stylish furniture and marketed to households. By 1925, 5.5 million radio sets were in use across America, and radio was a mass medium.

The RCA Partnership Unravels

In 1922, in a major power grab, AT&T, which already had a government-sanctioned monopoly in the telephone business, decided to break its RCA agreements in an attempt to monopolize radio as well. Identifying the new medium as the "wireless telephone," AT&T argued that broadcasting was merely an extension of its control over the telephone. Ultimately, the corporate giant complained that RCA had gained too much monopoly power. In violation of its early agreements with RCA, AT&T began making and selling its own radio receivers.

In the same year, AT&T started WEAF (now WNBC) in New York, the first radio station to regularly sell commercial time to advertisers. AT&T claimed that under the RCA agreements it had the exclusive right to sell ads, which AT&T called *toll broadcasting*. Most people in radio at the time recoiled at the idea of using the medium for crass advertising, viewing it instead as a public information service. In fact, stations that had earlier tried to sell ads received "cease and desist" letters from the Department of Commerce. But by August 1922, AT&T had nonetheless sold its first ad to a New York real-estate developer for $50. The idea of promoting the new medium as a public service, along the lines of today's noncommercial National Public Radio (NPR), ended when executives realized that radio ads offered another opportunity for profits. Advertising would in fact ensure profits long after radio-set sales had saturated the consumer market.

The initial strategy behind AT&T's toll broadcasting idea, however, was its effort to conquer radio. By virtue of its agreements with RCA, AT&T retained the rights to interconnect the signals between two or more radio stations via telephone wires. In 1923, when AT&T aired a program simultaneously on its flagship WEAF station and on WNAC in Boston, the phone company created the first **network**: a cost-saving operation that links, through special phone lines (and, later, satellite relays), a group of broadcast stations that share programming produced at a central location. By the end of 1924, AT&T had interconnected twenty-two stations in order to air a talk by President Calvin Coolidge. Some of these stations were owned by AT&T, but most of them simply consented to become AT&T "affiliates," agreeing to air the phone company's programs. These network stations informally became known as the *telephone group* and later as the Broadcasting Corporation of America (BCA).

In response, GE, Westinghouse, and RCA interconnected a smaller set of competing stations, known as the *radio group*. Initially, their network linked WGY in Schenectady, New York (then GE's national headquarters), and WJZ in Manhattan. The radio group had to use inferior Western Union telegraph lines when AT&T denied them access to telephone wires. By this time, AT&T had sold its stock in RCA and refused to lease its lines to competing radio networks. The telephone monopoly was now enmeshed in a battle to defeat RCA for control of radio. This, among other problems, eventually led to a government investigation and an arbitration settlement in 1925. In the agreement, the Justice Department, irritated by AT&T's power grab, redefined patent agreements. AT&T received a monopoly on providing the wires, known as *long lines*, to interconnect stations nationwide. In exchange, AT&T sold its BCA network to RCA for $1 million and agreed not to reenter broadcasting for eight years (a banishment that actually extended into the mid-1990s).

Sarnoff and NBC: Building the "Blue" and "Red" Networks

After Lee De Forest, David Sarnoff was among the first to envision the wireless as a modern mass medium. From the time he served as Marconi's fifteen-year-old personal messenger, Sarnoff rose rapidly at American Marconi. He became a wireless operator, helping to relay information about the *Titanic* survivors in 1912. Promoted to a series of management positions, Sarnoff was closely involved in RCA's creation in 1919, when most radio executives saw wireless merely as point-to-point communication. But with Sarnoff as RCA's first commercial manager, radio's potential as a mass medium was quickly realized. At age thirty, Sarnoff became RCA's general manager in 1921.

After RCA bought AT&T's telephone group network, Sarnoff created a new subsidiary in September 1926 called the National Broadcasting Company (NBC). Its ownership was shared by RCA (50 percent), General Electric (30 percent), and Westinghouse (20 percent). This loose network of stations would be hooked together by AT&T long lines. Shortly thereafter, the original telephone group became known as the NBC-Red network, and the radio group became the NBC-Blue network.

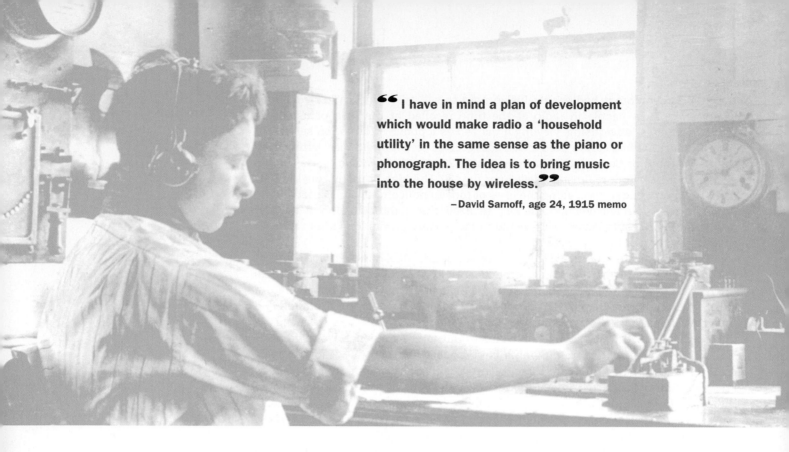

● A young David Sarnoff, who had taught himself Morse code and learned as much as possible in Marconi's experimental shop in New York, was given a job as wireless operator for the station on Nantucket Island. He went on to create NBC and network radio.

Although NBC owned a number of stations by the late 1920s, many independent stations also began affiliating with the NBC networks to receive programming. An affiliate station, though independently owned, signs a contract to be part of a network and receives money to carry the network's programs. In exchange, the network reserves time slots, which it sells to national advertisers. By 1933, NBC-Red had twenty-eight affiliates; NBC-Blue had twenty-four.

Recall that the rationale behind a network is an economic one: A network enables stations to control program costs and avoid unnecessary duplication. As early as 1923, AT&T had realized that it would be cheaper to produce programs at one station and broadcast them simultaneously over a network of owned or affiliated stations than for each station to generate its own programs. Such a network centralized costs and programming by bringing the best musical, dramatic, and comedic talent to one place, where programs could be produced and then distributed all over the country.

In fact, network radio may have helped modernize America by de-emphasizing the local and the regional in favor of national programs broadcast to nearly everyone. For example, when Charles Lindbergh returned from the first solo transatlantic flight in 1927, an estimated twenty-five to thirty million people listened to his welcome-home party on the six million radio sets then in use. At the time, it was the largest shared audience experience in the history of any mass medium.

David Sarnoff's leadership at RCA was capped by two other negotiations that solidified his stature as the driving force behind radio's development as a modern medium. In 1929, Sarnoff cut a deal with General Motors for the manufacture of car radios, which had been invented a year earlier by William Lear (later the designer of the Learjet), who sold the radios under the name Motorola. Sarnoff also merged RCA with the Victor Talking Machine Company. Afterward, until the mid-1960s, the company was known as RCA Victor, adopting as its corporate symbol the famous terrier sitting alertly next to a Victrola radio-phonograph. The merger gave RCA control over Victor's records and recording equipment, making the radio company a major player in the sound recording industry. In 1930, David Sarnoff became president of RCA. He ran the company for the next forty years.

Government Scrutiny Ends RCA's Monopoly

As early as 1923, the Federal Trade Commission had charged RCA with violations of antitrust laws but allowed the monopoly to continue. By the late 1920s, the government, concerned about NBC's growing control over radio content, intensified its scrutiny. Then, in 1930, when RCA bought out the GE and Westinghouse interests in the two NBC networks, federal marshals charged RCA/NBC with a number of violations, including exercising too much control over manufacturing and programming. Although the government had originally sanctioned a closely supervised monopoly for wireless communication, RCA products, its networks, and the growth of the new mass medium dramatically changed the radio industry by the late 1920s. After the collapse of the stock market in 1929, the public became increasingly distrustful of big business. In 1932, the government revoked RCA's monopoly status.

RCA acted quickly. To eliminate its monopolizing partnerships, Sarnoff's company bought out GE's and Westinghouse's remaining shares in RCA's manufacturing business. Now RCA would compete directly against GE, Westinghouse, and other radio manufacturers, encouraging more competition in the radio manufacturing industry. Ironically, in the mid-1980s, General Electric bought back RCA, a shell of its former self and no longer competitive with foreign electronics firms. GE was chiefly interested in RCA's brand-name status and its still-lucrative subsidiary, NBC.

Paley and CBS: Challenging NBC

Even with RCA's head start and its favored status, the company's two NBC networks faced competitors in the late 1920s. The competitors all found it tough going. One group, United Independent Broadcasters (UIB), even lined up twelve prospective affiliates and offered them $500 a week for access to ten hours of station time in exchange for quality programs. UIB was cash-poor, however, and AT&T would not rent the new company line services to link the affiliates. Enter the Columbia Phonograph Company, which was looking for a way to preempt RCA's merger with the Victor Company, then Columbia's major competitor. With backing from the record company, UIB and the new Columbia Phonograph Broadcasting System launched a wobbly sixteen-affiliate network in 1927, nicknamed CPBS. But after losing $100,000 in the first month, the record company pulled out. Later, CPBS dropped the word *phonograph* from the title, creating the Columbia Broadcasting System (CBS).

In 1928, William Paley, the twenty-seven-year-old son of Sam Paley, owner of a Philadelphia cigar company, bought a controlling interest in CBS to sponsor the cigar manufacturer's La Palina brand. One of Paley's first moves was to hire the public relations pioneer Edward Bernays, Sigmund Freud's nephew, to polish the new network's image. Paley and Bernays modified a concept called **option time**, in which CBS paid affiliate stations $50 per hour for an option on any portion of their time. The network provided programs to them and sold ad space or sponsorships to various product companies. In theory, CBS could now control up to twenty-four hours a day of its affiliates' radio time. Some affiliates received thousands of dollars per week merely to serve as conduits for CBS programs and ads. Because NBC was still charging some of its affiliates as much as $90 a week to carry network programs, the CBS offer was extremely appealing.

By 1933, Paley's efforts had netted CBS more than ninety affiliates, many of them defecting from NBC. Paley also concentrated on developing news programs and entertainment shows, particularly soap operas and comedy-variety series. In the process, CBS successfully raided NBC, not just for affiliates but for top talent as well. Throughout the 1930s and 1940s, Paley lured a number of radio stars from NBC, including Jack Benny, Frank Sinatra, George Burns and Gracie Allen, and Groucho Marx. During World War II, Edward R. Murrow's powerful firsthand news reports from bomb-riddled London established CBS as the premier radio news network, a reputation it carried forward to television. In 1949, near the end of big-time network radio, CBS finally surpassed NBC as the highest-rated network. Although William Paley had intended to run CBS only for six months to help get it off the ground, he ultimately ran it for more than fifty years.

A Cooperative Network:
The Mutual Broadcasting System

While the major networks were building their dynasties during the 1930s, not all radio stations sought affiliations with them; many stations were content to produce their own regional and local programs. In 1934, four powerful independent stations—WGN in Chicago, WOR in Newark, WLW in Cincinnati, and WXYZ in Detroit—formed the Mutual Broadcasting System. Sharing programs and functioning more as a cooperative venture than as a regular network, three of these stations operated fifty-thousand-watt "clear channels" that reached most of North America. Among the first AM stations established in the United States, clear channels claimed the most powerful AM signals. Other stations operating on the same channels were required to reduce their signal power at night, allowing clear channel stations to broadcast with a minimum of interference across distances of hundreds of miles, giving them huge potential audiences.

Mutual offered a small central news service and a few entertainment programs, and it mostly served smaller stations, often in remote areas that were ignored by NBC and CBS. In 1968, Mutual became the first network to offer a news service, the Mutual Black Network, which raised issues of interest to black listeners. Today, Mutual serves thousands of radio affiliates by providing a variety of national news services and other programs, including rebroadcasts of many old radio programs from the 1930s.

Bringing Order to Chaos with the Radio Act of 1927

In the 1920s, as radio moved from narrowcasting to broadcasting, the battle for more frequency space and less channel interference intensified. Manufacturers, engineers, station operators, network executives, and the listening public demanded action. Many wanted more sweeping regulation than the simple licensing function granted under the Radio Act of 1912, which gave the Commerce Department little power to deny a license or to unclog the airwaves.

Beginning in 1924, commerce secretary Herbert Hoover ordered radio stations to share time and to set aside certain frequencies for entertainment and news and others for farm and weather reports. To challenge Hoover, a station in Chicago jammed the airwaves, intentionally moving its signal onto an unauthorized frequency. In 1926, the courts decided that based on the existing Radio Act, Hoover had the power only to grant licenses, not to restrict stations from operating. Within the year, two hundred new stations clogged the airwaves, creating a chaotic period in which nearly all radios had poor reception. By early 1927, sales of radio sets had declined sharply.

In an attempt to restore order to the airwaves, Congress passed the **Radio Act of 1927**, the precursor to the **Federal Communications Act of 1934**. The 1927 act stated that licensees did not *own* their channels but could license them as long as they operated in order to serve the "public interest, convenience, or necessity." To oversee licenses and negotiate channel problems, the 1927 act created the **Federal Radio Commission (FRC)**, whose members were appointed by the president. Although the FRC was intended as a temporary committee, it grew into a powerful regulatory agency. In 1934, with passage of the Federal Communications Act, the FRC became

" Four years ago we were dealing with a scientific toy; today we are dealing with a vital force in American life. **"**

–Herbert Hoover, 1925

● During America's golden age of radio, millions tuned in to popular entertainment programs each week. Audiences thrilled to the suspenseful mysteries of Sherlock Holmes in 1939 and 1940. The detective was played by the dashing Basil Rathbone, who also played Holmes in a number of films.

the **Federal Communications Commission (FCC)**. Its jurisdiction covered not only radio but also the telephone and the telegraph (and later television, cable, and the Internet).

In 1941, an activist FCC went after the networks. Declaring that NBC and CBS could no longer force affiliates to carry programs they did not want, the government outlawed the practice of option time that Paley had used to build CBS into a major network. The FCC also demanded that RCA sell one of its two NBC networks. RCA and NBC claimed that the rulings would bankrupt them. The Supreme Court sided with the FCC, however, and RCA eventually sold NBC-Blue to a group of businessmen for $8 million in the mid-1940s. It became the American Broadcasting Company (ABC). These government crackdowns brought long-overdue reform to the radio industry. But they had not come soon enough to prevent considerable damage to noncommercial radio.

The Golden Age of Radio

Many ingredients in television today were initially formulated for radio. The term *veejay*, or *video jockey*, used on cable's MTV and VH1, derives from *deejay*, or *disc jockey*, a term first used in 1941 to describe someone who played recorded music on radio programs. In addition, the first weather forecasts and farm reports on radio began in the 1920s. Regularly scheduled radio news analysis started in 1927, with H. V. Kaltenborn, a reporter for the *Brooklyn Eagle*, providing commentary on AT&T's WEAF. The first regular *network* news analysis began on CBS in 1930, featuring Lowell Thomas, who would remain on radio for forty-four years. Thomas's first report began, "Adolf Hitler, the German fascist chief, is snorting fire. There are now two Mussolinis in the world, which seems to offer a rousing time."[6]

Radio in this golden age was not the portable medium it would later become, however. Prior to transistors and solid-state integrated circuits, most radio sets required large glass tubes housed in heavy wooden pieces of furniture. Like television today, the radio commanded a central position in most American living rooms in the 1930s and 1940s. At the time, only a handful of stations operated in most large radio markets, and popular stations were affiliated with either CBS or one of the two NBC networks. Many large stations employed their own in-house orchestras and aired live music daily. Listeners had favorite evening programs, usually fifteen minutes long, which they would tune in each night. Families gathered around the radio to hear such shows as *Amos 'n' Andy*, *The Shadow*, *The Lone Ranger*, *The Green Hornet*, and *Fibber McGee and Molly*, or one of President Franklin Roosevelt's fireside chats.

Among the most popular early forms on radio, the *variety show* served as the forerunner to such popular TV shows as the *Ed Sullivan Show*. The variety show, developed from stage acts and vaudeville, began with the *Eveready Hour* in 1923 on WEAF. Considered experimental, the program presented classical music, minstrel shows, comedy sketches, and dramatic readings. Stars from vaudeville, musical comedy, and New York theater and opera would occasionally make guest appearances.

By the 1930s, studio-audience *quiz shows*—*Professor Quiz* and the *Old Time Spelling Bee*—had emerged. Other quiz formats, used on *Information Please* and *Quiz Kids*, featured guest panelists. The quiz formats were later copied by television, particularly in the 1950s. *Truth or Consequences*, based on a nineteenth-century parlor game, began in 1940 and presented guests performing goofy stunts. It ran for seventeen years on radio and another twenty-seven on television, influencing TV stunt shows like CBS's *Beat the Clock* in the 1950s and NBC's *Fear Factor* in the early 2000s.

Dramatic programs, mostly radio plays that were broadcast live from theaters, developed as early as 1922. Historians mark the appearance of *Clara, Lu, and Em* on WGN in 1931 as the first *soap opera*. One year later, Colgate-Palmolive bought the program, put it on NBC, and began selling the soap products that gave this dramatic genre its distinctive nickname. Early "soaps" were fifteen minutes in length and ran five or six days a week. It wasn't until the mid-1960s on television that soaps were extended to thirty minutes, and by the late 1970s some had expanded to sixty minutes. Still a fixture on CBS, the *Guiding Light* actually began on radio in 1937 and moved to television in 1952 (the only radio soap to successfully make the transition). By 1940, sixty different soap operas occupied nearly eighty hours of network radio time each week.

The *situation comedy*, a major staple of TV programming today, also began on radio in the mid-1920s. By the early 1930s, the most popular comedy was *Amos 'n' Andy,* which started on Chicago radio in 1925 before moving to NBC-Blue in 1929. By today's standards, *Amos 'n' Andy* can be described as a nineteenth-century minstrel show that often stereotyped black characters as shiftless and stupid. Created as a blackface stage act by two white comedians, Charles Correll and Freeman Gosden, the program was criticized as racist. But NBC and the program's producers claimed that *Amos 'n' Andy* was as popular among black audiences as among white listeners.

A pioneering program in many ways, *Amos 'n' Andy* launched the idea of the *serial show*: a program that featured continuing story lines from one day to the next. The format was soon copied by soap operas and other radio dramas. *Amos 'n' Andy* aired six nights a week from 7:00 to 7:15 P.M. During the show's first year on the network, radio-set sales rose nearly 25 percent nationally. To keep people coming to restaurants and movie theaters, owners broadcast *Amos 'n' Andy* in lobbies, rest rooms, and entryways. Early radio research estimated that the program aired in more than half of all radio homes in the nation during the 1930–31 season, making it the most popular radio series in history. From 1951 to 1953, it made a brief transition to television (Correll and Gosden sold the rights to CBS for $1 million), becoming the first TV series to have an entirely black cast.

While *Amos 'n' Andy* was the most popular series in radio, the most famous single broadcast featured an adaptation of H. G. Wells' *War of the Worlds* on the radio series *Mercury Theater of the Air*. Orson Welles produced, hosted, and acted in this popular series, which adapted science fiction, mystery, and historical adventure dramas for radio. On Halloween eve in 1938, the twenty-three-year-old Welles aired the 1898 Martian invasion novel in the style of a radio news program. For people who missed the opening disclaimer, the program sounded like a real news report, with eyewitness accounts of pitched battles between Martian invaders and the U.S. Army.

The program created a panic that lasted several hours. In New Jersey, some people walked through the streets with wet towels around their heads for protection from deadly Martian heat rays. In New York, young men reported to their National Guard headquarters to prepare for battle. Across the nation, calls jammed police switchboards. Afterward, Orson Welles, once the radio voice of *The Shadow,* used the notoriety of this broadcast to launch a film career. Meanwhile, the FCC called for stricter warnings both before and during programs that imitated the style of radio news.

Most programs in those days had a single sponsor that created and produced each show. The networks distributed these programs live around the country, charging the sponsors advertising fees.

● On Halloween eve in 1938, Orson Welles' radio dramatization of *War of the Worlds* created a panic up and down the East Coast, especially in Grover's Mill, New Jersey—the setting for the fictional Martian invasion that many listeners assumed was real. Here, a seventy-six-year-old Grover's Mill resident guards a warehouse against alien invaders.

Many shows—the *Palmolive Hour, General Motors Family Party*, the *Lucky Strike Orchestra*, and the *Eveready Hour* among them—were named after the sole sponsor's product.

Radio Reinvents Itself

The history of American mass media reveals that older media forms do not disappear when confronted by newer forms. Instead, mass media adapt. Although radio threatened sound recording in the 1920s and television threatened radio in the 1950s, both older forms adjusted to the economic and social challenges posed by the arrival of a newer medium. Remarkably, the arrival of television in the 1950s marked the only time in media history in which a new medium virtually stole every national programming and advertising strategy from the older medium. Television snatched radio's advertisers, its program genres, its major celebrities, and its large evening audiences. In the process, the TV set physically displaced the radio as the living-room centerpiece across America.

New Technologies Bring Portability and Clarity to Radio

The story of radio's evolution and survival provides a fascinating look at the impact of one medium on another. This history is especially important today, as newspapers and magazines enter the information highway and as publishers produce books on tape and e-books for new generations of "readers." In contemporary culture, we have grown accustomed to such media convergence as the norm. To understand this blurring of the boundaries between media forms, it is useful to look at the 1950s and the ways in which radio responded to the advent of television.

● Amelia Earhart was one of a number of people to speak via radio with explorer Richard Byrd and his expedition team as they explored the Antarctic in 1929. These conversations were broadcast to the American public every two weeks. The Byrd expedition (1928–30) brought the novelty of advanced radio systems to a captivated home audience.

The Transistor: A Revolution of Small Proportions

A key development in radio's adaptation occurred with the invention of the transistor by Bell Laboratories in 1947. **Transistors**, like De Forest's vacuum tubes, were small electrical devices that could receive and amplify radio signals. They used less power and heat than vacuum tubes, and they were more durable and less expensive. Best of all, they were tiny. Transistors, which also revolutionized hearing aids, represented the first step in replacing bulky and delicate tubes, leading eventually to today's silicon-chip integrated circuits. Texas Instruments marketed the first transistor radios in 1953, at about $40 apiece. Using even smaller transistors, Sony introduced the pocket radio in 1957. But it wasn't until the 1960s that transistor radios became cheaper than conventional tube and battery radios. For a while, the term *transistor* became a synonym for a small, portable radio.

The development of transistors permitted radio to go where television could not—to the beach, to the office, into bedrooms and bathrooms, and into nearly all new cars. (Before the transistor, car radios were a luxury item.) By the 1960s, most radio listening actually took place outside the home. For economic reasons, radio turned to the recording industry for content to replace the shows it had lost to television.

Edwin Armstrong's FM Revolution

By the time the broadcast industry launched commercial television in the 1950s, many people, including David Sarnoff of RCA, were predicting radio's demise. To fund television's development and protect his radio holdings, Sarnoff had even delayed a dramatic breakthrough in broadcast sound, what he himself called a "revolution"—FM radio.

Edwin Armstrong, who first discovered and developed FM radio in the 1920s and early 1930s, is often considered the most prolific and influential inventor in radio history. He alone understood the impact of De Forest's vacuum tube, and he used it to invent an amplifying system that enabled radio receivers to pick up distant signals. Armstrong's innovations rendered obsolete the enormous alternators used for generating power in early radio transmitters. In 1922, he sold a "super" version of his circuit to RCA for $200,000 and sixty thousand shares of RCA stock, making him a millionaire as well as RCA's largest private stockholder.

Armstrong also worked on the major problem of radio reception—electrical interference. Between 1930 and 1933, the inventor filed five patents on **FM**, or frequency modulation. Offering static-less radio reception, FM supplied greater fidelity and clarity than AM, making FM ideal for music. **AM**, or amplitude modulation, stressed the volume, or height, of radio waves; FM accentuated the pitch, or distance, between radio waves (see Figure 4.2). Although David Sarnoff, by then the chairman of RCA, thought that television would replace the older medium, he helped Armstrong set up the first experimental FM station atop the Empire State Building in New York City. Eventually, though, the RCA chief thwarted FM's development (which he was able to do because RCA had an option on Armstrong's new patents). In 1935, Sarnoff threw RCA's considerable weight behind the development of television. With the FCC allocating and reassigning scarce frequency spaces, RCA wanted to ensure that channels went to television before they went to FM. But most of all, Sarnoff wanted to protect RCA's existing AM empire. Given the high costs of converting to FM and the revenue needed for TV experiments, Sarnoff decided to close down Armstrong's station.

Armstrong forged ahead without RCA. He founded a new FM station and advised other engineers, who started more than twenty experimental stations between 1935 and the early 1940s. In 1941, the FCC approved limited space allocations for

Figure 4.2 AM and FM Waves

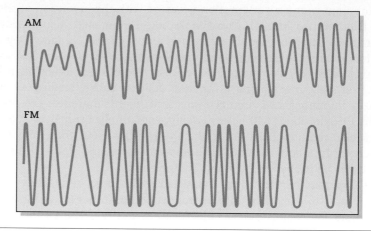

AM

FM

Source: Adapted from David Cheshire, *The Video Manual,* 1982.

● *Radio Broadcast* magazine (cover December 1926) was a trade magazine to disseminate information among industry insiders. Today mass media have similar trade magazines, such as *Broadcasting & Cable.*

commercial FM licenses. During the next few years, FM grew in fits and starts. Between 1946 and early 1949, the number of commercial FM stations expanded from forty-eight to seven hundred. But then the FCC moved FM's frequency space to a new band on the electromagnetic spectrum, rendering some 400,000 prewar FM receiver sets useless. FM's future became uncertain, and by 1954 the number of FM stations had fallen to 560.

On January 31, 1954, Edwin Armstrong, weary from years of legal skirmishes over patents, wrote a note apologizing to his wife, removed the air conditioner from his thirteenth-story New York apartment, and jumped to his death. A month later, David Sarnoff announced record profits of $850 million for RCA, with TV sales accounting for 54 percent of the company's earnings. In the early 1960s, the FCC opened up more spectrum space for the superior sound of FM, infusing new life into radio. Although AM stations had greater reach, they could not match the crisp fidelity of FM, which would gradually make FM the preferred broadcast medium for music. In the early 1970s, about 70 percent of listeners tuned almost exclusively to AM radio. By the 1980s, however, FM had surpassed AM in profitability. By the 1990s, more than 75 percent of all listeners reportedly preferred FM, and more than 5,500 commercial and 1,900 noncommercial FM stations were in operation. The expansion of FM represented one of the chief ways by which radio survived television and Sarnoff's gloomy predictions.

Changes in Programming

Live and recorded music had long been radio's single biggest staple, accounting for 48 percent of all programming in 1938. Although network affiliates in large markets carried many drama, comedy, and variety series, smaller independent stations had always relied heavily on music. As noted earlier, in the 1920s many stations even hired their own house bands and studio musicians. In the 1930s and 1940s, lean economic times forced more stations to play recorded music, either older music in the public domain (not under copyright) or music that was marginally popular and was not closely monitored by ASCAP. (See Chapter 3.)

Although live music on radio was generally considered superior to recorded music, early disc jockeys made a significant contribution to the latter. They demonstrated that music alone could drive radio. In fact, when television snatched radio's program ideas and national sponsors, radio's dependence on recorded music became a necessity and helped the medium survive in the 1950s.

The Rise of Format and Top 40 Radio

As early as 1949, station owner Todd Storz in Omaha, Nebraska, experimented with formula-driven radio, or **format radio**. Under this system, management rather than deejays controlled programming each hour. When Storz and his program manager noticed that bar patrons and waitresses repeatedly played certain favorite songs from the forty records available in a jukebox, they began researching record sales to identify the most popular tunes. From observing jukebox culture, Storz hit on the idea of **rotation**: playing the top songs many times during the day. By the mid-1950s, the management-control idea had combined with the rock-and-roll explosion. The *Top 40 format* was born. Although the term *Top 40* derived from the number of records stored in a jukebox, this format came to refer to the forty most popular hits in a given week as measured by record sales.

As format radio grew, program managers combined rapid deejay chatter with the best-selling songs of the day and occasional *oldies*—popular songs from a few months earlier. By the early 1960s, to avoid "dead air," managers asked deejays to talk over the beginning and the end of a song so that listeners would feel less compelled to switch stations. Ads, news, weather forecasts, and station identifications were all designed to fit a consistent station environment. Listeners, tuning in at any moment, would recognize the station by its distinctive sound.

In format radio, management carefully coordinates, or programs, each hour, dictating what the deejay will do at various intervals throughout each hour of the day (see Figure 4.3). Management creates a program log—once called a *hot clock* in radio jargon—that deejays must follow. By the mid-1960s, one study had determined that in a typical hour on Top 40, listeners could expect to hear about twenty ads; numerous weather, time, and contest announcements; multiple recitations of the station's call letters; about three minutes of news; and approximately twelve songs.

Radio managers further sectioned off programming into *day parts*, which typically consisted of time blocks covering 6 to 10 A.M., 10 A.M. to 3 P.M., 3 to 7 P.M., and 7 P.M. to 12 midnight. Each day part, or block, was programmed through ratings research according to who was listening. For instance, a Top 40 station would feature its top deejays in the morning and afternoon periods when audiences, many riding in cars, were largest. From 10 A.M. to 3 P.M., research determined that women at home and secretaries at work usually controlled the dial, so program managers, capitalizing on the gender stereotypes of the day, played more romantic ballads and less hard rock. Teenagers tended to be heavy evening listeners, so program managers often discarded news breaks at this time, since research showed that teens turned the dial when news came on.

Critics of format radio argued that only the top songs received play and that lesser-known songs deserving air time received meager attention. Although a few popular star deejays continued to play a role in programming, many others quit when managers introduced formats. Owners approached programming as if it were a science, but deejays considered it an art form. Program managers argued that deejays had different tastes than the average listener and therefore could not be fully trusted to know popular audience tastes. The owners' position, which generated more revenue, triumphed.

Payola Then and Now

According to management, format radio had another big advantage over deejays who simply played their favorite music: It helped curb **payola**, the practice by which record promoters paid deejays to play particular records. As we noted in Chapter 3, payola was rampant during the 1950s, as record companies sought to guarantee record sales. When management took control of programming, however, individual deejays had less impact on what records would be played and became less susceptible

> **❝** You go from town to town to town and you're hearing the same thing. It's like going to Kentucky Fried Chicken. **❞**
>
> —Ben Folds, of the band Ben Folds Five, 1998

Figure 4.3 Radio Program Log For an Adult Contemporary (AC) Station

```
MIX96                              8AM-9AM                    Thursday October 25, 2001

MIX MORNING SHOW W/JAMIE PHILIPS


  0:00   00137      COLLECTIVE SOUL                        :16/  4:06/COLD
                    DECEMBER

  4:06   01570      STAIND                                 :17/  4:22/COLD
                    IT'S BEEN AWHILE
---------------------------------------------------------------------------------
  8:28              STOP SET IF NEEDED                     4:00   (Sweep:  8:28)
---------------------------------------------------------------------------------
 12:28   00122      JOURNEY                                :17/  4:02/FADE
                    DON'T STOP BELIEVIN

 16:30   01173      FUEL                                   :10/  3:55/COLD
                    HEMORRHAGE (IN MY HANDS)

 20:25   01501      INCUBUS                                :21/  3:50/COLD
                    DRIVE
---------------------------------------------------------------------------------
 24:15              STOP SET IF NEEDED                     4:00   (Sweep: 11:47)
---------------------------------------------------------------------------------
 28:15   01428      SISTER HAZEL                           :11/  3:59/COLD
                    CHANGE YOUR MIND

 32:14   01590      JEWEL                                  :15/  4:23/FADE
                    STANDING STILL

 36:37   01489      LIFEHOUSE                              :08/  3:27/COLD
                    HANGING BY A MOMENT
```

Source: KCVM-FM, Waterloo/Cedar Falls, IA, 2001.

to bribery. In response to this situation, record promoters often showered their favors on a few influential, high-profile deejays, whose backing could make or break a record nationally, or on key program managers in charge of Top 40 formats in large urban markets.

Despite congressional hearings and new rules designed to eliminate the problem, payola persisted. In the 1970s, for example, payola scandals involved exchanging airplay for drugs as well as cash. Although a 1984 congressional hearing determined that there was "no credible evidence" of payola practices in the recording industry, NBC News broke a story in 1986 about independent promoters who had alleged ties to the Mafia. A subsequent investigation led major recording companies to break most of their ties with independent promoters. Prominent record labels had been paying such promoters up to $80 million per year to help records become hits.

Format radio may have eliminated the payola problem on a large scale, but charges of exchanging airplay for money, drugs, and sex continue to haunt both the radio and the recording industry. Most recently, Fonivisa Records, the largest independent Latin music label, and home to recordings by Enrique Iglesias and Marco Antonio Solis, was convicted in 1999 of funneling more than $1 million in payola cash to program directors at more than eighty Spanish music stations in the United States. The label and two of its executives paid heavy fines for tax fraud. The convictions were part of a continuing investigation of major music labels by the Justice Department's criminal division.

In 1998, a legal alternative to payola emerged that has been hotly debated in the radio and recording industries. The promotional strategy, called **pay-for-play**, typically involves up-front payments from record companies to radio stations to play a song a specific number of times.[7] Stations that use pay-for-play sidestep FCC regulations by broadcasting disclosures that state that the song has been sponsored or paid for by the record company. In effect, the time to play the song is being purchased, not unlike the paid programming of television infomercials. If the station's listeners ultimately like the pay-for-play song, the song can become part of the station's regular, unsponsored lineup. For example, Flip/Interscope Records paid a Portland, Oregon, radio station $5,000 to play a song by hip-hop/metal band Limp Bizkit fifty times during a five-week period. The band ultimately gained a listenership in the market, played a concert in Portland, and later gained a national fan base as other stations aired their music. Another form of pay-for-play involves a weekly, infomercial-like music program sponsored by a music label or department store that airs in several markets of a national radio chain. Although some see pay-for-play as a direct, honest way to introduce new music on radio stations, others object to having commercial interests blatantly tamper with playlists and the weekly *Billboard* music charts.

The Sounds of Radio Today

Contemporary radio sounds very different from its predecessors. In contrast to the few stations per market in the 1930s, most large markets today include more than forty receivable signals that vie for listener loyalty. With the exception of national network–sponsored news segments and nationally syndicated programs, most programming is locally produced and heavily dependent on the music industry for content. Although a few radio personalities, such as Howard Stern, Rush Limbaugh, Don Imus, Tom Joyner, Dr. Laura Schlessinger, and Jim Rome, are nationally prominent, local deejays and their music are the stars at most radio stations.

However, unlike listeners in the 1930s, who tuned in their favorite shows at set times, listeners today do not say, "Gee, my favorite song is coming on at 8 P.M., so I'd better be home to listen." Instead, radio has become a secondary, or background, medium that follows the rhythms of daily life. In the 1930s, radio often dictated those rhythms, particularly with its popular evening programs. Today, radio programmers worry about channel cruising—the habit listeners have of searching the dial until they find a song they like.

Today, stations are more specialized. Listeners in the 1940s were loyal to favorite programs, but now we are loyal to favorite stations, music formats, and even radio personalities. We generally listen to only four or five stations that target us, usually based on our age, gender, or race. In the 1930s, peak listening time occurred during evening hours—dubbed *prime time* in the TV era—when people were home from work and school. Nowadays, the heaviest radio listening occurs during **drive time**, those periods between 6 and 9 A.M. and 4 and 7 P.M., when people are commuting to and from work or school. Today, more than twelve thousand radio stations operate in the United States, customizing their sounds to reach mobile niche audiences. With radio as a truly portable medium, Americans are still tuning in, on average, for more than three hours on weekdays and nearly six hours on weekends.

The Economics of Broadcast Radio

More than 13 percent of all U.S. spending on media advertising goes to radio stations. Like newspapers, radio generates its largest profits by selling local and regional ads. Thirty-second radio-spot ads range from $1,500 or more in large markets to just a few dollars in the smallest markets. Gross advertising receipts were estimated to be $18.4 billion in 2001 (more than three-quarters of the revenues from local ad sales, with the remainder in national spot and network sales), up from about $12.4 billion in 1996. The industry is economically healthy, with approximately 13,200 stations

● Tom Joyner has the nation's No. 1 urban radio show, targeting African Americans between the ages of twenty-five and fifty-four with a mix of comedy, soap-opera sketches, social activism, and old-school R&B music. The syndicated program can be heard in more than a hundred broadcast markets, including Chicago, Dallas, Detroit, Miami, Washington, D.C., and Los Angeles.

(more than 4,800 AM stations, almost 6,200 FM stations, and more than 2,300 educational FM stations). Unlike television, where nearly 40 percent of a station's expenses goes to buy syndicated programs, local radio stations get much of their content free from the recording industry. Therefore, only about 20 percent of a typical radio station's budget goes to cover programming costs.

When radio stations want to purchase programming, they often turn to national network radio, which generates more than $910 million in ad sales annually by offering dozens of specialized services. For example, Westwood One, a major radio network service managed and owned by Viacom's Infinity Broadcasting, syndicates more than 150 programs, including regular news features (e.g., *CBS Radio News, Fox News Radio*), entertainment programs (e.g., *Country Countdown USA, Saturday Night All Request 80s*), talk shows to fill entire day parts (e.g., the *G. Gordon Liddy Show, Loveline,* and the *Tom Leykis Show*), and complete 24-hour formats (e.g., Adult Rock & Roll, Bright Adult Contemporary, Hot Country, Mainstream Country, and CNN Headline News). More than sixty companies offer national program and format services, typically providing local stations with programming in exchange for time slots for national ads. The most successful radio network programs are the shows broadcast by affiliates in the Top 20 markets, which offer advertisers half of the country's radio audience. As mergers and buyouts continue, creating huge national radio groups in the wake of the 1996 Telecommunications Act, national network radio is expected to produce a larger portion of radio revenues.

Commercial Radio and Format Specialization

Although Top 40 managers pioneered format radio, stations today use a variety of formats based on managed program logs and day parts, as explained earlier. All told, more than forty different radio formats, plus variations, serve diverse groups of listeners. To please advertisers, who want to know exactly who's listening, formats are usually targeted at audiences according to their age and income, gender, or race/ethnicity. Radio's specialization enables advertisers to reach smaller target audiences at costs that are much lower than those for television. This process has become extremely competitive, however, because there may be forty or fifty stations available in a large radio market. In the last decade, according to the Center of Radio Information, more than one thousand stations a year (roughly 10 percent of all stations) switched formats in an effort to find the formula that would generate more advertising money. Some stations, particularly those in large cities, have also been renting blocks of time to various local ethnic and civic groups; this enables the groups to dictate their own formats and sell ads.

The nation's fastest-growing format throughout much of the 1990s was the **news/talk format** (See "Case Study: Talk Radio Gets Personal" on page 130). In 1987, only 170 radio stations operated formats dominated by either news programs or talk shows, which tend to appeal to adults over age thirty-five (except for sports talk programs, which draw both younger and older, mostly male, sports fans). By 2002, buoyed by the notoriety and popularity of Dr. Laura Schlessinger and Rush Limbaugh, more than 1,100 stations used some combination of news and talk. With many of the most powerful AM stations in the country programming the format, and with a large portion of listeners being over age thirty-five, news/talk reigns as the most popular format in the nation. A news/talk format, though more expensive to produce than a music format, appeals to advertisers looking to target working- and middle-class adult consumers. Nevertheless, most radio stations continue to be driven by a variety of less expensive music formats. (See Figure 4.4.)

Just behind news/talk in popularity is the **adult contemporary (AC)** format. Known first as middle-of-the-road, or MOR, AC is among radio's oldest and most popular format, reaching about 15 percent of all listeners, most of them older than forty. In the early 1970s, *Broadcasting* magazine described AC's eclectic mix of news, talk, oldies, and soft rock music as "not too soft, not too loud, not too fast, not too slow, not too hard, not too lush, not too old, not too new."

Although Top 40 radio—also called **contemporary hits radio (CHR)**—is in decline, it still appeals to many teens and young adults, and advertisers continue to buy time from Top 40 stations. Since the mid-1980s, however, these stations have lost ground steadily as younger generations have followed music on MTV rather than on radio. In addition, Top 40 music has become so diverse, encompassing everything from gangsta rap to children's songs, that "no commercial radio station could ever play it all and hold on to an audience."[8]

The **country** format does not reach as many total listeners as news/talk, AC, or CHR radio, but country claims by far the most stations—more than 2,100 by 2002, about twice as many stations as those that have the news/talk format. Many of these stations are in tiny markets where country has traditionally reigned as the default format for communities with only one radio station. Country music has old roots in radio, starting in 1925 with the influential Grand Ole Opry program on WSM in Nashville. Although Top 40 drove country music out of many radio markets in the 1950s, the growth of FM in the 1960s brought it back as station managers looked for market niches not served by rock music. As diverse as rock, country music today includes such subdivisions as old-time, progressive country, country-rock, western swing, and country-gospel.

Many formats target by age or gender, but some also appeal to particular ethnic or racial groups. For example, formats featuring jazz, gospel, rhythm and blues, hip-hop, and dance music have targeted various audience segments of African American listeners over the years. In 1947, WDIA in Memphis was the first station to program exclusively for black listeners. Now called **urban**, this format targets a wide variety of African American listeners, primarily in large cities. Urban, which typically plays

Figure 4.4 Most Popular Radio Formats in the United States

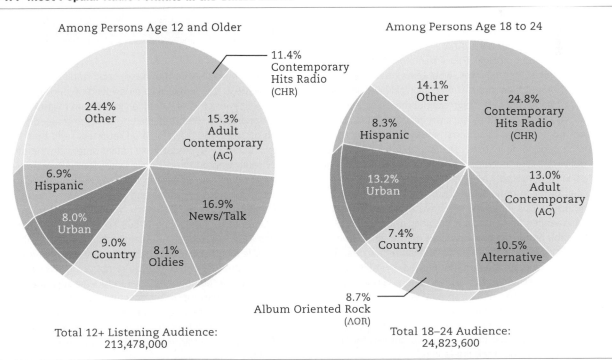

Source: Radio Advertising Bureau, *Radio Marketing and Fact Book for Advertisers*, 2001–2002 edition.

CASE STUDY

Talk Radio Gets Personal

In the late 1970s, when Ira Glass was nineteen, he interned at National Public Radio's Washington, D.C., headquarters. He was later hired on, and over the next seventeen years he eventually held about every radio position available at NPR, including work as a journalist for *Morning Edition* and fill-in host of *Talk of the Nation.* He made his mark, though, by filing quirky and memorable stories about peoples' lives. In 1995, when Glass was in his thirties, he was given the chance to start a new hour-long weekly program called *This American Life.* Produced at WBEZ in Chicago and syndicated by Public Radio International, the show became known as the documentary radio program for people who don't like documentaries. It was so personal, nonjudgmental, and experimental—void of the stiffness and formality that typifies documentaries—that *This American Life* became one of public radio's top programs, picked up by over three hundred stations and heard by over a million listeners each week.

For those who expect public radio to sound stodgy and elitist, *This American Life* comes as a big surprise. Glass has the most unlikely radio style as he introduces the show's weekly theme (e.g., Meet the Pros, Music Lessons, Fiasco, Jobs That Take Over Your Life) and the three or four stories that build around it. He speaks with a kind of casual, untailored style. His voice is flat and he often accelerates his sentences so they run into each other.

Other regular contributors to *This American Life* have their own signature styles. Sarah Vowell, who spins memorable and often hilarious stories about Thanksgiving dinner with her "odd" family or about life in the high school marching band, for example, has a voice that by her own account is like "a high-pitched, nasal, whiny, obnoxious, snotty drawl." Another regular, David Sedaris, is instantly recognizable by his dry and deadpan delivery as he recounts such experiences as working at a Macy's in New York City as one of Santa's Christmas elves, or the downside of being an American living in Paris.

Contributors to *This American Life* have a knack for sharing personal experiences and using the intimacy of the radio medium perhaps better than anyone else on the air. They comment on their miscalculations, their relationship fiascoes, and the general absurdities of modern life. Frequently, they intermix their personal narratives with conversations among ordinary people, talking simply and often poignantly about their own experiences and discoveries. "What we do on the show," says Glass, "is take people into the worlds of some people who are like them and some people who are not like them and just say, okay, here's what their life is like."

Some have likened the loose, nonformulaic, and confidential nature of the program to a new kind of journalism. "It gives you a glimmer of what American journalism might be like if you deported all the weak-kneed, homogenizing editors and TV producers, the lazy, tin-eared reporters, and then let the best, funniest, and most imaginative writers do the stories they really wanted to do," says writer Thane Peterson. "You would end up with something odd and individualistic that gives voice to all sorts of people and ideas you don't normally hear about."

"Journalism has a kind of seen-it-all world-weariness," Glass says. "Traditional journalism would hold that if you have strong feelings about the characters in the story or the situations, you're just a sap and you're not doing your job. Whereas I would argue the opposite, that in fact for anything interesting to come out of it, the writer doing it has to have a strong feeling about it." As radio becomes more and more homogenized with nationally syndicated voices, *This American Life* gives a national forum to the refreshingly unique voices of everyday people.

popular dance, rap, R&B, and hip-hop music (featuring performers like Usher, Ja Rule, and Mary J. Blige), also subdivides by age, featuring an Urban AC category with performers like Alicia Keys, Erykah Badu, and Maxwell.

Spanish-language radio, one of radio's fastest-growing formats, targets large Cuban populations in Miami, Puerto Rican and Dominican listeners in New York, and Mexican American audiences in Chicago, California, and Texas (where KCOR, the first all-Spanish-language station, originated in San Antonio in 1947). Besides talk shows and news segments in Spanish, Hispanic formats feature a variety of Spanish, Caribbean, and Latin American musical styles, including calypso, flamenco, mariachi, merengue, reggae, samba, salsa, and Tejano.

Resisting the Top 40

Accompanying the expansion of the FM spectrum in the mid-1960s, *progressive rock* emerged as an alternative to conventional formats. Many of the noncommercial stations broadcast from college campuses, where student deejays and managers, unencumbered by ads and format radio, rejected the commercialism associated with Top 40 tunes. Instead, they began playing lesser-known alternative music and longer album cuts. Until that time, most rock on radio had been consigned almost exclusively to Top 40 AM formats, with song length averaging about three minutes.

The expansion of FM created room for experimenting, particularly with classical music, jazz, blues, and non–Top 40 rock songs. Experimental FM stations, both commercial and noncommercial, served as a venue for Bob Dylan's 1965 song "Desolation Row," which ran eleven minutes. In 1967, the Doors' "Light My Fire," a No. 1 hit, featured a seven-minute version for FM and a three-minute Top 40 AM version. The same year, some FM stations played Arlo Guthrie's "Alice's Restaurant," an eighteen-minute satiric antiwar folk ballad. FM offered a cultural space for hard-edged political folk and for rock music that commented on the Civil Rights movement and protested America's involvement in the Vietnam War. By the 1970s, progressive rock had been copied, tamed, and absorbed by mainstream radio under the format label **album-oriented rock (AOR)**. By 1972, AOR-driven album sales already accounted for more than 85 percent of the retail record business. By the 1980s, as first-generation rock and rollers aged and became more affluent, AOR had become less political and played mostly white post-Beatles music featuring such groups as Pink Floyd, Led Zeppelin, Cream, and Queen.

A number of critics have denounced AOR for limiting the definition of rock music. They argue that the strictly controlled AOR format displaced progressive rock by aiming "programming at an extremely specific, limited listenership," mostly white males in the thirteen to twenty-five age range. AOR programming guidelines initially ignored most black and female performers, whom program directors claimed held little appeal for AOR's target audience. By discouraging certain kinds of music, it was claimed that AOR formats encouraged a type of "institutionalized racism and sexism." These guidelines were later adopted by MTV in its formative years, making it harder for black and female artists to crack the video scene in the early 1980s.[9]

Today, there are several spin-offs from AOR. *Classic rock* serves up rock oldies from the mid-1960s through the 1980s to the baby-boom generation and is aimed primarily at listeners who have outgrown the conventional Top 40. The *oldies* format serves adults who grew up on 1950s and early 1960s rock and roll. Begun in California in the mid-1960s, oldies formats recall the integrationist impulse of early rock as well as emphasizing soul and Motown music from the 1960s. Listening habits and record research indicate that most people identify closely with the music they listened to as adolescents and young adults. This tendency partially explains why oldies and classic rock stations combined have surpassed Top 40 stations today. It

also helps to explain the recent nostalgia for music from the 1980s and early 1990s. The *alternative music* format recaptures some of the experimental approach of the FM stations of the 1960s, albeit with much more controlled playlists, and has helped to break new artists such as Korn, Moby, and Blink-182.

Radio Ownership since 1996

In recent years, the rules concerning ownership of the public airwaves have changed substantially. With the passage of the **1996 Telecommunications Act**, the FCC eliminated most ownership restrictions on radio. As a result, in 1996 alone some 2,100 stations switched owners, as $15 billion changed hands. Between 1996 and 2000, more than half of U.S. radio stations changed owners, and the number of station owners declined by about 1,000.[10]

The FCC once tried to encourage diversity in broadcast ownership. From the 1950s through the 1980s, a media company could not own more than seven AM, seven FM, and seven TV stations nationally, and not more than one radio station per market. Just prior to the 1996 act, the ownership rules were relaxed to allow any single person or company to own up to twenty AM, twenty FM, and twelve television stations nationwide, and only two of these could be in the same market. But today the FCC embraces the consolidation schemes pushed by the powerful National Association of Broadcasters lobbyists in Washington, D.C., under which fewer and fewer owners control more and more of the airwaves.

The 1996 act allows individuals and companies to acquire as many stations as they want, with relaxed restrictions on the number of stations a single broadcaster may own in the same city: The larger the market or area, the more stations a company may own within that market. For example, in areas where forty-five or more stations are available to listeners, a broadcaster may own up to eight stations, but not more than five of one type (AM or FM). In areas with fourteen or fewer stations, a broadcaster may own up to five stations (three of any one type). In very small markets with a handful of stations, a broadcast company may not own more than half the stations. By 2000, more than 70 percent of radio stations were affiliated with other groups: either co-owned with other stations or under contract with a program supplier in a time-brokerage agreement (by which blocks of time are purchased to air certain programs), making stations that are independently owned and programmed increasingly rare.[11]

The consequences of the 1996 Telecommunications Act on radio ownership have been significant (see Table 4.1). Consider the cases of Clear Channel Communications and Viacom's Infinity Broadcasting, which had ballooned into the two largest radio chain owners by 2000.

Clear Channel Communications, which was formed in 1972 with one San Antonio station, entered 1996 just under the ownership limits of that time with 36 radio stations and 10 television stations in the United States, plus 8 radio stations in Aus-

● Deejay Furious George spins records at Free Radio Asheville, a pirate micro-power radio station in Asheville, North Carolina. Although threatened with closure several times by the FCC, the station regularly broadcasts community-oriented programs with a 20-watt transmitter (for a 5- to 6-mile radius) at 107.5 FM. Station supporters have also applied for a low-power FM license from the FCC.

● A long-time pirate station, Free Radio Berkeley was founded in 1993 but was shut down with a court injunction in 1998. The organization still offers radio technical support and training and maintains its Web site at <www.freeradio.org>. Free Radio Berkeley's efforts to "reclaim the airwaves" also feature the Information Libre logo that protesters of the 1968 Paris Revolution used against government-controlled radio.

● Table 4.1 The Largest Radio Groups in the United States, by Revenue

Radio Group (headquarters)	Number of Stations	Revenues ($ mil)	Major Stations
1. Clear Channel (San Antonio)	1,224	3,794	KFI-AM (Los Angeles), KOA-AM (Denver), WLW-AM (Cincinnati), WHO-AM (Des Moines)
2. Infinity Broadcasting (New York)	184	2,495	KLSX-FM (Los Angeles), WJFK-FM (Washington, D.C.), WNEW-FM (New York), WB-AM (Boston)
3. Cox Radio (Atlanta)	83	482	WSB-AM (Atlanta), KRMG-AM (Tulsa), WHIO-AM (Dayton), WSYR-AM (Syracuse), WDBO-AM (Orlando)
4. ABC Radio (Dallas)	50	457	KGO-AM (San Francisco), KABC (Los Angeles), WLS (Chicago), WABC-AM (New York), WJR (Detroit)
5. Entercom (Bala Cynwyd, PA)	95	392	KIRO-AM (Seattle-Tacoma), WWL-AM (New Orleans), KMBZ-AM (Kansas City), WBEN-AM (Buffalo)
6. Citadel Communications Corp. (Las Vegas)	204	368	WGRF-FM (Buffalo), KARN-AM/FM (Little Rock), KKOB-AM/FM (Albuquerque), KPRO-AM/FM (Providence)
7. Emmis Communications (Indianapolis)	24	285	KPWR-FM (Los Angeles), WRKS-FM (New York), WKQX-FM (Chicago), WIBC-AM (Indianapolis)
8. Radio One (Lanham, MD)	43	282	WMMJ-FM (Washington), WWIN-AM-FM (Baltimore), WDTJ-FM (Detroit), WCKX-FM (Columbus)
9. Hispanic Broadcasting (Dallas)	47	258	WRTO-FM (Miami), KLVE-FM (Los Angeles), WADO-AM (New York), WIND-AM (Chicago)
10. Susquehanna Radio Corp. (York, PA)	26	250	KLIF-AM (Dallas-Ft. Worth), WNNX-FM (Atlanta), KRBE-FM (Houston), WMOJ-FM (Cincinnati)

Source for revenues: Duncan's American Radio, <www.duncanradio.com>. Revenues are based on 2000 full-year billing estimates.

> 66 **Radio affects most people intimately, person-to-person, offering a world of unspoken communication between writer-speaker and listener. That is the immediate aspect of radio. A private experience.** 99
>
> —Marshall McLuhan, *Understanding Media,* 1964

tralia. In 1998, Clear Channel was the fourth-largest group owner. Then it swallowed up Jacor Communications, the fifth-largest radio chain, and became the nation's second-largest group, with 454 stations in 101 cities. In 1999, Clear Channel gobbled up another growing conglomerate, AMFM (formerly Chancellor Media Corporation), which had 463 stations and an estimated $1.6 billion in revenue. The deal broadened Clear Channel's operation to 874 stations in 187 U.S. markets (including all top 20 markets except Seattle), with access to more than 110 million listeners. By 2002, Clear Channel owned more than 1,225 radio stations, 37 television stations, 776,000 billboard and outdoor displays, and an interest in more than 240 stations internationally. With recent mergers, Clear Channel also distributes many of the leading syndicated programs, including *Dr. Laura, Rush Limbaugh, The Jim Rome Show, The Michael Reagan Talk Show,* and *The Bob & Tom Show.*

Viacom's Infinity Broadcasting is the second leading radio conglomerate, with 184 stations. It is also the leading outdoor advertising company in the nation. Whereas Clear Channel's stations are mostly in small and medium-sized markets, Infinity's stations dominate the nation's top markets and capture more than 25 percent of the radio revenue in twenty-seven major markets. Infinity also owns the Westwood One radio network, a leading programming syndicator.

Combined, Clear Channel and Infinity own more than 1,400 radio stations — about 12 percent of all U.S. stations — and control close to 40 percent of the entire radio industry's $18.4 billion revenue. Competing major radio groups that have grown in the recent radio industry consolidations include Cox, ABC Radio, Entercom, Citadel, and Emmis. As a result of the consolidations permitted by deregulation, in most American cities just two corporations dominate the radio market.

Nonprofit Radio and NPR

Although commercial radio (particularly those stations owned by huge radio conglomerates) dominates the radio spectrum, nonprofit radio maintains a voice. But the road to viability for nonprofit radio in the United States has not been easy. In the 1930s, the Wagner-Hatfield Amendment to the 1934 Communications Act was intended to set aside 25 percent of radio for a wide variety of nonprofit stations. When the amendment went down in defeat in 1935, the future of educational and noncommercial radio looked bleak. Many nonprofits had sold out to for-profit owners during the Depression. The stations that remained were often banished from the air during the evening hours or assigned weak signals by federal regulators who favored commercial owners and their lobbying agents. Still, nonprofit public radio survived. More than 1,700 such stations now operate, many of them low-wattage stations on college campuses.

During the 1960s, nonprofit broadcasting found a Congress sympathetic to an old idea: using radio and television as educational tools. As a result, **National Public Radio (NPR)** and the **Public Broadcasting Service (PBS)** were created as the first noncommercial networks. Under the auspices of the **Public Broadcasting Act of 1967** and the **Corporation for Public Broadcasting (CPB)**, NPR and PBS were mandated to provide alternatives to commercial broadcasting. Now, NPR's popular news and interview programs, *Morning Edition* and *All Things Considered,* draw three to four million listeners per day. Over the years, however, more time and attention have been devoted to public television than to public radio. When government funding tightened in the late 1980s and 1990s, television received the lion's share. In 1994, a conservative majority in Congress cut financial support and threatened to scrap the CPB, the funding authority for public broadcasting. Consequently, stations

> 66 **Although noncommercial radio seems to have turned the corner of public awareness, it has not yet overcome decades of disorganization and neglect and abuse by the federal government.** 99
>
> — Peter Fornatale and Joshua Mills,
> *Radio in the Television Age,* 1980

became more reliant than ever on private donations and corporate sponsorship. While depending on handouts, especially from big business, public broadcasters steered clear of some controversial subjects, especially those that critically examined corporations. (See "Applied Critical Process: Public Radio: Is the BBC Better Than NPR?" on page 136.)

Like commercial stations, nonprofit radio has also adopted the format style. Unlike commercial radio, however, the dominant style in public radio is a loose variety format whereby a station may actually switch from jazz, classical music, and alternative rock to news and talk during different parts of the day. Some college stations, too small to affiliate, have kept alive the spirit of early 1950s radio, when deejays chose the music. Noncommercial radio still remains the place for both tradition and experimentation, for programs that do not draw enough listeners for commercial success.

Although the proposed Wagner-Hatfield Amendment failed to redistribute radio resources in the mid-1930s, public and nonprofit radio have managed to maintain a presence on the radio dial. Two government rulings, both in 1948, aided nonprofit radio. First, the government began authorizing noncommercial licenses to stations not affiliated with labor, religion, education, or a civic group. The first license went to Lewis Kimball Hill, a radio reporter and pacifist during World War II who started the **Pacifica Foundation** to run experimental public stations. Pacifica stations, like Hill himself, have often challenged the status quo in radio as well as in government. Most notably, in the 1950s they aired the poetry, prose, and music of performers— considered radical, left-wing, or communist—who were blacklisted by television and seldom acknowledged by AM stations. Over the years, Pacifica has also been fined and reprimanded by the FCC and Congress for airing programs that critics considered inappropriate for public airwaves. In 2002, Pacifica had sixty affiliate stations.

Second, the FCC approved 10-watt FM stations, beginning in 1948. Prior to this time, radio stations had to have at least 250 watts to get licensed. A 10-watt station with a broadcast range of only about seven miles took very little capital to operate, so more people could participate in the new FM phenomenon. These stations not only promoted Edwin Armstrong's invention but became training sites for students interested in broadcasting. Although the FCC stopped licensing new 10-watt stations in 1978 (and didn't resume until a new class of low-power FM stations was approved in 2000), and although low-power stations aren't eligible for funding from the Corporation for Public Broadcasting, more than a thousand long-time 10-watters were still in operation in 2002.

Alternative Voices

As large corporations gained control of America's radio airwaves, activists in hundreds of communities across the United States in the 1990s protested the exclusivity of radio broadcasting by starting up their own noncommercial "pirate" radio stations. Broadcasting over a radius of just a few miles with low-power FM signals of one to ten watts, the pirate radio stations challenged corporate broadcasters' dominance of public airwaves. The National Association of Broadcasters (NAB) and other industry groups pressed to have the pirate broadcasters closed down, citing their illegality and their potential to create interference with existing stations. Between 1995 and 2000, more than five hundred illegal micropower radio stations were shut down. Still, an estimated one hundred to one thousand pirate stations are in operation in the United States, in both large urban areas and small rural towns.

The major complaint of pirate radio station operators was that the FCC had long ago ceased licensing low-power community radio stations. That problem was resolved in 2000 when the FCC, responding to tens of thousands of inquiries about the development of a new local radio broadcasting service, approved a new noncommercial **low power FM (LPFM)** class of stations in order to give voice to local groups lacking

Public Radio: Is the BBC Better Than NPR?

The United Kingdom's British Broadcasting Corporation (BBC) was established as a noncommercial, independent broadcasting service in 1922 and was funded by a radio receiver–set license fee. (BBC television and radio are now funded jointly by a monthly license fee of about $15 on all color TVs. If you own a color TV in Britain, you have to pay the fee or risk a steep fine.) The United States went a different route, not encouraging noncommercial public radio until 1967, with the creation of the Corporation for Public Broadcasting. National Public Radio began in 1970 as an outgrowth of the CPB, although NPR receives the bulk of its financing though member station dues and programming fees, contributions from private foundations, and corporate underwriting. Government funding accounts for only 2 percent of NPR's total revenues.

Description. Consider both NPR's and the BBC's program offerings. (The Web sites for each, <www.npr.org> and <www.bbc.co.uk/radio/>, are good starting points.) NPR, for example, has just one channel that it sends nationally, with news, talk shows, quiz shows, and music. The BBC has five radio channels, each with a specific niche. For example, from 4 to 5 P.M. on weekdays, most NPR affiliates are running *All Things Considered,* an award-winning in-depth news program. In the same hour BBC1 runs a popular music and interview program; BBC2 presents a program with music, news, sports, and commuter updates; BBC3 has Baroque and Renaissance music; BBC4 has a half-hour on books, then a half-hour on science and technology topics; and BBC5 carries a live news, sports, and commuter traffic program. The BBC also offers six digital channels.

Analysis. Looking for patterns and trends, make a list of program types and genres that are carried on NPR and the BBC. What kinds of program categories dominate? Can you detect what kinds of listeners the U.S. channel and the British counterparts imagine they are appealing to? Are there limitations on programming types based on the economic models of each country?

Interpretation. What do the patterns mean? Here, one might consider the history of public radio in each nation and the current funding of each. NPR has to struggle to make ends meet, and although it doesn't run advertising, it must run programming that can gain sufficient corporate and listener sponsorship. The BBC is well funded by license revenues and can bring a wider variety of channels and programming to listeners, without worrying about financial pressures.

Evaluation. Overall, which economic model creates better radio for the public good? Although the BBC might require more taxpayer funds, is it a worthwhile cost? Consider a third economic model by comparing the BBC's five noncommercial radio channels with the 100-plus channels (some commercial) of satellite radio services (see "Tracking Technology: Satellite Radio Goes Coast-to-Coast" on page 138). Is the public good better served with a publicly supported nationwide service like BBC radio, or should the users alone pay for such services, as in satellite radio and its monthly subscription costs (which are comparable to the monthly fee for BBC radio and television)?

access to the public airwaves. The LPFM service, which licenses 10- and 100-watt stations, planned to create one thousand new FM stations in the United States. The earliest LPFM station licensees included mostly religious groups but also high schools, colleges and universities, Native American tribes, labor groups, and museums.

The technical plans for LPFM located the stations in unused frequencies on the FM dial. Still, the NAB, the powerful Washington-based lobbying group representing commercial broadcasters, and National Public Radio fought to delay and limit the number of LPFM stations, arguing that such stations would cause interference with existing full-power FM stations. FCC chairman William E. Kennard, who fostered the LPFM initiative, responded: "This is about the haves—the broadcast industry—trying to prevent many have-nots—small community and educational organizations—

from having just a little piece of the pie. Just a little piece of the airwaves which belong to all of the people." [12] The NAB and NPR lobbyists prevailed, though, curtailing the number of new LPFMs to a few hundred in 2001.

Two alternative radio technologies also helped to bring more diverse sounds to listeners. First, **Internet radio** emerged in the 1990s, with the popularity of the Web. Internet radio stations come in two types: an existing station may "stream" a simulcast version of its on-air signal over the Web, or a station may be created exclusively for the Internet. Some of the most popular Internet radio stations are those that carry music formats unavailable on local radio, such as jazz, blues, and New Age music. But a decision by the Librarian of Congress in 2002 that established music royalty rates for Internet radio had an enormous chilling effect on Webcasters, which had grown to more than 40,000 stations. The ruling would require that commercial Webcasters pay a 0.07 cents royalty to the recording industry for each song played (and 0.02 cents per song for nonprofit Webcasters), a fee which corporate Webcasters like Yahoo! could afford but which would bankrupt low-revenue Webcasters on sites like Live365.com. (Interestingly, AM and FM radio broadcasters don't pay music performance fees, since airplay alone is considered to be of such high promotional value to the music industry.) Some members of Congress, fearing that most Webcasters would be forced off the Internet by thousands of dollars in royalty payments, responded with a bill that would exempt small and nonprofit Internet radio stations.

The other alternative radio technology added a third band—**satellite radio**—to AM and FM. (See "Tracking Technology: Satellite Radio Goes Coast-to-Coast" on page 138.) The two similar services, XM and Sirius, completed their national introduction by 2002 and offer more than one hundred digital music, news, and talk channels to the continental U.S. via satellite, at monthly prices ranging from about $10 (XM, with some commercial channels) to $13 (Sirius, with all music channels commercial-free). Channel programming ranges from all-reggae, Spanish Top 40, and opera, to NASCAR, National Public Radio, and comedy. By 2002, U.S. automakers (who are investors in the two competing satellite radio companies) began equipping most new cars with an XM or SAT satellite band, in addition to AM and FM, helping to ensure the adoption of satellite radio.

Radio and the Democracy of the Airwaves

The history of radio is also the history of broadcasting. In the United States, radio began as a crude but tremendously thrilling wireless communication tool of hobbyists and engineering students in engineering schools. As early inventors and entrepreneurs reconsidered radio as not just a wireless telegraph but as a medium for mass communication, broadcasting was born. The U.S. government also envisioned radio as a way for the United States to gain global communication dominance. It sanctioned RCA as a private monopoly, one that soon gained control of radio technology manufacturing.

In the decades before television, radio broadcasting experienced a golden age of programming, with high-quality variety, quiz, drama, comedy, and music shows carried on national networks like NBC and CBS. As network television overtook radio as the new American pastime, radio evolved into a portable medium for music. Format radio programming, which played Top 40 hits on an endless rotation, energized rock and roll in the 1950s and helped cultivate teen culture. In the 1990s, radio in the United States changed dramatically as government deregulation permitted unprecedented consolidation in ownership, with just a few corporations wielding great influence over the sound of radio.

Satellite Radio Goes Coast-to-Coast

It's coming from outer space, and it's going to take over your car radio.

At least, that's the plan of two companies who are vying for one of the hottest new broadcasting developments since a guy named Guglielmo Marconi figured out a way to wirelessly send telegraph signals.

It's called satellite radio, and if you think it's complicated, it isn't—the bottom line is it's a great new option for listening to radio on the road.

The two companies offering satellite radio service, XM and Sirius, each offer more than 100 channels of music, talk, sports, and news radio stations that are beamed via upper-atmosphere orbiters into your car (or even your home, for that matter). You can drive from Baltimore to Seattle and never lose the digital-quality sound of a Frank Sinatra broadcast. You can head cross-country and always be perfectly tuned to that obscure Mandarin Chinese music channel. . . .

There are pop music stations aplenty on satellite radio, of course, as well as classic rock, half a dozen country stations, a few New Wave channels, and a specialty station for just about any genre you can think of—African, reggae, heavy metal, Hindi, gospel, bluegrass, classical, and disco. And most of them have no commercial interruptions.

So what's the catch? Well, there's always money coming out of your pocket for anything good, and satellite radio is no exception.

On top of a one-time, purchase-and-installation fee for a radio, satellite antenna, and special receiver that will run you anywhere from $300 to $400, XM charges $10 a month for a subscription fee. Sirius, which has the same start-up costs, charges $12.95 a month. . . .

. . . [T]he basic premise of satellite radio should be understood. Sirius and XM are largely providing their own radio stations, being piped out of their own respective studios with their own DJs. In other words, there is almost no local programming available. . . .

That being said, it should also be noted that just about any satellite radio system you buy for your car would come with a standard AM/FM radio. This way you get the best of both worlds: local and satellite radio, with the latter essentially being an "add-on" to your car radio experience.

Also, XM and Sirius are two pretty distinct, independent entities. While both offer a huge variety of stations that cater to just about anyone, XM is more baby boomer and Sirius more hip-hop. It's no coincidence that XM's test radio provided to us came in a staid, brown Cadillac Deville DTS, while Sirius showcased its radio in a dark-blue Mustang with "SIRIUS ROCK" painted on the side, superimposed over a wild-looking guitar player. . . .

What the future holds for the two satellite radio companies will be interesting to watch. While the technology is terrific, the public is likely to have an initial adverse reaction to radio that comes with a price tag. . . . As satellite radios become more prevalent in new cars, though, public acceptance might follow. Even for $10 a month, satellite radio is a welcome alternative to the scant, static-interrupted selection we've all grown used to in the fast-aging world of AM/FM radio.

Source: Michael James, "High Flying Radio," *Baltimore Sun,* July 11, 2002, p. 11D.

Although the big radio chains control the largest share of radio's listeners, some critics charge that they have gotten even greedier. Along with deregulation of ownership, the 1996 Telecommunications Act also relaxed limits on radio advertising time, leading some formats, especially news/talk, to run up to thirty minutes of commercials each hour. Beginning in 1999, digital technology aided the drive to squeeze even more ads into each hour of radio. A small $12,000 audio processing device called Cash briefly delays live radio programs by a minute or two, shortens pauses between words, and clips long vowels before replaying the processed signal on air for listeners. The resulting digital compression speeds up the pace of the show and saves time for the insertion of up to four extra minutes of ads each hour. Listeners generally don't notice the tighter pace of the program, but they do notice the extra commercials. In fact, thousands of Rush Limbaugh's listeners complained about the additional commercials on his program. WABC in New York suspended the use of the technology for Limbaugh's show in that market, although many other stations continue to use it.[13]

Given broadcasters' reluctance to raise questions about these economic arrangements, public debate regarding radio as a special national resource has remained minuscule. Looking to the future, a big question remains to be answered: With a few large broadcast companies now permitted to dominate radio ownership nationwide, will this consolidation of power in any way restrict the number and kinds of voices permitted to speak over public airwaves? To ensure that mass-media industries continue to serve democracy, the public needs to play a role in developing the answer to this question.

Radio has managed to survive the economic threat posed by television, but its future in the twenty-first century is yet to be determined. With its specialized services, radio remains a diverse mass medium in which we can find our culture, our history, our politics, and our music represented. Radio's daily doses of news, talk, and song reverberate throughout the airwaves and across the Internet, helping to define areas of culture that are not readily acknowledged in mainstream newspapers or on prime-time television.

www.

To create an individualized study plan for Chapter 4, go to the interactive *Media and Culture* Online Study Guide at: bedfordstmartins.com/ mediaculture

REVIEW QUESTIONS

Early Technology and Development of Broadcasting

1. Why was the development of the telegraph important in media history? What were some of the disadvantages of telegraph technology?

2. How is the concept of the wireless different from that of radio?

3. What was Marconi's role in the development of the wireless?

4. What were Lee De Forest's contributions to radio?

5. Why was the RCA monopoly formed?

6. How did broadcasting, unlike print media, come to be federally regulated?

The Evolution of Commercial Radio

7. What was AT&T's role in the early days of radio?

8. How did the radio networks develop? What were the contributions of David Sarnoff and William Paley to network radio?

9. Why did the government-sanctioned RCA monopoly end?

10. What is the significance of the Communications Act of 1934?

Radio Reinvents Itself

11. How did radio adapt to the arrival of television?

12. What was Edwin Armstrong's role in the advancement of radio technology? Why did RCA hamper Armstrong's work?

13. How did music on radio change in the 1950s?

14. What was format radio, and why was it important to the survival of radio?

The Sounds of Radio Today

15. Why are there so many radio formats today?

16. Why did Top 40 radio diminish as a format in the 1980s and 1990s?

17. What is the state of nonprofit radio today?

18. What are the arguments that pirate radio operators use to justify the existence of their stations?

19. What are the reasons existing full-power radio broadcasters sought to delay and limit the emergence of low-power FM stations?

20. What are the current ownership rules governing American radio?

21. How do Internet radio and satellite radio present an alternative to broadcast radio?

22. What has been the main effect of the 1996 Telecommunications Act on radio-station ownership?

Radio and the Democracy of the Airwaves

23. Throughout the history of radio, why did the government encourage diversity among radio owners?

QUESTIONING THE MEDIA

1. Describe your earliest memories of listening to radio. Do you remember a favorite song? How old were you? Do you remember the station's call letters? Why did you listen?

2. Count the number and types of radio stations in your area today. What formats do they use? Do a little research and compare today's situation with the number and types of stations available in the 1930s and the 1950s. Describe the changes that have occurred.

3. If you could own and manage a commercial radio station, what format would you choose and why?

4. If you ran a noncommercial radio station in your area, what services would you provide that are not being met by commercial format radio?

5. How might radio be used to improve social and political discussions in the United States?

6. If you were the head of a large radio group, what arguments would you make in response to charges that your company limited the number of voices in the local media?

SEARCHING THE INTERNET

http://www.radio-locator.com

One of the most comprehensive listings of U.S. and worldwide radio station Web pages, including those stations that broadcast their audio signal on the Internet.

http://www.fcc.gov

A comprehensive government site, with sections on radio and the full text of the Telecommunications Act of 1996.

http://www.pri.org

PRI is a top provider of content for more than six hundred public radio stations, with programs such as Garrison Keillor's *A Prairie Home Companion,* Ira Glass's *This American Life,* and *World Cafe.*

http://www.npr.org

NPR's site includes audio files of special reports and hourly news updates, along with guides to other NPR programming.

http://www.live365.com

A leading site for thousands of live, "streaming" Internet radio stations.

http://www.xmradio.com and http://www.sirius.com

The Web sites for the two competing U.S. satellite radio services, XM and Sirius.

In Brief: Think-Pair-Share

Think: Take two minutes to write down answers to the following questions about your radio-listening habits: How much radio do you listen to? When do you listen? What attracts you to a particular station?

Pair: Turn to a neighbor and compare notes. Which radio formats (if any) do you agree on? What do you think the stations are doing that is "right"? Are there some aspects of radio programming that bother you? If so, what are they?

Share: Open up the discussion to the entire class. If you could envision the perfect radio station with the perfect format, what would it be? How would it be funded? Whom would it serve? What should be the purpose of this radio station in the community?

Critical Process: In Depth

This exercise examines radio-group ownership and format specialization. Assign each radio station of your market to individuals or small groups in the class. Listen to the same hour (e.g., 4 to 5 P.M.) during the day for each station.

Description. Use a chart and break down the hour into a program log, describing what you hear during the hour, including music, news, deejay chatter, ads, community announcements, station promotions, and contests. Describe the style of these broadcasts, as well as the time devoted to each category. Who do you think is the target audience? Who owns the station? Do the ad and promotion styles match the general flavor of the station?

Analysis. Compare program logs and other station information with classmates. What patterns emerge? Do the stations owned by the same radio group sound similar in certain ways (e.g., advertisers, newscasters, promotions)? Are there any locally owned stations, and do they operate differently in terms of programming? Which (if any) stations provide the best local news, events, and weather information? Which (if any) stations feature local artists? What did you like best of what you heard? What did you like least?

Interpretation. According to FCC rules, radio stations are trustees of public airwaves. Based on the limited hours you listened, were these stations doing a responsible job of serving the public? If some radio stations in a single market have similar formats, is that bad? Is there enough station differentiation in your market? Are there audience segments not targeted by the radio stations in your market? What are they, and why are they not being cultivated?

Evaluation. Does the radio industry give listeners what they want, or does it give listeners what the industry wants? Do you think radio companies are being responsible stewards of the public airwaves? What are some ways you'd like to see the state of radio today change?

KEY TERMS

telegraph, 107
Morse code, 107
electromagnetic waves, 108
radio waves, 108
wireless telegraphy, 110
wireless telephony, 110
broadcasting, 111
narrowcasting, 111
Radio Act of 1912, 112
Radio Corporation of America (RCA), 113
network, 115
option time, 117
Radio Act of 1927, 118

Federal Communications Act of 1934, 118
Federal Radio Commission (FRC), 118
Federal Communications Commission, 120
transistors, 123
FM, 123
AM, 123
format radio, 125
rotation, 125
payola, 125
pay-for-play, 126
drive time, 127
news/talk format, 128
adult contemporary (AC), 128

contemporary hits radio (CHR), 129
country, 129
urban, 129
album-oriented rock (AOR), 131
1996 Telecommunications Act, 132
National Public Radio (NPR), 134
Public Broadcasting Service (PBS), 134
Public Broadcasting Act of 1967, 134
Corporation for Public Broadcasting (CPB), 134
Pacifica Foundation, 135
low power FM (LPFM), 135
Internet radio, 137
satellite radio, 137

television

and the power of visual culture

CHAPTER 5

On a Sunday evening in December 2002, the notorious HBO gangster saga *The Sopranos* made TV history by beating the regular broadcast networks in audience ratings. This was unprecedented for a cable prime-time program, especially remarkable given that this premium cable service reaches only *one-third* of the total audience available to the "free" regular networks. But traditional network television has been in trouble now for a few years. The formerly dominant Big Three networks — ABC, CBS, and NBC — have lost more than half their audience over the last fifteen years, mostly to cable, DBS, VCR, and DVD viewing. For the past several years, HBO has garnered the bulk of the Emmy nominations (ninety-three in 2002 alone) for the best programming, while upstart networks UPN (United Paramount Network) and the WB (Warner Brothers) and cable alternatives Nickelodeon and MTV have siphoned away younger viewers. Even older faithful viewers have deserted the networks for cable alternatives A&E, C-Span, and the Weather Channel. Yet in spite of these shifts in allegiance, the Big Three have survived and mostly prospered. After all, they still attract the largest audiences

and, therefore, command the heftiest advertising rates from product companies that want to reach sizable audiences. TV is indeed a strange business when you can lose half your customer base and at the same time maintain—even increase—your ad revenues. How long this will last before cable and digital alternatives surpass the networks in audience size is yet to be determined.

In the history of television, the novelty of trendy programs eventually loses its allure. Thirty westerns were once on in prime time in the late 1950s, but today there are virtually none. Crime and cop shows dominated television in the 1970s and 1980s, and most of those have disappeared as well. For better clues into the ups and downs of television, it's probably best to look at programming with some staying power. Two programs in particular are representative of more telling shifts in network television—*The X-Files* and *Buffy the Vampire Slayer.* Both tapped into powerful and imaginative worlds and appealed to young viewers. *The X-Files* helped save a fledgling network, Fox, in the mid-1990s, and *Buffy*

best represents the new network strategy of taking young viewers away from the Big Three.

In 2002, *The X-Files* finished its final season on network television—nine years of tales about alien intruders, mutating monsters, government conspiracies, and citizen paranoia. Not only did *X-Files* help raise the national standing of the Fox network to the status of CBS, NBC, and ABC, but by 2000 the show's global presence had extended into more than ninety countries. With innovative and popular programs such as *The X-Files* and *The Simpsons,* the longest-running prime-time cartoon in history, the Fox network demonstrated that in a shrinking market—amid the VCR, DVD, cable, DBS, and Internet booms—a new network could evolve.

Following the Fox lead, in 1997 UPN launched *Buffy the Vampire Slayer.* A 1992 movie, *Buffy* mixed together supernatural themes with the ordinary world of teenagers—negotiating normal school experiences by day, slaying evil vampires by night. Joss Whedon, executive producer of *Buffy* (and also *Angel*), once told

a college audience that he intended the show as "a horror story about high school, and that's exactly what high school life is like . . . both literally and metaphorically." In fact, the program works because the stories stay grounded in everyday problems—identity issues, sexual tensions, popularity contests, and too much homework.

This strategy of creating programs that tap into the issues that are important to teens and young adults has enabled the newest networks to slowly gain a foothold in TV's prime-time hours. This strategy capitalized on perhaps the biggest failing of the Big Three over their many years of dominance—that in their quest to go for the largest possible audience and the adult consumer in the eighteen- to forty-nine age range, they generally failed to create enduring stories for younger viewers.

oday both the old and new networks are surviving and mostly prospering— by recycling old program ideas like the quiz show, by swiping concepts from European programmers (like *Survivor*), or just by stealing shows from each other. There is a long and storied history to all these techniques. After all, in the beginning, network television "borrowed" most of its best program ideas from radio. Throughout the 1950s, television snatched radio's national sponsors, program ideas, and even its **prime-time** audience. Old radio scripts began reappearing in TV form. In 1949, for instance, *The Lone Ranger* rode over to television from radio, where the program had originated in 1933. *Amos 'n' Andy*, a fixture on network radio since 1928, became the first TV series to have an entirely black cast in 1951. Jack Benny, Red Skelton, and George Burns and Gracie Allen, among the most prominent comedians of their day, all left radio for television. Symbolic of the times, the radio news program *Hear It Now* turned into TV's *See It Now*, and *Candid Microphone* became *Candid Camera*.

Since replacing radio in the 1950s as our most popular medium, television's social and cultural impact has repeatedly sparked arguments. During the 1990s, for example, teachers, clergy, journalists, and others waged a public assault on TV's negative impact on children. A 1995 *New York Times* poll suggested that most Americans blamed television as the biggest single factor underlying teenage sex and violence (although TV viewing during teenage years actually decreases).[1] During the 2000 presidential election campaign, television was targeted once again for reinforcing an outmoded two-party political system driven by big-money TV ads.

But there is another side to this story. In the 1960s, television was there to expose civil rights violations in the South, and in the 1980s it did the same in Eastern Europe and China. In the early 1990s, the televised Clarence Thomas–Anita Hill hearings triggered public debate about sexual harassment. In times of crisis, our fragmented and pluralistic society has turned to television as a touchstone, as common ground. We did this during the Army–McCarthy hearings on communism in the 1950s, in the aftermath of the Kennedy and King assassinations in the 1960s, and during the political turmoil of Watergate in the 1970s. In 1995, when 168 people died in the bombing of the Oklahoma City federal building, we again turned to television to make sense of senselessness. In 1998 and 1999, we followed the Clinton impeachment process. And in September 2001—in shock and horror—we all turned to television to learn that nearly 3,000 people had been killed in terrorist attacks on the World Trade Center and the Pentagon. For better or worse, television has woven itself into the cultural fabric of daily life.

In this age of increasing market specialization, television is still the one mass medium that delivers content millions can share simultaneously—everything from the Super Bowl to a network game show to the 1986 and 2003 space shuttle disasters. In this chapter, we will examine television's impact: the cultural, social, and economic factors surrounding the most influential media innovation since the printing press. We will begin by reviewing the early experiments with TV technology that led to the medium's development. We will then focus on the TV boom in the 1950s, including the downfall of sponsor-controlled content and the impact of the quiz-show scandals. Most of TV's major programming trends developed during this period, and we will investigate the most significant ones, including news, comedy, and drama. We will trace the audience decline that has affected the major networks and explore television as a prime-time money factory, examining various developments and costs in the production, distribution, and syndication of programs. Finally, we will look at television's impact on democracy.

> **❝** I wanted to see the type of drama that would unfold with these people stuck on an island. It's like *Real World* meets *Lord of the Flies*. And I wanted to see people eat rats. **❞**
>
> – Eric Robinson, age twenty-three, talent agent and *Survivor* fan

> **❝** I've watched many episodes in which Buffy wonders if she's smart enough for college, strong enough to beat up some baddies, and special enough for her friends' attention. Every teen has awesome abilities and potential, and just like Buffy, can't always see them. **❞**
>
> – Caitlin Campbell, age sixteen, *Television Quarterly*, 2001

> **❝** Television is the medium from which most of us receive our news, sports, entertainment, cues for civic discourse and, most of all, our marching orders as consumers. **❞**
> – Frank Rich, *New York Times*, 1998

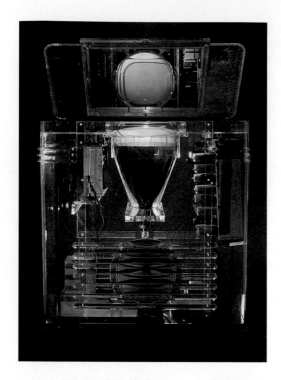

At the 1939 World's Fair in New York, the "guts" of a TV set featured a sealed glass device called a *cathode ray tube*. Such picture tubes were the technical standard in television for more than fifty years. Late in 1996, the FCC approved a new standard—digital, high-definition television.

The Origins and Early Development of Television

In 1948, only 1 percent of America's households had a television set; by 1953, more than 50 percent had one; and by the early 1960s, more than 90 percent of all homes had a TV set. With television on the rise throughout the 1950s, many feared that radio—as well as books, magazines, and movies—would become irrelevant and unnecessary. What happened, of course, is that both radio and print media adapted to this new technology. In fact, today more radio stations are operating and more books and magazines are published than ever before; and ticket sales for movies have remained fairly steady since the 1960s.

Early TV Technology

Although television achieved mass-media status in the 1950s, inventors from a number of nations had been toying with the idea of televised images for nearly a hundred years. Isolating TV and radio waves—part of the electromagnetic spectrum—required two ingredients: a photoelectric sensing material and a technique for encoding pictures for transmission via radio waves. Inventors needed a medium like film so that when light struck it, an electric current could be generated. In the late 1800s, the invention of the *cathode ray tube,* the forerunner of the TV picture tube, combined principles of the camera and electricity. Because television images could not physically float through the air, technicians and inventors developed a method of encoding them at a transmission point (a TV station) and decoding them at the reception point (a TV set). In the 1880s, German inventor Paul Nipkow developed the *scanning disk,* a large flat metal disk with a series of small perforations organized in a spiral pattern. As the disk rotated, it separated pictures into pinpoints of light that could be transmitted as a series of electronic lines. As the disk spun, each small hole scanned one line of a scene to be televised. For years, Nipkow's disk served as the foundation for experiments regarding the transmission of visual images.

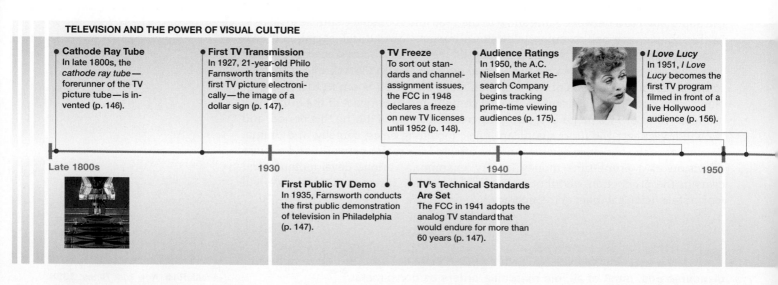

TELEVISION AND THE POWER OF VISUAL CULTURE

Cathode Ray Tube
In late 1800s, the *cathode ray tube*—forerunner of the TV picture tube—is invented (p. 146).

First TV Transmission
In 1927, 21-year-old Philo Farnsworth transmits the first TV picture electronically—the image of a dollar sign (p. 147).

TV Freeze
To sort out standards and channel-assignment issues, the FCC in 1948 declares a freeze on new TV licenses until 1952 (p. 148).

Audience Ratings
In 1950, the A.C. Nielsen Market Research Company begins tracking prime-time viewing audiences (p. 175).

I Love Lucy
In 1951, *I Love Lucy* becomes the first TV program filmed in front of a live Hollywood audience (p. 156).

Late 1800s   1930   1940   1950

First Public TV Demo
In 1935, Farnsworth conducts the first public demonstration of television in Philadelphia (p. 147).

TV's Technical Standards Are Set
The FCC in 1941 adopts the analog TV standard that would endure for more than 60 years (p. 147).

In 1907, Russian physicist Boris Rosing improved the mechanical scanning device, but it was his lab assistant, Vladimir Zworykin, and an Idaho teenager, Philo Farnsworth, who independently pioneered an electronic TV system. Zworykin left Russia for America in 1919 and went to work for Westinghouse, where he developed the *iconoscope,* the first TV camera tube to convert light rays into electrical signals. By breaking down and converting these signals into radio waves, transmitting them through the air, and reconstructing them in a receiver set, inventors made television a possibility by 1923.

At age sixteen, Farnsworth patented an electronic *image dissector* tube and figured out that mechanical scanning systems would not work for sending pictures through the air over long distances. In 1927, at age twenty-one, Farnsworth transmitted the first TV picture electronically—the image of a dollar sign. Finally, in 1930, he patented the first electronic television. RCA, then the world leader in broadcasting technology, challenged Farnsworth in a major patents battle. He would have to rely on his high-school notebooks as evidence to win against the company. After its court defeat, RCA had to negotiate to use Farnsworth's seventy-three patents. He later licensed these patents to RCA and AT&T for use in the commercial development of television. Farnsworth conducted the first public demonstration of television at the Franklin Institute in Philadelphia in 1935—four years *before* RCA's famous public demo at the 1939 World's Fair.

Setting Technical Standards

In the late 1930s, the National Television Systems Committee (NTSC), a group representing major electronics firms, began meeting to outline industry-wide manufacturing and technical standards. As a result of these meetings, in 1941 the Federal Communications Commission (FCC) adopted a 525-line image, scanned electronically at thirty frames per second (fps); this still is the standard for all TV sets produced in the United States until the new digital standard phases out old sets (see "Tracking Technology: Digital TV and the End of Analog" on page 150). About thirty countries, including Japan, Canada, Mexico, Saudi Arabia, and most Latin American nations, adopted the NTSC system. Great Britain and the former Soviet Union, however, waited for the technology to improve and eventually adopted a slightly superior 625-line, 25 fps system, used for decades throughout most of Europe and Asia. A third standard operated in France, Belgium, Algeria, and a few other countries.

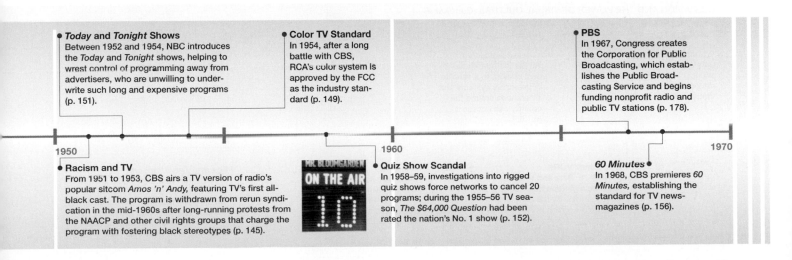

Today and Tonight Shows
Between 1952 and 1954, NBC introduces the *Today* and *Tonight* shows, helping to wrest control of programming away from advertisers, who are unwilling to underwrite such long and expensive programs (p. 151).

Color TV Standard
In 1954, after a long battle with CBS, RCA's color system is approved by the FCC as the industry standard (p. 149).

PBS
In 1967, Congress creates the Corporation for Public Broadcasting, which establishes the Public Broadcasting Service and begins funding nonprofit radio and public TV stations (p. 178).

1950

1960

1970

Racism and TV
From 1951 to 1953, CBS airs a TV version of radio's popular sitcom *Amos 'n' Andy*, featuring TV's first all-black cast. The program is withdrawn from rerun syndication in the mid-1960s after long-running protests from the NAACP and other civil rights groups that charge the program with fostering black stereotypes (p. 145).

Quiz Show Scandal
In 1958–59, investigations into rigged quiz shows force networks to cancel 20 programs; during the 1955–56 TV season, *The $64,000 Question* had been rated the nation's No. 1 show (p. 152).

60 Minutes
In 1968, CBS premieres *60 Minutes*, establishing the standard for TV newsmagazines (p. 156).

Fiddling with Frequencies and Freezing TV Licenses

A fundamental difference between broadcast television and cable is that traditional TV signals travel through the airwaves via the same electromagnetic spectrum that carries radio signals. This meant that the number of TV stations a city or market could support in television's early days (and today in some sparsely populated areas) was limited because airwave frequencies would interfere with one another. So a TV market could have a channel 2 and a channel 4 but not a channel 3, or a channel 5 and a channel 7 but not a channel 6. Cable systems don't have this problem because they download both regular wireless TV signals and satellite cable services and reassign them new channel allocations in a wired system. Frequency congestion and limited space is cleared up when over-the-air TV signals get reassigned to their own cable channels.

In the 1940s, the FCC began assigning certain channels in specific geographic areas to make sure there was no interference. (One consequence of this was that for years New Jersey had no TV stations because those signals would have interfered with all the New York stations.) The commission also set aside thirteen channels (1–13) on a **VHF** (very high frequency) band for black-and-white television. At this time, though, most electronics firms were converting to wartime production, so commercial TV development was limited: Only ten stations were operating when Pearl Harbor was attacked in December 1941. However, by 1948, the FCC had issued nearly a hundred television licenses. Due to growing concern about the allocation of a finite number of channels and with growing frequency interference problems as existing channels "overlapped," the FCC declared a freeze on new licenses from 1948 to 1952.

The Korean War prolonged the freeze. During this time, cities such as New York, Chicago, and Los Angeles had several TV stations, whereas other areas, including Little Rock, Arkansas, and Portland, Oregon, had none. Cities with TV stations saw a 20 to 40 percent drop in movie attendance during this period; more than sixty movie theaters closed in the Chicago area alone. But in non-TV cities, movie audiences increased. Taxi receipts and nightclub attendance also fell in TV cities, as did library book circulation. At the same time, radio listening declined; for example, Bob Hope's network radio show lost half its national audience between 1949 and 1951. By 1951, sales of television sets had surpassed sales of radio receivers.

After a second NTSC conference in 1952 sorted out technical problems, the FCC ended the licensing freeze and issued a major report finalizing technical standards,

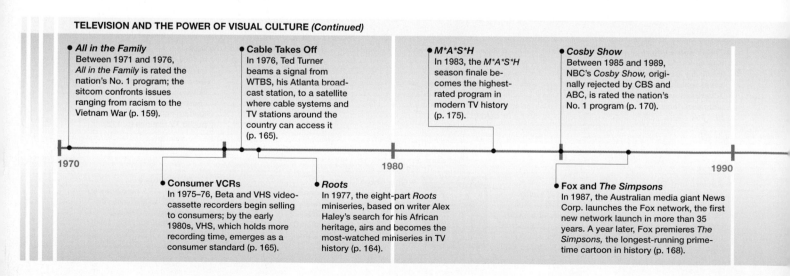

TELEVISION AND THE POWER OF VISUAL CULTURE *(Continued)*

● *All in the Family*
Between 1971 and 1976, *All in the Family* is rated the nation's No. 1 program; the sitcom confronts issues ranging from racism to the Vietnam War (p. 159).

● Cable Takes Off
In 1976, Ted Turner beams a signal from WTBS, his Atlanta broadcast station, to a satellite where cable systems and TV stations around the country can access it (p. 165).

● *M*A*S*H*
In 1983, the *M*A*S*H* season finale becomes the highest-rated program in modern TV history (p. 175).

● *Cosby Show*
Between 1985 and 1989, NBC's *Cosby Show*, originally rejected by CBS and ABC, is rated the nation's No. 1 program (p. 170).

1970

1980

1990

● Consumer VCRs
In 1975–76, Beta and VHS videocassette recorders begin selling to consumers; by the early 1980s, VHS, which holds more recording time, emerges as a consumer standard (p. 165).

● *Roots*
In 1977, the eight-part *Roots* miniseries, based on writer Alex Haley's search for his African heritage, airs and becomes the most-watched miniseries in TV history (p. 164).

● Fox and *The Simpsons*
In 1987, the Australian media giant News Corp. launches the Fox network, the first new network launch in more than 35 years. A year later, Fox premieres *The Simpsons*, the longest-running prime-time cartoon in history (p. 168).

many still in use today. Among its actions, the FCC set aside seventy new channels (14–83) on a **UHF** (ultrahigh frequency) band, although few manufacturers in the 1950s made TV sets equipped with UHF reception. As a result, UHF license holders struggled for years, until a 1964 law finally required manufacturers to equip sets with UHF reception. With the expansion of UHF slowed by technical snags, the FCC eventually "took back" channels 70–83 and reassigned those frequencies (plus VHF's channel 1) to other communication services, including new radio allocations and cellular phones. During this period, most major cities were assigned four to five VHF signals and maybe another five to six UHF signals.

In all the TV markets across the country, nearly 250 channels were initially set aside for educational or nonprofit status, most of them on the newly created UHF band. Commercial interests, as they did in radio, had gobbled up most of the early VHF assignments with the FCC's blessing. But the FCC did not establish a method for financing nonprofit stations, and a long economic struggle followed for many of the educational TV stations. Even with the creation of the Corporation for Public Broadcasting (CPB) in 1967, which funneled federal funds to nonprofit radio and public TV stations, the loose, decentralized network of stations that share Public Broadcasting Service (PBS) programming have had to beg listeners for much of their financial support. This has been especially true since the 1990s, when a more fiscally conservative Congress reduced much of the CPB's funding.

Another outcome of the freeze featured deliberations about the standards for a color TV system. In 1952, the FCC tentatively approved the experimental CBS system. Because its signal could not be received by black-and-white sets, however, the system was incompatible with those that most Americans owned. In 1954, RCA's color system, which could also receive black-and-white images, usurped CBS to become the color standard. Although NBC began broadcasting a few shows in color in the mid-1950s, it wasn't until 1966 that all three networks broadcast their entire evening lineups in color.

Almost thirteen hundred communities received TV-channel allocations from the FCC after the freeze ended. Because broadcast signals could interfere with one another, the FCC created a national map and tried to evenly distribute all available channels throughout the country. By the mid-1950s, there were more than four hundred television stations in operation, a 400 percent surge since the pre-freeze era. Today, about seventeen hundred TV stations are in operation, including more than three hundred nonprofit stations, which increasingly rely on corporate sponsorship and viewer donations for support.

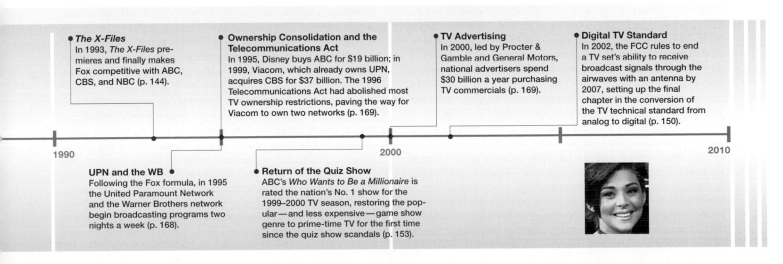

The X-Files
In 1993, *The X-Files* premieres and finally makes Fox competitive with ABC, CBS, and NBC (p. 144).

Ownership Consolidation and the Telecommunications Act
In 1995, Disney buys ABC for $19 billion; in 1999, Viacom, which already owns UPN, acquires CBS for $37 billion. The 1996 Telecommunications Act had abolished most TV ownership restrictions, paving the way for Viacom to own two networks (p. 169).

TV Advertising
In 2000, led by Procter & Gamble and General Motors, national advertisers spend $30 billion a year purchasing TV commercials (p. 169).

Digital TV Standard
In 2002, the FCC rules to end a TV set's ability to receive broadcast signals through the airwaves with an antenna by 2007, setting up the final chapter in the conversion of the TV technical standard from analog to digital (p. 150).

1990　　　　　　　　　　　　　2000　　　　　　　　　　　2010

UPN and the WB
Following the Fox formula, in 1995 the United Paramount Network and the Warner Brothers network begin broadcasting programs two nights a week (p. 168).

Return of the Quiz Show
ABC's *Who Wants to Be a Millionaire* is rated the nation's No. 1 show for the 1999–2000 TV season, restoring the popular—and less expensive—game show genre to prime-time TV for the first time since the quiz show scandals (p. 153).

Digital TV and the End of Analog

In 2002, the Federal Communications Commission (FCC) issued a ruling that would end a TV set's ability to receive broadcast signals through the airwaves with an antenna in 2007. So unless homes have cable or satellite service (or buy a $400 digital converter—which will be cheaper by 2007), about 15 to 20 percent of the 265 million existing analog TV sets now in use in the United States won't work.

Here's the story behind the analog-to-digital conversion:

Late in 1996, the FCC initiated the first fundamental changes in TV technology in more than fifty years.[1] Since the early 1960s, TV engineers had been searching to improve the clarity and resolution of the standard NTSC 525-line TV image established in the 1940s. Most experiments focused on improving existing **analog** transmission, in which images are sent as continuous signals through the airwaves on specific frequencies. By the 1980s, Japanese firms had developed high-definition television (HDTV) for their own markets; with 1,100-plus lines of resolution, HDTV was the far superior analog alternative to the old NTSC standard, which had only 525 lines of resolution. Some version of this early HDTV experiment seemed certain to become the new U.S. television standard.

In the late 1980s, however, HDTV ran into the digital revolution. After seeing an impressive Sony HDTV demonstration in 1987, the FCC set up a race among various companies to develop a new American standard that used **digital** technology, which converts images and text to computerized signals. Sony and other Japanese firms then created a hybrid of analog and digital HDTV innovations. To beat the Japanese challenge, in 1988 a consortium of broadcasters, electronics and computer manufacturers, and researchers from Europe and America—known as the Grand Alliance—began developing an all-digital system that surpassed the versatility of existing HDTV formats. The digital standard required less frequency space to store more images, channels, and computer data than analog or hybrid HDTV systems.

In late 1996, the FCC approved the Grand Alliance digital system. Under this plan, since analog and digital systems are incompatible without a converter, each existing station was allocated a second channel for roughly ten years as consumers convert to digital sets. During that time, each station would continue to broadcast programs using analog signals on its old channel, while many of the same programs would begin transmitting on a newly allocated digital channel. Because of the expense of digital conversion (roughly $1 million), by mid-2002

only about 400 of the nation's 1,300 commercial broadcast stations had begun digital transmissions. At the end of the adjustment period in 2007, though, local stations are supposed to surrender their old analog frequencies to the FCC, which will then auction them off—probably to various competing companies for use by cell phones or new TV services—formally ending analog broadcasting.

Analysts expect the pace of digital TV to pick up, projecting that three million digital TVs will be sold in the United States in 2003. But it is not likely Americans will quickly throw out their more than 265 million analog TV sets (which have about a ten-year life span) and 60 million–plus analog VCRs when the current analog NTSC broadcast system changes over to digital. Instead, most people without cable or satellite service will probably purchase set-top tuner/converters to pick up the digital signals. Even homes with cable or satellite hook-ups that can still use their analog TVs will not be able to get the full impact of superior digital pictures unless they have a digital TV or a converter. Moreover, analog broadcasts may not actually end in 2007 in some areas; a legal loophole allows a local station to keep its analog signal if less than 85 percent of homes in the station's area are equipped for digital TV.

As the conversion gets under way, in the 2001–2002 TV season the major TV networks began carrying partial digital schedules, with the expensive high-definition broadcasts typically underwritten by the digital setmakers. By 2002, though, the best medium for digital television was direct broadcast satellite systems like DirecTV, which offered a completely high-definition signal of HBO, plus another channel of special events in digital HDTV. Still, the majority of American TV households, the nearly 70 percent that watch broadcast TV via cable, were missing the crisp digital pictures. That is because although broadcasters were required to send digital signals, cable operators, limited by the technical capacities of their systems, often were unable to carry the broadcasters' digital programs. Interestingly enough, it may be DVDs and not digital broadcasts that have helped to push consumers to buy digital TV sets, since DVD movies look best on digital monitors. By 2002, about one-third of U.S. households had a DVD player, helping to pave the way to complete television's digital revolution. Additionally, the cost of a good digital set—like that of computers—has been dropping by half every two years or so. In 1999 the average price of a fully digital projection TV was $8,000, but by 2002 that price was less than $4,000.[2]

Sponsorship and Scandal—TV Grows Up

Although television was considered a novelty in the late 1940s and early 1950s, by the close of the 1950s the new technology had become a dominant mass medium and cultural force with more than 90 percent of U.S. households owning at least one set. Partly, television's new standing came as it moved away from the influence of radio and established a separate identity. Two important contributors to this identity were (1) a major change in the advertising and sponsorship structure of television, and, more significant, (2) a major cultural scandal.

The Rise and Fall of Sponsorship

Like radio in the 1930s and 1940s, early television programs were often conceived, produced, and supported by a single sponsor. Many of the top-rated programs in the 1950s even included the sponsor's name in the title: *Buick Circus Hour, Camel News Caravan, Colgate Comedy Hour, Gillette Cavalcade of Sports,* and *Goodyear TV Playhouse.* Today no regular program on network television is named after and controlled by a single sponsor.

Throughout the early 1950s, the broadcast networks became increasingly unhappy with the control sponsors exerted over program content, and they took steps to change things. With the growing popularity of television came opportunities to alter prior financial arrangements, especially given the high cost of producing programs on a weekly basis. In 1952, for example, a single one-hour TV show cost a sponsor about $35,000, a figure that rose to $90,000 by the end of the decade. These weekly costs became increasingly difficult for sponsors to bear.

David Sarnoff, then head of RCA/NBC, and William Paley, head of CBS, saw the opportunity to diminish the role of sponsors. Enter Sylvester "Pat" Weaver (father of actress Sigourney Weaver), who was appointed president of NBC by Sarnoff in 1953. A former advertising executive, Weaver was used to controlling radio content for his clients. When he made the switch to television, Weaver sought to retain that control—by forcing advertisers out of the content game. By increasing program length from fifteen minutes (standard for radio programs) to thirty minutes and longer, Weaver substantially raised program costs for advertisers. In addition, two new programming changes made significant inroads in helping the networks gain control of content. Both strategies involved producing ninety-minute to three-hour-long weekday programs, thus making it almost impossible for a single sponsor to foot the daily bill.

The first strategy featured the concept of a "magazine" program that included multiple segments—news, talk, comedy, music, and the like—similar to the content variety found in a general-interest or news magazine of the day, such as *Life* or *Time*. In January 1952, NBC introduced the *Today* show, which started as a three-hour morning talk-news program. Then in September 1954, NBC premiered the ninety-minute *Tonight Show*. Because both shows ran daily rather than weekly, studio production costs managed by a single sponsor were prohibitive. Rather than selling the whole concept to one sponsor, NBC sold spot ads within the shows: Advertisers paid the network for thirty- or sixty-second time slots. The network, not the sponsor, now owned the programs or bought them from independent producers. Fifty years later, the *Today* and *Tonight* shows remain fixtures on NBC.

The second strategy, known originally as the "spectacular," is today recognized by a more modest term, the *television special*. At NBC, Weaver bought special programs, like Laurence Olivier's filmed version

● NBC originally developed the *Today* show in 1952 as a strategy to wrest control away from sponsors. The 2003 version of *Today* stars newscaster Ann Curry, weatherman Al Roker, and co-hosts Matt Lauer and Katie Couric.

of *Richard III* and the Broadway production of *Peter Pan,* again selling spot ads to multiple sponsors. The 1955 TV version of *Peter Pan* was a particular success, watched by some sixty-five million viewers (compare CBS's *Survivor II,* watched at its peak by thirty million viewers in spring 2001). More typical specials featured music-variety shows hosted by top singers such as Judy Garland and Frank Sinatra. The combination of these programming strategies—and one juicy television scandal—ended sponsors' control over television content.

The Quiz-Show Scandals Seal Sponsorship's Fate

Corporate backers of quiz shows drove the final nail into the coffin of sponsor-controlled TV content. In the mid-1950s, the networks revived the radio quiz-show genre. CBS aired the *$64,000 Question,* originally radio's more modest *$64 Question*—symbolic of how much television had raised the economic stakes. Sponsored by Revlon, which bought a half-hour block of evening prime time from the network in 1955, the program ranked as the most popular TV show in America during its first year. As one historian has suggested: "It is impossible to explain fully the popular appeal of the *$64,000 Question.* Be it the lure of sudden wealth, the challenge to answer esoteric questions, happiness at seeing other people achieving financial success, whatever the program touched in the American psyche at mid-century, this was stunning TV."[2] By the end of the 1957–58 season, twenty-two quiz shows aired on network television.

Revlon followed its success with the *$64,000 Challenge* in 1956. At one point, Revlon's two shows were running first and second in the national ratings, and its name recognition was so enhanced that the company periodically ran out of prod-

● Quizmaster Jack Barry questions contestants on *Twenty-One* (NBC, 1956–58), the popular game show that was struck by scandal in 1958. In 1999, ABC scored a ratings hit with *Who Wants to Be a Millionaire,* the first new quiz show to appear on prime-time television since the scandal more than 40 years earlier. *Millionaire* was the most-watched program during the 1999–2000 TV season, but its ratings declined substantially during 2000–01.

ucts. In fact, the company's cosmetic sales skyrocketed from $1.2 million before its sponsorship of the quiz shows to nearly $10 million by 1959.

Compared with dramas and situation comedies (which we'll look at shortly), quiz shows were (and are today) cheap to produce, with inexpensive sets and mostly nonactors as guests. In addition, these programs offered the corporate sponsor the opportunity to have its name displayed on the set throughout the program. The problem was that most of these shows were rigged. To heighten the drama and get rid of guests whom the sponsors or producers did not find appealing, key contestants were rehearsed and given the answers. The most notorious rigging occurred on *Twenty-One*, a quiz show owned by Geritol (whose profits climbed by $4 million one year after deciding to sponsor the program in 1956). The subject of Robert Redford's 1994 film *Quiz Show*, *Twenty-One*'s most infamous contestant was Charles Van Doren, a Columbia University English professor from a famous literary family. In 1957, Van Doren won $129,000 during his fifteen-week run on the program; his fame then landed him a job on NBC's *Today* show. In 1958, after a series of contestants accused the morning show *Dotto* of being fixed, the networks quickly dropped twenty shows. Following further rumors, a *TV Guide* story, a New York grand-jury probe, and a congressional investigation in 1959 (during which Van Doren admitted cheating), big-money prime-time quiz shows ended—until ABC revived the format forty years later in *Who Wants to Be a Millionaire*. (In 2000, NBC tried but failed to bring back *Twenty-One*.)

Although often little more than a compelling footnote in many accounts of television's history, the impact of the quiz-show scandals was enormous. First, the pressure on TV executives to rig the programs and the subsequent fraud effectively put an end to any role sponsors might have had in creating television content. Second, although many Americans had believed in the democratic possibilities of television—bringing inexpensive information and entertainment into every household—this belief was undermined by the sponsors and TV executives who participated in the quiz-show fraud. During the 1950s, many people trusted that pictures were more honest than words. But the scandals provided the first dramatic indication that TV images could be manipulated. The seeds, then, for our contemporary cynicism about electronic culture had sprouted full-blown by the late 1950s. By the end of the decade, many middle-class parents were even refusing to allow their children to watch television.

The third, and most important, impact of the quiz-show scandals was that they magnified the separation between the privileged few and the general public, a division between high and low that would affect print and visual culture for at least the next forty years. That Charles Van Doren had come from a family of Ivy League intellectuals and "sold his soul" for fame and money drove a wedge between intellectuals and the popular new medium. At the time, many well-educated people aimed a wary skepticism toward television. This was best captured in the famous 1961 speech by FCC commissioner Newton Minow, who labeled game shows, westerns, cartoons, and other popular genres part of commercial television's "vast wasteland." Critics have used the wasteland metaphor ever since to admonish the TV industry for failing to live up to its potential. After the quiz-show scandal, non-network, independently produced programs like *Jeopardy* and *Wheel of Fortune*, now called *game shows*, made a strong comeback in late-afternoon time slots. Then cable services like MTV and Comedy Central (*Win Ben Stein's Money*) experimented with more comic game programs in evening hours. The major broadcast networks, however, remained reluctant to put game shows on again in prime time, even though they are much cheaper to produce than dramas or situation comedies. Finally, in 1999, ABC gambled that the nation was ready once again for a quiz show in prime time. The network, at least for a while, hit the jackpot with *Who Wants to Be a Millionaire*.

> **"** I was fascinated by the seduction of [Charles] Van Doren, by the Faustian bargain that lured entirely good and honest people into careers of deception. **"**
>
> — Robert Redford, director, *Quiz Show*, 1995

Major Programming Trends in the TV Age

The disappearance of quiz shows marked the end of most prime-time network programs originating from New York. From 1955 through 1957, the three major networks gradually moved their entertainment divisions to Los Angeles because of its proximity to Hollywood production studios. Network news operations, however, remained in New York. Symbolically, these cities came to represent the two major branches of TV programming: *entertainment* and *information*. Although there is considerable blurring between these categories today, at one time the two were more distinct.

TV Information: Our Daily News Culture

In television journalism, local broadcast stations, TV newsmagazines, and cable's CNN and Fox News have all made key contributions and generated their own controversies. But in this section our focus is on the traditional network evening news and the changes in TV news viewing ushered in by cable TV services. Interestingly, since the 1960s, broadcast journalism has consistently topped print news in national research polls that ask which news medium is most trustworthy. This fact alone makes the evening news a force to be reckoned with in our information culture.

NBC News

Featuring in the beginning a panel of reporters interrogating political figures, NBC's weekly *Meet the Press* (1947–) remains the oldest show on television. Daily evening newscasts, though, began on NBC in February 1948 with the *Camel Newsreel Theater*. Originally a ten-minute Fox Movietone newsreel that was also shown in theaters, this filmed news service was converted to a live broadcast one year later. Renamed the *Camel News Caravan* and anchored by John Cameron Swayze (who later became the major spokesperson for Timex watches), the NBC newscast showed Swayze reading short news items in a converted radio studio. Toward the end of the fifteen-minute show he would announce grandly, "Now let's go hopscotching the world for headlines!" and read a list of very brief reports, which were occasionally accompanied by whatever filmed newsreel footage the network could get that day.

Sponsored by a cigarette company and the first news show to air in color, *Camel News* was succeeded by the *Huntley-Brinkley Report* in 1956. With Chet Huntley in New York and David Brinkley in Washington, this coanchored NBC program became the most popular evening news show on television. To provide a touch of intimacy, the coanchors would sign off their broadcasts saying, "Good night, Chet."/"Good night, David." Chet and David, who were not close friends, served as the model for hundreds of local news broadcasts that eventually developed dual anchors to present the news. After Huntley retired in 1970, the program was renamed *NBC Nightly News* and struggled to compete with CBS's emerging star anchor, Walter Cronkite. A series of anchors and coanchors followed before Tom Brokaw settled in as NBC's sole anchor in September 1983.

CBS News

A second regular evening news show, *The CBS-TV News* with Douglas Edwards, premiered on CBS in May 1948. In 1956, the CBS program became the first news show videotaped for rebroadcast on **affiliate stations** (independently owned stations that sign contracts with a network and carry its programs) in western time zones. (Ampex had just developed the first workable videotape recorder.) Walter Cronkite succeeded Edwards in 1962, starting a nineteen-year run as anchor of the renamed

CBS Evening News. Formerly a World War II correspondent for a print wire service, Cronkite in 1963 anchored the first thirty-minute network newscast, which featured a live ocean-side interview with President John Kennedy, twelve weeks before his assassination. In 1968, Cronkite went to Vietnam to cover firsthand America's involvement in that civil war. Putting aside his role as a neutral news anchor, he concluded on the air that the American public had been misled about Vietnam and that U.S. participation in the war was a mistake. With such a centrist news personality now echoing the protest movement, public opinion against U.S. intervention mounted. In fact, partly because of the influence of Cronkite's criticisms, President Lyndon Johnson decided not to seek reelection in 1968.

Retiring from his anchor position in 1981, Cronkite was succeeded by Dan Rather, a former White House correspondent who had starred on CBS's respected TV news program *60 Minutes* since 1975. Despite a $22 million, ten-year contract, Rather could not sustain the program as the highest-rated evening newscast, however. To woo viewers and exude warmth, he tried wearing colorful sweater vests and briefly signed off with the slogan "Courage." But neither effort succeeded in increasing the size of his audience. In the mid-1990s, the network tried an experiment aimed at both recapturing viewers and responding to the long-standing criticism that male anchors controlled the daily network news: CBS paired Rather with former *Today* show host Connie Chung. Unlike CNN and many local news stations, which routinely use male and female news teams, women anchors on the networks have long been relegated to substitute or weekend duty. Ratings continued to sag, however, and CBS terminated Chung after just a few months. Into 2003, Rather continued on his own.

ABC News

Over the years, the ABC network tried many anchors and formats as it attempted to cut into the dominance of NBC in the 1960s and CBS in the 1970s. ABC premiered a daily program in 1948, but it folded when few affiliates chose to carry it. The network finally launched a daily news show in 1953, anchored by John Daly, the head of ABC News and also the host of CBS's evening game show *What's My Line?* After Daly left in 1960, a series of personalities sat behind the anchor desk, including John Cameron Swayze and, in 1965, a twenty-six-year-old Canadian, Peter Jennings, dubbed "anchor boy" by critics at the time. Another series of rotating anchors ensued, including Harry Reasoner and Howard K. Smith. Then, in 1976, the network hired Barbara Walters away from NBC's *Today* show, gave her a $1 million annual contract, and made her the first woman to regularly coanchor a network newscast. With Walters and Reasoner (the first reporter chosen in 1968 to launch *60 Minutes*) together, viewer ratings rose slightly, but the network was still behind CBS and NBC. In 1977, ABC sports director Roone Arledge took over as head of the newly combined ABC News and Sports division. In 1978, he launched *ABC World News Tonight,* featuring four anchors: Frank Reynolds in Washington, Jennings in London, Walters in New York, and Max Robinson in Chicago. Robinson was the first black reporter to coanchor a network news program. Walters decided to leave her anchor position in the early 1980s and focus on doing celebrity and political interviews. In 1983, ABC chose Jennings to return as the sole anchor. By the late 1980s, the ABC evening news had become the most-watched network newscast until, in 1996, it was dethroned by Brokaw's *NBC Nightly News,* which held on to a narrow ratings lead through 2002.

Contemporary Trends in Network and Cable News

Audiences watching the network news contributed to the demise of many afternoon daily newspapers (which have virtually disappeared in most large U.S. cities). By the 1980s, though, network audiences also began to decline. Facing competition from

● Walter Cronkite, the most respected and popular network newsman in TV history, anchored the *CBS Evening News* from 1963 to 1981. Cronkite ended his newscasts with his famous signature line, "And that's the way it is," followed by the day's date.

VCRs and cable, especially CNN, network advertising revenues flattened out. In response, the networks cut back staffs in the late 1980s and early 1990s, eliminating many national and foreign reporter posts. Unfortunately, these cutbacks would later hamper their ability to adequately cover global stories and international terrorism in the aftermath of 9/11.

In an effort to duplicate the financial success of *60 Minutes,* the most profitable show in TV history, the Big Three networks began developing relatively inexpensive **TV newsmagazines**. This format, pioneered in 1968 by *60 Minutes,* usually featured three stories per episode (rather than one topic per hour), alternating hard-hitting investigations of corruption or political intrigue with "softer" features on Hollywood celebrities, cultural trends, and assorted dignitaries. Copying this formula, ABC's *20/20* and *Primetime Live* (which was renamed as a second *20/20* in 1998) became moneymakers, and *20/20* aired three or four evenings a week by 2000. NBC's newsmagazine *Dateline* was appearing up to five nights a week by 2000—airing so often that critics accused NBC of trivializing the formula. By fall 2002, the program aired only two to three nights per week. Building on the success of *60 Minutes,* CBS launched *60 Minutes II* in January 1999 to compete with *Dateline* and other weeknight newsmagazines. In addition, independent producers developed a number of syndicated non-network newsmagazines for the local late-afternoon and late-night markets. These featured more than twenty breezy-sometimes-sleazy syndicated tabloids, including *Entertainment Tonight, Hard Copy,* and *A Current Affair.*

More recently, by 2000 the Fox network had started its own 24-hour news service on cable, and NBC, which already operated one cable news channel (CNBC), had teamed up with Microsoft to launch MSNBC, the first news channel available simultaneously on cable and the Web. Both cable and the Internet, offering 24-hour access to wire services and instant access to news about specific topics, continue the slow erosion of the traditional network news audience. Two important variations on the news have emerged in these programs. First, daily opinion programs such as MSNBC's *Hardball,* starring Chris Mathews, and Fox News' *The O'Reilly Factor,* starring Bill O'Reilly, proliferated on cable. Touting speculation and conjecture over traditional reporting based on verifying facts, these programs emerged primarily because of their inexpensive costs compared to traditional news: It is much cheaper to anchor your program around a single "talking head" personality and a few guests than to dispatch expensive equipment and field reporters to cover stories from multiple locations. Second, the demands of filling up time inexpensively during a 24-hour daily news operation have led to more viewer participation via studio audiences asking questions and call-in phone lines. CNN's long-running *Larry King Live* program and *Talk-Back Live* both allow selected viewers to participate in the news while at the same time keeping program costs down. We will return to these developments in Chapter 14.

TV Entertainment: Our Comic and Dramatic Culture

Even during the quiz-show boom of the mid and late 1950s, the primary staples of television entertainment were comedy and drama, both significantly influenced by New York radio, vaudeville, and theater. This period is often referred to as the "golden age" of television. While news divisions remained anchored in New York, the networks began to shift their entertainment divisions to Los Angeles, partly due to the success of the pioneering series *I Love Lucy* (1951–57). *Lucy's* owners and costars, Desi Arnaz and Lucille Ball, began filming the top-rated situation comedy in California near their home, although CBS originally wanted them to shoot in New York. Instead, in 1951, *Lucy* became the first TV program filmed in front of a live Hollywood audience. This was before the days of videotape, when the only way to preserve a live broadcast, other than by filming it like a movie, was through a technique called

kinescope. In this process, a film camera recorded a live TV show off a studio monitor. The quality of the kinescope technique was poor, and most series that were saved in this way have not survived. *I Love Lucy, Alfred Hitchcock Presents,* and the original *Dragnet* are among a handful of series from the 1950s that endured because they were originally shot and preserved on film.

Televised Comedy: From Sketches to Sitcoms

Television comedy then (as now) came in three varieties: the sketch comedy (the forerunner of programs such as *Saturday Night Live*), the situation comedy (or *sitcom*), and the domestic comedy. These comedy variations come from a rich history in popular culture that includes vaudeville stage comedy from the late 1800s, stand-up comedy routines that began in vaudeville and ended up in the comedy nightclubs that emerged in major cities after World War II, and the radio comedy programs that television would steal heavily from in its early days.

Sketch Comedy. Identified on occasion as *vaudeo,* or the marriage of vaudeville and video, **sketch comedy** was a key element in early vaudeville-like TV variety shows. These programs included singers, dancers, acrobats, animal acts, and ventriloquists as well as comedy skits. The shows "resurrected the essentials of stage variety entertainment" and played to noisy studio audiences.[3] Vaudeville performers dominated television's early history. Stars of sketch comedy included Milton Berle, TV's first major celebrity, in *Texaco Star Theater* (1948–67); Red Skelton in the *Red Skelton Show* (1951–71); and Sid Caesar, Imogene Coca, and Carl Reiner in *Your Show of Shows* (1950–54), for which playwright Neil Simon, filmmakers Mel Brooks and Woody Allen, and writer Larry Gelbart (*M*A*S*H*) all served for a time as sketch writers.

Sketch comedy had major drawbacks, though. Because skits were an integral part of the hour-long variety series, these programs were more expensive to produce than half-hour sitcoms. Skits on weekly variety shows, such as the *Perry Como Show* (1948–63), the *Dinah Shore Chevy Show* (1956–63), and the *Carol Burnett Show* (1967–79), also used up new routines very quickly. The ventriloquist Edgar Bergen (the father of *Murphy Brown* star Candice Bergen) once commented that "no comedian should be on TV once a week; he shouldn't be on more than once a month."[4]

With original skits and new sets required each week, production costs mounted, and the vaudeville-influenced variety series faded. The last successful program of this music-comedy type, *Barbara Mandrell & the Mandrell Sisters,* ended its two-year NBC run in 1982 due to the demanding schedule of doing music and comedy on a weekly basis. In this instance, it was Mandrell, not low ratings, who stopped production of the show. Mandrell said that musical numbers and sketch comedy, which could be used over and over for different audiences on the nightclub circuit, lasted only one week on television. Since the early 1980s, network variety shows have appeared only as yearly specials.

Situation Comedy. Over the years, the major staple on television has been the half-hour comedy series, the only genre represented in the Top 10–rated programs *every* year since 1949. (See Table 5.1.) One type of comedy series, the **situation comedy**, features a recurring cast. The story establishes a situation, complicates it, develops increasing confusion among its characters, and then alleviates the complications.[5] *I Love Lucy* from the 1950s, the *Beverly Hillbillies* from the 1960s, *Happy Days* from the 1970s, *Night Court* from the 1980s, *Seinfeld* from the 1990s, and now NBC's *Will & Grace,* Fox's *Malcolm in the Middle,* and HBO's *Curb Your Enthusiasm* (starring former *Seinfeld* producer Larry David as himself) are all part of this long tradition.

In most situation comedies, character development is downplayed in favor of zany plot twists and disruptions. Characters are usually static and predictable; they

generally do not develop much during the course of a series. Such characters "are never troubled in profound ways." Stress, more often the result of external confusion rather than emotional anxiety, "is always funny."[6] While watching situation-driven comedies, many viewers usually think of themselves as slightly superior to the characters who inhabit the sitcom world. Much like viewers who are attracted to soap operas, sitcom fans feel just a little bit smarter than the characters whose lives seem wacky and out of control.

Domestic Comedy. One spin-off of the sitcom form is the **domestic comedy**, in which characters and settings are usually more important than complicated predicaments. Although any given show might offer a wacky situation as part of a subplot, more typically the main narrative features a personal problem or family crisis that characters have to solve. There is a greater emphasis on character development than on reestablishing the order that has been disrupted by confusion. Domestic comedies take place primarily at home (*Leave It to Beaver; Everybody Loves Raymond*), at the workplace (*Just Shoot Me; Spin City*), or at both (*Frasier; Dharma & Greg*).

Although funny things happen in domestic comedies, the main emphasis is on how the characters react to one another. Family and workplace bonds are tested and strengthened by the end of the show. Generally, viewers identify more closely with

● Table 5.1 Selected Situation and Domestic Comedies Rated in the Top 10

The most durable genre in the history of television has been the half-hour comedy. It is the only genre that has been represented in the Nielsen rating Top 10 lists every year since 1949. Below is a selection of top-rated comedies at five-year intervals, spanning forty-five years.

1955–56	1980–81 (continued)
I Love Lucy (#2)	House Calls (tie #8)
Jack Benny Show (#5)	Three's Company (tie #8)
December Bride (#6)	
	1985–86
1960–61	
	Cosby Show (#1)
Andy Griffith Show (#4)	Family Ties (#2)
Real McCoys (#8)	Cheers (#5)
Jack Benny Show (#10)	Golden Girls (#7)
	Who's the Boss? (#10)
1965–66	
	1990–91
Gomer Pyle, U.S.M.C. (#2)	
Lucy Show (#3)	Cheers (#1)
Andy Griffith Show (tie #7)	Roseanne (#3)
Bewitched (tie #7)	A Different World (#4)
Beverly Hillbillies (tie #7)	Cosby Show (#5)
Hogan's Heroes (#9)	Murphy Brown (#6)
	Empty Nest (#7)
1970–71	Golden Girls (tie #10)
	Designing Women (tie #10)
Here's Lucy (#3)	
	1995–96
1975–76	
	Seinfeld (#2)
All in the Family (#1)	Friends (#3)
Laverne & Shirley (#3)	Caroline in the City (#4)
Maude (#4)	The Single Guy (#6)
Phyllis (#6)	Home Improvement (#7)
Sanford and Son (tie #7)	Boston Common (#8)
Rhoda (tie #7)	
	2000–01
1980–81	
	Friends (#3)
M*A*S*H (#4)	Everybody Loves Raymond (#4)
The Jeffersons (#6)	Will & Grace (#10)
Alice (#7)	

Sources: Tim Brooks and Earle Marsh, *The Complete Directory to Prime Time Network and Cable TV Shows*, 7th ed. (New York: Ballantine, 1999); *Times Almanac 1999* (Boston: Information Please LLC, 1998), 716; and A. C. Nielsen Media Research.

the major characters in domestic comedies. One example illustrates the difference between a sitcom and its domestic counterpart. In an early episode of the sitcom *Happy Days* (1974–84), the main characters were accidentally locked in a vault over a weekend. The plot turned on how they were going to free themselves, which they did after assorted goofy adventures. Contrast this with an episode from the domestic comedy *All in the Family* (1971–83), in which archconservative Archie and his ultra-liberal son-in-law Mike are accidentally locked in the basement. The physical predicament became a subplot as the main "action" shifted to the characters themselves, who reflected on their generational and political differences.

Today, many of these programs are a mix of both situation and domestic comedy. For example, an episode of *Friends* (1994–) might offer a character-driven plot about the generation gap and a minor subplot about a pet monkey gone berserk. Domestic comedies also mix dramatic and comedic elements. An episode of

Roseanne (1988–97), too, might juxtapose a dramatic scene in which a main character has a heart attack with another in which the Conner family intentionally offends their stuffy neighbors by decorating their home in a "white trash" holiday motif. This blurring of serious and comic themes marks a contemporary hybrid, sometimes labeled *dramedy*, which has included such series as *Moonlighting* (1985–89), the *Wonder Years* (1988–93), *Northern Exposure* (1990–95), *Ally McBeal* (1997–02), *Freaks and Geeks* (1999–00), and HBO's *Sex and the City* (1999–).

Televised Drama: Anthologies vs. Episodes

Because the production of TV entertainment was centered in New York in its early days, many of its ideas, sets, technicians, actors, and directors came from New York theater. Young stage actors, including Anne Bancroft, Warren Beatty, Ossie Davis, James Dean, Gene Hackman, Grace Kelly, Paul Newman, Sidney Poitier, Robert Red-ford, and Joanne Woodward, began their professional careers in early television, often because they could not find stage work in New York. The TV dramas that grew from these early influences fit roughly into two categories: the anthology drama and the episodic series.

Anthology Drama. In the early 1950s, television—like cable in the early 1980s—served a more elite and wealthier audience. **Anthology drama**, which brought live dramatic theater to television, entertained and often challenged that audience. In-fluenced by stage plays, anthologies offered new teleplays, casts, directors, writers, and sets from one week to the next. Because movie studios owned the rights to major stage plays of the day, anthology television was often based on original mate-rial. In fact, this genre launched the careers of such writers as Rod Serling (*Requiem for a Heavyweight*), William Gibson (*The Miracle Worker*), Reginald Rose (*Twelve Angry Men*), and Paddy Chayefsky (*Marty*). The teleplays of these writers were often later made into movies. Chayefsky, in fact, would go on to write the screenplay for the 1976 film *Network*, a biting condemnation of television.

> **❝ Despite the incredibly hostile treatment she has gotten in the press—because she's four things TV women are not supposed to be, working-class, loudmouthed, overweight, and a feminist—Roseanne became a success because her mission was simple and welcome: to take the schmaltz and hypocrisy out of media images of motherhood. ❞**
>
> —Susan Douglas, *Where the Girls Are*, 1994

In the 1952–53 season alone, there were eighteen anthology dramas competing on the networks. Programs such as *Kraft Television Theater* (1947–58 and actually created to introduce Kraft's Cheez Whiz product), *Studio One* (1948–58), *Goodyear TV Playhouse* (1951–57), the *U.S. Steel Hour* (1953–63), *Alfred Hitchcock Presents* (1955–65), *Playhouse 90* (1956–60), and the *Twilight Zone* (1959–64) mounted original plays each week. However, the demands on the schedule were such that many of these programs took more than a week to produce and had to alternate biweekly with other anthologies or with variety or news programs.

The commercial networks eventually stopped producing anthologies for economic and political reasons. First, although anthologies were popular, advertisers disliked them. Anthologies often presented stories that confronted complex human problems that were not easily resolved. Chayefsky had referred to these dramas as the "marvelous world of the ordinary."[7] The commercials that interrupted the drama, however, told upbeat stories in which problems were easily solved by purchasing a product: "a new pill, deodorant, toothpaste, shampoo, shaving lotion, hair tonic, car, girdle, coffee, muffin recipe, or floor wax."[8] By probing the psychology of the human condition, complicated anthologies made the simplicity of the commercial pitch ring false. Another aspect of the sponsors' dilemma was that these dramas often cast "non-beautiful heroes and heroines,"[9] unlike the stars of the commercials.

By 1954, sponsors and ad agencies were demanding more input into script revisions. For instance, Reginald Rose's teleplay *Thunder on Sycamore Street* was based on a real incident in which a black family moved into an all-white neighborhood and felt pressured to leave. CBS, pressured by advertisers who wanted to avoid public controversy, asked that the black family be changed to "something else." To make the teleplay more commercially palatable, Rose rewrote the script, abandoning the black family in favor of a white ex-convict. Faced with increasing creative battles with the writers and producers of these dramas, sponsors began to move toward less controversial programming, such as quiz shows and sitcoms.

A second reason for the demise of anthology dramas was that they were largely supported by a more affluent audience, particularly in the early 1950s. The people who could afford TV sets at this time could also afford tickets to a play. For these viewers, the anthology drama was an extension of their cultural tastes and simply brought theater directly into their homes. In 1950, fewer than 10 percent of American households had TV sets, with the heaviest concentration of ownership in New York. By 1956, however, 71 percent of all U.S. households had sets. As the production of TV sets rose during the post–World War II manufacturing boom, prices dropped as well. Working- and middle-class families were increasingly able to afford television. Anthology dramas were not as popular in this expanded market as they were with upscale theatergoers. When the networks began relocating their creative headquarters to Hollywood, such a geographical move also reduced theatrical influences. As a result, by the end of the decade, westerns, which were inexpensively produced by film studios on location near Los Angeles, had become the dominant TV genre.

Third, commercial networks stopped producing anthology dramas because they were expensive to produce—double the price of most other TV genres in the 1950s. In 1949, the average new sixty-minute drama cost around $10,000 (compared with $1.5 million today). Although variety series eventually became the most expensive genre, anthologies cost, on average, $35,000 per hour by 1955. In contrast, the average thirty-minute quiz show cost just over $10,000 to produce. For anthologies, each week meant a completely new story line, as well as new writers, casts, and expensive sets. Sponsors and networks came to realize that it would be cheaper to use the same cast and set each week, and it would also be easier to build audience allegiance with an ongoing program. In an anthology series of individual plays, there were no continuing characters with whom viewers could identify over time.

> **"** Aristotle once said that a play should have a beginning, a middle, and an end. But what did he know? Today, a play must have a first half, a second half, and a station break. **"**
>
> – Alfred Hitchcock, director

In addition, anthologies that dealt seriously with the changing social landscape were sometimes labeled "politically controversial." This was especially true during the witch-hunts provoked by Senator Joseph McCarthy and his followers to rid media industries and government agencies (including the army) of left-wing influences. (See Chapter 16 on blacklisting.) Ultimately, sponsors and networks came to prefer less controversial programming such as quiz shows and westerns over anthologies. By the early 1960s, this formerly dominant dramatic form had virtually disappeared from network television, although its legacy continues on American public television, especially with the imported British program *Masterpiece Theatre* (1971–).

Episodic Series. Abandoning anthologies, producers and writers increasingly developed **episodic series**, first used in radio in 1929, because it seemed best suited for the weekly grind of televised drama. In this format, main characters continue from week to week, sets and locales remain the same, and technical crews stay with the program. Story concepts in episodic series are broad enough to accommodate new adventures each week, creating an atmosphere in which there are ongoing characters with whom viewers can regularly identify.

The episodic series comes in two general types: chapter shows and serial programs. **Chapter shows** employ self-contained stories that feature a problem, a series of conflicts, and a resolution. This structure can be used in a wide range of dramatic genres, including adult westerns like *Gunsmoke* (1955–75); medical dramas like *Dr. Kildare* (1961–66) and *Marcus Welby, M.D.* (1969–76); police/detective shows like *Dragnet* (1951–59, 1967–70), *Magnum, P.I.* (1980–88), and *CSI: Crime Scene Investigations* (2000–); family dramas like *The Waltons* (1972–81) and *Little House on the Prairie*

● NBC's hybrid drama series *The West Wing* (1999–), starring Martin Sheen (center) as our nation's liberal president, was initially praised by critics for the complex way it addressed national issues such as health care and the death penalty. Declining ratings in 2002–03, however, led some critics to suggest that the program's creator, Aaron Sorkin, should have had the fake Democratic president lose a close election to a fake Republican president to draw in new viewers.

(1974–82); and fantasy/science fiction like *Star Trek* (1966–69) and some episodes of *The X-Files* (1993–2002).

Culturally, television dramas function as a window into the hopes and fears of the American psyche. In the 1970s, for instance, police/detective dramas became a chapter staple, mirroring the anxieties of many Americans regarding the urban unrest of the late 1960s. The 1970s brought more urban problems, which were precipitated by the loss of factory jobs and the decline of manufacturing. Americans' popular entertainment reflected the idea of heroic police and tenacious detectives protecting a nation from menacing forces that were undermining the economy and the cities. During this period, such shows as *The F.B.I.* (1965–74), *Ironside* (1967–75), *Mannix* (1967–75), *Hawaii Five-O* (1968–80), the *Mod Squad* (1968–73), *Kojak* (1973–75), and the *Rockford Files* (1974–80) all ranked among the nation's top-rated programs.

A recent spin-off of the police drama has been the law enforcement documentary-like program, sometimes called *cop docs*. Series like Fox's *Cops* (1989–) are cheap to produce, with low overhead and a big return on a minimal investment. Instead of hiring actors at $25,000 per episode, producers have their crews tag along with real police, whose supervisors—in exchange for TV publicity—often donate police cars and other equipment that the producers of conventional dramas usually have to rent or buy. Whereas an hour of a new conventional prime-time drama cost about $1.5 million to produce per episode in the late 1990s, an hour of crime reenactments cost less than half that amount. Cop docs, like many contemporary daytime talk shows, generally focus their stories on emotional situations and individual pathology rather than on a critical examination of the underlying social conditions that make crime and its related problems possible.

Prior to the rise of the cop was the reign of the cowboy, which marked an earlier period of change in America. The western served as one of the most popular chapter genres in television's early history. When movie studios such as Warner Brothers began dabbling in television in the 1950s, they produced a number of well-received series for ABC, such as *Cheyenne* (1955–63) and *Maverick* (1957–63). The popular western, with its themes of civilization confronting the frontier, apparently provided a symbol for many Middle Americans relocating to the suburbs—between the country and the city. Thirty prime-time westerns aired in the 1958–59 season alone. From this point through 1961, *Gunsmoke* (1955–75; TV's longest-running chapter series), *Wagon Train* (1957–65), and *Have Gun Will Travel* (1957–63) were the three most popular programs in America.

In contrast to chapter shows like westerns and police dramas, **serial programs** are open-ended episodic shows. That is, in these series most story lines continue from episode to episode. Cheaper to produce, usually employing just a few indoor sets, and running five days a week, daytime *soap operas* are among the longest-running serial programs in the history of television. Acquiring their name from soap-product ads that sponsored these programs in the days of fifteen-minute radio drama, popular soaps include *Guiding Light* (1952–), *As the World Turns* (1956–), *General Hospital* (1963–), *Days of Our Lives* (1965–), and *One Life to Live* (1968–).

With their cliff-hanging story lines and intimate close-up shots, which are well suited to television (a personal medium located in our living rooms and bedrooms), soap operas have been good at creating audience allegiance. Soaps also probably do the best job of any genre at imitating the actual open-ended rhythms of daily life.

The success of the daytime soap formula opened a door to prime time. Although the first popular prime-time serial, *Peyton Place* (1964–69), ran two or three nights a week, producers later shied away from such programs because they had less value as syndicated reruns. Most reruns of old network shows are **stripped**—that is, shown five days a week in almost any order, not requiring viewers to watch them on a daily basis. Serials, however, require that audiences watch every day so that they don't lose track of the multiple story lines.

> **"** The show's original spirit has become kind of the spirit of the country—if not the world. . . . With the Berlin Wall down, with the global nuclear threat gone, with Russia trying to be a market economy, there is a growing paranoia because . . . there are no easy villains anymore.**"**
>
> –Chris Carter,
> *The X-Files* creator, 1998

In the 1970s, however, with the popularity of the network *miniseries*—a serial that runs over a two-day to two-week period, usually on consecutive nights—producers and the networks began to look at the evening serial differently. The twelve-part *Rich Man, Poor Man,* adapted from an Irwin Shaw novel, ranked number three in national ratings in 1976. The next year, the eight-part *Roots* miniseries, based on writer Alex Haley's search for his African heritage, became the most-watched miniseries in TV history.

These miniseries demonstrated to the networks that viewers would watch a compelling, ongoing story in prime time. The success of these programs spawned such soap opera–style series as *Dallas* (1978–91), *Dynasty* (1981–89), *Knots Landing* (1979–92), and *Falcon Crest* (1981–90), which in the 1984–85 season all ranked among America's Top 10 most-viewed programs. In fact, as the top-rated shows in America in the early 1980s, *Dallas* and *Dynasty* both celebrated and criticized the excesses of the rich and spoiled. These shows reached their popular peak during the early years of the Reagan administration, a time when the economic disparity between rich and poor Americans began to widen dramatically.

Another type of contemporary serial is a *hybrid* form that developed in the early 1980s with the appearance of *Hill Street Blues* (1981–87). Mixing comic situations and grim plots, this multiple-cast show looked like an open-ended soap opera. On occasion, as in real life, crimes were not solved and recurring characters died. As a hybrid form, *Hill Street Blues* combined elements of both chapter and serial television. Juggling multiple story lines, *Hill Street* featured some self-contained plots that were brought to resolution in a single episode as well as other plot lines that continued from week to week. This technique was copied by several successful dramatic hybrids, including *St. Elsewhere* (1982–88), *L.A. Law* (1986–94), *The X-Files* (1993–2002), *Law and Order* (1990–), *NYPD Blue* (1993–), *ER* (1994–), *Buffy the Vampire Slayer* (1997–), *The Practice* (1997–), *The West Wing* (1999–), and *24* (2001–).

The Decline of the Network Era

Most historians mark the period from the late 1950s, when the networks gained control over TV's content, to the end of the 1970s as the **network era**. Except for British and American anthology dramas on PBS, this was a time when CBS, NBC, and ABC dictated virtually every trend in prime-time programming (see Figure 5.1). This network dominance was significant because it offered America's rich and diverse ethnic population a cultural center and common topics for daily conversation. Television is often credited, for example, with helping to heal the collective national consciousness after the assassination of President Kennedy in 1963 by creating time and space for shared mourning. During this period of supremacy, the networks collectively accounted for more than 95 percent of all prime-time TV viewing. By 2002, however, this figure had dropped to about 45 percent. So what happened? To understand the decline of the network era, we will look at three factors: technological changes, government regulations, and the development of new networks.

New Technologies Reduce Network Control

Two major technological developments contributed significantly to the erosion of network dominance: the arrival of communication satellite services for cable television and the home-video market. Prior to the early 1970s, broadcast lobbyists and

Figure 5.1
The Fall Prime-Time Schedule toward the End of the Network Era, 1978–79

Day	7	7:30	8	8:30	9	9:30	10	10:30	11 PM	Net
SUN	THE HARDY BOYS MYSTERIES 3		BATTLESTAR GALACTICA		MOVIE					ABC
	60 MINUTES 11		MARY		ALL IN THE FAMILY 9	ALICE 3	KAZ			CBS
	THE WONDERFUL WORLD OF DISNEY 25		THE BIG EVENT (I)				LIFELINE 2			NBC
MON			WELCOME BACK, KOTTER 4	OPERATION PETTICOAT 2	NFL MONDAY NIGHT FOOTBALL				9	ABC
			WKRP IN CINCINNATI	PEOPLE	M*A*S*H 7	ONE DAY AT A TIME 4	LOU GRANT		2	CBS
			LITTLE HOUSE ON THE PRAIRIE 5		MOVIE					NBC
TUE			HAPPY DAYS 6	LAVERNE AND SHIRLEY 4	THREE'S COMPANY 3	TAXI	STARSKY AND HUTCH		4	ABC
			THE PAPER CHASE		MOVIE					CBS
			GRANDPA GOES TO WASHINGTON		THE BIG EVENT (II)				2	NBC
WED			EIGHT IS ENOUGH 3		CHARLIE'S ANGELS 3		VEGA$			ABC
			THE JEFFERSONS 5	IN THE BEGINNING	MOVIE					CBS
			DICK CLARK'S LIVE WEDNESDAY		MOVIE					NBC
THU			MORK & MINDY 3	WHAT'S HAPPENING!!	BARNEY MILLER 5	SOAP 2	FAMILY		4	ABC
			THE WALTONS		HAWAII FIVE-0 11		BARNABY JONES		7	CBS
			PROJECT U.F.O. 2		QUINCY 3		W.E.B.			NBC
FRI			DONNY AND MARIE 4		MOVIE					ABC
			WONDER WOMAN 3		THE INCREDIBLE HULK 2		FLYING HIGH			CBS
			THE WAVERLY WONDERS	WHO'S WATCHING THE KIDS	THE ROCKFORD FILES 5		THE EDDIE CAPRA MYSTERIES			NBC
SAT			CARTER COUNTRY 2	APPLE PIE	THE LOVE BOAT 2		FANTASY ISLAND 2			ABC
			RHODA 5	GOOD TIMES 6	THE AMERICAN GIRLS		DALLAS 2			CBS
			CHiPS 2		SPECIALS		SWORD OF JUSTICE			NBC

1978-1979

Source: Alex McNeil, *Total Television: A Comprehensive Guide to Programming from 1948 to the Present*, 3rd ed. (New York: Penguin, 1991), 938.

local stations, fearing that competition would lead to the loss of advertising revenue, effectively limited the growth of cable television, which had been around since the late 1940s. But a series of moves by the FCC sprung cable loose in 1972. That same year, when Time Inc. launched HBO into satellite orbit, serving movies to hotels and motels, the first crack in the network dam appeared. In 1975, HBO became available to individual cable markets throughout the country, offering the "Thrilla from Manila"—the heavyweight boxing match between Muhammad Ali and Joe Frazier via satellite from the Philippines.

Then, in December 1976, Ted Turner beamed, or uplinked, the signal from WTBS, his Atlanta **independent station** (not affiliated with a network), to a satellite where cable systems and broadcast stations around the country could access, or downlink, it. To encourage interest, the signal was initially provided free, supported only by the ads Turner sold during WTBS programs. But as Turner expanded services, creating new channels like CNN, he also earned revenue by charging monthly fees for his cable services. In its early days, WTBS delivered a steady stream of old TV reruns, wrestling, and live sports from the Atlanta Hawks and the Atlanta Braves (both owned by Turner). Turner and a number of investors would eventually buy the MGM film library to provide additional movie programming. In the mid-1970s, only about 15 percent of American households received cable. As this figure grew steadily (to 70 percent in 2002), the TV networks, for the first time, began to face serious competition.

The second technological breakthrough also came in 1975–76 with the consumer marketing of **videocassette recorders (VCRs)**, which enabled viewers to tape-record TV programs and play them back later on the TV. Earlier in the 1970s, Japan's Sony Corporation had introduced the TV industry to a three quarter-inch-wide videocassette format that quickly revolutionized television news; until that time, TV news crews had relied solely on shooting film, which often took hours to develop and edit. Then, in 1975, Sony introduced consumers to a home version, *Betamax* (Beta for short), a half-inch format that enabled viewers to tape programs off the air for the first time. The next year, JVC in Japan introduced a slightly larger half-inch consumer format, *VHS* (Video Home System), which was incompatible with Beta. This triggered a marketing war, which helped drive the costs down and put VCRs in more and more homes.

Beta, though a smaller format and technically superior to VHS, ultimately lost the marketplace battle due to a cultural miscalculation by designers. Early Betamax tapes accommodated only about an hour and a half of programming. However, most American consumers used tapes primarily to record movies, usually two hours in length. This meant that two tapes, which cost around $15 apiece in the late 1970s, were necessary. When JVC developed the slightly larger VHS format, one standard tape accommodated two hours of programs, enough for an entire movie—or four sitcoms or soap operas. Even with technical improvements that compressed more programming onto a single tape, Betamax could never match the recording time or appeal of the longer VHS tapes.

The VCR also got a big boost from a failed suit brought against Sony by Disney and MCA (now Vivendi-owned Universal) in 1976: The two film studios alleged that home taping violated their movie copyrights. In 1979, a federal court ruled in favor of Sony and permitted home taping for personal use. In response, the defeated but industrious movie studios quickly set up videotaping facilities so that they could rent and sell movies via video stores, which exploded onto the scene in the early 1980s. By the mid-1980s, VHS had pretty much won the war for the video consumer market, and Sony concentrated on developing *Betacam*, a high-quality half-inch industrial format that in the late 1980s began replacing the bulkier three-quarter-inch format in TV newsrooms. Today, of course, the DVD format is slowly replacing VHS.

The impact of videocassettes on the networks was enormous. By 1997, nearly 90 percent of American homes were equipped with VCRs that were used for two major purposes: time shifting and movie rentals. **Time shifting** occurs when viewers tape shows and watch them later, when it is more convenient. Before VCRs, advertisers and networks worried that consumers used TV ad time to fix a snack or go to the bathroom. After VCRs, advertisers and networks had bigger things to worry about. For example, when consumers recorded TV programs for viewing at more convenient times, they produced more complex audience measurement problems. Along with the remote control, which enabled viewers to mute the sound during ads, time shifting made it possible to avoid ads altogether, either by *zapping*, or cutting, them out of the program with the pause button during recording or by *zipping*, or fast-forwarding, through the ads during the recorded viewing. On top of this was the lure of VCR movies: By the mid-1990s, more than half of all households in America watched a rented movie during prime time at least once a week. VCRs and movie rentals shook the TV industry; when viewers were watching a videotape—or the new DVD format—they weren't watching network shows or network ads.

At the outset of the twenty-first century, new technology may bring even greater challenges to traditional network control of viewers' television-watching habits and may also give potential advertisers more information about consumer preferences than ever before. New **"black box" technologies**—such as TiVo and Replay Networks—enable users to find and record specific shows and watch them at a later time. Unlike VCRs, however, hours of programming can be saved in the computer memory of the black box itself as opposed to storage on bulky tapes. Perhaps more important, the technology can seek out specific shows or even types of shows that appear on any channel connected to the box; for example, with one command a user could store or record all prime-time and syndicated versions of *ER* or any western movies the household receives. In fact, this technology can also suggest programs that users might wish to see based on previous viewing patterns. Some critics argue that this new system will completely shatter our current notion of prime-time television because viewers could watch whatever show they like at any time.

While offering greater flexibility for viewers, the black boxes would also watch the watchers, providing advertisers with almost complete information about what is viewed in each household using the technology. This could completely alter the ways in which television ratings are compiled and advertising dollars are divided, and it could also give rise to more niche advertising, specifically targeted at small but now accessible audiences.

Government Regulations Temporarily Restrict Network Control

By the late 1960s, a progressive and active FCC, increasingly concerned about the monopoly-like impact of the three networks, passed a series of regulations that began undercutting their power. The first, the passage of the *Prime-Time Access Rule* (PTAR) in April 1970, took the 7:30 to 8:00 P.M. slot (6:30 to 7:00 P.M. central) away from the networks and gave it exclusively to local stations in the nation's fifty largest TV markets. With this move, the FCC hoped to encourage local news and public-affairs programs. However, most stations simply acquired syndicated quiz shows *(The Joker's Wild; Wheel of Fortune)* or **infotainment** programs *(P.M. Magazine; Entertainment Tonight)*. These latter shows packaged human-interest and celebrity stories in TV news style, during which local affiliates sold lucrative regional ads.

In a second move, in 1970 the FCC created the Financial Interest and Syndication Rules—called **fin-syn**—which "constituted the most damaging attack against the network TV monopoly in FCC history."[10] Throughout the 1960s, the networks had run their own syndication companies. They sometimes demanded as much as 50 percent of the profits that producers earned from airing older shows as reruns in local TV markets. This was the case even though those shows were no longer on the networks and most of them had been developed not by the networks but by independent companies. The networks claimed that since popular TV series had gained a national audience because of their reach, production companies owed the networks compensation even after shows completed their prime-time runs. The FCC banned the networks from reaping such profits from program syndication.

A third and separate action was instituted by the Department of Justice in 1975. Reacting to a number of legal claims against monopolistic practices, the Justice Department limited the networks' own production of non-news shows to a few hours a week. Initially, the limit was three hours of prime-time entertainment programs per week, but this was raised to five hours by the late 1980s. In addition, ABC, CBS, and NBC were limited to producing eight hours per week of in-house entertainment or non-news programs outside prime time, most of which was devoted to soap operas (economical to produce and popular with advertisers). This meant that the networks were forced to continue licensing most of their prime-time programs from independent producers and film studios. Given that the networks could produce their own TV newsmagazines and select which programs to license, however, they still retained a great deal of power over the content of prime-time television.

With increasing competition from cable and home video in the 1990s, the FCC gradually phased out the ban limiting network production. In addition, beginning in 1995, the networks were once again allowed to syndicate and profit from rerun programs, but only the ones they had produced in-house. The elimination of fin-syn and other rules opened the door for megamerger deals. For example, Disney, which bought ABC in 1995, has been able to use its vast movie-production resources to develop more entertainment programming for its ABC network. This has reduced the opportunities for independent producers to create new shows and compete for prime-time slots on ABC. In fact, in fall 2000, ABC introduced only four new TV shows in prime time — the lowest number of new shows ever by a major network. Relying on multiple nights of its own *Who Wants to Be a Millionaire, 20/20,* and cheap "reality" shows like *The Bachelor,* ABC ignored many new series possibilities from independent sources. Just as networks may now favor running programs that they own, shows now also have a much shorter time to prove themselves. To cite an extreme example, in May 2000 ABC canceled the critically acclaimed show *Wonderland,* a drama set in a mental hospital, after only two episodes. (For more on this topic, see "Case Study: Anatomy of a TV 'Failure'" on page 176.) Indeed, many independent companies and TV critics fear the triumph of the oligopoly with Disney, Viacom, News Corp., and General Electric — the multinational corporations that now own the networks — increasingly dictating the program trends and economic terms for broadcast television.

Emerging Networks Target the Youth Market

In addition to the overwhelming number of cable services now available to consumers, the networks, which have lost about half of their audience since the 1980s, faced further challenges from the emergence of new networks. Rupert Murdoch, who heads the multinational company News Corp., launched the Fox network in April 1987 after purchasing several TV stations from another company and buying a major Hollywood film studio, Twentieth Century Fox. Not since 1955, when the old Dumont network collapsed, had there been an attempt to challenge the Big Three networks.

At first, Fox lost money because it had fewer than a hundred affiliated stations to carry its programs around the country. This was less than half the two-hundred-plus affiliates each that were contracted to ABC, CBS, and NBC. Originally presenting programs just two nights a week, the Fox network began targeting both young and black audiences with shows like *The Simpsons, Beverly Hills 90210, In Living Color, Martin, Roc,* and *Melrose Place.* By 1994, after outbidding CBS for a portion of pro-football broadcasts, Fox was competing every night of the week. It had managed to lure more than sixty affiliates away from the other networks or from independent status. Some of these stations were in major markets where traditional networks suddenly found themselves without affiliates. In fact, Fox's poaching forced CBS to spend millions to buy two unknown independent UHF stations — Channel 62 in Detroit and Channel 69 in Atlanta — to satisfy advertisers, who expected the network to reach audiences in all major markets. By the early 1990s, Fox was making money. By the mid-1990s, the new network's total number of affiliates rivaled that of the Big Three.

Fox's success continued the erosion of network power and spurred others who were interested in starting new networks. Paramount, which had recently been acquired by Viacom, and Time Warner, the world's largest media company, both launched networks in January 1995: UPN and the WB. Using the strategy initiated by Fox, the new networks offered original programs two nights a week in 1995, added a third night in 1996, and by 2000 they programmed every night except Saturday (the evening that generally draws the lowest audience ratings). Backed by multinational financing, these companies slowly began going after independent outlets and luring other stations away from their old network affiliations. However, their main strategy has been to target minority or young viewers with such programs as *Moesha, Buffy the Vampire Slayer, Angel, Felicity, Dawson's Creek, Charmed,* and *Gilmore Girls.* In December 2001, the network operations of UPN were consolidated with those of its "big sister" network, CBS, under Viacom's plan to cut costs and increase advertising revenue by developing more programs through its Paramount subsidiary rather than through independent producers.

● The cast from *CSI: Miami,* which premiered on CBS in 2002. This popular episodic cop-and-crime drama carries forward a tradition of "realistic" police shows that have included *Hill Street Blues* (NBC 1981–87), *NYPD Blue* (ABC 1993–), *Law and Order* (NBC 1995–), and *Miami*'s acclaimed ancestor, *CSI: Crime Scene Investigation* (CBS 2000–). The *CSI* franchise had become so popular that to counter it, ABC in 2003 resurrected a version of *Dragnet,* the genre's founding program that originally aired on NBC back in 1952.

The Economics of Television

Despite the erosion of their reach, the traditional networks have remained attractive investments in the business world. In 1985, General Electric, which once helped start RCA/NBC, bought back NBC. In 1995, Disney bought ABC for $19 billion; in 1999, Viacom acquired CBS for $37 billion.

Even though their audiences and profits may have declined, the networks continue to attract larger audiences than their cable or online competitors. But the business of television is not just about larger audiences. To understand the television business today, we need to examine the production, distribution, and syndication of programming, as well as the implications for audience share. At stake are $50 to $60 billion in advertising revenues each year. In fact, it would not be that much of a stretch to define TV programming as a system that delivers viewers to merchandise displayed in blocks of commercials. By 2002, national advertisers alone, led by Procter & Gamble and General Motors, were spending more than $30 billion a year in TV advertising.

Prime-Time Production

The key to the television industry's appeal resides in its ability to offer programs that American households will habitually tune in on a weekly basis. The networks, producers, and film studios spend fortunes creating programs that they hope will keep us coming back. In 1988, while film studios produced a large chunk of network television, more than half of the prime-time schedule was created by independent producers. These companies, such as Carsey-Werner (the *Cosby Show; A Different World; Roseanne; Cybill; Third Rock from the Sun*), license, or "rent," each episode to a network for two broadcasts, one in the fall or winter and one in the spring or summer. (Usually about twenty-two new episodes are produced in a TV season.)

Production costs in television generally fall into two categories: above-the-line and below-the-line. *Below-the-line* costs, which account for roughly 40 percent of a new program's production budget, include the technical, or "hardware," side of production: equipment, special effects, cameras and crews, sets and designers, carpenters, electricians, art directors, wardrobe, lighting, and transportation. More demanding are the *above-the-line,* or "software," costs, which include the creative talent: actors, writers, producers, editors, and directors. These costs account for about 60 percent of a program's budget, except in the case of successful long-running series (like *Friends* or *ER*), in which salary demands by actors drive up above-the-line costs.

❝ By 1960 television had become a mature and streamlined business, a great 'cash cow.' The focus now shifted from invention to convention, from carving out an acceptable social role for itself to counting the rewards of investment, planning, and monopoly. ❞

—J. Fred MacDonald, *One Nation under Television,* 1994

Risky Business: Deficit Financing and the Independents

Because of their high cost, many prime-time programs today are developed by independent production companies that are financed or backed by a major film studio such as Sony or Disney. In these arrangements, film studios serve as a bank (if they don't buy out the more successful independent producers), offering enough capital to carry producers through one or more seasons. In television, after a network agrees to carry a program, keeping it on the air is done through **deficit financing**. This means that the production company leases the show to a network for a license fee that is actually less than the cost of production. (The company hopes to recoup this loss later in lucrative rerun syndication.) Typically, in the late 1990s, the networks might lease an episode of a new half-hour sitcom for about $600,000 for two airings. Each episode, however, costs the producers about $800,000 to make, in which case they lose about $200,000 per episode. After two years of production (about forty-four episodes), an average half-hour sitcom builds up a deficit of over $8 million, and the average one-hour drama generates a deficit of $12 to $14 million. This is where film studios have been playing an increasingly crucial role: They finance the deficit. Film studios, which provide production facilities as well as money, have covered deficits totaling $350 to $400 million annually by bankrolling network prime-time television.

The key to erasing the losses generated by deficit financing is **rerun syndication**, the process by which programs that stay in a network's lineup long enough to build up enough episodes (usually four seasons' worth) are sold, or *syndicated,* to hundreds of TV stations in the United States and overseas (see "Applied Critical Process: TV and International Syndication" on page 171). With a successful program, the profits can be enormous. For instance, when Carsey-Werner's *Cosby Show,* the most-watched show in America from 1985 to 1989, sold its first three years into syndication in 1988, the producers netted more than $800 million. Because the show had already been produced and the original production costs were already covered, the syndication market at home and abroad became almost pure profit for the producers and their backers. It is for this reason that the practice of deficit financing endures. Although investors rarely hit the jackpot, when they do it can more than cover a lot of losses. By 1996, the *Cosby Show* had earned a record $1 billion in syndication.[11] Profits from the show (and from *Roseanne*) have enabled Carsey-Werner to function as a rare independent company that does not require the financial backing of a film studio.

Network Cost-Saving Strategies

Although the networks still purchase or license many prime-time TV programs, they create more of their own prime-time fare thanks to the relaxation of FCC rules in the mid-1990s. The production of TV newsmagazines and reality programs, for instance, became one major way for networks to save money and control content. Programs such as ABC's *The Bachelorette* or NBC's *Dateline* require only about half the outlay (between $600,000 and $800,000 per episode) demanded by an hour's worth of drama. In addition, the networks, by producing projects in-house, avoid paying license fees to independent producers.

Over the years, CBS's highly rated program *60 Minutes* has been a money machine. By 1980, a commercial minute on *60 Minutes,* the nation's highest-rated program that year, sold for a then record $230,000. By the late 1990s, *60 Minutes* commanded more than $400,000 per minute for its 7–8 minutes of national ad slots. (By comparison, a low-rated program brought in only a quarter of this amount per minute.) This meant that *60 Minutes* generally earned back its production costs and fees to local stations for carrying the program after selling just a couple of minutes of ad time. Even newsmagazines with low ratings still recoup their lower production costs fairly easily. Don Hewitt, the creator of *60 Minutes,* estimated that in its first twenty-five years on the air, his program grossed well over $1 billion for CBS.[12]

TV and International Syndication

The aftermath of the September 11 terrorist attacks in 2001 sparked numerous discussions about the cultural differences between the U.S. and other countries. Part of this conversation focused on the excesses and dominance of Western popular culture. In the last few years, for example, *Who Wants to Be a Millionaire* has been a major hit in India; bootleg reruns of the 1980s network soap *Dynasty* have become popular in China; and *Baywatch* retreads have made it big in Greece, the seat of civilization.[1] The popularity of U.S. TV poses a cultural dilemma: Nations that cannot afford to produce much original programming find it cheaper to buy made-in-America programs, thereby promoting Western culture over their own. U.S. producers, who have already paid for production costs and begun earning profits, can undercut most competition in foreign markets. What is the extent and impact of U.S. TV culture in other nations?

Description. Using the World Wide Web Virtual Library: Broadcasters <http://archive.museophile.sbu.ac.uk/broadcast/>, we were able to retrieve broadcast television schedules from a number of countries. For example, we looked at India's and New Zealand's schedules (easier, in part, because they are English-language Web sites). India's two television networks, DD1 and DD2, are government-controlled. Of New Zealand's four television networks, TV1, TV2 are state-owned enterprises, and TV3 and TV4 are privately owned.

Analysis. In focusing on patterns, we found that both India and New Zealand have strong government-financed TV networks. India's DD1 and DD2 feature Indian travel shows, Indian drama series, comedies, and police programs. There are a few time slots for U.S.-made cartoons (e.g., Mickey Mouse), but the bulk of Indian programming does not feature much U.S. TV content. In New Zealand, the two state-owned TV networks take different approaches. TV1 features mostly home-grown programming, including some Maori-language shows, and a few international programs. TV2 carries a few locally-produced programs, but is saturated with U.S. TV content, including *ER*, *The Sopranos*, *American Idol*, and *Alias*. TV3 and TV4 are also dominated by U.S. programming.

Interpretation. What might the findings mean? Government networks have a mission to serve local interests and support the cultural identity of their country. But their mission is dependent upon the health of their national film/TV production industry. In India's case, the nation has a thriving indigenous entertainment system. New Zealand has local production as well, but not enough to sustain more than one broadcast channel with a mostly New Zealand line-up.

Evaluation. In responding to television imports, nations have at least three options. First, they can close their broadcasting systems to TV imports. Second, they can let the market decide, a route that surely favors U.S. imports. Finally, they can coexist with imports, but with quotas that limit the percentage of air time available to imported programs, a strategy that encourages original, more culture-specific productions. Of course, another concern is satellite TV, which skirts foreign broadcast networks to bring U.S. programs and other imports directly to the screen.

Prime-Time Distribution

The networks have always been the main distributors of prime-time TV programs to their affiliate stations around the country. By 1997, ABC, CBS, NBC, and Fox were each allied with approximately two hundred stations. By 2000, UPN and WB had more than 150 affiliates each. The networks pay a fee to affiliate stations to carry their programs; in return, networks sell the bulk of advertising time and recoup their investments in these programs. In this arrangement, local stations receive national programs that attract large local audiences. In addition, some local ad spaces are allocated during prime time so that stations can sell their own time during these slots.

A common misconception is that TV networks own their affiliated stations. This is not usually true. Although networks own stations in major markets like New York, Los Angeles, and Chicago, throughout most of the country networks merely sign short-term contracts to rent time on local stations. For example, WDIV (Channel 4) in

Detroit has a contract to carry NBC programs but is owned by the Washington Post/Newsweek Company, based in Washington, D.C. Years ago, the FCC placed restrictions on network-owned-and-operated stations, called **O & Os**. Originally, networks and other companies were limited to owning five VHF and two UHF stations, but the limit was raised to twelve total stations during the 1980s. Hoping to ensure more diversity in ownership, the FCC during this time also mandated that an owner's combined TV stations could reach no more than 25 percent of the nation's ninety-million-plus TV households. Then, in 1996, the sweeping Telecommunications Act (which will be discussed in more depth in Chapter 6) abolished the twelve-station limit and most other ownership restrictions. By 2000, the FCC even allowed Viacom to own two networks—CBS and UPN. (Before this, the FCC and Congress had never allowed a single company to own more than one TV network.)

Although a local affiliate typically carries network programs, the station may preempt a network's offering by substituting other programs. According to *clearance rules,* established in the 1940s by the Justice Department and the FCC, all local affiliates are ultimately responsible for the content of their channels and must clear, or approve, all network programming.

Over the years, some of the circumstances in which local affiliates have rejected the network's programming have been controversial. For example, in 1956 Nat King Cole (singer Natalie Cole's father) was one of the first African American performers to host a network variety program. As a result of pressure applied by several white southern organizations, though, the program had trouble attracting a national sponsor. When some southern and northern affiliates refused to carry the program, NBC canceled it in 1957. In another instance, Norman Lear's popular CBS sitcom *Maude* (1972–78) aired two controversial episodes in which the title character, in her late forties, decided to abort an unwanted pregnancy. The episodes topped the ratings when they ran in 1972. However, when the episodes came up for network summer rebroadcast in 1973, a number of Catholic organizations led campaigns that generated seventeen thousand protest letters asking CBS to cancel the second airing. Although CBS refused, 39 of its 217 affiliates did not clear the episodes. Seven national sponsors also pulled their ads. The controversy generated an even bigger audience the second time around, as nearly sixty-five million people watched the two shows as reruns in 1973.

Syndication Keeps Shows Going and Going . . .

Syndication, selling TV stations the exclusive rights to air TV shows, is a critical component of the distribution process. Early each year, executives from thousands of local TV stations and cable firms gather at the world's main "TV supermarket" convention, the National Association of Television Program Executives (NATPE), to buy or barter for programs that are up for syndication. In so doing, they acquire the exclusive local market rights, usually for two- or three-year periods, to quiz shows, talk shows, and **evergreens**—popular old network reruns such as the *Andy Griffith Show* or *I Love Lucy*. In such a competitive arena, most TV managers become less concerned with the quality of programs and more concerned with keeping costs low, delivering viewers to advertisers, and drawing higher ratings than their competitors.

Although the networks have long dominated the selection and distribution of prime-time television, syndicators have played a large role in the hours outside prime time. The distribution/syndication company King World, for example, began in 1972 after the fin-syn rules banished the networks from syndication. Starting out by distributing *Little Rascals* film shorts from the 1930s, King World barely survived its first year. By the end of the 1980s, however, it had become the distributor of the top shows in syndication—*Wheel of Fortune, Jeopardy,* and the *Oprah Winfrey Show*—and grossed nearly $400 million per year. With the suspension of fin-syn and the networks once again allowed to syndicate programming, CBS-Viacom in 1999 bought King World for $5 billion.

In addition to companies like Viacom and King World, major syndicators of TV programming include film companies such as Twentieth Century Fox, Disney-Touchstone, and Time Warner, all of which are also involved in the production of TV shows. Networks usually select and distribute about three hours of programming each night (four on Sunday) during prime time and another three to four hours of daytime programming, but this still leaves a substantial number of hours to fill a local affiliate's schedule. Because it is often cheaper to buy syndicated programs than to produce local programs (other than news), many station managers take the most profitable path rather than originate topical shows that focus on issues that affect their own communities.

Off-Network and First-Run Syndication

For local affiliate stations, syndicated programs are often used or slotted in what is known as **fringe time**. This includes programming immediately before the evening's prime-time schedule, called *early fringe,* and the time following the local evening news or the network's late-night talk shows, called *late fringe.* Syndication to fill these slots comes in two forms. First, there is **off-network syndication**, in which older programs, no longer running during network prime time, are made available for reruns to local stations, cable operators, online services, and foreign markets. A local station may purchase old *Home Improvement* or *Simpsons* episodes as a lead-in to boost the ratings for its late-afternoon news, or it may purchase *Frasier* or *Seinfeld* to boost its ratings after the late-evening news.

A second type of syndication used to fill fringe time is **first-run syndication**, which is any program that is specifically produced for sale into syndication markets. Quiz programs such as *Jeopardy* and *Wheel of Fortune* and daytime talk shows like *Ricki Lake* and *Montel Williams* are made for syndication. The producers of these programs sell them directly to local markets around the country and the world. When the FCC established the Prime-Time Access Rule in 1971 to turn more prime time over to local stations, it created an immediate market for new non-network programs.

Hybrid Syndication

The newer *Star Trek* programs, which have included *The Next Generation* and *Deep Space Nine,* are examples of a hybrid form of first-run syndication. (Other *Star Trek* spin-offs—*Voyager* and *Enterprise*—were created as UPN network programs.) These new episodes are descended from the original *Star Trek*, which aired on NBC in the 1960s but was canceled after three years as a result of low ratings. Although network rejection ends the lives of most programs, on occasion a producer may decide to make new episodes for syndication.

Besides *Star Trek,* the most famous hybrid programs are *Hee Haw* and the *Lawrence Welk Show.* Beginning on CBS in 1969, *Hee Haw* was canceled in 1971 even though it was a Top 20 program during its two years on prime time. CBS, however, thought the show appealed to too many children and older rural viewers, who were not as likely to buy many of the network's advertised products. After cancellation, the show's producers continued making and syndicating *Hee Haw* for more than twenty years.

Lawrence Welk had a much longer network run, appearing on ABC for sixteen years before its cancellation in 1971 when network executives determined that the program's audience was too old to attract new ad revenue. Welk's production company, however, made 1,542 new episodes between 1971 and 1982 and sold them into first-run syndication. The show was one of the only series that ran in more TV markets (over 250) in first-run syndication than it did when it aired originally. In fact, PBS bought the syndication rights in the early 1990s, and in 2003 *Lawrence Welk* continued to run on more than two hundred noncommercial stations.

Barter vs. Cash Deals

Most financing of television syndication is based on either cash or barter. In a *cash deal,* the distributor of a program offers a series for syndication to the highest bidder in a market—typically a station trying to fill a particular time slot. Due to exclusive contractual arrangements, programs air on only one broadcast outlet per market. For example, Viacom, which distributes the *Cosby Show,* offers it in hundreds of television markets around the country. Whichever local station bids the most in a particular market gets the rights to that program, usually for a contract period of two or three years. A small-market station in Fargo, North Dakota, might pay a few thousand dollars to air a week's worth of episodes; in contrast, some Top 10 markets paid well over $150,000 a week for *Cosby* in the late 1980s.

One common variation of a cash deal is called *cash-plus.* For shows that are successful in syndication, distributors may retain some time to sell national commercial spots. When *Cosby* went into syndication, for example, Viacom, in addition to receiving cash for the show from various local outlets, also sold a minute of ad time to national advertisers. When the two-hundred-plus local stations received the programs, they already contained a minute's worth of national ads. Some syndicators use cash-plus deals to keep down the cost per episode; in other words, stations pay less per episode in exchange for giving up ad slots to a syndicator's national advertisers.

Although syndicators prefer cash deals, *barter deals* are usually arranged for new or untested programs. In a straight barter deal, no money changes hands between the local station and the syndicator. Instead, a syndicator offers a new program to a local TV station in exchange for a split of the advertising revenue. The program's syndicator will try to make an arrangement with the station that attracts the largest number of local viewers, though this is not always possible. The syndicator then sells some ads at the national level, charging advertisers more money if the program has been sold into a large number of markets. This guarantees the wide national distribution that the networks receive for prime-time shows.

As an example, in the early 1990s *Star Trek: The Next Generation* was offered by its producer-distributor, Paramount, in a 7/5 barter deal. Paramount did not charge cash per episode. Instead, during each airing it retained seven minutes of ad time to sell national spots and left stations with five minutes of ad time to sell local spots. The *Jenny Jones Show* also started out as a barter show. As it became a profitable product, its syndicator, Time Warner, repackaged the show as a cash-plus deal.

Measuring Television by Ratings and Shares

Although the networks wrested control of content from sponsors in the 1950s, advertising still drives the business. TV shows live or die based primarily on whether advertisers are satisfied with the quantity and quality of the viewing audience.

Since 1950, the major organization tracking prime-time viewing has been the A. C. Nielsen Market Research Company, which estimates what viewers are watching in the nation's major markets. During the 1950s and 1960s, before ratings were fine-tuned statistically, firms like Nielsen estimated only the mass numbers of households tuned to particular programs. By the 1970s, ratings services provided advertisers, networks, and local stations with much more detail about those viewers —from race and gender to age, occupation, and educational background.

In TV measurement a **rating** is a statistical estimate expressed as a percentage of households tuned to a program in the local or national market being sampled (see Table 5.2). By 2003, one Nielsen national ratings point represented just over 1.1 million

● **Table 5.2 The Top 10 Highest-Rated TV Series, Individual Programs (since 1960)**

Program	Network	Date	Rating
1. M*A*S*H (final episode)	CBS	2/28/83	60.2
2. Dallas ("Who Shot J.R.?" episode)	CBS	11/21/80	53.3
3. The Fugitive (final episode)	ABC	8/29/67	45.9
4. Cheers (final episode)	NBC	5/20/93	45.5
5. Ed Sullivan Show (Beatles' first U.S. TV appearance)	CBS	2/9/64	45.3
6. Beverly Hillbillies	CBS	1/8/64	44.0
7. Ed Sullivan Show (Beatles' second U.S. TV appearance)	CBS	2/16/64	43.8
8. Beverly Hillbillies	CBS	1/15/64	42.8
9. Beverly Hillbillies	CBS	2/26/64	42.4
10. Beverly Hillbillies	CBS	3/25/64	42.2

Note: The *Seinfeld* finale, which aired in May 1998, drew a rating of 41-plus; *Survivor*'s final first-season episode in August 2000 drew a rating of only 28—not quite Top 10 material.

Sources. The *World Almanac and Book of Facts 1997* (Mahwah, N.J.: World Almanac Books, 1996), 296; Corbett Steinberg, *TV Facts* (New York: Facts On File Publications, 1985); A. C. Nielsen Media Research.

Anatomy of a TV "Failure"

Television shows die early deaths for many reasons. And some, like David Lynch's 1999 TV pilot for ABC, which eventually became the critically acclaimed film *Mulholland Drive,* are stillborn. Lynch is best known for the frightening film noir *Blue Velvet* (1986) and the weird, wacky cult TV hit *Twin Peaks* (ABC 1990–92). His 1999 TV pilot for ABC, which explored the tension between innocence and evil along with the seamy underbelly of Hollywood, spooked some TV executives whose corporate parent just happened to be the Hollywood film studio Disney. Even after Lynch shortened the pilot by 40 minutes and cut out a scene in which a scary tramp covered in moss and dirt frightens a man to death, ABC dumped the show and its $7 million investment.[1]

Although TV executives killing pilots never seen by audiences is one way TV shows die, other factors doom a show once it does hit the air. Two of the most common are tough, competitive time slots and poor lead-in shows that fail to attract a big enough following. Then there's also the story of *Frank's Place* (1987–88), a critically acclaimed entry in the fall 1987 television lineup.

This series starred Tim Reid as a displaced history professor from Boston who inherited his estranged father's modest restaurant in a working-class area of New Orleans. The winner of three Emmys, *Frank's Place* was canceled by CBS just as it was set to produce new episodes for the 1988–89 TV season.

In fact, most new TV series fail. Even such successful series as *All in the Family, M*A*S*H, Hill Street Blues, Cheers,* and *60 Minutes* started out slowly, some at the bottom of the ratings. But they all got a second chance. Why not *Frank's Place*—especially after a strong premiere? In the first place, the show lacked a patient executive champion at the network level who would allow *Frank's Place* to "find" its audience gradually in a fixed time slot. During the show's first year, CBS programmers moved it to six different time slots on four different nights. In fact, the program moved so often that its co-producers, Reid and Hugh Wilson, said that their own mothers could no longer find it.[2] A second problem involved audience expectations. Instead of viewing *Frank's Place* as a series of short stories, as "individual little movies," viewers perhaps

● Combining a mystery drama with a reality show, *Push, Nevada* was canceled in October 2002 after seven episodes had aired.

wanted a more traditional comedy. Intrinsic to this problem were the following questions: Was *Frank's Place* too much about black culture to develop an audience among mainstream America? Though it was primarily a comedy, was it also viewed as too serious by tackling such issues as drugs, homelessness, corporate greed, alienation, and religion? No regular network dramatic series featuring a majority black cast had ever succeeded in prime time, although by 1993 there were nine sitcoms on television that had predominantly black casts.

In one of the show's early episodes, the older bartender, Tiger, tells a disconsolate Frank, who's not a great businessman, "White folks don't come down here much at night." Like the bar's clientele, not enough TV viewers, white or black, were even aware of the program. Unlike *Cosby,* essentially a show about social class, *Frank's Place* was a show about race as well as social class. Safer and less threatening, *Cosby* became one of the most popular shows in the history of television. *Frank's Place,* however, while it lasted, allowed mainstream America to see the viewpoints of characters who lived in a black working-class section of New Orleans—in the margins of America, a place where network prime-time television (as David Lynch also found out) has never been very comfortable.

> ❝ I found out in *Twin Peaks* that a lot of restrictions in television led to some very interesting things that were even better. . . . Sometimes the restrictions are great. And sometimes having no restrictions is great. ❞
>
> –Director David Lynch, 2001

television households. Another audience measure is the **share**, a statistical estimate of the percentage of homes tuned to a program, compared with those actually using their sets at the time of a sample. Let's say, for instance, that on a typical night, of the 5,000 metered homes sample-wired by Nielsen across the country, 4,000 of those households have their TV sets tuned in to assorted networks, pay channels, and cable channels. Of those 4,000, about 1,000 are tuned to *Friends* on NBC. The rating estimate for that show is 5,000 (number of sets monitored) divided by 1,000 (number of households watching *Friends*), which equals 20 percent. The share estimate is 4,000 (sets actually in use) divided by 1,000, which equals 25 percent.

Share measurements have become increasingly important because they tell advertising and TV executives approximately the number of viewers and the percentage of sets in use tuned to their programs in a competitive market. Shares are also good measures during fringe time, when most sets may be turned off. For example, on a given night, only 1,000 of the 5,000 sets may still be on for late-night viewing. If 500 of that 1,000 are tuned to the *Late Show,* its rating would be only 10 percent (5,000 divided by 500), but its share of the audience still tuned in would be 50 percent (1,000 divided by 500).

In the early 1970s, during the height of the network era, a prime-time series with a rating of 17 or 18 and a share of between 28 and 30 was generally a success. By 2000, though, with increasing competition from cable and VCRs, the threshold for success had dropped to a rating of 8 or 9 and a share of under 13 or 14. Expectations were even lower for the new Paramount (UPN) and Time Warner (WB) networks, which still had fewer affiliates than the four large networks.

The importance of ratings and shares to the survival of specific TV programs cannot be overestimated. (See "Case Study: Anatomy of a TV 'Failure'" on page 176.) Simply stated, audience measurement tells advertisers roughly how many people are watching. Even more important, it tells them what kind of people are watching. Prime-time advertisers are mainly interested in securing affluent eighteen- to forty-nine-year-old viewers, who account for most consumer spending. If a show is attracting viewers from that group, advertisers then decide if they want to buy time during that particular program and pay the network its asking price. In fact, television operates as an industry in which networks, producers, and distributors target, guarantee, and "sell" viewers in blocks to advertisers. About eight of ten new shows introduced each fall either do not attain the required ratings or fail to reach enough of the "right" viewers. The result is cancellation within the year. Unfortunately, over the years many popular programs also have been canceled because advertisers considered their audiences too young, too old, or too poor. (We will return to the economics of ratings in Chapter 13.)

Alternative Voices

Even though the major networks and their big-city affiliates have dominated mainstream television, alternative programming does exist—particularly at the small, low-power stations or on cable's public access channels. The king of "alt-TV" is probably Paper Tiger Television (PTTV), a loose and changing group of about one hundred producers, activists, artists, technicians, scholars, and "people-off-the-street" who have created more than two hundred half-hour programs since 1981. For more than fifteen years, PTTV has run a weekly half-hour commentary program on contemporary culture on Manhattan Cable. PTTV's focus has been providing programs on issues that have either been ignored by mainstream television or oversimplified by traditional news outlets. These mini–TV documentaries, often combining irreverent humor and detailed analysis, specialize in exploring the connections among production, audience, and sponsors: "Paper Tiger . . . aims to disrupt the TV beliefs of its viewers."[13]

PTTV's alternative catalogue includes "Super Barrio," a 1995 production documenting government injustices and economic conditions in Mexico, and "Torn Between Colors," a 1990 student production featuring African American and Latino high school teens who examine the media coverage of several high-profile crimes in New York. In their video (as in many PTTV productions), the students look at the role of language and image in shaping public opinion, using the medium of television to exert some control over their own lives and how they are portrayed. In 2001, the catalogue added "Who's Paying the Price?"—an examination of the effects of 9/11 on working people of New York City. Focusing on laid-off Marriott Hotel workers from the destroyed Twin Towers, this 28-minute documentary investigated "the contradictory glorification of workers in the immediate aftermath of the attacks and the near complete disregard of their needs in the ensuing national and local 'economic stimulus' packages."

The Public, Television, and Democracy

As we enter the new century, the dominant mass medium of the last half of the twentieth century has undergone significant transformations. In the 1950s, television's appearance significantly changed the media landscape—particularly the radio and magazine industries, both of which cultivated specialized audiences and markets to survive. But at the end of its dominant reign—with the coming of cable, the Internet, and even newer digital technologies—television changed too. While it still remains the main storytelling medium of our time, the news, comedy, and drama of television are increasingly controlled by larger and larger companies, most of which also own movie and recording studios and other media businesses. As in the sound recording business, it has become more difficult for independent producers to make their mark in network television as the major companies—like Disney (ABC), Viacom-Paramount (CBS, UPN), GE (NBC), and News Corp. (Fox)—have seized control of programming. The TV executives ruling over this concentration of storytelling power, however, have not figured out how to bring back viewers increasingly drawn to the more interactive and specialized terrain of cable and the Internet. Since the 1980s, the original Big Three networks have lost more than half their audience.

As the television industry works to re-imagine itself in the new century, it is important to remember that in the 1950s, television carried the anti-elitist promise that its technology could bypass traditional print literacy and reach all segments of society. In such a heterogeneous and diverse nation, the concept of a visual, affordable mass medium, giving citizens entertainment and information that they could all talk about the next day, held great appeal. However, since its creation, commercial television has tended to serve the interests of profit more than those of democracy. And networks have proved time and again that they are more interested in delivering audiences to advertisers than in providing educational and provocative programming to citizens and viewers.

Public television (PBS), which first aired in the late 1960s, has often filled the role of programming for viewers who are "less attractive" to commercial networks and advertisers. Besides providing programs for the over-fifty viewer, public television has played a key role in programming for viewers under age twelve—another demographic not valued by most advertisers and often neglected by the networks. Over the years, such children's series as *Mister Rogers' Neighborhood* (1967–2001), *Sesame Street* (1969–), and *Barney* (1991–) have been fixtures on PBS. With the exception of CBS's long-running *Captain Kangaroo* (1955–84), the major networks have pretty much abdicated the responsibility of developing educational series aimed at children under age twelve. In 1996, though, Congress did pass a law ordering the networks to offer three hours of children's educational programming per week. But the networks sidestepped this congressional mandate by claiming that many of their routine sitcoms, cartoons, and dramatic shows are educational.

By 2000, the future of PBS and noncommercial television remained cloudy. Ever since the late 1960s, when the Nixon administration began threatening funding cuts for any programming critical of status quo politics and values, our noncommercial system has occasionally been held hostage. Because the government never required wealthy commercial broadcasters to subsidize public television (as many other democracies do), politics has played an increasing role in the fate of PBS. As federal funding levels dropped in the 1980s, PBS depended more and more on corporate underwriting. By 2001, corporate sponsors funded more than 25 percent of all public television. While this development has supported many PBS programs, it has had a chilling effect on PBS's traditional independence from corporate America. As a result, PBS has sometimes rejected controversial programming and hard-hitting documentaries, such as *Deadly Deception,* the 1991 Oscar-winning film that criticized General Electric (which owns NBC) and the nuclear power industry.

In another example, in January 1998 PBS decided to "bury" *Surviving the Bottom Line,* a probing documentary produced by the journalist Hedrick Smith, by airing it on successive Friday evenings, which typically draw a smaller TV audience. This pre-Enron film offered "a provocative attack on the kind of Wall Street thinking that places short-term share-holder interests above the welfare of communities." Longtime PBS journalist (and former press secretary to President Johnson) Bill Moyers sharply criticized PBS's scheduling decision, which, he argued, placed the "life of business" before the "business of life."[14]

In addition to problems faced by our public broadcasting system, the original ideal of "universal" television programming serving as our cultural yardstick has also been undercut. The development of cable, the VCR and DVD, new networks, and individualized Internet services has fragmented us by appealing to our individual and special needs. As new technological

● The most influential children's show in TV history, *Sesame Street* (PBS, 1969–) has been teaching young children their letters and numbers for more than thirty years. The program has also helped break down ethnic, racial, and class barriers by introducing TV audiences to a rich and diverse cast of puppets and people.

changes and individualized online services provide more specialized and individual choices, they also weaken television's role as a national touchstone and our ability to think more broadly as citizens who are part of a larger community and nation.

But at the same time—supplementing PBS's role—diverse cable channels such as Nickelodeon, Comedy Central, and the Cartoon Network do appeal to one end of the age spectrum, while Lifetime, C-Span's Book TV, the History Channel, and Bravo serve the other end; each has built up loyal audiences that were not the main demographic target during the network era. To reinvigorate the ideal of television as a prevailing cultural center, local cable access channels and electronic "town hall" meetings—in which citizens participate directly in the programming process—have begun tentatively to restore the idea of a shared national culture. And certainly the enduring coverage of the aftermath of 9/11, the Washington-area sniper story in 2002, and the 2003 *Columbia* space shuttle tragedy demonstrated television's continuing ability to serve as a touchstone for important national events. Such developments at both the local and national levels offer a counter to the economic situation in television today in which a few large multinational companies are controlling the bulk of national and international TV programming. Although we certainly have a greater variety of consumer choices today, we still have very little say in what programs (or products) we might like to see.

● The first televised presidential debates took place in 1960, pitting Massachusetts Senator John F. Kennedy against Vice President Richard Nixon. Don Hewitt, who later created the long-running TV newsmagazine *60 Minutes,* directed the first debate and has argued that the TV makeup that Nixon turned down would have helped create a better appearance alongside his tanned opponent. In fact, one study at the time reported that a majority of radio listeners thought Nixon won the first debate while the majority of TV viewers believed Kennedy won.

The future of television is uncertain. Like the other print and broadcast media that it changed, television has also changed. Technologically, digital advances have already made flat-screen, wall-mounted television sets a reality in the twenty-first century. However, with Internet services now offering our favorite TV shows via computer screen, we no longer even need a traditional TV set. And yet companies are now marketing products that allow access to the World Wide Web through our TV sets. In the digital age, distinctions between computer and TV screens will eventually break down. Most television programs are created by a handful of companies, but the networks still rely—at least in part—on independent producers to supply them with the next new idea or story. Although the 1990s and early 2000s featured talk shows, wrestling, reality-based programs, and newsmagazines as hot trends (like quiz shows and westerns before them), these genres, too, will fade.

The mainstream allure of television is both its strength and its weakness. As a plus, television offers special moments—inaugurations, space disasters and conquests, football, *Roots,* the Olympics, impeachment hearings, the 2001 coverage of 9/11—that bring large heterogeneous groups together for shared information, triumphs, and mourning—for common experiences. One drawback, though, is that television does not easily explore or adapt to territory outside that common ground. When television aims for the great American middle, it can often mute points of view that are at the edges. As cultural activists and TV critics, we need to support the idea that many voices and views should have a place in the media market and on the screen.

> ❝ Those who complain about a lack of community among television viewers might pay attention to the vitality and interaction of TV sports watchers wherever they assemble. ❞
>
> –Barbra Morris, University of Michigan, 1997

www.

To create an individualized study plan for Chapter 5, go to the interactive *Media and Culture* Online Study Guide at: bedfordstmartins.com/mediaculture

REVIEW QUESTIONS

The Origins and Early Development of Television

1. What were the major technical standards established for television in the 1940s?

2. Why did the FCC freeze the allocation of TV licenses between 1948 and 1952?

3. How did the sponsorship of network programs change during the 1950s?

4. Why did it take forty years for the networks to put a quiz show—*Who Wants to Be a Millionaire*—back on the air in prime time?

Major Programming Trends in the TV Age

5. How did news develop at the networks in the late 1940s and 1950s?

6. What are the differences among sketch, situation, and domestic comedy on television?

7. Why did the anthology drama fade as a network programming staple?

8. What are the types of episodic TV series? Why did they survive as a TV staple?

The Decline of the Network Era

9. What were the technological changes that contributed to the decline of network control over television?

10. What rules and regulations did the government impose to restrict the networks' power?

11. How have new networks managed to grow over the last decade?

The Economics of Television

12. Why has it become more difficult for producers to independently create programs for television?

13. What are the differences between off-network and first-run syndication?

14. Why do syndicated American television shows have advantages in the global marketplace?

15. What is the difference between a rating and a share in audience measurement?

The Public, Television, and Democracy

16. How has television served as a national cultural center or reference point over the years?

17. What problems does traditional network television face in the early 2000s?

QUESTIONING THE MEDIA

1. Describe your earliest memories of watching television. What was your favorite show? Which shows did your family watch together? Were there shows that you were not allowed to watch? Which ones?

2. How much television do you watch today? Which programs do you try to watch regularly? What attracts you to your favorite program(s)?

3. If you were a network television executive, what changes would you try to make in the programs that America watches?

4. If you ran a public television station, what programming would you provide that isn't currently being supplied by commercial television? How would you finance such programming?

5. How could television be used to improve social and political life in the United States?

SEARCHING THE INTERNET

http://www.nab.org
Official Web site for the National Association of Broadcasters, the main trade association and lobbying body for the broadcast industry.

http://www.cpb.org
This Corporation for Public Broadcasting site provides information on PBS programs, member stations, and those who use public TV for education.

http://www.buttle.com/tv/schedule.htm
Buttle Broadcasting provides TV program guides from different nations around the world.

http://www.ultimatetv.com
Ultimate TV provides program information on all major networks and most local TV stations. It also provides information on what kinds of TV systems operate in various countries.

http://www.nbc.com

http://www.abc.com

http://www.cbs.com

http://www.fox.com

http://www.upn.com

http://www.thewb.com

These are the official national network Web sites. They contain information about their programs as well as listings of the local affiliates.

THE CRITICAL PROCESS

In Brief

Do you think television plays more of a role in uniting us as a culture or in separating us as individuals? Make two lists on the board (or in groups) and discuss them in class.

In Depth

Pick a fairly recent TV program that failed to survive on television for more than a year or two. Roughly following the steps in the critical process, write a four- to five-page examination of your program.

Description. Do as much research as you can on the program (use LexisNexis database to check old reviews). In your paper, give a brief description of the program—its storyline and major characters. Also, describe the history of the program: when it aired,

for how long, ratings information, and so forth. Discuss why you picked this program.

Analysis. After weeding through your research, identify three or four problems that may have contributed to your program's failure to stay on the air. Discuss whether these were problems with the program itself or problems with the industry in general.

Interpretation. What does this all mean? Why do you think the program failed? What's your interpretation of all the information you've examined?

Evaluation. Try to go beyond conventional "TV executive" thinking here to offer some fresh insights. Was your program a good one that deserved better? What made it good? Was it a weak program that deserved to fail? What made it weak? Or was it a mixture?

KEY TERMS

prime-time, 145
VHF, 148
UHF, 149
analog, 150
digital, 150
affiliate stations, 154
TV newsmagazines, 156
kinescope, 157
sketch comedy, 157
situation comedy, 157
domestic comedy, 158

anthology drama, 160
episodic series, 162
chapter shows, 162
serial programs, 163
stripped [syndicated reruns], 163
network era, 164
independent station, 165
videocassette recorders (VCRs), 165
time shifting, 166
"black box" technologies, 166
infotainment, 167

fin-syn, 167
deficit financing, 170
rerun syndication, 170
O & Os, 172
evergreens, 172
fringe time, 173
off-network syndication, 173
first-run syndication, 173
rating, 175
share, 177

cable

and the specialization of television

When MTV began on August 1, 1981, the first music video played was "Video Killed the Radio Star," by the Buggles. The song proved to be prophetic. But more than twenty years later, in 2002, video resurrected the radio star—in this case, an aging heavy-metal icon—with a show called *The Osbournes.* The program's introduction makes the show look like a fictional TV family sitcom. But the Osbournes are for real. Teenage children Jack and Kelly are making it through their awkward years with dyed hair and lots of black clothing. Mother Sharon, like most sitcom moms, clearly wields control over the household. She also generated strong viewer sympathy when the program revealed her battle with colon cancer. But the show's main attraction is father Ozzy Osbourne, the fifty-plus-year-old solo act and former lead singer of Black Sabbath. Osbourne is famous for such songs as "Crazy Train," "Paranoid," and "Iron Man" but perhaps even more famous for surviving his more youthful indiscretions, which include heavy drug use, alcoholism, biting the head off of a

bat on stage, and biting the head off of a dove at a meeting with record executives.

So, there was a certain appeal for viewers in seeing how the middle-aged, somewhat doddering heavy-metal star from Birmingham, England, copes as a suburban dad with his wife, two of their three children, and several poorly trained dogs and cats in their Beverly Hills mansion. And there was an unmistakable irony in many situations, including Ozzy dealing with a next-door neighbor who plays music too loud, and his two teenage children who stay out late at night. (A third child, the oldest daughter, declined to participate in the show's tapings.)

The Osbournes quickly generated great word-of-mouth buzz among viewers, and with just ten episodes in the spring of 2002 it became the biggest hit in MTV's history. It also led to multimillion-dollar agreements for twenty new episodes, a book deal, and DVD/videocassette releases worth about $30 million for the Osbournes. The show also recon-

firmed MTV's role as one of television's innovators. As the broadcast networks have struggled with declining audiences over the past two decades, MTV has more freely stretched the boundaries of conventional programming with reality programs such as *Real World* and *Road Rules,* shock stunt shows like *Jackass,* and satirical animation like *Beavis and Butt-head.* In fact, the idea for *The Osbournes* emerged from an appearance of the family on another MTV show—*Cribs,* which takes viewers through the

overdecorated homes of hip celebrities.

MTV programs like *The Osbournes* have been extremely successful in attracting the audience so desired by advertisers: people in the age twelve to thirty-four category. Thus, it was not surprising that the day after it premiered, NBC's chief programmer asked his staff to find similar material for his network.

Like many reality programs on network television, however, *The Osbournes'* star dimmed during its second season. It lost more than half its audience, dropping from close to 8 million viewers during its first season high to 6.5 million for its second season opener in November 2002 to fewer than 3.5 million by January 2003. The novelty of documenting the everyday life of an aging rock star's family apparently got old fast. Although the broadcast networks may want similar programming, they still face the reality that unscripted programs outside the creative control of writing teams—while cheaper to produce—are difficult to sustain.

although cable television is almost as old as broadcast television, broadcasters worked hard to stunt its growth throughout its first twenty-five years. Since the mid-1970s, however, when both HBO (Time Warner's premium movie service) and WTBS (Ted Turner's Atlanta TV station) became available to cable companies across the nation, cable television's growth has been rapid. In 1977, only 14 percent of all American homes received cable. By 1985, that number had climbed to 46 percent. By 2003, the figure had leveled off at about 70 percent.

The cable industry's emergence from the shadow of broadcast television and its rapid rise to prominence were due partly to the shortcomings of broadcast television. For example, cable generally improved signal reception in most communities. In addition, whereas prime-time broadcast television has traditionally tried to reach the largest possible audiences, cable channels—like magazines and radio—focused more on providing specialized services for smaller audiences that broadcasters often ignored. Furthermore, through its greater channel capacity, cable has provided more access. In many communities, various public, government, and educational channels have made it possible for anyone to air a point of view or produce a TV program. When it has lived up to its potential, cable has offered the public greater opportunities to more fully participate in the democratic promises of television.

We will begin this chapter by examining cable's technological development and traditional broadcasters' attempts to restrict its growth. We will discuss the impact of the various rules and regulations aimed at the cable industry, including the Telecommunications Act of 1996, which was the first major revision of communications law since 1934. We will then turn to various programming strategies, including basic service, premium cable, pay-per-view, video-on-demand, and cable music services, as well as the innovative contributions of CNN, MTV, and HBO. We will also explore an alternative technology—direct broadcast satellite—and its impact on cable. Finally, we will look at business and ownership patterns, particularly the influence of the largest cable operators, Comcast Corp. and Time Warner Cable, and investigate cable's role in a democratic society.

> **❝** New viewers are not coming to network television. How do you build for the future? If I was a young executive, I don't know if I would come into the network business. I'd probably rather program Comedy Central. **❞**
>
> –Leslie Moonves, president of CBS Television, 1998

Technology and the Development of Cable

Unlike recording, radio, and broadcast television, cable television's earliest technical breakthroughs came from a fairly anonymous and practical group of people. Originating in rural and small-town communities in the late 1940s, cable sprang from obstacles that appliance-store owners faced in selling TV sets to people who lived in remote areas. In an effort to increase sales in places where hills and mountains blocked broadcast signals, TV dealers and electronics firms built antenna relay towers on the outskirts of their communities to pick up blocked signals. They strung wire from utility poles and then ran cables from the towers into individual homes. Essentially, these individuals created a market for their products by ensuring clear TV reception for viewers.

Although today's technology is more advanced, cable TV continues to operate in pretty much the same way. The key technical distinction between cable and broadcasting remains: In cable, programs reach TV sets through signals transmitted via wire; in broadcasting, signals are transmitted over the air. The advantage of cable is that whereas the airwaves in any given community can accommodate fifteen or so VHF and UHF channels without electrical interference, cable wires can transmit hundreds of channels with no interference.

CATV—Community Antenna Television

The first small cable systems—called **CATV**, or community antenna television—originated in Oregon, Pennsylvania, and Manhattan (New York City), where mountains or tall buildings blocked TV signals. The early systems served roughly 10 percent of the country and, because of early technical and regulatory limits, contained only twelve channels. Even at this early stage, though, TV sales personnel, broadcasters, and electronics firms recognized the two big advantages of cable. First, by routing and reamplifying each channel in a separate wire, cable eliminated over-the-air interference. Second, by running signals through coaxial cable, channel capacity was increased.

In the early days, small communities with CATV often received twice as many channels as were available over the air in much larger cities. Because broadcast channels were generally regarded as a limited natural resource, CATV foreshadowed later developments in which cable-channel capacity grew dramatically and the need to operate a broadcast frequency diminished. In combination, the two early technological advantages of cable would soon propel the new cable industry into competition with conventional broadcast television. Unlike radio, which was intended to free mass communication from unwieldy wires, early cable technology sought to restore wires to improve the potential of television.

The Wires and Satellites behind Cable Television

With cable, TV signals are processed at a computerized nerve center, or *headend,* which operates various large satellite dishes that receive and process long-distance signals from, say, CNN in Atlanta or MTV in New York. In addition, the headend house's receiving equipment can pick up an area's local broadcast signals or a nearby city's PBS station. The headend relays each premium channel, local network affiliate, independent station, and public TV signal along its own separate line. These lines are made up of *coaxial cable, fiber optics,* or a combination of both. Until the 1980s, when scientists developed fiber-optic technology—sending coded information along beams of laser light—most cable systems transmitted electronic TV signals via coaxial cable, a solid core of copper-clad aluminum wire encircled by an outer axis of braided wires. These bundles of thin wire could accommodate fifty or more separate channels, or lines, running side by side with virtually no interference.

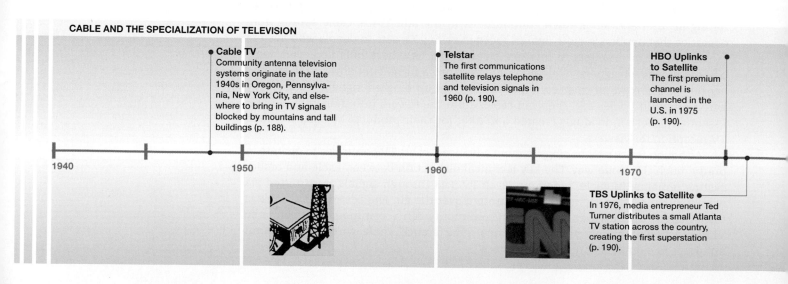

CABLE AND THE SPECIALIZATION OF TELEVISION

● Cable TV
Community antenna television systems originate in the late 1940s in Oregon, Pennsylvania, New York City, and elsewhere to bring in TV signals blocked by mountains and tall buildings (p. 188).

● Telstar
The first communications satellite relays telephone and television signals in 1960 (p. 190).

HBO Uplinks to Satellite
The first premium channel is launched in the U.S. in 1975 (p. 190).

1940　　　　　1950　　　　　1960　　　　　1970

TBS Uplinks to Satellite ●
In 1976, media entrepreneur Ted Turner distributes a small Atlanta TV station across the country, creating the first superstation (p. 190).

Figure 6.1 A Basic Cable Television System

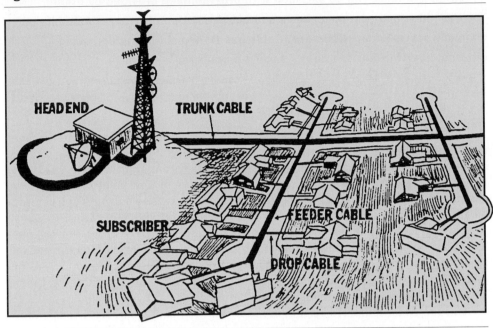

Source: Jennifer Stearns, *A Short Course in Cable* (Office of Communication, United Church of Christ, 1981), 9.

After "downlinking" various channels from satellites and pulling in nearby stations from the airwaves, headend computers relay them in the same way that telephone calls and electric power reach individual households. Most TV channels are relayed from the headend through *trunk* and *feeder cables* attached to existing utility poles. Cable companies rent space on these poles from phone and electric companies. Signals are then transmitted to *drop* or *tap lines* that run from the utility poles into subscribers' homes. TV signals either move from drop lines to cable-ready TV sets or pass through a cable converter box, which enables older TV sets to receive each channel. The newest set-top cable converter boxes can also bring the latest digital channels and services to subscribers. (See Figure 6.1.)

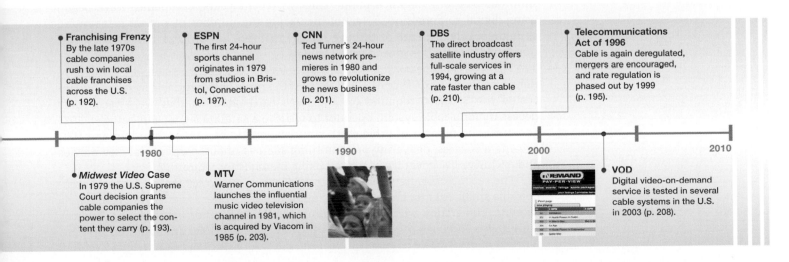

• **Franchising Frenzy**
By the late 1970s cable companies rush to win local cable franchises across the U.S. (p. 192).

• **ESPN**
The first 24-hour sports channel originates in 1979 from studios in Bristol, Connecticut (p. 197).

• **CNN**
Ted Turner's 24-hour news network premieres in 1980 and grows to revolutionize the news business (p. 201).

• **DBS**
The direct broadcast satellite industry offers full-scale services in 1994, growing at a rate faster than cable (p. 210).

• **Telecommunications Act of 1996**
Cable is again deregulated, mergers are encouraged, and rate regulation is phased out by 1999 (p. 195).

1980   1990   2000   2010

• *Midwest Video* **Case**
In 1979 the U.S. Supreme Court decision grants cable companies the power to select the content they carry (p. 193).

• **MTV**
Warner Communications launches the influential music video television channel in 1981, which is acquired by Viacom in 1985 (p. 203).

• **VOD**
Digital video-on-demand service is tested in several cable systems in the U.S. in 2003 (p. 208).

Advances in satellite technology in the 1970s dramatically changed the fortunes of cable by creating a reliable system for the distribution of programming to cable companies across the nation. In a few short years throughout the late 1970s and 1980s, cable television became popularized as dozens of new cable channels were launched. The idea for using space satellites for receiving and transmitting communication signals was literally right out of science fiction: In 1945, Arthur C. Clarke (who would later author dozens of sci-fi books, including 2001: *A Space Odyssey*) published the original theory for a global communication system based on three satellites equally spaced from each other, rotating with the earth's orbit. In the mid-1950s, these theories became reality as the Soviet Union and then the United States successfully sent satellites into orbit around the earth.

In 1962, AT&T launched Telstar, the first communication satellite capable of receiving, amplifying, and returning signals. Telstar received transmissions from the ground, beamed from an *uplink* facility, and retransmitted the signals to a receiving dish called a *downlink.* An active satellite, Telstar was able to process and relay telephone and occasional television signals between the United States and Europe. By the mid-1960s, scientists figured out how to lock a communication satellite into synchronous or geostationary orbit. Hovering 22,300 miles from the equator, satellites could travel at more than 6,800 mph and circle the earth at the same speed the earth revolves on its axis. For cable television, the breakthrough was the launch of domestic communications satellites, first with Canada's Anik satellite in 1972, followed by the United States' Westar in 1974.

The first satellites were capable of operating for seven or eight years and had twelve or twenty-four *transponders,* the relay points on a satellite that perform the receive-and-transmit functions. By the mid-1990s, the newest satellites had forty-eight transponders and lifetimes of more than fifteen years. Cable and DBS (direct broadcast satellite) program services such as MSNBC or the Discovery Network rent these transponders from satellite companies for million-dollar monthly fees. One conventional transponder can process one color-TV signal or about three thousand simultaneous long-distance phone calls. In recent years, companies have begun using digital compression, a way of increasing the number of signals transmitted simultaneously without disturbing image quality. This process has enabled one transponder to handle four to six TV signals.

The first cable network to use satellites for regular transmission of TV programming was Home Box Office (HBO) in 1975. At the time, only two cable systems had invested the $100,000 required for the large earth stations that were technically necessary for a cable system operator to retrieve a satellite signal. But between 1975 and 1980, the number of cable earth stations grew to seventeen hundred and HBO became a success, delivering programming such as uncut, commercial-free movies and exclusive live coverage of major boxing matches for a monthly fee.

The second cable network began in 1976, when media owner Ted Turner distributed his small, Atlanta broadcast TV station to cable systems across the country via satellite. The station was eventually renamed WTBS (Turner Broadcasting Service). Turner also launched the Cable News Network (CNN) in 1980 and followed it with a number of other cable channels.

Cable Threatens Broadcasting

Though the technology for cable existed as early as the late 1940s, cable's growth was effectively short-circuited by conventional broadcasters. For nearly thirty years, local broadcasters, the networks, and television's professional organization—the National Association of Broadcasters (NAB)—successfully lobbied to curb cable development in most cities. Throughout the 1950s and 1960s, the Federal Communications Commission (FCC) operated on behalf of the broadcast industry to ensure that cable would not compete with conventional television. Local broadcasters worried that if towns could bring in distant signals from more glamorous cities like Chicago or New York, viewers would reject their local stations—and their local advertisers—in favor of big-city signals. Early FCC rules therefore blocked cable companies from bringing distant TV stations into cities and towns with local channels.

There was one exception to these lobbying efforts: CATV service for sparsely populated communities. Because CATV generally served towns that had no TV stations of their own, the broadcast industry welcomed the distribution of distant signals to these areas via cable. After all, relaying a commercial signal to rural areas increased the audience reach and potential ad revenue of a broadcast station.

The FCC Reins In Cable's Growth

By the early 1970s, particularly with the advent of communication satellites, it was clear that cable's growth could no longer be limited to small, isolated communities. With cable's capacity for more channels and better reception, the FCC began to seriously examine industry issues. In 1972, the commission updated or enacted three main rules to regulate cable's expansion and protect conventional over-the-air television.

First, the FCC reaffirmed **must carry rules**, first established in 1965, which required all cable operators to assign channels to and carry all local TV broadcasts on their systems. This rule ensured that local network affiliates, independent stations (those not carrying network programs), and public television channels would benefit from cable's clearer reception. The FCC guidelines also allowed additional noncommercial channels to be introduced into bigger TV markets, but the guidelines limited the number of distant commercial TV signals to two or three independent stations per cable system. In addition, the guidelines prohibited cable companies from bringing in a network affiliate from another city when a local station already carried that network's programming. This ensured that a network affiliate in one market would not have to compete for viewers against a similar affiliate imported from another market.

Second, the FCC established **syndex rules**, which stands for "syndication exclusivity," and basically prohibited cable operators from importing off-network reruns like *Happy Days* and M*A*S*H from distant markets that would duplicate programming already available on local stations. These rules benefited local broadcasters, who each year competed with other local stations for exclusive syndication rights on specific programs. By applying syndex rules to cable, the FCC reaffirmed that cable could not undermine the programming choices of local stations. If cable systems did import duplicated shows, they were required to block them out—replace them with other programming—even if they filled a different time slot. Not surprisingly, the cable industry disliked this bothersome regulation.

Finally, the 1972 FCC rules required cable systems to carry their own original programming by mandating **access channels** in the nation's top one hundred TV markets. In other words, operators of cable systems were compelled to provide and

Figure 6.2 The Rise of Cable Systems, 1970–2005

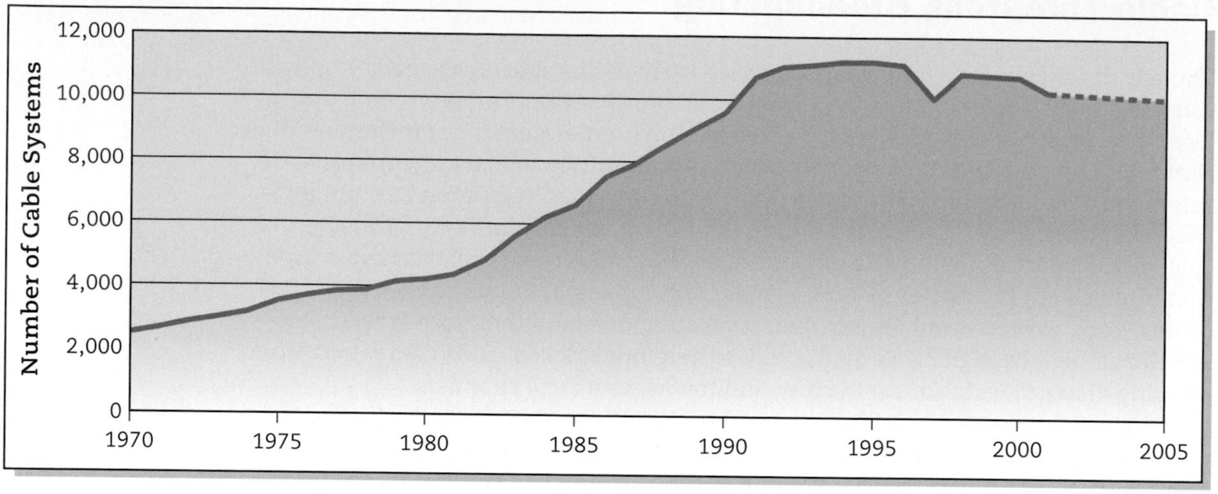

Source: National Cable Television Association (NCTA), <www.ncta.com>.

fund a tier of nonbroadcast channels dedicated to local education, government, and the public. The FCC required large-market cable operators to assign separate channels for each access service, whereas cable operators in smaller markets (and with fewer channels) could require education, government, and the public to share one channel. In addition to free public-access channels, the FCC called for **leased channels**. Citizens could buy time on these channels and produce longer programs or present controversial views.

Franchising Frenzy

By the end of the 1970s, the future of cable programming was clear, and competition over obtaining franchises to supply local cable service had become intense. Essentially, a cable franchise was a mini-monopoly awarded by a local community to the most attractive bidder, usually for a fifteen-year period. Although a few large cities permitted two companies to build different parts of their cable systems, in most cases communities granted franchises to only one company. Cities and states used the same logic that had been used in granting monopoly status to AT&T for more than a hundred years: They did not want more than one operator trampling over private property to string wire from utility poles or to bury cables underground.

The period from the late 1970s through the early 1990s constituted a unique, if turbulent, era in media history, for it was during this time that most of the nation's cable systems were built (see Figure 6.2). During the franchising process, a city (or state) would outline its cable system needs and request bids from cable companies. Then a number of companies—none of which could also own broadcast stations or newspapers in the community—competed for the right to install and manage the cable system. In the bid, a company would make a list of promises to the city, including information about construction schedules, system design, subscription rates, channel capacity, types of programming, financial backing, deadlines, and a *franchise fee:* the money the cable company would pay the city annually for the right to operate the local cable system.

Few rules or laws existed to regulate the process of franchise negotiations. During the franchising process, competing cable companies made attractive offers and promises to gain monopoly rights in certain areas. In the early 1980s, for example,

Sammon Communication bid for the Fort Worth, Texas, franchise by offering that city a multimillion-dollar community-access package that included three mobile television vans (for producing community programs), $50,000 for student-internship training programs, $175,000 as an annual budget for access channels, and $100,000 to modernize educational buildings and studios. Such offers were typical in large cable markets.

From the late 1970s through the 1980s, lots of wheeling and dealing transpired, along with occasional corruption. Cable companies sometimes offered far more than they could deliver, and some cities and suburbs occasionally made unfair demands on the franchise awardees. Often, battles over broken promises, unreasonable contracts, or escalating rates ended up in court.

New Rules Aid Cable's Growth

From the very beginning of cable, no one seemed to know who held legal jurisdiction over wired television. Because the 1934 Communications Act had not anticipated cable, its regulatory status was problematic during its early years. However, once cable began importing distant signals into bigger television markets, the FCC's interest perked up. By the mid-1980s, Congress, the FCC, and courts had repealed most early cable regulations, stimulating growth in the medium that had begun to acquaint the world with innovative programming like that carried on MTV and CNN.

Cable's Role: Common Carrier or Electronic Publisher?

Despite the 1972 ruling requiring cable firms to provide local access channels and a selection of leased channels to local bidders, the cable industry had long preferred to view its content (the programming provided on its cable systems) as similar to that provided by **electronic publishers**, with the same "publishing" freedoms and legal protections that broadcast and print media enjoy in selecting content. That meant that the cable companies felt entitled to pick and choose which channels to carry. The FCC argued the opposite: that cable systems should be **common carriers**—services that do not get involved in channel content. Like telephone operators, who do not question the topics of personal conversations ("Hi, I'm the phone company, and what are you going to be talking about today?"), the FCC argued that cable companies should offer part of their services on a first-come, first-served basis to whoever can pay the rate. In 1979, the debate over this issue ended in the landmark *Midwest Video* case, when

● Henry Winkler as Arthur "Fonzie" Fonzarelli, star of ABC's 1950s-nostalgia sitcom *Happy Days* (1974–84). Fonzie was initially written as a minor character, but his cool persona and trademark gesture (one or two thumbs up while saying "aaaayh!") made him immensely popular with audiences. *Happy Days*, now widely syndicated, was the first of several hit sitcoms, including the spin-off *Laverne & Shirley*, that propelled ABC into dominance among the networks in the 1970s.

the U.S. Supreme Court upheld the rights of cable companies to dictate their content and defined the industry as a form of "electronic publishing."[1] Although the FCC could no longer mandate channels, the Court said that it was still okay for communities to "request" access channels as part of contract negotiations in the franchising process. Access channels are no longer a requirement, but most cable companies continue to offer them in order to remain on good terms with their communities.

Soon thereafter, in 1980, to boost cable from its position as a struggling new industry, the FCC repealed its syndex rules. These rules had given local stations exclusive rights to syndicate TV programs, such as off-network reruns, that they had purchased. In exchange for the FCC's repeal of the syndex rules, cable companies agreed to pay copyright fees to broadcasters for imported distant signals. By the late 1980s, these fees amounted to more than $100 million, distributed mostly among the nation's three-hundred-plus independent TV stations. With the repeal of syndex, viewers could conceivably watch episodes of *Happy Days* and *M*A*S*H* five or six times a day on five or six different local and distant channels.

Deregulation and Re-Regulation with the Cable Acts of 1984 and 1992

The first major federal act governing cable was passed in 1984. Coming during the middle of the Reagan presidency, which had been favorable to deregulating business, the legislation represented a victory for the cable industry and a defeat for local communities. The act capped the annual franchise fee a city could charge a cable company at 5 percent of the company's gross revenues. The act further protected cable by making it difficult for cities to sign with a new company at the end of the regular fifteen-year franchise period. A more controversial aspect of the act called for a two-year phaseout of must-carry rules, a provision that upset local broadcasters who worried their stations might not be carried on local cable systems. In addition, it ended rate regulation. This meant that cable system operators, while constituting a local monopoly, could set their own unregulated monthly subscriber rates beginning in January 1987.

Between 1984 and 1990, the average rate for basic services (excluding premium movie channels like HBO) rose from about $9 to $17 a month. In addition, in 1984 cable operators effectively argued that must-carry rules violated their free-speech rights (because in many cases they had to assign one-third of their channels to existing broadcast stations). As a result, cable systems began dropping some PBS affiliates and weaker independent stations from their lineups. By the late 1980s, more than 150 public stations had been removed from local cable systems, and some 50 new independent UHF stations, licensed shortly after the 1984 act, were having difficulty getting a cable channel assigned to them. Some large cable companies dropped regular broadcast signals in favor of new satellite-delivered channels on which operators could run their own ads. Displeased with the act, broadcast lobbyists and consumer watchdog groups began calling for cable reform.

With the growing commercial success of cable and the rapid increase in subscription rates, a less sympathetic FCC and Congress changed the law in 1992, reinstating rate regulation. In the mid-1990s, the FCC surveyed the twenty-five largest cable companies, which served roughly 75 percent of all cable subscribers, and found that rates had decreased in fourteen of those systems but had increased in the other eleven systems. In most instances, loopholes allowed cable companies to raise rates on basic service but decrease rates for premium channels such as HBO and Showtime.

In terms of must-carry rules, the 1992 act required that every three years commercial broadcasters opt for either must-carry or **retransmission consent**. The latter option meant that broadcasters could now ask cable companies for fees to carry their channels. However, if broadcasters did this, they waived the right to be automatically carried on these cable systems. Alternately, local commercial broadcasters who chose must-carry gave up the right to be compensated for their channel but were guaranteed a channel assignment on their local cable system. By June 1993, each of the eleven-hundred-plus commercial U.S. TV stations (noncommercial stations could choose only must-carry) had to inform all cable system operators in their broadcast range whether they were opting for must-carry or retransmission. At the time, only low-rated independent stations on the fringes of a market opted for must-carry.

In 1993, the stations that chose retransmission consent did so because they correctly believed cable companies would not risk alienating customers by dropping the popular broadcast stations that carried network programs. In general, a broadcast station wanted either money from cable companies for carrying its signal or the right to advertise on more cable channels. A few large broadcast station owners, such as ABC, struck deals with cable companies that owned a large number of systems. For example, rather than ask for money, ABC requested that cable systems carry its new ESPN2 sports channel, which debuted in 1993. ABC's strategy successfully leveraged ESPN2 onto the lineups of major cable systems around the country. Similar tactics have been used by other broadcasters to launch cable channels such as FX and MSNBC.

The Telecommunications Act of 1996

After sixty-two years, Congress finally rewrote the nation's communications laws in the **Telecommunications Act of 1996**, bringing cable fully under the federal rules that had long governed the telephone, radio, and TV industries. In its most significant move, Congress used the Telecommunications Act to knock down regulatory barriers, allowing regional phone companies, long-distance carriers, and cable companies to enter one another's markets. For the first time, owners could operate TV or radio stations in the same market where they owned a cable system. Just as the Telecommunications Act allows cable companies to offer telephone services, it also permits phone companies to use fiber-optic wires to offer Internet services and to buy or construct cable systems in communities where there are fewer than fifty thousand residents. Before passage of the 1996 legislation, the phone and cable industries had long benefited from their regional and national monopoly status. Congress hoped that the new rules would spur competition and lower both phone and cable rates, although this did not usually happen.

While broadcasters fought steadily for must-carry rules over the years, cable companies continued to argue that these rules violated their free-speech rights by dictating what signals must be included among their cable offerings. The Telecommunications Act appeared to settle the issue by reaffirming broadcasters' need for must-carry rules. However, cable companies with limited channel capacity still objected to having to carry low-rated stations; operators could make more money carrying satellite-delivered movie services and specialty channels on topics such as history or health. The nation's cable companies continued to periodically ask the courts to repeal must-carry rules and free the cable companies to carry whatever channels best served their commercial interests. In 1997, however, broadcasting won a final victory when the Supreme Court upheld the constitutionality of must-carry rules, ensuring that most broadcasters would be carried by their local cable companies.

The 1996 act has had mixed effects for cable consumers. Cable companies argued that it would promote business mergers (such as the one announced in 1998 between telephone giant AT&T and cable giant TCI) that would lead to innovations in programming, services, and technology. But cable consumers often found themselves footing the bill for future interactive and video services that they did not

> **"** If this [telecommunications] bill is a blueprint, it's written in washable ink. Congress is putting out a picture of how things will evolve. But technology is transforming the industry in ways that we don't yet understand. **"**
>
> —Mark Rotenberg, Electronic Privacy Information Center, 1996

Figure 6.3 Market Share of Multichannel Video Program Distributors, Mid-Year 2002 (total multichannel subscribers: 93.4 million)

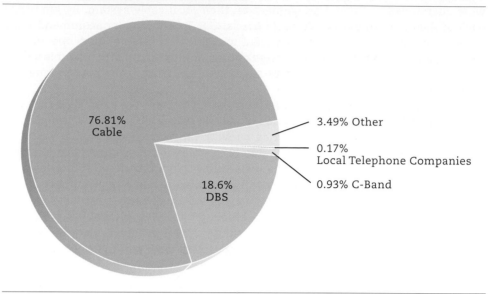

76.81%
Cable

3.49% Other

0.17%
Local Telephone Companies

0.93% C-Band

18.6%
DBS

Note: C-Band satellite service relies on large satellite dishes and serves mostly rural areas.

Source: Cable Television Industry Overview, mid-year 2002, <www.ncta.com>, 2002.

necessarily want. In fact, by the early 2000s, cable companies were investing billions of dollars a year in new services. By 2003, U.S. cable companies had signed up nearly seventeen million households to digital programming packages; more than nine million households had cable modem service, and more than two million households received cable-delivered telephone service.[2] Critics fear that more mergers will further eliminate rate competition in both the phone and cable businesses, and that there will be no government authority to step in and enforce rate freezes or cuts because the act required the FCC to end rate regulation in 1999. Cable rates in most markets are now determined solely by local monopoly cable companies.

The good news for cable subscribers is that the competition encouraged by the 1996 act—when it did occur—appeared to have some impact on cable rates. According to a 2002 FCC report, cable operators in noncompetitive markets charged an average of $37.13 a month to subscribers. In competitive markets—those in which another multichannel video programming distributor (e.g., another commercial cable company, a municipal cable company, or DBS service) held a significant market share—the average monthly charge was $34.93, or 6.3 percent less. Unfortunately for cable subscribers in the United States, only 368 of the more than 10,000 cable systems in the country face effective competition.[3] (See Figure 6.3.)

In terms of the act's impact on cable programs, advances in technology and new commercial interests will continue to increase the number of cable channels and add more specialized services, especially for affluent customers. As with other aspects of the information highway, of which cable is now a major thoroughfare, many new developments are likely to bypass poorer communities. Local governments and citizen advocate groups will need to play a strong role to ensure that new media developments reach the widest cross section of people in their communities. The cable industry itself has responded to such concerns with an initiative to provide schools and public libraries with free high-speed cable modems and Internet connections.

> **"Cable television rates have increased 45 percent since the federal government began deregulating the cable industry in 1996."**
>
> —The Consumers Union, 2002

Cable Comes of Age

Although its audience and advertising revenues remain smaller than those of the major TV networks, cable has emerged as a serious challenger to—and partner of—broadcasting. As the broadcast audience continued to erode throughout the 1990s, the major networks invested in cable. By 2003, each had developed or acquired several cable channels in order to capture some of the migrating viewers. NBC, for example, operated cable news services CNBC and MSNBC (with Microsoft) and entertainment channel Bravo. ABC owned ESPN and its many channels, along with portions of Lifetime, A&E, History, and E! CBS was the slowest to develop cable outlets, but its TNN (The National Network) and CMT (Country Music Television) channels have grown to be quite successful. Disney's purchase of ABC in 1995 and Viacom's purchase of CBS in 1999 paired the networks' cable channels with the more extensive cable properties of their corporate parents. The shifting balance of power between broadcasting and cable in the 1990s was even apparent in how the industry covered itself. *Broadcasting,* the trade magazine for television and an opponent of cable's early growth, became *Broadcasting & Cable* magazine in 1993.

During the old network era in television, ABC, CBS, and NBC accounted for more than 95 percent of prime-time viewing; independent stations and public television accounted for the rest. By the summer of 1997, basic cable channels had captured a larger prime-time audience than the broadcast networks, the first time that had ever happened. Considering the entire television viewing day, cable channels drew about 42 percent of the TV-viewing audience by 2002, up from less than 20 percent a decade earlier. Conversely, the old broadcast networks slid from a 58 percent share of the total television audience in 1989 to about 45 percent of television's total audience by 2002. The decline in the networks' viewer base appeared to be healthy for both competition and democracy. Yet with recent consolidations in media ownership, the companies that own the broadcast networks are often the same as those that control many of the leading cable channels. Thus the appearance of competition may at times be illusory.

In the new cable era, a redefined concept of **narrowcasting**—providing specialized programming for diverse and fragmented groups—has cut into broadcasting's large mass audience. For the advertising industry, cable programs provide access to specific target audiences that cannot be guaranteed in broadcasting (see, for example, "Case Study: ESPN's X Games Go to the Dogs" on page 198). For example, a golf-equipment manufacturer can buy ads on the Golf Channel and reach only golf enthusiasts. Because the audience is small and specialized, ads are a fraction of the cost of a network ad; they reach only the targeted viewers and not the larger general public. As cable channels have become more and more like specialized magazines or radio formats (see Figure 6.4), they have siphoned off network viewers. As a consequence, the networks' role as the chief programmer of the shared culture has eroded.

Cable consumers usually choose programming from a two-tiered structure: basic cable services are part of one monthly fee, and premium cable services are available individually to customers at an extra monthly or per-use fee. These services are the

> **❝** We used to think the possibility existed that the erosion was going to stop. We were silly. It's never going to stop. As you give consumers greater and greater choices, they are going to make more choices.**❞**
>
> —Robert A. Iger, president of ABC Inc., 1998

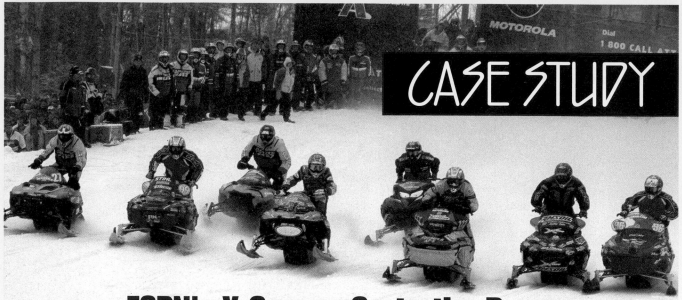

ESPN's X Games Go to the Dogs

Both the ESPN "X Games" and the ESPN "Great Outdoor Games" boast "Big Air" competitions. In the X Games version that aired in August 2002, "extreme" athletes on motorcycles and BMX bikes catapulted themselves off dirt hills and performed death-defying flips. In the Great Outdoor Games, broadcast a month earlier, Labrador retrievers launched themselves off a dock into a pond.

And which Big Air battle did more Americans watch?

That's right, the dogs. In fact, the Great Outdoor Games, the fledgling three-year-old Olympics of such sports as "hot sawing" and "speed tree climbing," earned slightly higher ratings on the main ESPN sports channel than the eight-year-old X Games, which did slightly better overall thanks to better time slots. X Games shows boasting Big Air competitions earned an average 0.75 Nielsen rating on ESPN, meaning it was seen in about 825,000 households. The Great Outdoor Games that included doggie Big Air contests earned an average 0.76.

Neither rating is much to write home about, of course. But the result underscores a little-recognized fact about the X Games, long seen as the Holy Grail of youth marketing: They aren't as popular as people think. And that has led the Disney-owned network to increasingly elbow skaters and snowboarders out of the picture and replace them with hunters, lumberjacks, and retrievers.

Initially panned by the athletes who participated in them for incorporating dubious sports like bungee jumping, the X Games have gained credibility as the extreme sports movement has flourished. Endorsement checks for the athletes — most notably those of skateboarders Tony Hawk and Andy Macdonald — soared. Official sponsorship fees, which buy some ads, jumped from less than $1 million the first year to more than $3 million apiece this year, when ESPN's collective sponsorship revenue for the X Games topped $30 million.

But ESPN has gradually whittled down its X Games telecast hours from forty-five in 1995 to twenty this year, and curtailed the reruns. There are no "up close and personal" athlete profiles, and ESPN provided little in the way of introduction to the events. In May, the company announced plans to extend the

franchise with an X Games global championship, which will pit national teams against one another, but ESPN has ended most of its non-X Games-related extreme sports programming and abandoned plans for a magazine on the genre.

These days, hunting and fishing increasingly account for programming on ESPN and sister cable channel ESPN2, which each reach more than 84 million households. Last year, the company inherited hundreds of hours of outdoor sport programming when it acquired the Bass Anglers Sportsmen Society in Huntsville, Alabama, for about $40 million.

Bass fishing may not sound as sexy as snowboarding or motorcycle jumping, but consider this: ESPN2 will be airing a show called "Fish On . . ." that is modeled after the E! Channel show "Wild On . . ." in which bikini-clad hostesses visit beaches around the world and report on the party scene. The ESPN2 show "stars three females and one male, accomplished anglers who happen to also be attractive people, who visit exotic locations and go fishing," says ESPN Outdoors spokesman George McNeilly. "And they partake in the nightlife."

The Outdoors division is also producing two other "sports entertainment" shows for ESPN2's Monday nights, including a reality-type show called "True Outdoor Adventures" and an updated version of the old "American Sportsman" show in which sportscaster Curt Gowdy went hunting and fishing with eminent sports figures.

The Great Outdoor Games are the centerpiece of ESPN's new push. Like the early X Games, the "GOGs" are a made-for-TV hodgepodge that includes both traditional pastimes like fishing and archery and more exotic competitions like speed tree-climbing and obstacle course races for dogs. The games, which generated nineteen hours of programming this year and earned a midday weekend broadcast on sister Disney network ABC, boasted double-digit ratings increases on all three channels that showed the event, including a 42 percent gain on ESPN2.

Source: Maureen Tkacik, " 'Extreme' Sports Programming Goes to Dogs," *Wall Street Journal,* August 30, 2002, p. B1.

Figure 6.4 The Top 20 Cable Networks, 2001 (Ranked by Number of Subscribers)

Note: Figures may include non-cable affiliates and/or subscribers. Broadcast viewership is not included.

Source: National Cable Television Association, <www.ncta.com>, June 2002.

production arm of the cable industry, supplying programming to the nation's approximately ten thousand cable operators, which function as program distributors to cable households.

Basic Cable Services

A typical **basic cable** system today includes a thirty-six- to seventy-two-channel lineup composed of local broadcast signals, nonbroadcast access channels (for local government, education, and general public use), a few regional PBS stations, and a variety of services retrieved from national communication satellites. These basic satellite services include ESPN, CNN, MTV, VH1, the USA Network, Bravo, Nickelodeon, Lifetime, ABC Family, Comedy Central, CNBC, C-Span and C-Span2, Black Entertainment Television, Telemundo, the Weather Channel, a home-shopping service, *superstations* (independent TV stations linked to a satellite) such as WGN (Chicago) or WPIX (New York), and ten to thirty additional channels depending on a cable system's capacity and regional interests.

Typically, local cable companies pay each of these satellite-delivered services between five cents (for low-cost, low-demand channels like C-Span) and more than $2 (for high-cost, high-demand channels like ESPN) a month per subscriber. That fee is passed along to consumers as part of their basic monthly cable rate. Unlike local broadcasters, which make money almost exclusively through advertising, cable companies earn revenue in a variety of ways: through monthly subscriptions for basic service, local ad sales, pay-per-view programming, and premium movie channels. Most basic satellite services, such as ESPN or Arts & Entertainment, block out time for inexpensive local and regional ads. These local ads are cheaply produced compared with national network ads and reach a smaller audience than do broadcast commercials. Cable, in fact, has permitted many small local companies—from restaurants to clothing stores—that might not otherwise be able to afford TV spots to use television as a means of advertising.

The 1990s witnessed a proliferation of new basic cable channels, increasingly specialized for smaller but more definable audiences. These include the popular Sci-Fi Channel (owned by the USA Network), the Cartoon Network (owned by AOL Time Warner), Comedy Central (owned by AOL Time Warner and Viacom), and FX (owned by News Corp.). Newer services featured channels devoted to history, health and fitness, books, games, parenting, pets, and therapy. In 1992, 87 cable networks were in business. By the end of 2002, that number had grown to more than 280.[4]

Cable system capacities continued to increase due to (1) the rebuilding of cable systems with high-bandwidth fiber-optic cable, and (2) the advent of digital cable services in the late 1990s, which have enabled cable companies to expand their offerings beyond the basic analog cable channels. Digital cable typically uses set-top cable boxes to offer interactive on-screen program guides, and dozens of additional premium, pay-per-view, and audio music channels, increasing total cable capacities to between 150 and 200 channels. By the end of 2002, more than seventeen million U.S. households subscribed to digital cable services.[5]

Battling with national cable networks are regional cable services, which target audiences geographically. About seventy-five regional channels exist in the United States, and nearly all of them are located in large metropolitan areas that can support such specialized programming. Many of the regional channels are news/talk formats modeled on CNN, but with coverage limited to a single media market. New York, for example, has New York 1 News, a 24-hour service that began in 1992. The New York region also has News 12 cable channels, which cover local markets outside the city. Similar services include BayTV (San Francisco), NorthWest Cable News (Seattle), Newschannel 8 (Washington, D.C.), and ChicagoLand Television News. Regional sports channels—many of them affiliates of the national Fox Sports Network—also thrive in many of the same top television markets and regions that are home to multiple professional sports teams.

The general success rate of new channels has been about 10 to 15 percent, which means that about 85 to 90 percent of new cable channels fail or are bought out by another cable service. The most difficult challenge new channels face is getting onto enough cable systems—many with limited channel capacity—to become profitable. Although several basic cable channels, such as the Discovery Channel and the USA Network (both with about eighty-six million cable subscribers), have been extremely successful, two basic channels—CNN and MTV—have made their mark both on American society and on global culture.

> **If Desert Storm fixed CNN's reputation, and O.J. did the same for Court TV, then the blizzard of '96 has put the Weather Channel solidly on the map.**
> —*Newsweek*, January 1996

> **MTV is popular fascism at its worst. MTV just doesn't care (and never has) about anything related to a big thing called talent!**
> —statement posted at <http://www.egroups.com/group/Anti-MTV>, an anti-MTV discussion site, 2000

CNN's Window to the World

Cable News Network (CNN), a 24-hour TV news channel, premiered in June 1980. CNN was the brainchild of Ted Turner, who helped revolutionize cable when he up-linked his small, independent Atlanta station (later named WTBS) to superstation stature. In 1982, Turner also launched Headline News, adapting the concept of format radio to TV news. Every thirty minutes, Headline News rotates brief versions of the top national and international news stories, followed by sports, business, and entertainment segments. Together, these two cable services—CNN and Headline News—lost nearly $80 million before turning a profit of $13 million in 1985. By the early 1990s, the two news channels were making more than $200 million in annual operating profits. In addition, CNN started a radio news service in 1992 that now provides news to five hundred radio affiliates in the United States. By 2003, CNN was available in more than eighty-six million U.S. homes and 890,000 hotel rooms worldwide. It was also carried part-time by more than 1,700 local broadcasters in the United States and Canada, and more than nine hundred worldwide.

CNN emerged as a serious news competitor to ABC, CBS, and NBC during the Persian Gulf War in 1991, when two of its reporters were able to maintain a live phone link from a downtown Baghdad hotel during the initial U.S. bombing of the Iraqi capital. Even Iraq's military leaders watched the channel to get the American point of view. CNN's ratings soared—from 930,000 U.S. households before the crisis to as many as ten million homes after the war began. About two hundred local broadcast stations with CNN agreements, including many network affiliates that ordinarily carried regular network coverage, switched to its crisis coverage. (Many of these local stations had already been carrying CNN during the night, when the networks did not offer news to affiliates.) Affecting more than network news, CNN's late-evening reports often made morning newspaper accounts obsolete because the newspapers had deadlines the previous evening.

Before Turner launched CNN in 1980 and well before the meteoric rise of the Internet, there were basically two major news cycles during a given day: in the morning, when many people read the day's newspaper or tuned in to a radio or TV news show; and in the evening, when people listened to the radio on the way home from work or watched the evening news on TV. Most industry experts thought CNN would

● CNN anchor Aaron Brown delivers the news from the cable network's headquarters in Atlanta, Georgia.

fail because they didn't believe most viewers wanted access to a twenty-four-hour news station.

Although economic loss characterized CNN's first five years, Turner eventually proved that his formula for delivering the news had some distinct advantages over the offerings of the broadcast networks. First, CNN emphasized the news itself and created a reporting style that refused to transform news anchors into celebrities. Second, unlike network news departments, which had to edit and condense the day's news into a handful of stories for a half-hour show, the 24-hour format enabled CNN to deliver more timely news in greater detail, often offering live, unedited coverage of news conferences, press briefings, and special events. Third, CNN mastered continuous coverage of breaking news events such as natural disasters, the 1989 student uprising in Beijing, and the 1991 Persian Gulf War. Liberated from the rigid program scheduling of the broadcast networks, viewers no longer had to wait for the revered evening network news to find a version of what was happening in the world.

CNN has also made a big impact on international news coverage, a topic most networks devote little time to. While the networks were cutting costs by closing foreign news operations in the 1980s and 1990s, CNN was opening them. Although CNN had started to back away from its international focus by 2000, it was still the only U.S. news network with correspondents in Afghanistan when terrorist attacks struck the United States on September 11, 2001. Today, CNN appears in more than 212 countries and territories around the globe; more than one billion people have access to a CNN service. In fact, CNN's growing presence in Europe expedited the development of a rival news service, EuroNews, in 1992. A consortium of eleven state-owned European TV groups, EuroNews emerged for cultural as well as economic reasons. One of its chief executives argued that "CNN is an American channel, an American point of view. The point of EuroNews is to give the viewer back his memories."[6] Though Turner's CNN brought the world its first 24-hour TV news service, it continues to reflect American viewpoints and values.

The success of CNN proved that there is both a need and a lucrative market for 24-hour news. Spawning a host of competitors in the United States and worldwide, CNN now battles for viewers with other 24-hour news providers, such as MSNBC, CNBC, Fox News Channel, EuroNews, Sky Broadcasting, and countless Web sites. But the legacy of CNN remains, and what was first dismissed as a silly idea is now considered a major force in the Information Age.

"I Want My MTV"

The second basic cable service to dramatically change the world's cultural landscape is MTV (the Music Television Network), launched by Warner Communications in 1981 and purchased by Viacom in 1985. Now a highly profitable subsidiary of the merger that joined Paramount and Viacom in 1994, MTV and its global offspring—including MTV Asia (including MTV Mandarin, MTV Southeast Asia, and MTV India), MTV Europe, MTV Brazil, MTV Japan, MTV Latin America, MTV Russia, and MTV Australia—reach about 400 million homes worldwide. When Poland became free of Soviet control in the late 1980s, its national television operation immediately began broadcasting MTV. By the late 1990s, more than a quarter of MTV's revenue came from international sources.

Although today MTV exerts a powerful influence on global culture, it was slow to develop in at least one significant way. In its formative years, MTV gave little airtime to African American artists. This history recalls the 1950s and the problems black rock and rollers faced in getting mainstream radio play. In the early 1980s, however, MTV's reluctance to play music videos by black artists was related not to racial tensions but to the economics of the cable system. At that time, most cable companies were operating primarily in affluent white communities in U.S. suburbs. These were the areas that could most easily afford cable. Because rock had been dominated by white male groups throughout the 1970s, MTV determined that white suburban teens probably wanted to see similar groups in their music videos. It took Michael Jackson's *Thriller* album in 1982 to break down music video's early color barrier. The album's large crossover appeal, coupled with the expansion of cable into more urban areas, opened the door to far more diverse videos. With hip-hop's rise in popularity throughout the 1980s and 1990s among both black and white audiences, MTV began to add more rap, soul, and R&B videos to the rotation, as well as programs like *Yo!* and *Jams Countdown*. Through its daily programming, MTV helped sell African American hip-hop culture—with its rap beats, baggy clothes, urban sensibility, and street language—to suburban America and the world at large.

Throughout the 1980s, MTV sought more and more control over music-video distribution and exhibition, employing two monopoly tactics to ensure dominance. First, MTV paid record companies for exclusive rights to the most popular music videos (for periods ranging from thirty days to one year), thereby preventing access by other music-video services. Although this was a form of payola, federal laws prohibiting this practice applied only to broadcasting, not to cable. According to *Billboard* magazine, MTV paid CBS Records $8 million in 1984, covering CBS's total music-video production costs for a two-year period. During the mid-1980s, MTV also signed exclusive deals with RCA Records, MCA, Geffen, Warner Music, Atlantic, PolyGram, and Capitol Records.[7]

Second, MTV signed agreements with the major cable companies to ensure that it would become the music-video network in all the main cable markets. Those cable companies with limited channel capacity were often reluctant to carry more than one music channel. Competing services, like Ted Turner's attempted music-video channel in 1984, were quickly countered by MTV's launch of VH1, which was geared toward the baby-boom generation and the parents of the MTV crowd. Within a month, MTV then bought out Turner's music-video channel; it also began to impose

● Fans of MTV's popular afternoon program *Total Request Live* cheer outside the network's studios in New York City. *TRL* features the most requested music videos, as well as interviews and live performances.

fees on cable companies if they refused to carry the new MTV–VH1 package. Late in the 1980s, a would-be competitor called Hit Video USA, trying to compete with MTV, charged that exclusive contracts constituted an MTV monopoly over music-video distribution and exhibition. The case was settled out of court, and by the late 1990s, MTV remained the only major player in rock videos.

Other countries and companies have tried to challenge MTV's dominance. To date, Canada's MuchMusic channel represents MTV's toughest competitor, due in large part to Canada's strict regulations that blocked MTV's access to many of the country's cable systems. MuchMusic, and its VH1-like counterpart, MuchMoreMusic, began offering service in the United States in 1994; by 2003, MuchMusic USA had twenty-seven million cable and DBS subscribers.

The major recording labels, spending as much as $50 million a year to produce videos in the 1990s, have grown dependent on MTV's power to certify a hit recording. These companies have also criticized the small group of MTV executives who wade through the hundreds of new videos released each week and judge which 10 to 15 percent are fit for MTV play. The recording companies want to see more of their products on MTV's regular music rotation, which usually accommodates about sixty recordings per week.

MTV began to stray from a rotation of music videos in the early 1990s to incorporate more original programming, including the reality-based soap opera *The Real World,* the cartoon *Beavis and Butt-head,* and the dating show *Singled Out*. The shift was an effort to provide advertisers with more regular audiences during specific viewing times, but it ended up infuriating record labels and many MTV viewers by further narrowing the channel's video playlists. By the end of the 1990s, the cable channel was attempting to put the music back into MTV by developing new programming that organized video airplay around artist promotion, band biographies, and fan interviews. For example, *Total Request Live* (TRL) features music videos requested by the young viewing audience via telephone and MTV's online site. The show's host, Carson Daly, has become a teen idol, as popular as the artists he introduces from his studio overlooking New York's Times Square. The MTV Music Video Awards have also become a significant MTV staple, rivaling the Grammy Awards as a television event. The retooling, along with an interactive Web site that allows users to sample videos online, join chat rooms, and submit comments to be read on the air, lifted ratings and reenergized the cable channel. MTV also created MTV2, a music video–only channel, as an additional response to its critics. By 2003, MTV2 had about thirty-seven million subscribers, mostly through direct broadcast satellite services.

As a subsidiary of Viacom, one of the world's largest media conglomerates, MTV actually draws more fire for its cultural than for its economic impact. Many critics worry that its influence has eroded local culture-specific traits among the world's young people and has substituted an overabundance of U.S. culture in its place. Others argue that MTV has contributed to the decline of conversation and civil discourse through its often sexually suggestive and rapid-fire style. Defenders of the network, however, point out that MTV and cable have created a global village, giving the world a common language. They also applaud a variety of MTV's special programs on issues ranging from drug addiction to racism and social activism. The visual style of MTV—from shaky camera footage and quick cuts to bright colors and dazzling visual innovations—has also had, and continues to have, an influence on the media landscape. Touching everything from movies to TV drama and commercials, the MTV style is one that constantly breaks rules and establishes new conventions. Besides turning to MTV for visual inspiration, Hollywood now looks to the channel as a

> ❝ MTV — Music Television. You may think of it as the channel that rattles your china . . . and hypnotizes your children, but what you may want to know is that MTV is responsible for a complete revolution in the music business. ❞
>
> –Diane Sawyer, *Primetime Live,* 1990

farm league of sorts for its hot new directors; indeed, a well-produced music video is considered an ideal audition reel. For many critics, however, MTV has become a virus, with its ceaseless succession of disconnected three-minute mini-musicals and compressed narratives infecting most major sound and visual media with plenty of style but little substance.

Beyond the world of music, one of MTV's major programming innovations has been the Nickelodeon channel. Tom Freston, chairman of Viacom's MTV Group, says Nickelodeon provides "as wide a variety of television for children as exists anywhere." Freston believes that Nickelodeon has changed the way children and teens think about television: "It's interesting—if you talk to kids who are nine years old, they don't see CBS, NBC, and ABC as being the big places. And that generation is going to grow up a generation in whose mind there's more parity between cable networks and broadcast networks."[8] In an era in which the major networks abandoned children's programming—except for cartoons—because they weren't lucrative enough, competitors such as PBS and Nickelodeon have tried to fill the gap. As Nickelodeon and MTV kids reach adulthood, they no longer view broadcast programs as superior to cable.

● MTV's biggest competitor is the Toronto-based MuchMusic music video channel. It features Canadian acts such as Barenaked Ladies, The Tragically Hip, and rapper Choclair, but it also presents south-of-the-border groups from the United States and elsewhere. Like MTV, MuchMusic has an annual awards program called the Juno Awards.

❝ **Sometimes you feel like you're sort of sitting in on a frat house party.** ❞
–NPR's Brian Naylor, about ESPN's *SportsCenter*, 2002

Premium Cable Services

Besides basic programming, cable offers a wide range of special channels, known as **premium channels**, and other services. These include movie channels, such as HBO and Showtime; pay-per-view (PPV) programs; and interactive (two-way) services that enable consumers to use their televisions to bank, shop, play games, and access the Internet. Subscribers to such services pay extra fees in addition to the fee for basic cable. In the early days of cable, there was only a single monthly charge; but with HBO providing movies, a new source of revenue—the premium, or deluxe, tier—was added to the subscription mix. In fact, luring customers to premium channels has plenty of incentives for cable companies: The cost to them is $4 to $6 per month per subscriber to carry a premium channel, but they then charge customers $10 or more per month and reap a nice profit.

The HBO Alternative

By far the oldest and most influential premium channel is Home Box Office (HBO), a subsidiary of AOL Time Warner, one of the nation's largest owners of cable companies. Although HBO reaches less than one-third the audience of a popular basic channel, it has remained the dominant premium channel, selling monthly subscriptions to more than 25 million homes by 2003. HBO and Cinemax, the second-highest rated premium channel, bring a combined total of about 38 million premium subscribers to parent corporation AOL Time Warner. Competing premium channels include Liberty Media's Encore, STARZ!, and MOVIEplex channels, which combined had 38 million subscribers in 2003; and Viacom's Showtime, the Movie Channel, and Flix, which had 31.3 million combined subscribers. New premium film channels such as the Sundance Channel (operated by Showtime and owned by actor Robert Redford, Universal Studios, and Showtime) and the Independent Film Channel emerged with the growing market of independent films in the mid-1990s.

The movie business initially feared that HBO would be a detriment to film attendance in theaters. Eventually, though, HBO and the other premium channels brought a lucrative source of income to the movie studios, which earn roughly a 15 percent share of premium cable's profits. With premium cable channels locking up the rights to feature-length movies after their initial theater runs, film companies recognized that they could recoup losses from a weak theater run by extending a film's life. This could be done not just via television or neighborhood second-run theaters but through lucrative arrangements with premium cable. Today, HBO runs more than ninety theatrical motion pictures a month.

In the early 1980s, when there was little competition, HBO dictated to movie studios which films it wanted and how much it was willing to pay. HBO and other premium channels ran into trouble, however, as videotapes became the preferred method of viewing movies after their theater runs. Both VCRs and PPV (pay-per-view) options brought competition to the movie channels. In the mid-1980s, film studios started releasing movies to PPV and to video stores before offering them to movie channels. The new competition forced the movie channels to expand their services. HBO, for example, began developing its own programming—from children's shows like *Fraggle Rock* to comedies like the *Larry Sanders Show,* an Emmy-winning satire of late-night talk shows. HBO's successes in original programming

● *The Sopranos,* starring James Gandolfini (center), and *Sex and the City,* starring Sarah Jessica Parker and Chris Noth, lead a group of critically acclaimed original series on HBO. Because these programs are not shown on broadcast networks, their stories are not subject to restrictions on sex, violence, or language.

continue today with critical praise for programs like *The Sopranos, Six Feet Under,* and *Sex and the City.*

What film studios clearly did not like was HBO's production of its own feature-length films. In 1982, HBO entered into an arrangement with CBS and Columbia Pictures (later bought by Sony) to form a new production house, TriStar Pictures. Many in the movie industry charged that HBO's movie productions constituted vertical integration, with involvement in production, distribution, and exhibition. They argued that when Time Inc. (before its merger with Warner) began making movies through HBO and TriStar, the media conglomerate was permitted to do something that film studios could not do. A Supreme Court decision in 1948 had broken up the film industry's vertical structure by forcing the major studios to sell their theaters, the exhibition part of their operations. Time Inc., on the other hand, was the second-largest owner of cable systems—the movie studio equivalent of owning theaters. Because so many cable companies and services existed, though, the government did not seriously challenge HBO's role in movie production.

Pay-per-View, Video-on-Demand, and Interactive Cable

Pay-per-view services, which began in 1985, allow customers to select a particular movie for a onetime $3 or $4 charge, payable to the local cable company, or $25 to $60 for a special onetime event, such as a championship boxing match, a professional wrestling event, or a rock concert. Approximately forty-eight million of the country's seventy million cable subscribers have PPV capacity. Generally, the movie studios make a hefty profit from PPV, asking as much as 50 percent of what the PPV and cable companies earn from subscribers who view the movies. The studios' cut from PPV is substantially higher than their share from home-movie rentals (about 20 percent) and premium movie channels (about 15 percent). In the 1990s, studios were so keen on the potential profits from PPV that they even started buying shares of PPV companies, but by the end of the decade it had become clear that consumers still preferred renting videos over viewing PPV movies. This is because video stores can typically release movies about a month and a half before pay-per-view services get a chance to offer them. Even though the PPV market still generates about $1.5 billion a year with movies, adult content, and special sporting events, it is unclear how long PPV will be around. By 2003, iN DEMAND (formerly Viewer's Choice) was the nation's largest PPV provider, reaching twenty-eight million households.

Unlike the limited schedules and titles of traditional cable PPV, **video-on-demand** services enable digital cable customers to select from hundreds of titles at roughly $4 per movie and download any of them for immediate viewing with VCR-like functionality. PPV company iN DEMAND is also the leading provider of video-on-demand (VOD) services, with an estimated 8.8 million active subscribers by 2003. In addition, premium cable channels such as HBO, Cinemax, Showtime, and The Movie Channel have begun to release their program libraries through on-demand channels. The rapid growth of VOD services is moving video fans closer to the day when ordering a movie off of television becomes better than driving to the local video store. (See "Tracking Technology: Video-on-Demand on the Cusp of Broad Release" on page 209.)

Another type of cable service features **interactive**, or two-way, **channels**. When equipped with two-way technology, such systems enable users to send signals upstream or back to the headend. (Most systems are one-way and can send signals only downstream to subscribers' homes.) Interactive cable can connect households to their banks, where customers can pay bills or transfer money. Some cable services also permit police burglary units and fire stations to monitor homes and apartments. Like the bulk of cable programming, the most frequent type of two-way serv-

Video-on-Demand on the Cusp of Broad Release

For years, video-on-demand has been a couch potato's dream. By pushing a few buttons on the remote control, a viewer would be able to order a movie and then sit back and watch as it unfolded immediately on the screen, pausing, rewinding or fast-forwarding at will. Movie-watching would be on the schedule set by the viewer, not the broadcaster or cable company. No need even to get up from the couch to insert a tape or DVD.

That has been the promise, and the technology to provide video-on-demand to television sets is well established. But the service is still very much in its infancy, and economic factors are largely to blame.

Viewers need better programming—like recent popular movies—before they will flock to video-on-demand. Studios need better security against video piracy before supplying their most popular movies, but quality encryption is costly and raises the price of the electronic components and set-top boxes that viewers need. And cable companies need more viewers to offset the expense of improving the technology for encryption, compression, and set-top boxes.

"I've seen various business models for V.O.D. and the numbers just don't add up, so no one is doing it in a large-scale way," said Bill Rosenblatt, president of GiantSteps/Media Technology Strategies, a New York consulting company.

There are currently four million cable customers who use video-on-demand, and another three million are expected to sign up by the end of the year, said Joe Boyle, vice president for corporate communications of iN DEMAND, a company that distributes content to cable operators. But there are about seventy million households with cable television in the United States, and analysts estimate that widespread adoption of video-on-demand by cable companies will take anywhere from three to ten years.

If companies can make it work, the projected market for first-run movies alone is about $640 million by 2006, according to Jupiter Research. So cable companies like AT&T Broadband, Comcast, Charter Communications, Time Warner Cable, Cox Communications, and Cablevision Systems are slowly testing or deploying video-on-demand as part of their digital cable services in some parts of the country.

Video-on-demand makes use of a server computer that contains video files and software to let more than one viewer have access to the video at a time. One model, the n4x made by nCube, a major provider of video-on-demand services, allows up to 53,000 viewers simultaneous access to the same movie or other video content. The video is sent by cable or fiber-optic connection from the servers to a set-top box connected to the home television.

Video files are compressed to take up less space and transfer faster. Currently, video is compressed according to MPEG-2 standards, although efforts are being made to advance to the MPEG-4 standard, which can be more than ten times as efficient.

The Internet is another conduit for video-on-demand, streaming delivery of television shows, music videos, and other programming to home computers. (On-demand delivery to hand-held devices, as well as via satellite or airwaves, is in the more distant future.) There are a number of relatively new video-on-demand sites like Intertainer, CinemaNow, and the forthcoming Movielink, an Internet video-on-demand venture from five major movie studios. But analysts say most viewers are unlikely to want to watch full-length movies on their computers or hand-helds. "Consumers are more likely to watch short-form content," said Lydia Loizides, a Jupiter Research senior analyst.

Instead of streaming, a cheaper and faster option is downloading video files to users' hard drives. But downloading also increases the potential that the file will be copied—a frightening prospect for movie studios. Video files can be encrypted, but encryption schemes can be overcome. "There is no such thing as hackproof encryption technology," Mr. Rosenblatt said. "The question is which type causes the least amount of damage once it is hacked."

Whether it is delivered to a television set, a computer or a palmtop, video-on-demand will depend on the quality of the content—beyond first-run movies—to be successful. The way that content is marketed will be important, too.

"Current fare is what drives traffic, so the question then becomes how to refresh old shows and movies," said T. S. Kelly, an analyst with Nielsen/NetRatings. "You need a middle ground between cable's airing movies in an exclusive window and the Internet's making information available anytime. There has to be significant marketing and promotion to make all this old programming an event. Otherwise it becomes just a dusty old library."

Source: Susan Karlin, "How It Works: Video-on-Demand Is Ready, But the Market Is Not," *New York Times,* October 10, 2002, p. G8.

ice involves entertainment. In 1991, Interactive Network began offering video games to cable consumers, including play-along versions of *Wheel of Fortune* and *Jeopardy*. It also provided services that allowed viewers to guess the next play during a football game or the identity of the villain in *Murder, She Wrote*. The limiting factor for interactive services, though, is bandwidth. Because interactive services require more space to send two-way information on cable (in contrast to the one-way communication of regular cable TV channels), most cable operators are unwilling to offer this feature at the expense of lucrative one-way channels.

Cable Music Services

In addition to movies and videos on request, many cable systems now offer CD-quality premium audio services. Routed through a consumer's stereo equipment, **cable music** companies like Music Choice and DMX Music provide 24-hour music channels uninterrupted by ads. Originally known as Digital Cable Radio in the 1980s, Music Choice was the first digital audio service. It featured separate audio channels playing all kinds of prepackaged musical styles ready for home audiotaping or as background music for business environments; by 2003, Music Choice had more than twenty-five million customers and offered fifty-four music channels, ranging from reggae to gospel. Such satellite-delivered channels are another example of media convergence; they link cable, sound recordings, and home-stereo units for a monthly fee of about $9, less than the price of a new CD.

For the home market, audio developments such as live-streaming Internet radio stations and free downloadable digital music files, as well as satellite radio services like Sirius and XM, threatened premium cable music services. But digital cable and direct broadcast satellite television, with their large channel capacity, helped to reinvigorate cable music services, as they were frequently bundled with digital programming packages.

Direct Broadcast Satellites: Cable without Wires

Because of its dependence on communication satellites, cable TV has always been on the cutting edge of technological developments. Now many of those advances are posing an economic threat to cable in the same ways that cable challenged traditional broadcasting in the 1970s. Of all the emerging technologies, including the Internet, **direct broadcast satellites (DBS)** present the biggest challenge to the existing cable and television industries.

The earliest earth-station antennas, or dishes—set up in the mid-1970s to receive cable programming—were large, measuring twenty to forty feet in diameter, and expensive (with FCC license fees adding to their high cost). From the beginning, however, engineers worked to reduce the size and cost of the receiving dishes in order to develop a consumer model. In regions and countries with rugged terrain, the installation of cable wiring was not always easy or possible.

To protect the fledgling cable business throughout the 1970s and 1980s, the FCC restricted the development of DBS companies, which get their programming from the same satellite channels (such as CNN, MTV, ESPN, and HBO) that supply the regular cable industry. In the United States, rural residents bypassed FCC restrictions by investing in seven- to ten-foot receiving dishes and downlinking, for free, the same channels that cable companies were supplying to wired communities. These home-satellite dishes, like early cable systems, appeared mostly in sprawling but sparsely populated areas that were too costly for cable companies to wire. Receiving dishes, visible from many interstate highways, began springing up on farms by the late 1970s. Initially, households could pick up channels once they had invested $2,000 to $3,000 in a large receiving dish. Not surprisingly, satellite programmers launched a flurry of legal challenges against farmers and small-town residents who were receiving their signals. Rural communities countered that they had the rights to the airspace above their own property; the satellite firms contended that their signals were being stolen. With the law being unclear, a number of cable channels began scrambling their signals. As a result, most satellite users had to buy or rent descramblers and subscribe to services, as cable customers did.

From home satellites, the DBS business developed. Signal scrambling spawned companies that provided both receiving dishes and satellite program services for a monthly fee. In 1978, Japanese companies, which had been experimenting with "wireless cable" alternatives for a number of years, launched the first DBS system in Florida. With gradual improvements in satellite technology, the diameters of satellite receiving dishes decreased from more than twenty feet to three feet in a few years. By 1995, consumers could order satellite dishes the size of a large pizza.

With the emergence of cable as a lucrative industry, the last FCC and technical obstacles gradually fell away, and full-blown DBS services began in 1994. Initially, the FCC authorized a French company, Thomson Consumer Electronics, which had acquired the RCA brand name from General Electric, to sell DBS dishes. After Thomson/RCA sold one million units, the FCC permitted Sony to enter the U.S. DBS market. Gradually, the commission let more licensees into the DBS game. Early rapid sales of Thomson/RCA's DBS systems ranked it among the fastest-starting technologies in media history.

Today, the two leading DBS companies—DirecTV and EchoStar (known as the DISH Network)—offer consumers most of the channels and tiers of service that cable companies carry, often at a slightly lower monthly cost (plus the initial investment of $0 to $300 for purchasing and installing the small-dish antenna system). In addition, DBS systems carry between 350 and 500 basic, premium, and pay-per-view channels, which can be purchased by customers in various packages. Thus DBS presents far more options than what is available on the three or four PPV movie channels offered on most conventional cable systems, which are limited by channel capacity. Buoyed by high consumer interest and competing in large cities as well as rural areas, DBS firms are challenging the long-standing monopoly status of most cable systems, offering distinct advantages—and disadvantages—compared with cable.

On the upside, DBS's digital technology is superior to standard cable and broadcast signals, providing digital-quality pictures and CD-quality sound. Another big drawing card for DBS is the ability to offer sports packages that give subscribers nationwide access to all the games of professional sports leagues—including football, baseball, soccer, and men's and women's basketball—that aren't carried locally on broadcast networks or basic cable channels.

On the downside, along with the initial start-up cost for consumers, DBS systems deliver one satellite signal at a time and do not allow consumers to tape a program on a VCR while they watch another show, or even to tune a second TV to another DBS channel. Another disadvantage of DBS systems was remedied in 1999, when Congress passed legislation allowing DBS to carry local broadcast channels. Until that time, DBS did not pick up an area's local broadcast signals, which were not uplinked to satellites. This meant that most subscribers had to use a local cable company, an outside TV antenna, or rabbit-ear antennas on their TV set to get the local PBS, independent, and broadcast network programming. The gradual addition of local broadcast signals to DBS's offerings across the United States since then has been a great catalyst for new DBS subscribers, increasing the number of DBS house-

Table 6.1 Top 10 U.S. Cable Operators, 2002

Rank	Company	Headquarters	Subscribers
1	Comcast Corp.	Philadelphia, Pa.	21,753,300
2	Time Warner Cable	Stamford, Conn.	12,847,000
3	Charter Communications	St. Louis, Mo.	6,783,900
4	Cox Communications	Atlanta, Ga.	6,250,000
5	Adelphia Communications	Coudersport, Pa.	5,845,900
6	Cablevision Systems Corporation	Bethpage, N.Y.	2,991,000
7	Mediacom LLC	Middletown, N.Y.	1,585,000
8	Insight Communications	New York, N.Y.	1,291,100
9	Cable One	Phoenix, Ariz.	731,700
10	RCN Corporation	Princeton, N.J.	506,700

Source: National Cable Television Association, <www.ncta.com>, June 30, 2002.

holds to more than seventeen million. DirecTV, the top DBS company, holds about 60 percent of the market, with ten million customers; EchoStar, at No. 2, has seven million subscribers, about 40 percent of the market. DBS's threat to cable has increased in the past few years, particularly with its ability to offer local broadcast signals via satellite. By 2001, about 70 percent of new DBS subscribers had access to cable but were choosing DBS.[9] Yet cable is responding, using digital compression technology to build systems that carry up to 500 channels, too. Cable's addition of high-speed Internet connections is also an advantage over DBS. But even here, DBS has responded with its own satellite-based broadband Internet connections, with comparable connection speeds and pricing.

Ownership and Business Issues in Cable

Although there are more than ten thousand cable systems in the United States, most of these systems are controlled by **multiple-system operators (MSOs)**, a shrinking number of large corporations that each owns many cable systems. Consolidation has happened quickly. For example, by 1998, the Top 12 MSOs controlled the lines into 70 percent of all households wired for cable. By 2002, the Top 10 MSOs served about 85 percent of all U.S. cable subscribers.[10] (See Table 6.1.) Once again, the economic trend points to an industry moving toward oligopoly, with a handful of megamedia firms controlling programming for future generations. Like the Internet, however, cable and DBS hold the promise of offering more specialized services on which the diverse needs of individuals and communities might be met.

Comcast and AOL Time Warner—The Major Players

For much of the 1980s and 1990s, two large companies—TCI (Tele-Communications, Inc.) and Time Warner Cable—dominated the acquisition of smaller cable companies and the accumulation of cable subscribers. But, by the late 1990s, cable became a coveted investment, not so much for its ability to carry television programming but for its infrastructure of households connected with high-bandwidth wires.

With increasing competition and declining long-distance revenues, AT&T, the nation's leading long-distance phone company, developed a new business plan in the 1990s to buy its way into the lucrative emerging broadband cable business. In 1998, AT&T purchased TCI, the leading cable MSO at the time with 13.1 million households, and renamed the cable division AT&T Broadband & Internet Services (BIS). In 2000, AT&T struck again, acquiring MediaOne, the third-largest cable firm, and boosting its direct subscriber base to 16 million.[11]

Ultimately, AT&T's appetite for acquisitions gave it a bad case of debt, and its stock lost half of its value in 2000. In late 2000, AT&T made a surprise announcement of its intention to voluntarily break the company into four components—consumer long distance, business services, wireless, and broadband services—by 2002. AT&T also spun off its cable programming subsidiary, Liberty Media. In late 2001, only three years after it ventured into the cable and broadband industry, AT&T got out of the business by merging its cable division in a $72 billion deal with Comcast, then the third-largest MSO. The new Comcast Corp. company became the instant cable industry behemoth, serving more than twenty-two million households—almost twice as many as the next largest MSO. Comcast's properties also include interests in QVC, E! Entertainment, and the Golf Channel.

Time Warner Cable, the second-largest MSO, is a division of the world's largest media company, Time Warner, a company that became even larger when it merged with America Online (the nation's largest Internet service provider) in 2000. Time Warner had 1.9 million subscribers in 1982. In 1995, when Time Warner bought Cablevision Industries—the eighth-largest MSO—it controlled cable circuits in 11.7 million homes. In 2003, AOL Time Warner had about 12.8 million cable subscribers.

Beyond its cable subscriber base, AOL Time Warner is also a major provider of programming services. In 1995, Time Warner buoyed its position as the world's

● The message televised on Time Warner Cable on May 2, 2000, the day after Disney-owned ABC pulled its programming off the cable network because of a contract dispute.

A Democracy of Channels?

For a new basic cable programming service to have a chance of financial viability, it needs to reach at least 50 percent of the cable audience. But what companies have the opportunity to create a successful cable channel?

Description. Take note of the top 20 cable networks, ranked by number of subscribers (see Figure 6.4 and also the Web site for the National Cable Television Association <http://www.ncta.com>).

Analysis. Compare ownership among the top channels. There should be clear patterns. For example, AOL Time Warner owns TBS, TNT, and CNN, among several other cable channels.

Interpretation. What do the patterns mean? As noted on page 194, cable television programming companies have leveraged retransmission consent regulations to get cable systems to adopt their new channel offerings. Thus, Disney owns not only ESPN but also highly rated ESPN2, ESPN News, and ESPN Classic. Other media corporations have been able to purchase larger shares of the cable audience. For example, Viacom owns MTV Networks (which operates MTV, Nickelodeon/Nick at Nite, VH1, and other channels) and gained TNN and CMT through its acquisition of CBS.

Evaluation. Does the fact that a handful of large media corporations control many of cable's most popular channels reduce cable's promise of a multiplicity of channels representing a wide range of voices? Are channels such as CNBC and MSNBC just an extension of NBC? Or does ownership not matter; do all of the top cable channels serve as independent, unique voices? How is the quality of programming affected?

largest media corporation by offering $6.5 billion to acquire Turner Broadcasting, which included superstation WTBS, CNN, Headline News, TNT, and CNN Radio. Although some FCC staffers raised concerns about sanctioning the extended economic power of Time Warner, the commission formally approved the deal in the fall of 1996. AOL Time Warner—with its magazine, movie, publishing, television, and music divisions—also produces content for its cable services. In addition to acquiring Turner and starting the WB television network, AOL Time Warner is the parent company of Cinemax and HBO, and it holds interests in Comedy Central and Court TV.

Three other cable companies count themselves among the major MSOs. Charter Communications grew quickly after its 1999 acquisition by multibillionaire investor Paul Allen, cofounder of Microsoft. Cox Communications, based in Atlanta, is part of the Cox Enterprises media empire, which has extensive interests in newspapers, television and radio stations, and automobile auctions across the country. Finally, Adelphia is headquartered in small-town Coudersport, Pennsylvania, where its first cable operation started in 1952. But in 2002, Adelphia's future was in doubt. The company filed for bankruptcy, as its major shareholders, the Rigas family, were charged on several felony counts and accused of borrowing more than $2.3 billion off the books.

A number of cable critics worry that the trend toward fewer owners will limit the number of viewpoints, options, and innovations available on cable. (See "Applied Critical Process: A Democracy of Channels?" above.) The response from the cable industry is that given the tremendous capital investment it takes to run cable, DBS, and other media enterprises, media conglomerates are necessary to buy up struggling companies and keep them afloat. This argument suggests that without today's MSOs, many smaller cable ventures in programming would not be possible.

Concerns have surfaced, though, that cable and telephone services will merge into giant communications overlords, fixing prices without the benefit of competition. These concerns raise an important question: In an economic climate in which fewer owners control the circulation of communication, what happens to new ideas or controversial views that may not always be profitable to circulate? Will crushing debt and declining stocks be enough to check these companies?

There is already evidence that large MSOs can wield their monopoly power unfairly. In May 2000, a business dispute between Disney and Time Warner erupted into a public spectacle as Time Warner dropped the ABC television network from 3.4 million of its cable customers in New York, Houston, Raleigh, and elsewhere for more than thirty hours. The conflict was over the renewal of the retransmission consent agreement for ABC on many Time Warner cable systems. Disney proposed that Time Warner expand carriage of existing channels and introduce its new SoapNet and Toon Disney channels, among other things, in return for allowing Time Warner to carry ABC on its cable systems. Talks broke down, Time Warner refused to grant Disney a contract extension, and Time Warner customers in affected areas who were trying to watch shows like *Who Wants to Be a Millionaire* saw only blue screens with messages such as: "Disney has taken ABC away from you." Time Warner was later found to be in violation of FCC rules, and it ultimately added SoapNet and Toon Disney to its digital channel lineup in New York.

The Business of Cable

In 1970, there were about 2,500 small cable systems operating in the United States; by 2003, slightly less than 10,000 systems were running. In 1976, there were two basic satellite-delivered services, two premium services, and no such thing as pay-per-view. Twenty years later, nearly 150 basic channels were competing for channel space with 43 premium services and 9 PPV companies. Since 1980, basic cable rates have grown fivefold, rising from about $/ per month to about $37. Monthly prices for premium services, however, have essentially remained the same—less than $9 a month per channel in 1980, and only a dollar or two more in 2003. By 2003, total revenues from cable rivaled those of broadcasting: $48 billion a year.

The cable industry employed about 23,000 people in 1978 and more than 130,000 by 2003. The cable workforce serves the production, distribution, and exhibition sectors of the industry. The production end includes the hundreds of providers who either make original programs or purchase older TV programming for national and global distribution. At the local level, production also includes staffers, volunteers, and student interns who create programming on access channels. The distribution sector includes the delivery systems and PPV services that transmit programming via satellite, then via coaxial or fiber-optic cable. The exhibition branch of the industry encompasses thousands of local cable systems, which require programming, sales, technical, and administrative divisions to operate.

Alternative Voices

After suffering through years of rising rates and limited expansion of service, some of the smallest cities in America have decided to challenge the private monopolies of cable giants by building competing, publicly owned cable systems. So far, the municipally owned cable systems number only in the hundreds and can be found in places like Glasgow, Kentucky; Lebanon, Ohio; Cedar Falls, Iowa; and Newnan, Georgia. In most cases, they're operated by the community-owned, nonprofit electric utilities. There are more than two thousand such municipal utilities across the United States, serving about 14 percent of Americans and creating the potential for more municipal utilities to expand into communications services. The municipal operations are less expensive for cable subscribers, too, with monthly cable rates averaging only $24.35, compared to the $36.99 average monthly price for all cable systems.[12]

Cities with public cable systems argue that with no competition, the private cable corporations have been slow to replace older coaxial cables with high-speed fiber-optic networks. Moreover, the lower population densities of small towns and rural areas mean that these towns are often the last places to get innovative cable services. By building municipal cable systems, these cities are making sure that they won't be the last stop on the information highway.

The first town to take on an existing private cable provider was Glasgow, Kentucky, which built its own municipal cable system in 1989. The town of fourteen thousand now has seven thousand municipal cable customers. William J. Ray, the town's Electric Plant Board superintendent and the visionary behind the municipal communications service, argues that this is not a new idea:

> Cities have long been turning a limited number of formerly private businesses into public-works projects. This happens only when the people making up a local government believe that the service has become so essential to the citizens that it is better if it is operated by the government. In colonial America, it was all about drinking water. . . . In the twentieth century, the issue was electric power and natural gas service. Now, we are facing the same transformation in broadband networks.[13]

For the customer, competition in the local cable market is beneficial. For example, in 1994 in Cedar Falls, Iowa, voters approved the creation of a new municipal broadband fiber-optic cable network, capable of carrying cable and Internet service. With the new challenges of competition, commercial provider TCI then decided to upgrade its own cable system in the city. The benefits of competition in Cedar Falls angered the nearby residents of Waterloo, Iowa, who were served only by TCI. In Waterloo, TCI offered only thirty-six channels for the same monthly fee that brought seventy-six channels to TCI customers in Cedar Falls. Only by threatening to build their own municipal cable system did Waterloo city officials get TCI to rebuild the Waterloo cable system and add more channels.

Almost a quarter of the country's two thousand municipal utilities plan to offer cable and high-speed Internet services. How will commercial cable operators fend off this unprecedented competition? William Ray of Glasgow, Kentucky, has the answer: "If cable operators are afraid of cities competing with them, there is a defense that is impregnable—they can charge reasonable rates, offer consummate customer service, improve their product, and conduct their business as if they were a guest that owes their existence to the benevolence of the city that has invited them in."[14]

 ## ★ Cable, DBS, and Implications for Democracy

When cable emerged to challenge traditional broadcasting in the 1970s, expectations were high, not unlike today's expectations for the Internet. When cable communication mushroomed in the 1980s, network supremacy over television ended. Offering more than new competition, cable's increased channel capacity provided the promise of access. With more channels, it was believed that access on cable would create vibrant debates, allowing ordinary citizens a voice via television. Access channels have, in fact, provided some opportunities for citizens to participate in democracy and even create their own programs. But by the late 1990s, major cities like Kansas City decided that public-access channels need not even be a requirement for cable franchises. For the most part, cable and DBS have come to follow the one-way broadcast model: Their operators choose the programming from a few service providers, with little input from citizens and consumers.

Most cable channels have become heavily dependent on recycling old television shows and movies to fill up their program schedules. In some ways, this has been beneficial. Cable, particularly through programming like Nickelodeon's *Nick at Nite* and *TVLand,* has become a repository for TV shows that are passed along from generation to generation. Ultimately, however, except for C-Span, local access channels, and some interactive services, cable still has not developed its potential to become a clear alternative to traditional broadcasting services. In fact, given that the television networks and many leading cable channels are owned by the same media conglomerates, cable has evolved into something of an ancillary service to the networks.

In the broadest sense, the development of cable has always posed a contradiction. On the one hand, cable has dramatically increased the number of channels and offered previously unserved groups the opportunity to address their particular issues on television. On the other hand, cable has undermined the network era during which television worked as a kind of social adhesive, giving most of the population a common bond, a set of shared programs. The concern remains: Does the onslaught of cable and developments such as the Internet create a fragmented culture in which individuals pursue narrow personal agendas at the expense of larger social concerns?

In the coming years, many communities will experience the convergence of computers and modems, satellites, fax machines, and television sets. Such convergence may make us homebound, freeing us from traditional participation in and travel to workplaces and schools. New technologies have the capacity, of course, to simultaneously bring us together in cyberspace and isolate us physically from one another. Another key issue democracies must face is the increasing control of a few giant media corporations over our means of communication: How will we direct cable, DBS, and new technologies to serve social agendas while they continue to meet consumer and business needs? As with the Internet, the gulf between the information-rich and the information-poor remains wide, increasing concerns about who will have access to—and who will be able to afford—cable and other new media technologies.

www.

To create an individualized study plan for Chapter 6, go to the interactive *Media and Culture* Online Study Guide at: bedfordstmartins.com/ mediaculture

REVIEW QUESTIONS

Technology and the Development of Cable

1. What is CATV, and what were its advantages over broadcast television?

2. How did satellite distribution change the cable industry?

Cable Threatens Broadcasting

3. How did cable pose a challenge to broadcasting, and how did the FCC respond to cable's early development?

4. What is the cable franchising process, and how did it work in the 1980s?

5. What were the syndex rules, and why were they repealed?

6. Why aren't cable companies treated more like a utility company and a common carrier?

7. What were the major differences between the cable acts of 1984 and 1992?

8. How did the Telecommunications Act of 1996 change the economic shape and future of the cable industry?

Cable Comes of Age

9. What are the differences between basic cable service and premium services?

10. How have CNN and MTV influenced culture worldwide?

11. How and why did HBO develop? How has HBO threatened the film industry?

12. What is video-on-demand, and how does it differ from pay-per-view services?

Direct Broadcast Satellites: Cable without Wires

13. What is DBS? How much of a threat are its services to the cable industry?

Ownership and Business Issues in Cable

14. Who are the biggest players in the cable business, and what has driven their recently acquired cable empires?

15. What are the three basic divisions in the organization of the cable business?

16. What are the main reasons some municipalities are building their own cable systems?

Cable, DBS, and Implications for Democracy

17. In terms of fostering democracy, what are cable's main advantages over traditional broadcasting?

QUESTIONING THE MEDIA

1. How many cable channels do you watch regularly? What programs do you watch? What attracts you to a certain channel?

2. If you controlled a cable public-access channel in your community, what would be your channel's goal? What could we do to make public-, government-, or educational-access programming more appealing? Should we?

3. Do you think the must-carry rules violate a cable company's First Amendment rights? Why or why not?

4. CNN and MTV have changed our society as well as the global culture. Have these changes been positive or negative? Explain.

5. Do you think DBS will eventually overtake cable in popularity? Why or why not?

6. Some critics argue that citizens no longer participate in traditional neighborhoods and that cable has played a role in fragmenting society, keeping us in our homes. Do you agree or disagree? What has cable done well, and in what ways has it adversely affected society?

SEARCHING THE INTERNET

http://www.ncta.com

The site for the cable industry's major trade association, the National Cable Television Association, details cable history, the latest developments in cable technology, and industry news.

http://www.cablecenter.org

A site funded by the cable industry, offering an excellent history of cable's development in the United States.

http://www.tvinsite.com/broadcastingcable

The online version of *Broadcasting & Cable,* a weekly magazine geared toward executives and managers of the television, radio, and cable industries.

http://www.mtv.com

MTV Online offers a comprehensive database of music videos, show information, music news, tips on where to find local bands, music reviews, and chat rooms.

http://www.cnn.com

One of the most sophisticated sites on the Web, CNN Interactive offers constantly updated news stories as well as news archives, a daily almanac, on-air transcripts, and other services.

http://www.dishnetwork.com

The Web site for EchoStar, one of the largest DBS companies in the United States.

THE CRITICAL PROCESS

In Brief

Working alone or in a group, propose a new cable channel that does two things: (1) It should find a unique market niche, and (2) it should be successful, meaning it should satisfy the demands of the television industry by drawing an audience that appeals to advertisers. Keep in mind that only 10 to 15 percent of new cable channels succeed. Lists of existing and planned cable channels are available online at the National Cable Television Association's Web site at <www.ncta.com>.

Consider the following questions while creating your proposal: What kinds of programs would run each day? What sort of audience would the channel try to reach? Why would this market be attractive to advertisers?

In Depth

Divide the class into groups of four to six. Each group should prepare an editorial for presentation on public-access cable. The editorial should be roughly four to five minutes in length (750–1,000 words) and should address a controversial or important public issue, such as equal access to the information highway, the state of media education, the impact of talk radio and television talk shows, or the advantages of wealth in the legal process.

Description. As a group, draft the editorial. Describe the issue in a compelling manner. Consult with your instructor for topic ideas and writing strategies. Rewrite the final copy of the editorial.

Analysis. Next, divide each group into subgroups of two or three. One subgroup should approach (by phone, mail, or face-to-face meeting) a local cable-access channel and request time to read the editorial. The other subgroup should approach a local commercial television station with the same editorial. Tell the station manager or news director that you would like to get your idea onto the public airwaves. Ask how your request might be accommodated. Note the patterns in how your proposal is received by each medium.

Interpretation. Designate a time for your entire group to meet and write a report about how your editorial was treated by the various media you approached. Address the following questions in your report:

- How easy or difficult was it to get access to traditional broadcasting as opposed to cable? How was your group treated?
- Based on your experience, do broadcast airwaves and cable services "belong" to the public? How democratic is the process of gaining access on cable?

Evaluation. During class, the various groups should share and compare reports and experiences. If you were permitted to cablecast or broadcast your editorial, share it with the class. Because television is the most pervasive medium, how important is it that citizens be able to express their views on significant public topics via cable and television? Are there certain topics that shouldn't be given such editorial airtime on broadcast or cable television? If so, why?

KEY TERMS

movies
and the impact of images

CHAPTER 7

In a June 6, 1977, review, *Box Office* magazine reported on a newly released science-fiction film. "The special effects are superb and can be the biggest draw," the review read. "But don't overlook the other elements . . . *Star Wars* should be a very big success." In retrospect, "a very big success" doesn't come close to measuring the huge impact that *Star Wars* has had on American movies and culture.

As film critic Roger Ebert explained: "*Star Wars* effectively brought to an end the golden era of early-1970s personal filmmaking and focused the industry on big-budget special-effects blockbusters, blasting off a trend we are still living through. . . . In one way or another all the big studios have been trying to make another *Star Wars* ever since."

Not only did *Star Wars* spawn a new blockbuster mentality in Hollywood, but it formed a new primary audience for those blockbusters—teenagers. Repeat attendance and positive buzz among young people made *Star Wars* the most successful movie

of its generation, grossing over $320 million in the United States in its original release and spawning an initial trilogy that included *The Empire Strikes Back* (1980) and *Return of the Jedi* (1983). Including the re-release of the trilogy in 1997, the three films earned a combined $1.3 billion at the box office. The youth-oriented focus of Hollywood begun by *Star Wars* is still evident today, with the largest segment of the U.S. movie audience—the twelve- to twenty-four-year-old age group—accounting for 39 percent of theater attendance.

Another part of the blockbuster mentality created by *Star Wars* and mimicked by other films is the way in which action-packed stories are made into big-budget summer or holiday releases with merchandising tie-ins and high potential for international distribution. George Lucas, the *Star Wars* writer and producer who also created the popular Indiana Jones film series, argues that

selling licensing rights is one of the ways he supports his independent filmmaking. By 1998, the *Star Wars* trilogy had generated an unprecedented $4 billion in merchandising—far more than the box-office revenues—as *Star Wars* images appeared on an astonishing array of products, from Lego's X-Wing fighter kits to Colgate's Darth Vader toothbrushes. Similar merchandising is evident in the *Harry Potter, Lord of the Rings,* and *Spider-Man* movie franchises.

The summer 1999 release of *The Phantom Menace,* the first of three *Star Wars* prequels (the original three films were actually episodes 4, 5, and 6 of a 9-part story), included the now-typical blockbuster characteristics of a summer or winter holiday release date, massive promotion, and lucrative merchandising tie-ins. In fact, prior to its release, people waited in line for weeks to obtain tickets and *The Phantom Menace* had already generated a reported

$1 billion in licensing revenue. It went on to earn $431 million in U.S. ticket sales.

With *The Phantom Menace,* Lucas again broke new ground in the film industry—this time becoming a technical force in the emerging era of digital filmmaking. Several scenes of the movie were not shot on film but on digital video, easing integration with the digital special effects of Lucas's renowned Industrial Light and Magic production house. The digital era in movie distribution also took its first steps when *The Phantom Menace* became the first full-length motion picture from a major studio to use digital electronic projectors at several movie theaters to replace standard film projectors. This change in exhibition technology will eventually move motion pictures away from the physical distribution of bulky and expensive film reels and toward a digital distribution system via satellite or optical disks.

The saga continued with *Star Wars: Episode II—Attack of the Clones,* released in 2002, twenty-five years after the very big success of the original *Star Wars.*

ating back to the late 1800s, American films have had a substantial social and cultural impact on society. Blockbuster movies such as *Star Wars, E.T., Jurassic Park, Titanic, The Sixth Sense,* and *Lord of the Rings* represent what Hollywood has become—America's storyteller. Telling cinematic tales that in 1909 drew us to a nickelodeon theater and last weekend to our local video store, Hollywood movies have long acted as contemporary mythmakers. At their best, they tell communal stories that evoke and symbolize our most enduring values and our secret desires. The most popular films often make the world seem clearer, more manageable, and more understandable.

Throughout the twentieth century, films helped moviegoers sort through experiences that either affirmed or deviated from their own values. Some movies allowed audiences to survey "the boundary between the permitted and the forbidden" and to experience, in a controlled way, "the possibility of stepping across this boundary."[1] Popular movies such as *Silence of the Lambs, American Beauty,* and *8 Mile* examined the distinctions between the normal and the abnormal—a moral border repeatedly fought over by religious leaders, politicians, and entrepreneurs as well as by teachers, parents, and the mass media.

Although the development and production time for films can often be two or more years, the movie industry as a whole must often react quickly to social events and cultural shifts. This was never more apparent than after the terrorist attacks of September 11, 2001. Hollywood studios suspended production or delayed the release of several movies with terrorism themes. Marketing campaigns were changed, and scenes with images of the World Trade Center towers were altered. In the midst of the horrors of terrorism, Americans stayed home and rented 40 percent more movie videos in the weeks after 9/11 compared to the same period in the previous year and also went out to the movies more often, making 2001 a record-breaking year for box-office revenue.

Over and above their immense economic impact (see Table 7.1), movies have always worked on several social and cultural levels. While they distract us from our

> **"** The movie is not only a supreme expression of mechanism, but paradoxically it offers as product the most magical of consumer commodities, namely dreams. **"**
>
> –Marshall McLuhan,
> *Understanding Media,* 1964

● Table 7.1 The Top 10 American Box-Office Champions, 2003*		
Rank	Title/Date	Domestic Gross** (millions)
1	Titanic (1997)	$601
2	Star Wars (1977)	461
3	E.T.: The Extra-Terrestrial (1982)	435
4	Star Wars: The Phantom Menace (1999)	431
5	Spider-Man (2002)	404
6	Jurassic Park (1993)	357
7	Lord of the Rings: The Two Towers (2002)	332
8	Forrest Gump (1994)	330
9	The Lion King (1994)	326
10	Harry Potter and the Sorcerer's Stone (2001)	318

*Most rankings of the Top 10 most popular films are based on American box-office receipts. If these were adjusted for inflation, *Gone with the Wind* (1939) would become No. 1 in U.S. theater revenue.

**Gross is shown in absolute dollars based on box-office sales in the United States and Canada.

Source: "Top 50+ All Time Highest Grossing Movies," March 10, 2003, <http://movieweb.com/movie/alltime.html>. © 2003 MovieWeb. All Rights Reserved.

● *Spider-Man*, with heavy promotion and merchandising, and expensive, eye-catching special effects, was the first blockbuster movie of the summer season in 2002. By the end of the year, it was the fifth-biggest-grossing film in domestic box office history and had become a major movie franchise for Sony's Columbia Pictures unit.

daily struggles, at the same time they encourage us to take part in rethinking contemporary ideas. We continue to be attracted to the stories that movies tell.

In this chapter, we will examine the rich legacy and current standing of Hollywood as a national and international mythmaker. We will begin by considering film's early technology and the evolution of film as a mass medium. We will look at the arrival of silent feature films, the emergence of Hollywood, and the development of the studio system with regard to production, distribution, and exhibition. We will then explore the coming of sound and the power of movie storytelling. In the context of Hollywood moviemaking, we will consider major film genres, directors, and alternatives to Hollywood's style, including foreign films and documentaries. Finally, we will look at the movie business today—its major players, economic clout, technological advances, and implications for democracy.

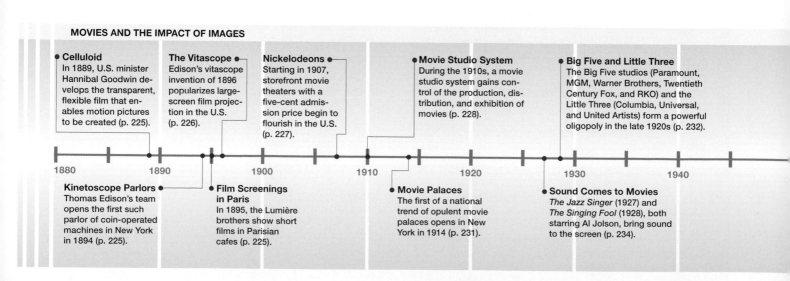

MOVIES AND THE IMPACT OF IMAGES

Celluloid
In 1889, U.S. minister Hannibal Goodwin develops the transparent, flexible film that enables motion pictures to be created (p. 225).

The Vitascope
Edison's vitascope invention of 1896 popularizes large-screen film projection in the U.S. (p. 226).

Nickelodeons
Starting in 1907, storefront movie theaters with a five-cent admission price begin to flourish in the U.S. (p. 227).

Movie Studio System
During the 1910s, a movie studio system gains control of the production, distribution, and exhibition of movies (p. 228).

Big Five and Little Three
The Big Five studios (Paramount, MGM, Warner Brothers, Twentieth Century Fox, and RKO) and the Little Three (Columbia, Universal, and United Artists) form a powerful oligopoly in the late 1920s (p. 232).

1880   1890   1900   1910   1920   1930   1940

Kinetoscope Parlors
Thomas Edison's team opens the first such parlor of coin-operated machines in New York in 1894 (p. 225).

Film Screenings in Paris
In 1895, the Lumière brothers show short films in Parisian cafes (p. 225).

Movie Palaces
The first of a national trend of opulent movie palaces opens in New York in 1914 (p. 231).

Sound Comes to Movies
The Jazz Singer (1927) and *The Singing Fool* (1928), both starring Al Jolson, bring sound to the screen (p. 234).

Early Technology and the Evolution of Movies

History often credits a handful of enterprising individuals with developing new technologies and new categories of mass media. Such innovations, however, are usually the result of extended and simultaneous investigations by a wide variety of people. In addition, the media innovations of both known and unknown inventors are propelled by economic and social forces as well as by individual abilities.[2]

The Development of Film

Solving the puzzle of making a picture move depended both on advances in photography and on the development of a flexible film stock to replace the heavy metal-and-glass plates used to make individual pictures in the 1800s. In 1889, an American minister, Hannibal Goodwin, developed a transparent and pliable film—called **celluloid**—that could hold a coating, or film, of chemicals sensitive to light. This breakthrough solved a major problem: It enabled a strip of film to move through a camera and be photographed in rapid succession, producing a series of pictures. In the 1890s, George Eastman (later of Eastman Kodak) bought Goodwin's patents, improved the ideas, and manufactured the first film used for motion pictures.

As with the development of sound recording, Thomas Edison takes center stage in most accounts of the invention of motion pictures. In the late 1800s, Edison initially planned to merge phonograph technology and moving images to create talking pictures (which would not happen in feature films until 1927). Because there was no breakthrough, however, Edison lost interest. But he directed an assistant, William Kennedy Dickson, to combine advances in Europe with the new celluloid to create an early movie camera, called the **kinetograph**, and a viewing system, called the **kinetoscope**. This small projection system housed fifty feet of film that revolved on spools (similar to a library microfilm reader). It was a kind of peep show in which viewers looked through a hole and saw images moving on a tiny plate. In 1894, a kinetoscope parlor, featuring two rows of coin-operated machines, opened in New York.

From the start, Edison envisioned movies only as a passing fad or an arcade novelty. Meanwhile, in France, Louis and Auguste Lumière, who ran a photographic equipment factory, were hard at work. The brothers developed a projection system

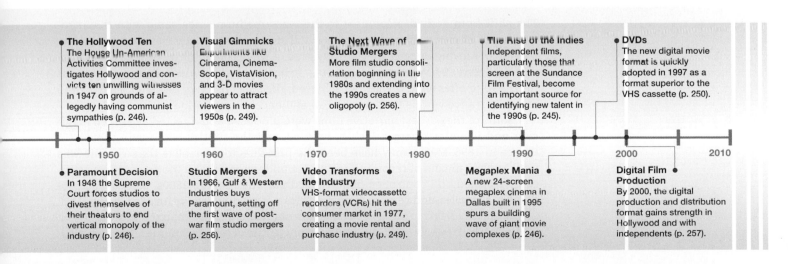

The Hollywood Ten
The House Un-American Activities Committee investigates Hollywood and convicts ten unwilling witnesses in 1947 on grounds of allegedly having communist sympathies (p. 246).

Visual Gimmicks
Enhancements like Cinerama, Cinema-Scope, VistaVision, and 3-D movies appear to attract viewers in the 1950s (p. 249).

The Next Wave of Studio Mergers
More film studio consolidation beginning in the 1980s and extending into the 1990s creates a new oligopoly (p. 256).

The Rise of the Indies
Independent films, particularly those that screen at the Sundance Film Festival, become an important source for identifying new talent in the 1990s (p. 245).

DVDs
The new digital movie format is quickly adopted in 1997 as a format superior to the VHS cassette (p. 250).

1950   1960   1970   1980   1990   2000   2010

Paramount Decision
In 1948 the Supreme Court forces studios to divest themselves of their theaters to end vertical monopoly of the industry (p. 246).

Studio Mergers
In 1966, Gulf & Western Industries buys Paramount, setting off the first wave of post-war film studio mergers (p. 256).

Video Transforms the Industry
VHS-format videocassette recorders (VCRs) hit the consumer market in 1977, creating a movie rental and purchase industry (p. 249).

Megaplex Mania
A new 24-screen megaplex cinema in Dallas built in 1995 spurs a building wave of giant movie complexes (p. 246).

Digital Film Production
By 2000, the digital production and distribution format gains strength in Hollywood and with independents (p. 257).

● Before the arrival of feature-length movies, audiences in the late 1890s were fascinated by the novelty of any moving image. This Edison kinetoscope reel from 1894 featured one of the first close-up shots ever recorded on film—a man sneezing.

so that more than one person at a time could see the moving images on a nine- by six-foot projection screen. In a Paris café on December 28, 1895, they projected ten short movies, for viewers who paid one franc each, on such subjects as a man falling off a horse and a child trying to grab a fish from a bowl. Within three weeks, twenty-five hundred people were coming each night to see how, according to one Paris paper, film "perpetuates the image of movement."

With innovators around the world dabbling in moving pictures, Edison's lab and kinetoscope company renewed its interest. Edison patented several inventions and manufactured a new large-screen system called the **vitascope**, which enabled film-strips of longer lengths to be projected without interruption. Unlike the kinetoscope, vitascope projection improved viewing for large audiences, hinting at the potential of movies as a future mass medium.

Staged at a music hall in New York in April 1896, Edison's first public showing of the vitascope featured shots from a boxing match and waves rolling onto a beach. The *New York Times* described the exhibition as "wonderfully real and singularly exhilarating." Some members of the audience were so taken with the realism of the film images that they stepped back from the screen's crashing waves to avoid getting their feet wet.

Early movie demonstrations such as these marked the beginning of the film industry. At this point, movies consisted of movement recorded by a single continuous camera shot. Early filmmakers had not yet figured out how to move the camera around or how to edit film shots together. Nonetheless, various innovators were beginning to see the commercial possibilities of film. By 1900, short movies had become a part of amusement arcades, traveling carnivals, wax museums, and vaudeville theater.

The Power of Stories in the Silent Era

The shift from early development to the mass-medium stage came with the introduction of **narrative films**: movies that tell stories. Once audiences understood the illusion of moving images, they quickly tired of waves breaking on beaches or vaudeville acts recorded by immobile cameras. To become a mass medium, the early silent films had to offer what books had achieved: the suspension of disbelief. They had to create narrative worlds that engaged an audience's imagination.

Some of the earliest narrative films were produced and directed by French magician and inventor Georges Méliès, who opened the first public movie theater in France in 1896. Méliès may have been the first director to realize that a movie was not simply a means of recording reality. He understood that a movie could be artificially planned and controlled like a staged play. By the late 1800s, Méliès was producing fairy tales and science-fiction stories—including *Joan of Arc, Red Riding Hood, Cinderella*, and *A Trip to the Moon*. These film shorts lasted less than ten minutes each. By the early 1900s, he had discovered camera tricks and techniques, such as slow motion and cartoon animation, that became key ingredients in future narrative filmmaking.

The first American filmmaker to adapt Méliès's innovations to narrative film was Edwin S. Porter. A cameraman who had studied Méliès's work in an Edison lab, Porter mastered the technique of editing diverse shots together to tell a coherent story. Early filmmakers plotted and recorded action in a long, continuous filmed sequence. But Porter shot narrative scenes out of order (for instance, some in a studio and some outdoors) and reassembled them in the editing process to make a story. In 1902, he made what is regarded as America's first narrative film, *The Life of an American Fireman.*

Porter also pioneered other innovations in filmmaking. First, he moved the camera and varied its distance from subjects and objects. *American Fireman,* for example, contained the first close-up shot in U.S. narrative film history—a ringing fire alarm. Until then, early moviemakers thought that close-ups cheated the audience of the opportunity to see an entire scene. Second, Porter's most important film, *The Great Train Robbery,* introduced the western as well as chase scenes. In this eleven-minute movie, Porter demonstrated the art of film suspense by alternating shots of the robbers with those of a posse in hot pursuit.

The Arrival of Nickelodeons

Another major development in the evolution of film as a mass medium was the arrival of movie theaters. They were called **nickelodeons**, a term that combines the admission price with the Greek word for "theater." According to media historian Douglas Gomery, these small and uncomfortable makeshift theaters were often converted cigar stores, pawnshops, or restaurants redecorated to mimic vaudeville theaters: "In front, large, hand-painted posters announced the movies for the day. Inside, the screening of news, documentary, comedy, fantasy, and dramatic shorts lasted about one hour."[3] Because they showed silent narrative film shorts that usually transcended language barriers, nickelodeons flourished during the great European immigration at the turn of the last century. These theaters filled a need for many newly arrived people struggling to learn English and seeking an inexpensive escape from the hard life of the city. Often managed by immigrants, nickelodeons required a minimal investment: just a secondhand projector and a large white sheet. Usually a piano player added live music, and sometimes theater operators used sound effects to simulate gunshots or loud crashes.

Although vaudeville theaters continued to feature movies, by 1908 nickelodeons had displaced the vaudeville circuit as the main showplace for films. Because they were less expensive than vaudeville shows and drew fewer well-to-do audiences, nickelodeons were labeled "democracy's theater." Between 1907 and 1909, the number of nickelodeons grew from five thousand to ten thousand. The craze had peaked by 1910, when entrepreneurs began to seek more affluent spectators, attracting them with larger and more lavish movie theaters.

● Italian-born Rudolph Valentino came to the United States in 1913, when he was 18. After finding his way to California, he quickly emerged as a star in the 1920s, appearing in 14 major films in only seven years. His sexy and passionate portrayal of Sheik Ahmed (opposite Agnes Ayres in *The Sheik,* 1921) earned him the nickname "Great Lover." Famous for his good looks and comic timing in silent films, he was also partially responsible for the popularity of the tango in the 1920s. Valentino died in 1926 at the age of 31.

The Power of the Studio System

By the late 1910s, the movie industry's three basic economic divisions—production, distribution, and exhibition—had been established. In its early phase, control of *production* meant control over camera and projector technology. But as narrative films became central to attracting consumers, production came to mean controlling the making of movies, from writing a script and hiring actors to raising money and filming the story. This is still the case today. *Distribution* constitutes the individuals or companies that deliver films into theaters in various regional, national, and international markets. Finally, *exhibition* refers to the places where films are displayed—the theaters themselves and the people and companies that own them. Much of film history, as well as the current state of moviemaking, has been significantly affected by the power struggles of film studios vying to dominate one or all of these industry divisions.

Among the first to try his hand at dominating the movie business, Thomas Edison had been observing the growing popularity of film. In 1908 he formed the Motion Picture Patents Company, a cartel of major U.S. and French film producers. Known as the *Trust*, Edison's company pooled patents in an effort to control film's major technology and, by default, the production of most movies. In addition, the Trust acquired most major film distributorships and signed an exclusive deal with George Eastman, who agreed to supply movie film only to Trust-approved companies.

However, some independent producers refused to bow to the Trust's terms. There was too much demand for films, too much money to be made, and too many ways to avoid the Trust's scrutiny. Some producers began to relocate from the early centers of film production in New York and New Jersey to Cuba and Florida. Ultimately, though, Hollywood became a movie magnet and the film capital of the world. Southern California offered cheap labor, diverse scenery for outdoor shooting, barns that could be converted into studios, and a mild climate suitable for year-round production. Geographically far from the Trust, independent companies could also easily slip over the border into Mexico to escape legal prosecution for patent violations.

Two Hungarian immigrants, Adolph Zukor, who would eventually run Paramount Pictures, and William Fox, who would found the Fox Film Corporation (which later became Twentieth Century Fox), played a role in the collapse of Edison's Trust. Zukor's early companies figured out ways to bypass the Trust, and a suit by Fox, a nickelodeon operator turned film distributor, resulted in the Trust's breakup for restraint of trade violations in 1917.

Ironically, although the Trust's monopoly efforts failed, entrepreneurs like Zukor went on to develop other tactics for controlling the industry. The new strategies, many of which are still used today, were more ambitious than just monopolizing patents and technology. They aimed at dominating the movie business at all three essential levels—production, distribution, and exhibition—in a **vertical integration** of power and control. The new tactics ultimately spawned a system that turned the film industry into an **oligopoly**, in which a few firms controlled the bulk of the business.

> **" The American cinema is a classical art, but why not then admire in it what is most admirable, i.e., not only the talent of this or that filmmaker, but the genius of the system."**
>
> —André Bazin, film theorist, 1957

Controlling Production

The first movies were sold or rented by the foot; one product was not differentiated from another. Films were novelties, and people were merely curious about the moving images. Gradually, however, producers and distributors recognized that fans sought not only particular kinds of stories—including dramas, westerns, and romances—but particular actors and actresses. This was not unlike what would occur in the 1950s, as radio-station managers noticed that teenagers listened to certain favorite performers again and again.

By 1910, film companies were receiving letters from fans inquiring about actors who were not named in the movie credits. (It was an early practice not to list actors in the credits.) Initially, companies were reluctant to identify these individuals for fear that their popularity would force higher salaries; most anonymous film actors were making only $5 to $15 per day. Eventually, though, film studios acknowledged that moviegoers went to certain films because of the performances of their favorite actors.

To meet the tastes of discerning audiences and to better compete against Edison's Trust, Adolph Zukor hired a number of popular actors, forming the Famous Players Company in 1912. Zukor's idea was to exert control over movie production, not through patents but through contracts with the most popular actors of the day. By this time, theater owners were already beginning to demand films featuring the performers who attracted the largest audiences. Zukor signed these performers to exclusive contracts, ensuring that they would make movies only for his company.

Zukor also understood the difference between film acting and theater acting, in which actors emphasized "the large gesture" and a "boldly sketched pantomime of emotions."[4] Film acting was more subtle, more intimate, and did not demand that an actor's voice reach the back of a cavernous theater. Film producers began developing talented performers such as Mary Pickford, who was "unspoiled" by a theater background and more suited to the new medium. Pickford became one of film's first movie stars. Known as "America's sweetheart" for her portrayal of spunky and innocent heroines, Pickford became so popular that audiences waited in line to see her movies, and producers had to pay her increasingly larger salaries to keep her services.

An astute businesswoman, Mary Pickford was the key figure in elevating the financial status and professional role of film actors. Whereas in 1910 Pickford made about $100 a week, by 1914 she earned $1,000 a week. Eventually, Zukor signed her to Famous Players (which later became part of Paramount Pictures). By 1917, Zukor was paying Pickford a weekly salary of $15,000. Having appeared in nearly two hundred films, Pickford was so influential that in 1919 she broke from Zukor to form her own company, United Artists. Joining her were actor Douglas Fairbanks (her future husband), comedian-director Charlie Chaplin, and director D. W. Griffith.

By the beginning of the 1920s, film production had evolved into the **studio system**. Pioneered by director Thomas Ince and his Hollywood company, Triangle, this system constituted a sort of assembly-line process for moviemaking. It organized a staff of the best technicians and directors schooled in the latest film techniques. According to the system, not only stars but directors, editors, writers, and others worked under exclusive contracts for the major studios. Indeed, those who weren't under contract with some movie company probably weren't working at all. Ince also developed the notion of the studio head; he gave up directing in 1915 and appointed producers to handle hiring, logistics, and finances so that he could more easily supervise many pictures at one time.

● With legions of fans, Mary Pickford became the first woman ever to make $1 million in a year and gained freedom to take artistic risks with her roles. She launched United Artists, a film distributing company, with Douglas Fairbanks and Charlie Chaplin.

66 No, I really cannot afford to work for only $10,000 a week. 99

– Mary Pickford to Adolph Zukor, 1915

Although United Artists represented a brief triumph of autonomy for a few powerful actors, by the 1920s the studio system firmly controlled creative talent in the industry. In 1927, for example, Paramount director Cecil B. DeMille required the actors playing Jesus and Mary in *The King of Kings* to refrain from such secular activities as playing cards or riding in convertibles off the set. The system was so efficient that each major studio was producing a feature film every week. Pooling talent, rather than patents, was a more ingenious approach for movie studios aiming to dominate film production.

Controlling Distribution

One of the early forms of movie distribution, *film exchanges* appeared around 1904 as movie companies provided vaudeville theaters with films and projectors. In exchange for their short films, shown between live acts, movie producers received a small percentage of the vaudeville ticket-gate receipts. Gradually, as the number of production companies and the popularity of narrative films grew, demand for a distribution system serving national and international markets increased as well. Because few regulations existed in these early days, movies were often stolen or copied. Edison's Trust represented, in part, an attempt to prevent film pirating and to manage the industry by withholding equipment from companies not willing to pay the Trust's patent-use fees.

However, emerging film companies and other independent firms looked to distribution strategies to gain a foothold in the fledgling industry. Early independents like Adolph Zukor, who opposed the Trust, developed several distribution techniques, including **block booking**. Under this system, to gain access to popular films exhibitors had to agree to rent new or marginal films with no stars. Zukor would

● Another era: a movie palace in Detroit. With ornate décor, air-conditioning, palatial restrooms, extensive concession stands, and large film screens, movie palaces became fixtures in major American cities in the 1920s. The palaces typically seated several thousand moviegoers, and often featured elaborate concert organs to accompany the films.

pressure theater operators into taking a hundred movies at a time to get the few Pickford titles they wanted. Such contracts enabled studios to test-market a new star without taking much financial risk. Although this practice was eventually outlawed as monopolistic, rising film studios used the tactic effectively to guarantee the success of their films in a competitive marketplace.

Another distribution strategy involved the marketing of American films in Europe. When World War I disrupted European film production, only U.S. studios were able to meet the demand. The war thus marked a turning point, making the United States the leader in the commercial movie business. Europe never regained its edge. After the war, no other film industry could compete economically with Hollywood. By the mid-1920s, foreign revenue from U.S. films totaled $100 million. Today, in any given week, when the industry trade magazine *Variety* ranks the top-grossing films in foreign countries, U.S. movies (especially easily translatable action/adventure features) continue to dominate the list. For example, in 2001, *Moulin Rouge!* emerged as a top box-office draw in Germany, Spain, Australia, France, and England.

Controlling Exhibition

When industrious theater owners began forming film cooperatives to compete with block-booking tactics, producers like Zukor conspired to dominate exhibition. By 1921, Zukor's company owned three hundred theaters, solidifying its ability to show the movies it created. In 1925, a business merger between Paramount and Publix (the country's largest theater chain at the time, with more than five hundred screens) gave Zukor enormous influence over movie exhibition.

Zukor and the heads of several major studios understood that they did not have to own all theaters to ensure that their movies were shown. Over time, the five major studios (which would eventually include MGM, RKO, Warner Brothers, Twentieth Century Fox, and Paramount) merely needed to own about 15 percent of the nation's twenty thousand movie houses. They needed only the first-run theaters, which premiered new films in major downtown areas in front of the largest audiences. Throughout the 1940s, ticket sales from these venues generated 85 to 95 percent of all film revenue.

Movie Palaces

Entrepreneurs ultimately realized that drawing the middle and upper-middle classes to movies required something more attractive than a sheet hung in an abandoned pawnshop. To provide a more hospitable moviegoing environment, exhibitors converted vaudeville theaters into full-time use as single-screen movie theaters. In 1914, the three-thousand-seat Strand Theatre, the first **movie palace**, opened in New York. With elaborate architecture, movie palaces lured spectators who enjoyed entertainment amid the elegant décor usually reserved for high-society opera, ballet, symphony, and live theater.

To work their magic on the outside, these theaters often evoked the grandeur of palaces, with massive electric-light displays that announced their presence from blocks away. Linking the moviegoing experience with the trappings of royalty created a powerful attraction. Inside the theater, customers meandered through lavish lobbies, plush promenades, and fancy waiting rooms. Movie exhibitors treated "the movie patron like a king or queen," with ushers, doormen, and services ranging from free child care to "smoking rooms and painting galleries."[5] Taking advantage of new air-cooling systems developed by Chicago's meatpacking industry, movie palaces also featured the first mechanically air-cooled theaters. This perquisite alone transformed summer moviegoing in Chicago into peak viewing time. Doctors even advised pregnant women to escape the heat by spending their afternoons at the movies.

● Visitors buy concessions at the nine-screen Magic Johnson Theatres complex in Harlem, New York. Since 1995, Magic Johnson has partnered with Loews Cineplex Entertainment to open movie theaters in urban neighborhoods in Los Angeles, Houston, Atlanta, Cleveland, and New York.

Mid-City Theaters

Another major innovation in exhibition was the development of mid-city movie theaters. The first wave of middle-class people moved from urban centers to city outskirts in the 1920s, and mass-transit systems emerged to shuttle these suburban-ites to and from work. Movie theaters soon followed, as exhibitors in Chicago began to locate theaters at major transportation intersections in outlying business areas rather than downtown. (For another view of exhibition, see "Case Study: Breaking through Hollywood's Race Barrier" on page 233.) This idea continues today, as **multi-plexes** featuring multiple screens lure middle-class crowds to interstate crossroads.

Throughout the 1920s, movie attendance climbed steadily. But the Depression hit the industry hard, and many customers turned to radio, a cheaper form of enter-tainment. To compete, theaters began holding contests and prize giveaways. They also offered double features—two movies for the price of one—and started selling candy, soda, and eventually popcorn (which, thanks to the movies, turned corn into a major farm crop in the late 1930s). With jobs restored during World War II, movie attendance surged during the 1940s. In 1946—the industry's all-time peak atten-dance year—ninety million people (out of a U.S. population of 141 million at that time) went to the movies *each week*.

By the late 1920s, the major studios had clearly established vertical integration in the industry. What had once been a fairly easy and cheap business to enter now was complex and capital-intensive. What had been many small competitive firms in the early 1900s now became a few powerful studios, including the **Big Five**—Paramount, MGM, Warner Brothers, Twentieth Century Fox, and RKO—and the **Little Three** (which did not own theaters)—Columbia, Universal, and United Artists. Together these eight companies formed a powerful oligopoly, which made it increasingly difficult for inde-pendent companies to make, distribute, and exhibit commercial films.

The Triumph of Hollywood Storytelling

Whereas early filmmakers like Edwin S. Porter and D. W. Griffith demonstrated the appeal of the film narrative, early stars like Mary Pickford and Charlie Chaplin re-vealed the audience's attraction to movie actors. Meanwhile, the studios searched for the next technical innovation to enliven the industry and further enhance film's storytelling capabilities. They found it by adding sound to moving images.

Breaking through Hollywood's Race Barrier

Despite inequities and discrimination, a thriving black cinema existed in New York's Harlem district during the 1930s and 1940s. Usually bankrolled by white business executives who were capitalizing on the black-only theaters fostered by segregation, independent films featuring black casts were supported by African American moviegoers, even during the Depression. But it was a popular Hollywood film, *Imitation of Life* (1934), that emerged as the highest-grossing film in black theaters during the mid-1930s. The film told the story of a friendship between a white woman and a black woman whose young daughter denied her heritage and passed for white, breaking her mother's heart.

Despite African Americans' long support of the film industry, their moviegoing experience has not been the same as that of whites. From the late 1800s until the passage of civil rights legislation in the mid-1960s, many theater owners discriminated against black patrons. In large cities, blacks often had to attend separate theaters where new movies might not appear until a year or two after white theaters had shown them. In smaller towns and in the South, blacks were often

able to patronize local theaters only after midnight. In addition, some theater managers required black patrons to sit in less desirable areas of the theater.[1]

Changes took place during and after World War II, however. When the "white flight" from central cities began during the suburbanization of the 1950s, many downtown and neighborhood theaters began catering to black customers in order to keep from going out of business. By the late 1960s and early 1970s, these theaters had become major venues for popular commercial films, even featuring a few movies about African Americans, including *Guess Who's Coming to Dinner?* (1967), *In the Heat of the Night* (1967), *The Learning Tree* (1969), and *Sounder* (1972).

Based on the popularity of these films, black photographer-turned-filmmaker Gordon Parks, who directed *The Learning Tree* (adapted from his own novel), went on to make commercial action/adventure films, including *Shaft* (1971, remade by John Singleton in 2000). Popular in urban theaters, especially among black teenagers, the movies produced by Parks and his son—Gordon Parks Jr. (*Super Fly,* 1972)—spawned a number of commercial imitators, labeled blaxploitation movies. These films were the subject of heated cultural debates in the 1970s; like some rap songs today, they were both praised for their realistic depictions of black urban life and criticized for glorifying violence. Nevertheless, these films reinvigorated urban movie attendance, reaching an audience that had not been well served by the film industry until the 1960s.

Although opportunities for black film directors expanded in the 1980s, during the 1990s mainstream Hollywood was still a formidable place for outsiders to crack. Even acclaimed director Spike Lee has had difficulty in getting large budgets from the studios. For example, in making *Get on the Bus* (1996), Lee asked a number of wealthy black men to bankroll $2 million for the film (made for one-tenth the cost of the average Hollywood movie at the time). The film depicted the October 1995 Million Man March on Washington, D.C., celebrating the kind of black self-reliance that Lee's own moviemaking has long illustrated.

● In 1927, Warner Brothers released *The Jazz Singer,* featuring vaudeville star Al Jolson in the first talkie. The film was supposed to be mostly silent with just a few musical numbers, but Jolson was so energetic and ex-citable that he couldn't re-sist talking between songs.

The "Sound" of Movies

With the studio system and Hollywood's worldwide dominance firmly in place, the next big challenge involved bringing sound to moving pictures. Various attempts at **talkies** had failed since Edison first tried to link phonograph and moving-picture technologies in the 1890s. During the 1910s, however, technical breakthroughs at AT&T's research arm, Bell Labs, produced prototypes of loudspeakers and sound am-plifiers. By the end of the decade, the idea of projecting clear sounds throughout large movie palaces was technically possible, although the cost of outfitting theaters with the necessary equipment remained high.

Experiments with ten-minute sound shorts continued during the 1920s. The four Warner brothers (Harry, Abe, Jack, and Sam), who ran a minor studio at the time, experimented with sound as a novelty, although they did not believe such films would replace silent movies. So Warner Brothers made short sound versions of vaudeville acts, featuring singers and comedians. The studio packaged them as a novelty along with silent feature films. Over time, Warner Brothers began outfitting theaters with the necessary sound equipment.

In 1927, Warner Brothers produced a feature-length film, *The Jazz Singer,* starring Al Jolson, a popular vaudeville singer. An experiment, *The Jazz Singer* was basically a silent film interspersed with musical numbers and brief dialogue. At first, there was only modest interest in the movie, which featured just 354 spoken words. But the film grew in popularity as it toured the Midwest, where audiences stood and cheered the short bursts of dialogue. The breakthrough film, however, was Warner Brothers' 1928 release *The Singing Fool,* which also starred Jolson. Costing $200,000 to make, the film took in $5 million and "proved to all doubters that talkies were here to stay."[6] *The Singing Fool* remained the box-office champ for more than ten years until 1939, when it was dethroned by *Gone with the Wind.*

By the mid-1920s, Bell Labs had developed the system used by Warner Brothers that coordinated sound on records with a film projector. Warner Brothers, however, was not the only studio forging into the technology of sound. In April 1927, five months before *The Jazz Singer* opened, the Fox studio premiered sound-film **news-reels.** Fox's newsreel company, Movietone, captured the first film footage, with sound, of the takeoff and return of Charles Lindbergh, who piloted the first solo, nonstop flight across the Atlantic Ocean in May 1927. Fox's Movietone system actu-ally photographed sound directly onto the film, running it on a narrow filmstrip that ran alongside the larger, image portion of the film. Superior to the sound-on-record system, the Movietone method eventually became film's standard sound system.

Meanwhile, Fox was sending camera crews around the world in search of talking news. By 1928, the success of newsreels, as popular as most silent features of the day, led to the full conversion to talking pictures. Boosted by the innovation of

sound, annual movie attendance in the United States rose from 60 million in 1927 to 110 million in 1929. By 1931, nearly 85 percent of America's twenty thousand theaters accommodated sound pictures, and by 1935, the world had adopted talking films as the commercial standard.

Classic Hollywood Cinema

By the time sound came to movies, Hollywood dictated not only the business but the style of most moviemaking worldwide. That style, or model, for storytelling developed with the studio system and continues to dominate American filmmaking today. The model serves up three ingredients that give Hollywood movies their distinctive flavor: the narrative, the genre, and the author (or director). The right blend of these ingredients—combined with timing, marketing, and luck—have led to **blockbuster** movie hits from *Gone with the Wind* to *Lord of the Rings: The Two Towers.* Major studios have historically relied on blockbusters to underwrite the 80 to 90 percent of films that fail at the box office.

Hollywood Narratives

American filmmakers from D. W. Griffith to Steven Spielberg have understood the allure of *narrative,* which always includes two basic components: the *story* (what happens to whom) and the *discourse* (how the story is told). Most movies, like most TV shows and novels, feature a number of stories that play out within the larger narrative of the entire film. For example, in Sam Mendes's Academy Award–winning film *American Beauty* (1999), the narrator is a character who is already dead—middle-aged father and husband Lester Burnham (played by Kevin Spacey). In this dark comedy, Lester recounts how his seemingly perfect suburban life was phony and unbearable. The movie's subplots—Lester's disconnected relationships with his daughter and wife, the unusual new neighbors next door, and Lester's obsession with his daughter's high-school girlfriend—culminate in Lester's redemption and demise.

Within Hollywood's classic narratives, filmgoers will find an amazing array of intriguing cultural variations. For example, *Spider-Man,* among the most lucrative films of all time, features the familiar narrative *conventions* of problems, heroes, villains, conflicts, and resolutions. However, the film *differentiates* itself through enhanced *inventions:* new levels of computer-generated imagery that had never been attempted before in a motion picture. This combination of convention and invention —standardized Hollywood stories and differentiated special effects—provides a powerful economic package that satisfies most audiences' appetites for both the familiar and the distinctive.

● Table 7.2 Hollywood Genres

Movies, especially contemporary films, are difficult to categorize because they often combine characteristics from different genres. In 1999, for example, *American Beauty* mixed elements from drama and comedy, and in 2002 *My Big Fat Greek Wedding* crossed the boundaries of comedy and romance. Shown below are the categories that are generally used by video stores to sort movies. Films from different decades represent the most familiar major genres.

Comedy

The Gold Rush (1925)
Horse Feathers (1932)
Arsenic and Old Lace (1944)
Some Like It Hot (1959)
Dr. Strangelove (1964)
Annie Hall (1977)*

A Fish Called Wanda (1988)
The Birdcage (1995)
American Beauty (1999)*
High Fidelity (2000)
Shrek (2001)

Drama

Grand Hotel (1932)
Gone with the Wind (1939)
Citizen Kane (1941)
On the Waterfront (1954)*
A Man for All Seasons (1966)*
One Flew over the Cuckoo's Nest (1975)*
Raging Bull (1980)

Do the Right Thing (1989)
Fried Green Tomatoes (1991)
Dead Man Walking (1996)
Good Will Hunting (1997)
Saving Private Ryan (1998)
Boys Don't Cry (1999)
A Beautiful Mind (2001)

Romance

It Happened One Night (1934)*
Casablanca (1943)*
Adam's Rib (1949)
Sabrina (1954)
Dr. Zhivago (1965)
The Graduate (1967)

The Goodbye Girl (1977)
Tootsie (1984)
Beauty and the Beast (1993)
Titanic (1997)*
Shakespeare in Love (1998)*
My Big Fat Greek Wedding (2002)

Action/Adventure

The Adventures of Robin Hood (1938)
Sands of Iwo Jima (1949)
Ben Hur (1959)*
The Great Escape (1963)
The Sting (1973)*

Die Hard (1988)
Thelma & Louise (1991)
The Lion King (1994)
Mission Impossible II (2000)
Daredevil (2003)

Mystery/Suspense

The Lady Vanishes (1938)
Rebecca (1940)*
North by Northwest (1959)
Psycho (1960)
Chinatown (1974)

Witness (1985)
Silence of the Lambs (1991)*
Seven (1996)
The Sixth Sense (1999)
The Others (2001)

(continued on next page)

Hollywood Genres

In general, Hollywood narratives fit a **genre**, or category, in which conventions regarding similar characters, scenes, structures, and themes recur in combination. Grouping films by category enables the industry to achieve two related economic goals: *product standardization* and *product differentiation*. By making films that fall into popular genres, the movie industry provides familiar models that can be imitated. It

Table 7.2 Hollywood Genres *(continued)*

Westerns

Cimarron (1931)*	The Outlaw Josey Wales (1976)
Stagecoach (1939)	Silverado (1985)
The Searchers (1956)	Unforgiven (1992)*
Butch Cassidy and the Sundance Kid (1969)	Maverick (1994)
Little Big Man (1970)	Texas Rangers (2001)

Gangster

Public Enemy (1931)	Scarface (1983)
Scarface (1932)	Goodfellas (1990)
High Sierra (1941)	Boyz N the Hood (1991)
Bonnie and Clyde (1967)	Menace II Society (1993)
The Godfather (1972)*	Donnie Brasco (1997)
The Godfather, Part II (1974)*	Ocean's Eleven (2001)

Horror

Phantom of the Opera (1925)	The Exorcist (1973)
Dracula (1931)	Nightmare on Elm Sreet (1985)
Bride of Frankenstein (1935)	Mary Shelley's Frankenstein (1994)
The Wolf Man (1941)	Scream (1996)
The Blob (1958)	The Blair Witch Project (1999)
The Birds (1963)	The Ring (2002)

Fantasy/Science Fiction

Metropolis (1926)	The Princess Bride (1987)
The Wizard of Oz (1939)	Terminator 2: Judgment Day (1991)
Invasion of the Body Snatchers (1956)	Independence Day (1996)
2001: A Space Odyssey (1968)	Armageddon (1998)
Star Wars (1977)	The Matrix (1999)
Blade Runner (1982)	The Lord of the Rings: The Two Towers (2002)

Musicals

Broadway Melody (1929)*	Jesus Christ Superstar (1973)
Top Hat (1935)	Annie (1982)
Meet Me in St. Louis (1944)	Evita (1997)
An American in Paris (1951)*	Moulin Rouge! (2001)
West Side Story (1961)*	Chicago (2002)
The Sound of Music (1965)*	

Film Noir

Double Indemnity (1944)	They Live by Night (1948)
Detour (1945)	Border Incident (1949)
The Postman Always Rings Twice (1946)	Sunset Boulevard (1950)
The Strange Love of Martha Ivers (1946)	L.A. Confidential (1997)
The Big Sleep (1946)	The Man Who Wasn't There (2001)
Key Largo (1948)	

*Won the Academy Award for that year's best picture.

is much easier for a studio to promote a film that already fits into a preexisting category with which viewers are familiar. Among the most familiar genres are comedy, drama, romance, action/adventure, mystery/suspense, fantasy/science fiction, musical, horror, gangster, western, and film noir. (See Table 7.2.)

> ❝ The thing of a musical is that you take a simple story, and tell it in a complicated way. ❞ –Baz Luhrmann, at the 2002 Academy Awards, on *Moulin Rouge!*

● A classic film noir, *Sunset Boulevard* (1950) explores the dark forces behind the Hollywood dream factory. Here, Norma Desmond is a faded silent-film star (played by Gloria Swanson, a real-life faded silent-film star) who takes in struggling Hollywood writer Joe Gillis (played by William Holden). The limousine driver is Max Von Mayerling, Desmond's former husband (played by Eric Von Stroheim, himself a silent-film director who found little directorial work after the advent of talkies). In film noir style, the movie ends in madness and death.

An enduring genre such as the western typically features "good" cowboys battling "evil" bad guys or resolves tension between the natural forces of the wilderness and the civilizing influence of a town. Romances present narratives in which women play more central roles and conflicts are mediated by the ideal of love. Another popular genre, mystery/suspense, usually casts "the city" as a corrupting place that needs to be overcome by the moral courage of a heroic detective. In these movies, the hero searches for clues of criminal violation, then confronts villains, victims, and bystanders, and finally explains and resolves the violation or transgression.[7]

Besides variations of dramas and comedies, which dominate film's long narrative history, another significant genre, the movie musical, added the innovation of on-screen music. Recently, however, the genre has fallen on hard times. Although such musicals as *Jesus Christ Superstar* (1973) and *Hair* (1979) were early influences on the music-video era, they have since been overwhelmed by MTV and other forms of popular music made visual.

Musicals are considered risky investments in the film industry today. By 2002, no live-action musicals ranked among the top-50-grossing films of all time. Although musicals like *Cats* have been popular as Broadway plays, the staged qualities of such shows are actually a negative when musicals are converted into movies. Because most Hollywood narratives try to create believable worlds, the artificial style of musicals is sometimes a disruption of what many viewers expect—although director Baz Luhrmann's acclaimed *Moulin Rouge!* (2001) created an intentionally unreal, hyperkinetic vision of nineteenth-century Paris. The movie musicals that have done the best at the box office are the ones with just a few musical numbers that accompany a spoken narrative story, appealing to both adults and children. Disney has skillfully employed this formula in creating a string of hybrid animation-musicals, including *Beauty and the Beast* (1991) and *The Lion King* (1994), both of which later resurfaced as successful Broadway shows after their film achievements.

Another fascinating genre is the horror film, which in 2002 counted only two movies among the top-50-grossing films of all time: *The Exorcist,* from 1973, and *The Mummy Returns,* from 2001. In fact, from *Psycho* (the original 1960 version) to *The Ring* (2002), in the history of the Academy Awards this lightly regarded genre has earned only one Oscar for best picture: *Silence of the Lambs*, a mystery/suspense-horror hybrid from 1991. Yet these movies are extremely popular with teenagers, among the largest theatergoing audience, who are in search of cultural choices distinct from those of their parents. Critics suggest that the teen appeal of such horror movies as

The Blair Witch Project (1999) is similar to the allure of gangsta rap or heavy-metal music. That is, the horror genre is a cultural form that often carries anti-adult messages or is so gross that no responsible adult would be caught within a mile of its performance. In other words, this genre repels parents while simultaneously attracting their children.

An interesting and relatively new genre is *film noir* (French for "black film"), which developed in the United States after World War II and continues to influence movies today. Using low-lighting techniques, few daytime scenes, and bleak urban settings that generate a chilling mood, films in this genre (such as *The Big Sleep*, 1946, and *Sunset Boulevard*, 1950) explore unstable characters and the sinister side of human nature. These films also often resist the conventional closure of the classic narrative. Although the French critics who first identified noir as a genre place these films in the 1940s, their influence resonates in contemporary films—sometimes called *neo-noir*—including *Raging Bull, Pulp Fiction, The Usual Suspects, Seven, L.A. Confidential,* and *Memento*.

Hollywood "Authors"

Film has generally been called a director's medium. Although commercial filmmaking requires hundreds of people to perform complicated tasks, from scriptwriting and casting to set design and editing, the director serves as the main "author" of a film. Certainly the names Steven Spielberg (*E.T.; Schindler's List; Jurassic Park; Saving Private Ryan*) and Spike Lee (*Do the Right Thing; Malcolm X; Get on the Bus; The Original Kings of Comedy*) attract many moviegoers to a film today.

D. W. Griffith, among the first "star" directors, paved the way for future filmmakers. Griffith refined many of the narrative techniques that are still in use today, including varied camera distances, close-up shots, multiple story lines, fast-paced editing, and symbolic imagery. His major work, *The Birth of a Nation* (1915), was a controversial three-hour Civil War epic. Although considered a technical masterpiece, the film glorified the Ku Klux Klan and stereotyped southern blacks. It is nevertheless the movie that triggered Hollywood's ongoing fascination with long narrative films. By 1915, more than 20 percent of films were feature-length (around two hours), and *The Birth of a Nation*, which cost filmgoers a record $2 admission, ran for a year on Broadway.

Successful directors, in general, develop a particular cinematic style or an interest in particular topics that differentiates their narratives from those of other directors. Alfred Hitchcock, for instance, redefined the suspense drama through editing techniques that heightened tension (*North by Northwest*, 1959; *Psycho*, 1960); and Frank Capra championed romantic characters who stood up for the common person (*Mr. Smith Goes to Washington*, 1939; *It's a Wonderful Life*, 1946).

The contemporary status of directors probably stems from two breakthrough films: Dennis Hopper's *Easy Rider* (1969) and George Lucas's *American Graffiti* (1973), which became surprise box-office hits. Their inexpensive budgets, rock-and-roll soundtracks, and big payoffs created opportunities for a new generation of directors. The success of these films exposed cracks in the Hollywood system, which was losing money in the late 1960s and early 1970s. Studio executives seemed at a loss to explain and predict the tastes of a new generation of moviegoers. Yet Hopper and Lucas had tapped into the anxieties of the postwar baby-boom generation in its search for self-realization, its longing for an innocent past, and its efforts to cope with the social turbulence of the late 1960s.

Trained in California or New York film schools and products of the 1960s, Francis Ford Coppola (*The Godfather*), Brian De Palma (*Carrie*), William Friedkin (*The Exorcist*), George Lucas (*Star Wars*), Martin Scorsese (*Taxi Driver; Raging Bull*), and Steven Spielberg (*Jaws; Raiders of the Lost Ark*) represented a new wave of Hollywood directors.

● Karyn Kusama was an award-winning film student at New York University. After years of odd jobs, she met director John Sayles in 1996 and became his personal assistant. With Sayles's help, Kusama financed her first feature-length film, *Girlfight* (1999), about a troubled high-school girl who finds self-respect and discipline in the boxing ring. The movie became a hit at the Sundance Film Festival, sharing the Grand Jury Prize for best dramatic film; Kusama also won Best Director.

> **"There are women in the Senate, women heading studios, and busloads of young women emerging from film school. So why are 96 percent of films directed by men?"**
>
> –Michelle Goldberg, Salon.com, 2002

Combining news or documentary techniques and Hollywood narratives, they demonstrated not only how mass-media borders had become blurred but also how movies had become more dependent on audiences that were used to television and rock and roll. These films signaled the start of a period that Scorsese has called "the deification of the director." A handful of successful men gained the kind of economic clout and celebrity standing that had belonged almost exclusively to top movie stars, and a few of these directors were transformed into big-time Hollywood producers.

Although the status of directors grew in the 1960s and 1970s, recognition for women directors of Hollywood features remained rare.[8] In the history of the Academy Awards, only two women have received an Academy Award nomination for directing a feature film: Lina Wertmuller in 1976 for *Seven Beauties* and Jane Campion in 1993 for *The Piano* (for which Campion won an Oscar for her original screenplay). It's worth noting that both Wertmuller and Campion are from outside the United States, where women directors often receive more funding opportunities for film development. When women in the United States do get an opportunity, it is often because their prominent standing as popular actors has given them the power to produce or direct. Barbra Streisand (*Yentl*, 1983; *The Mirror Has Two Faces*, 1996), Jodie Foster (*Little Man Tate*, 1991; *Home for the Holidays*, 1995), Penny Marshall (*A League of Their Own*, 1992; *Riding in Cars with Boys*, 2001), and Sally Field (*Beautiful*, 2000) all fall into this category. Other women have come to direct films via their script-writing successes. Respected essayist Nora Ephron, for example, wrote *Silkwood* in 1983, wrote and pro-

> **❝** Growing up in this country, the rich culture I saw in my neighborhood, in my family—I didn't see that on television or on the movie screen. It was always my ambition that if I was successful I would try to portray a truthful portrait of African Americans in this country, negative and positive. **❞**
>
> —Spike Lee, filmmaker, 1996

duced *When Harry Met Sally* in 1989, and then went on to direct *Sleepless in Seattle* and *You've Got Mail* in 1993 and 1998, each grossing more than $100 million.

Although women have made strong contributions in commercial movies as actors, editors, writers, artists, and designers, critics generally attribute their lack of power to the long history of male executives being atop the studio system. With the exception of Mary Pickford, the early studio moguls who ran Hollywood were men. Even by the late 1990s, among the major studio executives, only a few women held top posts. Independent filmmaker Julie Dash (*Daughters of the Dust*, 1992) has argued that women's best chances of controlling the movie process, apart from acting, remain outside the Hollywood system. But some women directors are proving otherwise. Directors such as Kasi Lemmons (*Eve's Bayou*, 1997; *The Caveman's Valentine,* 2001) and Julie Taymor (*Frida,* 2002) have begun to direct their own projects within the major studios.

Outside the Hollywood System

The contemporary film industry tends to focus on feature-length movies that command popular attention and most of the money. However, shorter narrative films and documentaries dominated cinema's first twenty years and continue to account for most of the movies made today. In addition, movie history has a long tradition in experimental, or avant-garde, films. These types of film, often produced outside the United States, provide opportunities for new filmmakers, both women and men. Below we will look at three alternatives to Hollywood: foreign films, documentaries, and independent films.

Foreign Films

Although U.S. films were earning more than 90 percent of global box-office revenues annually by 2000, they accounted for only 15 percent of the number of commercial films produced worldwide. Despite Hollywood's domination of global film distribution, other countries have a rich history in producing both successful and provocative short-subject and feature films. For example, German expressionism (1919–24), Soviet realism (1924–30), Italian neorealism (1942–51), French new-wave cinema (1959–60), and post–World War II Japanese cinema have all demonstrated alternatives to the Hollywood approach. Today, India has the world's largest film industry (nicknamed Bollywood, a play on words combining Bombay and Hollywood), producing a whopping 1,000 films a year—mostly romance or adventure musicals in a distinct style, but with Western influences.[9] In comparison, Hollywood moviemakers release 450 to 500 films a year.

Americans showed early interest in British and French short films and in experimental films such as Germany's *The Cabinet of Dr. Caligari* (1919). The studio moguls, however, held tight rein over the entry of foreign titles into the United States. Foreign-language movies did reasonably well throughout the 1920s, especially in ethnic neighborhood theaters in large American cities. For a time, Hollywood studios even dubbed some popular American movies into Spanish, Italian, French, and German for these theaters. But the Depression brought cutbacks, and by the 1930s the daughters and sons of turn-of-the-century immigrants—many of whom were trying to assimilate into mainstream American culture—preferred their Hollywood movies in English.[10]

Postwar prosperity and a rising globalism in the 1950s and 1960s saw a rebirth of interest in foreign-language films by such prominent directors as Sweden's Ingmar Bergman (*Wild Strawberries,* 1957), Italy's Federico Fellini (*La Dolce Vita,* 1960), France's François Truffaut (*Jules and Jim,* 1961), Japan's Akira Kurosawa (*Seven Samurai,* 1954), and India's Satyajit Ray (*Apu Trilogy,* 1955–59). In the 1950s, the gradual breakup of the studios' hold over theater exhibition stimulated the rise of art-house theaters, many specializing in foreign titles. Catering to academic audiences, art houses made a statement against Hollywood commercialism as they sought alternative movies.

Art houses numbered close to a thousand during their peak years in the late 1960s. By the late 1970s, though, the home-video market had emerged, and audiences began staying home to watch both foreign and domestic films. New multiplex theater owners also rejected the smaller profit margins of most foreign titles, which lacked the promotional hype of U.S. films. In addition, many viewers complained that English subtitles distracted them from devoting their attention to the visual images. As a result, between 1966 and 1990 the number of foreign films released annually in the United States dropped by two-thirds, from nearly three hundred to about one hundred titles per year.

With the growth of superstore video chains like Blockbuster in the 1990s, however, more shelf space opened up for diverse kinds of movies, including a larger selection of foreign-language titles. In 2001, the successes of *Amélie* (France), *Monsoon Wedding* (India), *Y Tu Mama Tambien* (Mexico), and *Italian for Beginners* (Denmark) illustrated that U.S. audiences are willing to watch subtitled films with non-Hollywood perspectives. Nevertheless, fewer than 5 percent of the nation's movie screens regularly show foreign-language films. Foreign films are even losing ground at these "alternative" screening sites, as they compete with the expanding independent American film market for screen space. (For a broader perspective on foreign film, see "The Global Village—Beyond Hollywood: Asian Cinema" on page 243.)

The Documentary Tradition

Both TV news and nonfiction films trace their roots to the movie industry's *interest films* and newsreels of the late 1890s. In Britain, interest films contained compiled footage of regional wars, political leaders, industrial workers, and agricultural scenes. These films accompanied fiction shorts as part of the early moviegoing experience. Pioneered in France and England, *newsreels* consisted of weekly ten-minute magazine-style compilations of filmed news events from around the world organized in a sequence of short reports. A number of international news services began supplying theaters and movie studios with newsreels, and by 1911 they had become a regular part of the moviegoing menu.

Early filmmakers also produced *travelogues,* which recorded daily life in various communities around the world. Travel films reached documentary status in Robert Flaherty's classic *Nanook of the North* (1922), which tracked a resourceful Eskimo family in the harsh Hudson Bay region of Canada. Flaherty edited his fifty-five-minute film to both tell and interpret the story of his subject. Flaherty's second film, *Moana* (1925), a Paramount-funded study of the lush South Pacific islands and a direct contrast to *Nanook,* inspired the term **documentary** in a 1926 film review by John Grierson, a Scottish film producer. Grierson defined Flaherty's work and the documentary form as "the creative treatment of actuality," or a genre that documents reality by recording real people and settings.

Crouching Tiger, Hidden Dragon

THE GLOBAL VILLAGE

Beyond Hollywood: Asian Cinema

● The Indian classic *Charulata (The Lonely Wife)*.

For those who think only U.S. films dominate the world's movie screens, consider the film industry in India, which produces about a thousand films a year, more than twice the number Hollywood does. Named "Bollywood" after the major filmmaking center in Bombay, the Indian film industry and its products are poised for broader world recognition. Part musical, part action, part romance, and part suspense, the epic films typically have fantastic sets, hordes of extras, plenty of wet saris, and symbolic fountain bursts (as a substitute for kissing and sex, which are prohibited from being shown). Indian movie fans regularly shell out from 75 cents to $5 to see these films, and the fans feel shortchanged if a Bollywood film is shorter than three hours.

With many films produced in less than a week, however, most of the Bollywood fare is cheaply produced and badly acted. The production aesthetics are changing, however. Bollywood moguls have begun to realize that with higher production values, their films can appeal to the middle and upper classes in India, to the twenty-five million Indians living abroad (mostly in England and the United States), and to Western audiences in general. Characters are increasingly dressed in Western clothes and many films are being shot abroad, with New Zealand sheep, English pubs, and Alaskan glaciers as backdrops. These efforts are working. The appetite for Bollywood films in England is so immense (due to the large Indian and Pakistani communities there) that multiplexes are setting aside screens to show Indian films exclusively. Meanwhile, Hollywood may become increasingly influenced by a Bollywood aesthetic as it employs Bollywood directors, producers, and actors. Bombay director Shekhar Kapur, for example, directed *Elizabeth* (1998), a stunning epic nominated for seven Oscars, including an Oscar for best picture, and *Four Feathers* (2002), an adventure story with epic battle scenes about a young British soldier.

Even though the influence of Bombay films and directors may be gaining in the first decade of the 2000s, Hong Kong films were the most talked about—and the most influential—film genre in cinema throughout the late 1980s and 1990s. The Hong Kong style of highly choreographed action with often breathtaking, ballet-like violence became hugely popular around the world, reaching American audiences and in some cases even outselling Hollywood blockbusters at the box office. In addition, Hong Kong directors like John Woo, Ringo Lam, and Jackie Chan (who also acts in his movies) arrived in Hollywood to direct action films; and Hong Kong stars like Jet Li (*Lethal Weapon 4; Romeo Must Die*), Chow Yun-Fat (*The Replacement Killers; Anna and the King*), and Malaysia's Michelle Yeoh (*Tomorrow Never Dies*) are landing leading roles in American movies.

Japanese cinema also seems to be in transition. Americans may be most familiar with low-budget monster movies like *Godzilla,* but the widely heralded films of the late director Akira Kurosawa have had an even greater impact: His *Seven Samurai* (1954) was remade by Hollywood as *The Magnificent Seven* (1960), and *The Hidden Fortress* (1958) was George Lucas's inspiration for *Star Wars*. New forces in Japanese cinema include Hayao Miyazaki, the country's top director of feature-length animated movies. Miyazaki's critically acclaimed *Princess Mononoke* (1997) trails only *Titanic* as Japan's biggest-grossing film ever. Although the movie had only limited release in the United States, devotees influenced by Miyazaki include John Lasseter (*Toy Story; A Bug's Life*) and Barry Cook and Tony Bancroft (*Mulan*). Animated films account for about 60 percent of film production in Japan.

Over time, the documentary developed an identity apart from its commercial presentation. As an educational, noncommercial form, the documentary usually required the backing of industry, government, or philanthropy to cover costs. In support of a clear alternative to Hollywood cinema, various governments began creating special units, such as Canada's National Film Board, to sponsor documentaries. In the United States, art and film received considerable support from the Roosevelt administration during the Depression. Such funding produced Pare Lorentz's *The Plow That Broke the Plains* (1936), which recounted the ecological abuse and erosion of the Great Plains in the 1930s. During World War II, the government continued to turn to filmmakers and to Hollywood to "sell" patriotism. Director Frank Capra produced the seven-part *Why We Fight* documentary series as propaganda to inspire support for the war effort against Germany and Japan.

By the late 1950s and early 1960s, the development of portable cameras had led to **cinema verité** (a French term for "truth film"). This documentary style allowed filmmakers to go where cameras could not go before and record fragments of everyday life more unobtrusively. Directly opposed to packaged, high-gloss Hollywood features, verité aimed to track reality, employing a rough, grainy look and shaky, handheld camerawork.

Among the key innovators in cinema verité were Drew and Associates, led by Robert Drew, a former *Life* magazine photographer. Through his connection to Time Inc. (which owned *Life*) and its chain of TV stations, Drew shot the groundbreaking documentary *Primary,* which followed the 1960 Democratic presidential primary race between Hubert Humphrey and John F. Kennedy. Drew's portable cameras went everywhere, capturing glimpses of the political process never seen before, including Humphrey directing rehearsals for a TV appearance and Kennedy in a Milwaukee hotel room nervously awaiting the results of the election.

Since the late 1960s, a leading American practitioner of cinema verité has been Frederick Wiseman, who has filmed a series of documentaries for public television on the misuses of power in American institutions. Unlike traditional TV news, in which the reporter's voice-over narration organizes the story, Wiseman used careful and clever editing to make his point without a reporter's comments. His work includes *Titicut Follies* (1967), which until 1993 was banned from public viewing in Massachusetts for its piercing look at a state-run mental health facility. Wiseman's films indirectly reveal institutional abuse and waste, and he and the verité tradition have been praised for bringing such issues to light. They have also been criticized, though, for offering few solutions to the institutional problems they expose.

The documentary form, both inside and outside the United States, extends from turn-of-the-century film shorts to Dziga Vertov's *Man with a Movie Camera* (1927), which demonstrated Soviet-sponsored innovations in film editing. In later eras, the documentary tradition included the French film *Night and Fog* (1955), which reported the atrocities of the Nazi death camps during World War II, and *Hoop Dreams* (1994), a three-hour examination of the rituals of college basketball recruiting in the United States.

Perhaps the major contribution of documentaries has been their willingness to tackle controversial or unpopular subject matter. For example, Michael Moore's *Roger and Me* (1989) presented a comic and controversial look at the complex relationship between the city of Flint, Michigan, and General Motors. More recently, Moore again created controversy with *Bowling for Columbine* (2002), which explored the predilection for violence with guns in the United States. Two of the most popular documentaries of recent years have humor at their heart: Spike Lee's *The Original Kings of Comedy* (2000) followed four African American stand-up comedians and won wide distribution in the United States. *Comedian* (2002) tracked Jerry Seinfeld's efforts to build an entirely new comedy routine after the end of his successful television sitcom, *Seinfeld.*

The Rise of Independent Films

The success of documentary films like *The Original Kings of Comedy* and *Hoop Dreams* dovetails with the rise of **indies**, or independently produced films. As opposed to directors working in the Hollywood system, independent filmmakers typically operate on a shoestring budget and show their movies in thousands of campus auditoriums and at hundreds of small film festivals. The decreasing costs of portable technology, including smaller cameras and digital computer editing, has kept many documentarists and other independent filmmakers in business. They make movies inexpensively, relying on real-life situations, stage actors and nonactors, crews made up of friends and students, and local settings outside the studio environment. Successful independents like Todd Solondz (*Welcome to the Dollhouse; Happiness*), Todd Haynes (*Velvet Goldmine; Far from Heaven*), and Mira Nair (*Salaam Bombay; Monsoon Wedding*) continue to find substantial audiences in college, art-house, and some mall theaters that promote work produced outside the studio system.

The rise of independent film festivals in the 1990s—especially the Sundance Film Festival held every January in Park City, Utah—has helped Hollywood rediscover low-cost independent films as an alternative to traditional movies with *Titanic*-size budgets. Films such as *Sex, Lies, and Videotape* (1989), *El Mariachi* (1993), *Shine* (1996), *The Full Monty* (1997), and *Real Women Have Curves* (2002) were all able to generate industry buzz and major studio distribution deals through Sundance screenings and became star vehicles for several directors and actors. One of the biggest successes of Sundance has been *The Blair Witch Project* (1999). The low-budget, low-tech, faux documentary was filmed by a team of University of Central Florida film school graduates for about $40,000. The young filmmakers sold the distribution rights for $1 million, and the movie went on to earn over $141 million at the box office, riding on a huge wave of buzz generated via the Internet, on college campuses, and eventually in the mainstream press. As with the recording industry, the major studios have recognized that in the 1990s, indies became a strong venue for discovering new talent. The studios have responded either by purchasing successful independent film companies (e.g., Disney's purchase of Miramax) or by developing in-house indie divisions (e.g., Sony's Sony Pictures Classics). Other independent filmmakers and writers gain wide exposure based on chance connections. For example, the ethnic comedy *My Big Fat Greek Wedding* (2002) was made for only $5 million but earned more than $240 million at the box office by February 2003 through positive word-of-mouth reviews, becoming the highest-grossing independent film ever in the United States. The movie was made possible in part by producer Rita Wilson and her husband, actor Tom Hanks, who saw the funny one-woman stage show by Nia Vardalos (who stars in the film) and helped bring her story based on her own Greek wedding to the screen.

> **"** After the success of *The Blair Witch Project* . . . it seemed that anyone with a dream, a camera and an Internet account could get a film made —or, at least, market it cheaply once it was made. **"**
>
> – Abby Ellin,
> *New York Times*, 2000

The Transformation of the Hollywood System

Beginning in 1946 and continuing over the next seventeen years, the movie industry lost much of its theatergoing audience. In 1951 alone, more than fifty theaters shut down in New York City. The ninety million people going to movies weekly in 1946 had fallen to less than twenty-five million by 1963. It seemed that the movie industry was in deep trouble, especially in light of television's ascent. Critics and observers began talking about the death of Hollywood. Although Hollywood had diminished as the geographic heart of the industry, a number of dramatic changes altered and eventually strengthened many aspects of the commercial movie business.

By the mid-1950s, significant cultural and social changes—such as suburbanization and the widespread availability of television—had begun to reshape the moviegoing experience. By 2002, Hollywood was coming off its biggest box-office revenues ever, as millions of moviegoers flocked to brand-new **megaplexes** (facilities with fourteen or more screens). Theaters, however, have been dramatically downsized from the five-thousand-seat movie palaces that reigned in the 1940s. But despite major social transformations, the commercial film industry remains controlled, as it was earlier, by a few powerful companies. Below, we will review the film industry's adjustments to changing conditions, particularly the impact of political and legal challenges, suburbanization, television, and other technological changes such as cable, VCRs, and DVDs.

The Hollywood Ten

In 1947, in the wake of the unfolding Cold War with the Soviet Union, conservative members of Congress began investigating Hollywood for alleged subversive and communist ties. That year, the aggressive witch-hunts for political radicals in the film industry by the House Un-American Activities Committee (HUAC) led to the famous **Hollywood Ten** hearings and subsequent trial. At the time, Congressman J. Parnell Thomas of New Jersey chaired HUAC, which included future president Richard M. Nixon, then a congressman from California, as one of five members of this powerful committee.

During the investigations, HUAC coerced prominent people from the film industry to declare their patriotism and to list those suspected of politically unfriendly tendencies. Upset over labor-union strikes and outspoken writers, many film executives were eager to testify. During the hearings, Jack L. Warner, of Warner Brothers, suggested that whenever film writers made fun of rich men or America's political system, they were engaging in communist propaganda. He reported that movies sympathetic to "Indians and the colored folks" were also suspect.[11] Film producer Sam Wood, who had directed Marx Brothers comedies in the mid-1930s, testified that communist writers could be spotted because they portrayed bankers and senators as villainous characters. Whether they believed it was their patriotic duty or they were afraid of losing their jobs, many film executives and prominent actors "named names" in 1947.

Eventually, HUAC subpoenaed ten unwilling witnesses who were questioned about their membership in various organizations. The so-called Hollywood Ten—nine screenwriters and one director—refused to discuss their memberships or to identify communist sympathizers. Charged with contempt of Congress in November 1947, they were eventually sent to prison. Ironically, two Hollywood Ten members went to the same prison as HUAC chairman Thomas, who would later be convicted of conspiracy to defraud the government in a phony payroll scheme. Although jailing the Hollywood Ten clearly violated their free-speech rights, in the atmosphere of the Cold War many seemingly well-intentioned people worried that "the American way" could be sabotaged via unfriendly messages planted in films.

Upon release from jail, the Hollywood Ten found themselves *blacklisted*, or boycotted, by the major studios, and their careers in the film industry were all but ruined. The national fervor over communism continued to plague Hollywood well into the 1950s.

The Paramount Decision

Coinciding with the political investigations, the government increased its scrutiny of the industry's aggressive business practices. By the mid-1940s, the Justice Department demanded that the five major film companies—Paramount, Warner Brothers,

Twentieth Century Fox, MGM, and RKO—end vertical integration. In 1948, after a series of court appeals, the Supreme Court ruled against the film industry in what is commonly known as **the Paramount decision**, forcing the studios to gradually divest themselves of their theaters.

Although the government had hoped to increase competition, the Paramount case never really changed the oligopoly structure of the commercial film industry. Initially, the 1948 decision did create opportunities in the exhibition part of the industry. In addition to art houses showing documentaries or foreign films, thousands of drive-in theaters sprang up in farmers' fields, welcoming new suburbanites who had left the city and embraced the automobile. Although drive-ins had been around since the 1930s, by the end of the 1950s more than four thousand existed. The Paramount decision encouraged other new indoor theater openings as well, but the major studios continued to dominate distribution. By producing the most polished and popular films, they still controlled consumer demand and orchestrated where the movies would play.

Moving to the Suburbs

Common sense might suggest that television alone precipitated the decline in post–World War II movie attendance, but the most dramatic drop actually occurred in the late 1940s—*before* most Americans even had TV sets.[12] In fact, with the FCC freeze on TV licenses between 1948 and 1952, most communities did not have TV stations up and running until 1954. By then, the theatergoing audience had already dropped by half.

The transformation of a wartime economy and an unprecedented surge in consumer production had a significant impact on moviegoing. With industries turning from armaments to appliances, Americans started cashing in their savings bonds for

● *Rebel Without a Cause* (1955), starring James Dean and Natalie Wood, was marketed in movie posters as "Warner Bros. Challenging Drama of Today's Teenage Violence!" James Dean's memorable portrayal of a troubled youth forever fixed his place in movie history. He was killed in a car crash a month before the movie opened.

household goods and new cars. Discretionary income that formerly went to movie tickets now went to acquiring consumer products. And the biggest product of all was a new house in the suburbs, far from the downtown theaters where movies still premiered. Relying on government help through Veterans Administration loans, people left the cities in record numbers to buy affordable houses in suburban areas where tax bases were lower. Home ownership in the United States doubled between 1945 and 1950, while the moviegoing public decreased just as quickly. According to census data, new housing starts, which had held steady at about 100,000 a year since the late 1920s, leaped to more than 930,000 in 1946 and peaked at 1,700,000 in 1950.

After World War II, the average age for couples entering marriage dropped from twenty-four to nineteen. Unlike their parents, many postwar couples had their first children before they turned twenty-one. The combination of social and economic changes meant there were significantly fewer couples dating at the movies. The suburban move altered spending patterns and had a far more profound impact on movie attendance than did television in the early 1950s. In terms of income, there was little left over for movies after mortgage and car payments. When television exploded in the late 1950s, there was even less discretionary income—and less reason to go to the movies.

Television Changes Hollywood

In the late 1940s, radio's popularity had a stronger impact than television on film's apparent decline. Not only were 1948 and 1949 high points in radio listenership, but with the shift to the suburbs, radio entertainment offered Americans an inexpensive alternative to the movies (as it had in the 1930s). As a result, many people stayed home and listened to radio programs until TV assumed this social function in the mid-1950s. Moviegoing was already in steep decline by the time television further eroded the annual number of movie tickets sold, which had peaked at four billion in 1946 but declined and then leveled off at around one billion by 1963.

By the mid-1950s, television had displaced both radio and movies as the medium of national entertainment. With growing legions of people gathering around their living-room TV sets, movie content slowly shifted toward more serious subjects. Although this shift may at first have been a response to the war and an acknowledgment of life's complexity, later movies started to focus on subject matter that television did not encourage. The shift in content began with the rise of film noir in the 1940s but continued into the 1950s as commercial movies, for the first time, explored larger social problems such as alcoholism (*The Lost Weekend*, 1945), anti-Semitism (*Gentleman's Agreement*, 1947), mental illness (*The Snake Pit*, 1948), racism (*Pinky*, 1949), adult–teen relationships (*Rebel Without a Cause*, 1955), and drug abuse (*The Man with the Golden Arm*, 1955).

Directors even explored sexual relationships that were formerly off-limits to film (in movies such as *Peyton Place*, 1957; *Butterfield 8*, 1960; and *Lolita*, 1962) and certainly off-limits to viewers of wholesome family television. Filmmakers also challenged the industry's own prohibitive Motion Picture Production Code (see Chapter 16), which had placed restrictions on film content to quiet public and political concerns about the movie business. Like sound recording executives in the early 1990s, movie administrators who worried about government regulation and public boycotts began planning a self-imposed ratings system. The explicit language and situations of *Who's Afraid of Virginia Woolf?* (1966), based on an Edward Albee play, led to the formation of the current ratings system in 1967. Nevertheless, filmmakers continued to make movies considered inappropriate for television as a way of holding on to under-thirty audiences, which had become the dominant group of theatergoers. By the 1980s and 1990s, however, with the baby-boom generation growing older and starting families, commercial opportunities emerged for popular feature-length cartoons and family movies, making Disney the most successful contemporary studio.

In terms of technology, Hollywood tried a number of approaches in an effort to appeal to the new TV generation. Technicolor, invented by an MIT scientist in 1917, had gradually improved, and it offered images that far surpassed those on a fuzzy black-and-white TV. Color advancement, though, was not enough for studio chiefs, who were increasingly alarmed by the popularity of television. Just as radio in the 1950s worked to improve sound to maintain an advantage over television, the film industry introduced a host of gimmicks to draw attention to the superiority of movie narratives.

In the early to mid-1950s, Cinerama, CinemaScope, and VistaVision all arrived in movie theaters, featuring striking wide-screen images, multiple synchronized projectors, and stereophonic sound. Then 3-D (three-dimensional) movies appeared, including Warner Brothers' horror film *House of Wax*, wildly popular in its first few weeks in theaters. But, like other experiments, 3-D required a large investment in new projection technology, plus special glasses distributed to all moviegoers. In addition, 3-D suffered from out-of-focus images; it wore off quickly as a novelty. Panavision, which used special Eastman color film and camera lenses that decreased the fuzziness of images, finally became the wide-screen standard throughout the industry. The new gimmicks, however, generally failed to address the movies' primary problem: the middle-class flight to the suburbs, away from downtown movie theaters.

Hollywood Adapts to Video

Just as nickelodeons, movie palaces, and drive-ins transformed movie exhibition in earlier times, the videocassette transformed contemporary movie exhibition. Despite the scope of Technicolor and wide-screen cinema, and despite theaters experimenting with five-story IMAX megascreens and surround sound, most people still prefer the convenience of watching movies at home. In fact, more than 50 percent of domestic revenue for Hollywood studios comes from the video/DVD rental and sales markets. Aside from videocassettes, pay-per-view and premium cable have also stolen parts of the theatergoing crowd, leaving box-office receipts accounting for just 20 percent of total film revenue by 2003. With the advent of videocassettes and cable, viewers are no longer required to catch a film in limited theatrical release—they can always view it later on. To keep their edge, TV manufacturers have introduced stereo sets and produced larger TV screens. New digital screens permit image projection the size of a living-room wall, more closely replicating a theater experience. As television monitors adopt the 16 : 9 aspect ratio that mimics the film screen (wider than the standard 4 : 3 dimension of television screens), the home-video experience feels even more like going to a movie theater.

Even though theater crowds have dwindled over the years, watching movies is a bigger business than ever. Film studios initially feared the coming of television in the 1950s—to the point of banning film actors from performing on the small screen—but television has, ironically, become a major second-run venue for many movies. In similar fashion, the movie industry tried to stall the arrival of the VCR in the 1970s—even filing suits to prohibit consumers from copying movies from television. But home-cassette and DVD rentals and purchases have turned into a bonanza for the movie business, extending the profitability of a movie product. For example, Disney/Pixar's *Monster's Inc.* earned $122 million during its first ten days at the box office. But just in the movie's first week as a for-purchase DVD in 2002, the movie grossed

> **❝ So TV did not kill Hollywood. In the great Hollywood whodunit there is, after all, not even a corpse. The film industry never died. Only where we enjoy its latest products has changed, forever.❞**
>
> –Douglas Gomery, *Wilson Quarterly,* 1991

far more in retail sales than its box-office take—$175 million. In just a month, *Monster's Inc.* DVD sales easily passed the film's total box-office sales of $256 million.[13]

By the beginning of 2003, about 92 percent of U.S. homes had VCRs and about 40 percent had DVD players; consumers were spending nearly $19 billion annually on prerecorded DVDs and videos. Also, with the growing popularity of the DVDs—which have a much higher purchase rate than VHS cassettes—sales of recorded video began to outweigh rentals. The home-video retail market maintains an edge over pay-per-view and premium cable channels by offering large libraries of titles. Viacom-owned Blockbuster dominates the industry, controlling 40 percent of the market with more than 6,000 stores in the United States (and 2,000 more stores outside of the United States). Its nearest competitor, Hollywood Video, has about 1,800 stores. As Blockbuster and Hollywood Video have grown, buying up smaller outlets and driving others out of business, the total number of video/DVD stores has decreased in recent years. Currently, about 24,300 retail video stores operate in the United States.

The introduction of the DVD format in 1997 helped reinvigorate the flat sales of the mature VHS video market, especially as people began to acquire new movie collections on DVD. Similar to the introduction of other technologies, such as the compact disc, DVD adoption rates were initially low because of expensive players ($500 or more) and limited content. But, by 2003, the price of many DVD players had plummeted to below $70, and thousands of new and classic movie titles were available for rent and purchase. Furthermore, the DVD format offers many advantages over VHS videocassettes: better visual quality, extra "outtake" scenes and movie information, multiple language subtitles from which to select, and the ability to cue the movie to any point. In fact, analysts predict that videocassettes will disappear from stores by 2007.

The Economics of the Movie Business

Despite the development of made-for-TV movies as well as the rise of the network era, cable television, pay-per-view, and home video, the movie business has continued to thrive. In fact, since 1963 Americans have purchased roughly one billion movie tickets each year, although by 2002 this jumped to about one-and-a-half billion tickets sold.[14] With first-run movie tickets in some areas rising gradually to more than $9.00 by 2003, gross revenues from box-office sales had climbed to more than $9 billion, up from $3.8 billion annually in the mid-1980s, as shown in Figure 7.1. In addition, video rentals and sales produced another $19 billion a year, more than doubling box-office receipts. To survive and flourish, the movie industry not only followed middle-class migration to the shopping malls but moved right into suburban homes. In other words, in 2003 more people watched commercial films on home-video and DVD players in one month than attended movie theaters for the entire year.

Production, Distribution, and Exhibition Today

It took until the 1970s for the movie industry to determine where the moviegoers had gone and how to catch up with them. Among the major "stars" in this effort were multiscreen movie complexes, called **multiplexes**, located either in shopping malls or at the crossroads of major highways. Throughout the 1970s, attendance by young moviegoers at the new multiplexes made megahits of *The Godfather* (1972), *The Exorcist* (1973), *Jaws* (1975), *Rocky* (1976), and *Star Wars* (1977). During this period, *Jaws*

Figure 7.1 Gross Revenues from Box-Office Sales, 1984–2002

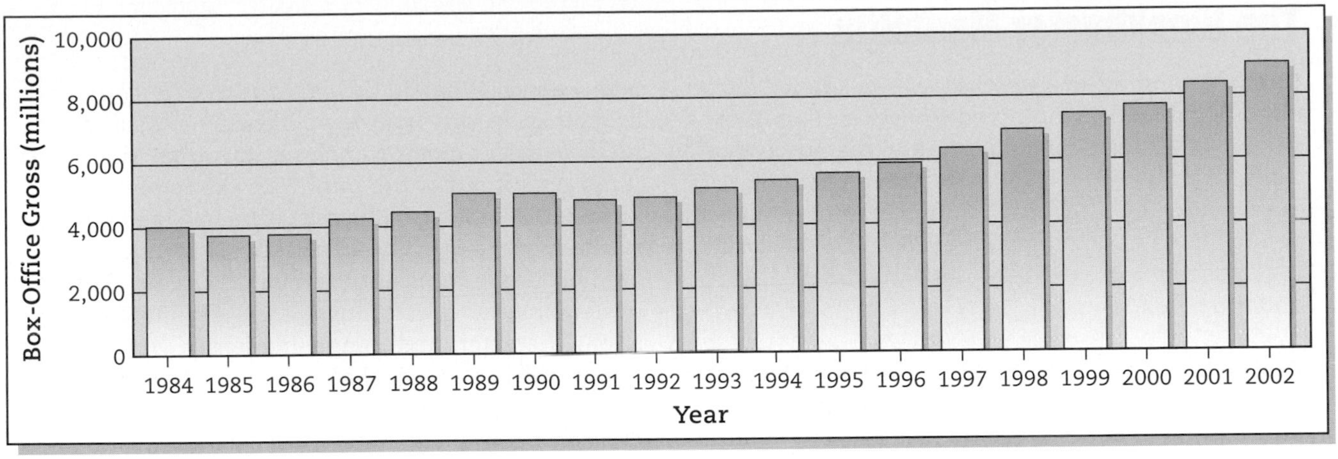

Sources: Motion Picture Association of America, *U.S. Economic Reviews,* 2001, <http://www.mpaa.com>, and Rick Lyman, "A big fat box office increase," *New York Times,* 30 December 2002, <http://www.nytimes.com>.

and *Star Wars* became the first movies to gross more than $100 million at the U.S. box office in a single year.

In trying to copy the success of these blockbuster hits, the major studios set in place economic strategies for future decades. With 80 to 90 percent of newly released movies failing to make money at the box office, the studios hoped for at least one major hit each year to offset losses on other films. By the 1980s, though, studios were already recouping box-office losses through the lucrative video market, as well as through foreign markets. For example, even though *The Beach* (2000), starring Leonardo DiCaprio, earned less than $40 million in the United States (well short of its $50 million in production and marketing costs), it went on to earn an additional $100 million in foreign markets and recorded an overall profit. (See "Applied Critical Process: The Blockbuster Mentality" on page 252.)

At the same time, movie studios were also confronting the escalating costs of making films. By 2001, a major studio film, on average, cost $47.7 million to produce. In that same year, marketing, advertising, and print costs increased 6.5 percent to $31.3 million per film, bringing the total average cost for major studio motion pictures to more than $78.7 million in 2001.[15]

With climbing film costs, creating revenue from a movie is a formidable task. Studios make money on movies from six major sources. First, the studios get a portion of the theater box-office revenue—about 40 percent of the box-office take goes to the producing studio, with 60 percent going to the theaters. Overall, box-office receipts provide studios with approximately 20 percent of a movie's domestic revenue. Second, video and DVD sales and rentals account for more than half of all domestic-film income for major studios. Third, the film is released to various cable and television outlets. After video stores get an exclusive "window," or period of time to offer a movie to customers, the studios then may release a movie to pay-per-view channels, video-on-demand channels, premium cable channels (such as HBO), network and basic cable channels, and, finally, the syndicated TV market. The price these cable and television outlets pay to the studios is negotiated on a film-by-film basis. Fourth, studios earn profits from distributing films in foreign markets. Fifth, studios make money by distributing the work of independent producers and filmmakers, who usually must hire the studios to gain wide circulation. Independents pay the studios between 30 and 50 percent of the box-office and video-rental money they make from

The Blockbuster Mentality

In the beginning of this chapter, we quoted film critic Roger Ebert, who noted Hollywood's shift toward a blockbuster mentality after the success of films like *Star Wars*. How pervasive is this blockbuster mentality, whose characteristics include young adults as the target audience, action-packed big-budget releases, heavy merchandising tie-ins, and the possibility of sequels?

Description. Consider a list of top 25 all-time highest grossing movies in the United States, such as the one on the Internet Movie Database http://indie .imdb.com/Charts/usatopmovies>.

Analyis. Note patterns in the list. For example, of these 25 top-grossing films, 23 target young audiences (*Forrest Gump* and *The Sixth Sense* are the only exceptions). Two-thirds of these top-grossing films feature animated or digitally composited characters (e.g., *Lion King*; *Shrek*; *Jurassic Park* dinosaurs) or extensive special effects (*Titanic*; *Spider-Man*). Two-thirds also either spawned or are a part of a series, like *Lord of the Rings*, *Batman*, *Home Alone*, and *Harry Potter*. Half of the films fit into the action movie genre. Nearly all of the top 25 had intense merchandising campaigns that featured action figures, fast-food tie-ins, and an incredible variety of products for sale. That is, nearly all weren't "surprise" hits.

Interpretation. What do the patterns mean? It's clear, economically, why Hollywood likes to have successful blockbuster movie franchises. But what kinds of films get left out of the mix? Hits like *Forrest Gump* and *The Sixth Sense*, which may have had big-budget releases but lack some of the other attributes of blockbusters, are clearly anomalies of the blockbuster mentality, although they illustrate that strong characters and compelling stories can carry a film to great commercial success.

Evaluation. It is likely that we will continue to see an increase in youth-oriented, animated/action movie franchises that are heavily merchandised and intended for wide international distribution. Indeed, Hollywood does not have a lot of motivation to put out other kinds of movies that don't fit these categories. Is this a good thing? Can you think of a film that you thought was excellent and that would have likely been a bigger hit with better promotion and wider distribution? Do you think independent successes like *My Big Fat Greek Wedding*—produced for $5 million and now in the top 30 of highest-grossing films—may mark a change in Hollywood storytelling?

● *My Big Fat Greek Wedding* (2002), a romantic comedy starring Nia Vardalos and John Corbett, started slowly at the box office but grew to be the biggest independent film in history, with more than $240 million in box-office revenue.

movies. As distributors, the film studios bear no production costs and charge independents for advertising and promoting their movies. Independents also pay distributors for making copies of the films sent to theaters and video stores. Because producers make money only after all distribution costs are paid, distributors can earn revenue even when the producers don't. Sixth, major studios are increasingly gaining revenue from merchandise licensing and product placements in their movies. In the earlier days of television and film, characters generally used generic products, or product labels weren't highlighted in shots. For example, Bette Davis's and Humphrey Bogart's cigarette packs were rarely seen in their movies. But with soaring film production costs, product placements are adding extra revenues while lending an element of authenticity to the staging. Famous product placements in movies include Reese's Pieces in *E.T.: The Extra-Terrestrial* (1982), Pepsi-Cola in *Back to the Future II* (1989), Dunkin' Donuts in *Good Will Hunting* (1997), and Starbucks in *Austin Powers: The Spy Who Shagged Me* (1999). The high profile of America Online in *You've Got Mail* (1998) netted between $3 and $6 million for Warner Brothers—the largest product placement deal yet.

Generally, major stars and directors receive separate fees and percentages totaling more than $30 million over and above the production costs for a blockbuster-

Table 7.3 Top 10 Movie Theater Chains in North America

Company	Headquarters	Number of Screens (Worldwide)	Sites
1. Regal Cinemas	Knoxville, TN	5,850	552
2. AMC Entertainment	Kansas City, MO	3,308	235
3. Carmike Cinemas	Columbus, GA	2,333	191
4. Cinemark USA	Plano, TX	2,241	191
5. Loews Cineplex	New York	2,161	226
6. National Amusements	Dedham, MA	1,087	96
7. Hoyts Cinemas	Boston, MA	922	102
8. Famous Players	Toronto, ON	841	91
9. Century Theatres	San Rafael, CA	822	76
10. Kerasotes Theatres	Springfield, IL	532	81

Source: National Association of Theatre Owners, "Top 10 Circuits (as of June 1, 2002)," <www.natoonline.org>.

type movie. Lesser-known actors and directors, assistant producers, screenplay writers, costume and set designers, film editors, music composers, and the cinematographers who physically shoot the movie, however, are paid a flat fee for their work and do not usually share in the net profits from a movie (although Dreamworks, Disney, Warner Brothers, and Columbia Pictures now write contracts that give cartoon animators and screenwriters a share of a film's profits).

Film exhibition, like distribution, is now controlled by a handful of theater chains. By 2002, several major consolidations and extensive theater expansion projects had left the top seven companies operating more than 50 percent of U.S. screens. The major chains—Regal Cinemas, AMC Entertainment, Carmike Cinemas, Cinemark USA, Loews Cineplex Entertainment, National Amusements, and Hoyts Cinema Group—own thousands of screens each in suburban malls and at highway crossroads, and most have expanded into international markets as well (see Table 7.3). Because distributors require access to movie screens, they do business with those chains that control the most screens. In a multiplex, an exhibitor can project a potential hit on two or three screens at the same time; films that do not debut well are relegated to the smallest theaters or bumped quickly for a new release.

The strategy of the leading theater chains during the 1990s was to build more megaplexes (facilities with fourteen or more screens), but with upscale concession services and luxurious screening rooms with stadium-style seating and digital sound to make moviegoing a special event. Still, going out to the movies appeals to only a specific market of people. Frequent moviegoers (people who attend at least twelve films per year) make up only 27 percent of the moviegoing population, but they account for 82 percent of ticket sales. In general, the theater audience for movies is young: Individuals under age thirty account for more than 50 percent of movie theater attendance.

In the past decade, the movie exhibition industry has been tapping into markets that are generally underserved. Notable is the partnership formed between Earvin "Magic" Johnson (formerly of the NBA's Los Angeles Lakers) and Sony Theatres in the 1990s to build Magic Johnson Theatres in urban minority communities in Los Angeles, Atlanta, Houston, and elsewhere. By building near existing shopping areas and hiring

❝ It is hard to mix business and culture. Business is going to win. ❞

— Jeremy Thomas, British Film Institute, 1996

from the surrounding community, these state-of-the-art multiplexes provide employment opportunities and foster local economic growth as well as offer entertainment.

Even with record box-office revenues, the major movie theater chains entered the 2000s in miserable financial shape. After several years of fast-paced building and renovations, beginning with a twenty-four-screen AMC megaplex in Dallas in 1995, the major chains had built an excess of screens and accrued an enormous debt. Although the attractive new megaplexes have pleased moviegoers, they have been expensive to build. In 2000, the cost to construct new theaters jumped to $1 million per screen, up from $500,000 per screen just five years earlier. By 2001, AMC was the only large theater chain that had not filed for—or was not on the verge of—bankruptcy.[16] But after closing hundreds of underperforming theaters and with a record finish to the box office in 2001, the movie exhibition business began to recover in 2002 (see Figure 7.2).

The Major Players

The American commercial film business and the classic Hollywood narrative remained dominant into the twenty-first century. Although MGM/UA (*Legally Blonde; Die Another Day*) was making a comeback after years of neglect and mismanagement, the industry was ruled primarily by six companies: Warner Brothers, Paramount, Twentieth Century Fox, Universal, Columbia Pictures, and Walt Disney. Except for Disney, all these companies are owned by large parent conglomerates (see Table 7.4). One new studio, Dreamworks, created in 1994 by Steven Spielberg, former Disney executive Jeffrey Katzenberg, and sound recording tycoon David Geffen, began to rival

Figure 7.2 Indoor Theater Screens in the United States, 1977–2001

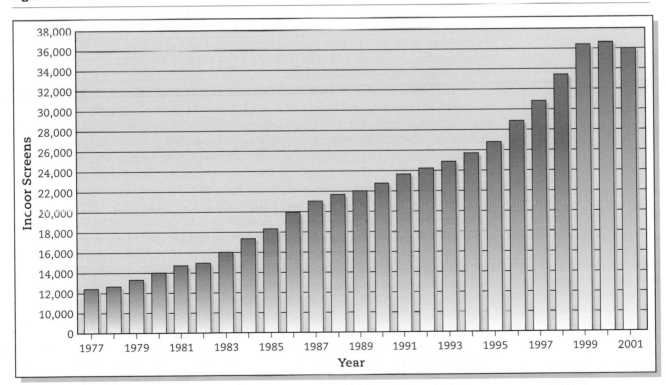

Source: Motion Picture Association of America, *U.S. Economic Reviews,* 2001, <http://www.mpaa.com>.
Note: Industry analysts predicted a continued reduction in the number of movie screens in 2002, to a total of about 32,500 by 2003.

Table 7.4 The Major Players in the Movie Business

Studio	Parent Company	Other Subsidiaries
Warner Brothers	AOL Time Warner (USA)	Turner Broadcasting, WB TV network, HBO, cable systems, magazines, records, D.C. Comics, books, Book-of-the-Month Club, theme parks
Walt Disney	Disney (USA)	ABC, theme parks, ESPN, broadcast stations, cable channels, books, magazines, newspapers, hockey team, baseball team
Columbia Pictures	Sony (Japan)	TV sets, VCRs, camcorders, CD-ROM drives, CD players, Walkman, videotapes, records, TV programs, movie theaters
Twentieth Century Fox	News Corp. (Australia)	Fox TV network, newspapers, broadcast stations, cable channels, books, satellite-delivery services, baseball team, rugby team
Paramount	Viacom (USA)	CBS, Blockbuster Video, UPN TV network, records, books, magazines, MTV, Nickelodeon, Showtime, movie theaters, broadcast stations
Universal	Vivendi Universal (France)	MCA Records, PolyGram Records, USA Networks, cable channels

Source: BOXOFFICE Magazine Special Report: Giants of Exhibition 2001, <www.boxoffice.com/giantstop.html>.

the production capabilities of the majors with films like *Saving Private Ryan, Gladiator,* and *Shrek.* Nevertheless, the six major studios accounted for more than 90 percent of the revenue generated by commercial films. They also controlled more than half the movie market in Europe and Asia, with nearly a third of the industry's annual box-office profits coming from overseas.

In the 1980s, to offset losses resulting from box-office failures, the movie industry began to diversify, expanding into other product lines and other mass media. This expansion included television programming, print media, sound recordings, and home videos/DVDs as well as cable and computers, electronic hardware and software, videocassettes, and theme parks such as Universal Studios. Indicative of the effectiveness of this strategy, in 1980 more than 80 percent of movie-studio revenue came from box-office receipts; in 2002, about 20 percent came from that source.

To maintain the industry's economic stability, management strategies today rely on both heavy advance promotion (which can double the cost of a commercial film) and the process of *synergy*—the promotion and sale of a product throughout the various subsidiaries of the media conglomerate. In other words, companies promote not only the new movie itself but its book form, soundtrack, calendars, T-shirts, Web site, toy action figures, and "the-making-of" story for distribution on television, cable, and home video. The Disney studio, in particular, has been successful with its multiple packaging of the company's youth-targeted movies, which includes comic books, toys, cable specials, fast-food tie-ins, and new theme-park attractions. Since the 1950s, this synergy has been the biggest change in the film industry and a key element in the flood of corporate mergers.

The first company to change hands in the atmosphere of postwar business mergers was Paramount, which was sold to Gulf & Western Industries in 1966. (Para-

● The first fully digital release from a major studio, *Time Code* (2000) offers frames of simultaneous action. The plot alternates between a love affair and the goings-on at a film-production company. Though sometimes overlapping, the soundtrack usually coincides with a single frame.

mount is now owned by Viacom, which originally made its mark by syndicating TV shows.) The next year Transamerica, an insurance and financial services company, bought United Artists (which merged with MGM in 1981). The biggest mergers, however, have involved the internationalization of the American film business. This began in 1985, when the Australian media conglomerate News Corp. paid nearly $1 billion for Twentieth Century Fox. Along with News Corp., the new players in Hollywood have been large Japanese electronics firms. First purchased by Coca-Cola in 1980, Columbia Pictures was absorbed by Sony for more than $4 billion in 1989. In the deal, Sony acquired a library of twenty-seven hundred films and twenty-three thousand TV episodes. In 1990, Matsushita paid $7 billion for MCA/Universal and in 1995 sold 80 percent of its Universal stock to Seagram, the Canadian beverage company. Universal changed hands once again in 2000, when Paris-based water and telecommunications utility Vivendi acquired it for $34 billion and renamed the newly created media giant Vivendi Universal.

Investment in American popular culture by the international electronics industry is particularly significant. This business strategy represents a new, high-tech kind of vertical integration—an attempt to control both the production of electronic equipment that consumers buy for their homes and the production/distribution of the content that runs on that equipment. Companies such as Sony in Japan or Philips in the Netherlands have sought to increase markets for their electronics hardware by buying "software," especially movies, recordings, and TV shows.

Even as foreign investment in the U.S. commercial film industry has increased, government policies in many nations have attempted to limit the influence of American films. Restrictions on importing U.S. films and TV programs are intended to promote the domestic film/TV industries in various countries and blunt the impact of U.S. popular culture. In 1989, for example, twelve European countries began placing a 50 percent quota on the amount of time they would allocate for the exhibition of American films and TV shows. With the expansion of cable and satellite-delivered television and movies, however, many countries still depend on inexpensive and abundant U.S. products to fill up channels.

Alternative Voices

The digital revolution in movie production is also a revolution in the cost and accessibility of high-quality production equipment. The revolution is really about a shift from celluloid film to digital video, as movie directors replace expensive and bulky 16-mm and

35-mm film cameras with less expensive, lightweight digital video cameras. For moviemakers, digital video also means seeing camerawork instantly instead of waiting for film to be developed, and being able to capture additional footage without concern for the high cost of film stock and processing.

By 2002, a number of major directors began testing the digital video format, including Steven Soderbergh, Spike Lee, Francis Ford Coppola, and Gus Van Sant. George Lucas, an early supporter of digital video with *The Phantom Menace* (1999), plans to go entirely digital for the remaining *Star Wars* episodes, but British director Mike Figgis more quickly reached the milestone of the first fully digital release from a major studio with *Time Code* (2000). The impact of the digital format on major movie productions is significant. Lucas estimates that in processing and distribution, digital video will ultimately pare as much as $15 million from the cost of a major motion picture.

But the greatest impact of digital technology is on independent filmmakers. The high cost of film has long acted as a gatekeeper to would-be directors, and only those with generous benefactors or investors have been able to work with the medium. Low-cost digital video opens up the creative process to countless new artists. With digital video camera equipment and computer-based desktop editors, short movies can now be made for just a few thousand dollars, a fraction of what the cost would be on film. For many new digital video makers, *The Blair Witch Project* (1999), made for about $40,000 with mostly digital equipment and grossing over $141 million in theaters, is their greatest inspiration. Digital filmmaking had clearly caught on by the 2002 Sundance Film Festival, where half of the documentary films and six of the sixteen films in the dramatic competition were shot digitally.

Because digital production puts movies in the same format as CD-ROMs and the Internet, independent filmmakers have new distribution venues beyond the short runs of film festivals. For example, AtomFilms.com, formed in 1998, has grown into one of the leading Internet sites for the screening and distribution of short films. The site also sells DVD and videocassette collections of independent short films. Other sites, such as IFILM.com, also offer independent directors opportunities to have their short films streamed to potentially millions of viewers, providing filmmakers with their most valuable asset—an audience.

★ Popular Movies and Implications for Democracy

Although alternative films may be hard to find, most other movies are readily available today—at the mall, on broadcast and cable television, in campus auditoriums, on videocassettes and DVDs, on pay-per-view, and in neighborhood theaters. However flawed, most of these are Hollywood films: the common currency in a global market.

At the cultural level, commercial U.S. films function as *consensus narratives*, a term that describes cultural products that become popular and command wide attention. For all their limitations, classic Hollywood movies, as consensus narratives, provide shared cultural experiences, operating across different times and cultures. In this sense, movies are part of a long narrative tradition, encompassing "the oral-formulaic of Homer's day, the theater of Sophocles, the Elizabethan theater, the English novel from Defoe to Dickens, . . . the silent film, the sound film, and television during the Network Era."[17] Consensus narratives—whether they are dramas, romances, westerns, or mysteries—speak to central myths and values in an accessible language that often bridges global boundaries.

At the international level, countries continue to struggle with questions about the influence of American films on local customs and culture. Like other media industries, the long reach of Hollywood movies is one of the key contradictions of contemporary life: Do such films contribute to a global village in which people throughout the world share a universal culture that breaks down barriers? Or does an American-based common culture stifle the development of local cultures worldwide and diversity in moviemaking? Clearly, the steady production of profitable action/adventure movies—whether they originate in the United States, Africa, France, or China—continues not only because these movies appeal to teens and young adults but because they translate easily into other languages.

With the rise of international media conglomerates, it has become more difficult to awaken public debate over issues of movie diversity and America's domination of the film business. In addition, technological innovations—whether they affect radio, television, film, cable, or the Internet—tend to outpace questions of legislation and regulation. Consequently, issues concerning greater competition and a better variety of movies sometimes fall by the wayside. As critical consumers, those of us who enjoy movies and recognize their cultural significance must raise these broader issues in public forums as well as in our personal conversations.

www.

To create an individualized study plan for Chapter 7, go to the interactive *Media and Culture* Online Study Guide at: bedfordstmartins.com/mediaculture

REVIEW QUESTIONS

Early Technology and the Evolution of Movies

1. How did film go from the novelty stage to the mass-medium stage?

2. Why were early silent films popular?

3. What contribution did nickelodeons make to film history?

The Power of the Studio System

4. Why did Hollywood end up as the center of film production?

5. Why did Thomas Edison and the patents Trust fail to shape and control the film industry, and why did Adolph Zukor of Paramount succeed?

6. How does vertical integration work in the film business?

The Triumph of Hollywood Storytelling

7. Why did a certain structure of film—called classic Hollywood narrative—become so dominant in moviemaking?

8. Why are genres and directors important to the film industry?

9. Why are documentaries an important alternative to traditional Hollywood filmmaking? What contributions have they made to the film industry?

The Transformation of the Hollywood System

10. What political and cultural forces changed the Hollywood system in the 1950s?

11. Explain how television changed the film industry.

12. How has the movie industry used television to its advantage?

The Economics of the Movie Business

13. What are the various ways in which major movie studios make money from the film business?

14. How do a few large film studios manage to control more than 90 percent of the commercial industry?

15. Why do U.S. movies remain popular worldwide while other countries have had great difficulty getting their films into the United States?

16. What is the current economic health of the movie industry, compared to previous eras?

Popular Movies and Implications for Democracy

17. Do films contribute to a global village in which people throughout the world share a universal culture? Or do U.S.-based films overwhelm the development of other cultures worldwide? Discuss.

QUESTIONING THE MEDIA

1. Describe your earliest memory of going to a movie. Do some research and compare this with a parent's or grandparent's earliest memory. Compare the different experiences.

2. Do you remember a movie you were not allowed to see? Discuss the experience.

3. How often do you go to movie theaters today? How often do you rent movies on video or DVD? Which experience do you prefer and why?

4. If you were a Hollywood film producer or executive, what kinds of films would you like to see made? What changes would you make in what we see at the movies?

5. Look at the international film box-office statistics in the latest issue of *Variety* magazine. Note which films are the most popular worldwide. What do you think about the significant role U.S. movies play in global culture? Should their role be less significant? Explain your answer.

SEARCHING THE INTERNET

http://us.imdb.com

The Internet Movie Database is a powerful, searchable movie database of more than 330,000 film titles.

http://www.hollywood.com

Hollywood.com includes film reviews, movie trailers and clips, soundtrack files, TV movies, Hollywood headlines, film release calendars, film festival reports, and an online store.

http://www.foreignfilms.com

A comprehensive Web site featuring news and information about classic foreign titles and the latest arthouse releases.

http://www.aint-it-cool-news.com

Movie reviews and humorous, critical industry-insider accounts written by Texas-based Harry Knowles.

http://movieweb.com

Movieweb contains listings of all motion-picture releases dating back to 1995, organized by year and by studio, as well as weekly box-office rankings.

http://www.indiewire.com

News about independent films and do-it-yourself moviemaking information.

http://www.sundance.org

Information on the Sundance Film Festival, and a searchable database of independent films.

In Brief

In class, make a tally of who prefers to attend movies in the theater and who prefers to watch movies at home on video or DVD. Discuss the advantages and disadvantages of both viewing habits. Discuss whether theatergoing will become obsolete in the next decade, given that increasingly more revenue is earned through video release than through box-office receipts.

What could be done to enhance moviegoing in theaters? Make a list. How might your ideas be reasonably financed? Would there be a payoff for theater owners?

In Depth

Pick a current popular film you have seen or one the class has seen together. Write a three- to four-page (750–1,000 word) movie critique either defending or attacking the movie as a form of popular culture (see Chapter 1). Include plenty of examples to support your argument, and focus on three or four significant points. Follow the four stages of the critical process to organize your critique:

Description. In preparing to write your paper, describe important plot, theme, or character points that are relevant to your argument. (This is essentially the note-taking part of your paper.)

Analysis. Analyze the particular patterns (the three or four significant points) that emerge from your Description step and that you have chosen to examine.

Interpretation. Interpret what all of this information might mean based on the evidence you provide.

Evaluation. Discuss the limits of your critique and offer evaluations of the film industry based on your evidence and your interpretations. Evaluate the movie by judging whether it works as high art or as popular culture. As part of your evaluation, cite reviews from other publications to support your point of view.

KEY TERMS

newspapers

and the rise of modern journalism

CHAPTER 8

In 1887, a young reporter left her job at the *Pittsburgh Dispatch* to seek her fortune in New York City. Although only twenty-three years old, she had grown tired of merely replying to letters and writing for the society pages. She wanted to be on the front page. In those days, however, it was considered unladylike for women journalists to use their real names, so the *Dispatch* editors changed her name from Elizabeth "Pink" Cochrane to Nellie Bly, a name adapted from a Stephen Foster song about the servant daughter of former slaves.

After four months of persistent job-hunting and freelance writing, Nellie Bly earned a tryout at Joseph Pulitzer's *New York World,* the nation's biggest paper. Her assignment: to investigate the deplorable conditions at the Women's Lunatic Asylum on Blackwell's Island. Her method: to get herself declared mad and committed to the asylum. After practicing the look of a disheveled lunatic in front of mirrors, wandering city streets dazed and unwashed, and terrifying her fellow boarders in a New York rooming house by acting

crazy, she succeeded in convincing doctors and officials to commit her. Other New York newspapers even reported her incarceration, speculating on the identity of this "mysterious waif," this "pretty crazy girl" with the "wild, hunted look in her eyes."[1]

Ten days later, an attorney from the *World* went in to get her out. Her two-part story appeared in October 1887 and caused a sensation in New York. She was the first reporter to have pulled off such a stunt. In the days before so-called objective journalism, Nellie Bly's dramatic first-person accounts documented harsh cold baths ("three buckets of water over my head—ice cold water—into my eyes, my ears, my nose and my mouth"); "cruel" attendants who abused and taunted patients; and newly arrived immigrant women, completely sane, who were committed to this "rat trap" simply because no one could understand them. After the series, Bly was famous. Pulitzer gave her a permanent job, and the city of New York committed $1 million toward upgrading the conditions of its asylums.

Within a year, Nellie Bly exposed a variety of shady scam artists, corrupt politicians and lobbyists, and unscrupulous business practices. Posing as an unwed mother with an unwanted child, she uncovered an outfit trafficking in newborn babies. Disguised as a sinner in need of reform, she revealed the appalling conditions at a home for "unfortunate women." And after stealing $50 from another woman's purse, she got herself arrested and then reported on how women were treated in New York jails.

A lifetime champion of women and the poor, Nellie Bly also pioneered what was called at the time *detective* or *stunt* journalism. Her work would inspire the whole twentieth-century practice of investigative journalism—from Ida Tarbell's exposés of oil corporations in the early 1900s to the award-winning *Wall Street Journal* investigations of big tobacco companies in the mid-1990s. From the vantage point of both the press and the public, this investigative tradition remains one of journalism's most revered contributions to democracy.

along with their watchdog role, newspapers play many parts in American culture. As chroniclers of daily life, newspapers both inform and entertain. They give assurances that communities are safe and nations are secure. Newspapers help readers make choices about everything from the kind of food to eat to the kind of leaders to elect. Comic strips and political cartoons find humor in everyday events. Opinion pages organize public debates and persuade readers to a particular point of view. Syndicated columnists offer everything from practical advice on raising children to political insight into the September 11, 2001, terrorist attacks.

Despite the importance of newspapers in daily life, in today's digital age the industry is losing both papers and readers at an alarming rate. Newspapers still garner a substantial portion of the nation's advertising dollars, but the loss of papers and readers raises significant concerns in a nation where daily news has historically functioned as a watchdog over democratic life. To provide some background for the current declines, we will trace the history of newspapers through a number of influential periods and styles. We will explore the eras of the early political-commercial press, the penny press, and yellow journalism. Turning to the modern era, we will examine the influence of the *New York Times* and twentieth-century journalism's embrace of objectivity. During this era, interpretive journalism emerged in the 1920s and 1930s to improve news practices, and the revival of literary journalism followed in the 1960s. We will also look at the evolution of contemporary newspapers and examine different ways of categorizing them. Finally, we will review issues of chain ownership, new technology, and the crucial role of newspapers in our democracy.

> **❝** There's almost no media experience sweeter . . . than poring over a good newspaper. In the quiet morning, with a cup of coffee — so long as you haven't turned on the TV, listened to the radio, or checked in online — it's as comfortable and personal as information gets. **❞**
>
> – Jon Katz,
> *Wired* magazine, 1994

The Evolution of American Newspapers

The idea of news is as old as language itself. The earliest news was passed along orally from family to family, from tribe to tribe, by community leaders and oral historians. The first written news accounts, or *news sheets,* were probably posted items distributed by local rulers and governments. The earliest known news sheet, *Acta Diurna* (Latin for "daily events"), was developed by Julius Caesar and posted in Rome in 59 B.C. Even in its oral and early written stages, news informed people on the state of their relations with neighboring tribes and towns. The development of the printing press in the fifteenth century greatly accelerated a society's ability to send and receive information. Throughout history, news has satisfied our need to know things we cannot experience personally. Newspapers today continue to document daily life and bear witness to both ordinary and extraordinary events.

Colonial Newspapers and the Partisan Press

The first newspaper produced in North America was *Publick Occurrences, Both Foreign and Domestick,* published on September 25, 1690, by Boston printer Benjamin Harris. The colonial government objected to Harris's negative tone regarding British rule, and local ministers were offended by a report that the king of France had had an affair with his son's wife. The newspaper was banned after one issue.

In 1704, the first regularly published newspaper appeared in the American colonies — the *Boston News-Letter,* published by John Campbell. Considered dull, it reported on mundane events that had taken place in Europe months earlier. Because European news took weeks to travel by ship, these early colonial papers were not very timely. In their more spirited sections, however, the papers did report local illnesses, public floggings, and even suicides. In 1721, also in Boston, James Franklin,

> **❝** Oral news systems must have arrived early in the development of language, some tens or even hundreds of thousands of years ago. . . . And the dissemination of news accomplishes some of the basic purposes of language: informing others, entertaining others, protecting the tribe. **❞**
>
> –Mitchell Stephens,
> *A History of News,* 1988

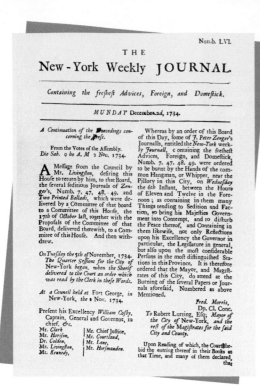

The older brother of Benjamin Franklin, started the *New England Courant*. The *Courant* established a tradition of running stories that interested ordinary readers rather than printing articles that appealed primarily to business and colonial leaders. In 1729, Benjamin Franklin, at age twenty-four, took over the *Pennsylvania Gazette,* which historians rate among the best of the colonial papers. Although a number of colonial papers operated solely on subsidies from political parties, the *Gazette* also made money by advertising products.

Another important colonial paper was the *New York Weekly Journal,* which appeared in 1733. John Peter Zenger had been installed as the printer of the *Journal* by the Popular Party, a political group that opposed British rule and ran articles that criticized the royal governor of New York. After a Popular Party judge was dismissed from office, the *Journal* escalated its attack on the governor. When Zenger shielded the writers of the critical articles, he was arrested in 1734 for *seditious libel*—defaming a public official's character in print. Championed by famed Philadelphia lawyer Andrew Hamilton, Zenger ultimately won his case in 1735. A sympathetic jury, in revolt against the colonial government, ruled that newspapers had the right to criticize government leaders as long as the reports were true. After the Zenger case, the British never prosecuted another colonial printer. Although the case did not substantially change sedition laws at the time, the Zenger decision would later provide a key foundation for the First Amendment to the Constitution—the right of a democratic press to criticize public officials.

By 1765, about thirty newspapers operated in the American colonies. The first *daily* paper began in 1784. These papers were of two general types: political or commercial. The development of both types was shaped in large part by social, cultural, and political responses to British rule and by its eventual overthrow. The gradual rise of political parties and the spread of commerce also played a significant role in the development of these early papers. Although the political and commercial papers carried both party news and business news, they had different agendas. Political papers, known as **partisan press**, generally pushed the plan of the particular political group that subsidized the paper. The more commercial press, on the other hand, served the leaders of commerce, who were interested in economic issues. Both types of journalism left a legacy. The partisan press gave us the editorial pages, and the

● During the colonial period, New York printer John Peter Zenger was arrested for libel. He eventually won his case, which established the precedent that today allows U.S. journalists and citizens to criticize public officials. In this 1734 issue, Zenger's *New York Weekly Journal* reported his own arrest and the burning of the paper by the city's "Common Hangman."

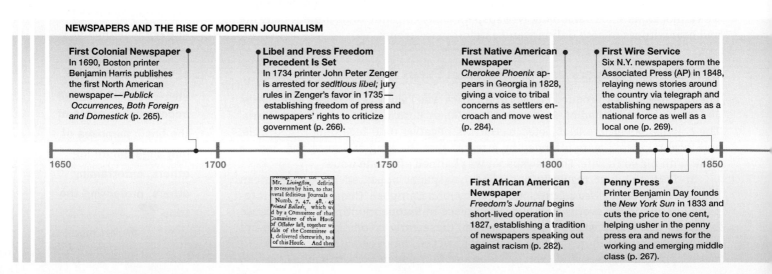

NEWSPAPERS AND THE RISE OF MODERN JOURNALISM

First Colonial Newspaper
In 1690, Boston printer Benjamin Harris publishes the first North American newspaper—*Publick Occurrences, Both Foreign and Domestick* (p. 265).

Libel and Press Freedom Precedent Is Set
In 1734 printer John Peter Zenger is arrested for *seditious libel;* jury rules in Zenger's favor in 1735—establishing freedom of press and newspapers' rights to criticize government (p. 266).

First Native American Newspaper
Cherokee Phoenix appears in Georgia in 1828, giving a voice to tribal concerns as settlers encroach and move west (p. 284).

First Wire Service
Six N.Y. newspapers form the Associated Press (AP) in 1848, relaying news stories around the country via telegraph and establishing newspapers as a national force as well as a local one (p. 269).

1650   1700   1750   1800   1850

First African American Newspaper
Freedom's Journal begins short-lived operation in 1827, establishing a tradition of newspapers speaking out against racism (p. 282).

Penny Press
Printer Benjamin Day founds the *New York Sun* in 1833 and cuts the price to one cent, helping usher in the penny press era and news for the working and emerging middle class (p. 267).

early commercial press was the forerunner of the business section in modern papers.

From the early 1700s to the early 1800s, even the largest of these papers rarely reached a circulation of fifteen hundred. Readership was confined primarily to educated or wealthy men who controlled local politics and commerce. During this time, though, a few pioneering women operated newspapers, including Elizabeth Timothy, the first American woman newspaper publisher. After her husband died of smallpox in 1738, Timothy took over the *South Carolina Gazette*, established in 1734 by Benjamin Franklin and the Timothy family, which included her eight children. Also during this period, Anna Maul Zenger ran the *New York Weekly Journal* throughout her husband's trial and after his death in 1746.[2] In general, though, the interests of women readers were not well addressed by either the political or the commercial press. By the 1830s, however, the Industrial Revolution and the rise of the middle classes had spurred the growth of literacy and set the stage for a more popular and inclusive press.

The Penny-Press Era: Newspapers Become Mass Media

By the late 1820s, the average newspaper cost six cents a copy and was sold not through street sales but through yearly subscriptions priced at $10 to $12. Because that price represented more than a week's salary for most skilled workers, newspaper readers were mostly affluent. The Industrial Revolution, however, spawned the conversion from expensive handmade to inexpensive machine-made paper. And when cheaper paper combined with increased literacy, **penny papers** soon began competing with conventional six-cent papers. In the 1820s, breakthroughs in technology, particularly steam-powered presses replacing mechanical presses, permitted publishers to produce as many as four thousand newspapers an hour. Subscriptions remained the preferred sales tool of many penny papers, although they began relying increasingly on daily street sales.

In 1833, printer Benjamin Day founded the *New York Sun*. After cutting the price to one penny, he also eliminated subscriptions. The *Sun* (whose slogan was "It shines for all") highlighted local events, scandals, and police reports. It also ran serialized stories, making legends of frontiersmen Davy Crockett and Daniel Boone and blazing the trail for the media's twentieth-century enthusiasm for celebrity news. In the tradition of today's tabloids, the *Sun* fabricated stories, including the famous moon hoax, which reported "scientific" evidence of life on the moon. Within six months,

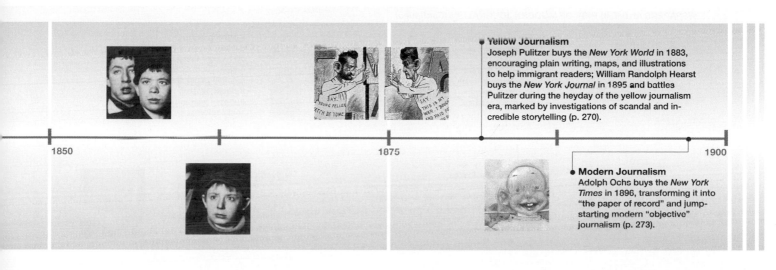

Yellow Journalism
Joseph Pulitzer buys the *New York World* in 1883, encouraging plain writing, maps, and illustrations to help immigrant readers; William Randolph Hearst buys the *New York Journal* in 1895 and battles Pulitzer during the heyday of the yellow journalism era, marked by investigations of scandal and incredible storytelling (p. 270).

1850   1875   1900

Modern Journalism
Adolph Ochs buys the *New York Times* in 1896, transforming it into "the paper of record" and jumpstarting modern "objective" journalism (p. 273).

● Newsboys sold Hearst and Pulitzer papers on the streets of New York in the 1890s. With more than a dozen dailies competing, street tactics were ferocious, and publishers often made young "newsies" buy the papers they could not sell.

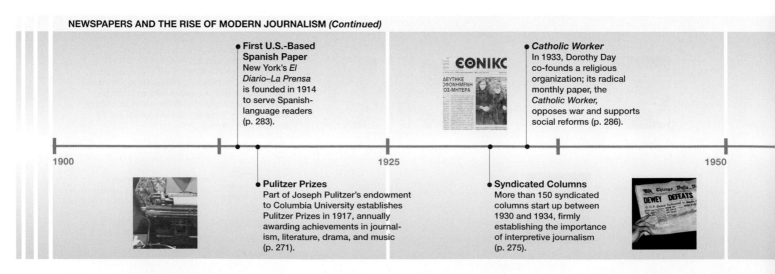

NEWSPAPERS AND THE RISE OF MODERN JOURNALISM *(Continued)*

● **First U.S.-Based Spanish Paper**
New York's *El Diario–La Prensa* is founded in 1914 to serve Spanish-language readers (p. 283).

● **Catholic Worker**
In 1933, Dorothy Day co-founds a religious organization; its radical monthly paper, the *Catholic Worker,* opposes war and supports social reforms (p. 286).

1900   1925   1950

● **Pulitzer Prizes**
Part of Joseph Pulitzer's endowment to Columbia University establishes Pulitzer Prizes in 1917, annually awarding achievements in journalism, literature, drama, and music (p. 271).

● **Syndicated Columns**
More than 150 syndicated columns start up between 1930 and 1934, firmly establishing the importance of interpretive journalism (p. 275).

the *Sun*'s lower price had generated a circulation of eight thousand, twice that of its nearest competitor.

The *Sun*'s success initiated a wave of penny papers that favored **human-interest stories**: news accounts that focus on the trials and tribulations of the human condition, often featuring ordinary individuals facing extraordinary challenges. These kinds of stories reveal journalism's ties to literary traditions (which today can be found in the horror or gangster news-story genres of urban drug and crime coverage).

The penny-press era also featured James Gordon Bennett's *New York Morning Herald*, founded in 1835. Bennett, considered the first U.S. press baron, aimed to free his newspaper from political parties. He wanted to establish an independent paper serving middle- and working-class readers as well as his own business ambitions. The *Herald* carried political essays and scandals, business stories, a letters section, fashion notes, moral reflections, religious news, society gossip, colloquial tales and jokes, sports stories, and later, reports from correspondents sent to cover the Civil War. In an era before modern "objective" journalism, Bennett's paper sponsored balloon races, financed safaris, and overplayed crime stories. After his first visit to America in the early 1840s, British writer Charles Dickens used the *Herald* as a model for the sleazy *Rowdy Journal*, the fictional newspaper in his novel *Martin Chuzzlewit*. By 1860, the *Herald* reached nearly eighty thousand readers, making it the world's largest daily paper at the time.

The penny papers were innovative. For example, they were the first to assign reporters to cover crime. In New York, where the penny-press competition was fierce, readers enthusiastically embraced the reporting of local news and crime. By gradually separating daily front-page reporting from overt political viewpoints on an editorial page, New York's penny papers shifted their economic base from political-party subsidies to the market—to advertising revenue, classified ads, and street sales. Although many partisan papers took a moral stand against advertising certain questionable products, the penny press became more neutral toward advertisers and printed virtually any ad. In fact, many penny papers regarded advertising as a kind of consumer news. The rise in ad revenues and circulation accelerated the growth of the newspaper industry. In 1830, 650 weekly and 65 daily papers operated in the United States, reaching 80,000 readers. By 1840, a total of 1,140 weeklies and 140 dailies attracted 300,000 readers.

In 1848, six New York newspapers formed a cooperative arrangement and founded the Associated Press (AP), the first major news wire service. **Wire services**

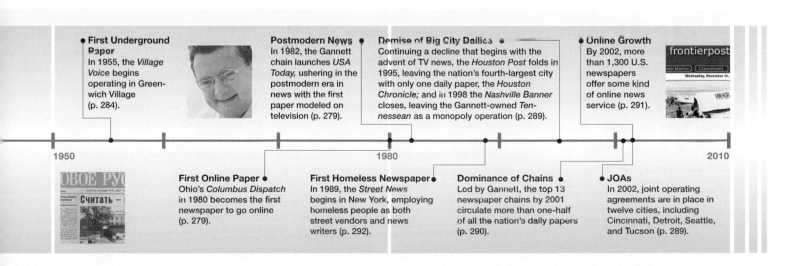

First Underground Paper
In 1955, the *Village Voice* begins operating in Greenwich Village (p. 284).

Postmodern News
In 1982, the Gannett chain launches *USA Today*, ushering in the postmodern era in news with the first paper modeled on television (p. 279).

Demise of Big City Dailies
Continuing a decline that begins with the advent of TV news, the *Houston Post* folds in 1995, leaving the nation's fourth-largest city with only one daily paper, the *Houston Chronicle*; and in 1998 the *Nashville Banner* closes, leaving the Gannett-owned *Tennessean* as a monopoly operation (p. 289).

Online Growth
By 2002, more than 1,300 U.S. newspapers offer some kind of online news service (p. 291).

1950   1980   2010

First Online Paper
Ohio's *Columbus Dispatch* in 1980 becomes the first newspaper to go online (p. 279).

First Homeless Newspaper
In 1989, the *Street News* begins in New York, employing homeless people as both street vendors and news writers (p. 292).

Dominance of Chains
Led by Gannett, the top 13 newspaper chains by 2001 circulate more than one-half of all the nation's daily papers (p. 290).

JOAs
In 2002, joint operating agreements are in place in twelve cities, including Cincinnati, Detroit, Seattle, and Tucson (p. 289).

began as commercial organizations that relayed news stories and information around the country and the world using telegraph lines and, later, radio waves and digital transmissions. In the case of the AP, the New York papers provided access to both their own stories and those from other newspapers. In the 1850s, papers started sending reporters to cover Washington, D.C., and in the early 1860s more than a hundred reporters from northern papers went south to cover the Civil War, relaying their reports back to their home papers via telegraph and wire services. The news-wire companies enabled news to travel rapidly from coast to coast and set the stage for modern journalism.

The combination of marketing news as a national and global product and using modern technology to dramatically cut costs gradually elevated newspapers to the status of a mass medium. By also adapting news content, penny papers captured the middle- and working-class readers who could now afford the paper and also had more leisure time to read it. As newspapers sought to sustain their mass appeal, news and "factual" reports about crimes and other items of human interest eventually superseded the importance of partisan articles about politics and commerce.

The Age of Yellow Journalism: Sensationalism and Investigation

The rise of competitive dailies and the penny press spawned the next significant period in American journalism. Labeled the era of **yellow journalism**, this late 1800s development emphasized profitable papers that carried exciting human-interest stories, crime news, large headlines, and more readable copy. This period is generally regarded as the age of sensationalism, the direct forerunner of today's tabloid papers and TV magazine shows like *Access Hollywood*. The era of yellow journalism featured two major characteristics. First were the overly dramatic—or sensational—stories about crimes, celebrities, disasters, scandals, and intrigue. The second, and sometimes forgotten, legacy is that the yellow press provided the roots for investigative journalism: news reports that hunted out and exposed corruption, particularly in business and government. Reporting increasingly became a crusading force for common people, with the press assuming a watchdog role on behalf of the public.

During this period, a newspaper circulation war pitted William Randolph Hearst's *New York Journal* against Joseph Pulitzer's *New York World*. A key player in the war was the first popular cartoon strip, "The Yellow Kid," created in 1895 by artist R. F. Outcault, who once worked for Thomas Edison. The phrase *yellow journalism* has since become associated with the cartoon strip, which shuttled between the Hearst and Pulitzer papers during their furious battle for readers in the mid to late 1890s.

Pulitzer and the *New York World*

After a brief career in St. Louis politics, Joseph Pulitzer, a Jewish-Hungarian immigrant, began his career in newspaper publishing in the early 1870s as part owner of the *St. Louis Post*. He then bought the bankrupt *St. Louis Dispatch* for $2,500 at an auction in 1878 and merged it with the *Post*. The *Post-Dispatch* became known for stories that highlighted "sex and sin" ("A Denver Maiden Taken from Disreputable House") and satires of the upper class ("St. Louis Swells"). Pulitzer also viewed the *Post-Dispatch* as a "national conscience" that promoted the public good. Pulitzer carried on the legacies of Bennett: making money and developing a "free and impartial" paper that would "serve no party but the people." Within five years, the *Post-Dispatch* had become one of the most influential newspapers in the Midwest.

In 1883, Pulitzer bought the *New York World* for $346,000. He encouraged plain writing and the inclusion of maps and illustrations to help immigrant and working-

> **❝** There is room in this great and growing city for a journal that is not only cheap but bright, not only bright but large . . . that will expose all fraud and sham, fight all public evils and abuses — that will serve and battle for the people. **❞**
>
> – Joseph Pulitzer, publisher, *New York World*, 1883

class readers understand the written text. In addition to running sensational stories on crime, sex, and cannibalism, Pulitzer instituted advice columns and women's pages. Like Bennett, Pulitzer treated advertising as a kind of news that displayed consumer products for readers. In fact, department stores became a major advertising source during this period. The revenue from these stores contributed directly to the expansion of consumer culture and indirectly to the acknowledgment of women as newspaper readers and to their eventual employment as reporters.

The *World* reflected the contradictory spirit of the yellow press. It crusaded for improved urban housing, better conditions for women, and equitable labor laws. It campaigned against monopoly practices by AT&T, Standard Oil, and Equitable Insurance. Such popular crusades helped lay the groundwork for tightening federal antitrust laws in the early 1910s. At the same time, Pulitzer's paper manufactured news events and staged stunts, such as sending star reporter Nellie Bly around the world in seventy-two days to beat the fictional record in the popular 1873 Jules Verne novel *Around the World in Eighty Days*.

Pulitzer created a lasting legacy by leaving $2 million to establish the graduate school of journalism at Columbia University in 1912. In 1917, part of Pulitzer's Columbia endowment launched the Pulitzer Prizes, the prestigious awards given each year for achievements in journalism, literature, drama, and music.

Hearst and the *New York Journal*

By 1887, the *World*'s Sunday circulation had soared to more than 250,000, the largest in the world. Eight years later, however, the paper faced its fiercest competition when William Randolph Hearst bought the *New York Journal*. Before moving to New York, Hearst had taken the reins of the *San Francisco Examiner* from his father, George Hearst, who had purchased the paper to further a political career. In 1887, when George was elected to the U.S. Senate, he turned the paper over to his twenty-four-year-old son, who had recently been expelled from Harvard for a practical joke he played on his professors. In 1895, with an inheritance from his father, the son bought the ailing *New York Journal* (a penny paper founded by Pulitzer's brother Albert) and then raided Joseph Pulitzer's paper for editors, writers, and cartoonists.

THE BIG TYPE WAR OF THE YELLOW KIDS.

Generally considered America's first comic-strip character, the Yellow Kid was created in the mid-1890s by cartoonist Richard Outcault. The cartoon was so popular that newspaper barons Joseph Pulitzer and William Randolph Hearst fought over Outcault's services, giving yellow journalism its name.

Taking his cue from Bennett and Pulitzer, Hearst focused on lurid, sensational stories and appealed (and pandered) to immigrant readers by using large headlines and bold layout designs. To boost circulation, the *Journal* invented interviews, faked pictures, and encouraged conflicts that might result in a story. One account of Hearst's tabloid legacy describes "tales about two-headed virgins" and "prehistoric creatures roaming the plains of Wyoming."[3] In promoting journalism as storytelling, Hearst reportedly said, "The modern editor of the popular journal does not care for facts. The editor wants novelty. The editor has no objection to facts if they are also novel. But he would prefer a novelty that is not a fact to a fact that is not a novelty."[4]

● This 1936 scene reveals the newsroom of Harlem's *Amsterdam News,* one of the nation's leading African American newspapers. Ironically, the Civil Rights movement and affirmative-action policies in the 1960s "helped" drain talented reporters from the black press by encouraging them to work for mainstream white newspapers.

Hearst is remembered as an unscrupulous publisher who once hired gangsters to distribute his newspapers. He was also, however, considered a champion of the underdog, and his paper's readership soared among the working and middle classes. In 1896, the *Journal*'s daily circulation reached 450,000, and by 1897 the Sunday edition of the paper rivaled the 600,000 circulation of the *World.* By the 1930s, Hearst's holdings included more than forty daily and Sunday papers, thirteen magazines (including *Good Housekeeping* and *Cosmopolitan*), eight radio stations, and two film companies. In addition, he controlled King Features Syndicate, which sold and distributed articles, comics, and features to many of the nation's 2,500 dailies. Hearst, the model for Charles Foster Kane, the ruthless and lonely publisher in Orson Welles' classic 1940 film *Citizen Kane,* operated the largest media business in the world—the AOL Time Warner of its day.

Competing Models of Modern Print Journalism

Over the years, the methods that journalists have used to convey information have varied. The early commercial and partisan presses were, to some extent, covering important events impartially. These papers often carried verbatim reports of presidential addresses, murder trials, or the annual statements of the U.S. Treasury. In the late 1800s, as newspapers pushed for greater circulation, newspaper reporting changed. Two distinct types of journalism were competing for readers: The penny papers and the yellow press focused on a story-driven model, dramatizing important events; the six-cent papers emphasized "the facts," an approach that appeared to package information more impartially.[5] Over the years, journalism has continued to try different venues of conveying stories and information. Overriding these efforts has been the notion of whether, in journalism, there is an ideal, attainable objective model or whether the quest to be objective actually conflicts with the traditional role of journalists to raise important questions about the abuses of power in a democratic society.

"Objectivity" in Modern Journalism

As the consumer marketplace expanded during the Industrial Revolution, facts and news became marketable products that could be sold to consumers. Throughout the mid-1800s, the more a newspaper appeared not to take sides, the more its readership base could be extended (although editorial pages were often rabidly supportive of particular political candidates). In addition, wire-service organizations were serving a variety of newspaper clients in different regions of the country. To satisfy all their clients and the wide range of political views, newspapers began to at least look more impartial.

Ochs and the *New York Times*

The ideal of an impartial, or informational, news model was reinvented by Adolph Ochs, who bought the *New York Times* in 1896. The son of immigrant German Jews, Ochs grew up in Ohio and Tennessee, where at age twenty-one he took over the *Chattanooga Times* in 1878. Known more for his business and organizational ability than for his writing and editing skills, he transformed the Tennessee paper. Ochs then moved to New York and invested $75,000 in the struggling *Times*. Through wise hiring, Ochs's staff of editors rebuilt the paper around substantial news coverage and provocative editorial pages. To distance themselves from the yellow press, the editors also downplayed entertainment news and sensational features, favoring the documentation of major events or issues.

Such distancing was partly a marketing strategy to counter the large circulations of the Hearst and Pulitzer papers. Ochs offered a distinct contrast to the more sensational newspapers: an informational paper that provided stock and real-estate reports to businesses, court reports to legal professionals, treaty summaries to political leaders, and theater and book reviews to intellectuals. Ochs's promotional gimmicks took direct aim at yellow journalism, advertising the *Times* under the motto "It does not soil the breakfast cloth." The strategy of the *Times* was similar to many TV marketing plans today that target upscale viewers who control a disproportionate share of consumer dollars.

With the Hearst and Pulitzer papers capturing the bulk of working- and middle-class readers, managers at the *Times* at first associated their straightforward reporting with people of higher social status. In 1898, however, Ochs lowered the paper's price to a penny. His thinking was that people bought the *World* and the *Journal* primarily because they were cheap, not because of their storytelling. As a result, the *Times* began attracting more middle-class readers who gravitated to the paper as a status marker for the educated and well informed. Between 1898 and 1899, its circulation rose from 25,000 to 75,000. By 1921, the *New York Times* had a daily circulation of 330,000 and 500,000 on Sunday. (For contemporary circulation figures, see Table 8.1.)

"Just the Facts, Please"

Early in the twentieth century, with reporters adopting a more "scientific" attitude to news- and fact-gathering, the ideal of objectivity began to anchor journalism. In **objective journalism**, which distinguishes factual reports from opinion columns,

● Table 8.1 The Nation's Largest Daily Newspapers

Newspaper	2002 Average Weekday Circulation*	Newspaper	2002 Average Weekday Circulation*
USA Today	2,231,000	Chicago Tribune	613,000
Wall Street Journal	1,801,000	New York Post	590,000
New York Times	1,113,000	(New York) Newsday	579,000
Los Angeles Times	965,000	Houston Chronicle	552,000
Washington Post	746,000	Dallas Morning News	522,000
(New York) Daily News	715,000	San Francisco Chronicle	512,000

*Average for six months ending September 30, 2002.

Source: Audit Bureau of Circulations; *New York Times*, November 6, 2002, sec. C, p. 3.

Figure 8.1 The Inverted-Pyramid Style of Reporting

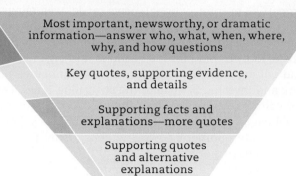

Most important, newsworthy, or dramatic information—answer who, what, when, where, why, and how questions

Key quotes, supporting evidence, and details

Supporting facts and explanations—more quotes

Supporting quotes and alternative explanations

Least important details

modern reporters strive to maintain a neutral attitude toward the issue or event they cover; they also search out competing points of view among the sources for a story. The writing and representation of this kind of reporting is often designated as the **inverted-pyramid style** (see Figure 8.1.). Civil War correspondents developed this style by imitating the terse, compact press releases that came from President Lincoln's secretary of war, Edwin M. Stanton.[6] Often stripped of adverbs and adjectives, inverted-pyramid reports began—as they do today—with the most dramatic or newsworthy information. They answer *who, what, where, when* (and, less frequently, *why* or *how*) questions at the top of the story and then tail off with less significant details. If wars or natural disasters disrupted the telegraph transmissions of these dispatches, the information the reporter chose to lead with in the story often had the best chance of getting through.

For much of the twentieth century, the inverted-pyramid style served as an efficient way to arrange a timely story. As one news critic pointed out, the wire services that used the inverted-pyramid style when distributing stories to newspapers nationwide "had to deal with large numbers of newspapers with widely different political and regional interests. The news had to be 'objective' . . . to be accepted by such a heterogeneous group."[7] Among other things, the importance of objectivity and the reliance on the inverted pyramid signaled journalism's break from the partisan tradition. Although difficult to achieve, the notion of objectivity nonetheless became (and in many ways remains) the guiding ideal of the modern press.

Despite the success of the *New York Times* and other modern papers, the more factual inverted-pyramid approach toward news has come under increasing scrutiny. As news critic Roy Peter Clark has noted: "Some reporters let the pyramid control the content so that the news comes out homogenized. Traffic fatalities, three-alarm fires, and new city ordinances all begin to look alike. In extreme cases, reporters have been known to keep files of story forms. Fill in the blanks. Stick it in the paper."[8] Although the inverted-pyramid style has for years solved deadline problems for reporters and enabled editors to cut a story from the bottom to fit available space, it has also discouraged many readers from continuing beyond the key details in the opening paragraphs. Studies have demonstrated that the majority of readers do not follow a front-page story when it continues, or "jumps," inside the paper.

By the 1920s, the *New York Times* had established itself as the official paper of record, the standard that other newspapers emulated and that libraries throughout the country stocked to document important daily occurrences. Filled with the texts of treaties, court reports, political speeches, and other national documents, the *Times* became more than a powerful alternative to the storytelling of earlier papers; it became the official model for journalism in the 1900s. The modern reporter evolved, ideally, as a detached observer who gathered information and adapted it to an informational or objective formula.

Interpretive Journalism Provides Explanation

By the 1920s, the more factual or "information" model of reporting had become the standard for most mainstream journalism. There was still a sense, however, especially after the trauma of World War I, that the impartial approach to reporting was insufficient for explaining complex national and global conditions. Partly as a result of "drab, factual, objective reporting," one news scholar contended that "the American people were utterly amazed when war broke out in August 1914, as they had no understanding of the foreign scene to prepare them for it."[9]

The Limits of Objectivity in Journalism

Modern journalism had undermined an early role of the partisan press—that of offering analysis and opinion. But with the world becoming more complex in the modern age, some papers began to re-explore the analytical function of news. The result was the rise of **interpretive journalism**, which tries to explain key issues or events and to place them in a broader historical or social context. According to one historian, this approach, especially in the 1930s and 1940s, was a viable way for journalism to address "the New Deal years, the rise of modern scientific technology, the increasing interdependence of economic groups at home, and the shrinking of the world into one vast arena for power politics."[10] In other words, journalism took an analytic turn in a world grown more interconnected and complicated.

Noting that objectivity and factuality *should* serve as the foundation for journalism, by the 1920s editor and columnist Walter Lippmann thought the press should do more. He ranked three press responsibilities: (1) "to make a current record," (2) "to make a running analysis of it," and (3) "on the basis of both, to suggest plans."[11] Indeed, reporters and readers alike have historically distinguished between informational reports and editorials, or interpretive pieces, that offer particular viewpoints or deeper analyses of the issues. The boundary between information and interpretation can be somewhat ambiguous. For this reason, American papers have traditionally placed news analysis in separate columns and opinion articles on certain pages so that readers do not confuse them with "straight news."

In the 1930s, the Depression and the Nazi threat to global stability helped news analysis take root in newsmagazines and radio commentary. First developed in the partisan era, editorial pages also made a strong comeback. More significant, however, was the growth of the political column. Although literary and humor columns existed prior to World War I, the political column was a new form. More than 150 syndicated columns developed between 1930 and 1934 alone. Moving beyond the informational and storytelling functions of news, journalists and newspapers began to extend their role as analysts.

The Press-Radio War

With the rise of radio in the 1930s, the newspaper industry became increasingly annoyed by broadcasters who took their news directly from papers and wire services. As a result, a major battle developed between radio journalism and the established power of print. Although they would eventually lose most of these cases in court, mainstream newspapers attempted to copyright facts reported in the news and even sued radio stations, which routinely used newspapers as their main sources (a common practice to this day). Editors and newspaper lobbyists argued that radio should be permitted to do only commentary. By conceding this interpretive role to radio, the print press temporarily protected its dominion over "the facts." It was amid the press-radio war that radio analysis began to flourish as a form of interpretive news. Lowell Thomas delivered the first daily network analysis for CBS on September 29, 1930, attacking Hitler's rise to power in Germany. By 1941, twenty regular network commentators were explaining their version of the world to millions of listeners.

In the 1930s, many print journalists and some editors believed that interpretive stories, rather than objective reports, could better compete with radio. They realized that interpretation was a way to counter radio's (and later television's) superior ability to report breaking news quickly. In 1933, the American Society of Newspaper Editors (ASNE) supported the idea of interpretive journalism, resolving to "devote a larger amount of attention and space to analytical and interpretative news and to presenting a background of information which will enable the average reader more adequately to understand the movement and the significance of events."[12]

Newspapers, however, did not fill their front pages with probing analysis during the 1930s. Even Walter Lippmann believed that news commentary and interpretation were misdirected without the foundation of facts and a "current record." As he put it, "the really important thing is to try and make opinion increasingly responsible to the facts."[13] Still, by the early 1930s, the ideals of objectivity and impartiality had shifted.

In Europe, interpretive news and partisan papers have long been the norm, but in American dailies explicit interpretation remains relegated to the two editorial and opinion pages in most papers. After World War II, interpretive journalism diminished substantially. It wasn't until the 1950s—with the Korean War, the development of atomic power, tensions with the Soviet Union, and the anticommunist movement—that reporting as analysis resurfaced in a new form on television. Interpretive journalism in newspapers grew at the same time, especially in such areas as the environment, science, agriculture, sports, health, and business. Today, stories favoring analysis over description frequently find their way onto most front pages, but the interpretive approach has not gained equal footing with the information model.

Literary Forms of Journalism

By the late 1960s, many people were criticizing America's major social institutions. Political assassinations, civil rights protests, the Vietnam War, the drug culture, and the women's movement were not easily explained. Faced with so much change and turmoil, many individuals began to lose faith in the ability of institutions to oversee and direct the social order. Members of protest movements as well as many middle- and working-class Americans began to suspect the privileges and power of traditional authority. As a result, key institutions—including journalism—lost much of the credibility they had previously commanded.

The Attack on Objectivity

Former *New York Times* columnist Tom Wicker has argued that in the early 1960s an objective approach to news remained the dominant model. According to Wicker, the "press had so wrapped itself in the paper chains of 'objective journalism' that it had little ability to report anything beyond the bare and undeniable facts."[14]

Throughout the 1960s, attacks on the detachment of reporters escalated. News critic Jack Newfield even indicted journalistic impartiality as "a figleaf for covert prejudice": "Objectivity is believing people with power and printing their press releases. Objectivity is not shouting 'liar' in a crowded country."[15] Consequently, the

❝ There are three kinds of lies: lies, damned lies, and statistics.❞

– Benjamin Disraeli,
British prime minister
(1868, 1874–80)

authority of experts and professionals in a variety of fields became suspect along with the ideal of objectivity.

A number of reporters responded to the criticism by rethinking the framework of conventional journalism. To improve on the older approach, they adopted a variety of alternative techniques. One of these was **advocacy journalism**, an approach in which the reporter actively promotes a particular cause or viewpoint. Following this approach, some women reporters displayed feminist points of view in their writing; they argued that merely recording events in a neutral way failed to confront the unequal arrangement of jobs and power in many institutions. **Precision journalism**, another technique, attempted to push news more in the direction of science. Precision journalists argued that only by applying rigorous social-science methods, such as using poll surveys and questionnaires, could they achieve a valid portrait of social reality.

Throughout the 1990s, major daily papers increasingly invested in training journalists in survey techniques and in hiring pollsters to do periodic research on key trends in their regions. However, critics charged that during the 2000 presidential campaign many newspapers and TV stations became too reliant on tracking polls. This reduced campaign coverage to "race-horse" journalism, telling "who's ahead" and "who's behind" stories rather than promoting substantial debates on serious issue differences among the candidates.

Journalism as an Art Form

Throughout the twentieth century's modern period, the story dimension of news reports—clouded by the abuses of yellow journalism—was downplayed to favor such conventions as the inverted pyramid and the separation of fact from opinion. Dissatisfied with these approaches, some reporters began reexploring and promoting journalism's ties to storytelling. This model of reporting, **literary journalism**—sometimes dubbed *new journalism*—adapted so-called fictional storytelling techniques to nonfictional material and in-depth reporting. In the United States, literary journalism's roots are evident in such novelists as Mark Twain, Stephen Crane, and Theodore Dreiser, all of whom started out as reporters in the nineteenth century. In

the late 1930s and 1940s, new journalism surfaced in literary reports: Journalists began to demonstrate how writing about real events could achieve an artistry often associated only with good fiction.

A leading practitioner, Tom Wolfe, argued that literary journalism mixed the *content* of reporting with the *form* of fiction to create "both the kind of objective reality of journalism" and "the subjective reality" of the novel.[16] Writers such as Wolfe (*The Electric Kool-Aid Acid Test*), Truman Capote (*In Cold Blood*), Joan Didion (*Slouching Towards Bethlehem*), and Norman Mailer (*Miami and the Siege of Chicago*) turned to literary journalism in the 1960s in an attempt to overcome the weaknesses they perceived in routine reporting. Their often self-conscious treatment of social problems gave their writing a perspective that conventional journalism did not offer.

The dilemmas and turmoil of the 1960s, according to critics, demanded a new journalistic form that could deal more effectively with social contradictions. After the tide of intense social upheaval ebbed, however, the new journalism subsided as well. In retrospect, literary reporting has often been criticized for being influenced by television or for blurring the lines between fact and fiction. Nevertheless, the legacy of literary journalism continues. Not only did it influence magazines like *Mother Jones* and *Rolling Stone*, but it affected the lifestyle and sports sections of most daily newspapers by emphasizing longer feature stories on cultural trends and social issues.

● **Table 8.2 Exceptional Works of American Journalism**

Working under the aegis of New York University's journalism department, thirty-six judges compiled a list of the Top 100 works of American journalism in the twentieth century. Published in 1999, the list took into account not just the newsworthiness of the event but the craft of the writing and reporting. What do you think of the Top 10 works listed below? What are some problems associated with making a list like this? Do you think newswriting should be judged in the same way we judge novels or movies?

Journalists	Title or Subject	Publisher	Year
1. John Hersey	"Hiroshima"	New Yorker	1946
2. Rachel Carson	*Silent Spring*	(Book)	1962
3. Bob Woodward/Carl Bernstein	Watergate investigation	Washington Post	1972–73
4. Edward R. Murrow	Battle of Britain	CBS Radio	1940
5. Ida Tarbell	"The History of the Standard Oil Company"	McClure's magazine	1902–04
6. Lincoln Steffens	"The Shame of the Cities"	McClure's magazine	1902–04
7. John Reed	*Ten Days That Shook the World*	(Book)	1919
8. H. L. Mencken	Coverage of the Scopes "monkey" trial	Baltimore Sun	1925
9. Ernie Pyle	Reports from Europe and the Pacific during World War II	Scripps-Howard newspapers	1940–45
10. Edward R. Murrow/Fred Friendly	Investigation of Senator Joseph McCarthy	CBS Television	1954

Source: New York University, Department of Journalism, New York, N.Y., 1999.

These reports reject the inverted-pyramid format by inviting readers into the stories through a more literary style that tries to set the scene using detailed description or dialogue. Today, writers such as Anna Quindlen (*Living Out Loud*) and John McPhee (*Annals of the Former World*) keep this tradition alive. (See Table 8.2 for top works in American journalism.)

Contemporary Journalism in the TV and Online Age

If Adolph Ochs and the *New York Times* planted the seeds of modern journalism in the late 1890s, a postmodern brand of journalism arose from two developments in the early 1980s. First, the *Columbus Dispatch* in 1980 became the first paper to go on-line and transmit its pages via computers and cable channels. By 2002, thirteen hundred U.S. papers were offering some kind of computerized news service. Second, the arrival of the colorful *USA Today* in 1982 radically changed the look of most major U.S. dailies. This new paper incorporated features closely associated with postmodern forms, including an emphasis on visual style over substantive news and the use of brief news items that appealed to readers' short attention span. Now the most widely circulated paper in the nation, *USA Today* represents the only successful launch of a new major U.S. daily newspaper in the last several decades. Showing its marketing savvy, *USA Today* was the first paper to acknowledge openly television's central role in mass culture: The paper designed its vending boxes to look like color TV sets. Today, even the writing style of *USA Today* news mimics TV news by casting many of its reports in the immediacy of the present tense rather than the past tense (which was the norm at most newspapers throughout the twentieth century).

Writing for *Rolling Stone* in March 1992, media critic Jon Katz argued that the authority of modern newspapers suffered in the wake of a variety of "new news" forms that combined immediacy, information, entertainment, persuasion, and analysis. Katz claimed that the news supremacy of most prominent daily papers, such as the *New York Times* and the *Washington Post*, was being disputed by "news" coming from talk shows, television sitcoms, popular films, and even rap music. In other words, we were passing from a society in which the transmission of knowledge depended mainly on books, newspapers, and magazines to a society dominated by a mix of print, visual, electronic, and digital information. In the process, the new forms of news began taking over the roles of traditional journalism, setting the nation's cultural, social, and political agendas. For instance, Matt Drudge, conservative Internet news source and gossip behind *The Drudge Report,* hijacked the national agenda in January 1998 and launched the Clinton-Lewinsky scandal when he posted a story claiming that *Newsweek* had backed off, or "spiked," a story about President Clinton having an affair with a White House intern. Although Drudge's report was essentially accurate, *Newsweek* delayed the story because its editors thought they needed more confirming sources before they could responsibly publish the allegations. Drudge effectively "outed" the *Newsweek* story prematurely, though critics debate whether his actions were legitimate or irresponsible.

Today, a fundamental tension exists between print and electronic conceptions of news. With news-reading habits among young people in decline, TV magazine programs, Internet sites, talk shows, sitcoms, movies, and popular music are sparking public conversation more often than are traditional newspapers. Add to this the speed at which personal computers can now transmit data. As Jon Katz wrote in *Wired:* "When in January 1994 a RadioMail subscriber used his wireless modem to flash news of the LA earthquake to the Net well before CNN or the Associated Press could report it, a new news medium was born."[17] With radio, television, film, music, and the Internet all competing with newspapers, their traditional roles are being challenged and changed. By 2002, more and more readers began their day by logging on to computers to scan a wide variety of the nation's online newspapers.

Categorizing News and U.S. Newspapers

In a visual and digital age, printed newspapers may have to fight harder to keep their readers, but they have not been abandoned. The nation's 1,465 daily papers still reach about sixty million readers each day. But this is down from 2,600 dailies in 1910, the high-water mark for daily newspapers in the United States.

In the news industry today, there are several kinds of papers. *National newspapers* (such as the *Wall Street Journal*, the *New York Times*, the *Christian Science Monitor*, and *USA Today*) serve a broad readership across the country. Other papers primarily serve specific geographic regions. Roughly 105 *metropolitan dailies* have a circulation of 100,000 or more. About 40 of these papers had a circulation of more than 250,000 in 2002. In addition, approximately 110 daily newspapers are classified as medium dailies with 50,000 to 100,000 in circulation. By far the largest number of U.S. dailies —about 1,250 papers—fall into the small daily category with circulations under 50,000. Whereas dailies serve urban and suburban centers, more than 8,000 nondaily and *weekly newspapers* (down from 14,000 in 1910) serve smaller communities and average just over 5,000 copies per issue.[18]

Consensus vs. Conflict: Newspapers Play Different Roles

Smaller nondaily papers tend to promote social and economic harmony in their communities. Besides providing community calendars and meeting notices, nondaily papers focus on **consensus-oriented journalism**, carrying articles on local schools, social events, town government, property crimes, and zoning issues. Recalling the partisan spirit of an earlier era, small newspapers are often owned by business leaders who may also serve in local politics. Because consensus-oriented papers have a small advertising base, they are generally careful not to offend local advertisers, who provide the financial underpinnings for many of these papers. At their best, these small-town papers foster a sense of community; at their worst, they can overlook or downplay discord and problems.

In contrast, national and metro dailies practice **conflict-oriented journalism** in which front-page news is often defined primarily as events, issues, or experiences that deviate from social norms. Under this news orientation, journalists see their role not merely as neutral fact-gatherers but as observers who monitor their city's institutions and problems. They often maintain an adversarial relationship with local politicians and public officials. These papers offer competing perspectives on such issues as education, government, poverty, crime, and the economy. It would be a conflict of interest for publishers, editors, or reporters on these papers to play a major role in community politics. In theory, modern newspapers believe their role in large cities is to keep a wary eye fixed on local and state intrigue and events— mostly from the day before.

In telling stories about complex and controversial topics, conflict-oriented journalists often turn such topics into two-dimensional stories, pitting one idea or person against another. This convention, often called "telling both sides of a story," allows a reporter to take the position of a detached observer. Although this practice offers the appearance of balance, it usually functions to generate conflict and sustain a lively news story; and sometimes reporters ignore the idea that there may be more than two sides to a story. But faced with deadline pressures, reporters often do not have the time—or the space—to develop a multifaceted and complex report or series of reports. (See "Applied Critical Process: Covering Business and Economic News" on page 281.)

Covering Business and Economic News

In 2001–2002 the collapse of Houston-based giant energy company Enron, the largest corporation to ever go bankrupt, put the spotlight on corporate corruption and journalism's coverage of this and similar issues. Over the years, critics have claimed that business news pages tend to favor issues related to management and downplay the role of everyday employees. Critics also charge that business news pages favor more positive business stories—such as which managers just got promotions—and minimize negative business news (unlike the front pages, which usually emphasize routine crime news). In the wake of Enron and other corporate scandals, check the business coverage in your local daily paper to see if these charges still seem accurate.

Description. Check a week's worth of business news reporting in your local paper. Examine both the business pages and the front and local sections for these stories. Devise a chart and create categories for sorting stories (e.g., promotion news, scandal stories, earnings reports, media-related news, etc.), and gauge whether these stories are positive or negative. If possible, compare this coverage to a week's worth of news from before the Enron scandal—during the business boom years of the 1990s. Or compare your local paper to business coverage in one of the nation's major dailies, such as the *New York Times* or *USA Today*. Or note how much coverage your paper devotes to media-related business stories.

Analysis. Look for patterns in the coverage. How many stories are positive? How many are negative?

Do the stories show any kind of gender favoritism (more men covered than women) or class bias (management favored over worker issues)? Compared to the local paper, are there differences in the frequency and kinds of coverage offered in the national newspaper? Does your paper routinely cover the business of the parent company that owns the local paper? How many stories are there on the business of newspapers and media in general?

Interpretation. What do some of the patterns mean? Did you find examples where the coverage of business seems comprehensive and fair? If business news gets more positive coverage than political news, what might this mean? If managers get more coverage than employees, what does this mean, particularly given that there are many more regular employees than managers at most businesses? What might it mean if men are more prominently featured than women in business stories? Considering the central role of media and news businesses in everyday life, what does it mean if these businesses are not being covered adequately by local and national news operations?

Evaluation. Determine which papers and stories you would judge as good and which ones would you judge as weaker models for how business should be covered. Are there some elements missing from coverage that should be included? If so, make suggestions.

Ethnic, Minority, and Oppositional Newspapers

Historically, small-town weeklies and daily newspapers have served predominantly white, mainstream readers. Exceptions to this include the various minority, foreign-language, and alternative papers, which have played a prominent role for Mexican and Cuban immigrants, Korean Americans, disabled veterans, retired workers, gay and lesbian communities, and the homeless. Most of these weekly and monthly newspapers serve some of the same functions for their constituencies as the "majority" papers. Minority papers, however, are often published outside the social mainstream. Consequently, they provide viewpoints that are different from the mostly middle- and upper-class white attitudes that have shaped the media throughout much of America's history.

The Immigrant and Ethnic Press

Since Benjamin Franklin launched the short-lived German-language *Philadelphische Zeitung* in 1732, newspapers aimed at ethnic groups have played a major role in initiating immigrants into American society. During the nineteenth century, Swedish- and Norwegian-language papers informed various immigrant communities in the Midwest. The early twentieth century gave rise to papers written in German, Yiddish, Russian, and Polish, which assisted the massive influx of European immigrants. In the 1980s, hundreds of small papers developed to serve immigrants from Cuba, Haiti, Pakistan, Laos, Cambodia, and China. More than fifty small U.S. papers are now printed in Vietnamese. Throughout the 1990s and into the twenty-first century, several hundred foreign-language daily and nondaily presses existed in at least forty different languages. Many are financially healthy today, supported by classified ads, local businesses, and increased ad revenue from long-distance phone companies and online computer services, which see the ethnic press as an ideal place to reach those customers most likely to use international phone services or the Internet.[19]

Ethnic papers help readers both adjust to foreign surroundings and retain ties to their traditional heritage. In addition, these papers often cover major stories that are downplayed in the mainstream press. For example, in the aftermath of 9/11, airport security teams detained thousands of Middle Eastern–looking men. The *Weekly Bangla Patrika*, a Long Island, New York, weekly with a circulation of twelve thousand, not only reported in detail on the one hundred people the Bangladeshi community lost in the World Trade Center attacks, but took the lead in the reporting on how it feels to be innocent yet targeted in ethnic profiling at New York's major area airports.[20]

African American Newspapers

Between 1827 and the end of the Civil War in 1865, forty newspapers directed at black readers and opposed to slavery struggled for survival. These papers faced not only higher rates of illiteracy among black slaves and citizens but also hostility from white society and the majority press of the day. The first black newspaper, *Freedom's Journal*, operated from 1827 to 1829 and opposed the racism of many New York newspapers. In addition, it offered a voice for a number of antislavery societies. Other notable papers included the *Alienated American* (1852–56) and the *New Orleans Daily Creole*, which began a short life in 1856 as the first black-owned daily in the South. The most influential oppositional newspaper at the time was Frederick Douglass's *North Star*, a weekly antislavery newspaper in Rochester, New York, that began in 1847 and reached a circulation of three thousand. Besides writing essays on slavery, Douglass, a former slave, addressed a variety of national and international topics.

Since 1827, more than three thousand newspapers have been edited and owned by blacks. These papers, with an average life span of nine years, took stands against race baiting, lynching, and the Ku Klux Klan. They promoted racial pride long before the Civil Rights movement of the 1950s and 1960s. The most widely circulated black-owned paper was Robert C. Vann's weekly *Pittsburgh Courier*, founded in 1910. Its circulation peaked at 350,000 in 1947 — the year professional baseball was integrated by Jackie Robinson, thanks in part to relentless editorials in the *Courier* that denounced the color barrier in pro sports. As they have throughout their history, these papers offer oppositional viewpoints to the mainstream press and record the daily activities of black communities by listing weddings, births, deaths, graduations, meetings, and church functions. More than 125 African American papers survive today and remain influential, including Baltimore's *Afro-American*, New York's *Amsterdam News*, and the Chicago *Defender*.

> **" Too long have others spoken for us. "**
>
> – *Freedom's Journal*, 1827

The circulation rates of most black papers have dropped sharply, however, particularly since the 1960s. The local and national editions of the *Pittsburgh Courier,* for instance, had a combined circulation of only twenty thousand by the early 1980s.[21] Several factors contributed to these declines. First, television and specialized black radio stations tapped into the limited pool of money that businesses allocated for advertising. Second, some advertisers, to avoid controversy, withdrew their support when the black press started giving favorable coverage to the Civil Rights movement in the 1960s. Third, the loss of industrial urban jobs in the 1970s and 1980s not only diminished readership but hurt small neighborhood businesses, which could no longer afford to advertise in both the mainstream and the black press. Finally, after the enactment of civil rights and affirmative-action laws, black papers were raided by mainstream papers seeking to integrate their newsrooms with good black journalists. Black papers could seldom match the offers from large white-owned dailies.

As civil rights legislation brought improved economic conditions for many working- and middle-class African Americans, the mainstream press began to court them as a consumer group, devoting weekly special sections to black issues and finding advertisers to support those sections. In siphoning off both ads and talent, a more integrated mainstream press diminished the status of many black papers—an ironic effect of the 1960s civil rights laws. By 2002, while 31 percent of the overall U.S. population was classified in a minority group, only 12 percent of the newsroom staffs at the nation's fifteen hundred daily papers were African American, Hispanic, Asian American, or Native American.[22]

Spanish-Language Newspapers

Bilingual and Spanish-language newspapers have long served a variety of Cuban, Mexican, Puerto Rican, and other Latino readerships. New York's *El Diario–La Prensa* has been serving Spanish-language readers since 1914. Los Angeles boasts *La Opinión,* the nation's largest Spanish-language daily. Other prominent publications are in Miami (*La Voz* and *Diario Las Americas*), Houston (*La Información*), Chicago (*El*

● Ethnic and foreign-language newspapers serve an important function, providing news and a sense of community to populations not targeted by mainstream papers. Pictured here are front pages from *Novoye Russkoye Slovo* (Russian), *Al-Ahram* (Arabic), the *National Herald* (Greek), and the *World Journal* (Chinese).

Mañana Daily News and *La Raza*), San Diego (*El Sol*), and New York (*Hoy, El Noticias del Mundo*). By 2002, some two hundred Hispanic newspapers reached more than 14 million readers nationwide, an increase of 2.7 million since 1984.

Until the late 1960s, Hispanic issues and culture were virtually ignored by mainstream newspapers. But with the influx of Mexican, Haitian, Puerto Rican, and Cuban immigrants throughout the 1980s and 1990s, many mainstream papers began to feature weekly Spanish-language supplements. The first was the *Miami Herald's* section, "El Nuevo Herald," introduced in 1976. Other mainstream papers also joined in, but many were folding their supplements by the mid-1990s. In 1995, the *Los Angeles Times* discontinued its supplement, "Nuestro Tiempo," and the *Miami Herald* trimmed budgets and staff for "El Nuevo Herald." Spanish-language radio and television had beaten the papers to these potential customers and to advertisers. By 2000, Spanish-language radio formats were thriving in many urban areas and taking advertisers with them. While many of the nation's mainstream papers were cutting their Spanish-language sections, TV advertising aimed at Hispanic markets jumped 25 percent and the number of Hispanics in U.S. TV newsrooms made up about 10 percent of those staffs.[23] However, on the print side Hispanic journalists accounted for slightly less than 4 percent of the newsroom work force at U.S. daily papers (compared to 5.3 percent for African Americans).[24]

Native American Newspapers

In mainstream journalism by 2002, Native American reporters and editors represented barely one-half of one percent of the 54,400 journalists working for the nation's daily papers.[25] (In 2000, the total Native American population was about one percent of the U.S. population.) As a result, much of the significant coverage of American Indian issues tends to come from other sources. An activist Native American press has provided oppositional voices to mainstream American media since 1828, when the *Cherokee Phoenix* appeared in Georgia. Another prominent early paper was the *Cherokee Rose Bud*, founded in 1848 by tribal women in the Oklahoma territory. The Native American Press Association has documented more than 350 different Native American papers, most of them printed in English but a few in tribal languages. Two national papers include *Akwesasne Notes*, a radical paper from the Mohawk nation published a few times a year, and *Wassaja*, a bimonthly paper of the American Indian Historical Society that promotes tribal pride and education.

To counter the lack of coverage of their culture's viewpoints in the mainstream press, Native American newspapers have helped educate various tribes about their heritage and build community solidarity. These papers also have developed stories on both the problems and progress among those Indian tribes that have opened gambling resorts over the past decade. Overall, these smaller papers provide a forum for debates on tribal conflicts and concerns that are generally overlooked in major papers, and they often signal the mainstream press on issues—such as gambling or hunting—that have significance for the larger culture.

The Underground Press

Another important historical development in the mid to late 1960s involved the explosion of alternative newspapers. Labeled the *underground press* at the time, these papers questioned mainstream political policies and conventional values. Generally running on shoestring budgets, they often voiced radical viewpoints and were erratic in meeting publication schedules. Springing up on college campuses and in major cities, underground papers were inspired by the writings of socialists and intellectuals from the 1930s and 1940s and, in their own time, by a new wave of thinkers and artists. Particularly inspirational were poets and writers (such as Allen

Ginsberg, LeRoi Jones, Jack Kerouac, and Eldridge Cleaver) and "protest" musicians (including Bob Dylan, Pete Seeger, and Joan Baez). In criticizing social institutions, alternative papers questioned the official reports distributed by public-relations agents, government spokespeople, and the conventional press (see "Case Study: The Alternative Journalism of Dorothy Day and I. F. Stone" on page 286).

During the 1960s, underground papers played a unique role in documenting social tension by including the voices of students, women, blacks, Native Americans, gay men and lesbians, and others whose opinions were often excluded from the mainstream press. The first and most enduring underground paper, the *Village Voice*, was founded in Greenwich Village in 1955. Among campus underground papers, the *Berkeley Barb* was the most influential, developing amid the free-speech movement in the mid-1960s.

Despite their irreverent and often vulgar tone, many underground papers turned a spotlight on racial and gender inequities and, on occasion, influenced mainstream journalism to examine social issues. Like the black press, though, most underground papers either lost circulation or folded after the 1960s. Given their radical outlook, it was difficult for them to generate sponsors or appeal to advertisers. In addition, like the black press, the underground press was raided by mainstream papers, which began expanding their coverage of culture by hiring the underground's best editors and writers.

Newspaper Operations:
Economic Demands vs. Editorial Duties

Today a weekly paper might employ only two or three people, whereas a major metro daily might have more than two thousand staffers. In either situation, however, most newspapers distinguish business operations from editorial or news functions. Journalists' and readers' praise or criticism usually rests on the quality of a paper's news and editorial components, but the business and advertising divisions drive today's industry.

Business and Advertising Decisions

Most major daily papers devote one-half to two-thirds of their pages to advertisements. Accounting for about 19 percent of all ad dollars spent annually in the United States, newspapers carry everything from expensive full-page spreads for prominent department stores to classifieds, which consumers can purchase for a few dollars to advertise everything from old cars to used furniture. In most cases, ads are positioned in the paper first. The space left over after ads are placed is called the **newshole**, which accounts for the remaining 35 to 50 percent of the context of daily newspapers—everything from front-page news reports to horoscopes and advice columns.

In addition to managing a paper's finances, business operations generally include departments of advertising, circulation, and promotion. Advertising staffs sell space to various companies and classified spots to individuals and small businesses. Circulation departments oversee distribution through street-corner boxes and newsstand sales, neighborhood paper routes, mail subscriptions, and, most recently, the Internet (although many papers now have separate Internet divisions). Promotion departments seek new readers and advertisers, paying particular attention to younger, hard-to-reach readers. Mechanical departments, supervised by a

The Alternative Journalism of Dorothy Day and I. F. Stone

Over the years, a number of unconventional reporters have struggled against the status quo to find a place for unheard voices and alternative ways to practice their craft. James Franklin stubbornly refused to get a news license during the early 1700s; Ida Wells fearlessly investigated violence against blacks for the *Memphis Free Speech* in the late 1800s; and the underground papers of the late 1960s made it possible for the voices of many groups to be heard. Newspaper lore offers a rich history of alternative journalists and their publications. Two such papers were Dorothy Day's *Catholic Worker* and *I. F. Stone's Weekly*.

In 1933, Dorothy Day (1897–1980) co-founded a radical religious organization with a monthly newspaper, *Catholic Worker,* that opposed war and supported social reforms. Like many young intellectual writers during World War I, Day was a pacifist; she also joined the Socialist Party. Quitting college at age eighteen to work as an activist reporter for socialist newspapers, Day participated in the on-going suffrage movement, which in 1920 helped pass the Nineteenth Amendment, giving women the right to vote. Throughout the 1930s, her Catholic Worker organization invested in thirty hospices for the poor and homeless, providing food and shelter for five thousand people a day. This legacy would endure into the twenty-first century, with the organization continuing to fund soup kitchens and homeless shelters throughout the country.

For more than sixty years, the *Worker* has consistently advocated personal activism to further social justice, opposing anti-Semitism, Japanese American internment camps during World War II, nuclear weapons, the Korean War, military drafts, and the communist witch-hunts of the 1950s. During the Cold War, Day was jailed four times for opposing military-style civil-defense drills in public schools. In the early 1970s, at age seventy-five, she was arrested for supporting migrant workers while she picketed with Cesar Chavez in California. The *Worker*'s circulation peaked in 1938 at 190,000, then fell dramatically during World War II, when Day's

pacifism was at odds with much of America. During the Vietnam War and the protest movements, however, it climbed again, to more than 100,000.

I. F. Stone (1907–1989) shared Dorothy Day's passion for social activism. He also started early, publishing his own monthly paper at the age of fourteen and becoming a full-time reporter by age twenty. He worked as a Washington political writer for the *Nation* in the early 1940s and later for the *New York Daily Compass*. Throughout his career, Stone challenged the conventions and privileges of both politics and journalism. In 1941, for example, he resigned from the National Press Club when it refused to serve his guest, the nation's first African American federal judge. In the early 1950s, he actively opposed Joseph McCarthy's rabid search to rid government and the media of alleged communists.

When the *Daily Compass* failed in 1952, the radical Stone was unable to find a newspaper job and decided to create his own newsletter, *I. F. Stone's Weekly*, which he published for nineteen years. Practicing interpretive and investigative reporting, Stone became as adept as any major journal-

ist at tracking down government records to discover contradictions, inaccuracies, and lies. Over the years, besides taking on McCarthy, Stone challenged the policies of J. Edgar Hoover's FBI, questioned decisions by the Supreme Court, investigated the substandard living conditions of many African Americans, and criticized political corruption. Working only with his wife and an occasional researcher, Stone guided the *Weekly* to a circulation that reached seventy thousand during the 1960s, when he probed American investments of money and military might in Vietnam.

I. F. Stone and Dorothy Day embodied a spirit of independent reporting that has been threatened by the decline in newspaper readership and the rise of chain ownership. Stone, who believed that alternative ideas were crucial to maintaining a healthy democracy, once wrote that "there must be free play for so-called 'subversive' ideas—every idea 'subverts' the old to make way for the new. To shut off 'subversion' is to shut off peaceful progress and to invite revolution and war."[1]

Alternative newspapers in the United States

Willamette Week Portland, OR

San Francisco Bay Guardian San Francisco

Denver Westward Denver, CO

City Pages Minneapolis/ St. Paul, MN

Chicago Reader Chicago

Boston Phoenix Boston

Village Voice New York City

Washington City Paper Washington, DC

Independent Raleigh/Durham/ Chapel Hill, NC

Los Angeles Independent L.A.

Private Eye Salt Lake City, UT

Austin Chronicle Austin, TX

The Riverfront Times St. Louis, MO

Gambit-New Orleans Weekly New Orleans, LA

Miami New Times Miami, FL

Creative Loafing Atlanta, GA

production manager, generally run the technical and computerized processes of assembling the pages of the paper and operating the printing presses.

News and Editorial Responsibilities

On the news and editorial side, the chain of command at most larger papers starts at the top, with the publisher and owner, and then moves to the editor in chief and managing editor, the persons in charge of the daily news-gathering and writing processes. Under the main editors, assistant editors and news managers run different news divisions, including features, sports, photos, local news, state news, and wire-service reports that contain much of the day's national and international news. In addition, copy editors check each story for accuracy, style, and grammar and write the headlines for each report.

Reporters work for editors and are generally grouped into two broad categories: *general assignment reporters,* who handle all sorts of stories that might emerge—or "break"—in a given day, and *specialty reporters,* who are assigned to particular beats (police, courts, schools, government) or topics (education, religion, health, environment, technology). On large dailies, *bureau reporters* file reports every day from other major cities—such as Washington or their state's capital. Daily papers also feature columnists and critics; these reporters have usually worked their way up the hierarchy and may review or analyze everything from fashion to foreign policy. By 2002, many newspapers employed a separate staff for their online operations, even though the vast majority of these operations were losing money.

Wire Services and Feature Syndication

Major daily papers might have between one hundred and two hundred local reporters and writers, but they still cannot cover the world or produce enough material to fill up the newshole each day. For this reason, newspapers rely on wire services and syndicated feature services to supplement local coverage. A few major dailies, such as the *New York Times,* run their own wire services, selling their reprinted stories to other papers. Other agencies, such as the Associated Press and United Press International (UPI), have hundreds of staffers stationed throughout major U.S. cities and the world capitals. They submit stories and photos each day for distribution to newspapers across the country. Some U.S. papers also subscribe to foreign wire services, such as Agence France-Presse in Paris or Reuters in London. Daily papers generally pay monthly fees for access to all wire stories, which are relayed by computer, satellite, and Teletype machines. Although they use only a fraction of what is available over the wires, editors carefully monitor wire services each day for important stories and ideas for local angles. Wire services have greatly expanded the national and international scope of news, but editors often must put their trust in a handful of powerful wire firms when they select a newsworthy issue or event for reprinting.

In addition, **feature syndicates,** such as United Features and Tribune Media Services, are commercial outlets that contract with newspapers to provide work from the nation's best political writers, editorial cartoonists, comic-strip artists, and self-help columnists. These companies serve as brokers, distributing horoscopes and crossword puzzles as well as the columns and comic strips that appeal to a wide audience. When a paper bids on and acquires the rights to a cartoonist or columnist, it signs exclusivity agreements with a syndicate to ensure that it is the only paper in the region to carry, say, Dilbert, Ellen Goodman, Molly Ivins, Bob Herbert, George Will, or Dear Abby. Feature syndicates, like wire services, wield great influence in determining which writers and cartoonists gain national prominence.

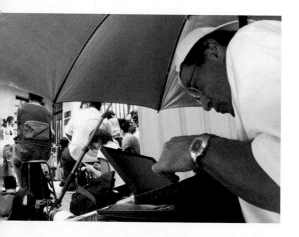

● Satellite technology and the Internet have made it possible to report from almost anywhere, even bypassing restrictions on press freedoms that some regimes try to impose on journalists. Here a Korean journalist reports from Kuala Lumpur on negotiations in 2000 between the United States and North Korea on restricting that communist nation's missile program.

Ownership, Economics, Technology, and Innovation

A number of tough issues face the newspaper industry as it adapts to changes in economics and technology. For publishers and journalists, no issues are more worrisome than the decline in newspaper readership and the failure of many papers to attract younger readers. Other problems persist as well, including the inability of most cities to support competing newspapers and the capability of online computer services and telephone and cable companies to vie with newspapers for lucrative classified advertising. Finally, the newspaper industry struggles to find its place on the Internet, trying to predict the future of printed and digital versions of the news.

Circulation Suffers as Readership Declines

Newspaper owners struggle daily with readership concerns. Between 1970 and 1990, yearly circulation flattened out at just over 60 million copies per day. By 2001, though, only 55 million copies circulated each day—59 million on Sunday, down also from 62 million in the early 1990s. Although the population increased during that period, the percentage of adults who read the paper at least once a week dropped from 78 percent in 1970 to 55.5 percent by 2001. This decline in readership actually began during the Depression and the rise of radio. Between 1931 and 1939, 600 newspapers ceased operation. Between the early 1940s and 2001, the number of daily papers in the United States dropped from 1,900 to 1,465.[26]

The biggest circulation crisis for newspapers occurred from the late 1960s through the 1970s. Both the rise in network television viewing and the competition from suburban weeklies intensified the decline in daily readership. In addition, with an increasing number of women working full-time outside the home throughout the 1970s, newspapers could no longer consistently count on one of their core readership groups. (In fact, by 2000 women made up only 45 percent of all daily newspaper readers.) Circulation dropped by more than 20 percent in the nation's twenty largest cities (even though the population declined by only 6 percent in those areas).[27]

Although some newspapers experienced circulation gains in the 1980s and mid-1990s, especially in more affluent suburban communities, readership in the United States generally declined or flattened out during this period. Increases at many suburban weekly papers actually siphoned off readers of large city dailies. By comparison, many other countries did not experience readership declines. For example, for every 1,000 people, Sweden sells 500 papers per day. In the United States that figure is fewer than 250 copies sold daily for every 1,000 people.[28] Countries such as Norway, Finland, Japan, South Korea, and Germany also have higher rates of readership.

Joint Operating Agreements and Declining Competition

In the past, antimonopoly rules prevented a single owner from controlling all the newspapers in a city or town. Today, however, such rules have little impact because just a single paper has survived to serve most communities. In addition, prior to the 1996 Telecommunications Act, the FCC prohibited newspaper owners from purchasing broadcast or cable outlets in the same markets where they publish newspapers. Such restrictions once encouraged more voices in the media marketplace.

Although regulation has lessened, in general the government continues to monitor the declining number of newspapers in various American cities as well as mergers in cities where competition among papers might be endangered. The Justice Department has allowed a number of mergers over the years, but it was not until 1970 that Congress passed the Newspaper Preservation Act, which enabled failing

> **“** Declining readership is a symptom well understood by the leaders of our industry. Only recently, however, have newspaper people come to agree that content is first among the many reasons readership is in decline. **”**
>
> – Robert Giles, former editor and publisher, *Detroit News*

papers to continue operating through a **joint operating agreement (JOA)**. Under a JOA, two competing papers keep separate news divisions while merging business and production operations for a period of years.

In 2002, JOAs were still in place in twelve cities, including Cincinnati, Seattle, and Tucson. Although JOAs and mergers encourage monopolistic tendencies, they have sometimes been the only way to maintain competition between newspapers in the Information Age. For instance, in the mid-1920s about five hundred American cities had two or more newspapers with separate owners. By 2000, fewer than twenty cities had independent, competing papers. In 1995, the *Houston Post* folded, leaving the nation's fourth-largest city with only one daily paper, the *Houston Chronicle*. In 1998, the *Nashville Banner* closed, leaving the Gannett-owned *Tennessean* as the only daily print game in town.

Until the 1990s, Detroit was one of the most competitive newspaper cities in the nation. The *Detroit News* and the *Detroit Free Press* both ranked among the ten most widely circulated papers in the country and sold their weekday editions for just fifteen cents a copy. But in the early 1990s, managers at the two papers began exploring joint ways to stabilize revenue declines. Claiming that in Detroit's depressed economy the death of one newspaper might result in substantial job losses, the papers asked for a JOA, which the government authorized. In the largest JOA to date, the *News*, owned by Gannett, and the *Free Press*, owned by Knight-Ridder, began sharing business and production operations, although the companies remained independently owned and staffed separate news and editorial departments.

On Saturday and Sunday, the two papers circulated one edition, which featured special sections from both papers. Beginning in the summer of 1995, a prolonged and bitter strike by several unions sharply reduced circulation, especially at the *News*, which had become a home-delivered afternoon daily under the terms of the JOA. One of the unions' concerns involved reduced competition under the JOA, which had allowed managers at both papers to cut costs and jobs to sustain high profits for stockholders. Before the 1995 strike, Gannett and Knight-Ridder—later accused of trying to break the labor unions in Detroit—had both reported profit margins of well over 15 percent on their other newspaper holdings.[29] By 2000, neither of the Detroit papers was ranked among the nation's top twenty papers, according to circulation figures. In fact, they had together lost half their circulation in ten years—a readership loss eight times higher than that of the industry as a whole.

Newspaper Chains Invest in TV

Another key economic change in the newspaper industry has been the rise of **newspaper chains**, companies that own several papers throughout the country. Edward Wyllis Scripps founded the first newspaper chain in the 1890s. By the 1920s, there were about thirty chains in the United States, each one owning an average of five papers. The emergence of chains paralleled the major business trend during the twentieth century: the movement toward oligopolies in which fewer and fewer corporations control each industry. By the 1980s, more than 130 chains owned an average of nine papers each, with the 12 largest chains accounting for 40 percent of the total circulation in the United States. By the mid-1990s, chains controlled nearly 80 percent of all daily newspapers, and by 2001 the top 13 chains circulated more than one-half of all the nation's daily papers. Gannett, for example, the nation's largest chain, owns more than ninety daily papers (and forty more nondailies), ranging from small suburban papers to the Nashville *Tennessean*, the *Detroit News*, and *USA Today*.

Similar to cable companies, newspapers operate as regional monopolies in most cities. Furthermore, many newspaper owners, instead of investing in investigative journalism or attracting new readers, have devoted their energies to buying radio and TV stations. Gannett, for instance, owns twenty TV stations. Rupert Murdoch's

News Corp., among the world's largest chains, now owns thirty-two U.S. television stations, the most in history. Right after the passage of the 1996 Telecommunications Act, the Tribune Company in Chicago paid more than $1 billion to acquire six more TV stations, now reaching into a third of all U.S. households.[30]

A disturbing trend in the 1990s found daily newspapers changing hands at a much faster rate than in previous years. For example, between 1993 and 1996, more than 250 of the nation's 1,500-plus daily papers were sold—usually to distant chains not headquartered in the community where the paper operates.[31] News critics fear that having only a few chain owners will make it more difficult for multiple viewpoints to be expressed in the news media. They are also concerned about whether out-of-town owners and newly installed editors will put the special needs of their communities below corporate interests and the bottom line. Increasingly, chains favor editors who are bottom line–oriented business managers over independent or progressive editors who seek to increase the newshole and the number of reporters and enterprising reports and series.

Incorporating Electronic and Digital Technology to Survive

Modern computer technology began radically revolutionizing newsrooms in the 1970s. VDTs (video display terminals), for instance, displaced typewriters, enabling reporters to easily change or share stories; editors could also measure headlines or design pages on their personal computer screens. As dramatic as this change was, however, it did not pose the challenges of the information highway and digital news, which brought a brand of competition that newspapers had never seen.

The 1996 Telecommunications Act spurred alliances among cable television and telephone companies in their quest to deliver digital data into homes via cable, copper, and fiber-optic wires. Hundreds of newspapers responded by developing online versions of their paper product. Most newspaper editors believe they can provide the best electronic versions of local community news and services, in contrast to the national services offered by cable or phone systems. Many newspapers now face competition with online computer services, cable companies, and phone services in the battle for lucrative local classified advertisements.

Because of their local monopoly status, many newspapers were slower than other media to confront the challenges of the electronic and digital revolution. Into the early part of the twenty-first century, however, newspapers were still the media leader in collecting advertising revenue. The nation's newspapers annually attract about 19 percent of all ad revenues spent in the United States, which is down from a 27 percent share in the late 1980s (see Figure 8.2).

Although some observers think newspapers are on the verge of extinction as the digital age eclipses the print era, the industry is no dinosaur. In fact, the history of communication demonstrates that older mass media have always adapted. Actually, with more than 1,300 papers now online, newspapers are tackling one of the industry's major economic headaches: the cost of newsprint. After salaries, purchasing newsprint from paper manufacturers is the industry's largest expense, typically accounting for more than 25 percent of a newspaper's total cost.

Figure 8.2 Newspapers' Slice of the U.S. Advertising Pie, 2001

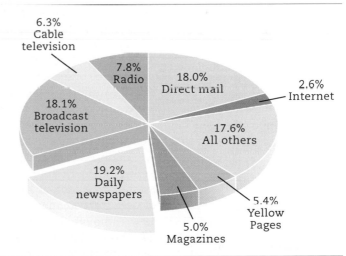

6.3% Cable television
7.8% Radio
18.0% Direct mail
2.6% Internet
18.1% Broadcast television
17.6% All others
19.2% Daily newspapers
5.0% Magazines
5.4% Yellow Pages

Source: Newspaper Association of America, Total U.S. Advertising Volume, <www.naa.org>, 2002.

In addition, online newspapers are truly taking advantage of the flexibility the Internet offers (see, for example, "Tracking Technology: Web Offers a Balanced Worldview" on page 293). Because space is not an issue, newspapers can post stories and reader letters online that they weren't able to print in the paper edition. They can also run longer stories with more in-depth coverage, as well as offer immediate updates to breaking news. For instance, during the Microsoft antitrust trial in the late 1990s and early 2000s, several newspapers devoted extra resources to their online coverage, and reporters posted stories to their Web sites several times a day. Online newspapers are also making themselves an invaluable resource to readers by offering hyperlinks to Web sites related to stories and by linking news reports to an archive of related articles. Free of charge or for a modest fee, a reader can search the newspaper's database from home and investigate the entire sequence and history of an ongoing story, such as the outcome of a trial over the course of several months. Taking advantage of the multimedia capabilities of the Internet, online newspapers offer readers the ability to download audio and video files—everything from presidential news conferences to sports highlights. Today's online newspapers offer readers a living rather than a static resource—one that does more than line the bottom of a birdcage a day after publication.

Alternative Voices

With most news organizations moving into the digital age and online editions, traditional printed newspapers found a new outlet in the 1980s with the development of *street papers*. Originally an idea for employing homeless people—both as street vendors and as news writers—the first such paper, *Street News,* emerged in New York in 1989. A number of urban imitators soon followed, including *Spare Change* in Boston and Toronto, *Street Sheet* in San Francisco, *Homeless Gazette News* in Dallas, and *Hard Times* in Los Angeles. These papers typically sell for 50 cents to $3, and the proceeds mostly go to the homeless. They cover such topics as the political and economic factors that contribute to homelessness, including the availability of inexpensive drugs like crack cocaine, the loss of urban manufacturing jobs, the downsizing of mental hospitals, and the gentrification of downtown areas. Featuring stories by and about the homeless, these papers often serve as a voice for the disenfranchised.

By 2001, fifty U.S. street papers were available, as well as another eighty worldwide. In addition to sporadic publishing schedules and financial woes, many street papers face bureaucratic obstacles that curtail distribution. For example, a New York Transit Authority regulation in the mid-1990s prohibited street vendors from selling papers on commuter trains, and in 1998 the Dallas public library system, a major gathering place for the homeless, declared a "temporary moratorium" on displaying free publications and street papers.

Oddly enough, in 1998 street papers in Los Angeles even found themselves competing with an international glossy general-interest publication, the *Big Issue.* Started in London in 1991 as a simple street paper and boasting a weekly circulation of over 250,000, mostly in England, the *Big Issue* launched an L.A. version in April 1998. Although the L.A. venture eventually failed, other versions, including Australian editions in Melbourne, Sydney, Brisbane, and Geelong, have been successful. (In fact, the color photos, celebrity profiles, and mainstream ads of the *Big Issue* remain the formula for contemporary street papers.) Designed to be sold by the homeless to middle-class youths under the motto "a good read and a good deed," these papers in 2002 directed $1.50 of the $3 price (it costs less in smaller cities) to homeless vendors. Even though homeless people have occasionally served as reporters and column writers, the success of the *Big Issue* in Europe and Australia has left many street-paper publishers questioning the value of a large-circulation street paper that generates money for the homeless at the expense of empowering them. Still, by 2002

> **❝ Selling the *Big Issue* helps my self-esteem, gives me a reason to get out of bed. Otherwise I'd sit home and get drunk, and I don't want to drink. Because I'm an alcoholic, you see, and I'm trying to kick that. ❞**
>
> – Jacki, homeless woman quoted in *The Australian,* July 2002

Web Offers a Balanced Worldview

by Todd Lappin

As the shock of the terrorist attacks of September 11, 2001, gives way to an American response, anyone with an Internet connection has access to sources of international news and opinion that were once the preserve of intelligence analysts and diplomats: local newspapers all over the world.

It is easy to find English-language newspapers, thanks to a site called The Paperboy (<www.thepaperboy.com>), which provides a directory of links to 5,288 newspapers in 176 countries. Searchable by country and by language, The Paperboy directory is free. For $2.95 a month, the site offers a subscription to options like machine-generated translations of some papers in other languages. The translations are far from perfect, but they are an improvement over utter indecipherability.

"In a case like this, the main reason for turning to the foreign media is to gain a balanced worldview," said Ian Duckworth, The Paperboy's creator, from his home in Perth, Australia. "U.S. media outlets are doing a fine job covering the story, but it's important to see how all the various players in the impending conflict are reporting it."

Mr. Duckworth said that The Paperboy counted 22,677 visitors on September 12, four times the norm for the site. It was the busiest day ever at The Paperboy, which was started up in 1997, and traffic remains high.

Many overseas news sites, of course, publish in English or offer English editions. . . .

As the investigation of the terrorist attacks enlists an international cast, British newspapers like *The Times* (<www.thetimes.co.uk>) and *The Guardian* (<www.guardian.co.uk>) are offering broad coverage of efforts by law-enforcement agencies to identify conspirators in Europe.

Grim speculation about possible military operations abounds at (<www.debka.com>), an Israeli site. Much of its information is attributed to unnamed "intelligence sources," but even skeptics may find certain headlines chilling, like "Iraq Trains Bin Laden's Men in Use of Weapons of Mass Destruction."

In Saudi Arabia, *Arab News* (<www.arabnews.com>) reflects the country's nervous attempt to juggle support for Islamic fundamentalism with support for the United States.

Nowhere is the tension between trying to support American policies and soothe Islamic constituencies more fraught than in Pakistan, which shares a long frontier with Afghanistan. Long ruled by the British, Pakistan is home to many English-language newspapers, among them *Dawn* (<www.dawn.com>), its most widely circulated English daily. Its opinion pages reflect the mood of Pakistan's dominant political establishment, cautious but generally favorable toward the United States.

For sheer proximity to a possible conflict zone, it is hard to beat *The Frontier Post* (<www.frontierpost.com.pk>), which is published in the Pakistani town of Peshawar, near the Afghan border. The area is home to many Islamic militants and is now thronged by Afghan refugees. Jalil Afridi, acting director of *The Frontier Post,* said that the site had been attracting 45,000 to 65,000 visitors a day since September 11, two to three times the average.

Each day *The Frontier Post* reports on the latest political developments among the Taliban and in Pakistan and on the flow of refugees and military activities in Afghanistan. The paper's Op-Ed commentaries, grouped under a link called Articles, reflect sentiments ranging from generous sympathy to fierce antagonism toward the United States.

After years of publishing in that volatile corner of the world, Mr. Afridi seems unfazed by the dangers ahead. "We started *The Frontier Post* during the war with the Soviet Union," he said, evoking the decade when Peshawar was a base for Afghan guerrillas fighting Soviet forces. "We have already been through some much more difficult times."

Source: Todd Lappin, "Turning the Page to a Fresh Worldview," *New York Times,* October 4, 2001, p. G9.

● The outcome of the 2000 presidential campaign was badly miscalled by the main TV and cable news networks. Many newspapers around the country repeated the mistake the next morning, although George Bush eventually did win the controversial election. Such media bungling brought back memories of the pre-TV 1948 election, in which the *Chicago Tribune* miscalled the race between eventual president Harry Truman and his Republican challenger Thomas Dewey.

street papers were a viable alternative voice to the mainstream press and TV networks, which generally stopped reporting on homelessness as major story by the mid-1990s.[32]

⦀⦀⦀★ Newspapers and Democracy

Of all mass media, newspapers have played the longest and strongest role in sustaining democracy. As a venue for the expression of ideas and the distribution of information, newspapers keep readers abreast of issues and events in their community, their nation, and their world. Over the years, newspapers have fought heroic battles in places that had little tolerance for differing points of view. During a ten-year period—from 1992 through 2001—389 reporters from around the world were killed trying to do their jobs. Of the 389, the international Committee to Protect Journalists reported that 298 were murdered, while another 62 were killed in cross fires as they were covering wars or civil uprisings.[33] In 2001 alone, 118 journalists were jailed and 37 died doing their work, including 9 in Afghanistan covering the U.S.-led military campaign. More journalists died at the outset of 2002, including Daniel Pearl, who was brutally killed in Pakistan by Islamic extremists; at the time, he was covering international terrorism for the *Wall Street Journal*. In various settings worldwide, journalists continue to face danger and articulate unpopular ideas, even when their lives are threatened.

Although newspapers remain a strong medium of communication, critics have raised a number of concerns about their future. For instance, some charge that newspapers have become so formulaic in their design and reporting styles that they may actually discourage new approaches to telling stories and reporting news. Another criticism is that many one-newspaper cities cover only issues and events of interest to middle- and upper-middle-class readers, thereby underreporting the experiences and events that affect poorer and working-class citizens. In addition, given the rise of newspaper chains, the likelihood of including new opinions, ideas, and information in mainstream daily papers may be diminishing. Although wealthy and powerful chains may keep smaller struggling papers solvent, such chains sometimes have little commitment to local communities beyond profits. Moreover, chain ownership tends to discourage watchdog journalism and the crusading traditions of newspapers. Like other business managers, many news executives prefer not to offend investors or outrage potential advertisers by running too many investigative reports, especially business probes. Indeed, reporters have generally undercovered the business and ownership arrangements in their own industry.

❝ Journalism, and specifically the newspaper, ought to become a support system for public life. ❞
—Jay Rosen, news scholar, 1992

Critics today have raised some important questions regarding the transformation from a modern print to a postmodern digital culture. For example, does such a transformation represent a cheapening of public discourse? Do "new news" forums and nonprint media offer opportunities to improve democracy by permitting public conversations that are not dependent on major newspapers? Also, what is the role of large corporations in this transformation? Do they allow enough different voices and viewpoints into the market? Do corporate owners prevent their newspaper divisions from reporting fully on the business aspects of journalism? (We will return to these questions and the public journalism movement in Chapter 14.)

By the late 1990s, the social definition and role of a reporter seemed in question. In reporting the latest White House gossip, weekly supermarket tabloids had a readership three and four times larger than that of the *New York Times,* which itself followed up on stories that first appeared in tabloids. Talk-show hosts were also performing news functions by bringing to light controversial issues. Giving third-party candidates like Ross Perot a platform, Larry King's talk show on CNN played a journalistic role in both the 1992 and the 1996 presidential campaigns. By 2001, the 24-hour cable news prime-time talk shows had become major venues for political discussion and national debate. The 1990s and early 2000s also saw furious competition for younger readers weaned on moving images in a highly visual culture. Because most major newspapers are now available via interactive computer services, the old battle lines between print and electronic culture need to be redrawn and remapped. For better or worse, journalism today encompasses a host of resources that perform news and entertainment functions. Newspapers are working to keep up as they compete in a world overloaded with information. The best of them continue to sustain journalism's democratic traditions: They make sense of important events and watch over our central institutions.

● Regarded as one of the best online newspapers, the *Mercury Center* is the Web-based extension of the *San Jose Mercury News.*

www.

To create an individualized study plan for Chapter 8, go to the interactive *Media and Culture* Online Study Guide at: bedfordstmartins.com/ mediaculture

REVIEW QUESTIONS

The Evolution of American Newspapers

1. What are the limitations of a press that serves only partisan interests? Why did the earliest papers appeal mainly to more privileged readers?

2. How did newspapers emerge as a mass medium during the penny-press era? How did content changes make this happen?

3. What are the two main features of yellow journalism? How have Joseph Pulitzer and William Randolph Hearst contributed to newspaper history?

Competing Models of Modern Print Journalism

4. Why did objective journalism develop? What are its characteristics? What are its strengths and limitations?

5. Why did interpretive forms of journalism develop in the modern era? What are the limits of objectivity?

6. How would you define literary journalism? Why did it emerge in such an intense way in the 1960s? How is literary journalism an attack on objective news?

Categorizing News and U.S. Newspapers

7. What is the difference between consensus- and conflict-oriented newspapers?

8. What role have ethnic, minority, and oppositional newspapers played in the United States?

9. Why have African American newspapers struggled to maintain their circulation levels over the past two decades?

Newspaper Operations: Economic Demands vs. Editorial Duties

10. Explain the distinction between the business and news operations of a newspaper.

11. What is a wire service? a feature syndication?

Ownership, Economics, Technology, and Innovation

12. What are the major reasons for the decline in newspaper circulation figures?

13. What is the impact of a JOA (joint operating agreement) on the business and editorial divisions of competing newspapers?

14. Why did newspaper chains become an economic trend in the twentieth century?

15. What major challenges does new technology pose to the newspaper industry?

Newspapers and Democracy

16. What is a newspaper's role in a democracy?

17. How has the definition of a reporter changed in the 1990s and early 2000s?

QUESTIONING THE MEDIA

1. What kinds of stories, topics, or issues are not being covered well by mainstream papers?

2. Why do you think people aren't reading daily newspapers as frequently as they once did? What can newspapers do to increase circulation?

3. Discuss whether newspaper chains are ultimately good or bad for the future of journalism.

4. Are Larry King or Oprah Winfrey practicing a form of journalism on their talk shows? Explain your answer.

5. Do newspapers today play a vigorous role as watchdogs of our powerful institutions? Why or why not?

6. Will 24-hour cable TV news and Internet news services eventually replace newspapers? Explain your response.

SEARCHING THE INTERNET

http://www.mediainfo.com

The official Web site of *Editor & Publisher,* the newspaper industry's top trade journal. This site offers statistics on the industry, links to national and international newspaper sites, library and research services, and major stories on the newspaper business.

http://www.nytimes.com

The site for the nation's best newspaper, the *New York Times,* not only offers a Web version of its daily newspaper but also updates major stories throughout the day.

http://www.wsj.com

The site for the nation's most widely circulated daily newspaper, the *Wall Street Journal.* Although parts of the site are by paid subscription only, free services allow readers to access current articles on a range of topics including the economy, financial markets, and politics.

http://www.latimes.com

The site for the nation's leading West Coast paper, the *Los Angeles Times,* offers main sections and updates of its print version, plus services similar to those offered by other leading national papers.

http://www.usatoday.com

The colorful site for the Web version of the nation's newest national paper, *USA Today,* founded in 1982, offers online counterparts to its four main print sections as well as a version of its famous full-color weather map.

http://www.washingtonpost.com

The site for one of the nation's most influential papers, the *Washington Post,* whose publisher also owns *Newsweek* magazine.

THE CRITICAL PROCESS

In Brief

In class, make several lists on the board regarding what sections of the newspaper you and your classmates read first, second, and/or not at all. Why do you make these choices? What do you think draws you to these particular sections? In terms of the whole class, which sections were people more likely to read first? Can you make any generalizations about your own newspaper-reading behavior and the newspaper-reading habits of your classmates?

In Depth

The purpose of this project is to extend your critical approach to news. Work with a partner or in a small group. Over a period of three weekdays, study the *New York Times, USA Today,* and one local daily paper. Devise a chart and a descriptive scheme so that you can compare how each of the three papers covers international news. You should consider international news to be any news story that is predominantly about a country other than the United States. Exclude the sports section of the papers. Follow these steps as you work on your project:

Description. Count the total number of international news stories in each paper. Which foreign cities are covered? Which countries? What are the subjects of these stories (civil wars, anti-Americanism, natural disasters, travelogue profiles, etc.)? Prepare a descriptive chart to show the differences among the three papers.

Analysis. Using your chart as a guide, write two or three paragraphs discussing patterns that emerge. What locales seem to get the most attention? What kinds of stories seem to appear most frequently? In other words, what kind of issue or event makes another country newsworthy? Do not try to summarize your chart here. Instead, just write about three or four intriguing patterns that you noticed.

Interpretation. Write a two- or three-paragraph critical interpretation of your findings. What does your analysis mean? Why do some countries appear more frequently than others? Why do certain kinds of stories seem to get featured?

Evaluation. Discuss the limitations of your study. Which paper seemed to do the best job of covering the rest of the world? Why? Do you think newspapers give us enough information about other people's cultures and experiences?

KEY TERMS

partisan press, 266
penny papers, 267
human-interest stories, 269
wire services, 269
yellow journalism, 270
objective journalism, 273

inverted-pyramid style, 274
interpretive journalism, 275
advocacy journalism, 277
precision journalism, 277
literary journalism, 277
consensus-oriented journalism, 280

conflict-oriented journalism, 280
newshole, 285
feature syndicates, 288
joint operating agreement (JOA), 290
newspaper chains, 290

magazines

in the age of specialization

CHAPTER 9

In 1991, Martha Stewart, the one-time fashion model, stockbroker, and caterer, was on the verge of creating an unprecedented media empire. Her magazine *Martha Stewart Living* had been successfully launched, and her reach expanded with new spin-off enterprises like books, videos, television shows, and a contract for a self-named line of housewares at Kmart. By 1999, she had gained control of her magazine and other media properties from Time Warner and had taken her company public on the stock exchange. Her personal fortune as the controlling shareholder of Martha Stewart Living Omnimedia ballooned to an estimated $1.27 billion. Still, her commercial success was based essentially on one simple thing: her own image as the flawless homemaker extraordinaire or (in her company's words) "America's most trusted guide to stylish living."

Building a media company on a famous personality has its advantages: Little effort is needed to build the brand name, and media publicity comes naturally. So, it's

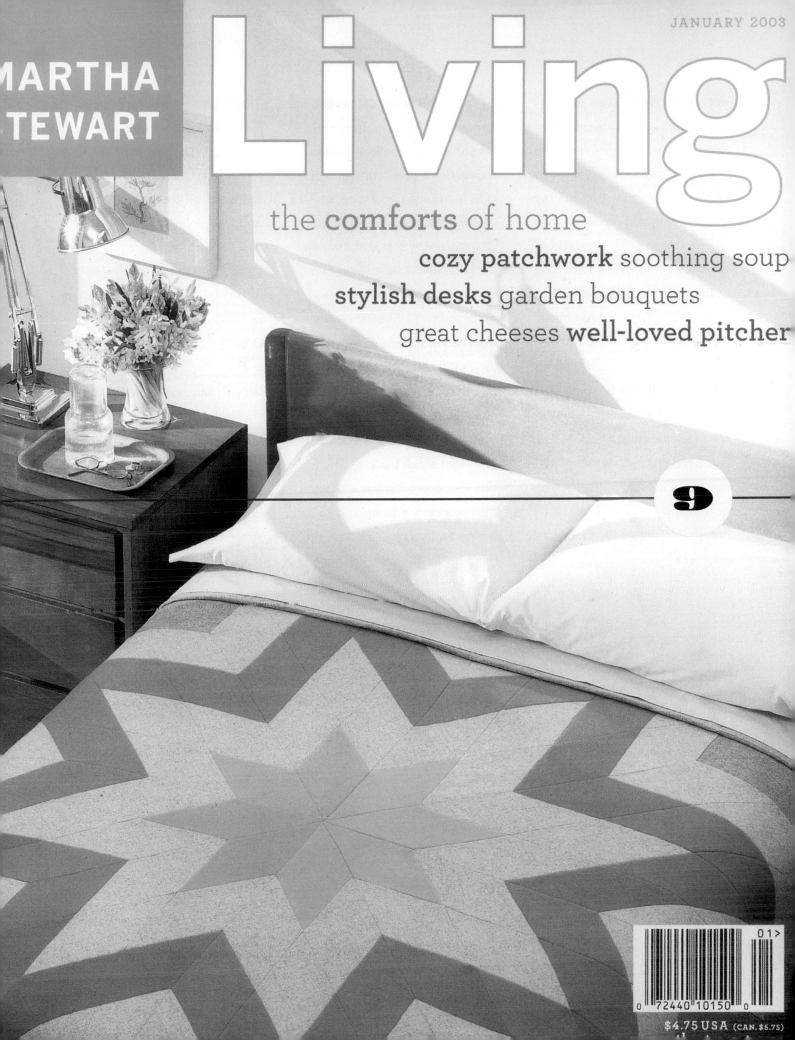

JANUARY 2003

MARTHA
STEWART

Living

the **comforts** of home

cozy patchwork soothing soup

stylish desks garden bouquets

great cheeses **well-loved pitcher**

9

0 72440 10150 0

01>

$4.75 USA (CAN. $5.75)

not surprising that two other magazines were subsequently launched in a similar fashion. In 2000, leading daytime talk show host Oprah Winfrey brought her name to her own new magazine, *O: The Oprah Magazine,* and it quickly became one of the best magazine introductions in years. Then, in 2001, publishing giant Bertelsmann partnered with its magazine unit Gruner + Jahr and another daytime talk host, Rosie O'Donnell, to revive its 125-year-old *McCall's* magazine, which had been perennially a top 10 magazine in circulation but was now losing up to $2 million a month. *McCall's* was relaunched as *Rosie.*

By the first half of 2002, branding a magazine on a single famous personality looked like a smart move. *Rosie* was fourteenth in U.S. magazine circulation, at 3.85 million copies, whereas *Martha Stewart Living* stood at thirtieth in circulation (2.32 million) and *O: The Oprah Magazine,* followed at thirty-first (2.76 million). But then two of the stars fell from their lofty perches. At *Martha Stewart Living,* living wasn't so easy as Stewart became the target of a federal investigation of insider stock trading, which dragged down the value of her own company's stock and sullied her perfect image. At *Rosie,* the relationship between O'Donnell and Gruner + Jahr soured quickly as they fought publicly over editorial control of the magazine.

Then, the namesake's public image shifted: In just a few short months, O'Donnell announced that she was a lesbian, ended her Emmy-award winning talk show, and then called her own magazine "boring." The magazine ended with the December 2002 issue and a flurry of lawsuit challenges between O'Donnell and Gruner + Jahr.

Only Oprah continued without scandal. But *O: The Oprah Magazine* and the rest of her media empire are certain to encounter difficulties when Oprah retires from her flagship talk show, which some expect her to do in 2006.

When television was on the rise in the early 1950s, many critics predicted the collapse of the magazine industry. But, like radio, the magazine industry showed remarkable resilience in adapting to a changing media landscape. In fact, by 2002 more than a thousand new consumer magazines, like O, were being launched annually.

Magazines adapted readily to the TV era. The introduction in 1953 of an inconspicuous publication—*TV Guide*—was a significant turning point in modern magazine history. That magazine capitalized instantly on TV's popularity. *TV Guide* was also an early example of media convergence: one medium devoting its content to another medium. It demonstrated one way the magazine industry could survive television, which would soon digest ever-larger portions of the national advertising pie.

Traditional national magazines discovered they would have to retool rapidly; television was snatching away sponsors and displacing general-circulation magazines as the dominant family medium. As a result, many magazines started developing market niches, appealing to advertisers who wanted to reach specific audiences defined by gender, age, race, class, or social and cultural interests.

Since the 1740s, magazines have played a key role in our social and cultural lives. More than newspapers, which have been mainly local and regional in scope, magazines became America's earliest national mass medium. They created some of the first spaces for discussing the broad issues of the age, including public education, the abolition of slavery, women's suffrage, literacy, and the Civil War. Early publications provided a political forum for debates among the colonial elite. In addition, many leading literary figures used magazines to gain public exposure for their essays and fiction.

In the nineteenth century, magazines became an important educational forum for women, who were barred from higher education and from active participation in the nation's political life. At the turn of the twentieth century, magazines contained probing reports that would influence a century of investigative print and broadcast journalism. From an economic perspective, magazines helped reorient households toward advertised products, hastening the rise of a consumer society. From a cultural perspective, magazines pioneered the use of engraving and photography, providing the earliest hints of the visual culture to come.

Today—despite movies, radio, television, and cable—magazines still give us voices that are not readily heard in mainstream electronic culture. Certainly, newsmagazines such as *Time* and *Newsweek* play a pivotal role in determining what consumers think about. But outside the mainstream, specialized magazines cover everything from radical politics to unusual hobbies. These publications bring information and viewpoints to readers who are not being served by the major media channels.

More than twelve thousand commercial and alternative magazines, and an additional thirteen thousand noncommercial publications and newsletters, are published in the United States annually. Like newspapers and television, magazines continue to both reflect and construct portraits of American life. They are catalogues for daily events and experiences. They show us the latest products, putting our consumer culture on continuous display. Just as we delve into other forms of culture, we read and view our favorite magazines to learn something about our community, our nation, our world, and ourselves.

In this chapter we will investigate the history and health of the magazine industry, highlighting the colonial and early American eras, the arrival of national magazines, and the development of engraving and photography. Turning to the modern American magazine, we will also focus on the age of muckraking and the rise of general-interest publications and consumer magazines. We will then look at the

> **"** No matter how Net-savvy they might be, readers just want paper. That's good news for [magazine] publishers. . . . **"**
>
> *– Minneapolis Star Tribune,* **2001**

decline of mass-market magazines and TV's impact on the older print medium. We will see how magazines have specialized in order to survive in a fragmented market and adapt in the Information Age. Finally, we will investigate the organization and economics of magazines and their function in a democracy.

The Early History of Magazines

The first magazines probably developed in seventeenth-century France, originating from bookseller catalogues and notices that book publishers inserted into newspapers. The word *magazine* derives from the French term *magasin,* meaning "storehouse." The earliest magazines were indeed storehouses of contemporary writing and reports taken mostly from newspapers. Today, the word **magazine** broadly refers to collections of articles, stories, and advertisements appearing in nondaily (such as weekly or monthly) periodicals that are published in tabloid style rather than newspaper style.

The first political magazine, called the *Review,* appeared in London in 1704. Edited by political activist and novelist Daniel Defoe (author of *Robinson Crusoe*), the *Review* was printed sporadically until 1713. Like the *Nation, National Review,* and the *Progressive* in the United States today, early European magazines were channels for political commentary and argument. These periodicals looked like newspapers, but they appeared less frequently and were oriented more toward broad domestic and political issues than toward recent news.

In the eighteenth century, regularly published magazines or pamphlets, such as the *Tatler* and the *Spectator,* also appeared in England. They offered poetry, politics, and philosophy for London's elite, and they served readerships of a few thousand. The first publication to use the term *magazine* was *Gentleman's Magazine,* which appeared in London in 1731 and consisted of reprinted articles from newspapers, books, and political pamphlets. Later the magazine began publishing original work by such writers as Defoe, Samuel Johnson, and Alexander Pope.

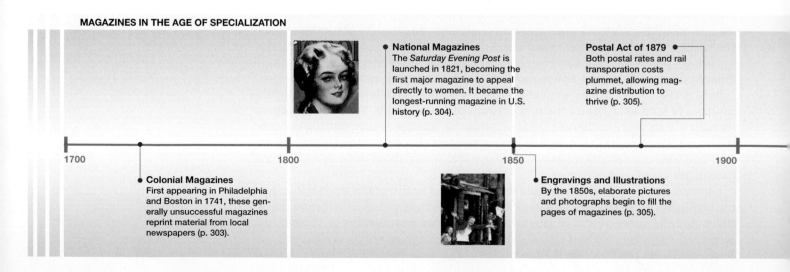

MAGAZINES IN THE AGE OF SPECIALIZATION

National Magazines
The *Saturday Evening Post* is launched in 1821, becoming the first major magazine to appeal directly to women. It became the longest-running magazine in U.S. history (p. 304).

Postal Act of 1879
Both postal rates and rail transporation costs plummet, allowing magazine distribution to thrive (p. 305).

1700   1800   1850   1900

Colonial Magazines
First appearing in Philadelphia and Boston in 1741, these generally unsuccessful magazines reprint material from local newspapers (p. 303).

Engravings and Illustrations
By the 1850s, elaborate pictures and photographs begin to fill the pages of magazines (p. 305).

Colonial Magazines

With neither a substantial middle class nor advanced printing technology, magazines developed slowly in the United States. Like partisan newspapers, magazines served politicians, the educated, and the merchant classes, interpreting their political, commercial, and cultural world. Paid circulations were slight—between one hundred and fifteen hundred. In the late 1700s, reading magazines was not a habit among the working classes; most adults were illiterate. However, early magazines did document a new nation coming to terms with issues of taxation, state versus federal power, Indian treaties, public education, and the end of colonialism. George Washington, Alexander Hamilton, and John Hancock all wrote for magazines, and Paul Revere worked as a magazine illustrator for a time.

The first colonial magazines appeared in Philadelphia in 1741, about fifty years after the first newspapers. Andrew Bradford started it all with *American Magazine, or A Monthly View of the Political State of the British Colonies*. Three days later, Ben Franklin's *General Magazine and Historical Chronicle* appeared. Bradford's magazine lasted only three months and three issues. It faced circulation and postal obstacles that Franklin, who had replaced Bradford as Philadelphia's postmaster, put in its way. For instance, Franklin mailed his magazine without paying the high postal rates that he subsequently charged others. Franklin's magazine primarily duplicated what was already available in local papers. After six months he, too, stopped publication.

Following the Philadelphia experiments, magazines emerged in other colonies as well. Several magazines were produced in Boston beginning in the 1740s. The most successful publications simply reprinted articles from leading London periodicals, keeping readers abreast of European events. Magazines such as the *Independent Reflector* also sprang up in New York, featuring poetry as well as cultural and political essays. The *Pennsylvania Magazine,* edited by activist Thomas Paine, helped rally the colonies against British rule. While editing the magazine, Paine worked on his famous 1776 pamphlet *Common Sense,* which made the intellectual case for American independence. By 1776, about a hundred colonial magazines had appeared and disappeared. Although historians consider them dull and uninspired, these magazines did launch a new medium that ultimately caught on after the Revolution.

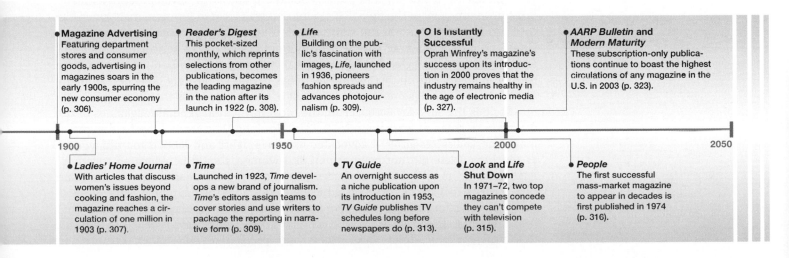

● **Magazine Advertising**
Featuring department stores and consumer goods, advertising in magazines soars in the early 1900s, spurring the new consumer economy (p. 306).

● **Reader's Digest**
This pocket-sized monthly, which reprints selections from other publications, becomes the leading magazine in the nation after its launch in 1922 (p. 308).

● **Life**
Building on the public's fascination with images, *Life,* launched in 1936, pioneers fashion spreads and advances photojournalism (p. 309).

● **O Is Instantly Successful**
Oprah Winfrey's magazine's success upon its introduction in 2000 proves that the industry remains healthy in the age of electronic media (p. 327).

● **AARP Bulletin and Modern Maturity**
These subscription-only publications continue to boast the highest circulations of any magazine in the U.S. in 2003 (p. 323).

1900   1950   2000   2050

● **Ladies' Home Journal**
With articles that discuss women's issues beyond cooking and fashion, the magazine reaches a circulation of one million in 1903 (p. 307).

● **Time**
Launched in 1923, *Time* develops a new brand of journalism. *Time*'s editors assign teams to cover stories and use writers to package the reporting in narrative form (p. 309).

● **TV Guide**
An overnight success as a niche publication upon its introduction in 1953, *TV Guide* publishes TV schedules long before newspapers do (p. 313).

● **Look and Life Shut Down**
In 1971–72, two top magazines concede they can't compete with television (p. 315).

● **People**
The first successful mass-market magazine to appear in decades is first published in 1974 (p. 316).

The First U.S. Magazines

The early growth of magazines in the United States was steady but slow. Delivery costs remained high, and some postal carriers even refused to carry magazines because they added so much weight to a load. Twelve magazines operated in 1800. By 1825, about a hundred magazines existed, although another five hundred or so had failed in the first twenty-five years of the nineteenth century. By the early 1800s, most communities had their own weekly magazines, but much of the material was still reprinted from other sources. These magazines featured essays on local issues, government activities, and political intrigue. They sold some advertising but were usually in precarious financial straits because of their small circulations.

The idea of specialized magazines devoted to certain categories of readers developed throughout the nineteenth century. Many early periodicals, for instance, were overtly religious. Published by various denominations, religious magazines boasted the largest readerships in their day. The Methodist *Christian Journal and Advocate,* for example, claimed 25,000 subscribers by 1826. Literary magazines also emerged. The *North American Review,* for example, established the work of important writers such as Ralph Waldo Emerson, Henry David Thoreau, and Mark Twain. Besides religion and literature, magazines addressed various professions, lifestyles, and topics, including agriculture (*American Farmer*), education (*American Journal of Education*), law (*American Law Journal*), medicine (*Medical Repository*), and science (*American Journal of Science*). Such specialization spawned the modern trend of reaching readers who share a profession, a set of beliefs, cultural tastes, or a social identity.

In 1821, two young Philadelphia printers, Charles Alexander and Samuel Coate Atkinson, launched the *Saturday Evening Post,* which became the longest-running magazine in U.S. history. The printers operated their venture from the same printing plant that formerly published Franklin's newspaper, the *Pennsylvania Gazette.* Like most magazines of the day, the early *Post* included a few original essays by its own editors but "borrowed" many pieces from other sources. Eventually the *Post* developed into one of the leading magazines of the nineteenth century, featuring news, poetry, essays, and play reviews. Its editors published the writings of such prominent popular authors as Nathaniel Hawthorne and Harriet Beecher Stowe. It was the first major magazine to appeal directly to women, starting the "Lady's Friend," a column that addressed women's issues. During the 1800s, the weekly *Post* became the first important general-interest magazine aimed at a national audience.

The Arrival of National Magazines

With increases in literacy and public education, and with developments in faster printing technology in the mid-1880s, a market was created for more magazines like the *Post.* Improvements in rail transportation also made it possible to ship magazines and other consumer products easily from city to city. Whereas in 1825 a hundred magazines struggled for survival, by 1850 nearly six hundred magazines were being produced. During this twenty-five-year period, publishers launched as many as five thousand magazines, although most of them lasted less than a year.

Besides the *Saturday Evening Post,* the most influential general magazines of the day were targeted at women. In 1828, Sarah Josepha Hale started the first women's magazine, *Ladies' Magazine.* It advocated women's rights and schools to train women as teachers. (Hale did not believe men and women should be educated together.) After nine years and marginal success, Hale merged her magazine with its main rival, *Godey's Lady's Book* (1830–98), which she edited for the next forty years. By 1850, *Godey's,* known for its colored fashion illustrations, had a circulation of 40,000, at that time the biggest ever for a U.S. magazine. By 1860, circulation swelled to 150,000. Hale's magazine, a champion of women's property rights, played a central role in educating working- and middle-class women, who were denied access to higher education throughout the nineteenth century.

Other magazines also marked the shift to national periodicals. *Graham's Magazine,* published in Philadelphia from 1840 to 1858, was one of the most influential and entertaining magazines in the country. Also important at the time was the precursor of the *New Yorker, Knickerbocker* (1833–64), which drew from such literary talent as Washington Irving, James Fenimore Cooper, and Nathaniel Hawthorne. The magazine introduced the "Editor's Table," a breezy and often humorous column that discussed current topics and was later imitated by the *New Yorker.* Also emerging during this period was the *Nation,* founded in 1865 by E. L. Godkin. The oldest surviving American political opinion magazine, the *Nation* continues to serve mostly an educated readership whose politics are left of center. In addition, the weekly *Youth's Companion* (1826–1929) became one of the first successful magazines for younger readers. It, too, sought to extend the reach of magazines beyond local boundaries.

Pictorial Pioneers

Like the first newspapers, many early magazines were dull and gray in appearance, totally dependent on the printed word. By the mid-1850s, though, drawings, engravings, woodcuts, and other forms of illustration had become major features of magazines. During this time, *Godey's Lady's Book* employed up to 150 women to color-tint its magazine illustrations and stencil drawings. *Harper's New Monthly Magazine,* founded in 1850, published the work of top American and British writers but also offered extensive woodcut illustrations with each issue. During the Civil War, many readers relied on *Harper's* for its elaborate battlefield sketches. Publications like *Harper's* married visual language to the printed word, helping to transform magazines into a popular national mass medium.

Bringing photographs to magazines took a bit longer. Mathew Brady and his employees, whose thirty-five hundred photos documented the Civil War, had popularized photography by the 1860s. But it was not until the 1890s that newspapers and magazines had the technology to adapt photos to print media. (For more on this topic, see "Case Study: The Evolution of Photojournalism" on page 310.)

The Development of Modern American Magazines

In 1870, about twelve hundred magazines were produced in the United States. By 1890, the number of magazines reached forty-five hundred; by 1905, more than six thousand existed, most of them intended for local and regional audiences. The rate of failure, however, was high. Although publishers launched approximately seventy-five hundred magazines between 1895 and 1905, more than half of them died or merged with other magazines.[1] Part of this surge in titles and readership was facilitated by the Postal Act of 1879, which assigned magazines lower postage rates and put them on an equal footing with newspapers delivered by mail.

While lower postal rates and better rail transportation were reducing magazines' distribution costs, advances in modern technology were lowering production costs. By the end of the nineteenth century, advances in mass-production printing, conveyor systems, assembly lines, and faster presses made large-circulation national magazines possible.[2] These technological improvements enabled magazine entrepreneurs to slash the prices of magazines, which ran about thirty-five cents a copy in the late 1880s. As prices dropped to fifteen and then to ten cents, the working classes were gradually able to purchase national publications. By 1905, there

> **❝** They spring up as fast as mushrooms, in every corner, and like all rapid vegetation, bear the seeds of early decay within them . . . and then comes a 'frost, a killing frost,' in the form of bills due and debts unpaid. . . . The average age of periodicals in this country is found to be six months. **❞**
>
> *– New-York Mirror, 1828*

● Launched in 1886 as a magazine for "first-class families," *Cosmopolitan* began as a literary publication, offering both general-interest and fiction articles. It was not until the 1960s that *Cosmopolitan* began to focus on young, career-oriented women and adopted the credo "Fun Fearless Female." *Cosmo*'s editor at that time, Helen Gurley Brown (who came to fame with her popular book *Sex and the Single Girl*), shaped the publication into one of the best-selling magazines in the United States and worldwide. Today, *Cosmopolitan* has 41 international editions.

● Norman Rockwell's 322 cover illustrations for the *Saturday Evening Post* between 1916 and 1963 included a series of 11 covers featuring a young World War II GI named Willie Gillis. The character was modeled after a Vermont neighbor of Rockwell's who posed for the artist and later went to war himself. In the final Willie Gillis cover illustration, in 1945, the soldier returns home to his mother.

were about twenty-five national magazines, available from coast to coast and serving millions of readers.[3]

As magazine circulation started to skyrocket, publishers began deriving higher ad revenues from companies eager to sell their wares in the expanding market. Ad pages in national magazines soared. *Harper's,* for instance, devoted only seven pages to ads in the mid-1880s, nearly fifty pages in 1890, and more than ninety pages in 1900.[4] By the turn of the century, advertisers increasingly used national magazines to capture consumers' attention and build a national marketplace. In addition, the dramatic growth of drugstores and dime stores, supermarkets, and department stores offered new venues and shelf space for selling consumer goods, including magazines. As jobs and the population began shifting from farms and small towns to urban areas, magazines helped readers to imagine themselves as part of a nation rather than as individuals with only local or regional identities.

One magazine that took advantage of these changes was *Ladies' Home Journal,* begun in 1883 by Cyrus Curtis. Prior to *LHJ,* many women's magazines had been called cookie-and-pattern publications because they narrowly confined women's concerns to baking and fashion. *LHJ* broadened the scope of magazines as its editors and advertisers realized that women consumers constituted a growing and lucrative market. Publishing popular fiction and sheet music as well as the latest consumer ads, *LHJ* had a circulation of half a million by the early 1890s—the highest of any magazine in the country. In 1903, it became the first magazine to reach a circulation of one million.

Social Reform and the Muckrakers

The economics behind the rise of popular magazines was simple: A commercial publisher could dramatically expand circulation by dropping the price of an issue below the actual production cost for a single copy. The publisher recouped the loss through ad revenue, guaranteeing large readerships to advertisers who were willing to pay more to reach more readers. Throughout the twentieth century, many commercial magazines adopted this principle. However, simply lowering costs from twenty-five or thirty-five cents to a dime wasn't enough. Like the penny press, magazines had to change content as well.

Besides being attracted to the ten-cent price tag, readers were drawn to the issues that magazines addressed. While printing the fiction and essays of good writers of the day, magazines also engaged in one aspect of yellow journalism—crusading for social reform on behalf of the public good. In the early 1890s, for example, Curtis's *LHJ* and its editor, Edward Bok, led the fight against unregulated patent medicines (which often contained nearly 50 percent alcohol). Other magazines joined the fight against phony medicines, poor living and working conditions, and unsanitary practices in various food industries.

The rise in overall magazine circulation coincided with the search for better jobs. In the move from farms to factories, hundreds of thousands of Americans and new immigrants poured into cities. Thus, the nation that journalists and magazines wrote about had grown increasingly complex by the turn of the century. Some reporters became dissatisfied with conventional journalism and turned from newspapers to magazines, where they were able to write in greater depth about broader issues. They wrote both factual and fictional accounts on such topics as corruption in big business and government, urban problems faced by immigrants, conflicts between labor and management, and race relations. Angry with so much negative reporting, President Theodore Roosevelt in 1906 dubbed these reporters *muckrakers,* because they were willing to crawl in society's muck to uncover a story. **Muckraking** was a label that Roosevelt used with disdain, but it was worn with pride by reporters such as Ray Stannard Baker, Frank Norris, Lincoln Steffens, and Ida Tarbell.

In 1902, *McClure's* magazine (1893–1933) touched off this investigative era in magazine reporting with a series of probing stories on business monopolies, life-insurance frauds, political dishonesty in city governments, and the problems of labor and working people. The muckrakers distrusted established institutions and undertook to protect ordinary citizens from corruption. First serialized in *McClure's,* Ida Tarbell's *The History of the Standard Oil Company* took on John D. Rockefeller's big oil monopoly. Lincoln Steffens's "Shame of the Cities" series for *McClure's* tackled urban problems. Steffens said of his own investigations, "When I set out to describe the corrupt systems of certain typical cities, I meant to show simply how the people were deceived and betrayed."[5]

In 1906, *Cosmopolitan* (1886–), recently purchased by William Randolph Hearst, joined the muckraking parade with a series called "The Treason of the Senate." *Collier's* (1888–1957) developed "The Great American Fraud" series, focusing on patent medicines (whose ads accounted for 30 percent of the profits made by the American press by the 1890s). Influenced by Upton Sinclair's novel *The Jungle*, a fictional account of Chicago's meatpacking industry, and by *Collier's* and *LHJ*'s muckraking reports, Congress passed the Pure Food and Drug Act in 1906.

The Rise of General-Interest Magazines

The heyday of the muckraking era lasted into the mid-1910s. Then national social crusades and reforms became less significant, as America and journalism were gradually drawn into the first major international war. After World War I the prominent publications were **general-interest magazines**, which offered occasional investigative articles but covered a wide variety of topics aimed at a broad national audience. A key to these magazines, predominant from the 1920s into the 1950s, was the pioneering influence of **photojournalism**—the use of photos to document the rhythms of daily life (see "Case Study: The Evolution of Photojournalism" on page 310). With their high-quality photos, national picture magazines gave the industry at least one advantage over radio, which was developing into the most popular medium of the day.

Saturday Evening Post

The first widely popular general-interest magazine was the *Saturday Evening Post*. When Cyrus Curtis bought the *Post* in 1897 for $1,000, it had a circulation of approximately ten thousand. Curtis's strategy for reinvigorating the magazine included printing popular fiction and romanticizing American virtues through words and pictures (a *Post* tradition best depicted in the three hundred–plus cover illustrations by Norman Rockwell). Curtis also featured articles that celebrated the business boom of the 1920s. This reversed the journalistic direction of the muckraking era, in which business corruption was often the focus. By the 1920s, the *Post* had reached two million in circulation, the first magazine to hit that mark. By 1920, about fifty-five magazines fit the general-interest category; by 1946, more than a hundred such magazines competed with radio networks for the national audience.

Reader's Digest

The most widely circulated general-interest magazine during this period was *Reader's Digest*. Started in 1922 by Dewitt Wallace and Lila Acheson Wallace for $5,000 in a Greenwich Village basement, *Reader's Digest* championed one of the earliest functions of magazines: printing condensed versions of selected articles from other magazines. In the magazine's early years, the Wallaces refused to accept ads and sold the *Digest* only through subscriptions. The *Digest*'s circulation was just over 100,000 by the late 1920s, when it began to appear on newsstands. With its inexpensive production costs and low price, the magazine's circulation climbed to one million in 1935 during the depths of the Great Depression. By 1946, *Reader's Digest* was the nation's most popular magazine, with a circulation of nine million. Its pocket-size format made it popular both at home and for travel. By 1963, the *Digest* had a circulation of more than fourteen million, five million more than its nearest rival, *TV Guide*.

For years the *Digest* selected articles based on three criteria: "applicability" (articles relevant to readers' daily lives); "lasting interest" (articles that could still be read the next year); and "constructiveness" (articles that had an optimistic, upbeat outlook on life).[6] Although over the years *Reader's Digest* has been both chastised and praised for its conservative viewpoints and occasionally pious moral tone, by the mid-1980s it had become the most popular magazine in the world. At its peak, it

● Table 9.1 The Top 10 Magazines (ranked by paid U.S. circulation, 1972 vs. 2002)

1972		2002*	
Rank/Publication	Circulation	Rank/Publication	Circulation
1 Reader's Digest	17,827,661	1 AARP Bulletin	21,712,410
2 TV Guide	16,410,858	2 Modern Maturity	17,538,189
3 Woman's Day	8,191,731	3 Reader's Digest	12,212,040
4 Better Homes and Gardens	7,996,050	4 TV Guide	9,072,609
5 Family Circle	7,889,587	5 Better Homes and Gardens	7,602,575
6 McCall's	7,516,960	6 National Geographic	6,890,852
7 National Geographic	7,260,179	7 Good Housekeeping	4,708,964
8 Ladies' Home Journal	7,014,251	8 Family Circle	4,671,052
9 Playboy	6,400,573	9 Woman's Day	4,167,933
10 Good Housekeeping	5,801,446	10 Time	4,114,137

*Circulation for first six months of 2002.

Source: Magazine Publishers of America, <http://www.magazine.org>.

reached a circulation of twenty million in America and another ten to twelve million in 160 other countries. (See Table 9.1 for the circulation figures of the Top 10 U.S. magazines.)

Time

During the general-interest era, national newsmagazines such as *Time* were also major commercial successes. Begun in 1923 by Henry Luce and Britton Hadden, *Time* developed a magazine brand of interpretive journalism, assigning reporter-researcher teams to cover stories over a period of several weeks. A rewrite editor would then put the whole project together in narrative form and provide an interpretive point of view. Luce believed that journalistic objectivity was a myth and sought instead to be fair. Critics, however, charged that *Time* became increasingly conservative politically as the magazine grew more successful in the 1940s and 1950s. *Time* had a circulation of 200,000 by 1930, increasing to more than three million by the mid-1960s.

Time's success encouraged prominent imitators, including *Newsweek* (1933–   ) and *U.S. News & World Report* (1948–   ). When the major weekly general-interest magazines *Life* and *Look* failed in the early 1970s, newsmagazines took over photojournalism's role in news reporting, visually documenting both national and international events. By 2002, the three major newsmagazines had circulations ranging from *Time*'s 4.1 million to *Newsweek*'s 3.2 million and *U.S. News*'s 2.1 million.

Life

Despite the commercial success of *Reader's Digest* and *Time*, these two magazines did not come to symbolize general-interest publications during the 1930s. That honor belongs to the oversized pictorial weeklies *Look* and, especially, *Life*. More than any other magazine of its day, *Life* developed an effective strategy for competing with

The Evolution of Photojournalism

By Christopher R. Harris

● Jacob Riis, "The Tramp," c. 1890. Riis, who emigrated from Denmark in 1870, lived in poverty in New York for several years before becoming a photojournalist. He spent much of his later life chronicling the lives of the poor in New York City. Courtesy: The Jacob A. Riis Collection, Museum of the City of New York.

. . . What we now recognize as photojournalism started with the assignment of photographer Roger Fenton, of the *Sunday Times of London,* to document the Crimean War in 1856. Technical limitations did not allow *direct* reproduction of photodocumentary images in the publications of the day, however. Woodcut artists had to interpret the photographic images as black-and-white-toned woodblocks that could be reproduced by the presses of the period. Images interpreted by artists therefore lost the inherent qualities of photographic visual documentation: an on-site visual representation of facts for those who weren't present.

Woodcuts remained the basic method of press reproduction until 1880, when *New York Daily Graphic* photographer Stephen Horgan invented half-tone reproduction using a dot-pattern screen. This screen enabled metallic plates to directly represent photographic images in the printing process; now periodicals could bring exciting visual reportage to their pages.

In the mid-1890s, Jimmy Hare became the first photographer recognized as a photojournalist in the United States. Taken for *Collier's Weekly,* Hare's photoreportage on the sinking of the battleship *Maine* in 1898 near Havana, Cuba, established his reputation as a newsman traveling the world to bring back images of news events. Hare's images fed into growing popular support for Cuban independence from Spain and eventual U.S. involvement in the Spanish-American War.

In 1888, George Eastman opened photography to the working and middle classes when he introduced the first flexible-film camera from Kodak, his company in Rochester, New York. Gone were the bulky equipment and fragile photographic plates of the past. Now families and journalists could more easily and affordably document gatherings and events.

As photography became easier and more widespread, photojournalism began to take on an increasingly important social role. At the turn of the century, the documentary photography of Jacob Riis and Lewis Hine captured the harsh working and living conditions of the nation's many child laborers, including crowded ghettos and unsafe mills and factories. Reaction to these shockingly honest photographs resulted in public outcry and new laws against the exploitation of children. Photographs also brought the horrors of World War I to people far from the battlefields.

In 1923, visionaries Henry Luce and Britton Hadden published *Time,* the first modern photographic newsweekly; *Life* and *Fortune* soon followed. From coverage of the Roaring Twenties to the Great Depression, these magazines used images that changed the way people viewed the world.

Life, with its spacious 10- by 13-inch format and large photographs, became one of the most influential magazines in America, printing what are now classic images from World War II and the Korean War. Often, *Life* offered images that were unavailable anywhere else: Margaret Bourke-White's photographic proof of the unspeakably horrific concentration camps; W. Eugene Smith's gentle portraits of the humanitarian Albert Schweitzer in Africa; David Duncan's gritty images of the faces of U.S. troops fighting in Korea.

Television photojournalism made its quantum leap into the public mind as it documented the assassination of President Kennedy in 1963. In televised images that were broadcast and rebroadcast, the public witnessed the actual assassination and the confusing aftermath, including live coverage of the murder of alleged assassin Lee Harvey Oswald and of President Kennedy's funeral procession.

Photojournalism also provided visual documentation of the turbulent 1960s, including aggressive photographic coverage of the Vietnam War — its protesters and supporters. Pulitzer Prize–winning photographer Eddie Adams shook the emotions of the American public with his photographs of a South Vietnamese colonel's summary execution of a suspected Vietcong terrorist. Closer to home, shocking images of the Civil Rights movement culminated in pictures of Birmingham police and police dogs attacking civil rights protesters.

In the 1970s, new computer technologies emerged that were embraced by print and television media worldwide. By the late 1980s, computers could transform images into digital form, easily manipulated by sophisticated software programs. In addition, any photographer can now transmit images around the world almost instantaneously by using digital transmission, and the Internet allows publication of virtually any image, without censorship. In 1999, a reporter in war-torn Kosovo could take a picture and within minutes send that picture to news offices in Tokyo, Berlin, and New York; moments later, the images could be posted on the Internet or used in a late-breaking TV story.

Digital technology is likely to revolutionize photojournalism, perhaps even more than the advent of roll film did in the late nineteenth century. Because of rapid delivery times, competition among print publications, television networks, and online news providers is heightened, as each can run late-breaking images transmitted from anywhere in the world.

There is a dark side to digital technology as well. Because of the absence of physical film, there is a resulting loss of proof, or veracity, of the authenticity of images. Original film has qualities that make it easy to determine whether it has been tampered with. Digital images, by contrast, can be easily altered, but such alteration can be very difficult to detect.

A relatively recent example of image-tampering involved mug shots taken of O. J. Simpson after his arrest in 1994. Both *Newsweek* and *Time* ran one of these shots on their covers; *Newsweek* ran the image as photographed, whereas *Time* artificially darkened the image so that Simpson appeared more menacing. Accusations of foul play from the public and the media forced *Time* to address the issue and apologize. Nonetheless, this event gives a small indication of the dangers of altering photographs.

Photojournalists and news sources are now confronted with unprecedented concerns over truth-telling. In the past, trust in documentary photojournalism rested solely on the verifiability of images as they were used in the media. Just as we must evaluate the words we read, at the start of a new century we must also view with a more critical eye these images that mean so much to so many.

Christopher R. Harris is a professor in the Department of Electronic Media Communication at Middle Tennessee State University.

popular radio by advancing photojournalism. Launched as a weekly by Henry Luce in 1936, *Life* combined the public's fascination with images (invigorated by the movie industry), radio journalism, and the popularity of advertising and fashion photography. By the end of the 1930s, *Life* had a **pass-along readership**—that is, the total number of people who come into contact with a single copy of a magazine—of more than seventeen million, rivaling the ratings of popular national radio programs.

Life's first editor, Wilson Hicks, formerly a picture editor for the Associated Press, built a staff of renowned photographer-reporters who chronicled the world's ordinary and extraordinary events from the late 1930s through the 1960s. Among them were Margaret Bourke-White, the first woman war correspondent to fly combat missions during World War II, and Gordon Parks, who later became Hollywood's first African American director of major feature films. *Life*—child of the turn-of-the-century pictorial magazines and parent to *People, Us,* and *Entertainment Weekly*—used an oversized format featuring ninety-six pages of pictures with a minimum of written text.

The Fall of General-Interest Magazines

In 1970, *Life*'s circulation peaked at 8.5 million, with an estimated pass-along readership of nearly 50 million. *Life*'s chief competitor, *Look,* founded by Gardner Cowles in 1937, reached 2 million in circulation by 1945 and 4 million by 1955. It climbed to almost 8 million in 1971. Dramatically, though, both magazines suspended publication. The demise of these popular periodicals at the peak of their circulations seems inexplicable, but their fall illustrates a key economic shift in media history as well as a crucial moment in the conversion to an electronically oriented culture.

TV Guide Is Born

While *Life* and *Look* were just beginning to make sense of the impact of television on their audiences, *TV Guide* appeared in 1953. Taking its cue from the pocket-size format of *Reader's Digest* and the supermarket sales strategy used by women's magazines, *TV Guide,* started by Walter Annenberg's Triangle Publications, soon rivaled the success of *Reader's Digest* by specializing in TV listings and addressing the nation's growing fascination with television. The first issue sold a record 1.5 million copies in ten urban markets. The next year, *TV Guide* featured twenty-seven regional editions, tailoring its listings to TV channels in specific areas of the country. Because many newspapers were not yet listing TV programs, *TV Guide's* circulation soared to 2.2 million in its second year. In 1962, the magazine became the first weekly to reach a circulation of 8 million with its seventy regional editions.

TV Guide would rank among the nation's most popular magazines from the late 1950s into the twenty-first century. However, with increased competition from newspaper TV supplements and thousands of new magazines, *TV Guide's* prominence and circulation began flattening out in the 1980s. Then, in 1988, media baron Rupert Murdoch acquired Triangle Publications for $3 billion. Out of this magazine group (which included *Seventeen* and the *Daily Racing Form*), Murdoch kept only *TV Guide*. Murdoch's News Corp. already owned the new Fox network, and buying *TV Guide* ensured that the fledgling network would have its programs listed. Prior to this move, many predicted that no one would be able to start a new network because ABC, CBS, and NBC exercised so much control over television. By the mid-1990s, however, Fox was using *TV Guide* to promote the network's programming in the magazine's 100-plus regional editions. The other networks occasionally complained that their programs were not treated as well and even threatened to pull their ads.

The *TV Guide* story illustrates a number of key trends in the magazine business. First, in exploiting Americans' shared interest in television, *TV Guide* emerged as a wildly successful magazine just as general magazines like *Life* and *Look* began their economic decline. Second, *TV Guide* demonstrated the growing sales power of the nation's checkout lines, which also sustained the high circulation rates of women's magazines and supermarket tabloids. Third, News Corp.'s ownership of *TV Guide* underscored the fact that magazines were facing the same challenges as other mass media: Large media companies were strategically buying up smaller media outlets and applying the economic synergy of using one medium to promote another.

After the Fox network became firmly established, and as *TV Guide's* circulation began to decline, Murdoch's News Corp. looked for ways to expand the publication's reach. In 1999, Murdoch struck a $2 billion deal with United Video Satellite Group, owner of cable television's Prevue Channel. The deal allowed *TV Guide's* print listings to combine with the Prevue Channel's program listings. The Prevue Channel became the TV Guide Channel, and the new company was called TV Guide, Inc., with the News Corp. maintaining a portion of the ownership. Besides offering television listings in print and electronic form, TV Guide, Inc. aimed to create both online and interactive television listings—in short, a *TV Guide* that would try to avoid becoming obsolete in the new electronic media environment.

Before those plans developed in full, however, Murdoch's *TV Guide* franchise morphed again in 2000 when Gemstar International acquired TV Guide, Inc. in a $7 billion merger. Because Gemstar controls all the patents that make interactive electronic TV guides possible, the new company—Gemstar–TV Guide International, Inc.—plans to become the search engine of all television programming. With its interactive potential, Gemstar–TV Guide viewers will be able to search for shows by name, automatically select them by pushing a button, receive recommendations about upcoming shows based on their viewing habits, and order food and merchandise advertised on the screen. Analysts are projecting that the interactive TV guide

IN A HAREM

BEACH EXERCISE

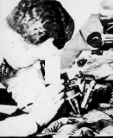

SCIENTIFIC G-MEN

YOUR FUTURE

OIL WELL FIRE

LOok

10¢

JULY 19, 1938

MARLENE DIETRICH'S TROUBLES EXPOSED!

services have the potential to be one of the most valuable media assets ever created. Not surprisingly, Murdoch is in on the deal, controlling 22 percent of the venture.

The rise of *TV Guide* as a specialized service paralleled the decline of the weekly general-interest magazines that had dominated the industry for thirty years. By 1957, both *Collier's* (founded in 1888) and *Woman's Home Companion* (founded in 1873) had folded. Each magazine had a national circulation of more than four million the year it died. No magazine with this kind of circulation had ever shut down before. Together, the two publications brought in advertising revenues of more than $26 million in 1956. Although some critics blamed poor management, both magazines were victims of changing consumer tastes, rising postal costs, falling ad revenues—and television, which began usurping the role of magazines as the preferred family medium.

Life and *Look* Expire

Although *Reader's Digest* and women's supermarket magazines were not greatly affected by television, other general-interest magazines were. The weekly *Saturday Evening Post* folded in 1969, *Look* in 1971, and *Life* in 1972. At the time, all three magazines were rated in the Top 10 in terms of paid circulation; each had a readership that exceeded six million per issue. To maintain these figures, however, their publishers were selling the magazines for far less than the cost of production. For example, by the early 1970s a subscription to *Life* cost a consumer twelve cents an issue, yet it cost the publisher more than forty cents per copy to make and mail a single issue.

Eventually, the national advertising revenue pie that helped make up the cost differences for *Life* and *Look* had to be shared with network television—and magazines' slices were getting smaller. *Life*'s high pass-along readership meant that it had a larger audience than many prime-time TV shows. But it cost more in 1971 to reach that general audience with a single full-page ad in *Life* than it did to buy a minute of time during evening television. National advertisers were often forced to choose between the two, and in the late 1960s and early 1970s television seemed a slightly better buy to many general advertisers looking for the biggest audience.

● With large pages, beautiful photographs, and compelling stories on celebrities like Marlene Dietrich, *Look* entertained millions of readers from 1939 to 1971, emphasizing photojournalism to compete with radio. By the late 1960s, however, TV lured away national advertisers, postal rates increased, and production costs rose, forcing *Look* to fold despite a readership of more than six million.

● Debuting amidst much hype in 1999, *Talk* offered celebrity profiles, political articles, and New York gossip. This new general-interest magazine expected great success with veteran editor Tina Brown, who had resurrected both *Vanity Fair* and the *New Yorker* in the 1980s and 1990s, at the helm. But in January 2002, *Talk* suspended production after losing financial backing from Hearst Magazines and Miramax co-chairman Harvey Weinstein. Closure of the high-profile magazine attracted attention to an industry weakened by the economic downturn and loss of advertising.

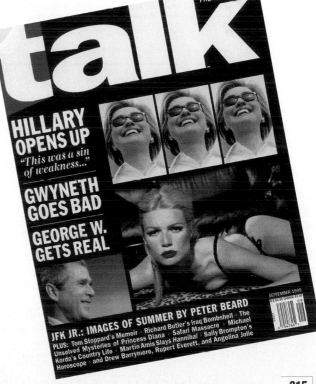

The failure of prominent general magazines was complicated by other problems as well. Essentially, both distribution and production costs (especially paper) were rising, whereas national magazine ad sales had flattened out. Also, the *Saturday Evening Post, Life,* and *Look* still relied more on subscriptions than on supermarket and newsstand sales. Dramatic increases in postal rates, however, had a particularly negative effect on oversized publications (those larger than the 8- by 10.5-inch standard for most magazines). In the 1970s, postal rates increased by more than 400 percent for these magazines. The *Post* and *Life* cut their circulations drastically to save money. The *Post* went from producing 6.8 million to 3 million copies per issue; *Life,* which lost $30 million between 1968 and 1972, cut circulation from 8.5 million to 7 million. The economic rationale here was that limiting the number of copies would reduce production and postal costs, enabling the magazines to lower their ad rates to compete with network television. But, in fact, with decreased circulation, these magazines became less attractive than television for advertisers trying to reach the largest general audience.

The general magazines that survived the competition for national ad dollars tended to be women's magazines, such as *Good Housekeeping, Better Homes and Gardens, Redbook, Ladies' Home Journal,* and *Woman's Day.* These publications were in smaller formats and depended primarily on supermarket sales rather than on expensive mail-delivered subscriptions. However, the most popular magazines, *TV Guide* and *Reader's Digest,* benefited not only from supermarket sales but from their larger circulation (twice that of *Life*), their pocket size, and their small photo budget. Although the *Saturday Evening Post* and *Life* later returned as downsized monthlies, their failure as oversized weeklies ushered in a new era of specialization.

People Puts *Life* Back into Magazines

In March 1974, Time Inc. launched *People,* the first successful mass-market magazine to appear in decades. With an abundance of celebrity profiles and human-interest stories, *People* showed a profit in two years and reached a circulation of more than two million within five years. By 2000, *People* ranked second behind *TV Guide* in revenue from advertising and circulation sales—more than $1.1 billion a year.

The success of *People* is instructive, particularly because only two years earlier television had helped kill *Life* by draining away national ad dollars. Instead of using a bulky oversized format and relying on subscriptions, *People* downsized and generated most of its circulation revenue from newsstand and supermarket sales. For content, it took its cue from our culture's fascination with celebrities. Supported by plenty of photos, its articles were short, with about one-third as many words as those of a typical newsmagazine.

Time Inc. used *People* as the model for reviving *Life* in 1978. As a standard-size supermarket monthly, *Life* maintained a steady circulation of around 1.5 million by the late 1990s; still, *Life*'s new life was short, lasting from 1978 until 2000, when parent company Time Warner terminated it because of low profit margins.

Although *People* has not achieved the broad popularity that *Life* once commanded, it does seem to defy the contemporary trend of specialized magazines aimed at narrow but well-defined audiences, such as *Tennis World, Teen,* and *Hispanic Business.* One argument suggests that *People* is not, in fact, a mass-market magazine but a specialized publication targeting people with particular cultural interests: a fascination with music, TV, and movie stars. If *People* is viewed as a specialty magazine, its financial success makes much more sense in a world dominated by electronic mass media.

> ❝ Starting a magazine is an intensely complicated business, with many factors in play. You have to have the right person at the right time with the right ideas. ❞
>
> —Tina Brown, former editor of the defunct *Talk* magazine, 2002

The Domination of Specialization

The general trend away from mass-market publications and toward specialty magazines coincided with radio's move to specialized formats in the 1950s. With the rise of television in that decade, magazines ultimately reacted the same way radio did: They adapted, trading the mass audience for smaller, discrete audiences that could be guaranteed to advertisers. Two major marketing innovations also helped ease the industry into a new era: the development of regional and demographic editions.

Regional Editions

As television advertising siphoned off national ad revenues, magazines began introducing **regional editions**: national magazines whose content is tailored to the interests of different geographic areas. For example, *Reader's Digest* for years had been printing different language editions for international markets. Largely by necessity, *TV Guide* also developed special editions for each major TV market in the country. Produced on a cheaper grade of paper, different regional listings were inserted into a glossy national section that featured the same photos and articles across the country. *TV Guide* today has more than two hundred regional editions to suit various markets.

Even though magazine content shifted in these regional editions, ads generally remained the same. Other magazines, however, soon adapted this idea to advertising variations and inserts. Often called **split-run editions**, these national magazines tailor ads to different geographic areas. Most editions of *Time* and *Newsweek*, for example, contain a number of pages of regional ads. The editorial content remains the same, but the magazine includes a few pages of ads purchased by local or regional companies in various areas of the country. By the end of the 1960s, nearly 250 magazines featured split-run editions. This strategy has been enhanced by the growth of regional printing centers, which enable publishers to download national magazines from communications satellites for printing near their distribution points. The local ads are inserted at the various regional production sites.

Another innovation in computer technology, called **ink-jet imaging**, enables a magazine publisher or advertiser to print personalized messages to individual subscribers. In this technique, a national news story on political elections might contain the individual subscriber's own voting district in a special inset within the larger national story. In other words, the same technology that enables magazines to encode names and addresses on magazine covers makes it possible to print names inside the magazine as well. The technique is frequently used to personalize an ad. Publishers Clearing House and other direct-mail advertisers have long used this technology to identify consumers by name as potential sweepstakes winners.

Demographic Editions

Another variation of specialization includes **demographic editions**, which target particular groups of consumers. In this strategy, market researchers identify subscribers primarily by occupation, class, and zip-code address. In an experiment conducted in 1963, *Time* pioneered demographic editions by carrying advertising from a drug company that was inserted into copies of its magazine. These editions were then sent to only sixty thousand doctors chosen from *Time*'s subscription rolls. By the 1980s, aided by developments in computer technology, *Time* had also developed special editions for top management, high-income zip-code areas, and ultrahigh-income professional/managerial households. Certain high-income zip-code editions,

> **"** Demographics should be the province of marketers and advertisers, not magazine editors. **"**
>
> –Matt Goldberg, former editor of the defunct magazine *Swing*, 1998

for instance, would include ads for more expensive consumer products. *Newsweek,* too, began to use demographic specialization. One annual edition, for example, targets college campuses with special inserts featuring articles on college life and ads aimed only at students.

The economic strategy behind regional and demographic editions guaranteed advertisers a particular magazine audience at lower rates. Because these ads would run only in special editions, advertisers had to purchase only part of the total audience. Not only is this less expensive than buying access to a publication's entire readership, but it also links a national magazine with local retailers. The magazine can then compete with advertising in regional television or cable markets and in newspaper supplements. Because of the flexibility of special editions, new sources of income opened up for national magazines. Ultimately, these marketing strategies permitted the massive growth of magazines in the face of predictions that television would cripple the magazine industry.

Magazine Types: *Playboy* to *Modern Maturity*

Although regional and demographic editions provided specific strategies for financial survival, the magazine industry ultimately prospered by fragmenting into a wide range of choices and categories. (See Table 9.2.) Given their current variety, magazines are not easily classified by type, but one method has been to divide them by advertiser type: consumer magazines *(Newsweek; Maxim),* which carry a host of general consumer product ads; business or trade magazines *(Advertising Age; Progressive Grocer),* which include ads for products and services for various occupational groups; or farm magazines *(Dairy Herd Management; Dakota Farmer),* which contain ads for agricultural products and farming lifestyles. Grouping by advertisers further distinguishes commercial magazines from noncommercial magazine-like periodicals. The noncommercial category includes everything from activist newsletters and scholarly journals to business newsletters created by companies for distribution to employees. Magazines such as *Ms.* and *Consumer Reports,* which rely solely on subscription and newsstand sales, also accept no advertising.

As we have seen, during the 1950s radio, film, and magazines arrived at a crossroads as they encountered television. In their own ways, all three media shifted to specialization. Radio developed formats for older and younger audiences, for rock fans and classical fans. At the movies, filmmakers focused on more adult subject matter that was off-limits to television's image as a family medium. The depiction of language, violence, and sexuality all changed as movies sought an identity apart from television.

Magazines also used such strategies as they searched for niche audiences that were not being served by the new medium. In the magazine industry, publications targeted older and younger readers, tennis buffs, and quilting enthusiasts. Magazine content changed, too. *Playboy,* started in 1953 by Hugh Hefner, undermined the conventional values of pre–World War II America and emphasized subject matter that was taboo on television in the 1950s. Scraping together $7,000, Hefner published his first issue, which contained a nude calendar reprint of actress Marilyn Monroe together with an attack on alimony payments and gold-digging women. With the financial success of that first issue, which sold more than fifty thousand copies, Hefner was in business.

Circulation gradually climbed, and Hefner introduced advertising in 1956. *Playboy's* circulation peaked in the 1960s, at more than seven million, but fell gradually throughout the 1970s as the magazine faced competition from imitators and video, as well as criticism for "packaging" women for the enjoyment of men. Throughout the 1970s and 1980s, government commissions and religious groups succeeded in eliminating the sale of *Playboy* and similar magazines at military bases and in many local retail chains.

Table 9.2 Number of New Consumer Magazine Launches by Interest Categories, 2002

Category	Number	Category	Number
Miscellaneous	40	Entertainment/Performing Arts	3
Metro/Regional/State	39	Media Personalities	3
Crafts/Games/Hobbies	25	Aviation	3
Sports	19	Fitness	3
Home Service/Home	13	Gay Interest	2
Computers	13	TV/Radio/Communications	2
Sex	12	Religious/Denominational	2
Children's	12	Dogs/Pets	2
Black/Ethnic Interest	11	Gaming	2
Fashion/Beauty/Grooming	9	Literary Reviews/Writing	2
Fishing/Hunting	8	Nature/Ecology	2
Music	7	Military/Naval	2
Automotive	7	Political/Social Topics	2
Business/Finance	5	Women's	1
Teen	5	Photography	1
Epicurean	5	Science/Technology	1
Arts/Antiques	5	Dress	1
Health	5	Camping/Outdoor	1
Men's	4	Babies	1
Travel	4	Gardening	1
Pop Culture	3	TOTAL	291
Comics/Comic Technique	3		

Note: This list represents weekly, bimonthly, monthly, and quarterly titles only and has been edited to meet MPA criteria.

Source: Magazine Publishers of America, <http://www.magazine.org>, 2002.

Playboy's early financial success demonstrated to the magazine industry that specialty magazines aimed at men could achieve large circulation figures. Women's publications sold in supermarkets had long demonstrated that gender-based magazines were highly marketable and that women wielded enormous economic clout. *Better Homes and Gardens, Good Housekeeping, Ladies' Home Journal, Family Circle,* and *Woman's Day* have all ranked among the Top 12 for years, with circulations ranging from 4 to 7.6 million by 2002. But these numbers are the exception rather than the norm. Of the eighteen thousand or so consumer magazines published in the United States today, fewer than ninety have a circulation of more than one million. Most contemporary magazines and newsletters aim at smaller communities of readers who share values, interests, or social identity—from Asian Americans to disabled veterans and politically conservative students. Indeed, in 2002 the Magazine Publishers of America trade organization listed more than forty special categories of

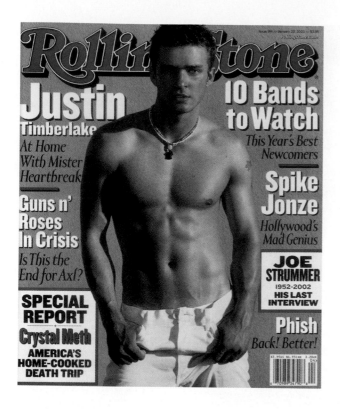

● With a circulation of more than 3.2 million and a readership of nearly 21 million adults weekly, *Sports Illustrated* is the leading sports publication. In addition to *Sports Illustrated for Women* and *Sports Illustrated for Kids,* the *SI* franchise also includes CNN/SI, a 24-hour sports news network, *SI* Development, which produces books, calendars, and collectibles, and *SI* International, which markets the *SI* brand globally.

● *Rolling Stone* magazine, which began in 1967 by chronicling rock and roll's counterculture, remains one of the leading music magazines, with a circulation of 1.25 million. But the magazine has faced increasing competition in recent years, particularly from *Vibe, Spin, Blender,* and *Entertainment Weekly.*

consumer magazines, illustrating the fragmentation of the industry. These include magazines organized around sports and leisure activities, travel and geography, lifestyle and age, and race and ethnicity.

Leisure, Sports, and Music Magazines

The television age spawned not only *TV Guide* but a number of specialized leisure magazines. For example, *Soap Opera Digest* updates viewers on the latest plot twists and their favorite characters. In the age of specialization, magazine executives have developed multiple magazines for fans of soap operas, running, tennis, golf, hunting, quilting, antiquing, surfing, and video-game playing, to name only a few. Within categories, magazines specialize further, targeting older or younger runners, men or women golfers, duck hunters or bird-watchers, and midwestern or southern antique collectors.

The most popular sports and leisure magazine is *Sports Illustrated,* which took its name from a failed 1935 publication. Launched in 1954 by Henry Luce's Time Inc., *Sports Illustrated* was initially aimed at well-educated, middle-class men. It has become the most successful general sports magazine in history, covering everything from major-league sports and mountain climbing to fox hunts and snorkeling. Although frequently criticized for its popular but exploitative yearly swimsuit editions, *Sports Illustrated* over the years has done major investigative pieces—for example, on racketeering in boxing and on land conservation. Its circulation climbed from more than half a million in its first year to 2 million by 1980 and more than 3.2 million by 2002.

Another popular magazine type that fits loosely into the leisure category includes magazines devoted to music—everything from rap's *The Source* to country's *Country Weekly.* The all-time circulation champ in this category is *Rolling Stone,* started in 1967 as an irreverent, left-wing political and cultural magazine by twenty-one-year-old Jann Wenner. Once considered an alternative magazine, by 1982 *Rolling*

Stone had paddled into the mainstream with a circulation approaching 800,000—with half of its ninety-six-plus pages devoted to high-gloss fashion and consumer ads. By 2002 *Rolling Stone,* still famous for its personality profiles and occasionally radical feature articles on economics or politics, had a circulation of more than 1.2 million. Many fans of the early *Rolling Stone,* however, disappointed with its move to increase circulation and reflect mainstream consumer values, turned to less high-gloss alternatives such as *Spin* and *Blender.*

Travel and Geography Magazines

In 1992 and 1993, capitalizing on the increasing longevity of the American population and retirees interested in travel, publishers introduced thirty new travel magazines. Periodicals such as *Discover, Smithsonian, AAA Going Places, Travel & Leisure,* and *Condé Nast Traveler* have all ranked among the nation's Top 200 magazines. Some accompany subscriptions to museum organizations or travel clubs, like the American Automobile Association (AAA). Others are devoted to exploring distant cultures or planning trips to various locales.

The undisputed champion in this category is *National Geographic.* Boston lawyer Gardiner Green Hubbard and his famous son-in-law, Alexander Graham Bell, founded the magazine in 1888 along with the nonprofit National Geographic Society. From the outset, *National Geographic* relied for its content on a number of distinguished mapmakers, naturalists, explorers, geologists, and geographers. Bell, who became the society's director in 1889, referred to the magazine as "a vehicle for carrying the living, breathing human-interest truth about this great world of ours to the people."[7] Promoted as "humanized geography," *National Geographic* helped pioneer color photography in 1910. It was the first publication to publish both undersea and aerial color photographs. It remains one of the few magazines that subscribers save from year to year and also pass along from generation to generation. In addition, many of *National Geographic*'s nature and culture specials on television, which began in 1965, rank among the most popular programs in the history of public television. *National Geographic*'s popularity grew slowly and steadily throughout the twentieth century, reaching one million in circulation in 1935 and ten million in the 1970s. In the late 1990s, its circulation of paid subscriptions slipped to under nine million, prompting the staid National Geographic Society to diversify and lend its name to for-profit ventures such as CD-ROMs, television miniseries, a cable channel, and a line of road maps and atlases. The other media ventures provided new revenue as circulation for the magazine continued to slide, falling to six million by 2003.

● Launched in January 1998, *Teen People* complements the WB television network as part of AOL Time Warner's strategy to reach the demographic group aged twelve to nineteen.

Magazines for the Ages

For years, magazines have targeted readers by economic class and lifestyle, usually distinguishing the mass appeal of *People* and *Reader's Digest* from the more sophisticated appeal of, say, the *New Yorker* or the *Economist.* In the age of specialization, however, magazines have further delineated readers along ever-narrowing age lines, appealing more and more to very young and to older readers, groups that have often been ignored by mainstream television.

APPLIED CRITICAL PROCESS
Uncovering American Beauty

How does the United States' leading fashion magazine define "beauty"? One way to explore this question is by critically analyzing the covers of *Cosmopolitan*.

Description. If you review a number of *Cosmopolitan* covers, you'll notice that they typically feature a body shot of a female model, surrounded by blaring headlines—often using words like "Hot" and "Sex" to lure readers inside the magazine. The cover model is dressed provocatively and is positioned against a solid color background. She looks confident. Everything about the cover is loud and brassy.

Analysis. What are some *significant* patterns here? If you look at issue after issue, all of these models look incredibly alike: They're tall, they've got a sassy expression, and they're white. It's as if they are all the same person, recast with every issue. In fact, with a little more research, you would discover that *Cosmopolitan* has used only two black models since 1990 (Naomi Campbell in 1990 and Halle Berry in 2002) and only five black models since the magazine began using cover photos in 1964.

Interpretation. What does this mean? *Cosmopolitan's* covers do not even come close to reflecting the racial composition of the United States, which is 30 percent nonwhite. Indeed, the magazine narrowly defines beauty as almost exclusively white. Halle Berry is biracial; both Berry and Naomi Campbell appeal to the fashion and advertising industries' narrow mainstream standard of beauty.

Evaluation. Perhaps *Cosmo's* lack of diversity on its covers is due to a lack of diversity within the magazine's editorial and publishing departments. The magazine industry on the whole is only 6.1 percent nonwhite. Perhaps this broad-circulation magazine is scared of alienating its audience of Middle Americans by featuring a cover girl who does not look like them. Either way, *Cosmo* seems to be increasingly out of touch. There could also be a generation gap. Teen magazines are increasingly presenting more diverse notions of beauty; magazines like *YM* and *Teen People* featured 25 percent nonwhite cover subjects in 2002.

The first children's magazines appeared in New England in the late 1700s. Ever since, magazines such as *Youth's Companion, Boy's Life* (the Boy Scouts' national publication since 1912), *Highlights for Children,* and *Ranger Rick* have successfully targeted preschool and elementary-school children. The ad-free *Highlights for Children,* which can only be obtained through subscription, led the top children's magazine category in 2003, with a circulation of more than 2.5 million.

In the popular arena, the leading female teen magazines showed substantial growth in the late 1990s; the top magazines for thirteen- to nineteen-year-olds included *Seventeen* and *YM,* both with circulations of around 2 million in 2002. Several established magazines responded to the growing popularity of the teen market by introducing specialized editions, such as *Teen Vogue, Teen People,* and *Cosmo Girl.* Targeting young men in their twenties, *Maxim,* launched in 1997, was one of the fastest-growing magazines of the late 1990s; it reached a circulation of more than 2.5 million in 2002. *Maxim's* covers boast the magazine's obsession with "sex, sports, beer, gadgets, clothes, fitness," a content mix that helped it eclipse rivals like *GQ* and *Esquire.*

Especially in the beauty and fashion segments, marketing magazines toward age groups continues through the lifespan. For example, women ages eighteen to forty-nine are targeted with titles such as *Cosmopolitan, Vogue, Glamour, Elle, Harper's Bazaar, Self,* and *Allure.* (For more on women's fashion magazines, see "Applied Critical Process: Uncovering American Beauty" above.)

In targeting audiences by age, the most dramatic success has come from magazines aimed at readers over age fifty, America's fastest-growing age segment. These publications have tried to meet the cultural interests of older Americans, who historically have not been prominently featured in mainstream consumer culture. The American Association of Retired Persons (AARP) and its magazine, *Modern Maturity*, were founded in 1958 by retired California teacher Ethel Percy Andrus, who eleven years earlier had established the National Retired Teachers Association (NRTA). For years, both groups published newsletters—which they later merged into the *AARP Bulletin* — keeping older citizens current on politics, health, and culture.

Subscriptions to the bimonthly *Modern Maturity* and the monthly *AARP Bulletin* have always carried a modest membership fee ($10 in 2003). By the early 1980s, *Modern Maturity*'s circulation approached seven million. However, with the AARP signing up thirty thousand new members each week by the late 1980s, both *Modern Maturity* and the newsletter overtook *TV Guide* and *Reader's Digest* as the top circulated magazines. By 2000, both had circulations of about twenty million, far surpassing the circulations of all other magazines. Not available at newsstands, *Modern Maturity* also did not carry advertising during its first ten years. The conventional wisdom in many ad agencies, dominated by staffers under age fifty, suggested that people over fifty were loyal to certain brand names and were difficult to influence through ads. Research demonstrated, however, that many in this group are more affluent than eighteen- to forty-nine-year-olds and have consumer interests increasingly in line with the thirty-nine to forty-nine age bracket. Today, *Modern Maturity* still carries few consumer ads, relying mostly on inexpensive subscriptions, the growth of its target age group, and its readers' continuing interest in the printed word.

In 2001, the AARP further refined the targeting of its members by redesigning *Modern Maturity* and creating two editions of it: one for readers ages fifty-six to sixty-five, and another for those older than sixty-five. For its youngest members, baby boomers between ages fifty and fifty-five, the AARP also introduced a new magazine called *My Generation*. With an initial circulation of 3.1 million—the largest magazine launch ever—*My Generation* absorbed the youngest subscribers of *Modern Maturity*, which dropped to a circulation rate of 17.5 million in 2003.

Elite Magazines and Cultural Minorities

In his important 1964 study, *Magazines in the Twentieth Century*, historian Theodore Peterson devoted a chapter to cultural minorities. In the mid-1960s, though, the term *cultural minorities* referred to elite readers who were served mainly by non-mass-market political and literary magazines such as *Atlantic Monthly*, *Kenyon Review*, the *Nation*, *National Review*, the *New Republic*, the *New Yorker*, *Partisan Review*, and *Poetry*. In general, these political and literary magazines appealed to formally educated readers who shared political ideas, aesthetic concerns, or social values. To their credit, the editors and publishers of these magazines have often struggled financially to maintain the integrity of their magazines in an industry dominated by advertising and mass-market publications.

The *New Yorker*

The most widely circulated "elite" magazine in the twentieth century was the *New Yorker*. Launched in 1925 by Harold Ross, the *New Yorker* became the first city magazine aimed at a national upscale audience. In some ways, the *New Yorker* was the magazine equivalent of the *New York Times*, cultivating an affluent and educated audience and excluding general readers. Snubbing the Midwest, Ross once claimed, "The *New Yorker* will be the magazine which is not edited for the old lady in Dubuque. It will not be concerned in what she is thinking about."[8] Over the years, the *New Yorker* featured many of the twentieth century's most prominent

biographers, writers, reporters, and humorists, including A. J. Liebling, Dorothy Parker, Lillian Ross, John Updike, E. B. White, and Garrison Keillor, as well as James Thurber's cartoons and Ogden Nash's poetry. It introduced some of the finest literary journalism of the twentieth century, devoting an entire issue to John Hersey's *Hiroshima* and serializing Truman Capote's *In Cold Blood*.

By the mid-1960s, the *New Yorker*'s circulation hovered around 500,000. Just as the *New York Times* became known as the nation's best newspaper, the *New Yorker* made promotional claims as the country's best magazine. By the 1960s, the magazine even had a hundred subscribers in Dubuque, Iowa, including a number of "old ladies." In 1985, the *New Yorker* was acquired for $168 million by Advance Publications, the Newhouse newspaper-publishing conglomerate. By 2003, the magazine's circulation had reached 925,000 and was experiencing its first profitable year since Advance purchased it.

Redefining Cultural Minorities

By the 1980s and 1990s, the term *cultural minority* had taken on different connotations. It referred to distinctions regarding gender, age, race, ethnicity, and sexual orientation. Since the late 1960s, with attention drawn to many discriminatory practices, a number of magazines have developed to address concerns that were often ignored by mainstream magazines. Historically, one key magazine has been the *Advocate,* which began in 1967 as a twelve-page newsletter addressing issues

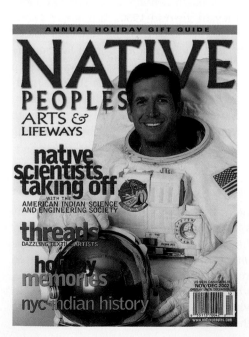

about homosexuality. By the mid-1980s the magazine had a circulation of nearly 100,000, and by the early 1990s more than fifteen new magazines aimed at gay men or lesbians had been launched. The *Advocate* has published some of the best journalism on AIDS, antigay violence, and policy issues affecting homosexual communities. In some instances, its reporting has led to increased coverage of important issues by the mainstream press.

In general, the term *cultural minority* has been more closely associated with racial and ethnic groups that have often been misrepresented or underrepresented in America's popular media. To counter white mainstream conceptions, African American magazines, for example, date to antislavery publications such as the *Emancipator, Liberator,* and *Reformer* during the pre–Civil War era. In the modern age, the major magazine publisher for African Americans has been John H. Johnson, a former Chicago insurance salesman who started *Negro Digest* in 1942 on $500 borrowed against his mother's furniture. By 1945, with a circulation of more than 100,000, the *Digest*'s profits enabled Johnson and a small group of editors to start *Ebony*, a picture-text magazine modeled on *Life* but serving chiefly black readers. The Johnson Publishing Company has since successfully introduced *Jet*, a pocket-size supermarket magazine that originally contained shorter pieces left over from *Ebony*. By 2003, *Jet*'s circulation was close to one million.

Johnson's publications were among the first places where people could see black images on a weekly basis in American popular culture. Originally criticized for favoring light-skinned over dark-skinned black faces, *Ebony* has developed over the years into the leading popular magazine forum for black politics and social life in the United States. In fact, Johnson's publications were among the first forums to help clarify what it meant to be black and middle-class in America after World War II. By the late 1970s, *Ebony*'s circulation had reached 1.3 million; by 2003, it had nearly 1.8 million paid subscribers. In 1970, the first successful magazine aimed at black middle-class women, *Essence*, was started by Edward Lewis. It enjoyed a circulation of 1 million by 2003.

With increases in Hispanic populations and immigration, magazines appealing to Spanish-speaking readers have developed rapidly since the 1980s. In 1983, the De Armas Spanish Magazine Network began distributing Spanish-language versions of mainstream American magazines, including *Cosmopolitan en Español*, *Harper's Bazaar en Español*, and *Ring*, the prominent boxing magazine. In 1989, Casiano Communications launched *Imagen*, a glossy upscale publication for middle- and upper-middle-class Hispanic readers. By the early 1990s, however, the best-selling Spanish-language magazine was *Selecciones del Reader's Digest*, with more than 150,000 paid subscriptions in the United States alone. In the late 1990s, a new wave of magazines was released, some in Spanish, some in English, and some in a combination of both languages to reflect the bilingual lives of many Americans of Hispanic descent. The involvement of major media corporations signaled that the Hispanic magazine audience had arrived for major advertisers: The bilingual *Latina* magazine was started with the help of Essence Communications in 1996, media giant Time Warner launched *People en Español* nationally in 1997, and Condé Nast and Ideas Publishing Group introduced *Glamour en Español* in 1998. Other recent start-ups include *Latina Bride*, *MiGente*, *Moderna*, *Latina Style*, *Estylo*, and *Gusto!* The new magazines are targeted at the most upwardly mobile segments of the growing American Latino population, which numbered more than 38.6 million —about 13.4 percent of the U.S. population—by 2003.

Supermarket Tabloids

Partly due to the bad reputation of **supermarket tabloids**, neither the newspaper nor the magazine industry likes to claim them as part of its domain. With headlines like "J. Lo Meltdown!," "Condit's Plan to Get Rid of Body," "JonBenet Secret Video Evidence," and "Al Qaeda Breeding Killer Mosquitos," tabloids push the limits of both decency and credibility. Although they are published on newsprint, the Audit Bureau of Circulations, which checks newspaper and magazine circulation figures to determine advertising rates, counts weekly tabloids as magazines. Tabloid history can be traced to newspapers' use of graphics and pictorial layouts in the 1860s and 1870s, but the modern U.S. tabloid dates from the founding of the *National Enquirer* by

> **66** It's wonderful. I love talking to witches and Satanists and vampire hunters, and people who have been kidnapped by UFOs—it sure beats covering zoning board meetings. **99**
>
> –Cliff Linedecker, former associate editor, *National Examiner*

William Randolph Hearst in 1926. The *Enquirer* struggled until it was purchased in 1952 by Generoso Pope, who had worked in the cement business and for his father's New York–based Italian-language newspaper, *Il Progresso*. Also a former intelligence officer for the CIA's psychological warfare unit, Pope intended to use the paper to "fight for the rights of man" and "human decency and dignity."[9] In the interest of profit, though, he settled on the "gore formula" to transform the paper's anemic weekly circulation of seven thousand: "I noticed how auto accidents drew crowds and I decided that if it was blood that interested people, I'd give it to them."[10]

By the mid-1960s, Pope had built the *Enquirer*'s circulation to one million through the use of bizarre human-interest stories, gruesome murder tales, violent accident accounts, unexplained phenomena stories, and malicious celebrity gossip. Later, the *Enquirer* incorporated some of yellow journalism's crusading traditions, reporting government cover-ups and stories of bureaucratic waste. By 1974, the magazine's weekly circulation topped four million, where it remained for several years. In 1977, its edition covering the death of Elvis Presley included a controversial picture of Presley in his open coffin and sold more than 6.6 million copies, still a tabloid record.

In 1974, Rupert Murdoch's News Corp. launched the *Star*, built on the "circus-poster layout, garish headlines, and steamy prose" traditions of Great Britain's tabloid press. Among the *Star*'s announced objectives: to "not be politically committed, not be a killjoy, not be bullied, not be boring."[11] The *Star* and a third major tabloid player, the *Globe* (founded in 1954), cut into the *Enquirer*'s circulation and set the tone for current trends in tabloid content, including stories on medical cures, astrological predictions, alien mutants, celebrity gossip, and the occult.

Between 1990 and 1996, the three largest tabloids lost about 30 percent of their circulation. The *National Enquirer* fell from 4 to 2.7 million, the *Star* from 3.6 to 2.5 million, and the *Globe* from 1.3 million to under 1 million. Not only did imitators like the *National Examiner,* the *Sun,* and the *Weekly World News* offer competition, but *People, Us,* new entertainment magazines, newsmagazines, and talk shows also began claiming part of the tabloid audience.[12] At the same time, occasional investigative and political stories started appearing in tabloids and influencing coverage by major newspapers and newsmagazines. Tabloid editors, however, have tried to avoid most political stories: Circulation apparently declines when political intrigue graces their front pages.[13] Ironically, one of the biggest "tabloid" stories of the late 1990s had to do with politics. The Bill Clinton–Monica Lewinsky affair, which was covered by virtually all news media, left tabloids with the dilemma of finding other stories that would be more eye-catching. Although their popularity peaked in the 1980s, tabloids continue to specialize in reaching audiences not served by mainstream media.

Webzines and Media Convergence

The Internet's flexibility and vast, inexpensive distribution capabilities make it an attractive area of investment for companies and individuals looking to create a successful magazine. Most print magazines have a Web site that offers a few stories online while encouraging readers to subscribe or buy the magazine at the newsstand.

The World Wide Web also offers a solution to some of the distribution problems associated with magazines. With production costs much lower than those of glossy print publications, and with the potential for a graphic-rich (albeit computer monitor–based) appearance and widespread distribution, the Web provides an alternate route to maintaining our culture's connection to words, analysis, and ideas. **Webzines** such as *Salon* and *Slate,* which are magazines that appear exclusively on the Web, have made the Web a legitimate site for breaking news and discussing culture and politics. Although some Webzines, such as Microsoft's *Slate,* have big corporate backers, most original Webzines have more modest beginnings and arise out of an interest in creating a cultural or political forum. For example, *Salon* magazine was founded in 1995 by five former reporters from the *San Francisco Examiner* who wanted to break from the traditions of newspaper publishing and build "a different kind of newsroom" to create well-developed stories and commentary. With the help of positive word-of-mouth comments, *Salon* became the leading Webzine, claiming 3.8 million monthly users by 2003. Yet stand-alone, advertising-supported Webzines have yet to find great financial success. As *Slate* discovered in 1999, Web readers aren't likely to pay for subscriptions. *Salon's* problems in 2000 were even more serious, as the magazine cut editorial staff in an attempt to become profitable. In 2001, two of the most long-running and critically acclaimed Webzines, *Feed* and *Suck*, suspended publication due to financial shortcomings.

In the meantime, many media companies viewed the magazine industry as an area of growth. In 1998, ESPN cable sports network launched *ESPN the Magazine,* and Yahoo!, one of the most popular Internet portals, licensed its name for *Yahoo! Internet Life.* Publishers also exploited the synergies of daytime television programs and magazines. Media mogul and icon Martha Stewart promotes her magazine *Martha Stewart Living* through her syndicated television show, along with a radio program, newspaper column, and Internet site. Similarly, Oprah Winfrey's talk show and other media outlets provide constant support and new subscribers for *O: The Oprah Magazine.*

The Organization and Economics of Magazines

Given the great diversity in magazine content and ownership, it is hard to offer a common profile of a successful magazine. Unlike a broadcast station or a daily newspaper, a small newsletter or magazine can begin cheaply via the computer-driven technology of **desktop publishing**, which enables one aspiring publisher-editor to write, design, lay out, and even print a modest publication. Such self-published magazines — sometimes called **zines** (pronounced "zeens") — are also mushrooming on the World Wide Web.

Departments and Duties

Throughout the 1990s, electronic alternatives did not slow the growth of printed magazines. Despite the rise of inexpensive desktop publishing, most large commercial magazines still operate several departments, which employ hundreds of people.

Production and Technology

The magazine unit most concerned with merging old and new ideas is the production and technology department, which maintains the computer and printing hardware necessary for mass-market production. Because magazines are usually printed weekly, monthly, or bimonthly, it is not economically practical for most magazine publishers to maintain expensive print facilities. As with *USA Today,* many national magazines are now able to digitally transport magazine copy via satellite to various regional printing sites for the insertion of local ads and for faster distribution.

To attract advertisers and audiences over the years, magazines have deployed other technological innovations: from *National Geographic's* pioneering 3-D color holograph cover to digitized full-color versions of magazines on the World Wide Web. Today they have developed special inserts, called *selective edits,* for specific customers. For example, *Sports Illustrated* identified 400,000 serious golfers among its readers and began a "Golf Plus" insert for those copies sent to golfing enthusiasts.[14]

Editorial Content

The lifeblood of a magazine is the editorial department, which produces its content, excluding advertisements. Like newspapers, most magazines have a chain of command that begins with the publisher and extends to the editor-in-chief, the managing editor, and a variety of subeditors. These subeditors oversee such editorial functions as photography, illustrations, reporting and writing, copyediting, and layout and design. Writing staffs for magazines generally include contributing writers, who are specialists in certain fields. Magazines also hire professional, nonstaff *freelance writers,* who are assigned to cover particular stories or a region of the country. Many magazines, especially those with small budgets, also rely on well-written unsolicited manuscripts to fill their pages. Most commercial magazines, however, reject more than 95 percent of unsolicited pieces.

Advertising and Sales

The advertising and sales department of a magazine secures clients, arranges promotions, and places ads. Industrywide, this unit has pioneered innovations such as the scent strip in perfume ads, pop-up ads, and ads on computer microchips that emit sounds when a page is turned. Besides stuffing magazines with the ever-present subscription-renewal postcards, this department also conducts market research to study trends and changes in magazine-reading habits.

Magazines generate about half their annual revenue from selling ads, with the remaining money coming from single-copy and subscription sales (see Figure 9.1). (Another source of magazine revenue—but one that the magazine industry rarely wishes to discuss with the general public—is the sale of subscription lists to advertisers and marketers.) Like radio and TV stations, consumer magazines offer advertisers rate cards, which list what a magazine charges for an ad. For example, a top-rated consumer magazine might charge $64,000 for a full-page color ad and $20,000 for a one-third page, black-and-white ad. However, in today's competitive world most rate cards are not very meaningful: Almost all magazines offer 25 to 50 percent rate discounts to advertisers.[15]

Although fashion and general-interest magazines carry a higher percentage of ads than do political-literary magazines, the average magazine contains about 50 percent ad copy and 50 percent editorial material. This figure has remained fairly constant over the past twenty-five years.

A few contemporary magazines, such as *Highlights for Children,* have decided not to carry ads and rely solely on subscriptions and newsstand sales instead. To protect the integrity of its various tests and product comparisons, for instance, *Consumer Reports* carries no advertising. To strengthen its editorial independence, *Ms.* magazine abandoned ads in 1990 after years of pressure from the food, cosmetics, and fashion industries to feature recipes and more complementary copy. Some advertisers and companies have canceled ads when a magazine featured an unflattering or critical article about a company or industry.[16] In some instances, this practice has put enormous pressure on editors not to offend advertisers. The cozy relationships between some advertisers and magazines have led to a dramatic decline in investigative reporting, once central to popular magazines during the muckraking era (see "Examining Ethics: Is a Magazine without Ads Possible? *Ms.* Thinks So." on page 329).

> **"If you don't acknowledge your magazine's advertisers, you don't have a magazine."**
> —Anna Wintour, editor of *Vogue* (quoted by the *Guardian,* July 17, 2000)

Is a Magazine without Ads Possible? *Ms.* Thinks So.

Gloria Steinem doesn't think much of American women's magazines.

"Most women's magazines started out as catalogs," Steinem said in a phone interview from the Beverly Hills offices of *Ms.* magazine. "They put a few articles in to get the readers to purchase the catalog. . . . You buy them as consumers looking for products, but not as a magazine reader."

Steinem, a co-founder of *Ms.* who remains a consulting editor, believes that the *Ms.* brand of serious, feminist journalism can rise again, even in a magazine world dominated by *Vogue, Glamour, Cosmopolitan, Oprah* and *Martha Stewart.*

During the magazine's bumpy history, it has been owned by nonprofits and for-profit companies, and it ceased publication in 1998. But Steinem led a group of feminists who bought the magazine, revived it and then sold it in 2001 to the Feminist Majority Foundation, which returned *Ms.* to bimonthly publication in 2003.

Steinem and company are no less enthusiastic about their prospects today than they were 30 years ago. She believes "the need for *Ms.* has never been greater than it is right now. The media is more in control of advertising and corporate concentration is greater than when we started. There were more fiction, poetry and political articles in women's magazines then than now."

The modern women's magazines have editorial content polluted by the need for advertising, Steinem said. "To get ads for food, they put recipes with the articles," Steinem said. "To get ads for shampoo, they put in articles about how to wash your hair. *Ms.* readers don't need articles about how to wash your hair." . . .

Making the challenge somewhat more daunting, at least as it's envisioned now, *Ms.* won't take any commercial advertising. In its Oct. 1, 2002 issue, *Ms.* had only 15 pages of ads—in a 100-page issue—and all of the ads came from like-minded nonprofit organizations.

Talk about breaching the church-state wall between editorial and advertising—at *Ms.,* the editorial mission [rules] what ads will be accepted.

It's a similar strategy, albeit more extreme, to that employed by other magazines published by nonprofit foundations, such as *Mother Jones.* (*Ms.* may ultimately take ads from companies it deems acceptable, just as *Mother Jones* has ads from firms like the Body Shop.)

"We want to make sure the products themselves are credible, and are not made in sweatshops or hurting animals or polluting the environment," said Katherine Spillar, executive vice president of the Feminist Majority Foundation, the nonprofit group that owns *Ms.* "We're very selective. We do want the ads to be informative. *Ms.* has tremendous credibility among its readership. If a company is advertising in *Ms.,* the readership can trust that company."

In some ways, *Ms.* faces an even bigger challenge: The women's movement that spawned *Ms.* magazine 30 years ago no longer carries the same urgent force in American life. "A lot of issues that were so important 30 years ago have become part of the mainstream mind-set," said Gene Ely, editor and publisher of *Media Life,* a magazine that covers the media marketplace for ad buyers. "What are they going to say that's different and attract a new readership? . . . How many more remakes can it do before it runs out of gas?"

The new editor, Tracy Wood, who was previously investigations editor at the *Orange County Register,* said she believes strongly in the need and demand for *Ms.* She particularly wants to reach young feminists.

Wood cites a 1995 Harris Poll in which an overwhelming number of college-aged women identified themselves as feminists. "There are 800 women's studies programs on college campuses in the U.S. alone," she said. "Thirty years ago there were none. Those numbers are so strong that it shows how women coming into adulthood view themselves."

Source: Dan Fost, "*Ms.* Ready for Latest Makeover," *San Francisco Chronicle,* July 17, 2002, p. B1.

Figure 9.1 The Changing Balance of Magazine Circulation: Subscription vs. Single-Copy Sales

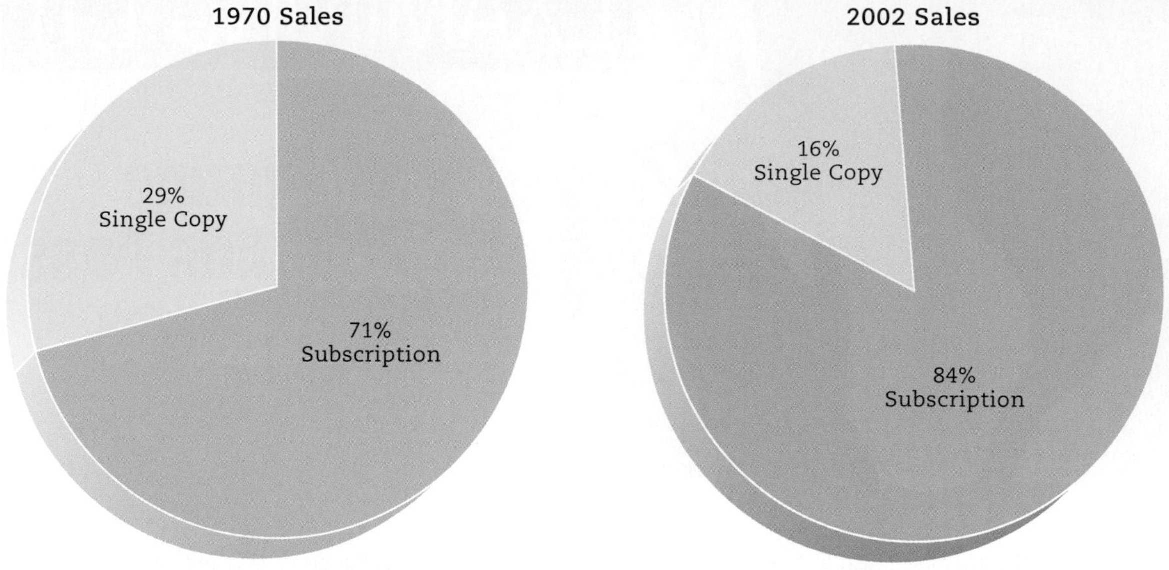

1970 Sales

29% Single Copy

71% Subscription

2002 Sales

16% Single Copy

84% Subscription

Source: Magazine Publishers of America, 2002.

Circulation and Distribution

The circulation and distribution department of a magazine monitors single-copy and subscription sales. Subscriptions, which dominated the industry's infancy, have made a strong comeback. For example, toward the end of the general-interest era in 1950, single-copy sales at supermarkets and newsstands accounted for about 43 percent of magazine sales and subscriptions constituted 57 percent. By 2001, single-copy sales had fallen to 16 percent whereas subscriptions had risen to 84 percent (see Figure 9.1). One tactic used by circulation departments is to encourage consumers to renew well in advance of their actual renewal dates. Magazines can thus invest and earn interest on early renewal money as a hedge against consumers who drop their subscriptions each year. Another strategy is "evergreen" subscriptions, those that automatically renew on a credit card account unless subscribers request that the automatic renewal be stopped.

Magazines circulate in two basic ways: paid or controlled. *Paid circulation* simply means that consumers either pay for a regular subscription to the magazine or buy individual copies at a newsstand or supermarket. Most consumer magazines depend on paid circulation as well as advertising. *Controlled circulation* provides readers with the magazine at no charge and generally targets captive audiences such as airline passengers or association members. Many business or technical magazines and newsletters, which depend on advertising or corporate sponsorship, are distributed free to members or loyal customers. Major magazine publishing company Hachette Filipacchi developed new titles in the 1990s by producing custom-controlled circulation magazines for specific organizations, such as *Trump Style* for guests of Donald Trump's casinos.[17]

Studies by the Magazine Publishers of America suggest that more than 80 percent of all American households either subscribe to a magazine or purchase one on a regular basis. The average household typically purchases at least six different titles during a given year. Although the magazine industry was generally regarded as economically healthy throughout the 1980s, some signs worry editors and publishers.

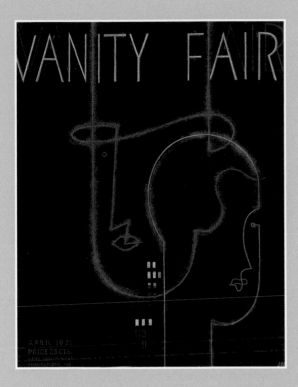

● Originally launched in the United States in 1914 by Condé Nast, *Vanity Fair* featured top writers such as Dorothy Parker and P. G. Wodehouse. In 1922, it helped to identify the "flapper" style emerging among young women. The magazine folded in 1936 but was revived in its current form by Condé Nast in 1983. It is now known for its mix of social and political commentary, celebrity profiles, fiction, fashion, and arts coverage. Today's contributors include photographer Annie Leibovitz and writers James Wolcott, Christopher Hitchens, David Halberstam, and Leslie Bennetts.

For instance, in 1990, for the first time since the Great Depression, the number of consumer-magazine titles declined. In addition, a decline in operating pretax profit margins for magazines, which began in the early 1990s, plagued the industry. In part, the decline was attributed to the proliferation of specialized cable television channels and new personal-computer and Internet services that competed for the same advertisers. The magazine industry boomed through the late 1990s, but by 2001, as the U.S. economy slowed, the magazine industry quickly felt the pinch of declining ad sales.

Major Magazine Chains

In terms of ownership, the commercial magazine industry most closely resembles the cable television business, which actually patterned its specialized channels on the consumer-magazine market. About twelve thousand commercial magazine

Table 9.3 Major Magazine Chains (selected holdings as of 2003)

Advance Publications (Staten Island, NY)

Condé Nast Group

Allure	Golf Digest
Architectural Digest	Gourmet
Bon Appétit	GQ
Bride's	Self
Condé Nast Traveler	Vanity Fair
Glamour	Vogue
House & Garden	Teen Vogue
Modern Bride	Wired
New Yorker	

Jane
W

Bertelsmann (Gütersloh, Germany)

Child	Parents
Family Circle	YM
Fitness	

Hachette Filipacchi, a subsidiary of Lagardère Groupe (Paris)

Car and Driver	Metropolitan Home
Cycle World	Premiere
Elle	Road & Track
Elle Decor	Woman's Day

Hearst Corporation (New York, NY)

Cosmopolitan	Marie Claire
Country Living	O: The Oprah Magazine
Esquire	Popular Mechanics
Good Housekeeping	Redbook
Harper's Bazaar	Town & Country
House Beautiful	

(continued on next page)

titles appear each year—many of them independently owned—just as roughly ten thousand cable systems now operate in the United States. Also, as in the cable industry, large companies or chains increasingly dominate the magazine business. This raises yet unanswered questions about the impact of a handful of powerful magazine owners on the ideas that circulate in the commercial marketplace.

AOL Time Warner, the world's largest media conglomerate and the nation's largest Internet service provider, also runs a magazine subsidiary, Time Inc., a major player among magazine-chain operators with more than sixty-four titles. (See Table 9.3.) Cross-division synergies at AOL Time Warner have been particularly helpful to its magazines. For example, pop-up boxes on America Online generated 1.1 million subscriptions for Time Inc. magazines in less than a year.

Other important commercial players include Mortimer Zuckerman, who owns the *Atlantic Monthly* and *U.S. News & World Report,* and the Meredith Publishing Company, which specializes in women's magazines. The Hearst Corporation, the leading

Meredith Corporation (Des Moines, IA)

Better Homes and Gardens	Ladies' Home Journal
Country Home	Successful Farming
Do It Yourself	Wood

PRIMEDIA (New York, NY)

American Baby	Soap Opera Digest
American History	Soap Opera Weekly
Guns & Ammo	Truckin'
New York	Snowboarder
Seventeen	

Rodale Press (Emmaus, PA)

Backpacker	Mountain Bike
Bicycling	Prevention
Men's Health	Runner's World

Time Inc. (New York, NY)

Asiaweek	Progressive Farmer
Entertainment Weekly	SI for Kids
FORTUNE	Sports Illustrated
InStyle	Sunset
Life	Teen People
Money	This Old House
Parenting	Time

Sources: Hoover's Online, <www.hoovers.com>; *Advertising Age,* Ad Age DataCenter, <http://www.adage.com/datacenter.cms>.

magazine chain early in the twentieth century, still remains a formidable publisher. New York City–based PRIMEDIA (formerly K-III Communications, and owned by investment firm Kohlberg Kravis Roberts) publishes 220 magazine titles, ranging from *Lowrider* to *Seventeen,* and also controls the school-based Channel One news.

Long a force in upscale consumer magazines, Condé Nast is now a division of Advance Publications, which operates the Newhouse newspaper chain. The Condé Nast group controls several key magazines, including *Vanity Fair, GQ,* and *Vogue.* Advance Publications also owns *Parade* magazine, the popular Sunday newspaper supplement that goes to 36 million homes each week. Because Sunday supplements come with newspaper subscriptions, they are not counted among most official magazine tallies. Nevertheless, *Parade* and its closest rival, *USA Weekend* (23.5 million weekly circulation), reach far more readers than the leading popular magazines.

International companies like Paris-based Hachette Filipacchi are also major players in the U.S. magazine industry. Hachette owns more than two hundred magazine titles worldwide, including about twenty in the United States. Its holdings include *Elle, Woman's Day, Premiere,* and *Car and Driver.* Germany's Bertelsmann (whose Gruner + Jahr magazine subsidiary includes titles like *Fitness* and *YM*).

In addition, a number of American magazines have carved out market niches worldwide. *Reader's Digest, Cosmopolitan, Newsweek,* and *Time,* for example, all produce international editions in several languages. In general, though, most American magazines are local, regional, or specialized and therefore less exportable than this country's movies and television. Of eighteen thousand titles, only about two hundred magazines from the United States circulate routinely in the world market. Such magazines, however, like exported American TV shows and films, still play a key role in determining the look of global culture.

Alternative Voices

With fewer than 90 of the almost 18,000 American commercial, trade, and farm magazines reaching circulations that top one million, the great bulk of alternative publications struggle to satisfy small but loyal groups of readers. Of these more modest periodicals, alternative magazines number more than 2,000, with many failing and others starting up from month to month.

Alternative magazines have historically defined themselves in terms of politics—published either by the Left (e.g., the *Progressive; In These Times;* the *Nation*) or the Right (e.g., *National Review; American Spectator; Insight*). However, what constitutes an alternative magazine has broadened far beyond politics to include just about any publication considered "outside the mainstream," ranging from politics to punkzines—the magazine answer to punk rock. The *Utne Reader,* widely regarded as "the *Reader's Digest* of alternative magazines," has defined *alternative* as any sort of "thinking that doesn't reinvent the status quo, that broadens issues you might see on TV or in the daily paper."

Occasionally, alternative magazines have become marginally mainstream. For example, during the conservative Reagan era in the 1980s, William F. Buckley's *National Review* saw its circulation swell to more than 100,000—enormous by alternative standards. In the late 1980s, the *Review* even ran slick TV ads featuring actors such as Charlton Heston, Tom Selleck, and Ronald Reagan. On the Left, *Mother Jones* (named after labor organizer Mary Harris Jones), which continues to champion the muckraking tradition of investigative journalism, had a circulation of more than 200,000 in 2002.

Most alternative magazines, however, are content to swim outside the mainstream. These are the small magazines that typically include diverse political, cultural, religious, international, environmental, and humorous alternative publications such as *Against the Current; Punk Planet; Christianity and Crisis; Jewish Currents; Asia Book Club Review; Whole Earth Review; Yellow Silk: Journal of Erotic Arts; Hysteria: Women, Humor and Social Change;* and the *Journal of Polymorphous Perversity* ("a social scientist's answer to *Mad* magazine").

 ★ # Magazines in a Democratic Society

Like other mass media whose product lines have proliferated, magazines are a major part of the cluttered media landscape. To keep pace, the magazine industry has become fast-paced and high-risk. Of the eight hundred to one thousand new magazines that start up each year, fewer than two hundred will survive longer than a year.

As an industry, magazine publishing—like advertising and public relations—has played a central role in transforming the United States from a producer to a consumer society. Since the 1950s, though, magazines have not been the powerful national voice they once were, uniting separate communities around important issues such as abolition and suffrage. Today, with so many specialized magazines appealing to distinct groups of consumers, magazines play a much-diminished role in creating a sense of national identity.

On the positive side, magazine ownership is more diversified than ownership in other mass media. More magazine voices circulate in the marketplace than do broadcast or cable television channels. Moreover, many new magazines still play an important role in uniting geographically dispersed groups of readers, often giving cultural minorities or newly arrived immigrants a sense of membership in a broader community.

Contemporary commercial magazines provide essential information about politics, society, and culture, thus helping us think about ourselves as participants in a democracy. Unfortunately, however, these magazines have often identified their readers as consumers first and as citizens only secondarily. With magazines' growing dependence on advertising, controversial content sometimes has difficulty finding its way into print. More and more, magazines define their readers merely as viewers of displayed products and purchasers of material goods.

At the same time, magazines arguably have had more freedom than other media to encourage and participate in democratic debates. In addition, because magazines are distributed weekly, monthly, or bimonthly, they are less restricted by the deadline pressures of daily newspapers or evening broadcasts. Released from this burden, good magazines can usually offer more analysis of and insight into society than other media outlets can. In the midst of today's swirl of images, magazines and their advertisements certainly contribute to the commotion. But good magazines also maintain our connection to words, sustaining their vital role in an increasingly electronic and digital culture.

www.

To create an individualized study plan for Chapter 9, go to the interactive *Media and Culture* Online Study Guide at: bedfordstmartins.com/ mediaculture

REVIEW QUESTIONS

The Early History of Magazines

1. Why did magazines develop later than newspapers in the American colonies?

2. Why did most of the earliest magazines have so much trouble staying financially solvent?

3. How did magazines become national in scope?

The Development of Modern American Magazines

4. What role did magazines play in social reform at the turn of the twentieth century?

5. When and why did general-interest magazines become so popular?

6. Why did some of the major general-interest magazines fail in the twentieth century?

The Domination of Specialization

7. What triggered the move toward magazine specialization?

8. What are the differences between regional and demographic editions?

9. What are the most useful ways to categorize the magazine industry? Why?

The Organization and Economics of Magazines

10. What are the four main departments at a typical consumer magazine?

11. What are the major magazine chains, and what is their impact on the mass-media industry in general?

Magazines in a Democratic Society

12. In what ways do magazines serve a democratic society?

QUESTIONING THE MEDIA

1. What are your earliest recollections of magazines? Which magazines do you read regularly today? Why?

2. What role did magazines play in America's political and social shift from being colonies of Great Britain to becoming an independent nation?

3. Why is the muckraking spirit—so important in popular magazines at the turn of the twentieth century—generally missing from magazines today?

4. Imagine that you are the marketing director of your favorite magazine. What would you do to increase circulation?

5. Think of stories, ideas, and images (illustrations and photos) that do not appear in mainstream maga-

zines. Why do you think this is so? (Use the Internet, LexisNexis, or the library to compare your list with Project Censored, an annual list of the year's most underreported stories.)

6. Discuss whether your favorite magazines define you primarily as a consumer or as a citizen. Do you think magazines have a responsibility to educate their readers as both? What can they do to promote responsible citizenship?

7. Do you think cable television, the World Wide Web, and other specialized computer technology will eventually displace magazines? Why or why not?

SEARCHING THE INTERNET

http://www.adage.com/datacenter.cms

The *Advertising Age,* Ad Age Datacenter provides data on the advertising industry: information on the top-selling magazines, circulation rankings, the top U.S. advertisers, the top media companies, the top global advertising markets, and the top-selling brand products.

http://www.magazine.org

The site of the Magazine Publishers of America, the industry association for consumer magazines, loaded with magazine facts and data.

http://www.aarp.org

The American Association of Retired Persons (AARP) is a nonprofit association founded in 1958 and dedicated to aging issues. The site includes links to AARP's *Bulletin, Modern Maturity,* and *My Generation* publications.

http://www.nationalgeographic.com

An extensive site that includes articles, discussion forums, a children's page, map resources, and links to other National Geographic Society publications and activities.

http://www.oprah.com

The popular site for Oprah Winfrey's synergistic media empire, including links to *O: The Oprah Magazine.*

http://www.utne.com

An online version of the *Utne Reader,* with in-depth reports in the following departments: Culture, Society, Spirit, Body, Media, and New Planet. The site also includes the popular Café Utne Web discussion forum.

THE CRITICAL PROCESS

In Brief

Using a few sample magazines in class, consider the following issues related to magazine advertisements:

- Are ads placed in proximity to editorial content of a related topic (e.g., suntan lotion or sunglasses ads next to an article about beach vacations)?
- How aesthetically similar are the ads and editorial content (e.g., the style of a magazine's photo shoot and its fashion ads)?
- Are there ads that seem to be at odds with the editorial content (e.g., cigarette ads in a youth-oriented magazine)?
- Do ad pages outnumber editorial-content pages?
- Do ad pages make it hard to find the magazine's table of contents?

Discuss the following questions: Do advertisements add a positive experience to magazine reading? Do advertisements seem to influence magazine content? Can a magazine's credibility be damaged by too much adherence to advertiser values? Are there some magazines that are purchased largely for the advertisements?

In Depth

The purpose of this project is to offer a particular type of critical approach to magazines. Work with a partner or in small groups. (This project could also be converted into a formal argument paper.)

Description. Take any recent issues of *Time* and *Newsweek*. (Other magazines may be substituted, or contemporary issues may be compared with issues from earlier decades.) Review all photos in the two magazines, counting the men and women represented. For each magazine, keep a separate count of the number of men and women depicted in the ads and the number shown in the news photos that accompany the stories. (*Option:* You might also break down your count by race and age. When these categories are difficult to determine, create a category called Unknown.)

Analysis. Devise a rough chart to organize your findings. What patterns emerge? Are men treated differently from women? If so, in what ways? (Document your evidence.)

Interpretation. Do the content, photos, and ads in these magazines make you think of yourself as a consumer or as a citizen? Who do the magazine editors think their readers are? Based on your limited analysis, sketch a profile of the typical reader of each magazine. (*Option:* Now call the research department at various magazines and see if they will give you a profile sketch of their typical reader. Compare your profile with theirs.)

Evaluation. How would you judge the overall quality of these magazines? Also, explain the limits of simply counting gender depictions in ad and news photos. What issues cannot be addressed by such a method? How might we go about doing a fuller study of issues raised in this project?

KEY TERMS

books

and the power of print

As it turns out, the Muggles do have special powers. For those who haven't read any of the Harry Potter books, "Muggles" are mere mortals, those without any magical powers. Yet hordes of book-buying Muggles have turned the book industry upside down. In a world where children seem to be spending more and more time with electronic media, a series of books about a young wizard boy named Harry Potter has captured the attention of millions of readers in the United States and around the world.

British writer J. K. Rowling began the first book, *Harry Potter and the Sorcerer's Stone* (1998), as a struggling, recently divorced mother living on public assistance in Edinburgh, Scotland. Her books since have become a stunning success, with the first four books (in a series that will ultimately include seven) selling more than 75 million copies in the United States. In fact, the cross-country excitement over the release of Rowling's fourth Harry Potter book drew comparisons to Beatlemania, the British cultural invasion of a previous generation.

Children and adults—often in costume as the books' characters—lined up hundreds deep outside of bookstores across the United States for the release of *Harry Potter and the Goblet of Fire* at precisely 12:01 A.M. on July 8, 2000. The book flew out of stores almost magically, with the then record-setting first printing of 3.8 million copies selling out so quickly that its U.S. publisher, Scholastic Books, rushed a second printing of 3 million more.

The Harry Potter phenomenon extends beyond the United States and the United Kingdom; by 2003 more than 192 million copies of the first four books were in print worldwide, in 55 languages. Just the announcement of the June 2003 release of the fifth book of the series, *Harry Potter and the Order of the Phoenix,* generated 600,000 preorders at Amazon.com, a record that surpassed that of book four.

The universal quality of the Harry Potter stories (not unlike the appeal of the *Star Wars* movie series) is breaking down age barriers. Almost a third of the Harry Potter books have been purchased for readers age thirty-five and older. As *Time* magazine critic Richard Corliss noted, "Reading the books, kids feel more mature, adults feel younger. And all become part of a community where age doesn't matter."[1]

O
ver the past two decades, the interdependence between print and visual forms of popular media has become commonplace. Apart from economics, however, a cultural gulf between the two genres remains. Public debate continues to pit the "superior" quality of print media—usually represented by serious books—against the "inferior" fluff of television. Even within print culture itself, a mini-version of the high-low cultural gulf is apparent. It pits high-quality literature against such popular forms as the newest legal thriller, a supermarket romance novel, or a children's fantasy like a Harry Potter book.

As individuals and as a society, we continue to create cultural classifications that distinguish good from bad, organizing the world through simple black-and-white categories. We also make critical judgments about the kinds of culture that best entertain, inform, and serve a democracy. Because the lines between print and electronic culture have become blurred, we need to look at the developments that have made these media more interdependent. On the one hand, book publishers and video-stocked libraries use talk shows, TV advertising, and public-service announcements to promote reading. On the other hand, the networks follow made-for-TV movies, special miniseries, and even NBA basketball games with promotions for books and libraries.

In the 1950s and 1960s, cultural forecasters thought that the popularity of television might spell the demise of a healthy book industry. It did not happen. In 1950, more than eleven thousand new book titles were introduced, and by 2001 publishers were producing about ten times that number—more than 110,000 titles per year (see Table 10.1). Despite the trend toward the absorption of small publishing houses by big media corporations, more than twenty thousand different publishers—most of

> **66** In 50 years today's children will not remember who survived *Survivor* . . . but they will remember Harry [Potter].**99**
>
> –Anna Quindlen, *Newsweek,* July 2000

● Table 10.1 Annual Numbers of New Book Titles Published, Selected Years

Year	Number of Titles	Year	Number of Titles
1778	461	1935	8,766 (drop during the Great Depression)
1798	1,808		
1880	2,076	1940	11,328
1890	4,559	1945	6,548 (drop during World War II)
1900	6,356		
1910	13,470 (peak until after World War II)	1950	11,022
		1960	15,012
		1970	36,071
1915	8,202	1980	42,377
1919	5,714 (low point as a result of World War I)	1990	46,473
		1996	68,175
1925	8,173	2001	114,487*
1930	10,027		

Sources: Figures through 1945 from John Tebbel, *A History of Book Publishing in the United States,* 4 vols. (New York: R. R. Bowker, 1978); figures after 1945 from various editions of *The Bowker Annual Library and Book Trade Almanac* (R. R. Bowker).

*A change in the *Bowker Annual*'s methodology in 1997 resulted in a more accurate count of annual book title production in the United States, and this accounts for the statistical jump since that year.

them small independents—issue at least one title a year. Still, economic trends in the book industry are similar to those in other media industries: Several large publishing firms, distribution companies, and bookstore chains control the commercial end of the business and claim the bulk of the profits.

The bottom line is that the book industry has met the social and cultural challenges of television. Books have managed to maintain a distinct cultural identity, partly because of the book industry's willingness to capitalize on TV's reach, and vice versa. As one example, when Oprah Winfrey announced in 2002 that she would end her popular Oprah's Book Club segments on her TV talk show, NBC's *Today Show* filled the void by creating a monthly segment that features the works of lesser-known authors.

Our oldest mass medium is still our most influential and our most diverse. The very portability and compactness of books make them a preferred medium in many situations, including relaxing at the beach, passing lunch hour in the park, resting in bed, and traveling to work on city buses or commuter trains. Most important, books and print culture enable individuals and nations to store knowledge from the past. In their key social role, books are still the main repository of human history and everyday experience, passing along stories, knowledge, and wisdom from generation to generation.

In this chapter, we will trace the history of the book from its earliest roots in Egyptian papyrus plants to its evolution as a paperback, a CD-ROM, and a downloadable electronic file. After examining the development of the printing press, we will investigate the rise of the book industry. We will look first at publishing in Europe

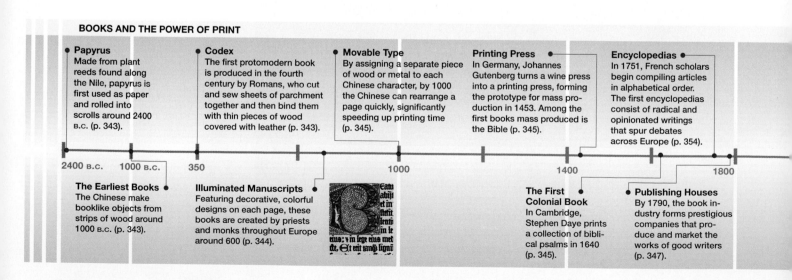

BOOKS AND THE POWER OF PRINT

Papyrus
Made from plant reeds found along the Nile, papyrus is first used as paper and rolled into scrolls around 2400 B.C. (p. 343).

Codex
The first protomodern book is produced in the fourth century by Romans, who cut and sew sheets of parchment together and then bind them with thin pieces of wood covered with leather (p. 343).

Movable Type
By assigning a separate piece of wood or metal to each Chinese character, by 1000 the Chinese can rearrange a page quickly, significantly speeding up printing time (p. 345).

Printing Press
In Germany, Johannes Gutenberg turns a wine press into a printing press, forming the prototype for mass production in 1453. Among the first books mass produced is the Bible (p. 345).

Encyclopedias
In 1751, French scholars begin compiling articles in alphabetical order. The first encyclopedias consist of radical and opinionated writings that spur debates across Europe (p. 354).

2400 B.C.   1000 B.C.   350   1000   1400   1800

The Earliest Books
The Chinese make booklike objects from strips of wood around 1000 B.C. (p. 343).

Illuminated Manuscripts
Featuring decorative, colorful designs on each page, these books are created by priests and monks throughout Europe around 600 (p. 344).

The First Colonial Book
In Cambridge, Stephen Daye prints a collection of biblical psalms in 1640 (p. 345).

Publishing Houses
By 1790, the book industry forms prestigious companies that produce and market the works of good writers (p. 347).

and colonial America and later at the development of publishing houses in the nineteenth and twentieth centuries. As part of this discussion, we will review the various types of books and the economic issues facing the book industry, particularly the growth of book clubs, bookstore chains, and publishing conglomerates. Finally, we will consider trends in the industry, including books on tape, electronic books, and book preservation. Influencing everything from educational curriculums to popular movies, books continue to play a pivotal role in media culture and democratic life. They are still our central storehouse of personal stories and public knowledge.

The History of Books from Papyrus to Paperbacks

Ever since the ancient Babylonians and Egyptians began experimenting with alphabets some five thousand years ago, people have found ways to preserve their written symbols. Initially, pictorial symbols and letters appeared on wood strips or clay tablets, tied or stacked together to form the first "books." As early as 2400 B.C., the Egyptians wrote on **papyrus** (from which the word *paper* is derived) made from plant reeds found along the Nile River. They rolled these writings in scrolls, much as builders do today with blueprints. This method was adopted by the Greeks in 650 B.C. and by the Romans (who imported the papyrus from Egypt) from 300 to 100 B.C.

Around 1000 B.C., the Chinese made booklike objects from strips of wood and bamboo tied together in bundles. At about the time the Egyptians started using papyrus, the Babylonians began pressing symbols and marks into small tablets of clay. These stacked tablets recorded business transactions, government records, favorite stories, and local history. Gradually, **parchment**—treated animal skin—replaced papyrus. Parchment was stronger, smoother, more durable, and less expensive, because it did not have to be imported from Egypt.

Although the Chinese began making paper in A.D. 105, paper made by hand from cotton and linen did not replace parchment in Europe until the thirteenth century. Paper was not as strong as parchment, but it was cheaper. The first protomodern book was probably produced in the fourth century by the Romans, who created the

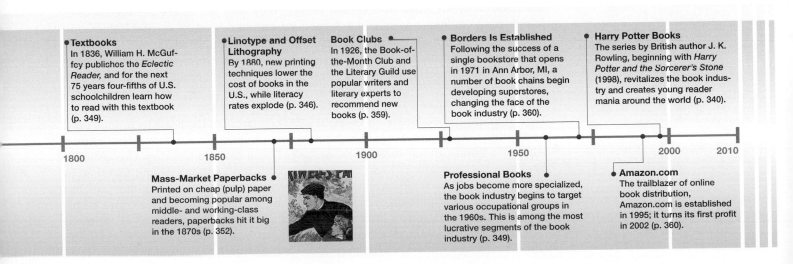

Textbooks
In 1836, William H. McGuffey publishes the *Eclectic Reader,* and for the next 75 years four-fifths of U.S. schoolchildren learn how to read with this textbook (p. 349).

Linotype and Offset Lithography
By 1880, new printing techniques lower the cost of books in the U.S., while literacy rates explode (p. 346).

Book Clubs
In 1926, the Book-of-the-Month Club and the Literary Guild use popular writers and literary experts to recommend new books (p. 359).

Borders Is Established
Following the success of a single bookstore that opens in 1971 in Ann Arbor, MI, a number of book chains begin developing superstores, changing the face of the book industry (p. 360).

Harry Potter Books
The series by British author J. K. Rowling, beginning with *Harry Potter and the Sorcerer's Stone* (1998), revitalizes the book industry and creates young reader mania around the world (p. 340).

1800　1850　1900　1950　2000　2010

Mass-Market Paperbacks
Printed on cheap (pulp) paper and becoming popular among middle- and working-class readers, paperbacks hit it big in the 1870s (p. 352).

Professional Books
As jobs become more specialized, the book industry begins to target various occupational groups in the 1960s. This is among the most lucrative segments of the book industry (p. 349).

Amazon.com
The trailblazer of online book distribution, Amazon.com is established in 1995; it turns its first profit in 2002 (p. 360).

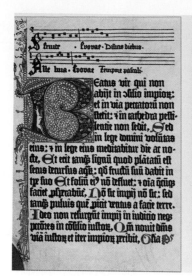

● Probably the most revolutionary development in media history, the printing press and the mass production of books paved the way for both a consumer market and the democratic spread of knowledge. This page from the *Psalter,* or *Book of Psalms,* was printed by Gutenberg's partner, Johann Fust, in 1457. Beside it is a recreation of a plate that could have been used to print it.

codex, a type of book cut into sheets of parchment and sewn together along the edge, then bound with thin pieces of wood and covered with leather. Whereas scrolls had to be wound, unwound, and rewound, codices could be opened to any page, and their configuration allowed writing on both sides of a page.

Manuscript Culture

During the Middle Ages (A.D. 400 to 1500), the Christian clergy strongly influenced what has become known as **manuscript culture**, a period in which books were painstakingly lettered, decorated, and bound by hand. During this time, priests and monks advanced the art of bookmaking; in many ways, they may be considered the earliest professional editors. Known as *scribes,* they "wrote" most of the books of this period, making copies of existing philosophical tracts and religious books, especially versions of the Bible. Through tedious and painstaking work, scribes became the chief caretakers of recorded history and culture.

Many works from the Middle Ages were **illuminated manuscripts**. These books featured decorative, colorful designs and illustrations on each page. Their covers were made from leather, and some were inscribed with precious gems or gold and silver trim. During this period, scribes developed rules of punctuation and made distinctions between small and capital letters; they also put space between words, which made reading easier. Older Roman writing had used all capital letters, and words ran together on a page, making reading a torturous experience.

The oldest printed book still in existence is China's *Diamond Sutra* by Wang Chieh, from A.D. 868. It consists of seven sheets pasted together and rolled up in a scroll. To make copies of pages, early Chinese printers developed **block printing**, a technique using sheets of paper applied to a block of inked wood with raised surfaces in hand-carved letters and sketches. This constituted the basic technique used in printing newspapers, magazines, and books throughout much of modern history. Although hand-carving each block, or "page," was time-consuming, this printing breakthrough enabled multiple copies to be produced and then bound together. In 1295, explorer Marco Polo introduced these techniques to Europe after his excursion to China. The first handmade printed books appeared in Europe during the 1400s, and demand for them began to grow among the literate middle-class populace emerging in large European cities.

The Gutenberg Revolution

The next step in printing was the radical development of movable type, first invented in China around the year 1000. Movable type featured Chinese characters made from reusable pieces of wood or metal. Printers arranged or moved letters into various word combinations, greatly speeding up the time it took to make a page. This process, also used in Korea as early as the thirteenth century, developed independently in Europe in the 1400s. Then, in Germany, between 1453 and 1456, Johannes Gutenberg used movable type to develop a **printing press**, which he adapted from a wine press. Gutenberg's staff of printers produced the first so-called modern books, including two hundred copies of a Latin Bible, twenty-one copies of which still exist. The Bible required six presses, many printers, and several months to produce. It was printed on fine handmade paper, a treated animal skin called **vellum**. The pages were hand-decorated, and the use of woodcuts made illustrations possible.

Essentially, Gutenberg and his printing assistants had not only found a way to carry knowledge across geographic borders but had also formed the prototype for mass production. Printing presses spread rapidly across Europe in the late 1400s and early 1500s. Chaucer's *Canterbury Tales* became the first English work to be printed in book form. Many early books were large, elaborate, and expensive, taking months to illustrate and publish. They were usually purchased by aristocrats, royal families, religious leaders, and ruling politicians. Printers, however, gradually reduced the size of books and developed less expensive grades of paper, making books cheaper so more people could afford them.

The social and cultural transformations ushered in by the spread of printing presses and books cannot be overestimated. As historian Elizabeth Eisenstein has noted, when people could learn for themselves by using maps, dictionaries, Bibles, and the writings of others, they could differentiate themselves as individuals; their social identities were no longer solely dependent on what their leaders told them or on the habits of their families, communities, or social class. The technology of printing presses permitted information and knowledge to spread outside local jurisdictions. Gradually, individuals had access to ideas far beyond their isolated experiences, and this permitted them to challenge the traditional wisdom and customs of their tribes and leaders.[2]

Book Production in the United States

In colonial America, English locksmith Stephen Daye set up a print shop in the late 1630s in Cambridge, Massachusetts. In 1640, Daye and his son Matthew printed the first colonial book, *The Whole Booke of Psalms* (known today as *The Bay Psalm Book*). This collection of biblical psalms sold out its printing of 1,750 copies even though fewer than 3,500 families lived in the colonies at the time. By the mid-1760s, all thirteen colonies had printing shops.

> 66 **For books, issuing from those primal founts of heresy and rebellion, the printing presses have done more to shape the course of human affairs than any other product of the human mind because they are the carriers of ideas and it is ideas that change the world.** 99
>
> –John Tebbel, *A History of Book Publishing in the United States*, 1972

● Paperback books, which originated in Europe, were first published in the United States in the early 1830s. In the 1860s, paperback "dime novels" (sold for five or ten cents) became a dominant form. By 1870, dime novels had sold seven million copies. The weekly paperback series *Tip Top Weekly,* which was published between 1896 and 1912, featured stories of the most popular dime novel hero of the day, the fictional Yale football star and heroic adventurer Frank Merriwell. This issue, from 1901, followed Frank's exploits in the wilds of the Florida Everglades.

In 1744, Benjamin Franklin imported *Pamela; or, Virtue Rewarded,* the first novel reprinted and sold in colonial America. *Pamela* had been written four years earlier by Britain's Samuel Richardson, who helped pioneer the novel as a literary form. *Pamela* and Richardson's second novel, *Clarissa; or, The History of a Young Lady* (1747), connected with the newly emerging and literate middle classes, especially with women, who were just starting to gain a social identity as individuals apart from the men they were married to or worked for. Still restricted from active participation in politics and professional education, women were drawn to these novels for their glimpses into new social worlds. Richardson's novels, overly long and sentimental by current standards, were among the earliest mass-media works to portray women in subordinate roles. Richardson also, however, depicted women triumphing over tragedy, so he is credited as one of the first popular writers to take the domestic life of women seriously.

By the early 1800s, the demand for books among both literate women and men was growing. Machine-made paper supplanted more expensive handmade varieties in the 1830s. The use of cloth rather than leather covers also helped reduce book prices. By the mid-1800s, **paperback books** made with cheaper paper covers had been introduced in the United States from Europe. In 1860, Erastus and Irwin Beadle pioneered paperback **dime novels**. Magazine editor–writer Ann Stephens authored the Beadles' first dime novel, *Malaeska: The Indian Wife of the White Hunter,* which was actually a reprint of a serialized magazine story she had written in 1839 for the *Ladies' Companion.*[3] By 1885, one-third of all books published in the United States were popular paperbacks and dime novels, sometimes identified as **pulp fiction**, a reference to the cheap, machine-made pulp paper they were printed on.

The printing process also became quicker and more mechanized. The introduction of **linotype** machines in the mid-1880s finally enabled printers to set type mechanically using a typewriter-style keyboard. The introduction of steam-powered machines and high-speed rotary presses also permitted the production of more books at lower costs. Another printing development in the early 1900s, **offset lithography**, allowed books to be printed from photographic plates rather than metal casts. Reducing the cost of color and illustrations, offset printing accelerated production and eventually led to computerized typesetting.

The early history of publishing demonstrated that books could widely disseminate and preserve culture and knowledge over time. Even if a paperback fell apart, another version usually existed in a public library or a personal book collection. Oral culture depended on information and values passed down through the wisdom and memories of a community's elders or tribal storytellers, and sometimes these rich traditions were lost. Print culture and the book, however, gave future generations different and often more enduring records of particular authors' words at particular periods in history.

Modern Publishing and the Book Industry

Throughout the 1800s, the rapid spread of knowledge and literacy as well as the Industrial Revolution spurred the emergence of the middle class. New professions developed in areas such as the social sciences, business management, and journalism. The demand for books also promoted the development of a class of publishing professionals, who capitalized on increased middle-class literacy and widespread compulsory education. Many of these early publishers were less interested in applying skillful marketing strategies than in finding quality authors. But with the growth of advertising and the rise of a market economy in the latter half of the nineteenth century, publishing gradually became more competitive and more concerned with the sales value of titles and authors.

The Formation of Publishing Houses

The modern book industry developed gradually throughout the nineteenth century with the formation of the early prestigious **publishing houses**: companies that tried to identify and produce the works of good writers.[4] These companies professionalized the book industry by dividing into discrete tasks the jobs of acquiring, publishing, and marketing books. Among the oldest American houses established in the 1800s (although all of them are now part of media conglomerates) were J. B. Lippincott (1792); Harper & Bros. (1817), which became Harper & Row in 1962 and HarperCollins in 1990; Houghton Mifflin (1832); Little, Brown (1837); G. P. Putnam (1838); Scribner's (1842); E. P. Dutton (1852); Rand McNally (1856); and Macmillan (1869). Out of this group, Scribner's—known more for its magazines in the late 1800s than for its books—became the most prestigious literary house of the 1920s and 1930s, publishing the first novels of F. Scott Fitzgerald (*This Side of Paradise,* 1920) and Ernest Hemingway (*The Sun Also Rises,* 1926).

Between 1880 and 1920, as the center of social and economic life shifted from rural farm production to an industrialized urban culture, the demand for books and bookstores grew. Helped by the influx of European immigrants, the book industry acclimated newcomers to the English language and to American culture. In fact, 1910 marked a peak year in the number of new titles produced—13,470—a record that would not be challenged until the 1950s.

The turn of the twentieth century also marked the next wave of prominent publishing houses, as entrepreneurs began to better understand the marketing potential of books. These houses included Doubleday (1897), McGraw-Hill (1909), Prentice-Hall (1913), Alfred A. Knopf (1914), Simon & Schuster (1924), and Random House (1925). After World War II, Doubleday became the world's largest publishing firm for a time. Unlike radio and magazines, however, book publishing sputtered from 1910 into the 1950s. Book-industry profits were adversely affected by the two world wars and the Great Depression. Radio and magazines fared better because they were generally less expensive and could more immediately cover topical issues during times of crisis.

Types of Books

The division of the modern book industry, a $25 billion business in the United States in 2002, comes from economic and structural categories developed by publishers and by trade organizations such as the Association of American Publishers (AAP) and the American Booksellers Association (ABA). The categories include trade books

Figure 10.1 2001 Publishers' Net Sales

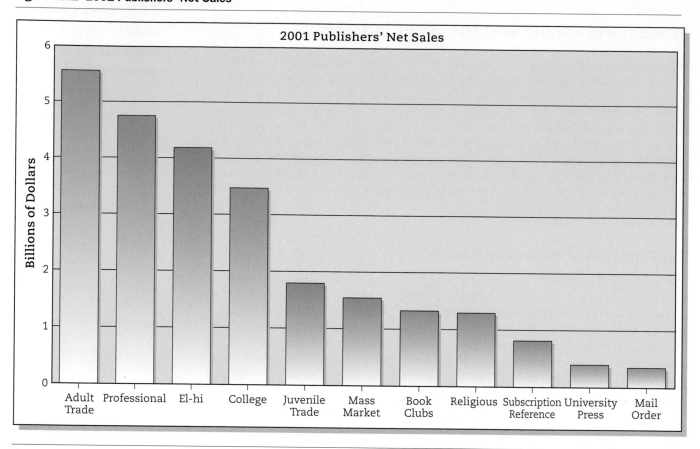

2001 Publishers' Net Sales

Source: American Association of Publishers, <http://www.publishers.org/industry/index.cfm>, 2002.

(both adult and juvenile); professional books; elementary, high-school, and college textbooks; mass-market paperbacks; religious books; reference works; and university press books. An additional category—comic books—also exists but is not acknowledged by most conventional publishers (see "Case Study—Comic Books: Alternative Themes, but Superheroes Prevail" on page 350).

Trade Books

One of the most lucrative parts of the industry, **trade books** include hardbound and paperback books aimed at general readers and sold at various retail outlets (see Figure 10.1). The industry distinguishes between adult and juvenile trade divisions. Adult trade books include hardbound fiction; current nonfiction and biographies; literary classics; books on hobbies, art, and travel; popular science, technology, and computer publications; self-help books; and cookbooks. (*Betty Crocker's Cookbook,* first published in 1950, has sold more than twenty-two million copies in hardcover trade editions.) Like most of the book industry, fiction and nonfiction trade books have experienced long-term growth in the electronic age.

Juvenile book categories range from preschool picture books to young-adult or young-reader books, such as Bantam's Sweet Valley adventure series, Pocket Books' Fear Street series, and Scholastic's Harry Potter series. In fact, the Harry Potter series alone provided an enormous boost to the segment, helping create a nearly 16 percent surge in children's book sales in 1999 and another 14 percent increase in 2000. Another surge is likely with the publication of the fifth book in the series in 2003.

Professional Books

The counterpart to trade publications in the magazine industry, **professional books** target various occupational groups and are not intended for the general consumer market. This area of publishing mirrors the growth of professional and technical specialties that has characterized the job market, particularly since the 1960s. Traditionally, the industry has subdivided professional books into the areas of law, business, medicine, and technical-scientific works. These books are sold mostly through mail order or by sales representatives knowledgeable about various subject areas. This segment of the book industry has found profitable market niches by capitalizing on the expansion of job specialization.

Textbooks

During the mid-1800s, William H. McGuffey, Presbyterian minister and college professor, sold more than 100 million copies of his *Eclectic Reader*, which taught most nineteenth-century elementary school children to read—and to respect their nation's political and economic systems. Ever since the McGuffey reader, **textbooks** have served a nation intent on improving literacy rates and public education. Elementary school textbooks found a solid market niche in the nineteenth century, but college textbooks boomed in the 1950s, when the GI Bill enabled hundreds of thousands of working- and middle-class men, returning from World War II, to attend college. The demand for textbooks further accelerated in the 1960s, as opportunities for women and other minorities expanded.

Textbooks are divided into elementary–high school, known as *el-hi*; vocational education; and college texts. In most states, local school districts determine which el-hi textbooks are appropriate for their students. Texas and California, however, use statewide adoption policies that control text selections. In such situations, only a small number of texts are mandated by the state. If individual schools choose to use books other than those mandated, they are not reimbursed by the state for their purchases. Some teachers and publishers have argued that such sweeping authority undermines the local autonomy of districts, which have varied educational needs and problems. The statewide system of adoptions also enables a few states, which are courted heavily by publishers, to virtually determine the content of the texts sold to every state in the nation. In addition, when publishers aim textbooks at a broad nationwide audience, they tend to water down the content by eliminating regional material or controversial ideas that might offend a group of adopters or a local selection committee.

Unlike el-hi texts, which are subsidized by various states and school districts, hardbound and softcover college texts are paid for by individual students (and parents). At some time during most students' experience, in fact, disputes erupt on campuses about the increasing cost of textbooks, the mark-up on used books, and the profit margins of local college bookstores, which in many cases face no on-campus competition. According to a 2002 survey, the average college student spends between $727 and $807 on textbooks and supplies each year.[5] (See Figure 10.2.)

Today, more than 3,600 college bookstores in the United States sell both texts and trade books. In the late 1990s several new online booksellers, modeled on Amazon.com but specializing in college textbooks, promoted themselves as an alternative to local college bookstores. By 2003, big e-commerce sites like Amazon.com, BarnesandNoble.com, and Walmart.com, along with start-ups like ecampus.com, accounted for about 6 percent of the total college textbook market.[6] Other enterprising students have developed swap sites on the Web to trade and resell books. Meanwhile, the majority of traditional college stores have developed "clicks and mortar" strategies, with their own Web sites that enable students to purchase texts online and pick them up at the local store.

Comic Books: Alternative Themes, but Superheroes Prevail

By Mark C. Rogers

At the precarious edge of the book industry are comic books, which are sometimes called *graphic novels* or simply *comix*. A medium that neither conventional book nor magazine publishers will claim as their own, comics have long integrated print and visual culture. They remain a paradoxical medium, existing as both collectibles and consumables.

They are perhaps the medium most open to independent producers—anyone with a pencil and access to a Xerox machine can produce mini-comics. Nevertheless, two companies—Marvel and DC—have dominated the commercial industry for more than thirty years, publishing the routine superhero stories that have been so marketable.

Comics are a relatively young mass medium, first appearing in their present format in the 1920s in Japan and in the 1930s in the United States. They began as simple reprints of newspaper comic strips, but by the mid-1930s most comic books featured original material. Comics have always been published in a variety of genres, but their signature contribution to American culture has been the superhero. In 1938, Jerry Siegel and Joe Shuster created Superman for DC comics. Bob Kane's Batman character arrived the following year. In 1941, Marvel comics introduced Captain America to fight Nazis, and except for a brief period in the 1950s, the superhero genre has dominated the history of comics.

After World War II, comic books moved away from superheroes and began experimenting with other genres, most notably crime and horror (e.g. *Tales from the Crypt*). With the end of the war, the reading public was ready for more moral ambiguity than was possible in the simple good-versus-evil world of the superhero. Comics became increasingly graphic and lurid as they tried to compete with other mass media, especially television and mass-market paperbacks.

In the early 1950s, the popularity of crime and horror comics led to a moral panic about their effects on society. Frederic Wertham, a prominent psychiatrist, campaigned against them, claiming they led to juvenile delinquency. Wertham was joined by many religious and parent groups, and Senate hearings were held on the issue in 1954. In October 1954, the Comics Magazine Association of America adopted a code of acceptable conduct for publishers of comic books. One of the most restrictive examples of industry self-censorship in mass-media history, the code kept the government from legislating its own code or restricting the sale of comic books to minors.

The code had both immediate and long-term effects on comics. In the short run, the number of comics sold in the United States declined sharply. Comic books lost many of their adult readers because the code confined comics' topics to those suitable for children. Consequently, comics have rarely been taken seriously as a mass medium or as an art form; they remain stigmatized as the lowest of low culture—a sort of literature for the subliterate.

In the 1960s, Marvel and DC led the way as superhero comics regained their dominance. This period also gave rise to underground comics, which featured more explicit sexual, violent, and drug themes—for example, R. Crumb's *Mr. Natural* and Bill Griffith's *Zippy the Pinhead.* These alternative comics, like underground newspapers, originated in the 1960s counterculture and challenged the major institutions of the time. Instead of relying on newsstand sales, underground comics were sold through record stores, at alternative bookstores, and in a growing number of comic-book specialty shops.

In the 1970s, responding in part to the challenge of the underground form, "legitimate" comics began to increase the political content and relevance of their story lines. In 1974, a new method of distributing comics—direct sales—developed, catering to the increasing number of comic-book stores. This direct-sales method involved selling comics on a nonreturnable basis but with a higher discount than was available to newsstand distributors, who bought comics only on the condition that they could return unsold copies. The percentage of comics sold through specialty shops increased gradually, and by the early 1990s more than 80 percent of all comics were sold through direct sales.

The shift from newsstand to direct sales enabled comics to once again approach adult themes and also created an explosion in the number of comics available and in the number of companies publishing comics. Spurred by direct sales and by a rise in speculation, the industry's sales reached historic highs in the early 1990s but plummeted by the mid-1990s, falling to less than half of their peak. Although DC and Marvel still control the majority of this market, worth about $500 million annually, some smaller companies have made significant cuts into their shares. For example, Image and Dark Horse, together with Marvel and DC, controlled about 75 percent of the comic-book market in the late 1990s, leaving another 150 smaller firms to split the remaining quarter share. Despite

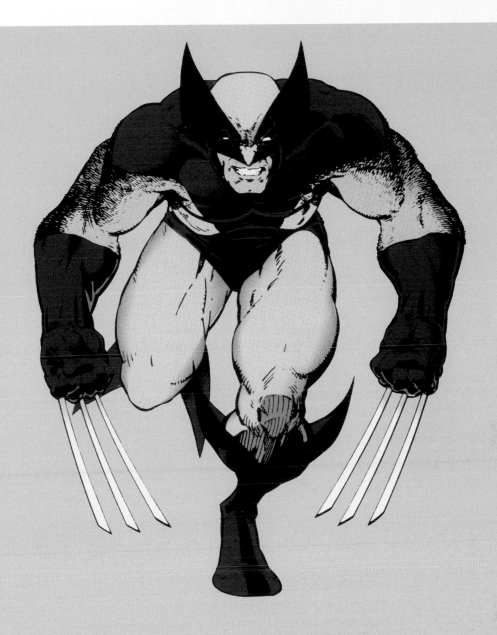

recent sales declines, superheroes still sell the best. Comics continue to represent virtually every genre, including autobiography *(Self-Loathing Comics)*, nonfiction journalism *(Palestine)*, and historical fiction *(Berlin)*. Mainstream comics include traditional juvenile and superhero fare as well as more experimental material, such as DC's Vertigo line of horror and fantasy comics *(Sandman)* for "mature readers."

In the wake of the 1980s success of *Teenage Mutant Ninja Turtles* (who began life in an alternative comic book), many independent companies have been purchased by or have entered into alliances with larger media firms that want to exploit particular characters or superheroes. DC, for example, is owned by AOL Time Warner, which has used the DC characters, especially Superman and Batman, to build successful film and television properties. Marvel also got into the licensing act with film versions of Spiderman and X-Men.

In 1992, comics' flexibility was demonstrated in *Maus: A Survivor's Tale* by Art Spiegelman, cofounder and editor of *Raw* (an alternative magazine for comics and graphic art). The first comic-style book to win a Pulitzer Prize, Spiegelman's two-book fable merged print and visual styles to recount his complex relationship with his father, a Holocaust survivor.

As print media face more competition from electronic media, comics seem well suited in the long run to adapt and survive, appearing frequently in electronic form, on CD-ROM, and on the World Wide Web. In an early victory for electronic comics, *Maus* has appeared in CD-ROM form. In the year 2000, Stan Lee, the creative mind behind many of Marvel's signature characters, produced his own online comic, and underground comic author Scott McCloud wrote the manifesto *Reinventing Comics* and posted many comics on the Web at <www.scottmccloud.com>.

As other writers and artists continue to adapt the form to both fictional and nonfictional stories, comics endure as part of popular and alternative culture.

Mark C. Rogers teaches communication at Walsh University. He wrote his doctoral dissertation on the comic-book industry.

Figure 10.2 Where the New Textbook Dollar Goes* . . .

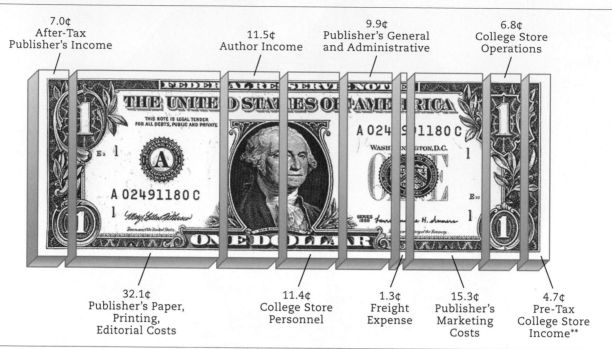

7.0¢
After-Tax
Publisher's Income

11.5¢
Author Income

9.9¢
Publisher's General
and Administrative

6.8¢
College Store
Operations

32.1¢
Publisher's Paper,
Printing,
Editorial Costs

11.4¢
College Store
Personnel

1.3¢
Freight
Expense

15.3¢
Publisher's
Marketing
Costs

4.7¢
Pre-Tax
College Store
Income**

*The statistics in this illustration reflect the most current 2001–2002 financial data gathered by the National Association of College Stores and financial data provided by the Association of American Publishers. The average cost of a college textbook is $66.08.

***Note:* The amount of federal, state and/or local tax, and therefore the amount and use of any after-tax profit, is determined by the store's ownership, and usually depends on whether the college store is owned by an institution of higher education, a contract management company, a cooperative, a foundation, or by private individuals.

These numbers are averages and do not represent a particular publisher or store.

Source: © 2002 by the National Association of College Stores, <www.nacs.org/common/research/textbook$.pdf>.

Mass-Market Paperbacks

Unlike larger trade paperbacks, which are sold mostly in bookstores, **mass-market paperbacks** are sold off racks in drugstores, supermarkets, and airports as well as in bookstores. Mass-market paperbacks—often the work of blockbuster authors such as Stephen King, Danielle Steel, Patricia Cornwell, and John Grisham—represent the second-largest segment of the industry in terms of units sold, but because the books are low-priced (under $10) they generate less revenue than trade books. Moreover, mass-market paperbacks have had declining sales in recent years, as big bookstore chains display and heavily promote the more expensive and higher quality (in terms of paper and packaging) paperback and hardbound trade books (see Figure 10.3).

Paperbacks did not hit it big until the 1870s, when they became popular among middle- and working-class readers. This phenomenon sparked fear and outrage among those in the professional and educated classes, many of whom thought that reading cheap westerns and crime novels might ruin civilization. Some of the earliest paperbacks ripped off foreign writers, who were unprotected by copyright law and did not receive royalties for the books they sold in the United States. This changed with the International Copyright Law of 1891, which mandated that all authors' works could be reproduced only with their permission.

The popularity of paperbacks hit a major peak in 1939 with the establishment of Pocket Books under the leadership of Robert de Graff. Revolutionizing the paperback industry, Pocket Books lowered the standard book price of fifty or seventy-five cents to twenty-five cents. To accomplish this, de Graff cut bookstore discounts from 30 to

Figure 10.3 Consumer Adult Book Purchasing, by Outlet

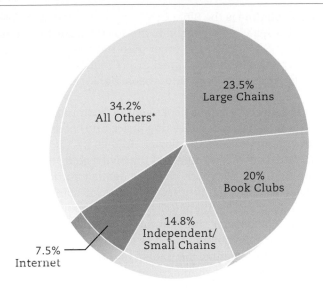

23.5%
Large Chains

34.2%
All Others*

20%
Book Clubs

14.8%
Independent/
Small Chains

7.5%
Internet

*For a complete listing of "Other" book outlets, see Table 10.3.

Source: © 2002 American Booksellers Association, <http://news.bookweb.org/news/444.html>.

20 percent. The book distributor's share was trimmed from 46 to 36 percent of the cover price, and author royalty rates went from 10 to 4 percent. In its first three weeks in business, Pocket Books sold 100,000 books in New York City alone. Among its first titles was *Wake Up and Live* by Dorothea Brande, a 1936 best-seller on self-improvement that ignited an early wave of self-help books. In testing the market with both nonfiction and fiction, Pocket Books also published paperbacks of *The Murder of Roger Ackroyd* by Agatha Christie; *Enough Rope,* a collection of poems by Dorothy Parker; *Five Great Tragedies* by Shakespeare; and *Bambi* by Felix Salten, which became a children's classic three years before Walt Disney released the film version. Pocket Books' success spawned a series of imitators, including Dell, Fawcett, and Bantam Books.[7]

A major innovation of paperback publishers was the **instant book**, a marketing strategy that involves publishing a topical book quickly after a major event occurs. Pocket Books produced the first instant book, *Franklin Delano Roosevelt: A Memorial,* six days after FDR's death in 1945. Similar to made-for-TV movies that capitalize on contemporary events, instant books enable the industry to better compete with journalism and magazines. Such books, however, like their TV counterparts, have been accused of exploiting tragedies for quick profits.

Bantam began dominating this field in 1964 with *The Report of the Warren Commission on the Assassination of President Kennedy,* the first Bantam "extra" edition. (*Extra* is a term borrowed from daily newspapers, which produced extra editions to tell important breaking news stories in the pre-TV era.) After receiving the 385,000-word report on a Friday afternoon, Bantam staffers began editing the Warren Report on the way to the airport; the book was produced within a week. The publisher, in a joint venture with the *New York Times,* ultimately sold 1.6 million copies.

Today, instant books continue to capitalize on a variety of contemporary events, from the death of Princess Diana in 1997 to President Bush's address about the terrorist attacks of September 11, 2001. Although instant books make fast money for their publishers, they often sacrifice the kind of in-depth analysis and historical perspective that the book medium has generally brought to important social events.

● J.R.R. Tolkien's mythical fantasy *The Hobbit*, first published in 1937, reappeared as a mass-market best-seller in 2001, as the Harry Potter series and a heavily marketed Tolkien film trilogy (premiering in December 2001) energized sales. Del Rey/Ballantine Books also packaged the mass-market paperback editions of *The Hobbit* with Tolkien's follow-up *Lord of the Rings* trilogy—$27.95 for the four-book boxed set.

Religious Books

The best-selling book of all time is the Bible, in all its diverse versions. Over the years the success of Bible sales spawned a large industry for **religious books**, now divided into four categories: Bibles, hymnals, and other materials related to religious observances; spiritual or inspirational books aimed at lay readers; professional publications focusing on the work of clergy and theologians; and religious-education textbooks.

After World War II, sales of religious books soared. Historians attribute the sales boom to economic growth and a nation seeking peace and security while facing the threat of "godless communism" and the Soviet Union.[8] By the 1960s, though, the scene had changed dramatically. The impact of the civil rights struggle, the Vietnam War, the sexual revolution, and the youth rebellion against authority led to declines in formal church membership. Not surprisingly, sales of some types of religious books dropped as well. To compete, many religious-book publishers extended their offerings to include serious secular titles on such topics as war and peace, race, poverty, gender, and civic responsibility.

Throughout this period of change, the publication of fundamentalist and evangelical literature remained steady. It then expanded rapidly during the 1980s, when the Republican Party began making political overtures to conservative groups and prominent TV evangelists. The popularity of conservative and tradition-bound publications stabilized religious publishing during turbulent social times. From 2001 to 2002, for example, the total book industry grew by 1 percent, but the sales of religious and spiritual books grew by 4.7 percent, an increase attributed to the aftermath of the terrorist attacks of 9/11. By 2002, the religious-book segment accounted for over $1.3 billion in sales and 5.2 percent of all book sales (see Figure 10.1 on page 348).

Reference Books

Another major division of the book industry includes all sorts of **reference books**, including dictionaries, encyclopedias, atlases, and a number of substantial volumes directly related to particular professions or trades, such as legal casebooks and medical manuals.

The idea of developing encyclopedic writings to document the extent of human knowledge is attributed to Aristotle. Pliny the Elder (A.D. 23–79) wrote the oldest reference work still in existence, *Historia Naturalis*, detailing in Latin thousands of facts about animals, minerals, and plants. But it wasn't until the early 1700s that the compilers of reference works began organizing articles in alphabetical order and relying on specialists to contribute essays in their areas of interest. Between 1751 and 1771, a group of French scholars produced a twenty-eight-volume set of encyclopedias. The circulation of these volumes, full of new and often radical ideas, encouraged support for the French Revolution against aristocratic rule later in that century.

The oldest English-language encyclopedia still in production, the *Encyclopaedia Britannica* (*EB*), was first published in Scotland in 1768. Significant U.S. encyclopedias followed, including *Encyclopedia Americana* (1829), *The World Book Encyclopedia* (1917), and *Compton's Pictured Encyclopedia* (1922), bought by *EB* in 1961. *EB* produced its first U.S. edition in 1908. Purchased by Sears in 1920 and later by a U.S. ad agency, *EB* was eventually run as a nonprofit venture for the University of Chicago. *EB* contributed more than $125 million to the university over the years. However, its sales fell from 117,000 sets in 1990 to 51,000 in 1994 due to competition from electronic encyclopedias (which many critics considered inferior in quality) bundled with many home computers. Eventually, the company was forced to reorganize and disband its famous door-to-door sales force. *EB* was much slower to adapt to the electronic environment than were other reference firms. In 1995, it finally issued a CD-ROM version

that sold for $995 (a traditional bound set ran about $1,500), a price targeted at libraries and other institutional buyers. By this time, though, Microsoft was already selling a CD-ROM Funk & Wagnalls encyclopedia for $99, a price tailored to mass-market buyers. *EB*, Microsoft's *Encarta*, and *World Book* are the leading CD-ROM encyclopedias today, and they range in price from about $20 to $70. *EB* and *World Book* have also developed online versions of their encyclopedias (*World Book* is available on a one-year subscription basis), and the *Encarta* CD-ROM connects to "premium" online content available only through the *Encarta* CD package.

Dictionaries have also accounted for a large portion of reference sales. Like encyclopedias, the earliest dictionaries were produced by Greek and Roman writers attempting to document specialized and rare words. During the manuscript period in the Middle Ages, however, European scribes and monks began creating glossaries and dictionaries to help people understand Latin. In 1604, a British schoolmaster prepared a three-thousand-word English dictionary. A sixty-thousand-word English dictionary was produced in 1721, followed by Samuel Johnson's *Dictionary of the English Language* in 1755. Describing rather than prescribing word usage, Johnson was among the first to understand that language changes—that words and usage cannot be fixed for all time. Johnson's dictionary served as the model and standard for English dictionaries into the mid-1800s. In the United States in 1828, Noah Webster, using Johnson's work as a model, published the seventy-thousand-word, two-volume *American Dictionary of the English Language*, differentiating between British and American usages and simplifying spelling (for example, *colour* became *color* and *musick* became *music*).

Other reference works include the atlases and almanacs that have become so popular in schools, homes, offices, and libraries. Media trade organizations publish their own reference works, such as *Editor & Publisher International Year Book* and *Broadcasting & Cable Yearbook*. Each year, R. R. Bowker publishes *Books in Print* and *Paperbound Books in Print*, which list all new and available book titles. *The Bowker Annual Library and Book Trade Almanac* reprints articles and compiles statistics on the book industry.

University Press Books

The smallest unit in the book industry is the noncommercial **university press**, which publishes scholarly works for small groups of readers interested in specialized areas. Professors often try to secure book contracts from reputable university

● The New York Public Library's reference room, where computers and printers have displaced books as the main reference tool.

presses to increase their chances for tenure, a lifetime teaching contract. Some university presses are very small, producing as few as ten books a year. The largest, the University of Chicago Press, regularly publishes more than two hundred titles a year. Among the oldest and most prestigious of these presses are Yale University Press, established in 1908, and Harvard University Press, formally founded in 1913 but claiming roots that go back to 1640, when Stephen Daye published the first colonial book in a small shop located behind the house of Harvard's president.

University presses traditionally have not faced pressure to produce commercially viable books, so they can encourage innovative writers and thinkers. Large commercial trade houses are often criticized for encouraging only blockbuster books, but university presses often suffer an opposite criticism—that they produce subsidized books that only a handful of scholars read. Nonetheless, many scholars believe that university presses need to protect narrowly focused, specialized, noncommercial publications. Others argue that it is time to declare "an end to scholarly publications as a series of guarded conversations between professors."[9]

University press books typically sell fewer than a thousand copies each, most of which are sold to libraries. Although they bring academic institutions a certain prestige, university presses routinely lose money. Even academic books written in accessible language rarely attract the interest of the general public because university presses have little money for marketing and promotion. Increasingly, administrators are reducing subsidies, requiring presses to show more profit. This has led to a decrease in the number of books university presses can publish. To offset costs and increase revenue, some presses are trying to form alliances with commercial houses to help promote and produce academic books that have wider appeal.

The Organization and Ownership of the Book Industry

Compared with the revenues earned by other mass-media industries, the steady growth of book publishing has been relatively modest. From the mid-1980s to 2002, total revenues went from $9 billion to $25 billion. Within the industry, the concept of who or what constitutes a publisher varies widely. A publisher may be a large company that is a subsidiary of a global media conglomerate and occupies an entire office building, or a publisher may be a one-person home-office operation using a desktop computer. Unlike commercial television and film, small book publishers can start up relatively easily because of advances in personal computer technology.

The Structure of Book Publishing

Medium-size and large publishing houses employ hundreds of people and share certain similarities. Most of the thousands of small houses, however, have staffs of fewer than twenty. In the larger houses, divisions usually include acquisitions and development; copyediting, design, and production; marketing and sales; and administration and business. Unlike newspapers but similar to magazines, most publishing houses contract independent printers to produce their books.

Most publishers employ **acquisitions editors** to seek out and sign authors to contracts. In the trade-fiction area, this might mean discovering talented writers by reading hundreds of unsolicited manuscripts. In nonfiction, editors might examine manuscripts and letters of inquiry or actively match a known writer to a particular topic or project (such as a celebrity biography). Acquisitions editors also handle **subsidiary rights** for an author—that is, selling the rights to a book for use in other

● As a retired general, Colin Powell received an enormous $6.5 million advance from Random House to write *My American Journey,* published in 1995. In 2000, Powell joined the administration of George W. Bush as secretary of state.

media forms, such as a mass-market paperback or e-book, or as the basis for a movie screenplay.

As part of their contracts, writers sometimes receive advance money, which is actually an early payment against royalties to be earned later. New authors may receive little or no advance from a publisher, but commercially successful authors can receive millions. For example, *Interview with a Vampire* author Anne Rice hauled in a $17 million advance from Knopf for three more vampire novels. First-time authors who are nationally recognized, such as political leaders, sports figures, or movie stars, can also command large advances from publishers who are banking on the well-known person's commercial potential. For example, retired general (now secretary of state) Colin Powell, who directed military operations during the Persian Gulf War and was the first African American to head the Joint Chiefs of Staff, received a $6.5 million advance from Random House for his autobiography. U.S. senator Hillary Clinton received one of the largest advances ever—$8 million—from Simon & Schuster in 2000 to write a book about her years as first lady. A year later, former

Table 10.2 How Trade Books Lose Money

Publishing is hit-driven; most books lose money. Here is a hardcover priced at $25 ($11.75 goes to the publisher) with initial sales of 24,000, of which retailers send back 36%.

Net Sales (after returns)	$180,000
Printing	−84,000
Author's royalty (at 10% of net sales)	−18,000
Unearned royalty (from $25,000 advance)	−7,000
Write-offs from returned books (at $3 each)	−26,000
Direct marketing	−25,000
Overhead (shipping, warehousing, sales commission, etc.)	−54,000
Net Loss	−$34,000

Source: Albert N. Greco, Fordham University.

president Bill Clinton signed a record deal reportedly worth more than $10 million with Knopf to publish his memoirs. Typically, an author's royalty is between 5 and 15 percent of the net price of the book. But before a royalty check is paid, advance money is subtracted from royalties earned during the sale of the book (see Table 10.2).

After a contract is signed, the acquisitions editor guides the manuscript through several stages. In educational publishing, a major text may also be turned over to a **developmental editor**, who provides the author with feedback, makes suggestions for improvements, and obtains advice from knowledgeable members of the academic community. If a book is illustrated, editors work closely with photo researchers to select appropriate photographs and pieces of art. After the development stage, copy-editing, design, and production people enter the picture. While **copy editors** attend to specific problems in writing or length, production and **design managers** work on the look of the book, making decisions about type style, paper, cover design, and layout.

Simultaneously, plans are under way to market and sell the book. Decisions generally need to be made concerning number of copies to print, how to best reach potential readers, and costs for promotion and advertising. For trade books and some scholarly books, publishing houses may send early or advance copies of a book to appropriate magazines and newspapers with the hope of receiving favorable reviews that can be used later in promotional material. Prominent trade writers typically sign autographs at selected bookstores and travel the radio and TV talk-show circuit to promote their new books. Unlike trade publishers, college-textbook firms rarely sell directly to bookstores. Instead, they contact instructors through either direct-mail brochures or sales representatives assigned to various geographic regions. As noted earlier, el-hi salespeople may deal with local school districts or state adoption committees.

Large trade houses spend millions of dollars promoting new books. To help create a best-seller, trade houses often distribute large cardboard bins, called dumps, to thousands of stores to display a book in bulk quantity. Like food merchants who buy eye-level shelf placement for their products in supermarkets, large trade houses buy shelf space from major chains to ensure prominent locations in bookstores. For example, to have copies of one title placed in a front-of-the-store dump bin or table at all the Borders bookstore locations costs about $10,000 for two weeks.[10] Publishers also buy ad space on buses and billboards and in newspapers and magazines. Some trade houses now routinely purchase ads on television and radio.

The final part of the publishing process involves the business and order-fulfillment stages—getting books to market and shipping and invoicing orders to thousands of commercial outlets and college bookstores. Warehouse inventories are monitored to ensure that enough copies of a book will be available to meet demand. Anticipating such demand, though, is a tricky business. No publisher wants to get stuck with books it cannot sell or be caught short if a book becomes more popular than originally predicted. Publishers must absorb the cost of returned books. Independent bookstores, which tend to order more carefully, return about 20 percent of books ordered; in contrast, mass merchandisers such as Wal-Mart and Costco, which routinely overstock popular titles, often return up to 40 percent. Returns this high can seriously impact a publisher's bottom line.

Book Clubs and Mail Order

In terms of selling books, two alternative strategies have worked for a number of years—book clubs and mail order. Book clubs, similar to music clubs, entice new members with offers such as five books for $1, then require regular purchases from their list of recommended titles. Mail-order services typically market specialized titles directly to readers. Both sales strategies have in many cases sustained publishers during the changeover from a print-based to an electronically influenced culture. The two tactics also helped the industry in earlier times when bookstores were not as numerous as they are today. Modeled on the turn-of-the-century catalogue sales techniques used by retailers such as Sears, direct-mail services brought books to rural and small-town areas that had no bookstores.

The Book-of-the-Month Club and the Literary Guild both started in 1926. Using popular writers and literary experts to recommend new books, the clubs were successful immediately. Book clubs have long served as editors for their customers, screening thousands of titles and recommending key books in particular genres. Occasionally, though, important books have been overlooked by clubs, including Steinbeck's *The Grapes of Wrath* and Hemingway's *The Sun Also Rises*.

During the 1980s, as book clubs experienced declining sales, they became more susceptible to pressure from major publishers. Indeed, the outside experts for the clubs began complaining not only that their recommendations were frequently bypassed by club editors but that the clubs were stressing commercially viable authors without regard to literary merit.

Besides screening new books for consumers, clubs have offered incentives, such as free books and occasional price reductions, to compete with bookstores. Book clubs offer the same advantages as a cable home-shopping network: You can order from the comfort of your home and avoid "mall madness" or the congestion of downtown shopping. Although AOL Time Warner operates the Book-of-the-Month Club (the largest single club, with more than one million members), Doubleday remains the most active publisher in the book-club business. In the late 1990s, Doubleday owned and operated both the Literary Guild and Doubleday Book Club as well as several specialty clubs, including the Mystery Guild, the Military Book Club, the Science Fiction Book Club, and the Black Expressions Book Club for African American literature.

In 2000, the Book-of-the-Month Club, the Literary Guild, and Doubleday combined their online efforts with a partnership called Bookspan. The alliance offers such benefits as discussion forums, live chats with authors, bulletin boards, reviews, and book excerpts from upcoming selections.[11] This strategy was intended to make book clubs more competitive with online booksellers, which had been making significant inroads into book club sales.

Mail-order bookselling is used primarily by trade, professional, and university press publishers. The mail-order strategy offers many of the benefits of book clubs in terms of immediately notifying readers about new book titles. Mail-order book-selling was pioneered in the 1950s by magazine publishers. They created special sets of books, such as Time-Life Books, focusing on science, nature, household maintenance, cooking, and so forth. These series usually offered one book at a time (unlike encyclopedias) and sustained sales through direct-mail flyers and newspaper, magazine, radio, and television advertising. To enhance their perceived value and uniqueness, most of these sets could be obtained only through the mail. Although such sets are more costly due to advertising and postal charges, mail-order books still appeal to customers who prefer the convenience of mail to the hassle of shopping. Others like the privacy of mail order (particularly if they are ordering sexually explicit books or magazines).

Bookstores

Although the book industry remains the most diverse of all mass media, the same media trend toward large chain ownership prevails. In 2001, nearly 26,000 outlets sold books in the United States, including traditional bookstores, department stores, drugstores, used-book stores, and toy stores (see Table 10.3). Book sales, however, were dominated by two large chains: Borders-Walden and Barnes & Noble, which includes B. Dalton stores. These chains operate hundreds of stores each and account for about one-quarter of all book sales. The two next-largest chains are Books-A-Million and Crown Books.

Shopping-mall bookstores have boosted book sales since the late 1960s. But the trend currently reinvigorating the business began in the 1980s with the development of superstores. The idea was to adapt to the book trade the large retail-store concept, such as Home Depot in home improvement or Wal-Mart in general retail. Following the success of a single Borders store in Ann Arbor, Michigan, a number of book chains began developing **book superstores** that catered to suburban areas and to avid readers. A typical superstore now stocks about 150,000 titles, compared with the 20,000 or 40,000 titles found in older B. Dalton or Waldenbooks stores. As superstores expanded, they also started to sell recorded music and to feature coffee shops, restaurants, and live performances. By 2002, Borders had grown from only 14 superstores in 1991 to more than 385 superstores in addition to 800 Waldenbooks stores. With 25 new stores in places like Australia, New Zealand, Singapore, and the United Kingdom, Borders was also growing abroad. Similarly, Barnes & Noble was operating 606 superstores and 286 smaller B. Dalton bookstores.

The rise of book superstores severely cut into independent bookstores' business, which dropped from a 31 percent market share in 1991 to about 15 percent today. Yet independents have maintained their 15 percent market share for more than three years, suggesting that their business has stabilized. Despite the control that chains have over commercial trade books, the majority of bookstores today remain small and independent. For example, more than 2,500 used- and rare-book stores operate nationwide. To oppose chains, many independents have formed regional or statewide groups to plan survival tactics. For instance, independents in Madison, Wisconsin, countered the arrival of a new Borders superstore by redecorating, extending hours and services, creating newsletters, and offering musical and children's performances.

Online Bookstores

In just a few short years, online booksellers have created an entirely new book-distribution system on the Internet. The trailblazer is Amazon.com, established in 1995 by then-thirty-year-old Jeff Bezos, who left Wall Street to start a Web-based business. Bezos realized books were an untapped and ideal market for the Internet,

Table 10.3 Bookstores in the United States, 2001

Category of Store	Number	Category of Store	Number
Antiquarian general	1,566	Mail-order general	313
Antiquarian mail order	523	Mail-order specialized	714
Antiquarian specialized	249	Metaphysics, New Age, and occult	248
Art supply store	73	Museum store and art gallery	586
College general	3,445	Nature and natural history	198
College specialized	121	Newsdealer	92
Comics	243	Office supply	57
Computer software	964	Other§	1,980
Cooking	170	Paperback‡	250
Department store	1,986	Religious*	3,849
Educational*	341	Self-help/Development	41
Federal sites†	235	Stationer	11
Foreign language*	38	Toy store	112
General	6,267	Used*	594
Gift shop	388	Total	25,916
Juvenile*	262		

*Includes mail-order shops for this topic, which are not counted elsewhere in this survey.

†National historic sites, national monuments, and national parks.

§Stores specializing in subjects or services other than those covered in this survey.

‡Includes mail order. Excludes used-paperback bookstores, stationers, drugstores, or wholesalers handling paperbacks.

Source: The Bowker Annual Library and Book Trade Almanac, 2002 (New Providence, N.J.: R. R. Bowker).

with more than three million publications in print and plenty of distributors to fulfill orders. Therefore he moved to Seattle and started Amazon.com, so named because Web search engines like Yahoo! listed categories in alphabetical order, putting Amazon near the top of the list.

In 1997, Barnes & Noble, the leading retail store bookseller, launched its heavily invested and carefully researched bn.com Web site (of which publishing giant Bertelsmann bought 50 percent in the following year when it canceled plans to start its own online store). The Web site's success, however, remains dwarfed by Amazon. In 1999, the American Booksellers Association also launched BookSense.com to help more than one thousand independent bookstores create an online presence. By 2002, online booksellers controlled about 7.5 percent of the retail book market, and their share of the market was projected to grow to 12.4 percent of consumer book sales by 2005.[12] The strength of online sellers lies in their convenience, low prices, and especially their ability to offer backlist titles and the works of less famous authors that even 150,000-volume superstores don't carry on their shelves. Online customers are also drawn to the interactive nature of these sites, which allow them to post their own book reviews, read those of fellow customers, and receive

> 66 The stores are clean and comfortable. It's a safe environment. Sometimes we find students sprawled out on the floor studying. It's cool to be seen in a bookstore. 99
>
> —Debra Williams, director of communications for Barnes & Noble, *New York Times,* 1999

● Employees filling Christmas orders in Amazon.com's Seattle distribution warehouse.

book recommendations based upon book searches and past purchases. The chief business strategy of online booksellers is to buy exclusive listings with the most popular World Wide Web portals. For example, bn.com signed a multimillion-dollar deal with Microsoft to be the "buy books" button on MSN.com, and it is the exclusive bookseller on America Online. Similarly, Amazon.com has marketing agreements with the busy Yahoo! and Excite Web sites and is the exclusive music retailer on MSN.com.

Ownership Patterns

Like most mass media, commercial publishing is dominated by a handful of major corporations with ties to international media conglomerates such as Viacom/Paramount (which now owns Simon & Schuster), AOL Time Warner, Newhouse's Advance Publications, and Bertelsmann, which began by publishing German Bibles in the 1700s. Since the 1960s and 1970s—when CBS acquired Holt, Rinehart & Winston; Popular Library; and Fawcett— mergers and consolidations have driven the book industry. Germany's Bertelsmann purchased Dell in the late 1970s for $35 million and in the 1980s bought Doubleday for $475 million. In 1998, Bertelsmann shook up the book industry by adding Random House, the largest U.S. book publisher, to its fold. With the $1.4 billion purchase of Random House from Advance Publications, Bertelsmann gained control of about one-third of the U.S. trade-book market (about 10 percent of the total U.S. book market) and became the world's largest publisher of English-language books.[13] Bertelsmann's book companies include the Bantam Dell Publishing Group, the Doubleday Broadway Publishing Group, the Ballantine Publishing Group, the Knopf Publishing Group, the Random House Trade Publishing Group, and the Random House imprints of Modern Library and Fodor's Travel Publications, among others (see Table 10.4).

A number of concerns have surfaced regarding conglomerates' control over the publishing industry. The distinctive styles of older houses and their associations with certain literary figures and book types no longer characterize the industry. Of special concern has been the financial struggle of independent publishers and booksellers, who are often undercut in price and promotion by large corporations and bookstore chains. Large houses also tend to favor blockbusters or best-sellers and do not aggressively pursue more modest or unconventional books.

From the corporate point of view, book-industry executives argue that large companies can financially support a number of smaller struggling firms and that the editorial ideas of these firms can remain independent from the parent corporation. Executives also tout the advantages of *synergy*: the involvement of several media subsidiaries under one corporate umbrella, all working to develop different versions of a similar product. One writer commented on these synergistic possibilities when Time and Warner merged in 1989: "Theoretically, this unprecedented corporate fusion makes it possible for a title to be published in hardcover by Little, Brown (a division of Time Inc.), featured as a Book-of-the-Month Club main selection, reviewed by *Time* magazine, issued in paperback by Warner Books, made into a major motion picture, and turned into a TV series by Warner television."[14] Still, authors and critics worry that book ideas that lack such multimedia potential may be rejected in the trend toward large corporate control.

On one level, the industry appears healthy, with thousands of independent presses still able to make books using inexpensive production techniques and desktop computer publishing. Many independents, however, struggle against the few large conglomerates that define the direction of much of the industry.

● **Table 10.4** *New York Times* **Best-seller Scorecard**
Hardcover Nonfiction Best-sellers, 2001

Rank/Publisher	Titles	Wks	Rank/Publisher	Titles	Wks
1. Random House	**31**	**274**	**4. Hyperion**	**6**	**59**
Random House	8	72	Hyperion	4	26
Doubleday	6	67	Talk Miramax/Hyperion	2	33
Knopf	5	62			
Broadway	4	25	**5. Penguin Putnam**	**5**	**47**
Crown	2	15	Dutton	1	18
Bantam	1	15	Lipper/Viking	1	5
Harmony	1	1	Putnam	1	15
Nan A. Talese/Doubleday	1	2	Riverhead	1	8
Pantheon	1	3	Viking	1	1
Villard	1	8			
Modern Library	1	4	**6. Holtzbrink**	**4**	**33**
			Farrar, Straus & Giroux	1	1
2. Simon & Schuster	**20**	**124**	Holt	1	18
Simon & Schuster	10	91	Metropolitan/Holt	1	13
Scribner	4	21	St. Martin's Press	1	1
Free Press	3	6			
Pocket Books	2	4	**7. Regnery**	**3**	**17**
Lisa Drew/Scribner	1	2			
			8. Time Warner	**3**	**13**
3. HarperCollins	**16**	**74**	Little, Brown	1	3
HarperCollins	4	21	Warner	1	2
ReganBooks	4	24	Warner Business	1	8
Morrow	3	11			
HarperBusiness	2	8	**9. Houghton Mifflin**	**2**	**24**
HarperResource	1	3			
ReganBooks/HarperCollins	1	4	**10. Norton**	**2**	**7**
ReganBooks/HarperPerennial	1	3			

Source. Adapted from SIMBA Information Inc. analysis of the 2001 *New York Times* best-seller lists through Sunday, November 18, 2001.

Trends in Book Publishing

A number of technological changes in the publishing industry demonstrate the blurring of print and electronic cultures. The book industry has adapted successfully in the digital age by using computer technology to effectively lower costs: Everything from an author's word-processing program to printing and distribution is digitized.[15] Leading distributors, publishers, and bookstores have all begun using digital technology to print books on demand, reviving books that would otherwise go out of print and avoiding the inconveniences of carrying unsold books or being unable to respond to limited demand for a book.

Digitized manuscripts can also be downloaded from the Internet as **e-books** (electronic books), reaching interested readers directly and transforming the entire book industry. Superstar author Stephen King has been a key force in pushing more reading material toward electronic book formats. His first experiment involved his 66-page novella *Riding the Bullet* (2000), which his publisher, Simon & Schuster, made available only on the Internet as an encrypted document that could not be copied. *Riding the Bullet,* selling for $2.50 (and given away for free as a promotion by some book sites), was the first online release by a big-name author, and it resulted in 400,000 downloads in the first twenty-four hours alone, pointing to the potential market for e-books. Soon thereafter, Random House published blockbuster novelist Michael Crichton's thriller *Timeline* as a free e-book for users of the Microsoft Reader operating system—a deal with Microsoft to popularize the company's new handheld reading device software. Simon & Schuster subsequently released fifteen Star Trek titles, also as free Microsoft Reader downloads.

Because e-books make possible such low publishing and distribution costs, **e-publishing** has also enabled authors to sidestep traditional publishers. A new breed of Internet-based publishing house, such as Xlibris, iUniverse, and 1stbooks, design and distribute books for a comparatively small price ($99 to $1,600, depending on the level of services) for aspiring authors wanting to self-publish a title. The companies then distribute the books in both print and e-book formats through Internet sellers such as Amazon.com and BarnesandNoble.com. Although sales are typically low for such books, the low overhead costs allow higher royalty rates for the authors and lower retail prices for readers.

The digital age has also inspired some authors to circumvent traditional and Internet publishers completely. After *Riding the Bullet* became an e-book success under Simon & Schuster, Stephen King began another e-book experiment in 2000, this time without his publisher. Releasing installments of his new novel, *The Plant,* on his own Web site, King brought his serial novel directly to his fans and merely requested that his readers pay a dollar (later $2) per downloaded chapter on an honor code system. As long as 75 percent of the downloads were paid for, King would add subsequent installments. "My friends," King wrote on his Web site, "we have a chance to become Big Publishing's worst nightmare."[16] Yet by the fourth and fifth installments, at least half of the downloaders were freeloaders, leading King to suspend the unfinished project after installment six. After the honor system of payments failed, some critics concluded that self-publishing on the Internet would never be viable, especially if Stephen King couldn't do it. Yet the project ultimately made $500,000 in sales for King, who said that the Internet may serve authors as a site for serializing novels before publication. Such prepublication revenues are much greater than the $10,000 to $50,000 that authors might earn from a magazine that prints book excerpts. *The Plant,* which is ironically about a creeping "vampire" plant that takes over a publishing company, would later be published in book form, King said.

Meanwhile, there is also a battle over the platforms and devices on which people will read electronic books. Computers present one popular medium, but they can't claim the portability that books have long offered (see "Applied Critical Process: E-books vs. the Printed Word," page 365). Portable e-book reading devices, which are book-size lightweight monitors that can hold several e-books at a time, have been retail failures in recent years even as prices have dropped below $200. Part of the problem has been the proprietary text formats and the scarcity of e-book titles offered for the devices. The three technology companies still vying for dominance in the portable e-book market are Gemstar, which has its own e-book reading device, and Microsoft and Adobe Systems, which have tailored their existing computer software to run e-books on handheld personal digital assistants.

Influences of Television and Film

Through their vast television exposure, books by TV anchors and actors such as Tom Brokaw, Peter Jennings, Ellen DeGeneres, and Jerry Seinfeld have sold millions of copies—enormous sales in a business where 100,000 in sales constitutes remarkable success. In national polls conducted in the 1980s and 1990s, nearly 30 percent of respondents said they had read a book after seeing the story or a promotion on television.

In fact, Brokaw's book, *The Greatest Generation,* and Jennings's elaborately illustrated *The Century* both ranked as best-sellers throughout much of 1998 and early

E-books vs. the Printed Word

Humans have been putting written words on paper since the first papyrus scrolls in 2400 B.C. In the past few years, e-books have mounted a challenge against traditional books by displaying works on computer screens. Yet the paper-based word seems to have won the early battles. To investigate why, comparatively analyze the two book media.

Description. Describe the qualities of the traditional printed book and various forms of the e-book, including those that appear on computers and on portable e-book reading devices. Consider qualities that would be relevant to readers (such as cost, ease of use, and aesthetics), libraries (cost, accessibility, and archival/storage ability), bookstores (product aesthetics and cost), and publishers (cost and protection of intellectual property).

Analysis. What important patterns and differences emerge? E-books generally cost as much as printed books, even though they don't carry the same expenses of printing, binding, and distribution. E-books can be portable, but the reader would need to invest a few hundred dollars in a portable reading device, which can display only those e-books offered by the device manufacturer. Also, readers tend to still find the printed word to be more user-friendly. Indeed, libraries have experienced a four-fold increase in paper demand in recent years because so many people want to have their digital documents on paper. Yet e-books also help libraries to expand their holdings without increasing shelf space. In terms of library distribution, e-books can't get lost, be turned in late, or get damaged in circulation either.

Interpretation. E-books have yet to offer major advantages for readers, particularly in terms of cost and utility. For libraries, though, digital e-books solve many cost and circulation problems. For bookstores, e-books don't offer much in terms of savings or in terms of aesthetics. Booksellers know that oftentimes people do judge a book (and buy it) based on its cover. For publishers, e-books present the cautionary lesson of the music and movie industries—how does the industry protect copyrights once computer users discover how to illegally copy and distribute digital content?

Evaluation. Clearly, e-books aren't a wholesale improvement over printed books. It is much more likely that e-books will gradually expand their reach into specific niches, such as special library holdings.

1999. Interest in these books was enormously enhanced by network/publisher cross-promotions and cross-media ventures. A special on NBC's *Dateline* and a profile of Brokaw's project on *NBC Nightly News* both promoted his book (NBC owns nearly a 25 percent interest in the book). Jennings's book grew out of a twelve-part ABC documentary project on the twentieth century. The book's publisher, Doubleday (a subsidiary of Random House, which also published Brokaw's book), developed a Web site linking ABC to the publisher and sponsored a fifteen-hour History Channel series for cable based on the book. Even though some critics frowned at network anchors using network time to promote their own books, Thomas Rosenstiel, former *Los Angeles Times* media critic and director of the Project for Excellence in Journalism, disagreed: "If you're able to communicate things of substance to people and that

● Jim Carrey's perform-
ance in *How the Grinch
Stole Christmas* trans-
formed a long-popular children's book and television
special into 2000's top-
grossing movie.

dribbles into *Dateline* instead of the newest celebrity book on one-liners or 'How I Got to Be a Sitcom Star,' then I think the culture is better off."[17]

Even before the development of Oprah's Book Club in 1996, Oprah Winfrey's afternoon talk show had become a major power broker in selling books. In 1993, for example, Holocaust survivor and Nobel Prize recipient Elie Wiesel appeared on *Oprah*. Afterward, his 1960 memoir, *Night*, which came out as a Bantam paperback in 1982, returned to the best-seller lists. In 1996, novelist Toni Morrison's nineteen-year-old book *Song of Solomon* became a paperback best-seller after Morrison appeared on *Oprah*. In 1998, Winfrey, as actor and producer, brought another of Morrison's novels—the Pulitzer Prize–winning *Beloved*—to movie screens. The film version inspired new interest in the book, putting *Beloved* on the best-seller lists. The success of Oprah's Book Club had extended far beyond anyone's expectations. Each selection became an immediate best-seller, generating tremendous excitement within the book industry.

Television and film continue to get many of their story ideas from books. Michael Crichton's *Jurassic Park* and John Irving's *The Cider House Rules* became major motion pictures. *Bridget Jones's Diary,* Helen Fielding's novel about a woman's quest for self-improvement, inspired the 2001 film of the same name, starring Renée Zell-

weger, Colin Firth, and Hugh Grant. Even nineteenth-century novels still translate to the screen. For example, the popular 1994 film version of *Little Women*, written in 1868 by Louisa May Alcott, sent the Random House reissue of the novel to the top of the juvenile best-seller list. Children's books also translate to the screen. Scholastic's successful *Clifford* books about a lovable big red dog, first published by Norman Bridwell in 1963, became an animated television series in 2000, giving Scholastic a boost in book sales and paving the way for other TV tie-ins. The half-hour episodes are viewed by millions in more than twenty languages in fifty countries. The Dr. Seuss children's classic of 1957, *How the Grinch Stole Christmas*, has had even greater resonance, inspiring first a 1966 television special narrated by Boris Karloff and then a feature-length film starring Jim Carrey in 2000.

Blockbusters and Licenses

Since Harriet Beecher Stowe's abolitionist novel *Uncle Tom's Cabin* sold fifteen thousand copies in fifteen days back in 1852 (and three million total copies prior to the Civil War), many American publishers have stalked the best-seller. As in the movie business, large publishers are always searching for the blockbuster. To ensure popular success, publishers often pay rights to license popular film and television programs, especially in the juvenile book trade. For instance, the Disney Company's resurgence in animated films since the 1980s generated a wave of successful book titles based on its movies.

The drive to create blockbusters in the book industry also led to a number of overpriced book advances to media figures without much writing talent. Although Ellen DeGeneres, Jerry Seinfeld, and the professional wrestlers "The Rock" and "Mankind" had best-selling books, readers apparently do not find the written work of all entertainers to be compelling reading. Whoopi Goldberg received a whopping $6 million advance for a book that sold poorly, and Paul Reiser nearly matched that with $5.6 million for an under-performing second book. Jay Leno's publisher took a beating after Leno's $4 million advance resulted in 400,000 returned unsold copies of his book. The O. J. Simpson trial created the biggest bidding frenzy, as publishers tried to find books with juicy insider information but ended up with duds like Paula Barbieri's memoir of boyfriend O. J., a book that failed to recoup its $3 million advance.

Talking Books

Another major development in publishing has been the merger of sound recording with publishing. Audio books, or books on tape, generally feature actors or authors reading abridged versions of popular fiction and nonfiction trade books. Indispensable to many sightless readers and older readers whose vision is diminished, talking books are also popular among regular readers who do a lot of commuter driving or who want to listen to a book at home while doing something else. A 1999 study by the Audio Publishers Association reported that about 45 percent of all audio-book use took place in cars, and that listening while exercising is becoming an increasingly popular use. Recent award-winning audio books include 'Tis by Frank McCourt (read by the author), The Screwtape Letters by C. S. Lewis (read by actor/comedian John Cleese), and The Corrections by Jonathan Franzen (read by actor Dylan Baker). The number of books on tape borrowed from libraries soared in the 1990s, and small bookstore chains such as Talking Book World and Earful of Books developed to cater to the audio-book niche. Audio books also began to be released on CDs in the late 1990s, as compact-disc players became more commonplace in automobile sound systems.

Book Preservation

Another recent trend in the book industry involves the preservation of older books, especially those from the nineteenth century printed on acid-based paper. Ever since the conversion to machine-made publishing materials during the Industrial Revolution, paper had been produced by using chemicals that gradually deteriorate over time. At the turn of the twentieth century, research provided evidence that acid-based paper would eventually turn brittle and self-destruct. This research, initiated by libraries concerned with losing valuable older collections, was confirmed by further studies in the 1940s and 1950s. The paper industry, however, did not respond. In the 1970s, leading libraries began developing techniques to de-acidify book pages in an attempt to halt any further deterioration (although this process could not restore books to their original state). Meanwhile, more and more books were removed from circulation and were available to the public only on microfilm and microfiche, which were difficult to read.

Despite evidence that alkaline-based paper was easier on machinery, produced a whiter paper, and caused less pollution, the paper industry did not change. But by the early 1990s, motivated almost entirely by economics rather than by the cultural value of books, the industry finally began producing paper that was acid-free.

Libraries and book conservationists, however, still had to focus attention on older, at-risk books. Although clumsy, hard-to-read microfilm remained an option, some institutions began photocopying original books onto acid-free paper to make copies available to the public. Libraries then stored the originals, which were treated to halt further wear.

More recently, pioneering projects in digital technology by Xerox and Cornell University have produced electronic copies of books through computer scanning. Other companies, such as netLibrary, have eschewed scanning, which they say produces too many errors, and have enlisted armies of typists in China, India, and the Philippines to convert books into electronic form. The Colorado-based company, a division of the nonprofit Online Computer Library Center, digitizes about two hundred books a day. By 2002, netLibrary offered more than forty thousand e-books through more than one thousand public, corporate, and academic libraries. Library patrons can "check out" the digitized books over the Internet, although only one title per library is accessible at a time.

Alternative Voices

Even though the book industry is dominated by large book conglomerates and superstores, there are still major efforts to make books freely available to everyone. The idea is not a new one. In the late nineteenth and early twentieth centuries, industrialist Andrew Carnegie used millions of dollars from his vast steel fortune to build more than 2,500 libraries in the United States, Britain, Australia, and New Zealand. Carnegie believed that libraries created great learning opportunities for citizens, and especially for immigrants like himself.

In 2002, a partnership of the Internet Archive, the University of Maryland's Human-Computer Interaction Lab, and government, corporate, and private philanthropists unveiled the prototype for the International Children's Digital Library (ICDL). The goal of the library in its first five years is to build a globally accessible online collection of ten thousand books in their original languages drawn from one hundred cultures around the world. The books, available at www.icdlbooks.org, are literature for children ages three to thirteen. According to the organization, "The goal of ICDL is to revisit [Carnegie's] vision, using technological advancements to strengthen the dream by providing all children with direct access to the resources that are essential to enlightened citizenship: literature, knowledge, and information."[18]

● James Joyce's novel *Ulysses* was embroiled in a famous and lengthy censorship battle between 1918 and 1933. The book used many radical literary techniques and forms to depict a single day in the lives of characters living in Dublin, Ireland, but it also riled up censors who judged *Ulysses* obscene. After it began appearing serially in *The Little Review,* an American literary magazine, between 1918 and 1920, censors successfully used the courts to stop any further printing of *Ulysses* in the United States. Then Sylvia Beach (shown here with Joyce), an American expatriate living in Paris, risked prosecution to publish the controversial novel in 1922. It was not until 1933, however, that the ban on *Ulysses* was lifted in the United States. According to one reactionary critic of the day, "*Ulysses* is not pornographic, but it is more indecent, obscene, scatological, and licentious than the majority of pornographic books."

Censorship Issues in Book Publishing

Over the years, small communities and large nations have successfully kept certain books out of the hands of their citizens. In 1929, for instance, Edgar Rice Burroughs's Tarzan series was pulled from the Los Angeles public library system because Tarzan and Jane lived together but were not married. In 1989, the Ayatollah Khomeini of Iran not only banned Salman Rushdie's novel *The Satanic Verses* for blaspheming the Islamic religion but also ordered Rushdie killed, forcing the author into hiding for several years. In 1998, censorship of a different kind revolved around *East and West,* a book critical of the Chinese government written by former Hong Kong governor Chris Patten. Chinese officials expressed deep opposition to the book, and the book's publisher, HarperCollins, was directed by parent company News Corp. and its chairman, Rupert Murdoch, to cancel publication because the book threatened the corporate giant's considerable business interests in China.

Books have faced innumerable cultural and social challenges. Censorship campaigns have often attempted to remove certain books from libraries and classrooms. The American Library Association (ALA), which represents more than sixty-four thousand librarians and associates nationwide, documents between four hundred and eight hundred reported censorship attempts annually.

One of the most celebrated censorship cases involved Walt Whitman's *Leaves of Grass.* The book became the center of a legal battle in the early 1880s and was eventually banned in Boston. Because of their provocative sexual themes and language, the full versions of D. H. Lawrence's *Lady Chatterley's Lover* (1928) and Henry Miller's *Tropic of Cancer* (1934) were banned in the United States until the early 1960s.

During the 1980s and 1990s, the books most frequently challenged in school libraries and curriculums included either controversial language or sexual themes. In New York City in 1998, parents targeted the book *Nappy Hair*—a children's text written by an African American woman that celebrates kinky, nappy hair—as racially insensitive. As a result, the teacher who chose the book for her classroom was transferred and a nationwide discussion in the media on the purpose of books in education was revived. Censorship campaigns—initiated by both liberal and conservative groups—have sometimes tried to "protect" preteens and teenagers from significant works of literature. Often these books contain common street language or introduce adolescents to complex personal and social themes that some adults believe are inappropriate for young people.

Censorship campaigns have targeted everything from John Steinbeck's *Of Mice and Men* to all the books in J. K. Rowling's Harry Potter series (for allegedly promoting witchcraft and Satanism). But the most censored book has been Mark Twain's *Adventures of Huckleberry Finn,* an 1884 classic that still sells tens of thousands of copies a year in paperback. The novel routinely uses the word *nigger* the way it was used in everyday language in nineteenth-century America. Most high-school teachers are taught how to handle the sensitive racial issues raised in the book. Occasionally, though, parent groups and some civil rights organizations have argued that the frequent appearance of the offensive word gives the book racist overtones.

IMPORTANT HISTORICAL BANNED BOOKS

Ulysses, by James Joyce

The Scarlet Letter, by Nathaniel Hawthorne

Leaves of Grass, by Walt Whitman

The Diary of a Young Girl, by Anne Frank

Lolita, by Vladimir Nabokov

To Kill a Mockingbird, by Harper Lee

I Know Why the Caged Bird Sings, by Maya Angelou

Are You There God? It's Me, Margaret, by Judy Blume

The Color Purple, by Alice Walker

The Satanic Verses, by Salman Rushdie

THE TOP 15 MOST FREQUENTLY CHALLENGED BOOKS OF THE 1990s

1. Scary Stories (series), by Alvin Schwartz
2. *Daddy's Roommate,* by Michael Willholte
3. *I Know Why the Caged Bird Sings,* by Maya Angelou
4. *The Chocolate War,* by Robert Cormier
5. *The Adventures of Huckleberry Finn,* by Mark Twain
6. *Of Mice and Men,* by John Steinbeck
7. *Forever,* by Judy Blume
8. *Bridge to Terabithia,* by Katherine Paterson
9. *Heather Has Two Mommies,* by Leslea Newman
10. *The Catcher in the Rye,* by J. D. Salinger
11. *The Giver,* by Lois Lowry
12. *My Brother Sam Is Dead,* by James Lincoln Collier and Christopher Collier
13. *It's Perfectly Normal,* by Robie Harris
14. Alice (series), by Phyllis Reynolds Naylor
15. Goosebumps (series), by R. L. Stine

Note: According to the American Library Association, a *challenge* is an attempt to remove or restrict materials, based upon the objections of a person or group. A *banning* is the removal of those materials.

★ Books and the Future of Democracy

As we enter the digital age, the book-reading habits of children and adults are a social concern. After all, books have played an important role not only in spreading the idea of democracy but in connecting us to new ideas beyond our local experience. In surveys taken in the 1990s, however, only about 27 percent of middle-school students indicated that they read for pleasure each day (although they reported watching about three hours of television per day). Adults also reported sporadic reading habits. For instance, only about 50 percent of U.S. adults said that they read at least one book a year. Likewise, 40 percent of young adults between ages nineteen and twenty-one reported that they did not read books. Yet studies also suggest that reading habits are generally more evident among the young than among older people; 60 percent of all avid or regular book readers, for example, are under the age of forty. Overall, the share of regular book readers in the population is about 25 percent, a figure that has remained steady since the 1930s.

Although our society is being dramatically influenced by electronic and digital culture, the impact of our oldest mass medium—the book—remains immense. Without the development of printing presses and books, the idea of democracy would be hard to imagine. From the impact of Stowe's *Uncle Tom's Cabin,* which helped bring an end to slavery in the 1860s, to Rachel Carson's *Silent Spring,* which led to reforms in the pesticide industry in the 1960s, books have made a difference. They have told us things that we wanted—and needed—to know.

Over time, the wide circulation of books gave many ordinary people the same opportunities to learn that were once available to only a privileged few. However, as societies discovered the power associated with knowledge and the printed word, books were subjected to a variety of censors (see "Examining Ethics: Censorship Issues in Book Publishing" on page 370). Imposed by various rulers and groups intent on maintaining their authority, the censorship of books often prevented people from learning about the rituals and moral standards of other cultures. Political censors sought to banish "dangerous" books that promoted radical ideas or challenged conventional authority. Some versions of the Bible, Karl Marx's *Das Kapital* (1867), *The Autobiography of Malcolm X* (1965), and Salman Rushdie's *The Satanic Verses* (1989) have all been banned at one time or another. In fact, one of the triumphs of the Internet is that it allows the digital passage of banned books into nations where printed versions have been outlawed.

Beyond censorship issues, other concerns have surfaced regarding the limits that democratic societies place on books. For example, the economic clout of publishing houses run by large multinational corporations has made it more difficult for new authors and new ideas to gain a foothold in commercial publishing. Often, editors and executives prefer to invest in commercially successful writers or authors who have a built-in television, sports, or movie audience.

Another issue is whether the contemporary book industry, in its own way, has contributed to entertainment and information overload. For example, in his book *The Death of Literature,* Alvin Kernan argues that serious literary work has been increasingly overwhelmed by the triumph of consumerism. In other words, people accumulate craftily marketed celebrity biographies and popular fiction but seldom read serious works. Kernan's critique reflects the long-standing view that "superior" cultural taste is associated with reading literature. He contends that cultural standards have been undermined by marketing ploys that divert attention away from serious books and toward mass-produced works that are more easily read.[19]

Because democracies generally depend on literate populations to sift through cultural products and make informed decisions, the abundance of media products raises other important questions. Of particular concern is the apparent decline in juvenile reading levels as measured by standardized tests over the past few decades.

Indeed, the increase in published book titles since the 1950s does not mean that we have become a more literate society. The adult illiteracy rate has remained fairly constant at about 10 percent over the years. And today children have multiple electronic and digital distractions and options competing for their leisure time.

Yet books and reading have survived the challenge of visual and digital culture. Developments such as word processing, books on tape, children's pictorial literature, and online computer services have integrated aspects of print and electronic culture into our daily lives. Most of these new forms carry on the original legacy of books: transcending geographic borders to provide personal stories, world history, and general knowledge to all who can read.

Despite a commercial book industry that has increasingly developed its own star system of authors, approximately a thousand new publishers enter the business each year. Tensions persist, however, between businesspeople who publish books as a moneymaking enterprise and authors who try to write well and advance knowledge—or between authors who seek fame and fortune and editor-publishers who are interested in wisdom and the written word. Some argue that the industry balanced these conflicts better before corporate takeovers tipped the scales heavily toward profit motives. As our society's oldest media institution, the book industry bears the weight of these economic and cultural battles perhaps more than any other medium.

Given our increasing channels of specialized media, people can zero in on their own interests. Books, however, are one medium that takes us in other directions. Since the early days of the printing press, books have helped us to understand ideas and customs outside our own experiences. For democracy to work well, we must read. When we examine other cultures through books, we discover not only who we are and what we value but who others are and what our common ties might be.

www.

To create an individualized study plan for Chapter 10, go to the interactive *Media and Culture* Online Study Guide at: bedfordstmartins.com/ mediaculture

REVIEW QUESTIONS

The History of Books from Papyrus to Paperbacks

1. What distinguishes the manuscript culture of the Middle Ages from both the oral and print eras in communication?

2. Why was the printing press such an important and revolutionary invention?

3. Why were books considered so dangerous to colonial rulers and other leaders during the early periods of American history?

Modern Publishing and the Book Industry

4. Why did publishing houses develop?

5. Why have instant books become important to the paperback market?

6. What are the major issues that affect textbook publishing?

7. Why have religious books been so successful historically?

8. What has hampered the sales of subscription reference encyclopedias?

The Organization and Ownership of the Book Industry

9. What are the general divisions within a typical publishing house?

10. Why have book clubs and mail-order strategies continued to flourish despite the rapid growth of mall stores and superstores?

11. Why have book superstores been so successful over the past few years?

12. What are the strengths of the online bookstore industry?

13. What are the current ownership patterns in the book industry? How have these trends affected independent stores?

Trends in Book Publishing

14. What are the main ways in which digital technologies have changed the publishing industry over the past few years?

15. Why did paper manufacturers convert to acid-free paper in the late 1980s and early 1990s?

Books and the Future of Democracy

16. What have book publishers and sellers done to keep pace with changes in technology and society?

17. What have been the major contributions of books to democratic life?

QUESTIONING THE MEVIA

1. What are your earliest recollections of books? Do you read for pleasure? If yes, what kind of books do you enjoy? Why?

2. What can the book industry do better to ensure that we are not overwhelmed by a visual and electronic culture?

3. If you were opening an independent bookstore in a town with a chain store, such as a Borders or a Barnes & Noble, how would you compete?

4. Imagine that you are on a committee that oversees book choices for a high school library in your town. What policies do you think should guide the committee's selection of controversial books?

5. Why do you think the availability of television and cable hasn't substantially decreased the number of new book titles available each year? What do books offer that television doesn't?

SEARCHING THE INTERNET

http://www.bookweb.org

The Web home of the American Booksellers Association, the trade association representing independent bookstores in the United States.

http://www.publishersweekly.com/

The online version of *Publishers Weekly,* the book industry's trade magazine.

http://www.publishers.org/

Home site for the Association of American Publishers, the principal trade association of the book-publishing industry.

http://www.gutenberg.net

Founded in 1971, Project Gutenberg is a nonprofit database that makes hundreds of public-domain literature titles (from Jane Austen to Tolstoy) available to Internet users for free.

http://www.amazon.com

Established in 1995, this online bookseller claims to be the world's largest bookstore. Competing online bookstores include bn.com (Barnes & Noble).

http://www.nytimes.com/pages/books/index.html

This Web site features the *New York Times*'s book reviews, best-seller lists, first chapters, art news, and book forums. (It's a free site, but registration is required.)

http://www.ala.org/bbooks

Part of the American Library Association's Web site, this page provides information about censorship and banned books.

THE CRITICAL PROCESS

In Brief

This "think-pair-share" exercise focuses on the publishing and sales of college and university textbooks.

Think: On your own, spend two to three minutes writing down:

- money you spent this semester on textbooks and cost of each book
- if you returned any books last semester, how much money you got back
- what choices are available at your university or college for purchasing textbooks

Pair: With a partner, discuss your observations for a few minutes and consider these questions: Which types of books seem to be most expensive? Why do you think these books cost so much? What do you typically do with textbooks at the end of a semester—keep them or sell them back—and why? Who do you think is responsible for pricing the books? Who do you think reaps the most profit from textbook sales?

Share: As a class, consider the college-textbook publishing business. Who in the class spent the most money? If a book is more expensive, are you more or less likely to buy it? Should professors tie lectures closely to the texts, or should the required reading be done independently by the student? If you didn't spend your money on textbooks, what do you think you would do with the money? What are some of the factors in the production and distribution of textbooks that account for their cost?

In Depth

In small groups, investigate a college bookstore in your area and then compare it with competing college bookstores in the same area or at other colleges or universities in your state. Look at the National Association of College Stores Web site for information, <www.nacs.org>, and see Figure 10.2, "Where the New Textbook Dollar Goes" (page 352). In your investigation, follow the four steps in the critical process:

Description. Describe each store and the variety of products sold. How does the bookstore make most of its money? Is the bookstore operated by the college or university, a private franchise that contracts to manage the store for the university, or is it independently owned? Does the bookstore have any competitors? How does the bookstore price its textbooks? What is the bookstore's policy on returning/reselling used textbooks? Is warehousing and handling used books an expensive operation for the bookstore? What factors can affect the store's bottom line?

Analysis. Make a chart to organize your comparisons of the college bookstores. What sort of patterns emerge? Are textbook sale and return policies and prices similar? Are supplies, computer products, trade books, and insignia merchandise important business segments for this store? Are local residents significant customers, too?

Interpretation. Critically interpret the findings. For example, does competition (or lack of it) have an impact on the pricing and strategies of the stores?

Evaluation. How would you evaluate the college bookstore industry based on your observations and experiences? Can you envision creative ways for existing or new bookstores to discount textbooks to students, yet still be reasonably profitable?

KEY TERMS

advertising

and commercial culture

In his 1996 novel *Infinite Jest,* David Foster Wallace writes of a time in the not-so-distant future when entire calendar years will be sponsored by corporations. So a letter dated 17 November Y.D.A.U. means it was written in the Year of the Depend Adult Undergarment. Other twelve-month periods are renamed the Year of Dairy Products from the American Heartland, the Year of the Trial-Size Dove Bar, and the Year of the Whopper.

Wallace's jesting is not far from today's reality. College-football bowl games are rarely named after regional flowers or agricultural goods these days. Instead, we have the Nokia Sugar Bowl, the Tostitos Fiesta Bowl, the Insight.com Bowl, and the Chick-Fil-A Peach Bowl, among others. The sites for sporting events, too, may be past the day when they would be named for an esteemed coach or player, or for the host city. Instead, naming goes to the highest bidder. Today, major-league baseball and NBA games can be found in places like Coors Field, the United Center, the Bank One Ballpark, and Qualcomm

Stadium. This trend backfired all over the United States in 2001 and 2002 in the wake of a series of corporate scandals. In Houston and Nashville, for example, after both Enron and Adelphia Communications declared bankruptcy, the Astros' baseball team and the Titans' NFL franchise purged the corporate names from Enron Field and Adelphia Coliseum.

Still, the trend toward corporate sponsorship has not ebbed; it is catching on at colleges and universities, too. Syracuse has the Carrier Dome, Louisville has the Papa John's Cardinal Stadium, and Ohio State has the Value City Arena (with an athletics hall of fame sponsored by Kroger grocery stores and a special Huntington Bank club for luxury box-seat holders). College athletes are billboards for products as well, with the ubiquitous Nike swoosh logo on the uniforms of nearly every NCAA Division I sports powerhouse. The commercial battle for students' eyes and minds even extends to secondary and elementary schools, particularly as Coke and Pepsi sign exclusive agreements with school districts that allow the beverage companies to cover schools with vending machines and advertisements.

Some people wonder if the commercialization of everyday life has gone too far. In 1998, a high-school student in Georgia was suspended not for violent behavior or drug use but for wearing a Pepsi shirt on his school's official "Coke Day." In 2000, babies became unwitting corporate icons for life when the Internet Underground Music Archive, <www.iuma.com>, in a national promotion, paid ten families $5,000 each for naming their newborns IUMA. Iuma Thornhill (a boy) of Kansas, meet Iuma Godfrey (a girl) of California. And in 2001, two seniors from a New Jersey high school offered themselves as "spokesguys" to any corporation willing to pay their way through college. The two, now attending universities in Southern California, each receive $40,000 a year from a credit card company for making personal appearances, publicizing the company on a Web page, and wearing the corporate logo on their clothes and surfboards.

Yet the relationship with advertising and its symbols around the world is more complicated than sponsorship agreements and corporate sellouts. Millions of people happily purchase and don clothing decorated with Nike swooshes, soft-drink logos, NFL sports team symbols, college and university names, Disney characters, or the clothing's designer name. Others delight in a McDonald's jingle or Budweiser's "Wassup?" ads, admire the daring design of Calvin Klein print ads, and feel comforted by the homespun familiarity of Saturn's commercials. Advertising can be an annoying, even oppressive, intrusion into our lives, but it also seems to have become a natural part of our popular culture's landscape.

today, ads are scattered everywhere—and they are multiplying. Chameleon-like, advertising adapts to many media forms. At local theaters and on home videos, advertisements now precede the latest Hollywood movies. Corporate sponsors spend millions for product placement: buying spaces for their particular goods to appear on a TV or movie set or in the background as supporting props. Ads are also part of every deejay's morning patter, and they routinely interrupt our favorite television and cable programs. By 2001, an hour of prime-time network television contained an average of 16 minutes, 8 seconds of ads—three minutes more than in 1991.

Ads take up more than half the space in most daily newspapers and consumer magazines. They are inserted into trade books and textbooks. They clutter Web sites on the Internet. They fill our mailboxes and wallpaper the buses we ride. Dotting the nation's highways, billboards promote fast-food and hotel chains while neon signs announce the names of stores along major streets and strip malls. According to the Food Marketing Institute, the typical supermarket's shelves are filled with 30,000 to 50,000 different brand-name packages, each functioning like miniature billboards. Consumers can also order products displayed on cable home-shopping networks and on the World Wide Web twenty-four hours a day. In sum, each day the American consumer comes into contact with thousands of different kinds of advertising urging him or her to purchase something.

Advertising comes in many forms, from classified ads to business-to-business ads, providing detailed information on specific products. In this chapter, however, we will concentrate on the more conspicuous advertisements that shape product images and brand-name identities. Because so much consumer advertising intrudes into daily life, ads are often viewed in a negative light. Although business managers agree that advertising is the foundation of a healthy media economy—far preferable to government-controlled media—citizens routinely complain about how many ads they are forced to endure. Accordingly, the national cynicism about advertising has caused advertisers to become more competitive. And ad agencies, in turn, create ads that not only seem natural but also stand out in some way. To get noticed, ads routinely include celebrities, humor, computer animation, music-video devices, and Hollywood movie special effects.

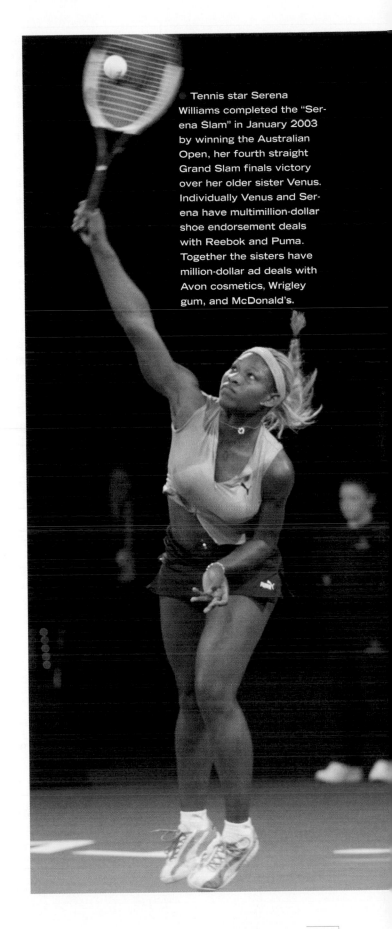

Tennis star Serena Williams completed the "Serena Slam" in January 2003 by winning the Australian Open, her fourth straight Grand Slam finals victory over her older sister Venus. Individually Venus and Serena have multimillion-dollar shoe endorsement deals with Reebok and Puma. Together the sisters have million-dollar ad deals with Avon cosmetics, Wrigley gum, and McDonald's.

"You can tell the ideals of a nation by its advertisements." –Norman Douglas, *South Wind*, 1917

Given the public's increasing sophistication regarding visual culture, companies have to work hard to get our attention. The ad industry's annual CLIO awards recognize the best TV commercials as forms of contemporary art. But consumers have found a variety of ways to dodge ads they dislike: remote controls, mute buttons, VCRs, and digital television recorders. Advertisers try to counter the new technology with computer tricks and technological wizardry of their own. To ensure that we pay attention, advertisers also spend enormous sums to associate their products with celebrities. For example, by his mid-twenties Tiger Woods had become the leading sports spokesperson, providing endorsements for a growing list of companies, including Nike, American Express, Electronic Arts video games, Golf Digest, All Star Café, Rolex, Wheaties, CBS SportsLine, ABC, ESPN, Warner Books, TLC Laser Eye Centers, Buick, and Asahi Beverages in Japan. Now the most recognizable sports figure on the planet, Woods amassed $54 million in 2001, more than the $45 million that basketball star Michael Jordan made in his best year of endorsements.

The cultural and social impact of advertising has been extensive. By the early 1900s, advertising had helped transform American society from agrarian, small-town customs to urban, consumer-driven lifestyles. The same kind of social transformations occurred with the fall of the communist governments in Europe in the 1980s and 1990s. When Poland became free of Soviet influence in the late 1980s, TV ads and billboards proliferated—announcing Poland's leap into a market-driven economy. For generations, advertisers have informed society about "new and improved" products, both satisfying consumers' desires and creating needs we never knew we had. Advertising, finally, has taught us to imagine ourselves as consumers before thinking of ourselves as citizens.

Without consumer advertisements, mass-communication industries would cease to function in their present forms. Advertising is the economic glue that holds most media industries together. Yet despite advertising's importance to the economy, many of us remain skeptical about its impact on American life. In this chapter, we will examine the historical development and role of advertising—an industry that helped transform a number of nations into consumer societies. We will look at the first U.S. ad agencies, early advertisements, and the emergence of packaging, trademarks, and brand-name recognition. Then we will consider the growth of advertising in the last century, scrutinizing the increasing influence of ad agencies and the shift to a more visually oriented culture. In keeping with our goal of developing critical skills, we will outline the key persuasive techniques used in consumer advertising. In addition, we will investigate ads as a form of commercial speech and

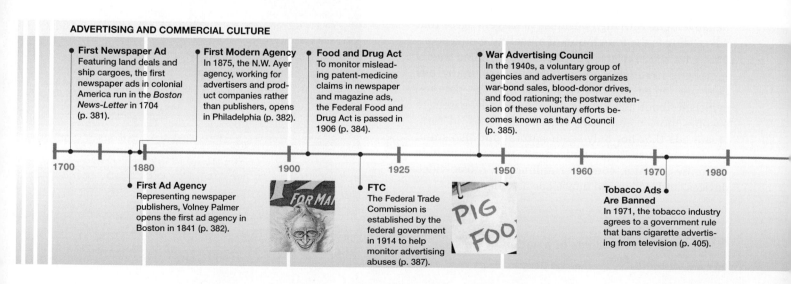

ADVERTISING AND COMMERCIAL CULTURE

First Newspaper Ad Featuring land deals and ship cargoes, the first newspaper ads in colonial America run in the *Boston News-Letter* in 1704 (p. 381).

First Modern Agency In 1875, the N.W. Ayer agency, working for advertisers and product companies rather than publishers, opens in Philadelphia (p. 382).

Food and Drug Act To monitor misleading patent-medicine claims in newspaper and magazine ads, the Federal Food and Drug Act is passed in 1906 (p. 384).

War Advertising Council In the 1940s, a voluntary group of agencies and advertisers organizes war-bond sales, blood-donor drives, and food rationing; the postwar extension of these voluntary efforts becomes known as the Ad Council (p. 385).

1700   1880   1900   1925   1950   1960   1970   1980

First Ad Agency Representing newspaper publishers, Volney Palmer opens the first ad agency in Boston in 1841 (p. 382).

FTC The Federal Trade Commission is established by the federal government in 1914 to help monitor advertising abuses (p. 387).

Tobacco Ads Are Banned In 1971, the tobacco industry agrees to a government rule that bans cigarette advertising from television (p. 405).

discuss the measures aimed at regulating advertising. Finally, we will look at political advertising and its impact on democracy.

Early Developments in American Advertising

Advertising has existed since 3000 B.C., when shop owners in ancient Babylon first began hanging outdoor signs carved in stone and wood so that customers could spot their stores. Merchants in early Egyptian society hired town criers to walk through the streets, announcing the arrival of ships and listing the goods on board. When archaeologists were searching for Pompeii, the ancient Italian city destroyed when Mount Vesuvius erupted in A.D. 79, they turned up advertising messages painted on walls. By the year 900, many European cities featured town criers who not only called out the news of the day but directed customers to various stores.

The earliest media ads were in the form of handbills, posters, and broadsides (long newsprint-quality posters). English booksellers printed brochures and bills announcing new publications as early as the 1470s, when posters advertising religious books were tacked on church doors. In 1622, print ads imitating the oral style of criers began appearing in the first English newspapers. Announcing land deals and ship cargoes, the first newspaper ads in colonial America ran in the *Boston News-Letter* in 1704.

To distinguish themselves from the commercialism of newspapers, early magazines refused to carry advertisements. By the mid-1800s, though, most magazines contained ads and most publishers started magazines hoping to earn advertising dollars. About 80 percent of early advertisements covered three subjects: land sales, transportation announcements (stagecoach and ship schedules), and "runaways" (ads placed by farm and plantation owners whose slaves had fled).[1]

The First Advertising Agencies

Until the 1830s, little need existed for elaborate advertising. Prior to the full impact of manufacturing plants and the Industrial Revolution, few goods and products were even available for sale. Demand was also low because 90 percent of Americans lived in isolated areas and produced most of their own tools, clothes, and food. The

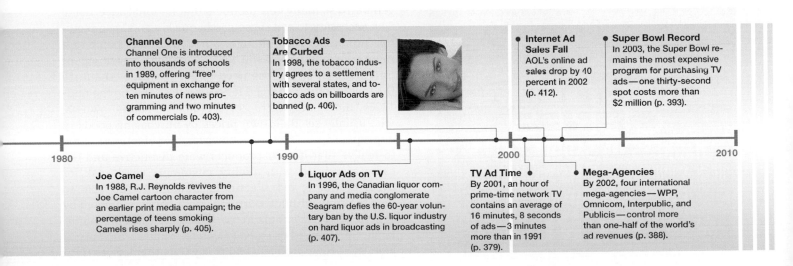

Channel One Channel One is introduced into thousands of schools in 1989, offering "free" equipment in exchange for ten minutes of news programming and two minutes of commercials (p. 403).

Tobacco Ads Are Curbed In 1998, the tobacco industry agrees to a settlement with several states, and tobacco ads on billboards are banned (p. 406).

Internet Ad Sales Fall AOL's online ad sales drop by 40 percent in 2002 (p. 412).

Super Bowl Record In 2003, the Super Bowl remains the most expensive program for purchasing TV ads—one thirty-second spot costs more than $2 million (p. 393).

1980   1990   2000   2010

Joe Camel In 1988, R.J. Reynolds revives the Joe Camel cartoon character from an earlier print media campaign; the percentage of teens smoking Camels rises sharply (p. 405).

Liquor Ads on TV In 1996, the Canadian liquor company and media conglomerate Seagram defies the 60-year voluntary ban by the U.S. liquor industry on hard liquor ads in broadcasting (p. 407).

TV Ad Time By 2001, an hour of prime-time network TV contains an average of 16 minutes, 8 seconds of ads—3 minutes more than in 1991 (p. 379).

Mega-Agencies By 2002, four international mega-agencies—WPP, Omnicom, Interpublic, and Publicis—control more than one-half of the world's ad revenues (p. 388).

minimal advertising that did exist usually featured local merchants selling goods and services in their own communities. National advertising, which initially focused on patent medicines, didn't start in earnest until the 1850s. At that point, railroads first linked towns from the East Coast to the Mississippi River and began carrying newspapers, handbills, and broadsides—as well as national consumer goods—across the country.

The first American advertising agencies were really newspaper **space brokers**, that is, individuals who purchased space in newspapers and sold it to various merchants. Newspapers, accustomed to a 25 percent nonpayment rate from advertisers, welcomed the space brokers, who paid up front. In return, brokers usually received discounts of 15 to 30 percent and would sell the space to advertisers at the going rate. In 1841, Volney Palmer opened the first ad agency in Boston; he had been retained by newspaper publishers to sell space to advertisers for a 25 percent commission.

Advertising in the 1800s

The first so-called modern ad agency, N. W. Ayer, worked primarily for advertisers and product companies rather than for publishers. Opening in 1875 in Philadelphia, the agency helped create, write, produce, and place ads in selected newspapers and magazines. To this day, under a payment structure that began in the nineteenth century, the agency collects a fee from its advertising client for each ad placed; the fee covers the price that each media outlet charges for placement of the ad. Typically, the agency then keeps 15 percent of this fee for itself and passes on the rest to the appropriate mass media. For example, if a local TV station charges $1,000 for a 30-second commercial, the ad agency tacks on 15 percent; it then charges the client $1,150, passes on $1,000 to the station, and pockets $150 for its services. The more ads an agency places, the larger the agency's revenue. Thus agencies have little incentive to buy fewer ads on behalf of their clients. Since the beginning of space brokerage in the 1840s, few have seriously challenged this odd relationship, which drives up costs, adds clutter to the media landscape, and does not always represent the best interests of the client.

Trademarks and Packaging

Some historians contend that the Industrial Revolution generated so many new products that national advertising was necessary to sell these goods quickly and keep factories humming. Now, though, other historians point to a more fundamental reason for advertising's development on a national scale: "the need to get control of the price the manufacturer charged for his goods."[2] During the mid-1800s, most manufacturers served retail-store owners, who usually set their own prices by purchasing goods in large quantities. Over time, however, manufacturers came to realize that if their products were distinctive and became associated with quality, customers would ask for them by name; manufacturers would then be able to dictate prices without worrying about being undersold by generic products or bulk items. To achieve this end, manufacturers began to use advertising to establish the special identity of their products and to separate themselves from

● Unregulated patent medicines, such as the one represented in this 1880 ad for Pratts Healing Ointment, created a bonanza for nineteenth-century print media in search of advertising revenue. After several muckraking magazine reports about deceptive patent medicine claims, Congress created the Federal Drug Administration in 1906.

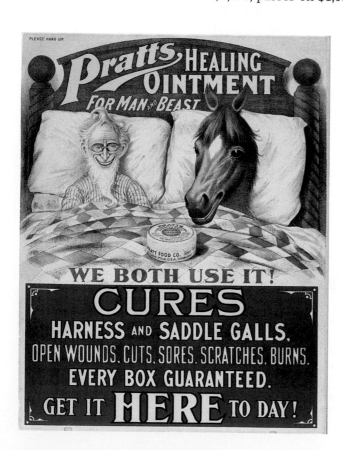

competitors. Like many ads today, nineteenth-century advertisements for patent medicines and cereals often created the impression of significant differences among products when in fact very few differences actually existed. But when consumers began demanding certain products—either because of quality or because of advertising—manufacturers seized control of pricing. With ads creating and maintaining brand-name recognition, retail stores had to stock the desired brands.

One of the first brand names, Smith Brothers, has been advertising cough drops since the early 1850s. Quaker Oats, the first cereal company to register a trademark, has used the image of William Penn, a Quaker who founded Pennsylvania in 1681, to project a company image of honesty, decency, and hard work since 1877. Other early and enduring brands include Campbell Soup, which came along in 1869, Levi Strauss overalls in 1873, Ivory Soap in 1879, and Eastman Kodak film in 1888. Many of these companies packaged their products in small quantities, thereby distinguishing them from the generic products sold in large barrels and bins.

Packaging also enabled manufacturers to add preservatives and to claim less contamination and more freshness than might be found in loose food barrels at the local general store. For example, Quaker Oats developed the folding carton, which could be printed with color displays and recipes before it was filled with cereal. This marketing strategy represented "the beginning of the end of selling cereal to retailers in bulk."[3] Product differentiation associated with brand-name packaged goods represents the single biggest triumph of advertising. Studies suggest that although most ads are not very effective in the short run, over time they create demand by leading consumers to associate particular brands with quality.

Not surprisingly, building or sustaining brand-name recognition is the focus of many product-marketing campaigns. But the costs that packaging and advertising add to products generate many consumer complaints. The high price of many contemporary products results from advertising costs. For example, designer jeans that cost $40 or $50 (or more) today are made from the same inexpensive denim that has outfitted farmworkers since the 1800s. The difference now is that more than 90 percent of the jeans' costs go toward advertising and profit.

Patent Medicines and Department Stores

By the end of the 1800s, patent medicines and department stores dominated advertising copy, accounting for half of the revenues taken in by ad agencies. During this period, one-sixth of all print ads came from patent-medicine and drug companies. Such ads ensured the financial survival of numerous magazines, as "the role of the publisher changed from being a seller of a product to consumers to being a gatherer of consumers for the advertisers."[4] Bearing names like Lydia Pinkham's Vegetable Compound, Dr. Lin's Chinese Blood Pills, and William Radam's Microbe Killer, patent medicines were often made with water and 15 to 40 percent concentrations of ethyl alcohol. One patent medicine—Mrs. Winslow's Soothing Syrup—actually contained morphine. The alcohol and other powerful drugs in these medicines went a long way toward explaining why people felt "better" after taking them; at the same time, they triggered lifelong addiction problems for many customers.

Table 11.1 The Top Ten National Advertisers

Rank	Advertiser	Headquarters	2001 Advertising Expenditures (in $ billions)	% Change from 2000
1	General Motors	Detroit, MI	3.37	−14.5
2	Procter & Gamble	Cincinnati, OH	2.54	−2.8
3	Ford Motor	Dearborn, MI	2.41	+2.7
4	PepsiCo	Purchase, NY	2.21	+4.5
5	Pfizer	New York	2.19	−3.0
6	DaimlerChrysler	Stuttgart, Germany/ Auburn Hills, MI	1.98	−8.2
7	AOL Time Warner	New York	1.86	+6.2
8	Philip Morris	New York	1.82	−7.7
9	Walt Disney	Burbank, CA	1.76	−3.4
10	Johnson & Johnson	New Brunswick, NJ	1.62	+1.0

Source: *Advertsing Age,* Ad Age Datacenter, "100 Leading National Advertisers," <www.adage.com/datacenter.cms>, November 17, 2002.

Many contemporary products, in fact, originated as medicines. Coca-Cola, for instance, was initially sold as a medicinal tonic and even contained traces of cocaine until 1903, when that drug was replaced by caffeine. Early Post and Kellogg's cereal ads promised to cure stomach and digestive problems. Many patent medicines made outrageous claims about what they could cure, leading ultimately to increased public cynicism. As a result, advertisers began to police their ranks and develop industry codes to restore customer confidence. Partly to monitor patent-medicine claims, the Federal Food and Drug Act was passed in 1906.

Along with patent medicines, department-store ads were also becoming prominent in newspapers and magazines. By the early 1890s, more than 20 percent of ad space was devoted to department stores and the product lines they carried. At the time, these stores were frequently reviled for undermining small shops and businesses, which depended on shopkeepers to direct people to store items. The more impersonal department stores allowed shoppers to browse and find brand-name goods themselves. Because these stores purchased merchandise in large quantities, they could generally sell the same products for less. With increased volume and less money spent on individualized service, department-store chains, like Kmart and Wal-Mart today, undercut small local stores and put more of their profits into ads.

With the advent of the Industrial Revolution, "continuous-process machinery" kept company factories operating at peak efficiency, helping to produce an abundance of inexpensive packaged consumer goods.[5] The companies that produced those goods were some of the first to advertise, and they remain major advertisers today (although many of these brand names have been absorbed by larger conglomerates). They include Procter & Gamble, Colgate-Palmolive, Heinz, Borden, Pillsbury, Eastman Kodak, Carnation, and American Tobacco (see Table 11.1). A few firms, such as Hershey's Chocolate, chose not to advertise initially yet still rose to national prominence through word-of-mouth reputations. By the 1880s, however, the demand for newspaper advertising by product companies and retail stores had significantly changed the ratio of copy at most newspapers. Whereas in the mid-1880s papers featured 70 to 75 percent news and editorial material and only 25 to 30 percent advertisements, by the early 1900s more than half the space in daily papers was devoted to advertising. This trend continues today, with more than 60 percent of the space in large daily newspapers consumed by ads.

Promoting Social Change and Dictating Values

As U.S. advertising became more pervasive, it contributed to major social changes in the twentieth century. First, it significantly influenced the transition from a producer-directed to a consumer-driven society. By stimulating demand for new products, advertising helped manufacturers create new markets and recover product start-up costs quickly. From farms to cities, advertising spread the word—first in newspapers and magazines and later on radio and television. Second, advertising promoted technological advances by showing how new machines, such as vacuum cleaners, washing machines, and cars, could improve daily life. Third, advertising encouraged economic growth by increasing sales. To meet the demand generated by ads, manufacturers produced greater quantities, which reduced their costs per unit, although they did not always pass these savings along to consumers.

By the early 1900s, advertisers and ad agencies believed that women, who constituted 70 to 80 percent of newspaper and magazine readers, controlled most household purchasing decisions. (This is still a fundamental principle of advertising today.) Ironically, more than 99 percent of the copywriters and ad executives at that time were men, primarily from Chicago and New York. They emphasized stereotyped appeals to women, believing that simple ads with emotional and even irrational content worked best. Thus early ad copy featured personal tales of "heroic" cleaning products and household appliances. The intention was to help consumers feel good about defeating life's problems—an advertising strategy that endured throughout much of the twentieth century.

Although ad revenues fell during the 1930s, World War II marked a rejuvenation for advertising. For the first time, the federal government bought large quantities of advertising space to promote U.S. involvement in a war. These purchases helped offset a decline in traditional advertising, as many industries had turned their attention and production facilities to the war effort. Also during the 1940s, the industry began to actively deflect criticism that advertising created consumer needs that ordinary citizens never knew they had. To promote a more positive image, the industry developed the War Advertising Council—a voluntary group of agencies and advertisers that organized war-bond sales, blood-donor drives, and the rationing of scarce goods.

The postwar extension of advertising's voluntary efforts became known as the Ad Council, praised over the years for its Smokey the Bear campaign ("Only you can prevent forest fires"), its fund-raising campaign for the United Negro College Fund ("A mind is a terrible thing to waste"), and its "crash dummy" spots for the Department of Transportation, which

● During World War II, the federal government engaged the advertising industry to create messages to support the U.S. war effort. Advertisers promoted the sale of war bonds, conservation of natural resources such as tin and gasoline, and even saving kitchen waste so it could be fed to farm animals.

substantially increased seat-belt use. Choosing a dozen worthy causes annually, the Ad Council continues to produce pro bono *public-service announcements* (PSAs) on a wide range of topics, including literacy, homelessness, drug addiction, antismoking, and AIDS education.

After the Great Depression and World War II, the advent of television dramatically altered advertising. With this new visual medium, ads increasingly intruded on daily life. Criticism of advertising grew as the industry appeared to be dictating American values as well as driving the economy. Critics discovered that some agencies used **subliminal advertising**. This term, coined in the 1950s, refers to hidden or disguised print and visual messages that allegedly register on the subconscious and fool people into buying products. Only a few examples of subliminal ads actually exist (for example, a "Drink Coca-Cola" ad embedded in a few frames of a movie, or hidden sexual activity drawn into liquor ads), and research has suggested that such ads are no more effective than regular ads.

Early Ad Regulation

During the early 1900s, the emerging clout of ad agencies and revelations of fraudulent advertising practices led to the formation of several watchdog organizations. Partly to keep tabs on deceptive advertising, advocates in the business community in 1913 created the nonprofit Better Business Bureau, which by the 1990s had more than two hundred branch offices in the United States, Canada, and Israel. At the same time, advertisers wanted a formal service that tracked newspaper readership, guaranteed accurate audience measures, and ensured that papers would not overcharge agencies and their clients. As a result, publishers formed the Audit Bureau of Circulation (ABC) in 1914. That same year, the government created the Federal Trade Commission (FTC), in part to help monitor advertising abuses. Thereafter, the industry urged self-regulatory measures in order to keep government interference at bay. The American Association of Advertising Agencies (AAAA), for example, established in 1917, tried to minimize government oversight by urging ad agencies to refrain from making misleading product claims.

The Shape of U.S. Advertising Today

Most of the history of modern advertising has been influenced by the print media and the facility of copywriters, who create the words in advertisements. Until the 1960s, the shape and pitch of most U.S. ads were determined by a **slogan**, the phrase that attempts to sell a product by capturing its essence in words. With slogans such as Clairol's "Does she or doesn't she?" and "Only her hairdresser knows for sure," the visual dimension of ads was merely a complement. Eventually, however, through the influence of movies, television, and European design, images asserted themselves and visual style began to dictate printed substance in U.S. advertising as megaagencies dominated and boutique agencies emerged.

The Influence of Visual Design

Just as a postmodern design phase developed in art and architecture during the 1960s and 1970s, an era of stunning image fragments began to affect advertising at the same time. Part of this visual revolution was imported from non-U.S. schools of design; indeed, ad-rich magazines such as *Vogue* and *Vanity Fair* increasingly hired European designers as art directors. These directors tended to be less tied to U.S.

● Most advertising companies devote some of their time to creating public-service announcements or working with nonprofit organizations such as the World Wildlife Fund. This ad encourages readers to learn more about the WWF and to support threatened animals such as the polar bear.

word-driven radio advertising, because most European countries had government-sponsored radio systems with no ads.

By the early 1970s, agencies had developed teams of writers and artists: Images and words were granted equal status in the creative process. By the mid-1980s, the visual techniques of MTV, which initially modeled its videos on advertising, influenced many ads and most agencies. MTV promoted a particular visual aesthetic — rapid edits, creative camera angles, compressed narratives, and staged performances. Video-style ads soon saturated television and featured such prominent performers as Paula Abdul, Ray Charles, Michael Jackson, and Elton John. The popularity of MTV's visual style also started a trend in the 1980s to license hit songs for commercial tie-ins. Warner Music, for example, aggressively pitched its music catalogue for use by advertisers. By 2002, a wide range of short, polished musical performances and familiar songs — including the work of Sting (for Jaguar cars), Fatboy Slim (for Mercedes-Benz), 'NSYNC (for McDonald's), Backstreet Boys (for Burger King), and Britney Spears and Shakira (for Pepsi) — were routinely used in TV ads to encourage consumers not to click the remote control.

The Mega-Agency

Although more than thirteen thousand ad agencies currently operate in the United States, advertising revenue worldwide is dominated by **mega-agencies**, large ad firms that are formed by merging several individual agencies that maintain worldwide regional offices. In addition to providing both advertising and public relations services, these agencies usually operate their own in-house radio and TV production studios. By 2002, four mega-agencies controlled more than one-half of the world's ad revenues.[6] The largest mega-agency is the London-based WPP Group, which had its beginnings as a British company named Wire & Plastic Products. WPP grew quickly in the 1980s with the 1987 purchase of J. Walter Thompson, the largest U.S. firm at the time, and Hill and Knowlton, one of the largest U.S. public relations agencies, and the 1989 acquisition of Ogilvy & Mather Worldwide, another significant U.S. agency. In 2000, WPP Group acquired another U.S. Top 5 agency, Young & Rubicam. By 2002, WPP had grown to include more than 65,000 employees with offices in more than ninety countries. WPP Group's top competitors are two New York–based mega-firms — the Omnicom Group and the Interpublic Group, also huge international holding companies, each with dozens of advertising and marketing firms operating around the globe and each with more than 50,000 employees. The fourth mega-agency, the Paris-based Publicis Groupe, in 2002 acquired the number seven ranked U.S.-based Bcom3 Group (which includes both the Leo Burnett and the D'Arcy Masius Benton & Bowles agencies). Publicis, which also owns the top British agency, Saatchi & Saatchi, employed more than 38,000 people worldwide in 2002 (see Table 11.2).

The mega-agency trend has stirred debate among consumer and media watchdog groups. Some consider large agencies a threat to the independence of smaller firms, which are slowly being bought out. An additional concern is that four firms now control more than half the distribution of advertising dollars globally. As a re-

Table 11.2 The World's Largest Advertising Agencies, 2002

Rank	Company	Headquarters	2001 Income (in $ billions)
1	WPP Group (includes J. Walter Thompson, Ogilvy & Mather, Young & Rubicam)	London	$8.17
2	Interpublic Group (includes McCann-Erickson, Campbell-Ewald)	New York	7.81
3	Omnicom Group (includes BBDO, DDB, TBWA Worldwide)	New York	7.40
4	Publicis Groupe SA (includes Leo Burnett, D'Arcy Masius Benton & Bowles, Saatchi & Saatchi)	Paris	4.77
5	Dentsu (includes DCA)	Tokyo	2.80
6	Havas Advertising	Paris	2.73
7	Grey Global Group	New York	1.86
8	Cordiant Communications Group	London	1.17

Source: Advertising Age, Ad Age Datacenter, "World's Top 100 Advertising Organizations," <http://adage.com/datacenter.cms>, November 17, 2002.

sult, the cultural values represented by U.S. and European ads may undermine or overwhelm the values and products of developing countries.

The Boutique Agency

The visual revolutions in advertising during the 1960s elevated the standing of designers and graphic artists, who became closely identified with the look of particular ads. Breaking away from bigger agencies, many of these creative individuals formed small **boutique agencies** to devote their talents to a handful of select clients. Offering more personal services, the boutiques prospered, bolstered by innovative ad campaigns and increasing profits from TV accounts. By the 1980s, large agencies had bought up many of the boutiques. Nevertheless, they continued to operate as fairly independent subsidiaries within multinational corporate structures.

One boutique agency in Portland, Oregon, Weiden & Kennedy, made its name by winning the Nike sneaker account in the 1980s and developing the slogan "Just do it." Like other boutique agencies at the time, the firm experimented with merging television imagery and popular music to appeal to the baby-boom generation. Weiden & Kennedy gained notoriety in 1987 with a Nike ad driven by the beat of the 1968 Beatles protest song "Revolution." The agency has since signed long-term contracts with Coke, Miller Brewing Company, and ESPN. One of Weiden & Kennedy's recent successes is its series of "Nike Freestyle" commercials, which feature unknown street athletes skillfully dribbling basketballs to a hip-hop beat. Shot in a stark studio setting, the 2½-minute music video version attained cult status after several airings on MTV in 2001.[7]

The Structure of Ad Agencies

The nation's agencies, regardless of their size, generally divide the labor of creating and maintaining advertising campaigns among four departments: market research, creative development, media selection, and account services. A separate administrative unit, besides handling employee salaries, pays each media outlet that runs ads and collects an agency's fees. As previously mentioned, agencies typically take a 10 to 15 percent commission on total ad costs and send the remaining 85 to 90 percent on to the media outlet for payment. Expenses incurred for producing the ads are part of a separate negotiation between the agency and the advertiser. As a result of this commission arrangement, it generally costs most large-volume advertisers no more to use an agency than it does to use their own staff.

Market Research and VALS

Before an agency can pay bills or collect commissions, a great deal of planning and research takes place. Because computer technology now enables companies to gather intimate data about consumers, the **market research** department plays a significant role in any agency. This department assesses the behaviors and attitudes of consumers toward particular products long before any ads are created. It may study everything from possible names for a new product to the size of the copy for a print ad. Research is conducted not only on toothpastes and cereals but on books, television comedies, and Hollywood action films. In trying to predict customers' buying habits, researchers also test new ideas and products on groups of consumers to get feedback before developing final ad strategies. In addition, some researchers contract with outside polling firms, which are better equipped to conduct regional and national studies of consumer preferences.

As the economic stakes in advertising have grown, agencies have employed scientific methods to study consumer behavior. In 1932, Young & Rubicam first used statistical techniques developed by pollster George Gallup. By the 1980s, most large agencies retained psychologists and anthropologists to advise them on human nature and buying habits. The earliest type of market research, **demographics**, mainly studied and documented audience members' age, gender, occupation, ethnicity, education, and income. Early demographic analyses provided advertisers with data on people's behavior and social status but revealed less about feelings and attitudes. Today, demographic data are much more specific. They make it possible for not only advertisers but Internet heavyweights like Amazon.com and phone giants like AT&T to locate consumers in particular geographic regions—usually by zip code. This enables advertisers and product companies to target ethnic neighborhoods or affluent suburbs for direct mail, point-of-purchase store displays, or specialized magazines and newspaper inserts.

By the 1960s and 1970s, television had greatly increased advertising revenues, allowing agencies to expand their research activities. Advertisers and agencies began using **psychographics**, a research approach that attempts to categorize consumers according to their attitudes, beliefs, interests, and motivations. Psychographic analysis often relies on **focus groups**, a small-group interview technique in which a moderator leads a discussion about a product or an issue, usually with six to twelve people. Because focus groups are small and less scientific than most demographic research, the findings from such groups may be suspect.

In 1978, the Stanford Research Institute (SRI), now called SRI Consulting Business Intelligence, instituted its **Values and Lifestyles (VALS)** strategy, which divides consumers into types. Using questionnaires, VALS researchers parceled the public

> **❝** The best advertising artist of all time was Raphael. He had the best client — the papacy; the best art director — the College of Cardinals; and the best product — salvation. And we never disparage Raphael for working for a client or selling an idea. **❞**
> —Mark Fenske, Creative director, N. W. Ayer, 1996

into clusters and measured psychological factors, including how consumers think and feel about products. VALS classified people according to three broad categories: *inner-directed, outer-directed,* and *need-driven.* Each of these groups also had several subclassifications, such as *achievers, experiencers, societally conscious, belongers,* and *survivors.* Many advertisers adopted VALS to help focus their sales pitch, trying to get the most appropriate target audience for their dollars. VALS research assumed that not every product suited every consumer, encouraging advertisers to vary their sales slants to find their specific market niches.

In the late 1980s, VALS 2 was launched; it not only classified people by values and lifestyles but also considered the ways consumers achieve (or do not achieve) the lifestyles to which they aspire (see Figure 11.1). VALS 2 distinguished *principle-oriented, status-oriented,* and *action-oriented* consumer types. The principle-oriented group, for instance, includes *fulfilleds*—"mature, satisfied, comfortable, reflective people who value order, knowledge, and responsibility." These consumers apparently like products that are functional, fairly priced, and durable. Also in this group, *believers* have "modest but sufficient" income and education; they are generally considered "conservative, conventional people with concrete beliefs based on traditional, established codes." VALS and similar research techniques ultimately provide advertisers with microscopic details about which consumers are most likely to buy which products.

Agencies and clients—particularly auto manufacturers—have relied heavily on VALS to determine the best placement for TV and magazine ads. VALS data suggest, for example, that *achievers* and *experiencers* watch more sports and news programs; these groups prefer luxury cars or sport-utility vehicles like the Jeep Grand Cherokee and the Ford Explorer. *Fulfilleds,* on the other hand, favor TV dramas and documentaries. In cars, they like the functionality of minivans or the gas efficiency of Hondas. VALS researchers do not claim that most people fit neatly into a category. But many agencies believe that VALS research can give them an edge in markets where few differences in quality may actually exist among top-selling brands, whether they are headache medicines or designer jeans. Consumer groups, wary of such research, argue that too many ads promote only an image and provide little information about a product's price, its content, or the work conditions under which it was produced.

Creative Development

The creative aspects of the advertising business—teams of writers and artists—make up its nerve center. Many of these individuals regard ads as a commercial art form. For print ads, the creative department outlines the rough sketches for newspaper, magazine, and direct-mail advertisements, developing the words and graphics. For radio, the creative side prepares a working script, generating ideas for everything from choosing the narrator's voice to determining background sound effects. For television, the creative department develops a **storyboard**, a sort of blueprint or roughly drawn comic-strip version of the potential ad.

Just as tension has always existed between network executives and the creative people who develop TV programs, advertising has its own version of this battle. Often the creative side of the business (the copywriters who create jingles and the graphic artists who design the look of an ad) finds itself in conflict with the research side (the marketers who collect the consumer data to target an ad campaign). In most cases, however, both sides share the responsibility for successful or failed ad campaigns. In the 1960s, for example, both Doyle Dane Bernbach (DDB) and Ogilvy & Mather downplayed research; they championed the art of persuasion and what "felt right." Yet DDB's simple ads for Volkswagen Beetles in the 1960s were based on weeks of intensive interviews with VW workers as well as on creative instincts. The campaign was remarkably successful in establishing the first niche for a foreign-car

Figure 11.1 VALS Types and Characteristics

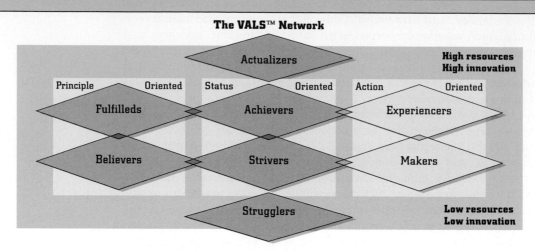

VALS™ Types and Characteristics

Actualizers Actualizers are successful, sophisticated, active, take-charge people with high self-esteem and abundant resources. They are interested in growth and seek to develop, explore, and express themselves in a variety of ways—sometimes guided by principle, and sometimes by a desire to have an effect, to make a change.

Fulfilleds Fulfilleds are mature, satisfied, comfortable, reflective people who value order, knowledge, and responsibility. Most are well-educated and in (or recently retired from) professional occupations. They are well-informed about world and national events, and are alert to opportunities to broaden their knowledge. Content with their career, families, and station in life, their leisure activities tend to center around the home.

Achievers Achievers are successful career- and work-oriented people who like to—and generally do—feel in control of their lives. They value consensus, predictability, and stability over risk, intimacy, and self-discovery. They are deeply committed to work and family. Work provides them with a sense of duty, material rewards, and prestige. Their social lives reflect this focus and are structured around family, church, and career.

Experiencers Experiencers are young, vital, enthusiastic, impulsive, and rebellious. They seek variety and excitement, savoring the new, the offbeat, and the risky. Still in the process of formulating life values and patterns of behavior, they quickly become enthusiastic about new possibilities but are equally quick to cool. At this stage in their lives, they are politically uncommitted, uninformed, and highly ambivalent about what they believe.

Believers Believers are conservative, conventional people with concrete beliefs based on traditional, established codes: family, church, community, and the nation. Many Believers express moral codes that are deeply rooted and literally interpreted. They follow established routines, organized in large part around home, family, and social or religious organizations to which they belong.

Strivers Strivers seek motivation, self-definition, and approval from the world around them. They strive to find a secure place in life. Unsure of themselves and low on economic, social, and psychological resources, Strivers are concerned about the opinions and approval of others.

Makers Makers are practical people who have constructive skills and value self-sufficiency. They live within a traditional context of family, practical work, and physical recreation and have little interest in what lies outside that context. Makers experience the world by working on it—building a house, raising children, fixing a car, or canning vegetables—and have enough skill, income, and energy to carry out their projects successfully.

Strugglers Strugglers have constricted lives, with limited economic, social, and emotional resources. Because their resources are so limited, Strugglers show no evidence of a strong self-orientation but are focused mostly on meeting the needs of the present moment. Strugglers are cautious consumers. They represent a very modest market for most products and services but are loyal to favorite brands.

Source: SRI Consulting Business Intelligence, 2001, <http://future.sri.com/vals/vals.segs.shtml>.

The Lemon ad text (small print within image):

Lemon.

This Volkswagen missed the boat.

The chrome strip on the glove compartment is blemished and must be replaced. Chances are you wouldn't have noticed it; Inspector Kurt Kroner did.

There are 3,389 men at our Wolfsburg factory with only one job: to inspect Volkswagens at each stage of production. 3000 Volkswagens are produced daily; there are more inspectors than cars.)

Every shock absorber is tested (spot checking won't do), every windshield is scanned. VWs have been rejected for surface scratches barely visible to the eye.

Final inspection is really something! VW inspectors run each car off the line onto the Funktionsprufstand (car test stand), tote up 189 check points, gun ahead to the automatic brake stand, and say "no" to one VW out of fifty.

This preoccupation with detail means the VW lasts longer and requires less maintenance, by and large, than other cars. (It also means a used VW depreciates less than any other car.)

We pluck the lemons; you get the plums.

● The New York ad agency Doyle Dane Bernbach created a famous series of print and television ads for Volkswagen beginning in 1959, and helped to usher in an era of creative advertising that combined a single-point sales emphasis with bold design, humor, and honesty. Arnold Communications, a Boston agency, continued the highly creative approach with its clever, award-winning "Drivers Wanted" campaign for the New Beetle.

manufacturer in the United States. Although sales of the VW "bug" had been growing before the ad campaign started, the successful ads helped Volkswagen preempt the Detroit auto industry's entry into the small-car field.

The cost of advertising, especially on network television, increases each year. The Super Bowl remains the most expensive program for purchasing television advertising, with thirty seconds of time costing more than $2 million in 2003. But just creating television commercials in general is expensive; the average cost for producing a thirty-second national television spot was $343,000 in 1999, nearly twice as much as the $180,000 production costs ten years earlier.[8] Running a thirty-second ad during a national prime-time TV show can cost from $100,000 to more than $500,000, depending on the popularity and ratings of the program. Moreover, even with their greater emphasis on market research, both the creative and research sides of the business acknowledge that they cannot predict with any certainty which ads and which campaigns will succeed. They say ads work best by slowly creating brand-name identities—by associating certain products over time with quality and reliability in the minds of consumers. Some economists, however, believe that much of the money spent on advertising is ultimately wasted because it simply encourages consumers to change from one brand name to another. Such switching may lead to increased profits for a particular manufacturer, but it has little positive impact on the overall economy.

Media Selection and Buying Ads

Another integral department in an ad agency, media selection, is staffed by **media buyers**: people who choose and purchase the types of media that are best suited to carry a client's ads and reach the targeted audience. For instance, a company like Procter & Gamble, one of the world's leading advertisers, displays its more than three hundred major brands—most of them household products like Crest toothpaste and Huggies diapers—on TV shows viewed primarily by women. To reach male viewers, however, media buyers encourage beer advertisers to spend their ad budgets on cable and network sports programming, evening talk radio, or sports magazines. Buyers pay particular attention to the relative strengths and weaknesses of print and electronic forms of advertising. For example, ad campaigns aimed at supermarket shoppers effectively use newspapers, direct mail, and magazine inserts, all of which encourage the tradition of coupon clipping; local news programs, which do not have many teenage viewers, might not be a good buy for a client selling rap music or snack food.

Along with the typical 10 to 15 percent commission, advertisers often add incentive clauses to their contracts with agencies, raising the fee if sales goals are met and lowering it if goals are missed. With incentive clauses, it is in the agencies' best interests to conduct repetitive **saturation advertising**, in which a variety of media are inundated with ads aimed at target audiences. The initial Miller Lite beer campaign ("Tastes great, less filling"), which used humor and retired athletes to reach its male audience, became one of the most successful saturation campaigns in media history. It ran from 1973 to 1991 and included television and radio spots, magazine and newspaper ads, and billboards and point-of-purchase store displays. The excessive repetition of the campaign helped light beer overcome a potential image problem, that of being viewed as watered-down beer unworthy of "real" men.

Account and Client Management

Ad agencies also include a department composed of client liaisons, or **account executives**: individuals responsible for bringing in new business and managing the accounts of established clients. Generally, this department oversees new ad campaigns in which several agencies bid for the business of a client. Account managers coordinate the presentation of a proposed campaign and various aspects of the bidding process, such as what a series of ads will cost a client. Account executives function as liaisons between the advertiser and the creative team that produces an ad. Because most major companies maintain their own ad departments to handle everyday details, account executives also coordinate activities between their agency and a client's in-house personnel.

The advertising business tends to be volatile, and account departments are especially vulnerable to upheavals. For instance, when True North Communications (acquired by Interpublic in 2001) lost its portion of the $2.4 billion DaimlerChrysler account in 2000 to BBDO's Worldwide (owned by Omnicom), it had to lay off the three

> **"** Ads seem to work on the very advanced principle that a very small pellet or pattern in a noisy, redundant barrage of repetition will gradually assert itself. **"**
>
> –Marshall McLuhan, *Understanding Media*, 1964

hundred staffers who worked on the account. Clients routinely conduct **account reviews**, the process of evaluating and reinvigorating a product's image by reviewing an existing ad agency's campaign or by inviting several new agencies to submit new campaign strategies, which may result in the product company switching agencies.[9] One industry study conducted in the mid-1980s indicated that client accounts stayed with the same agency on average for about seven years, but since the late 1980s clients have changed agencies much more often. There are a few exceptions, however; Campbell-Ewald (also owned by Interpublic) has held GM's Chevrolet account since 1922—more than eighty years—and Chicago's Leo Burnett agency (now owned by Publicis) has managed the Green Giant (now a subsidiary of Pillsbury) account since 1935, when it was one of Burnett's original clients. In addition to the Jolly Green Giant, Leo Burnett also created the Pillsbury Doughboy, the Marlboro Man, the Keebler Elves, and Kellogg's Tony the Tiger.

Persuasive Techniques in Contemporary Advertising

Ad agencies and product companies often argue that the main purpose of advertising is to inform consumers about available products in a straightforward way. In fact, many types of advertisements, like classified ads in newspapers, are devoted primarily to delivering price information. Most consumer ads, however, merely create a mood or tell stories about products without revealing much about prices. Because national advertisers generally choose to buy a one-page magazine ad or a thirty-second TV spot to deliver their pitch, consumers get little information about how a product was made or how it compares with similar brands. In managing space and time constraints, advertising agencies engage in a variety of persuasive techniques. We will look briefly at some specific techniques and then focus on the association principle, a key technique employed by advertisers trying to persuade consumers.

Conventional Persuasive Strategies

One of the most frequently used advertising approaches is the **famous-person testimonial**, whereby a product is endorsed by a well-known person, such as comedian Jerry Seinfeld touting the American Express credit card or singer Britney Spears starring in Pepsi commercials. Another technique, the **plain-folks pitch**, associates a product with simplicity. Over the years, Volkswagen ("Drivers wanted"), General Electric ("We bring good things to life"), and Microsoft ("Where do you want to go today?") have each used slogans that stress how new technologies fit into the lives of ordinary people. By contrast, the **snob-appeal approach** attempts to persuade consumers that using a product will maintain or elevate their social status. Advertisers selling jewelry, perfume, clothing, and luxury automobiles often use snob appeal. For example, upscale ads for Lexus sedans in 2002 promoted its "ultra luxury selection" package with phrases like "a tranquil sea of supple leather upholstery," "true luxury . . . can be found in an automobile" and "the passionate pursuit of perfection."

Another approach, the **bandwagon effect**, points out in exaggerated claims that *everyone* is using a particular product. Brands that refer to themselves as "America's favorite" or "the best" imply that consumers will be left out—or that they are not hip—if they ignore these products. A different technique, the **hidden-fear appeal**, plays on consumers' sense of insecurity. Deodorant, mouthwash, and dandruff-shampoo ads frequently invoke anxiety, pointing out that only a specific product could relieve embarrassing personal hygiene problems and restore a person to normalcy.

A final ad strategy, used more in local TV and radio campaigns than in national ones, has been labeled **irritation advertising**: creating product-name recognition by being annoying or obnoxious. Although both research and common sense suggest that irritating ads do not work very well, there have been exceptions. In the 1950s and 1960s, for instance, an aspirin company ran a TV ad showing a hammer pounding inside a person's brain. Critics and the product's own agency suggested that people bought the product, which sold well, to get relief from the ad as well as from their headaches. For years, Charmin tissue used the annoying Mr. Whipple, a fussy store clerk who commanded customers, "Please don't squeeze the Charmin." One study found that people hated the ad but bought the product anyway. The new millennium brought us the annoying Carrot Top, the orange-haired comedian in the AT&T 1-800 commercials. On the regional level, irritation ads are often used by appliance discount stores or local car dealers, who dress in outrageous costumes and yell at the camera.

The Association Principle

Historically, American car advertisements have displayed automobiles in natural settings — on winding back roads that cut through rugged mountain passes or across shimmering wheat fields. These ads rarely contain images of cars on congested city

● **Table 11.3 Estimated Advertising Revenue Lost during Four Days Following a Major National Event:**

1941 (Pearl Harbor), 1963 (John F. Kennedy assassination), 2001 (New York/Pentagon terrorist attacks)

($ millions)	1941	1963	2001
Total advertising revenue for the year	$1,869.0	$10,424.0	*$174,985.0
(Adjusted for inflation to 2001 $)	$22,568.0	$60,459.0	
Average advertising revenue over four-day period	$20.7	$115.5	$1,917.6
(Adjusted for inflation to 2001 $)	$250.0	$670.0	
Actual advertising revenue lost over four days following major event	$9.3	$75.5	$779.6
(Adjusted for inflation to 2001 $)	$112.4	$437.9	
Percentage of total advertising revenue lost during four days following major event	45%	65%	41%

*Projected total advertising revenue for year 2001.

Note: Actual average advertising revenue lost in 2001 equals more than 40 percent of all the advertising done in 1941. Percentage of total advertising revenue lost in 2001 is lower than those of 1941 and 1963 due to new media outlets that continued normal day-to-day operations and advertising practices.

Sources: Leo Kivijarv, Ph.D., Veronis Suhler Stevenson: Veronis Suhler Communications Industry Forecast, 2001; McCann-Erikson.

streets or in other urban settings where most driving actually occurs. Instead, the car—an example of advanced technology—merges seamlessly into the natural world.

This type of advertising exemplifies the **association principle**, a persuasive technique used in most consumer ads. Employing this principle, an ad associates a product with some cultural value or image that has a positive connotation but may have little connection to the actual product. For example, many ads displayed visual symbols of American patriotism in the wake of the September 11, 2001, terrorist attacks in an attempt to associate products and companies with national pride. In trying "to convince us that there's an innate relationship between a brand name and an attitude,"[10] agencies and advertisers may associate products with nationalism, happy families, success at school or work, natural scenery, or humor.

Of course, association can have a negative effect. Because of its omnipresence in the mass media, advertising can be immediately affected by economic and social factors, especially in times of national tragedy (see Table 11.3). The terrorist attacks of Septemeber 11, 2001, resulted in the suspension of advertising for several days on the major television networks and in many publications. Even after advertising resumed, many ad campaigns had to be revised to fit the more somber national mood.

Over the years, one of the more controversial uses of the association principle has been the linkage of products to stereotyped caricatures of women. In numerous instances, women have been portrayed either as sex objects or as clueless housewives who, during many a daytime TV commercial, needed the powerful offscreen voice of a male narrator to instruct them in their own kitchens (see "Case Study — Idiots and Objects: Stereotyping in Advertising" on page 398).

Another strong association used in advertising is nature. For years, Philip Morris's Marlboro brand used the association principle to link its cigarettes to nature and completely transform the product's initial image. In the 1920s, Marlboro began as a fashionable woman's cigarette. Back then, the company's ads equated smoking with emancipation and a sense of freedom, attempting to appeal to women who had just won the right to vote. Marlboro, though, did poorly as a women's product, and new campaigns in the 1950s and 1960s transformed the brand into a man's cigarette. In these campaigns, powerful images of active, rugged men dominated the ads. Often, Marlboro associated its product with the image of a lone cowboy roping a calf, building a fence, or riding over a snow-covered landscape. Ironically, over the years two of the Marlboro Man models died of lung cancer associated with smoking. Still, in 2002 the international branding consultancy, Interbrand (owned by Omnicom), called Marlboro the world's ninth "most valuable brand name," having an estimated worth of $24 billion (Coca-Cola and Microsoft were the top two rated brands in 2002, worth $69 and $64 billion, respectively).[11]

As a response to corporate merger mania and public skepticism toward large impersonal companies, a *disassociation corollary* has emerged as a recent trend in advertising. The nation's largest winery, Gallo, pioneered the idea in the 1980s by establishing a dummy corporation, Bartles & Jaymes, to sell jug wine and wine coolers, thereby avoiding the Gallo corporate image in ads and on its bottles. The ads featured Frank and Ed, two low-key, grandfatherly types, as "co-owners" and ad spokesmen. On the one hand, the simulated entrepreneurship in the ad was "a way to connect with younger consumers who yearn for products that are handmade, quirky, and authentic."[12] On the other hand, this technique, by concealing the Gallo tie-in, also allowed the wine giant to *disassociate* from the negative publicity of the 1970s—a period when labor leader Cesar Chavez organized migrant workers in a long boycott of Gallo after the company signed a contract with the Teamsters, which eventually won a workers' election that Chavez and his union—the United Farm Workers—opposed.

CASE STUDY

Idiots and Objects: Stereotyping in Advertising

Over the years, critics and consumers alike have complained about stereotyping in mainstream advertising. *Stereotyping* refers to the process of assigning people to abstract groups, whose members are assumed to act as a single entity—rather than as individuals with distinct identities—and to display shared characteristics, which often have negative connotations. Today, particularly in beer ads, men are often stereotyped as inept or stupid, incapable of negotiating a routine day or a normal conversation unless fortified—or dulled—by the heroic product. Throughout advertising history, men have often been portrayed as doofuses and idiots when

Hmmm.
10 A.M.
So much for being
a morning person.

M A R T E X
THE BARE NECESSITIES

Our Soft & Cozy sheets are 100% cotton and pre-washed for extra softness.
And don't you just hate morning people, anyway.

More? 1-800-458-3000

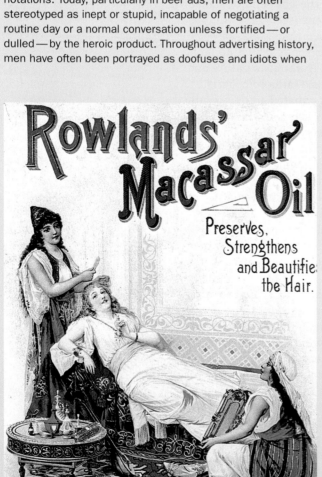

Rowlands'
Macassar Oil

Preserves,
Strengthens
and Beautifies
the Hair.

A. ROWLAN

confronted by ordinary food items or a simple household appliance.

On the other hand, in the early history of product ads on television, women were often stereotyped as naïve or emotional, needing the experienced voice of a rational male narrator to guide them around their own homes. Ads have also stereotyped women as brainless or helpless or offered them as a man's reward for drinking a particular beer, wearing cool jeans, or smoking the right cigarette. Worst of all, women, or even parts of women—with their heads cut from the frame—have been used as objects, merely associated with a particular product (e.g., a swimsuit model holding a new muffler or wrapped around a bottle of Scotch). Influenced by the women's movement and critiques of advertising culture, such as Betty Friedan's *The Feminine Mystique* (1963), ads depicting women have changed. Although many sexist stereotypes still persist in advertising, women today are more often portrayed in a variety of social roles.

In addition to ads that have stereotyped men and women, there is also *invisible stereotyping.* This occurs when whole segments of the population are ignored—particularly African, Arab, Asian, Latin, and Native Americans. Advertising—especially in its early history—has often faced criticism that many segments of the varied and multicultural U.S. population have been underrepresented in the ads and images that dominate the landscape. In the last several years, however, conscious of how diverse the United States has become, many companies have been doing a much better job of representing that diversity in their product ads.

In the 1990s, the disassociation strategy was also used by Miller Brewing Company's Red Dog beer, sold under the quaint Plank Road Brewery logo, and by R. J. Reynolds's Moonlight Tobacco Company, which began selling local brand cigarettes such as City and North Star. In addition, General Motors, reeling from a declining corporate reputation, "disassociate[d] itself from its innovative offspring, the Saturn," and tried to package the Saturn as "a small-town enterprise, run by folks not terribly unlike Frank and Ed" who provide caring, personal service.[13] As an advertising strategy, disassociation links new brands in a product line to eccentric or simple regional places rather than to the image conjured up by giant conglomerates.

In our increasingly technology-dependent environment, shaped by corporate giants, many consumers have come to value products that claim associations with "the real" and "the natural"—possibly the two most familiar adjectives associated with advertising. For example, Coke sells itself as "the real thing," and the cosmetics industry offers synthetic products that make us look "natural." The twin adjectives—*real* and *natural*—saturate American ads yet almost always describe processed or synthetic goods. Most advertisers do not expect consumers to accept without question the stories they tell or the associations they make in their ads; they do not "make the mistake of asking for belief."[14] Instead, ads are most effective when they create attitudes and reinforce values. They operate then like popular fiction, encouraging us to suspend our disbelief. Although most of us realize that ads create a fictional world, we can get caught up in their thirty-second stories and reassuring associations. Unfortunately, however, most consumer advertisements do not provide much useful information about products. Instead, they try to reassure us that through the use of familiar brand names and positive associations, everyday anxieties and problems can be managed (see "Applied Critical Process: Myth Analysis," on page 400).

Commercial Speech and Regulating Advertising

In 1791, Congress passed the First Amendment to the U.S. Constitution, promising, among other guarantees, to "make no law . . . abridging the freedom of speech, or of the press." Over time, we have developed a shorthand label for the First Amendment, misnaming it the free-speech clause. The amendment ensures that citizens and reporters can generally say and write what they want, but it says nothing directly about speech that is not free. What, then, about **commercial speech**—any print or broadcast expression for which a fee is charged to organizations and individuals buying time or space in the mass media? Whereas freedom of speech refers to the right to express thoughts, beliefs, and opinions in the abstract marketplace of ideas, commercial speech supports the right to circulate goods, services, and images in the concrete marketplace of products. Although most people can buy some commercial speech inexpensively, such as a classified newspaper ad, only very wealthy citizens (like Ross Perot or Steve Forbes), established political parties, and multinational companies can routinely afford speech that reaches millions.

New forms of commercial speech and advertising continue to crowd the media landscape. Cable television offers several home-shopping networks, with nonstop banter about must-have goods. Late-night television is also filled with long-form spots advertising sex talk and fortune-telling to the lonely, the young, and the curious via pay telephone numbers that charge outrageous per-minute rates.

Infomercials represent another substantial growth area in cable and broadcast television. These thirty-minute, late-night and daytime programs usually feature fading TV and music celebrities who advertise a product or service in a format that

Myth Analysis

Most ads, especially on television, are packaged as narratives with stories to tell and social conflicts to resolve. As narratives, then, another way to critique ads is through **myth analysis**. The term *myth* is not used here in a pejorative sense, referring to an untrue story or outright falsehood. Rather, cultural myths help define relationships among people, organizations, and social norms; they contain the stories a society constructs to bring order to the conflicts and contradictions of everyday life.

Three common mythical elements are found in many types of ads: (1) Ads incorporate myths in mini-story form, featuring characters, settings, and plots; (2) most stories in ads involve conflicts, pitting one set of characters or social values against another; and (3) such conflicts are negotiated or resolved by the end of the ad, usually by applying or purchasing a product. In advertising, the product and those who use it often emerge as the heroes of the story.

Using myth analysis, select a visually interesting TV ad featuring either a car or a beer brand for your critique. Once again, use the four steps in the critical process:

Description. What is the plot; that is, what happens? Does the ad pose a particular problem that needs to be resolved? What is the setting (a congested city street, a mountainous back road, a fraternity party)? Who are the characters? Besides the actors used, remember that in commercials off-screen narrators and musicians can function as characters; in addi-

tion, products are often the stars of the story. Is there conflict in the story? Remember that this can work at a more abstract level—for example, nature versus technology, old versus new, tradition versus change, male versus female, and so on.

Analysis. What are the key patterns that emerge in your ad? Is nature used in a particular way? How is technology viewed in the ad? Are men or women in the ad stereotyped in particular ways? Is the car or beer personified at all; that is, are human characteristics attributed to the product? Does the ad produce anxiety or fear about anything? What seems to be the central tension or conflict in the story of your ad?

Interpretation. What does the ad mean at a mythic level; that is, how is the major conflict(s) resolved? For example, if a car ad pits nature against technology, is this tension resolved by having the car (a symbol of technology) blend seamlessly into nature, or is nature overcome in the ad by the sheer power of the car? If a beer ad suggests some kind of reward for using the product, how does the reward manifest itself?

Evaluation. Does the ad work or not? Does it promote particular values? What are they? Does the ad say something about the way men or women are? If so, is this good or bad? Make a judgment about the ad based on the best evidence you have found.

looks like a laid-back talk show. Even on regular talk shows, guests generally appear when they have a book to sell or a movie to promote. Paid a fee by the program to boost ratings, such guests use their celebrity status and allotted time as a commercial forum to promote themselves and a cultural product they are selling.

Although the mass media have often not hesitated to carry product- and service-selling advertisements in publications and have embraced the concept of program-length infomercials and even 24-hour cable shopping channels, they have also refused certain issue-based advertising that might upset their traditional advertisers. For example, although corporations have easy access in placing paid ads, many labor unions have had their print and broadcast ads rejected as "controversial." The nonprofit Adbusters Media Foundation, based in Vancouver, Canada, has also had difficulty getting networks to air its "uncommercials." One of its spots promotes the Friday after Thanksgiving (traditionally, the beginning of the holiday buying season) as "Buy Nothing Day."

YOU'RE RUNNING
BECAUSE YOU WANT THAT RAISE,
TO BE ALL YOU CAN BE.
BUT IT'S NOT EASY
WHEN YOU
WORK
SIXTY HOURS A WEEK
MAKING SNEAKERS IN AN
INDONESIAN FACTORY
AND YOUR FRIENDS
DISAPPEAR
WHEN THEY
ASK FOR A RAISE.
SO THINK
GLOBALLY BEFORE YOU DECIDE
IT'S SO COOL
TO WEAR

NIKE

● The Adbusters Media Foundation, a nonprofit organization based in Canada, says its spoof ads, like the one shown here, are designed to "put out a better product and beat the corporations at their own game." Besides satirizing the advertising appeals of the fashion, tobacco, alcohol, and food industries, the Adbusters Media Foundation sponsors Buy Nothing Day, an anticonsumption campaign that annually falls on the day after Thanksgiving—the busiest shopping day of the year.

Critical Issues in Advertising

In his 1957 book *The Hidden Persuaders,* Vance Packard expressed concern that advertising was manipulating helpless consumers, attacking our dignity, and invading "the privacy of our minds."[15] According to this view, the advertising industry was considered to be all-powerful. Although consumers have historically been regarded as dupes by many critics, research reveals that the consumer mind is not as easy to predict as some advertisers once thought. In the 1950s, for example, Ford could not successfully sell its midsize car, the Edsel, which was aimed at newly prosperous Ford customers looking to move up to the latest in push-button window wipers and antennas. After a splashy and expensive ad campaign, Ford sold only 63,000 Edsels in 1958 and just 2,000 in 1960, when the model was discontinued. Similarly, in the 1960s, the Scott paper company predicted that its disposable clothing line would challenge traditional apparel, but despite heavy advertising, throwaway apparel never caught on.

More recently, one of the most disastrous campaigns ever featured the now famous "This is not your father's Oldsmobile" spots that began running in 1989 and starred celebrities like former Beatle drummer Ringo Starr and his daughter. Established in 1897 and the nation's oldest carmaker, Oldsmobile (which became part of General Motors in 1903) and its agency, Leo Burnett, decided to market to a younger generation after sales declined from a high of 1.1 million vehicles in 1985 to only 715,000 in 1988. But the campaign backfired, apparently alienating its older loyal customers (who may have felt abandoned by Olds and its catchy new slogan) and failing to lure younger buyers (who probably still had trouble getting past the name "Olds"). In 2000, Oldsmobile sold only 260,000 cars, and that same year GM decided to phase out its Olds division by 2004–05.[16]

As these examples illustrate, most people are not easily persuaded by advertising. Over the years, studies have suggested that between 75 and 90 percent of new consumer products typically fail because they are not embraced by the buying public.[17] But despite public resistance to many new products and the cynical eye we cast on advertising, the ad industry has made contributions, including raising the American standard of living and financing most media industries. Yet serious concerns over the impact of advertising remain. Watchdog groups worry about the expansion of advertising's reach, and critics continue to condemn ads that associate products with sex appeal, youth, and narrow definitions of beauty. Some of the most serious concerns involve children, teens, and health.

Children and Advertising

Children and teenagers, living in a culture dominated by TV ads, are often viewed as "consumer trainees." For years, groups such as Action for Children's Television (ACT) worked to limit advertising aimed at children. In the 1980s, ACT fought particularly hard to curb program-length commercials: thirty-minute cartoon programs (such as *G.I. Joe, My Little Pony and Friends, The Care Bear Family,* and *He-Man and the Masters of the Universe*) developed for television syndication primarily to promote a line of toys. This commercial tradition continues today with programs such as *Pokémon* and *The Powerpuff Girls.*

In addition, parent groups have worried about the heavy promotion of products like sugar-coated cereals during children's programs. Pointing to European countries, where children's advertising is banned, these groups have pushed to limit advertising directed at children. Congress, faced with the protection that the First Amendment offers commercial speech, has responded weakly. The Children's Television Act of 1990 mandated that networks provide some educational and informational children's programming, but the act has been difficult to enforce and did little to restrict advertising aimed at kids. Because children and teenagers influence up to $500 billion a year in family spending—on everything from snacks to cars— they are increasingly targeted by advertisers.[18] A recent Stanford University study, however, found that a single thirty-second TV ad can influence the brand choices of children as young as age two. In addition, very young children cannot distinguish between a commercial and the TV program that the ad interrupts. Still, methods for marketing junk food to children have become increasingly seductive. For example, producers of the 2001 blockbuster movie *Spider-Man* licensed the popular superhero's image for use on Froot Loops cereal boxes and inside Eggo waffles in the form of Day-Glo stickers.[19]

Advertising in Schools

Among the most controversial developments in recent years was the introduction of Channel One into thousands of schools during the 1989–90 school year. The brainchild of Whittle Communications, Channel One offered "free" video and satellite equipment (tuned exclusively to Channel One) in exchange for a twelve-minute package of current events programming that included two minutes of commercials. If school districts decided to curtail or limit the program, Whittle could reclaim its "free" equipment. In 1994, Channel One was acquired by K-III Communications, which is now known as PRIMEDIA (also publisher of *Weekly Reader, Seventeen,* and *Soap Opera Digest*). By 2002, Channel One, available in more than twelve thousand of the nation's junior high and high schools and reaching a captive audience of eight million students, grossed more than $800,000 each school day.

Over the years, the National Dairy Council and other organizations have also used schools to promote products, providing free filmstrips, posters, magazines, folders, and study guides adorned with corporate logos. Teachers, especially in underfunded districts, have usually been grateful for the support. Channel One, however, has been viewed as a more intrusive threat, violating the implicit cultural border between an entertainment situation (watching commercial television) and a learning situation (going to school). One study showed that schools with a high concentration of low-income students were more than twice as likely as affluent schools to receive Channel One.[20] Some individual school districts have banned Channel One, as have the states of New York and California. These school systems have argued that Channel One provides students with only slight additional knowledge about current affairs; but students find the products advertised—sneakers, cereal, and soda, among others—more worthy of purchase because they are advertised in educational environments.[21] A similar commercial in-school news program, the Youth News Network (YNN), was launched in Canada in the late 1990s, generating a great deal of controversy.

A 1998 settlement between the tobacco industry and the government now bans cigarette ads from billboards. (Cigarette ads on TV have been banned since the early 1970s.) The contemporary ad pictured here replaces the popular Joe Camel campaign, since the 1998 agreement also prohibits tobacco companies from using cartoon characters to appeal to young smokers. The tobacco industry also agreed in 1998 to pay state governments $256 billion dollars to help with health costs long associated with smoking and lung cancer.

Health and Advertising

Advertising has a powerful impact on the standards of youthful beauty in our culture. A long-standing trend in advertising is the association of certain products with ultra-thin female models, promoting a style of "attractiveness" that girls and women are invited to emulate. Even with the popularity today of resistance training and more shapely bodies, most fashion models remain much thinner than the norm. Some forms of fashion and cosmetics advertising actually pander to individuals' insecurities and low self-esteem. Such advertising suggests standards of style and behavior that may be not only unattainable but also harmful, leading to eating disorders such as anorexia and bulimia. In fact, some female models became so skinny that critics began referring to the style of their ads as "heroin chic" because the models looked like victims of prolonged drug use. To their credit, many ad agencies refused to do this type of advertising, which was then usually produced by the fashion industry's own in-house staff. Throughout history, however, many companies have capitalized on consumers' unhappiness and insecurity by promising relief or the kind of body that is currently fashionable.

Along with criticism of promoting skeleton-like beauty, probably the most sustained criticism of advertising is its promotion of alcohol and tobacco consumption. Opponents of such advertising have become more vocal in the face of grim statistics. Each year, on average 400,000 Americans die from diseases related to nicotine addiction and poisoning; 100,000 die from alcohol-related diseases; and another 15,000 to 18,000 die in car crashes involving drunk drivers.

Tobacco ads disappeared from television in 1971, under pressure from Congress and the FCC, and the hard-liquor industry voluntarily banned TV and radio ads for many decades. Still, staggering amounts of money are spent each year to encourage these habits. According to the Federal Trade Commission (FTC), by 1998, the year that the tobacco industry agreed to an enormous settlement with state attorneys general in the United States, tobacco companies spent a record $6.73 billion on advertising—even though no money went to television.

Over the years, numerous ad campaigns have appealed to teenage consumers of cigarettes. In 1988, for example, R. J. Reynolds, a subdivision of RJR Nabisco, revived its Joe Camel cartoon character from an earlier campaign, outfitting him with hipper clothes and sunglasses. Spending $75 million annually, the company put the new Joe on billboards and store posters and in sports stadiums and magazines. One study revealed that before 1988 fewer than 1 percent of teens under age eighteen smoked Camels. After the ad blitz, however, 33 percent of this age group preferred Camels. In response, the ad industry's trade journal, *Advertising Age,* raised some serious questions. For example, shouldn't cigarette advertisers' profit interests be balanced against their "unique social responsibility" in light of the health risks of smoking?

● These billboards along Sunset Boulevard in Los Angeles are symbolic of the pervasiveness of advertising. From towering billboards to people's T-shirts, sales pitches and product messages constantly bombard us. Leo Burnett's successful Marlboro Man images, which associate the cigarette with stoic masculinity and rugged individualism, are considered part of the most successful ad campaign in history. Since this photograph was taken, billboard advertising for cigarettes has been made illegal.

UNITED COLORS OF BENETTON.

● From 1983 to 2000, former fashion photographer Oliviero Toscani developed one of the most talked-about ad campaigns of the late twentieth century, as creative director for clothing manufacturer Benetton. Toscani's "United Colors of Benetton" poster-style images featured few words and no Benetton clothing. Instead, the ads carried frank, often controversial socio-political images such as a white infant nursing at a black woman's breast, a nun kissing a priest, Jewish and Arab boys embracing, dying AIDS patients, and U.S. death row prisoners.

In addition to young smokers, the tobacco industry has targeted other groups. In the 1960s, for instance, the advertising campaigns for Eve and Virginia Slims cigarettes (reminiscent of ads during the suffrage movement in the early 1900s) associated their products with women's liberation, equality, and slim fashion models. And in 1989, Reynolds introduced a cigarette called Uptown, targeting African American consumers. The ad campaign fizzled, however, due to public protests by black leaders and government officials. When these leaders pointed to the high concentration of cigarette billboards in poor urban areas and the high mortality rates among black male smokers, the tobacco company withdrew the brand from the market.

The government's position regarding the tobacco industry began to change in the mid-1990s, when new reports revealed that some tobacco companies had known that nicotine was addictive as early as the 1950s and had withheld that information from the public. In 1998, after four states won settlements against the tobacco industry and the remaining states threatened to bring more expensive lawsuits against the companies, the tobacco industry agreed to an unprecedented settlement that carried significant limits on advertising and marketing tobacco products. The agreement's provisions included banning cartoon characters in advertising, thus ending the use of the Joe Camel character; prohibiting the industry from targeting youths in ads and marketing, including free samples, tobacco-brand clothing, and other merchandise; and ending outdoor billboard and transit advertising. The agreement also banned tobacco-company sponsorship of concerts and athletic events, and it strictly limited other corporate sponsorships by tobacco companies.

Antismoking advocates charged that tobacco companies still targeted youths even after the 1998 agreement. Under pressure, Philip Morris, the largest tobacco corporation, agreed in 2000 to withdraw its ads from about forty magazines—including *Rolling Stone* and *Sports Illustrated*—with a 15 percent readership younger than age eighteen. By 2002, other tobacco companies, including R. J. Reynolds, were still placing their ads in general audience magazines with young readers.

Many of the same complaints regarding tobacco advertising are also being directed at alcohol ads. For example, one of the most popular beer ad campaigns of the late 1990s, featuring the trio of Budweiser frogs (which croak Bud-weis-errrr) and two envious lizards, has been accused of using cartoonish animal characters to appeal to young viewers. In fact, the Budweiser ads would be banned under the standards of the tobacco settlement, which prohibits the attribution of human characteristics to animals, plants, or other objects.

Alcohol ads have also targeted minority populations. Malt liquors, which contain higher concentrations of alcohol than beers do, have been touted in high-profile television ads for such labels as Colt 45, PowerMaster, and Magnum. Featuring actors such as Billy Dee Williams, these ads have usually been shown during programs that appeal to a high percentage of black viewers.

College students, too, have been heavily targeted by alcohol ads, particularly by the beer industry. Although colleges and universities have outlawed "beer bashes" hosted and supplied directly by major brewers, both Coors and Miller, a unit of Philip Morris, still employ student representatives to help "create brand awareness." These students notify brewers of special events that might be sponsored by and linked to a specific beer label. The images and slogans in alcohol ads often associate the products with power, romance, sexual prowess, or athletic skill. In reality, though, alcohol is a chemical depressant; it diminishes athletic ability and sexual performance, triggers addiction in roughly 10 percent of the U.S. population, and is a factor in many spousal-abuse cases.

Watching over Advertisers

In 1996, Seagram, a Canadian liquor company and media conglomerate, defied the sixty-year voluntary ban by the American liquor industry on hard liquor advertising in broadcasting. (Such ads had been banned from radio since 1936 and from television since 1948.) Faced with declining sales, the company argued that wine and beer, which have long been advertised on television and radio, had an unfair market advantage over the hard liquor industry. To promote its Crown Royal Canadian whiskey, Seagram (which sold Crown Royal to Diageo in 2000) began testing regional TV ads in Texas. Executives at Seagram called the old ban "obsolete." They pointed to other countries that featured liquor ads on television and noted the escalating World Wide Web sites devoted to marketing liquor. In 1996, following Seagram's lead, the Distilled Spirits Council of the United States, the liquor industry's trade association, voted to lift its voluntary ban on broadcast ads. In late 2001, NBC became the first TV network to accept liquor advertising when it ran ads from Smirnoff vodka on *Saturday Night Live*. In early 2002, though, NBC, under pressure from politicians and health advocates, reinstated the voluntary network ban. But then in fall 2002, Scotland's Diageo Group, the world's largest liquor company (whose brands include Smirnoff, Guinness, Johnnie Walker, and J&B), resumed talks with the major networks even as their ads were already appearing locally on more than three hundred regional broadcast stations and cable outlets nationwide.[22]

Advertisers and agencies have generally had their commercial-speech rights protected by the First Amendment. But the Seagram and NBC moves touched off renewed activity at both state and federal levels to pass legislation restricting alcohol advertising. In addition to legislation aimed at controversial products, oversight agencies—such as the Better Business Bureau, the National Fraud Information Center, and the FTC—have long monitored deceptive and false ads. During the Reagan administration in the 1980s, however, the FTC underwent sizable staff cuts, going from more than seventeen hundred employees to fewer than nine hundred. With these reductions and a relatively small budget, the FTC has become a less effective watchdog agency over the past twenty years.

THE GLOBAL VILLAGE

Smoking Up the Global Market

By 2000, the status of tobacco companies and their advertising in the United States had hit a low point. A $206 billion settlement between tobacco companies and state attorneys general ended tobacco advertising on billboards and severely limited the ways in which cigarette companies can promote their products in the United States. Advertising bans and antismoking public-service announcements contributed to a growing disfavor about tobacco in America, with smoking rates dropping from a high of 42.5 percent of the population in 1965 to 25 percent more than thirty years later.

As Western cultural attitudes have turned against tobacco, the large tobacco multinationals have shifted their global marketing focus, targeting Asia in particular. So while smoking has declined by 13 percent in developed countries over the last decade, it has increased by 20 percent in China, which now boasts an estimated 350 million smokers.[1] Underfunded government health programs and populations that generally admire American and European cultural products make Asian nations ill-equipped to deal with cigarette marketing efforts. For example, even though Vietnam strengthened its ban on print, broadcast, and billboard ads in 1994, nearly three-fourths of Vietnamese men smoke, the highest smoking rate for men in the world. In China, 63 percent of males over age eighteen now smoke; in Malaysia, 30 percent of boys between the ages of twelve and eighteen

408

now smoke; and across Asia in general, 40,000 to 50,000 teens a day light up for the first time.

Advertising bans have actually forced tobacco companies to find alternative and, as it turns out, better ways to promote smoking. Philip Morris, the largest private tobacco company, and its global rival, British American Tobacco (BAT), practice "brand stretching," linking their logos to race-car events, soccer leagues, youth festivals, disco parties, rock concerts, TV shows, and popular cafés. The higher price for Western cigarettes in Asia has the effect of increasing their prestige, and it makes packs of Marlboros symbols of middle-class aspirations.

The unmistakable silhouette of the Marlboro Man is ubiquitous throughout developing countries, and particularly in Asia. In Hanoi, Vietnam, almost every corner boasts a street vendor with a trolley cart, the bottom half of which carries the Marlboro logo or one of the other premium foreign brands. Vietnam's Ho Chi Minh City has two thousand such trolleys. Children in Malaysia are especially keen

on Marlboro clothing, which, along with watches, binoculars, radios, knives, and backpacks, they can win by collecting a certain number of empty Marlboro packages. (It is now illegal to sell tobacco-brand clothing and merchandise in the United States.)

Sporting-event sponsorship has proved to be an especially successful brand-stretching technique with men, who smoke the majority of cigarettes in Asia. Philip Morris pumps close to $80 million a year into Formula One race-car sponsorship, which is now broadcast to 130 countries, and many observers argue that much of the popularity of Marlboro cigarettes in China derives from Philip Morris's sponsor-

ship of the Marlboro soccer league there. Throughout Asia, attractive young women wearing tight red Marlboro outfits cruise cities in red Marlboro minivans, frequently stopping to distribute free cigarettes, even to minors.

Some critics suggest that the same marketing strategies will make their way into America and other Western countries, but that's unlikely. Tobacco companies are mainly interested in developing regions like Asia for two reasons. First, China alone accounts for nearly a third of the world's cigarette smoking, with people there consuming 1.7 trillion cigarettes a year. Because only one in ten cigarettes now sold in China is a foreign brand, the potential market is staggering. Second, the majority of smokers in countries like China—whose government officially bans tobacco advertising—are unaware that smoking causes diseases like lung cancer. In fact, 3.5 million people—nearly 10,000 per day—now die from tobacco-related diseases. For tobacco companies like Philip Morris, ignorance is bliss.

In addition to oversight groups, professions like medicine and law have long had uneasy relationships with advertising and often try to limit ads through their professional organizations. For example, bar associations actually prohibited lawyers from advertising until 1978, when the Supreme Court ruled that lawyers have a First Amendment right to promote their services. (The Supreme Court has since outlined some limits, ruling in 1995 that states may prevent lawyers from sending direct-mail ads within thirty days of an accident for the purpose of soliciting victims or survivors as clients.) Nonetheless, although prestigious law and medical practices have traditionally shunned advertising, many firms advertise to jump-start a new business or to reinvigorate a sagging practice.

Comparative Advertising

For years it was considered taboo for one advertiser to mention a competitor by name in its ads. Industry guidelines discouraged such advertising, and TV networks prohibited it. The government and networks feared that comparative ads would degenerate into unseemly name-calling, and advertisers believed they should not give free time or space to competitors. This led to the development of so-called Brand X products, which identified a competing brand without using a real name. The FTC, however, began encouraging comparative advertising in 1971. The agency thought such ads would help consumers by providing more product information. Subsequently, various food industries started taste-test wars specifically targeting each other in their ads. Burger King took on McDonald's, and Pepsi challenged Coke. As comparative ads became the norm, Japanese and American auto manufacturers began to compare prices, gas mileage, safety records, and repair and recall rates in their ads.

In 2002, comparative advertising even led to an international legal showdown over bunnies and batteries. A court case in Australia featured Eveready batteries, famous for its Energizer bunny ads, challenging the misleading claims of Duracell batteries (owned by Gillette), which created its own cartoon bunny, who routinely outlasted Eveready's bunny in a race across the desert. Although Eveready initially won an injunction that forced Duracell to alter the ads, an appeals court reversed the injunction and told Eveready it should use its own ads to address the issue of which types of batteries lasted the longest.[23]

Puffery and Deceptive Ads

Since the days when Lydia Pinkham's Vegetable Compound promised "a sure cure for all female weakness," false and misleading claims have haunted advertising. Over the years, the FTC has played an investigative role in substantiating the claims of various advertisers. A certain amount of *puffery*—ads featuring hyperbole and exaggeration—has usually been permitted, particularly when a product says it is "new and improved." However, when a product claims to be "the best," "the greatest," or "preferred by four out of five doctors," the FTC has often asked for supportive evidence.

Typical of deceptive advertising over the years were the Campbell Soup ads that used marbles in the bottom of a soup bowl to push more bulky ingredients—and less water—to the surface. In another instance, a 1990 Volvo commercial featured a monster truck driving over a line of cars and crushing all but the Volvo; the company later admitted that the Volvo had been specially reinforced and the other cars' support columns had been weakened. A more subtle form of deception featured the Klondike Lite ice-cream bar—"the 93 percent fat-free dessert with chocolate-flavored coating." The bars were indeed 93 percent fat-free, but only after the chocolate coating was removed.[24]

In 2002, the FTC went after diet pill companies making claims such as "Lose up to eight to ten pounds per week—no dieting, no strenuous exercise" and "No exercise and eat as much as you want—the more you eat, the more you lose, we'll show you how." Such deceptive weight-loss ads besieged consumers on television, radio, the Internet, and in magazines and newspapers. Arguing that these types of unsubstantiated claims were proliferating (generating $35 billion in sales in 2000 alone), the FTC charged a Canadian corporation operating in the United States (under the name Bio Lab) with deceiving consumers through its advertisements for Quick Slim and another product. The ads for Quick Slim, a dietary supplement sold as a "fat blocker," appeared in inserts that were distributed in prestigious news outlets, including the *Phildelphia Inquirer,* the *Los Angeles Times,* and the *Washington Post,* among other major papers.[25] When the FTC discovers deceptive ads, it usually requires advertisers to change their ads or remove them from circulation. Although the FTC does not have the power to assess financial penalties, it occasionally requires an advertiser to run spots to correct the deceptive ads.

Advertising's Threat to Journalism

Much of the power advertising wields is subtle and difficult to monitor. One problem, particularly troubling for newspapers during economic recessions, occurs when reporters cover news issues that reflect poorly on a newspaper's major advertisers. Local real-estate firms or car dealers, for instance, are no longer so dependent on newspapers as their main advertising channel. Companies can now take their ad business to direct mail, cable, and the Internet if they are unhappy with negative stories in the local newspaper. With many dailies facing financial difficulties in the 1990s and the early 2000s, some editors turned their investigative eyes away from controversial business stories in order to keep advertisers happy.

In the early 1990s, a report by the nonprofit Center for the Study of Commercialism investigated fifty news stories that were allegedly "killed or downplayed by news media to appease advertisers."[26] The *Portland Oregonian,* for example, Oregon's largest daily paper, destroyed thousands of copies of a Sunday edition in 1989 after a salesperson in the advertising department complained to editors about a real-estate story. The story advised readers on how to sell a home without the help of a real-estate agent. The editor responsible for publishing the article was later demoted. In 1990, car dealers in Hartford, Connecticut, withdrew advertising from the *Hartford Courant* over an article that urged consumers to be wary of shady dealers. After the *Courant*'s publisher apologized to the dealers, they ended their boycott, but many readers in the community were upset that the paper backed down. Two years later, one dealer in suburban Hartford reported that he had seen no more negative articles about dealers: "Consumer reporting is virtually nonexistent now."

By the early 2000s, despite deceptive ad practices by auto dealers nationwide, virtually no daily newspapers were initiating investigative stories on local and regional car dealerships; more often, papers merely reported on local government investigations. For example, the state of New York in 2001 reached out-of-court settlements with nearly fifty dealers accused of deceptive ads. Some dealers were offering $2,500 to customers for trade-ins but then adding that cost to the price of a new car; other dealers put so many qualifications in fine print that customers could rarely qualify for the advertised low prices or interest rates. In the New York settlement, the dealers denied wrongdoing but agreed to pull the ads.[27]

Occasionally, newspapers stand up to their advertisers. Nordstrom, a large department-store retailer, reduced its advertising in the *Seattle Times* in the early 1990s after the paper criticized the company's labor difficulties. In this case, the newspaper did not back down. Michael Fancher, then the executive editor of the *Times,* told the *Wall Street Journal:* "You can't just sell your soul in little bits and pieces and expect that readers will understand it. A lot of newspapers don't understand that."[28] Local television news outlets are also subject to advertiser pressure. A survey by the nonprofit Project for Excellence in Journalism in 2000 found that one-third of television news directors had been pressured by advertisers or station management to do positive stories, or kill negative stories, about advertisers.[29]

Advertising and the Internet

Worldwide Internet advertising is expected to climb from $1 billion in 1998 to $28 billion by 2005. The earliest major form of Web advertising featured banner ads, the rectangular ads that load at the top of a Web page. But banner ads were losing favor by 2001, as click-through rates on the ads had fallen below 1 percent. To achieve higher click-through rates, the Interactive Advertising Bureau agreed on seven new larger "skyscraper" and "large rectangle" ad formats, which were embedded within the Web-page text much like a newspaper layout. These larger ads were accompanied by a surge in pop-up, pop-under, and flash multimedia ads—all provocative attempts to produce brand awareness and entice Web users to interact with the advertisement. Marketing analysts expect the ad-editorial mix on many Internet sites—like their newspaper counterparts—will soon settle at about the 60–40 range, although unlike their print counterparts, these ads will be blinking, moving, and demanding more attention.[30] Other forms of Internet advertising are less obvious. Search engines, for example, regularly give top billing in search-result lists to companies that pay for prominence, and Web directories subtly steer users to shopping sites.

Another form of Web advertising is through affiliate referrals on the Web. A Web site becomes an affiliate when it carries a hot button for an Internet business on its page; the affiliate then earns a commission—typically 7 to 15 percent—for any sales that it creates for the Web business. Amazon.com and CDNow, both of which actively seek affiliates on their Web sites, have more than 500,000 affiliate Web pages that carry their hot-button logos to refer customers to buy books, music, and other offerings. Other forms of Internet advertising include classified ads, unsolicited e-mail ads—known as **spam**—and **interstitials**, ads that intrusively pop up in new screen windows as the user attempts to access a new Web site.

The lure of the Internet to advertisers is its unique ability to record and track online users. Most ads are placed by Internet advertising agencies and are served to hundreds of client sites by the agencies' computers. The agencies then track ad impressions (how often the ads are seen) and click-throughs. By 2002, the leading Web ad agencies were DoubleClick, Engage, Inc., and 24/7 Media. Each of these businesses tracks millions of consumers by developing information profiles that help them to direct targeted advertisements to Web-site visitors. By 2000, DoubleClick, the top Internet advertising and marketing firm, had "already assembled profiles of the habits, tastes, and vital statistics of 100 million Americans."[31] Internet user information is gained through cookies and online surveys—for example, an ESPN.com contest required users to fill out a survey to be eligible to win sports tickets—or through sites such as Nytimes.com, which requires users to provide demographic information for free access to that newspaper's site. Online and in-store retail sales data can be added to Internet user profiles as well, creating an unprecedented database of consumer information, but one that disturbs privacy advocates.

Even with all the technical innovations spurred by the Internet, the failure of so many dot-com companies and the stock market slide in the early 2000s dramatically affected online advertising. For example, AOL Time Warner, the world's largest media company, reported that AOL's online ad sales fell 40 percent during 2002. In addition to the economic downturn, all the digital ad gimmicks of the Internet were still not enough to win over substantial numbers of new Internet consumers. In fact, at the

> 66 Web surfers are becoming increasingly immune to the shriek of banner ads, the online equivalent of freeway billboards dotting the cyber landscape. 99
>
> – Jonathan Gaw,
> *Los Angeles Times*, 1999

outset of 2003, many product companies, Web sites, and ad agencies worried about how effective Internet advertising would ultimately be and whether consumers would pay attention to the glut of online ads arranged before them.

Alternative Voices

One of the provisions of the government's multibillion-dollar settlement with the tobacco industry in 1998 established a nonprofit organization with the mission to counteract tobacco marketing and reduce youth tobacco use. That mission became a reality in 2000, when the American Legacy Foundation launched its antismoking/ anti–tobacco-industry ad campaign.

Working with a coalition of ad agencies, a group of teenage consultants, and a $300 million budget, the foundation created a stylish, gritty print and television campaign that uses teen voices and actors. The TV ads, which have appeared on NBC, MTV, UPN, WB, Fox, BET, and during the 2002 Olympics, deconstruct the images that have long been associated with cigarette ads—macho horse country, carefree beach life, sexy bar scenes, and daring skydives. Instead of glamorizing these settings, they show teens dragging, piling, or heaving body bags across the beach or onto a horse, and holding up signs that say "What if cigarette ads told the truth?" Other ads target the tobacco industry itself. Teens are shown piling body bags in front of Philip Morris's headquarters and delivering a lie detector to tobacco company market executives. The point of all these ads is clear: Addictive and deadly, tobacco use has social consequences, and the tobacco industry must be held accountable for deceptive advertising.

The TV and print ads prominently reference the Foundation's Web site, <www.thetruth.com>, which offers statistics, discussion forums, and outlets for teen creativity. For example, the site provides information on "how to market an addictive product ethically" and data on how much money the two largest cigarette-makers— Philip Morris and R. J. Reynolds Tobacco—gave to politicians between 1989 and 2002: $29 million. Text from the Web site's message boards is also incorporated into the ad campaign, such as in the following exchange:

> DD: More carcinogens come out of an automobile's tailpipe than a cigarette.

> Erin: Yeah, but car manufacturers don't run $5 billion a year in ads making it look sexy to suck on the tailpipe, okay, DD?

With its jarring messages and cross-media platform, "The Truth" antitobacco campaign is one of the most memorable collections of advocacy ads in years.

Advertising, Politics, and Democracy

Advertising as a profession came of age in the twentieth century, facilitating the transformation of U.S. society from production-oriented small-town values to consumer-oriented urban lifestyles. With manufacturers developing the products and advertisers producing the consumers, advertising became the central economic support system for our mass-media industries. Through its seemingly endless supply of pervasive and persuasive strategies, advertising today saturates the cultural landscape. Its ubiquity raises serious questions about our privacy and the ease with which companies can gather data on our consumer habits. But an even more serious issue is the influence of advertising on our lives as democratic citizens. With fewer and fewer large media conglomerates controlling advertising and commercial speech, what is the effect of this trend on free speech and political debate? In the future, how easy will it be to get heard in a marketplace where only a handful of large companies control access to that space?

As advertising has become more pervasive and consumers more discriminating, ad practitioners have searched for ways to weave their work more seamlessly into the social and cultural fabric. Products now blend in as props or even as "characters" in TV shows and movies. In addition, almost every national consumer product now has its own site on the World Wide Web, which displays advertising on computers around the globe. With today's video technology and digital graphics, producers can even generate a TV advertising image on a wall or a flat surface—as Fox did on the seating façade behind the batter's box during the 2002 World Series—when in reality no image exists.

Among the more intriguing efforts to become enmeshed in the culture are the ads that exploit, distort, or transform the political and cultural meanings of popular music. In the 1990s and through the early 2000s, for instance, a number of formerly radical or progressive rock songs made their way into TV ads, muddying the boundary between art and commerce. "Revolution" (1968) promoted Nike shoes; more recently, The Beatles' "Come Together" (1969) morphed into the commercial theme for Nextel, and "Getting Better" (1967) accompanied Philips Electronics TV ads. Buffalo Springfield's "For What It's Worth" (1967) sold Miller beer—with the commercial stopping just short of the band's Vietnam War protest lyric, "There's a man with a gun over there." David Bowie's "Heroes" (1977) and the Rolling Stones' "Start Me Up" (1981) peddled Microsoft software, and Sly and the Family Stone's "Everyday People" (1969) sold Toyota cars.

A much more straightforward form of cultural blending is **political advertising**, the use of ad techniques to promote a candidate's image and persuade the public to adopt a particular viewpoint. Since the 1950s, political consultants have been imitating market-research and advertising techniques to sell their candidates. In the early days of television, politicians running for major offices either bought or were offered half-hour blocks of time to discuss their views and the significant issues of the day. As advertising time became more valuable, however, local stations and the networks became reluctant to give away time in large chunks. Gradually, TV managers began selling thirty-second spots to political campaigns just as they sold time to product advertisers.

In the late 1980s, a research team at the University of Pennsylvania's Annenberg School of Communication began critiquing political advertisements that reduce a candidate's ideas to a thirty-second advertising pitch. The research revealed that in using powerful visual images, these ads often attack other candidates and distract viewers through misleading verbal messages. Since the early 1990s, the major networks have been using the school's techniques in a news segment called Ad Watch. After critiquing a political ad, a commentator labeled it "true," "correct but . . . ," "misleading," or "false." As a result of Ad Watch, media consultants began paying more attention to the veracity of their ads. Ad Watch pieces, however, usually ran only once, so they were viewed mainly by people who regularly watch the evening news.[32]

During the 1992 and 1996 presidential campaigns, third-party candidate Ross Perot restored the use of the half-hour time block when he ran political infomercials on cable and the networks. However, only very wealthy candidates can afford such promotional strategies because television does not usually provide free airtime to politicians. Questions about political ads continue to be asked: Can serious information on political issues be conveyed in thirty-second spots that many candidates can barely afford? Do repeated attack ads, which assault another candidate's character, so undermine citizens' confidence in the electoral process that they stop voting?[33] And how does a society ensure that alternative political voices, which are not so well financed or commercially viable, still receive a hearing in a democratic society?

Although broadcasters use the public's airwaves, they have long opposed providing free time for political campaigns and issues. Critics charge that the clear reason is because political advertising is big business for television stations. TV broadcasters earned $400 million in the 1996 election year and took in another $605 million from political ads in 2000.[34]

Although commercialism—through packaging both products and politicians—has generated cultural feedback that is often critical of advertising's pervasiveness, the growth of the industry has not diminished. Ads continue to fascinate. Many consumers buy magazines or watch the Super Bowl just for the advertisements. Adolescents decorate their rooms with their favorite ads and identify with the images certain products convey. For the year 2001, an estimated $500 billion worldwide ($250 billion of that in the United States) was spent on advertising—enough money to finance the operation of several small countries. A number of factors have made possible advertising's largely unchecked growth. Many Americans tolerate advertising as a necessary "evil" for maintaining the economy, but many others dismiss advertising as not believable and even trivial. As a result, because we are willing to downplay its centrality to global culture, many citizens do not think advertising is significant enough to monitor or reform. Such attitudes have ensured advertising's pervasiveness and suggest the need to escalate our critical vigilance.

As individuals and as a society, we have developed an uneasy relationship with advertising. Favorite ads and commercial jingles remain part of our cultural world for a lifetime. But we detest irritating and repetitive commercials, using the remote control to mute the offenders on television. We realize that without ads many mass media would need to reinvent themselves. At the same time, we should remain critical of what advertising has come to represent: the overemphasis on commercial acquisitions and cultural images, and the disparity between those who can afford new products and those who cannot.

> 66 Corporations put ads on fruit, ads all over the schools, ads on cars, ads on clothes. The only place you can't find ads is where they belong: on politicians. 99
>
> —Molly Ivins,
> syndicated columnist, 2000

www.

To create an individualized study plan for Chapter 11, go to the interactive *Media and Culture* Online Study Guide at: bedfordstmartins.com/ mediaculture

REVIEW QUESTIONS

Early Developments in American Advertising

1. Whom did the first ad agents serve?

2. How did packaging and trademarks influence advertising?

3. Explain why patent medicines and department stores figured so prominently in advertising in the late 1800s.

4. What role did advertising play in transforming America into a consumer society?

The Shape of U.S. Advertising Today

5. What influences did visual culture exert on advertising?

6. What are the differences between boutique and mega-agencies?

7. What are the major divisions at most ad agencies? What is the function of each department?

8. What causes the occasional tension between the research and creative departments at some agencies?

Persuasive Techniques in Contemporary Advertising

9. How do the common persuasive techniques used in advertising work?

10. How does the association principle work, and why is it an effective way to analyze advertising?

11. What is the disassociation corollary?

Commercial Speech and Regulating Advertising

12. What is commercial speech?

13. What are three serious contemporary issues regarding health and advertising? Why is each issue controversial?

14. What is comparative advertising?

15. What aspect of Internet advertising concerns privacy advocates?

Advertising, Politics, and Democracy

16. What are some of the major issues involving political advertising?

17. What role does advertising play in a democratic society?

QUESTIONING THE MEDIA

1. What is your earliest recollection of watching a television commercial? Do you have a favorite ad? A most-despised ad? What is it about these ads that you particularly like or dislike?

2. Why are so many people critical of advertising?

3. If you were (or are) a parent, what strategies would you use to explain an objectionable ad to your child or teenager? Use an example.

4. Should advertising aimed at children be regulated? Support your response.

5. Should tobacco (or alcohol) advertising be prohibited? Why or why not? How would you deal with First Amendment issues regarding controversial ads?

6. Would you be in favor of regular advertising on public television and radio as a means of financial support for these media? Explain your answer.

7. Is advertising at odds with the ideals of democracy? Why or why not?

SEARCHING THE INTERNET

http://www.adcouncil.org

The site of the nonprofit Ad Council, which uses the pro bono work of top ad agencies to create public-service announcements on topics such as education and preventive health care.

http://www.adbusters.org

Satire with a sharp anti-consumerist critique, including spoofs of many advertisements, is the style of the Vancouver-based Adbusters Media Foundation, publisher of *Adbusters* magazine.

http://www.adage.com

Advertising Age is the leading advertising trade journal, with a large data portfolio of agency and brand rankings.

http://www.adweek.com

The online version of *Adweek,* a top advertising, marketing, and media publication.

http://www.clioawards.com

The official site for the advertising industry's major awards competition.

http://www.sric-bi.com/VALS

The site for the online VALS questionnaire, which categorizes adult consumers on the basis of their psychological characteristics and several key demographic factors.

In Brief

As a class, consider the impact of advertising on your college campus. Are any buildings or sports facilities named after advertisers? Are any on-campus dining facilities run by fast-food franchises? Who has the soda franchise on your campus and how much do they pay? What are the dominant companies that advertise on your campus and where do they place their ads? Should college campuses be free of advertisements? Why or why not? Are there any places in society that are free of ads and corporate sponsorship?

In Depth

From a business perspective, magazine ads function to promote advertisers' goods or services over competing brands and to place these goods or services before consumers so that they can make informed buying decisions. We know, however, that ads mean more than what advertisers intend, because readers form their own opinions. We know, too, that ads function as popular culture. They operate on a symbolic level to affirm cultural values.

In a three- or four-page analysis, compare and critique three magazine ads. The ads should all feature the same type of product but should be taken from contrasting magazines (for example, three alcohol ads from women's and men's magazines, or three clothing ads from various kinds of publications).

Description. Take notes on your three choices, laying out what is going on in the ads. Briefly describe each ad. Is a narrative apparent here (setting, characters, conflict, etc.)? What different persuasive strategies seem to be at work?

Analysis. Figure out common patterns or differences that emerge among the three ads, and then develop an argument that you want to prove. For example, you may notice that one ad demonstrates more social responsibility than the others or provides better consumer information. In your critique, use the association principle to deal with the ads' cultural meanings. Your analysis should go beyond the issue of whether the ads successfully market their products.

Interpretation. Now think about these questions in regard to the ads you have chosen: What's going on? What different sets of values are being sold (e.g., ideas about patriotism, family, sex, beauty, technology, tradition)? Are the ads selling a vision (or stereotype) of what it means to be male or female? of what it means to be young, old, or middle-class? of what it means to be a member of a particular racial or ethnic group?

Evaluation. Make a judgment about which ad works best and why. Which ad is the best at treating both the product and consumer fairly and responsibly? Are any of the ads deceptive or irresponsible?

Again, your paper should have a central argument or thesis, drawing on evidence from your ads. To this end, organize your paper around an idea that is worth proving. For example, pointing out that your ads "sell their products in different ways" is not an argument. But if you state that an ad sells "the American dream as equal opportunity for all," or that it is racist or sexist, these arguments are worth proving.

KEY TERMS

space brokers, 382
subliminal advertising, 387
slogan, 387
mega-agencies, 388
boutique agencies, 389
market research, 390
demographics, 390
psychographics, 390
focus groups, 390
Values and Lifestyles (VALS), 390

storyboard, 391
media buyers, 394
saturation advertising, 394
account executives, 394
account reviews, 395
famous-person testimonial, 395
plain-folks pitch, 395
snob-appeal approach, 395
bandwagon effect, 395
hidden-fear appeal, 395

irritation advertising, 396
association principle, 397
commercial speech, 399
infomercials, 399
myth analysis, 400
spam, 412
interstitials, 412
political advertising, 414

public relations

and framing the message

CHAPTER 12

Early Developments in Public Relations

The Practice of Public Relations

Tensions between Public Relations and the Press

Public Relations, Social Responsibility, and Democracy

● The delinquent in jeans: Marlon Brando in *The Wild One* (1953).

In the mid-1950s, the blue-jeans industry was in deep trouble. After hitting a postwar peak in 1953, jeans sales began to slide. The durable one-hundred-year-old denim product had become associated with rock and roll and teenage troublemakers. Popular movies, especially *The Wild One* and *Blackboard Jungle,* featured emotionally disturbed, blue-jeans-wearing "young toughs" terrorizing adult authority figures. A Broadway play about juvenile delinquency was even entitled *Blue Denim.* The worst was yet to come, however. In 1957, the public school system in Buffalo, New York, banned the wearing of blue jeans for all high-school students. Formerly associated with farmers, factory workers, and an adult work ethic, jeans had become a reverse fashion statement for teenagers—something many adults could not abide.

In response to the crisis, the denim industry waged a public relations (PR) campaign to eradicate the delinquency label and rejuvenate denim's image. In 1956, the nation's top blue-jeans manufacturers formed the national Denim Council "to put schoolchildren back in blue jeans

through a concerted national public relations, advertising, and promotional effort."[1] First the council targeted teens, but its promotional efforts were unsuccessful. The manufacturers soon realized that the problem was not with the teens but with the parents, administrators, teachers, and school boards. It was the adults who felt threatened by a fashion trend that seemed to promote disrespect through casualness. In response, the council hired a public relations firm to turn the image of blue jeans around. Over the next five years, the firm did just that.

The public relations team determined that mothers were refusing to outfit their children in jeans because of the product's association with delinquency. To change this perception among women, the team encouraged fashion designers to update denim's image by producing new women's sportswear styles made from the fabric. Media outlets and fashion editors were soon inundated with news releases about the "new look" of durable denim.

The PR team next enlisted sportswear designers to provide new designs for both men's and women's work and utility clothes, long the backbone of denim sales. Targeting business reporters as well as fashion editors, the team transformed the redesign effort into a story that appealed to writers in both areas. They also planned retail-store promotions nationwide, including "jean queen" beauty contests, and advanced positive denim stories in men's publications.

The team's major PR coup, however, involved an association with the newly formed national Peace Corps. The brainchild of the Kennedy administration, the Peace Corps encouraged young people to serve their country by working with people from developing nations. Envisioning the Peace Corps as the flip side of delinquency, the Denim Council saw its opening. In 1961, it agreed to outfit the first group of two hundred corps volunteers in denim. As a result of all these PR efforts, by 1963 manufacturers were flooded with orders, and sales of jeans and other denim goods were way up. The delinquency tag disappeared, and jeans gradually became associated with a more casual, though not antisocial, dress ethic.

● The good citizen in jeans: former president Jimmy Carter, working with Habitat for Humanity.

he blue-jeans story illustrates a major difference between advertising and public relations: Advertising is controlled publicity that a company or an individual buys; public relations attempts to secure favorable media publicity (which is more difficult to control) to promote a company or client. In advertising, clients buy space or time for their products or services, and consumers know who paid for the messages. But with public relations the process is more subtle, requiring news media to accept the premise or legitimacy of a PR campaign and to use it as news. The transformation of denim in the public's eye was achieved primarily without the purchase of advertising. The PR team restyled denim's image mainly by cultivating friendly relations with reporters who subsequently wrote stories associating the fabric with a casual, dedicated, youthful America.

Publicity refers to one type of PR communication: messages that spread information about a person, corporation, issue, or policy in various media. Public relations today, however, involves many communication strategies besides publicity. In fact, much of what PR specialists do involves dealing with negative or unplanned publicity. For example, when documents and audiotapes surfaced in the fall of 1996 revealing that certain top executives at Texaco had made racist remarks, an intense PR campaign began. It employed a range of tactics, including paid TV advertising, major news conferences, and meetings with regional Texaco distributors. The Denny's chain of restaurants encountered similar negative publicity throughout the 1990s, particularly after six African American Secret Service agents were refused service in one of the restaurants in 1993. However, by 2002 the chain had improved its image so much that *Fortune* magazine listed it as the country's best company for minority employees two years in a row.

Because it involves multiple forms of communication, **public relations** is difficult to define precisely. It covers a wide array of actions, such as shaping the image of a politician or celebrity, repairing the image of a major corporation, establishing two-way communication between consumers and companies, and molding wartime propaganda. Broadly defined, *public relations* refers to the entire range of efforts by an individual, an agency, or any organization attempting to reach or persuade audiences.[2]

The social and cultural impact of public relations, like that of advertising, has been immense. In its infancy, PR helped convince many American businesses of the value of nurturing the public, who had been redefined as purchasers rather than as producers of their own goods. PR also set the tone for the corporate image-building that characterized the economic environment of the twentieth century and transformed the profession of journalism by complicating the way "facts" could be interpreted. Perhaps PR's most significant effect, however, has been on the political process in which individuals and organizations—on both the Right and the Left—hire *spin doctors* to shape their media images.

Without public relations, the news profession would be hard-pressed to keep up with every upcoming event or complex issue. Although reporters and editors do not like to admit it, PR departments and agencies are a major source of story ideas and information. In this chapter, we will examine the impact of public relations and the historical conditions that affected its development as a modern profession —how it helped transform America into a more image-conscious society. We will begin by looking at nineteenth-century press agents and the role that railroads and utility companies played in developing corporate PR. We will then consider the rise of modern PR, particularly the influences of former reporters Ivy Lee and

> **"** An image . . . is not simply a trademark, a design, a slogan or an easily remembered picture. It is a studiously crafted personality profile of an individual, institution, corporation, product or service.**"**
>
> –Daniel Boorstin, *The Image*, 1961

Edward Bernays. In addition, we will explore the major practices and specialties of public relations, the reasons for the long-standing antagonism between journalists and members of the PR profession, and the social responsibilities of PR in a democracy.

Early Developments in Public Relations

At the beginning of the twentieth century, the United States slowly shifted to a consumer-oriented, industrial society that fostered the rapid spread of advertising and publicity for new products and services. During this gradual transformation from farm to factory, PR emerged as a profession, partly because businesses needed to fend off increased scrutiny from muckraking journalists and emerging labor unions.[3]

Prior to this time, the first PR practitioners were simply theatrical **press agents**: those who sought to advance a client's image through media exposure, primarily via stunts staged for newspapers. The potential of these early PR techniques soon became obvious to business executives and to politicians. For instance, press agents were used by people like Daniel Boone, who engineered various land-grab and real-estate ventures, and Davy Crockett, who in addition to heroic exploits was also involved in the massacre of Native Americans. Such individuals often wanted to repair and reshape their reputation as cherished frontier legends or as respectable candidates for public office.

P. T. Barnum, Buffalo Bill, and the Railroads

The most notorious theatrical agent of the 1800s was Phineas Taylor (P. T.) Barnum, who used gross exaggeration, fraudulent stories, and staged events to secure newspaper coverage for his clients, his American Museum, and later, his circus. Barnum's best-known acts included the "midget" General Tom Thumb, Swedish soprano Jenny Lind, Jumbo the Elephant, and Joice Heth, who Barnum claimed was the 161-year-old nurse of George Washington (although she was actually 80 when she died). These performers became some of the earliest nationally known celebrities because of

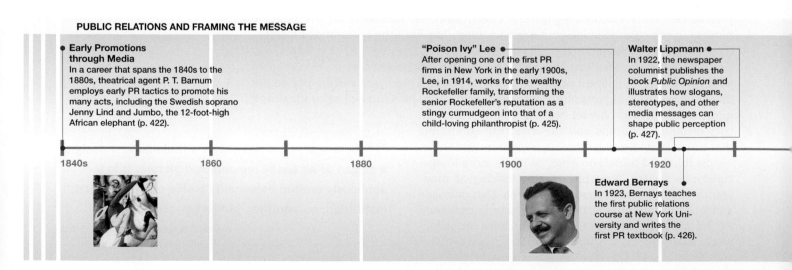

PUBLIC RELATIONS AND FRAMING THE MESSAGE

Early Promotions through Media
In a career that spans the 1840s to the 1880s, theatrical agent P. T. Barnum employs early PR tactics to promote his many acts, including the Swedish soprano Jenny Lind and Jumbo, the 12-foot-high African elephant (p. 422).

"Poison Ivy" Lee ●
After opening one of the first PR firms in New York in the early 1900s, Lee, in 1914, works for the wealthy Rockefeller family, transforming the senior Rockefeller's reputation as a stingy curmudgeon into that of a child-loving philanthropist (p. 425).

Walter Lippmann ●
In 1922, the newspaper columnist publishes the book *Public Opinion* and illustrates how slogans, stereotypes, and other media messages can shape public perception (p. 427).

1840s   1860   1880   1900   1920

Edward Bernays ●
In 1923, Bernays teaches the first public relations course at New York University and writes the first PR textbook (p. 426).

Barnum's skill in using the media for promotion. Decrying outright fraud and cheating, Barnum understood that his audiences liked to be tricked. In newspapers and on handbills, he later often revealed the strategies behind his more elaborate hoaxes.

From 1883 to 1916, former army scout William F. Cody, who once killed buffalo for the railroads, promoted himself in his "Buffalo Bill's Wild West and Congress of Rough Riders" traveling show. Cody's troupe—which featured bedouins, cossacks, and gauchos as well as "cowboys and Indians"—re-created dramatic gunfights, the Civil War, and battles of the Old West. The show employed sharpshooter Annie Oakley and Lakota medicine man Sitting Bull, whose own legends were partially shaped by Cody's nine publicity agents. These agents were led by John Burke, who promoted the show for its thirty-four-year run. Burke was one of the first PR agents to use a variety of media channels: promotional newspaper stories, magazine articles and ads, dime novels, theater marquees, poster art, and early films. Burke's efforts successfully elevated Cody's show, which was seen by more than fifty million people in a thousand cities in twelve countries.[4] Burke and Buffalo Bill shaped many of the lasting myths about rugged American individualism and frontier expansion. Along with Barnum, they were among the first to use publicity to elevate entertainment-centered culture to an international level.

During the 1800s, America's largest industrial companies, particularly the railroads, also employed press agents to win favor in the court of public opinion. Initially, government involvement in railroad development was minimal; local businesses raised funds to finance the spread of rail service. Around 1850, however, the railroads began pushing for federal subsidies, complaining that local fundraising efforts took too long. In its drive for government support, for example, Illinois Central promoted the following public strategy: "The railroad line would be expensive to construct; it would open up new land for economic development; without subsidy, the line might not be built; with subsidy the public interest would be served."[5] Illinois Central was one of the first companies to use government lobbyists to argue that railroad service between the North and the South would ease tensions, unite the two regions, and prevent a war.

● Buffalo Bill's Wild West and Congress of Rough Riders of the World show, depicted in this 1899 poster, was internationally popular as a touring show for more than thirty years. William Frederick Cody (1846–1917) became popularly known as "Buffalo Bill" through dime-store novel stories adapted from his life by E. Z. C. Judson (under the pen name Ned Buntline). Prior to his fame as an entertainer, he worked as a Pony Express rider at age 14, and later as a buffalo hunter for the Kansas Pacific Railroad.

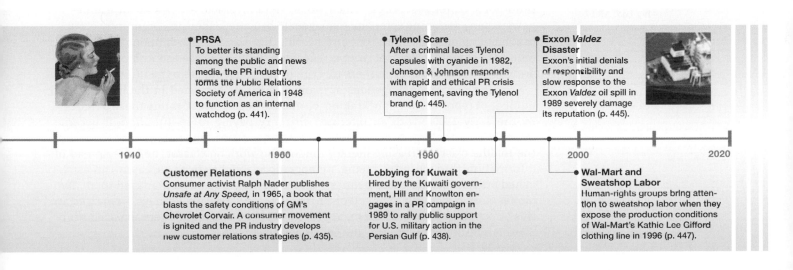

● **PRSA**
To better its standing among the public and news media, the PR industry forms the Public Relations Society of America in 1948 to function as an internal watchdog (p. 441).

● **Tylenol Scare**
After a criminal laces Tylenol capsules with cyanide in 1982, Johnson & Johnson responds with rapid and ethical PR crisis management, saving the Tylenol brand (p. 445).

● **Exxon *Valdez* Disaster**
Exxon's initial denials of responsibility and slow response to the Exxon *Valdez* oil spill in 1989 severely damage its reputation (p. 445).

1940   1960   1980   2000   2020

Customer Relations ●
Consumer activist Ralph Nader publishes *Unsafe at Any Speed,* in 1965, a book that blasts the safety conditions of GM's Chevrolet Corvair. A consumer movement is ignited and the PR industry develops new customer relations strategies (p. 435).

Lobbying for Kuwait ●
Hired by the Kuwaiti government, Hill and Knowlton engages in a PR campaign in 1989 to rally public support for U.S. military action in the Persian Gulf (p. 438).

● **Wal-Mart and Sweatshop Labor**
Human-rights groups bring attention to sweatshop labor when they expose the production conditions of Wal-Mart's Kathie Lee Gifford clothing line in 1996 (p. 447).

The railroads successfully campaigned for government support by developing some of the earliest publicity tactics. Their first strategy was simply to buy favorable news stories through direct bribes. By the late 1880s, this practice was so common that a Chicago news reporter published his tongue-in-cheek rates: "For setting forth of virtues (actual or alleged) of presidents, general managers, or directors, $2 per line. . . . For complimentary notices of the wives and children of railroad officials, we demand $1.50 per line. . . . Epic poems, containing descriptions of scenery, dining cars, etc., will be published at special rates."[6] In addition to planting favorable articles in the press, the railroads engaged in *deadheading*: the practice of giving reporters free rail passes with the tacit understanding that they would write glowing reports about rail travel. Eventually, wealthy railroads received federal subsidies and increased their profits, while the public shouldered much of the financial burden for rail expansion.

In terms of power and influence, companies like Illinois Central and the Pennsylvania Railroad in the late 1800s were comparable to American automakers in the 1950s. Having obtained construction subsidies, the larger rail companies turned their attention to bigger game—lobbying the government to control rates and reduce competition, especially from smaller, aggressive regional lines. Railroad lobbyists argued that federal support would lead to improved service and guaranteed quality, because the government would be keeping a close watch. These lobbying efforts, accompanied by favorable publicity, led to passage of the Interstate Commerce Act in 1881, authorizing railroads "to revamp their freight classification, raise rates, and eliminate fare reduction."[7] Historians have argued that, ironically, the PR campaign's success actually led to the decline of railroads: Artificially maintained higher rates and burdensome government regulations forced smaller firms out of business and eventually drove many customers to other modes of transportation.

The Modern Public Relations Agent

Along with the railroads, utility companies such as Chicago Edison and AT&T also used PR strategies in the late 1800s to derail competition and eventually attain monopoly status. In fact, although both local and regional competitors existed at the time, AT&T's PR and lobbying efforts were so effective that they eliminated all telephone competition—with the government's blessing—until the 1980s.

The tactics of the 1880s and 1890s, however, would haunt public relations as it struggled to become a respected profession. In addition to buying the votes of key lawmakers, the utilities used a number of shady practices. These included hiring third-party editorial services, which would send favorable articles about utilities to newspapers; assigning company managers to become leaders in community groups; producing ghostwritten articles (often using the names of prominent leaders and members of women's social groups, who were flattered to see their names in print); and influencing textbook authors to write histories favorable to the utilities.[8]

As the promotional agendas of many companies escalated in the late 1800s, a number of reporters and muckraking journalists began investigating these practices. By the early 1900s, with an informed citizenry paying more attention, it became more difficult for large firms to fool the press and mislead the public. With the rise of the middle class, increasing literacy among the working classes, and the spread of information through print media, democratic ideals began to threaten the established order of business and politics—and the elite groups who managed them. Two pioneers of public relations—"Poison Ivy" Lee and Edward Bernays—emerged in this atmosphere to popularize an approach to public opinion that emphasized shaping the interpretation of facts and "engineering consent."

> **❝Since crowds do not reason, they can only be organized and stimulated through symbols and phrases.❞**
>
> —Ivy Lee, 1917

"Poison Ivy" Lee

Most nineteenth-century corporations and manufacturers cared little about public sentiment. By the early 1900s, though, executives realized that their companies could sell more products if they were associated with positive public images and values. Into this public space stepped Ivy Ledbetter Lee, considered one of the founders of modern public relations. Lee understood the undercurrents of social change. He counseled clients that honesty and directness were better PR devices than the deceptive corporate practices of the 1800s, which had fostered suspicion and an anti–big-business sentiment.

A minister's son and once an economics student at Princeton University, Lee, a former reporter, opened one of the first New York PR firms with a colleague in the early 1900s. Lee quit the firm in 1906 to work for the Pennsylvania Railroad, which, following a rail accident, wanted him to help downplay unfavorable publicity. Lee's advice, however, was that Penn Railroad admit its mistake, vow to do better, and let newspapers in on the story. These suggestions ran counter to what the utilities and railroads had been doing, yet Lee argued that an open relationship between the press and business would lead to a more favorable public image. In the end, Penn adopted Lee's strategies.

In 1914, Lee went to work for John D. Rockefeller, who by the 1880s controlled 90 percent of the nation's oil industry (Rockefeller once said, "It is my duty to make money and still more money").[9] Rockefeller suffered from periodic image problems, particularly after Ida Tarbell's powerful muckraking series in *McClure's* magazine about Rockefeller's Standard Oil trust. Despite his philanthropic work, Rockefeller was often depicted in the press as a tyrant, as were other corporate bosses. The Rockefeller and Standard Oil reputations reached a low point in April 1914, when tactics to stop union organizing erupted in tragedy at a fuel and iron company in Ludlow, Colorado. During a violent strike, fifty-three workers and their family members, including thirteen women and children, died.

Lee was hired to contain the damaging publicity fallout. He immediately distributed a series of "fact" sheets to the press, telling the corporate side of the story and discrediting the United Mine Workers, which had been trying to organize the Ludlow workers. As he had done for Penn Railroad, Lee brought in the press and staged photo opportunities. John D. Rockefeller Jr., who by then ran his father's

● Public relations pioneer Edward Bernays and his business partner and wife, Doris Fleischman, worked on behalf of a client, the American Tobacco Company, to make smoking socially acceptable for women. For one of American Tobacco's brands, Lucky Strike, they were also asked to change public attitudes toward the color green. (Women weren't buying the brand because surveys indicated that the forest-green package clashed with their wardrobes.) Bernays and Fleischman organized events such as green fashion shows and sold the idea of a new trend in green to the press. By 1934, green had become the fashion color of the season, making Lucky Strikes the perfect accessory for the female smoker. Interestingly, Bernays forbade his own wife to smoke, flushing her cigarettes down the toilet and calling smoking a nasty habit.

company, donned overalls and a miner's helmet and posed with the families of workers and union leaders. While Lee helped the company improve conditions for workers, the publicity campaign also kept the union out of the Ludlow coal mines. This was probably the first use of a PR campaign in a labor-management dispute. Over the years, Lee completely transformed the wealthy family's image, urging the discreet Rockefellers to publicize their charitable work. To improve his image, the senior Rockefeller took to handing out dimes to children wherever he went—a strategic ritual that historians attribute to Lee.

Called "Poison Ivy" by newspaper critics and corporate foes, Lee had a complex understanding of facts. He realized, better than most journalists of his day, that facts were open to various interpretations. For Lee, facts were elusive and malleable, begging to be forged and shaped. Interpreting facts so as to shine the best light on a client was not viewed as a particularly honorable practice, however. In the Ludlow case, for instance, Lee noted that the women and children who died while retreating from the charging company-backed militia had overturned a stove, which caught fire and caused their deaths. His PR fact sheet implied that they had, in part, been victims of their own carelessness.

In the 1930s, Ivy Lee was investigated by Congress for counseling German industries during the Nazi regime and for fraternizing with the Soviet Union under Joseph Stalin. Some critics thought that Lee's interest in a communist nation represented a curious contradiction for an avowed capitalist. In Lee's earlier work for railroads and utilities, however, he had advocated an anticompetition, pro-consolidation theme that he believed was in the best interests of his clients. Lee had argued for corporate-controlled monopolies, which benefited from protective government regulation. Thus Lee did share some common ground with foreign governments that ran state-controlled, anticompetitive business monopolies.

Edward Bernays

The nephew of Sigmund Freud, former reporter Edward Bernays inherited the public relations mantle from Ivy Lee and dressed it up with modern social science. Bernays, who died in 1995 at age 103, was the first person to apply the findings of psychology and sociology to the business of public relations. He also referred to himself as a "public relations counselor" rather than as just a publicity agent. Over the years, Bernays's client list included General Electric, the American Tobacco Company, General Motors, *Good Housekeeping* and *Time* magazines, Procter & Gamble, RCA, the government of India, and the city of Vienna. In addition, he served as an adviser to President Coolidge in the 1920s, helping the president revamp his stiff, formal image.

Bernays made key contributions to public relations education.[10] He taught the first class called *public relations*—at New York University in 1923—and wrote the field's first textbook, *Crystallizing Public Opinion*. For many years, his definition of PR was a standard: "Public relations is the attempt, by information, persuasion, and adjustment, to engineer public support for an activity, cause, movement, or institution." Bernays worked for the Committee on Public Information (CPI) during World War I, developing propaganda that supported America's entry into that conflict. Later, CPI helped create the image of President Woodrow Wilson as a peacemaker, among the first full-scale governmental attempts to mobilize public opinion.

Hired by the American Tobacco Company after World War I, Bernays was asked to develop a campaign that would make smoking more publicly acceptable for newly liberated women who had recently won the right to vote. Among other strategies, Bernays staged an event: placing women smokers in New York's 1929 Easter parade. He labeled cigarettes "torches of freedom" and encouraged women to smoke as a symbol of their newly acquired suffrage and independence from men. He also asked the women he placed in the parade to contact newspaper and newsreel companies in advance—to announce their symbolic protest. The campaign received plenty of free publicity from newspapers and magazines. Within five weeks of the parade, men-only smoking rooms in New York theaters began opening up to women.

Through much of his writing, Bernays suggested that emerging forms of social democracy threatened the established hierarchical order. He thought it was important for experts and leaders to keep business and society pointed in the right directions: "The duty of the higher strata of society—the cultivated, the learned, the expert, the intellectual—is therefore clear. They must inject moral and spiritual motives into public opinion."[11] Bernays saw a typical public relations campaign giving shape to public opinion—what he termed the "engineering of consent." Bernays believed that for any PR campaign to work, securing the consent of the people was the crucial ingredient.

Both Ivy Lee and Edward Bernays thought that public opinion was pliant and not always rational: In the hands of the right experts, leaders, and PR counselors, public opinion was ready for shaping in forms that people could rally behind.[12] Walter Lippmann, the newspaper columnist who wrote *Public Opinion* in 1922, also believed in the importance of an expert class to direct the more irrational twists and turns of public opinion. But he saw the development of public relations as "a clear sign that the facts of modern life [did] not spontaneously take a shape in which they can be known."[13] Lippmann lamented that too often PR professionals with hidden agendas, rather than detached reporters, were giving only their own meaning to the facts.

Throughout Bernays's most active years, his business partner and later his wife, Doris Fleischman, worked on many joint projects as a researcher and coauthor. Beginning in the 1920s, she was one of the first women to work in advertising and public relations. She edited a pamphlet called *Contact*, which explained the emerging profession of public relations to America's most powerful leaders. Because it was a new quasi-profession not claimed entirely by men, PR was one of the few professions—apart from teaching and nursing—that were accessible to women who chose to work outside the home. Today, women outnumber men by more than three to one in the profession.

Pseudo-Events and Manufacturing News

Armed with its new understanding of public psychology, modern public relations changed not only the relationship between corporations and the public but also that among corporations, politics, and journalism. In his influential book *The Image*, historian Daniel Boorstin coined the term **pseudo-event** to refer to one of the key contributions of PR and advertising in the twentieth century. Basically, a pseudo-event is any circumstance created for the purpose of gaining coverage in the media. In other words, if no news media show up, there is no event.[14]

Typical pseudo-events are interviews, press conferences, TV and radio talk shows, the Super Bowl pregame show, or any other staged activity aimed at drawing public attention and media coverage. Such events depend on the participation of clients and performers and on the media's recording of the performances. With regard to national politics, Theodore Roosevelt's administration set up the first White House pressroom and held the first presidential press conferences in the early 1900s. In the 1990s, Vice President Al Gore championed White House Internet sites, making it possible for larger public audiences to interact with reporters and leaders in electronic press conferences.

As powerful companies, savvy politicians, and activist groups became aware of the media's susceptibility to pseudo-events, these activities proliferated. For example, to get free publicity, companies began staging press conferences to announce new product lines. During the 1960s, antiwar and civil rights protesters began their events only when the news media were assembled. One anecdote from that era aptly illustrates the principle of a pseudo-event: A reporter asked a student leader about the starting time for a particular protest; the student responded, "When can you get here?"

Politicians running for national office have become particularly adept at scheduling press conferences and interviews around 5 or 6 P.M. They realize that local TV news is live during these times, so they stage pseudo-events to take advantage of TV's appetite for live remote feeds and breaking news.

The Practice of Public Relations

Today, there are more than 2,900 PR firms worldwide, including 2,200 in the United States; thousands of companies and organizations also have in-house departments devoted to public relations functions. Especially since the 1980s, the formal study of public relations has grown significantly at colleges and universities. As certified PR programs have expanded (often featuring journalism as a minor), the profession has relied less and less on the ranks of reporters for its workforce. At the same time, new courses in professional ethics and issues management have called on future practitioners to be more responsible.

The growth of formal PR education has been fairly dramatic. In the 1970s, the majority of students in communications and journalism programs indicated in surveys that they intended to pursue careers in news or magazine writing. By the late

● **Table 12.1 The Top 15 Public Relations Firms, 2001
(by Worldwide Net Fees in U.S. $)**

Rank	Firm (parent firm)	2001 Fees*
1	Weber Shandwick Worldwide (Interpublic)	$426.6
2	Fleishman-Hillard (Omnicom)	345.1
3	Hill and Knowlton (WPP Group)	325.1
4	Burson-Marsteller (WPP Group)	290.7
5	Incepta (Incepta Group)	266.0
6	Edelman PR Worldwide (independent)	223.7
7	Porter Novelli (Omnicom)	186.3
8	Ketchum (Omnicom)	185.2
9	GCI Group/APCO Worldwide (Grey)	151.1
10	Ogilvy PR Worldwide (WPP Group)	145.9
11	Euro RSCG (Havas)	124.2
12	Manning, Selvage & Lee (Publicis Groupe)	116.0
13	Golin/Harris Int'l (Interpublic)	113.2
14	Cordiant Communications Group (Cordiant)	90.7
15	Ruder Finn Inc. (independent)	80.3

*Dollars are in millions.

Source: AdAge.com, 2002, <www.adage.com/page.cms?pageid=888>.

1980s, however, similar surveys indicated that the majority of students wanted to enter public relations or advertising, both of which had higher entry-level salaries than journalism positions. By 2002, the Public Relations Student Society of America (PRSSA) had more than 7,000 members and 227 chapters in colleges and universities. Such growth parallels the general rise of business schools and majors throughout the 1970s and 1980s.

Approaches to Organized Public Relations

In 1988, the Public Relations Society of America (PRSA) offered this useful definition of PR: "Public relations helps an organization and its publics adapt mutually to each other." To carry out this mutual communication process, the PR industry follows two main approaches. First, many agencies function as independent companies whose sole job is to provide various clients with PR services. (During the 1980s and 1990s, though, many large ad agencies acquired independent PR firms as subsidiaries.) Second, most companies, which may or may not buy the services of independent PR firms, maintain their own in-house staffs to handle routine PR tasks, such as writing press releases, managing various media requests, staging special events, and dealing with the public.

Independent Agencies

About 2,200 American companies identify themselves exclusively as public relations counseling firms. Two of the biggest, Burson-Marsteller and Hill and Knowlton, are now subsidiaries of the same global ad agency, the WPP Group (see Table 12.1). Founded in 1953, Burson-Marsteller remains one of PR's top-ranking firms, with revenue of close to $300 million annually. It has about 89 offices operating in 35 countries and lists Boeing and McDonald's among its major clients.

Hill and Knowlton maintains 170 offices in 36 countries. Its clients have included Microsoft, Motorola, Nintendo, Pepsi, Procter & Gamble, Xerox, former president Richard Nixon, and the royal family of Kuwait. By the late 1990s, most of the largest PR firms were owned by or affiliated with multinational ad agencies, such as WPP, Omnicom, and Interpublic, which have long provided PR as a part of their full-service operations.

In-House Services

In contrast to independent agencies, the most common type of public relations is done in-house by individual companies and organizations. Although about a third of America's largest companies retain an external PR firm, almost every company involved in a manufacturing or service industry has an in-house department. Such departments are also a vital part of many professional organizations, such as the American Medical Association, the AFL-CIO, and the National Association of Broadcasters, as well as large nonprofit organizations, such as the American Cancer Society, the Arthritis Foundation, and most universities and colleges.

Performing Public Relations

Public relations, like advertising, pays careful attention to the various audiences and clients that it interacts with or serves. These groups include not only consumers and the general public but company

● During World War I, PR pioneer Edward Bernays (1891–1995) worked for the federal Committee on Public Information (CPI). One of the main functions of the CPI was to create the poster art and print ads that would persuade reluctant or isolationist Americans to support the war effort against Germany.

employees, shareholders, media organizations, government agencies, and community and industry leaders. Among potential clients, which constitute another public, are politicians, small businesses, industries, and nonprofit organizations (see "Case Study: The 20 Top PR Campaigns Ever?" on page 432).

Public relations involves a multitude of practices and techniques. The PRSA identifies a number of general activities associated with PR: publicity, communication, public affairs, issues management, government relations, financial PR, community relations, industry relations, minority relations, advertising, press agentry, promotion, media relations, and propaganda. This last activity, **propaganda**, is communication strategically placed, either as advertising or as publicity, to gain public support for a special issue, program, or policy, such as a nation's war effort.

The practice of public relations encompasses a wide range of activities. PR personnel produce employee newsletters, manage client trade shows and conferences, conduct historical tours, appear on news programs, organize damage control after negative publicity, and analyze complex issues and trends that may affect a client's future. Basic among these activities, however, are writing and editing, media relations, special events, research, and community and government relations. PR practice is generally divided into two roles: PR technicians, who handle daily short-term activities, and PR managers, who counsel clients and manage activities over the long term.

Writing and Editing

One of the chief day-to-day technical functions in public relations is composing news releases, or **press releases**: announcements, written in the style of news reports, that give new information about an individual, company, or organization and pitch a story idea to the news media (see Figure 12.1). In issuing press releases, often called *handouts* by the news media, PR agents hope that their client information will be picked up and transformed into news. Through press releases, PR firms manage the flow of information; they often control which media get what material in which order. (Sometimes a PR agent will reward a cooperative reporter through the strategic release of information.)

News editors and broadcasters sort through hundreds of releases daily to determine which ones contain the most original ideas or the most currency for their readers and viewers. The majority of large media institutions rewrite and double-check the information in news releases, but small media companies and small-town newspapers often use them verbatim, especially if their own editorial resources are limited or if they are under deadline constraints. Usually, the more closely a press release resembles actual news copy, the more likely it is to be used, which is why newspaper work is a good training ground for PR.

Since the 1970s and the introduction of portable video equipment, PR agencies and departments have been using **video news releases (VNRs)**, which are thirty- to ninety-second visual PR stories packaged to mimic the style of a broadcast news report. Many large companies now operate their own TV studios, which enable them to produce training videos for their employees and to create VNRs for their clients. Broadcast news stations in small TV markets regularly use video material from VNRs. Although large stations with more resources may get story ideas from VNRs, their news directors do not like to use video material obtained directly from PR sources; they prefer to assemble their own reports in order to maintain their independence. On occasion, news stations have been criticized for using bits of video footage from a VNR without acknowledging the source.

In addition to issuing press releases, nonprofit groups also produce **public-service announcements (PSAs)**: fifteen- to sixty-second reports or announcements for radio

> **"** PR expands the public discourse, helps provide a wide assortment of news, and is essential in explaining the pluralism of our total communication system. **"**
>
> – John C. Merrill, *Media Debates*, 1991

Figure 12.1 Differences between a Press Release and a News Story

News reporters can be heavily dependent on public relations for story ideas. Here is a press release about an upcoming art exhibit written by PR staff at the University of Northern Iowa Gallery of Art, and an excerpt of a news story from the *Waterloo–Cedar Falls Courier* based on information in the release.

Sources: (a) Courtesy Office of University Marketing & Public Relations, University of Northern Iowa; (b) Courtesy *Waterloo–Cedar Falls* (IA) *Courier.*

and television that promote government programs, educational projects, volunteer agencies, or social reform. As part of their requirement to serve the public interest, broadcasters historically have been encouraged to carry free PSAs. Since the deregulation of broadcasting began in the 1980s, however, there has been less pressure and no minimum obligation for TV and radio stations to air PSAs. When PSAs do run, they are frequently scheduled between midnight and 6 A.M., a less commercially valuable time slot with relatively few viewers or listeners.

The writing and editing part of PR also involves creating brochures and catalogues as well as company newsletters and annual reports for shareholders. It may include writing and editing speeches that aim to boost a politician's image or a company's stature. Major politicians and business leaders today seldom write their own speeches. Instead, they hire speechwriters or PR specialists.

CASE STUDY

The 20 Top PR Campaigns Ever?

Editor's Note: PRWeek magazine asked ten public relations experts to select their ten favorite campaigns of all time. Those campaigns with the most votes were compiled into this list of what *PRWeek* calls "20 phenomenal campaigns that highlight the broad scope, history, and power of the PR profession."

Boston Tea Party

The Boston Tea Party was a favorite of all the judges who recognized Samuel Adams's mastery of opinion-swaying techniques. When American colonists threw crates of tea leaves from a British trade ship into Boston Harbor to protest excessive British taxation, the action was significant—but the message it sent was more important still.

Jenny Lind, "The Swedish Nightingale"

Celebrity publicists could learn a lesson from entertainment entrepreneur P. T. Barnum, whose national tour for Swedish soprano Jenny Lind made her a pop icon even before the start of the Civil War. Barnum fueled "Lindomania" by scheduling appearances nationwide and negotiating product endorsements, all the while promoting her virtuous personality. "It's a terrific celebrity tour model," said Norma Lee.

Henry Morrison Flagler Promotes Florida

The founding father of travel and tourism PR turned a muggy, mosquito-infested swamp into vacation paradise. At the turn of the twentieth century, Florida rail and hotel owner Henry Morrison Flagler hired a New York firm to convince Americans of the merits of visiting the east coast of Florida, ultimately establishing the tradition of the Florida Vacation.

Ed Bernays's Campaign for the Ballet

In a time when ballet was considered a scandalous form of entertainment, Bernays used magazine placement, created a publicity guide, and used overseas reviews to make men in tights respectable and put ballerina dreams into the heads of little girls.

Macy's Thanksgiving Day Parade

For the past seventy-five years, Americans across the country have witnessed hundred-foot helium balloons of cartoon characters floating among Manhattan skyscrapers and Rockettes tap dancing in Herald Square, thanks to a publicity campaign so successful that it is recognized by many as the official kick-off to the holiday shopping season.

Olympic Torch Relay

The International Olympic Committee understood that strong symbols and high visibility are key to great PR and have created an emblem that is arguably the most recognizable in the world. The Torch Relay program, executed in the months before the Winter and Summer Games, has generated publicity for the Olympics, the runners, and sponsors on a global stage since 1936.

March of Dimes

Established in 1938 by polio survivor Franklin Delano Roosevelt, the March of Dimes was originally part of a larger PR movement to eradicate the virus. Radio celebrities encouraged Americans to mail dimes to the president on his birthday, and the campaign raised $268,000 in its first year.

Lucky Strike Green Has Gone to War

While many judges recognized the PR prowess of anti-smoking campaigns that have resulted in heavy fines for tobacco companies, one of the greatest PR campaigns actually contributed to the popularity of cigarettes. The campaign, which publicized the redesign of Lucky Strike's packaging, is now known as one that made smoking fashionable among women.

Martin Luther King Jr.'s Civil Rights Campaign

Every PR pro knows that good speechwriting and delivery are essential tools to a successful campaign, and few would argue that they have ever been better used than in Martin Luther King Jr.'s 1963 civil rights campaign—which is to say nothing of this great man's letter-writing skills, lobbying, or ability to stage effective nonviolent protests.

NASA

Ever since Houston's Johnson Space Center director Chris Kraft insisted that television cameras be placed on the lunar lander in 1969 and reporters invited inside mission control during the *Apollo 13* mission, the public has closely witnessed NASA activities—both awe-inspiring and tragic alike. Those historic moments have helped the public overlook the huge taxpayer expenses and numerous technical debacles that could otherwise have jeopardized the future of the organization.

Cabbage Patch Kids

PR efforts that led up to the national launch of the Cabbage Patch Kids created hysteria among the media, kids, and parents looking to get their hands on the elusive adoptable dolls. The PR efforts set a standard for the creation of a toy fad on this scale.

Traffic Safety

In the 1980s, the U.S. automotive industry saved lives and got the nation to buckle up entirely through PR and lobbying for better safety-belt laws—no advertising was used. Tactics included winning the support of the news media across the country, interactive displays, celebrity endorsements, letter-writing campaigns, and several publicity events, like buckling a 600-foot-wide safety belt around the Hollywood sign.

Hands across America

The largest human gathering in history was a PR stunt that saw everyone from bikers to Boy Scouts and ball players come together for a worthy cause in a huge show of support orchestrated through media outreach by Weber Shandwick. On May 26, 1986, more than seven million people, including President Ronald Reagan, joined hands in a human chain across sixteen states to raise money for the hungry and homeless in the United States.

StarKist Tuna

When negative coverage threatened the tuna industry because dolphins were getting caught in fishermen's nets, Edelman and H. J. Heinz's StarKist led the way in changing fishing practices, with conferences, videos, and an Earth Day coalition. This campaign was not just about changing perception but about changing reality, with commercial tuna fishermen everywhere following StarKist's lead.

Tylenol Crisis

When Johnson & Johnson discovered that several people had died from cyanide-laced Tylenol capsules, a national panic erupted, and many thought that the company would never recover from the damage caused by the tamperings. Tylenol's PR pros ignored short-term profit losses and issued a complete recall of the product, with the company ultimately becoming a leader in the redesign of medicinal packaging.

Windows 95 Launch

In the pantheon of modern product launches, Microsoft's Windows 95 invaded the minds of the American public and consumed the media, resulting in an unprecedented 99 percent awareness level among all audiences before the product even hit store shelves.

Understanding AIDS

Arguably the most successful health-education campaign ever, the national AIDS mailing "Understanding AIDS" changed the way the disease was perceived by Americans and caused a sexual revolution. Dictated by the U.S. Congress in 1987, the Ogilvy PR campaign also included grassroots activities that specifically targeted black and Hispanic Americans in order to curb the epidemic's spread.

Making BP Beyond

British Petroleum is currently enjoying success that runs counter to most trends in the energy market, and much of that is due to a repositioning that started with this impressive internal branding campaign. BP's 1999 global initiative defined the brand as innovative and environmentally aware while building confidence, performance, and unity among the company's several thousand employees.

Human Genome Project

It's not difficult to get publicity for a controversial scientific discovery, but with a lot of preparation, an early press conference, and some excellent education programs, the PR pros at the Whitehead Institute made sure that the complicated science of the human genome project was not lost in politics and scandal.

Justice for East Timor

In a literally revolutionary campaign, Amnesty International, Initiatives for International Dialogue (IID), and the East Timor Action Network succeeded in liberating East Timor from Indonesia with a precedent-setting and phenomenally powerful Internet campaign. After the 1991 massacre of Timorese citizens by the Indonesian army, human-rights advocates took notice and employed new global technology to draw attention to the injustice quickly and effectively. Using tactics that involved exposing human-rights violators and lobbying through mass e-mails, organizing committees in chat rooms, and educating the East Timorese, IID proved the power of the Internet by successfully deposing those who abused their own power.

Source: Melanie Shortman and Jonah Bloom, "The Greatest Campaigns Ever?" *PRWeek*, July 15, 2002, p. 14.

Media Relations

Through publicity, PR managers specializing in media relations promote a client or organization by securing favorable coverage in the news media. Media specialization often requires an in-house PR person to speak on behalf of an organization or to direct reporters to experts who can provide the best, or at least official, sources of information.

Media-relations specialists also perform *damage control* or *crisis management* when negative publicity occurs. Occasionally, in times of crisis—such as a virus outbreak at a hospital, a scandal at a university, or a safety recall by a car manufacturer—a PR spokesperson might be designated as the only source of information available to news media. Although journalists often resent being cut off from higher administrative levels and leaders, the institution or company wants to ensure that rumors and inaccurate stories do not circulate in the media. In these situations, a game often develops in which reporters attempt to circumvent the company spokesperson and induce a knowledgeable insider to talk *off the record,* providing background details without being named directly as a source.

PR agents who specialize in media relations also recommend advertising to their clients when it seems appropriate. Unlike publicity, which is sometimes outside a PR agency's control, paid advertising may help to focus a complex issue or a client's image. Publicity, however, carries the aura of legitimate news and thus has more credibility than advertising. In addition, media specialists cultivate associations with editors, reporters, freelance writers, and broadcast news directors to ensure that press releases or VNRs are favorably received.

Special Events

Another public relations specialty involves coordinating special events. Since the late 1960s, for instance, the city of Milwaukee has run Summerfest, a ten-day music and food festival that attracts about a million people each year. As the festival's popularity grew, various companies sought to become sponsors of the event. Local manufacturers and the beer industry, for example, signed up to support different musical venues. The Miller Brewing Company sponsored a festival stage devoted to jazz. In exchange for sponsorship, the stage carried the Miller name, which also accompanied many items connected with Summerfest. In this way, Miller received favorable publicity by showing a commitment to the city that serves as the company's corporate headquarters.[15]

More typical of special-events publicity is the corporate sponsor that aligns its company image with a cause, or an organization that has positive stature among the general public. For example, for more than thirty years Mobil Oil (now ExxonMobil) has underwritten special programming such as *Masterpiece Theatre* on PBS. At the local level, companies often sponsor a community parade or a charitable fund-raising activity. When a new professional sports team arrives in a community, a host of local companies may compete to associate themselves with the new franchise. In this kind of situation, a team's PR specialist attempts to identify those companies that will provide the most favorable publicity for the client.

Research

Just as advertising is driven today by demographic and psychographic research, PR uses similar strategies to project a client's image to the appropriate audience. The research area is PR's fastest-growing segment as the profession attempts to bring new social-science techniques to its audience studies and image campaigns. Because historically it has been difficult to determine why particular campaigns succeed or fail, research has become the key ingredient in PR forecasting. Like advertising studies, PR research targets specific audiences. It makes use of mail and telephone surveys to get a fix on an audience's perceptions of a client's reputation.

As in advertising research, focus groups have become prominent in public relations campaigns. Although such groups are often unreliable because of small sample size, they are fairly easy to set up and do not require elaborate statistical designs. In 2001, for example, a social justice organization called the Catholic Campaign for Human Development used focus groups to assess poverty awareness in the United States. After working with a series of focus groups in key cities across the country, the organization found that most people felt compassion for those living in poverty and believed that they had a responsibility to help the poor. But the focus group data also indicated that United States citizens will only do something about poverty when they're confronted with the problem. One of the most jarring facts discovered in other research is that 32 million people in the United States live in poverty—more people than the population of many states. So, the organization launched its campaign with the theme "Welcome to Poverty, USA." The media campaign introduced a fifty-first state called "Poverty" and asked audiences to visit its Web site at <www.povertyusa.org> and collect souvenirs that say "Poverty lives here—in numbers larger than you ever imagined." The campaign generated nearly seven hundred news stories nationwide and resulted in Americans being more likely to believe that education is key to breaking the cycle of poverty and less likely to label the poor as lazy and unmotivated.[16]

Community and Consumer Relations

Two other PR activities involve building relationships between companies and their communities. Companies have learned that sustaining close ties with their neighbors not only enhances their image but promotes the idea that the companies are good citizens. Such ties expose a business to potential customers through activities such as plant tours, open houses, participation in town parades, and special events such as a company's anniversary.

Besides encouraging client employees to get involved in community activities, many PR firms like their clients to make charitable donations that build local bonds. Some companies offer their work sites to local groups for meetings and help in fundraising efforts. More progressive companies get involved in unemployment and job-retraining programs, and others donate equipment and workers to urban revitalization projects such as Habitat for Humanity.

In terms of customer relations, PR has become much more sophisticated since 1965, when Ralph Nader's *Unsafe at Any Speed* revealed safety problems concerning the Chevrolet Corvair. Nader's book gave General Motors a corporate migraine that resulted in the discontinuance of the Corvair line. More important, however, Nader's book lit the fuse that ignited a vibrant consumerism movement. During the 1960s, consumers became more sophisticated and, consequently, unwilling to readily accept the claims of those in power—including corporate leaders. Contributing to this movement was the trend toward large multinational corporate mergers and the rise of impersonal chain stores, both of which signaled a decreasing accountability to consumers.

For a while, the consumerism movement drew media attention. Many newspapers and TV stations hired consumer reporters, who tracked down the sources of customer complaints and often embarrassed companies by putting them in the media spotlight. Firms that were PR savvy responded by paying more attention to customers, establishing product and service guarantees and ensuring that all calls and mail from customers were answered promptly. Some companies even produced

AMERICA'S ECONOM

Carefully staged presidential appearances are just one instance in which politics and PR intersect. This event in 2003 featured President Bush in a trucking company warehouse in St. Louis unveiling his strategy to revive the economy and illustrate his connection with American small businesses. The staging of the event, however, undermined the message when reporters revealed the façade: the wall of boxes bearing the "Made in U.S.A." slogan behind the president was actually a painted backdrop. The real boxes in front of the President's podium, hidden in this photo, were also hiding something: their "Made in China" lettering had been covered with tape. The embarrassed Bush administration attributed the taped boxes to an "overzealous volunteer."

consumer-education literature about specific products and developed close ties with local consumer groups.

Today, the impact of the consumer movement is especially evident in the resources devoted to carefully training employees in good customer relations. Many product and service companies have also developed customer-satisfaction questionnaires and "consumer creeds." For example, many restaurants and department stores go beyond asking consumers for advice, outlining what treatment customers should expect and what they should do when those expectations are not met. PR professionals routinely advise clients that satisfied customers mean not only repeat business but new business, based on a strong word-of-mouth reputation about a company's behavior and image.

Government Relations and Lobbying

Public relations also entails maintaining connections with government agencies that have some say in how companies operate in a particular community, state, or nation. The PR divisions of major firms are especially interested in making sure that government regulation neither becomes burdensome nor reduces their control over their businesses. Specialists in this area often develop self-regulatory practices, which either keep governments at some distance or draw on them for subsidies, as the railroads and utilities did in the nineteenth century. Such specialists also monitor new and existing legislation, create opportunities to ensure favorable publicity, and write press releases and direct-mail letters to educate the public on the pros and cons of new regulations.

In many firms, government relations has developed into **lobbying**: the process of attempting to influence the voting of lawmakers to support an organization's or an industry's best interests. In seeking favorable legislation, some PR agents lobby government officials on a daily basis. In Washington, D.C., alone, more than twenty thousand registered lobbyists write speeches, articles, and position papers in addition to designing direct-mail campaigns, buying ads, and befriending editors.

Today, most major corporations, trade associations, labor unions, consumer groups, professional organizations, religious groups, and even foreign governments

● Corporations, trade associations, labor unions, and special-interest groups are among the organizations that help to mobilize citizens to lobby government agencies and politicians to support their causes. For example, the Texas Motorcycle Rights Association directs its members to attend press conferences and legislative hearings that might concern motorcycle regulations.

employ lobbyists. For instance, prior to the Persian Gulf War, lobbyists tried to justify U.S. and UN military action against Iraq, which had invaded Kuwait in 1990. To that end, the Kuwaiti royal family (who went into exile before Iraq invaded Kuwait) hired Hill and Knowlton to help rally public support for U.S. military intervention. The firm developed the idea of a "congressional human rights caucus," which in October 1990 reported acts of barbarism perpetrated by Iraqis on Kuwaitis. Later it was discovered that one witness, a fifteen-year-old Kuwaiti girl who testified at the caucus to seeing acts of cruelty, was the daughter of the Kuwaiti ambassador to the United States and "had been witness to no such events." In January 1991 the United States invaded Iraq, with the majority of Americans, according to opinion polls, supporting the intervention.[17]

Public relations firms have had a hand in the public's understanding of a number of other international situations as well. For example, the Chinese government retained Hill and Knowlton to repair its image after the 1989 Tiananmen Square massacre that left more than 150 unarmed civilian protesters dead. More recently, the Saudi Arabian government began paying the PR firm Qorvis Communications about $200,000 a month to help repair its image with the American public after the September 11, 2001, terrorism attacks on the United States.[18]

Tensions between Public Relations and the Press

In 1932, Stanley Walker, an editor at the *New York Herald Tribune,* identified public relations agents and publicity advisers as "mass-mind molders, fronts, mouthpieces, chiselers, moochers, and special assistants to the president."[19] Walker added that newspapers and public relations agencies would always remain enemies, even if PR professionals adopted a code of ethics (which they did in the 1950s) to "take them out of the red-light district of human relations."[20] Walker's tone captures the spirit of one of the most mutually dependent—and antagonistic—relationships across mass media.

Much of this antagonism, directed at public relations from the journalism profession, is historical. Reporters have long considered themselves part of an older public-service profession, whereas many regard PR as a pseudo-profession created to distort the facts that reporters work so hard to gather. Over time, reporters and editors developed a nationwide derogatory term for a PR agent—**flack**—which continues in usage to this day. The term derives from the military word *flak,* meaning the antiaircraft artillery shells fired to deflect aerial attack, and from the related flak jacket, the protective military attire worn to ward off enemy fire. For journalists, the word *flack* has come to mean PR people who insert themselves between their employers/clients and members of the press.

In the 1960s, an Associated Press manual for editors defined a flack as "a person who makes all or part of his income by obtaining space in newspapers without cost to himself or his clients." The AP depiction continued: "A flack is a flack. His job is to say kind things about his client. He will not lie very often, but much of the time he tells less than the whole story. You do not owe the PR man anything. The owner of the newspaper, not the flack, pays your salary. Your immediate job is to serve the readers, not the man who would raid your columns." This description, however, belies journalism's dependence on public relations. Many editors, for instance, admit that more than half of their story ideas each day originate with PR people.

Elements of Professional Friction

The relationship between journalism and PR is an important and complex one. Although journalism lays claim to independent traditions, the news media have become ever more reliant on public relations because of the increasing amount of information now available. Staff cutbacks at many papers, combined with television's need for local newscast events, have also expanded the news media's need for PR story ideas.

Further depleting journalism, PR firms routinely raid the ranks of reporting for new talent. Because most press releases are written in a style that imitates news reports, the PR profession has always sought good writers who are well connected to sources and savvy about the news business. For instance, the fashion industry likes to hire former style or fashion news writers for its PR staff, and university information offices seek reporters who once covered higher education. It is interesting to note that although reporters frequently move into PR, public relations practitioners seldom move into journalism; the news profession rarely accepts prodigal sons or daughters back into the fold once they have left reporting for public relations. According to many reporters and editors, any profession that shapes images is considered manipulative or self-serving—and its practitioners may not be redeemable. Nevertheless, the professions remain co-dependent: PR needs journalists for publicity, and journalism needs PR for story ideas and access. Several historical explanations shed light on this type of discord and on the ways in which different media professions interact.

Undermining Facts and Blocking Access

Modern public relations redefined and complicated the notion of facts. PR professionals demonstrated that the same set of facts can be spun in a variety of ways, depending on what information is emphasized and what is downplayed. As Ivy Lee noted in 1925: "The effort to state an absolute fact is simply an attempt to achieve what is humanly impossible; all I can do is to give you *my interpretation* of the facts."[21] With practitioners like Lee showing the emerging PR profession how facts and news could be manipulated, the journalist's role as a custodian of accurate information became much more difficult. In fact, a 2000 survey of PR professionals gave some credence to public relations' worst image: "25 percent admit to lying on the job, 39 percent say they had exaggerated the truth, and 44 percent were uncertain of the ethics of the task they were required to perform."[22]

Journalists have also objected to PR flacks who block press access to key leaders. At one time, reporters could talk to such leaders directly and obtain quotable information for their news stories. Now, however, PR people insert themselves between the press and the powerful, thus disrupting the old ritual in which reporters would vie for interviews with top government and business leaders. If PR agents today want to manipulate or use reporters, they may give information to journalists who are likely to cast a story in a favorable light in return for getting the information first. On rarer occasions, a reporter's access to key sources might be cut off altogether if that journalist has written unfavorably about a PR agency's client.

Promoting Publicity and Business as News

Another explanation for the professional friction between the press and PR involves simple economics. The trade journal *Editor & Publisher* once called public relations agents "space grabbers"; what editors and publishers feared actually became a reality: PR agents helped companies "promote as news what otherwise would have been purchased in advertising."[23]

As Ivy Lee wrote to John D. Rockefeller after the oil magnate gave money to Johns Hopkins University: "In view of the fact that this was not really news, and that the newspapers gave so much attention to it, it would seem that this was wholly due to the manner in which the material was 'dressed up' for newspaper consumption. It seems to suggest very considerable possibilities along this line."[24] Many newspeople react strongly to this sort of manipulation. Critics worry that public relations is taking media space and time away from those who do not have the financial resources or the sophistication to become readily visible in the public eye. Beyond this lies another issue: If public relations can secure publicity for clients in the news, the added credibility of a journalistic context gives clients a status that the purchase of advertising cannot confer.

Today, however, something more subtle underlies journalism's contempt for public relations: Much of journalism actually functions in the same way. For instance, politicians, celebrities, and PR firms with abundant resources are clearly afforded more coverage by the news media than are their lesser-known counterparts. For example, workers and union leaders have long argued that the money that corporations allocate to PR leads to more favorable coverage for management positions in labor disputes. Standard news reports may feature subtle language choices, with "rational, cool-headed management making *offers*" and "hot-headed workers making *demands*." Walter Lippmann saw such differences in 1922 when he wrote: "If you study the way many a strike is reported in the press, you will find very often that [labor] issues are rarely in the headlines, barely in the leading paragraph, and sometimes not even mentioned anywhere."[25] Most newspapers now have business sections that focus on the work of various managers, but few have a labor, worker, or employee section. In fact, most large metro papers have eliminated the specialty beat of labor reporting.[26]

Business, economic, and stock "news" reports generated by corporate PR agents inundate newspapers and the evening news. A single business reporter at a large metro daily sometimes receives as many as a hundred press releases a day—far outnumbering the fraction of handouts generated by organized labor or grassroots organizations. This imbalance is particularly significant in that the great majority of workers are neither managers nor CEOs, and yet these workers receive little if any

media coverage on a regular basis. Essentially, as a number of critics have pointed out, mainstream journalism best serves managers and the business status quo.

Managing the Press

Public relations, by making reporters' jobs easier, has often enabled reporters to become lazy. PR firms now supply what reporters used to work hard to gather for themselves. Instead of going out to beat the competition, many journalists have become content to wait for a PR handout or a good tip before following up on a story. Small community groups, social activists, and nonprofit organizations often cannot afford elaborate publicity. These groups argue that because of PR, large corporations and well-connected politicians enjoy easier access to reporters and receive much more frequent news coverage. Occasionally, also because of PR, powerful firms and individuals receive less critical scrutiny. Some members of the news media, grateful for the reduced workload that occurs when they are provided with handouts, may be hesitant to criticize a particular PR firm's clients.

Dealing with both a tainted past and journalism's hostility has often preoccupied the public relations profession, leading to the development of several image-enhancing strategies. Over the years, for example, as public relations has subdivided itself into specialized areas, it has used more positive descriptive phrases, such as "institutional relations," "corporate communications," and "news and information services." With the development of its own professional organization in 1948, PRSA, the PR industry has also enhanced its standing among the public and even the news media.[27] PRSA functions as an internal watchdog group that accredits individuals, maintains a code of ethics, and publishes newsletters and trade publications. Most PRSA local chapters and national conventions also routinely invite reporters and editors to speak to PR practitioners about what the news media expect from their rival professionals. In addition, independent agencies, devoted to uncovering shady or unethical public relations activities, publish their findings in publications like PR Tactics, PRWeek, or PR Watch. Ethical issues have become a major focus of the PR profession, with self-examination of these issues routinely appearing in PR textbooks as well as in various professional newsletters (see Table 12.2).

Public relations' best press strategy, however, may be the limitations of the journalism profession itself. For most of the twentieth century, many reporters and editors clung to the ideal that journalism is, at its best, an objective institution that gathers information on behalf of the public. Reporters have only occasionally turned their pens, computers, and cameras on themselves to examine their own practices or their vulnerability to manipulation. Thus, by not challenging PR's more subtle strategies, many journalists have allowed PR professionals to interpret "facts" to their clients' advantage.

Limited by its reluctance or failure to identify and evade savvy public relations tactics, conventional journalism remains vulnerable. Consider this hypothetical situation: A wealthy and powerful development corporation decides to raze a homeless shelter to build a condo. The firm uses public relations resources that overwhelm the protests of a few homeless activists. The major newspaper in town attempts to remain neutral on the issue. However, the strength of the corporation's PR unit has already tipped the balance of the issue in all of the town's media outlets. To recenter the scales, the newspaper in this case would have to take an advocacy position on behalf of the activists. But in conventional journalism, detachment prohibits this, and thus the corporate point of view typically triumphs—or, at least, gains most of the space and time in the news coverage. Although many alternative newspapers and advocacy reporters do a fine job of critiquing the limits of some questionable public relations activities, conventional journalism has few mechanisms for rebalancing the scales tipped by PR embellishment, whether advanced by government or business leaders.

Crude oil from the tanker Exxon *Valdez* swirls on the surface of Alaska's Prince William Sound on April 9, 1989, 16 days after the tanker ran aground, spilling millions of gallons of oil and causing widespread environmental damage.

Alternative Voices

Because public relations professionals work so closely with the press, their practices are not often the subject of media reports or investigations. Indeed, the multibillion-dollar industry remains virtually invisible to the public, most of whom have never heard of Burson-Marsteller, Hill and Knowlton, or Ketchum. John Stauber and Sheldon Rampton, investigative reporters who work for the Center for Media and Democracy in Washington, D.C., are concerned about the invisibility of PR practices and have sought to expose the hidden activities of large PR firms. As editors of *PR Watch,* a quarterly publication they launched in 1995, they publish investigative reports on the PR industry that never appear in mainstream mass media outlets. "PR

APPLIED CRITICAL PROCESS
The Invisible Hand of PR

In 1997, John Stauber of the industry watchdog *PR Watch* described the PR industry as "a huge, invisible industry, probably over a $10-billion-a-year entity that's really only available to wealthy individuals, large multinational corporations, politicians and government agencies."[1] How true is this? Is the PR industry so invisible?

Description. We've decided to test the PR industry's so-called invisibility and see how often it is discussed in TV news. Using LexisNexis, we searched television, cable, and radio news transcripts over the entire year of 2002 for any mention of the three enormous PR firms Weber Shandwick Worldwide, Fleishman-Hillard, and Burson-Marsteller. All are among the top five largest PR firms in the world. We found 4 stories about Weber Shandwick, 98 about Fleishman-Hillard, and 9 about Burson-Marsteller.

Analysis. What are the patterns that emerged from these 111 stories? First, nearly all of the programs on which these stories appeared were business-oriented networks or programs (e.g., CNNfn, CNBC, PBS's *Nightly Business Report,* Minnesota Public Radio's syndicated *Marketplace,* and Boston's "Business 1060" radio station). Second, 75 percent of the 111 stories mentioned one of the PR firms only because the news program had invited a PR executive from one of the firms to be an expert studio guest— this especially accounted for the high number of Fleishman-Hillard mentions. Third, only two stories in a year of news transcripts connected one of the PR firms with its client. In one case, *60 Minutes*

reporter Leslie Stahl mentioned that Burson-Marsteller worked on behalf of the Iraqi National Congress (INC), an exiled Iraqi resistance group trying to topple Saddam Hussein. In the other case, ABC's *20/20 Downtown* reported on a California family who hired Fleishman-Hillard in the wake of their daughter's abduction. Fleishman-Hillard, according to *20/20 Downtown,* was helping the family deal with intense media coverage during the search for their daughter.

Interpretation. The PR industry spends a good deal of effort placing positive stories about their clients in the news media. But clearly, reports *about* the PR industry itself do not exist in U.S. news coverage. Weber Shandwick, Fleishman-Hillard and Burson-Marsteller alone managed to accumulate more than $10 billion in profits in 2002, but as enormous conglomerates, they are largely invisible to the American public.

Evaluation. PR firms—such as the heavyweights we examined—have enormous power in influencing the public images (and hence the practices) of both global and local corporations, entire nations, and important public policy initiatives in the United States and abroad. PR firms also have enormous influence over news content, generating tens of thousands of news stories each year. Yet the U.S. mass media is silent on this influence. Public relations firms certainly aren't going to be more public about their power, but should journalism be more public about its role as a publicity vehicle for PR?

Watch seeks to serve the public rather than PR," they explain. "With the assistance of whistleblowers and a few sympathetic insiders, we report about the secretive activities of an industry which works behind the scenes to control government policy and shape public opinion."[28] (See "Applied Critical Process: The Invisible Hand of PR" above.)

Stauber and Rampton have also written books targeting public relations practices having to do with industrial waste *(Toxic Sludge Is Good for You: Lies, Damn Lies, and the Public Relations Industry),* mad cow disease *(Mad Cow USA: Could the Nightmare Happen Here?),* and PR uses of scientific research *(Trust Us, We're Experts!: How Industry Manipulates Science and Gambles with Your Future).* The work of Stauber and Rampton helps to bring an alternative angle to the well-monied battles over public opinion. "You know, we feel that in a democracy, it's very, very critical that everyone knows who the players are, and what they're up to," Stauber says.[29]

Public Relations, Social Responsibility, and Democracy

From the days of its origins in the early 1900s, many people—especially journalists—have been skeptical of communications originating from public relations professionals. Yet early PR practitioners such as Ivy Lee and Edward Bernays were often very effective, and journalists have grown to rely on the public relations profession for information and ideas. Today, most public relations activity emerges from small in-house services, but the largest corporate clients and governments are usually served by the multinational PR subsidiaries of global communications firms.

Although the image of public relations professionals may not be as negative as that of advertisers, a cynical view of the profession nonetheless exists beyond the field of journalism. Given the history of corporate public relations, many concerned citizens believe that when a company or an individual makes a mistake or misleads the public, too often a PR counsel is hired to alter the image rather than to admit the misdeed and correct the problem. For example, in the aftermath of one of the largest environmental disasters of the twentieth century—the Exxon *Valdez* oil spill along the Alaska coast in 1989—the multinational corporation eventually changed the name of the tanker *Valdez* to *Mediterranean* in the 1990s. The name change was just a small tactic in a series of damage-control strategies that Exxon enacted to cope with the oil spill. Disaster management may reveal the worst—or best—attributes of the PR profession. How to enhance a company's image and, at the same time, encourage the company to be a socially responsible corporate citizen remains a major challenge for public relations (see "Examining Ethics: Levi Strauss and Anti-Sweatshop Public Relations" on page 446).

The Exxon *Valdez* case was a corporate as well as an environmental disaster, despite the company's outlay of $2 billion to clean up both its image and the spill. When eleven million gallons of crude oil spilled into Prince William Sound, contaminating fifteen hundred miles of Alaskan coastline and killing countless birds, otters, seals, and fish, Exxon was slow to react to the crisis and even slower to accept responsibility. Although its PR advisers had encouraged a quick response, the corporation failed to send any of its chief officers immediately to the site to express concern. Many critics believed that Exxon was trying to duck responsibility by laying the burden of the crisis on the shoulders of the tanker's captain. A former president of NBC News, William Small, maintained that Exxon "lost the battle of public relations" and suffered "one of the worst tarnishings of its corporate image in American history."[30]

A decidedly different approach was taken in the 1982 tragedy involving Tylenol pain-relief capsules. Seven people died in the Chicago area after someone tampered with several bottles and laced them with poison. Like the oil spill, the case was a major news story. Discussions between the parent company, Johnson & Johnson, and its PR and advertising representatives focused on whether withdrawing all Tylenol capsules might send a signal that corporations could be intimidated by a single deranged person. Nevertheless, Johnson & Johnson's chairman, James E. Burke, and the company's PR agency, Burson-Marsteller, opted for full disclosure to the media and the immediate recall of the capsules nationally, costing the company an estimated

> **"** The Exxon *Valdez* Story: How to Spend a Billion or Two and Still Get a Black Eye in Public. **"**
>
> –Business school conference title, Fordham University, 1990

> **"** The burden is on us to earn your trust all over again. But it will take more than words. It will only be through our actions that people will once again think well of Firestone. **"**
>
> –John Lampe, CEO, Bridgestone/Firestone, 2000

REAL GAP KIDS
N CLOTHES FOR
56¢
AN HOUR

New York,
New York
a helluva town
costs go up &
wages go down!

Support the
"Living Wage Bill!"

UNITE!

● Thousands rally in New York City in a National Labor Committee protest against sweatshops and child labor.

Levi Strauss and Anti-Sweatshop Public Relations

In the late 1990s, a growing tide of Americans focused on the problems of outsourcing: using the production, manufacturing, and labor resources of foreign companies to produce American brand-name products, sometimes under deplorable working conditions. Since 1998, more than 180 university chapters of United Students Against Sweatshops have formed, and at several universities—including Duke, Georgetown, the University of Wisconsin, and some Ivy League schools—students staged rallies and sit-ins to urge administrators to take a hard line against companies that use overseas sweatshops to make apparel bearing university logos. At many of these schools, administrators complied by instituting tougher guidelines for overseas licensing.

In 1996, outsourcing was pushed into the public eye after major media attention focused on morning talk-show host Kathie Lee Gifford when human-rights groups revealed that part of her clothing line, made and distributed by Wal-Mart, came from sweatshops in New York and Honduras. The sweatshops paid less than minimum wages, and some employed child laborers. Human-rights activists claimed that in the overseas sweatshops in particular, children were being exploited in violation of international child-labor laws.

New York, New York a helluva town costs go up & wages go down!

Support the "Living Wage Bill!"

Many global companies now comply with international guidelines that protect children and pay workers living wages. Many countries, however, including the United States, still tolerate sweatshop conditions in which workers take home minimal pay, sometimes less than a dollar an hour for working ten- to twelve-hour shifts six days a week.

As labor unions, the national media, and human-rights groups began tracking the problem of sweatshops, stories about worker exploitation were exposed. One U.S. firm, Levi Strauss & Company, pioneered an institutional public relations program to guard against sweatshop practices. With more than seven hundred sewing contractors making jeans and other clothing in fifty countries, Levi Strauss developed the first set of international, anti-sweatshop guidelines for its contractors. The guidelines were the company's response to early criticism about its moving some of its manufacturing overseas in search of low-cost labor markets.

The Levi Strauss plan focused on balancing "the company's merchandising and production needs with corporate social responsibility." Managers at Levi Strauss studied various ways of dealing with the cultural values and differences in the countries where they had manufacturing interests.[1]

To execute the plan, Levi Strauss instituted a training program involving more than a hundred "in-country" managers who understood the language, culture, and values of their workforces. The company met with apparel workers' unions to get input and support; the trained managers then regularly monitored and audited their plants. The Levi Strauss media plan succeeded in positioning the company as a leader in global business practices while "distinguishing itself from other companies as the 'bright spot' in otherwise negative sourcing stories."[2]

By 1993, all of Levi Strauss's worldwide contractors had been audited. About 70 percent met the anti-sweatshop standards set by company policy. About 25 percent of the contractors promised to make mandated improvements in the treatment of their workers. Five percent of the contractors were dropped for violating anti-sweatshop agreements. The company withdrew outsourcing from both Burma and China after human-rights violations persisted. It also suspended its contract with Peruvian plants because of employee safety concerns. In 1993, *Fortune* magazine ranked Levi Strauss as "America's most admired apparel company," and *Business Ethics* magazine honored the jeans company with its Award for Excellence in Ethics.

In 2002, even as sales of Levi's clothing had fallen, the company's executives held fast to their code of conduct. "Levi Strauss & Co. is committed to ensuring compliance with our code of conduct at all facilities that manufacture or finish our products around the world," executives said. "If a contractor fails to meet the corrective action plan commitment, Levi Strauss & Co. will terminate the business relationship."[3] Meanwhile, several other clothing sellers, including Wal-Mart, still struggled with charges that they use sweatshop labor in hundreds of garment factories in places like China, Saipan, Bangladesh, and Honduras.[4]

$100 million. Before the incident, Tylenol had a market share of 37 percent, making it the leading pain-relief medicine. After the capsule withdrawal, Tylenol's share was cut nearly in half.

As part of its PR strategy to overcome the negative publicity and to restore Tylenol's market share, Burson-Marsteller tracked public opinion nightly through telephone surveys and organized satellite press conferences to debrief the news media. In addition, emergency phone lines were set up to take calls from consumers and health-care providers, who altogether sent two million messages to Johnson & Johnson. When the company reintroduced Tylenol three months after the tragedy began, it did so with tamper-resistant bottles that were soon copied by almost every major drug manufacturer. Burson-Marsteller, which received PRSA awards for its handling of the crisis, found that the public thought Johnson & Johnson had responded admirably to the crisis and did not hold Tylenol responsible for the deaths. In fewer than three years, Tylenol recaptured its former share of the market.

> **" In politics, image [has] replaced action. "**
>
> – Randall Rothenberg, *Where the Suckers Moon*, 1994

The Exxon and Tylenol incidents—and the more recent crisis of the Bridgestone/Firestone–Ford Explorer tire problems—demonstrate both dim and bright aspects of public relations, a profession that continues to provoke concern. The bulk of the criticism leveled at public relations argues that the crush of information produced by PR professionals overwhelms traditional journalism. In one example, former president Richard Nixon, who resigned from office in 1974 to avoid impeachment hearings regarding his role in the Watergate scandal, hired Hill and Knowlton to restore his post-presidency image. Through the firm's guidance, Nixon's writings, mostly on international politics, began appearing in Sunday op-ed pages. Nixon himself started showing up on *Nightline* and spoke frequently before groups such as the American Newspaper Publishers Association and the Economic Club of New York. In 1984, after a media blitz by Nixon's PR handlers, the *New York Times* announced: "After a decade, Nixon is gaining favor," and *USA Today* trumpeted: "Richard Nixon is back." Before his death in 1994, Nixon, who never publicly apologized for his role in Watergate, saw a large portion of his public image shift from that of an arrogant, disgraced politician to that of a revered elder statesman.[31] Many media critics have charged that the press did not balance the scales and treated Nixon too reverently after the successful PR campaign.

In terms of its immediate impact on democracy, the information crush delivered by public relations is at its height during national election campaigns. In fact, PR's most significant impact may be on the political process, especially when organizations hire spin doctors to favorably shape or reshape a candidate's media image. During the 1998 governor's race in Minnesota, former pro wrestler and navy SEAL Jesse "the Body" Ventura successfully combined a third-party PR and ad campaign to defeat the leading Democratic and Republican candidates. Ventura's strategy—which targeted independent voters and young adults—transformed his image as an evil, cross-dressing, "dumb rassler" into that of a patriotic, rugged individualist. Minnesota's registered-voter turnout—more than 60 percent—was the highest in the nation in 1998.

Public relations has long been firmly ensconced in the White House as well. One of George W. Bush's closest advisers as Texas governor and in the first two years of his presidency was Karen Hughes, his public relations counselor. A number of events—from Bush's tee-ball games on the White House lawn to his long summer "working vacations" at his remote Texas ranch—were engineered by the White House communications staff to create an image that would differentiate Bush from his predecessor, Bill Clinton.

Though public relations often provides political information and story ideas, the PR profession probably bears only part of the responsibility for manipulating the news media; after all, it is the job of an agency to spin the news favorably for the individual or group it represents. PR professionals should certainly police their own ranks (and often do) for unethical or irresponsible practices, but the news media should also monitor the public relations industry, as they do other government and business activities. This media vigilance should be on behalf of citizens, who are entitled to robust, well-rounded debates on important social and political issues.

In a democracy, journalism and public relations need to retain their guarded posture toward each other. But journalism itself may need to institute changes that will make it less dependent on PR and more conscious of how its own practices play into the hands of spin strategies. Especially during elections, journalists need to become more vigilant in monitoring questionable PR tactics. A positive example of change on this front is that many major newspapers and news networks now offer regular critiques of the facts and falsehoods contained in political advertising.

Like advertising and other forms of commercial speech, publicity campaigns that result in free media exposure raise a number of questions regarding democracy and the expression of ideas. Large PR agencies and product companies, like well-financed politicians, have money to invest to figure out how to obtain favorable publicity. The question is not how to prevent that but how to ensure that other voices, less well financed and less commercial, receive an adequate hearing. To that end, journalists need to become less willing conduits in the distribution of publicity. PR agencies, for their part, need to show clients that participating in the democratic process as responsible citizens can serve them well and enhance their image.

www.

To create an individualized study plan for Chapter 12, go to the interactive *Media and Culture* Online Study Guide at: bedfordstmartins.com/ mediaculture

REVIEW QUESTIONS

Early Developments in Public Relations

1. What did people like P. T. Barnum and Buffalo Bill Cody contribute to the development of modern public relations in the twentieth century?

2. How did railroads and utility companies give the early forms of corporate public relations a bad name?

3. What contributions did Ivy Lee make toward the development of modern PR?

4. How did Edward Bernays affect public relations?

5. What is a pseudo-event? How does it relate to the manufacturing of news?

The Practice of Public Relations

6. What are two approaches to organizing a PR firm?

7. What are press releases, and why are they important to reporters?

8. What is the difference between a VNR and a PSA?

9. What special events might a PR firm sponsor to build stronger ties to its community?

10. Why have research and lobbying become increasingly important to the practice of PR?

Tensions between Public Relations and the Press

11. Explain the historical background of the antagonism between journalism and public relations.

12. How did PR change old relationships between journalists and their sources?

13. In what ways is conventional news like public relations?

14. How does journalism as a profession contribute to its own manipulation at the hands of competent PR practitioners?

Public Relations, Social Responsibility, and Democracy

15. What are some socially responsible strategies that a PR specialist can use during a crisis to help a client manage unfavorable publicity?

16. In what ways does the profession of public relations serve democracy? In what ways can it impede democracy?

QUESTIONING THE MEDIA

1. What do you think of when you hear the term *public relations*? What images come to mind? Where did these impressions come from?

2. What might a college or university do to improve public relations with homeowners on the edge of a campus who have to deal with noisy student parties and a shortage of parking spaces?

3. What steps can reporters and editors take to monitor PR agents who manipulate the news media?

4. Can and should the often hostile relationship between the journalism and PR professions be mended? Why or why not?

5. Besides the Exxon *Valdez* and Tylenol cases cited in this chapter, investigate and research a PR crisis (such as the Bridgestone/Firestone–Ford Explorer tire problems, the mad cow disease beef scare in Europe, the contamination of Odwalla fruit juice, or any number of campaigns described by PRWatch.org). How was the crisis handled?

SEARCHING THE INTERNET

http://www.prsa.org

The official site of the Public Relations Society of America, the leading U.S. professional PR organization. Provides information on membership, awards, conferences, PR publications, and links to other PR-related sites.

http://www.prssa.org

This site of the Public Relations Student Society of America gives information on local student chapters around the United States.

http://www.prmuseum.com

The Web site for the New York-based museum, which was established in 1997, includes interesting histories of Edward Bernays and other important figures in PR history.

http://www.odwyerpr.com

This site, linked to an influential and independent publisher of PR news and directories of PR firms, includes information about the field and statistics on numerous firms. Some parts of the site require a fee for access.

http://silveranvil.org

A resource center and archive for case studies of award-winning PR campaigns.

http://www.prwatch.org

This site is the online presence of the Center for Media and Democracy, a nonprofit, public interest organization dedicated to investigative reporting on the PR industry.

THE CRITICAL PROCESS

In Brief

Imagine that you work for a high-powered PR firm, and a controversial client (e.g., a tobacco company, Bridgestone/Firestone, the government of Saudi Arabia, etc.) hires your firm to reshape the client's image. To perform this job, what are the strategies you would employ and why? (Before you begin, your class may want to discuss clients you would refuse to work for.)

In Depth

What influence do press releases have? To find out, track three to five press releases, from the time they are released through any resulting news stories. First, check with a public relations organization that issues releases. For example, you can check with your university's public relations office or the athletic department's sports information office. Both offices may post their press releases on a Web site as well. On the day the press releases are issued, track the local print news stories that are generated. (Alternatively, you could track broadcast news stories.)

Description. Describe your list of stories. How many stories are there? Which newspaper(s) used the press release?

Analysis. What kinds of patterns emerge? Do most publications and broadcasts seem to be willing to print the information in the press release? Did the reporters do any additional investigation, or did they take the point of view of the release? Did certain types of releases fail to get any coverage? What kinds of stories received more prominence and coverage?

Interpretation. What changes, if any, were made between each public relations release and the corresponding news story? Why do you think these changes were made? Do newspapers ever print releases verbatim? Should they? Which version represented the best story—the press release or the news story? Why? (Keep in mind that each story has a different purpose and audience.)

Evaluation. How much should press releases drive a newspaper's coverage of an institution like a local college or university? Are there potentially significant stories on campus that don't get reported because they are not likely to be suggested to the press via a press release?

KEY TERMS

publicity, 421
public relations, 421
press agents, 422
pseudo-event, 427

propaganda, 430
press releases, 430
video news releases (VNRs), 430

public-service announcements
  (PSAs), 430
lobbying, 437
flack, 438

media economics

and the global marketplace

CHAPTER 13

Analyzing the Media Economy

The Transition to an Information Economy

Social Issues in Media Economics

The Media Marketplace and Democracy

Enron, the Houston-based energy trading firm that pumped up its stock price with phony accounting and later collapsed (but not before its executives made off with millions of dollars), became the metaphor for a wave of corporate accounting scandals that came to light beginning in 2001.

As it turns out, several major media corporations that were reporting on the multibillion-dollar meltdowns of corporations like Enron, Worldcom, and Tyco got "Enronized" themselves. That is, investors lost confidence in the corporations' grand growth

and synergy schemes and shaky accounting practices. In fact, the scandals shook the very foundations of global stock markets.

Just a few years earlier, global media corporations giddily tried to outdo each other with rounds of media acquisitions. *Business Week* magazine called them the "moguls who shopped till they dropped."[1] And drop they did. AOL Time Warner president Bob Pittman, Bertelsmann CEO Thomas Middlehoff, and Vivendi Universal CEO Jean-Marie Messier were all fired in 2002, with Messier undergoing the

↓

18

additional consequence of having his home raided by French police investigating his role in the possible falsification of Vivendi Universal accounts to inflate its stock price. In 2003, Steve Case, the embattled chairman of the biggest media firm, AOL Time Warner, resigned in a storm of criticism and federal investigations of his company's finances. Shortly afterward, Ted Turner—vice chairman of AOL Time Warner and a stern critic of the 2001 AOL-Time Warner merger—resigned as well. Turner's resignation came just after AOL Time Warner announced that its net losses for 2002 totaled nearly $100 billion—the largest corporate loss ever posted in the U.S.

Richard Parsons, the new chairman and CEO at AOL Time Warner, vowed to do "no more silly deals" as he attempted to stabilize the giant firm. Bertelsmann was left to sell many of its recent acquisitions at below-purchase prices. Vivendi, a French utility company that billed itself as Europe's rival to AOL Time Warner when it bought Universal in 2000, entered 2003 with losses of $25.6 billion (the largest corporate loss in French history) and plans to sell off all of its Universal entertainment assets.

The failure of these media conglomerates to capitalize on potential corporate synergies of their far-flung divisions doesn't mean an end to global media empire building, but instead just a reshuffling of the rankings. In fact, Viacom, News Corp., and others waited patiently to buy up parts of the debt-ridden media conglomerates at discount prices to make themselves even larger.

the rash of media mergers over the last two decades has made our world very distinct from that of earlier generations—at least in economic terms. In this chapter, we will explore the issues and tensions that have contributed to current economic conditions. We will look at the rise of the Information Age, distinguished by flexible, global, and specialized markets. We will discuss the breakdown of economic borders, focusing on media consolidation, corporate mergers, synergy, deregulation, and the emergence of an economic global village. We will also take up ethical and social issues in media economics, investigating the limits of antitrust laws, the concept of consumer control, and the threat of cultural imperialism. Finally, after examining the role of journalism in monitoring media economics, we will consider the impact of media consolidation on democracy and on the diversity of the marketplace.

Analyzing the Media Economy

Given the sprawling scope of the mass media, the study of their economic conditions poses a number of complicated questions. For example, does the government need to play a stronger role in determining who owns what mass media and what kinds of media products should be manufactured? Should the government step back

● Kenneth Lay, the former Enron CEO, is sworn in before the Senate Committee on Commerce, Science and Transportation February 12, 2002, in connection with his role in Enron's financial collapse. Lay exercised his fifth amendment right and did not testify.

and let competition and market forces dictate what happens to mass-media industries? Should citizen groups play a larger part in demanding that media organizations help maintain the quality of social and cultural life? Does the rapid spread of American culture worldwide smother or encourage the growth of democracy and local cultures? Does the increasing concentration of economic power in the hands of several international corporations restrict or expand the number of players and voices in media markets? Answers to such questions span the economic spectrum. On the one hand, critics express concerns about the increasing power and reach of large media conglomerates. On the other hand, many free-market advocates maintain that as long as these structures ensure efficient operation and generous profits, they measure up as quality media organizations. In order to probe economic issues from different perspectives, we need to understand key economic concepts in two broad areas: media structure and media performance.[2]

The Structure of the Media Industry

In economic terms, three common structures characterize the media business: monopoly, oligopoly, and limited competition. First, a **monopoly** occurs when a single firm dominates production and distribution in a particular industry, either nationally or locally. At the national level, for example, until the mid-1980s AT&T ran a rare government-approved and -regulated monopoly—the telephone business. Software giant Microsoft, accused of monopolistic practices throughout much of the 1990s, was ordered by a federal judge in 2000 to split into two separate companies. But Microsoft ultimately prevailed, and in 2002 it agreed to a court settlement that imposed restrictions on its business dealings with personal computer makers but left the company intact. On the local level, monopoly situations have been more plentiful, occurring in any city that has only one newspaper or one cable company. Until the 1996 Telecommunications Act, the government had historically encouraged owner diversity by prohibiting a newspaper from operating a broadcast or cable company in the same city. Many individual local media monopolies, though, have been purchased by national and international firms. For instance, TCI and Time Warner—for years the nation's largest cable operators—own hundreds of small cable monopolies. And in 1999 AT&T swallowed TCI, a multibillion-dollar deal that married the world's largest phone company and the world's largest cable TV operation. Likewise, in the newspaper business, chain operators like Gannett own more

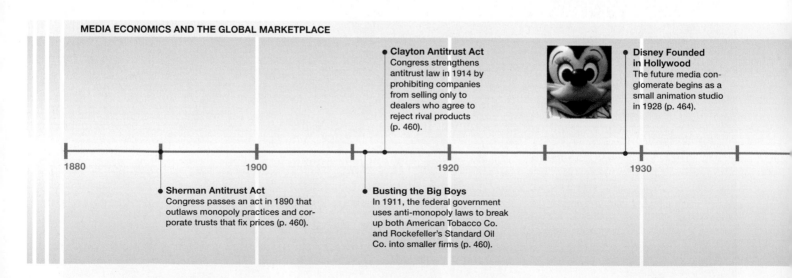

MEDIA ECONOMICS AND THE GLOBAL MARKETPLACE

● **Clayton Antitrust Act**
Congress strengthens antitrust law in 1914 by prohibiting companies from selling only to dealers who agree to reject rival products (p. 460).

● **Disney Founded in Hollywood**
The future media conglomerate begins as a small animation studio in 1928 (p. 464).

1880   1900   1920   1930

● **Sherman Antitrust Act**
Congress passes an act in 1890 that outlaws monopoly practices and corporate trusts that fix prices (p. 460).

● **Busting the Big Boys**
In 1911, the federal government uses anti-monopoly laws to break up both American Tobacco Co. and Rockefeller's Standard Oil Co. into smaller firms (p. 460).

than a hundred papers, most of which constitute a newspaper monopoly in their communities.

Second, an **oligopoly** describes an economic situation in which just a few firms dominate an industry. The commercial sound-recording and feature-film businesses are both oligopolies. Each has five or six major players that control the production and distribution of more than 90 percent of that industry. Since 2000, three multinational firms—Vivendi Universal of France (which acquired Seagram and Universal Studios late in 2000), Sony of Japan, and AOL Time Warner of the United States—have been major players in both the movie and the music oligopolies. Usually conducting business only in response to each other, such companies face little economic competition from small independent firms. Oligopolies often add new ideas and product lines by purchasing successful independents.

Third, **limited competition**, sometimes called *monopolistic competition,* characterizes a media market with many producers and sellers but only a few differentiable products within a particular category.[3] For instance, although the 1996 Telecommunications Act encouraged consolidation by lifting ownership restrictions on radio, hundreds of independently owned stations still operate in the United States. Most of these commercial stations, however, feature a limited number of formats—such as country, classic rock, and contemporary hits—from which listeners may choose. Because commercial broadcast radio is now a difficult market to enter, requiring an FCC license and major capital investment, most station managers play the few formats that attract sizable audiences. Under these circumstances, fans of blues, alternative country, or classical music may not be able to find the radio product that matches their interests. Given the high start-up costs of launching a commercial media business, diverse players offering alternative products are becoming more rare as we begin the twenty-first century.

The Performance of Media Organizations

A second important area in media economics involves analyzing the behavior and performance of media companies. Economists pay particular attention to the two ways the media collect revenues: through direct and indirect methods. **Direct payment** involves media products supported primarily by consumers, who pay directly for a book, a music CD, a movie, an online computer service, or a cable TV subscription. **Indirect payment** involves media products supported primarily by advertisers,

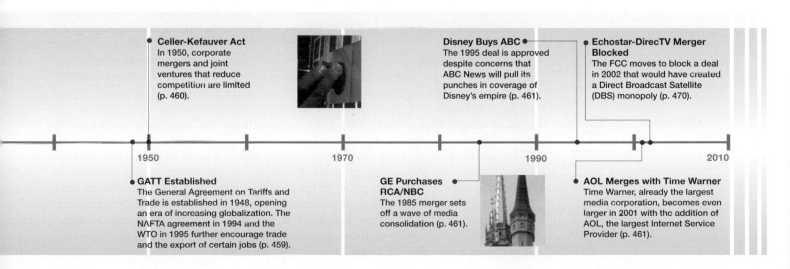

Celler-Kefauver Act
In 1950, corporate mergers and joint ventures that reduce competition are limited (p. 460).

Disney Buys ABC
The 1995 deal is approved despite concerns that ABC News will pull its punches in coverage of Disney's empire (p. 461).

Echostar-DirecTV Merger Blocked
The FCC moves to block a deal in 2002 that would have created a Direct Broadcast Satellite (DBS) monopoly (p. 470).

1950   1970   1990   2010

GATT Established
The General Agreement on Tariffs and Trade is established in 1948, opening an era of increasing globalization. The NAFTA agreement in 1994 and the WTO in 1995 further encourage trade and the export of certain jobs (p. 459).

GE Purchases RCA/NBC
The 1985 merger sets off a wave of media consolidation (p. 461).

AOL Merges with Time Warner
Time Warner, already the largest media corporation, becomes even larger in 2001 with the addition of AOL, the largest Internet Service Provider (p. 461).

Table 13.1 Consumer Spending per Person per Year on Selected Media, 1996–2000 (in $)

Year	Broadcast Radio/ Television	Cable & Satellite	Home Video	Movies in Theaters	Recorded Music	Newspapers	Consumer Books	Consumer Magazines	Internet
1996	$0.00	$138.96	$85.98	$27.11	$57.47	$52.84	$72.68	$39.51	$13.24
1997	0.00	153.11	85.63	28.88	55.51	52.81	72.26	40.33	20.87
1998	0.00	165.56	92.38	31.23	61.67	53.30	75.62	40.57	27.63
1999	0.00	179.89	95.39	33.11	65.13	53.65	80.43	40.30	41.77
2000	0.00	192.82	109.22	32.49	62.80	53.32	77.64	39.50	50.63

Hours per Person per Year Using Consumer Media, 1996–2000

Year	Radio	Network-Affiliated Stations	Cable & Satellite	Home Video	Movies in Theaters	Recorded Music	Daily Newspapers	Consumer Books	Consumer Magazines	Internet
1996	973	809	573	54	12	292	162	100	112	10
1997	964	750	620	53	13	270	159	95	112	34
1998	936	710	667	55	13	283	156	97	111	61
1999	967	706	720	55	13	289	154	98	110	99
2000	961	801	771	59	12	263	151	90	107	124

Source: Veronis Suhler Communications Industry Forecast, 15th Edition, July 2001.

who pay for the quantity or quality of audience members that a particular medium delivers. Over-the-air radio and TV broadcasting, daily newspapers, and consumer magazines rely on indirect payments for the majority of their revenue. Through direct payments, consumers communicate their preferences immediately. Through indirect payments of advertiser-supported media, "the client is the advertiser, not the viewer or listener or reader."[4] Advertisers, in turn, seek media that persuade customers with discretionary income to acquire new products or switch brand loyalty. Many forms of mass media, of course, generate revenue both directly and indirectly, including newspapers, magazines, World Wide Web services, and cable systems, which charge subscription fees in addition to selling commercial time to advertisers (see Table 13.1).

In reviewing other behaviors of the media, economists look at many elements of the commercial process, including program or product costs, price setting, marketing strategies, and regulatory practices. For instance, marketers and media economists determine how high a local newspaper can raise its weekly price before enough disgruntled readers drop their subscriptions and offset the profits made from the price increase. Let's look at another example. In 1996, critics and government agencies began reviewing the artificially inflated price of CDs. They demonstrated that the **economies of scale** principle, which refers to the practice of increasing production levels so as to reduce the overall cost per unit, should have driven down the price of a CD in the same way that the price of blank videotapes and movie videos dropped in the 1980s. By 2003, however, CD prices have remained inflated, largely as a result of the oligopoly formed by the five major recording conglomerates and their rigid control of distribution.

Over the years, economists, media critics, and consumer organizations have asked the mass media to meet certain performance criteria. Following are some of the key expectations of media organizations: introducing new technologies to the marketplace; making media products and services available to all economic classes; facilitating free expression and robust political discussion; acting as public watchdogs over wrongdoing; monitoring times of crisis; playing a positive role in education; and maintaining the quality of culture.[5] Although media industries live up to some of these expectations better than others, economic analyses permit consumers and citizens to examine the instances when the mass media fall short. For example, when corporate executives at the networks trimmed TV news budgets in the early 1990s to make their businesses leaner and increase profit margins, their decision jeopardized the networks' role as watchdog on the rest of society.

The Transition to an Information Economy

During the last half of the twentieth century, a number of key economic changes affected the media. The 1950s, for instance, marked a transitional period in which the machines that drove the modern Industrial Age changed gear in the new Information Age. With offices displacing factories as major work sites, centralized mass production gave way to decentralized and often temporary service work. Indeed, by the early 1990s, the temporary-employment agency Manpower surpassed General Motors for a time as the largest U.S. private employer.

A major global change, which continues to unfold, accompanied this transformation. Bolstered in the past two decades by the passage of NAFTA (North American Free Trade Agreement), GATT (General Agreement on Tariffs and Trade), and the WTO (World Trade Organization), which succeeded GATT in 1995, global cooperation fostered the breakdown of economic borders. Transnational media corporations executed business deals across international terrain. Global companies took over high-profile brand-name industries, particularly the electronic equipment formerly associated with the United States. In 1995, for example, Matsushita, at the time the world's seventeenth-largest company according to *Fortune* magazine, produced VCRs under the General Electric, Magnavox, Sylvania, and J. C. Penney labels.

The first half of the twentieth century emphasized mass production, the rise of manufacturing plants, and the intense rivalry of one country's products against another's. The contemporary era, however, emphasizes information distribution and retrieval as well as transnational economic cooperation. The major shift to an information-based economy began in the 1950s as various mass-media industries were able to market music, movies, television programs, and computer software on a global level. During this time, the emphasis on mass production shifted to the

> **66** Had anyone in 1975 predicted that the two oldest and most famous corporate producers and marketers of American recorded music [the RCA and CBS labels] would end up in the hands of German printers and publishers [Bertelsmann] and Japanese physicists and electronic engineers [Sony], the reaction in the industry would have been astonishment. **99**
>
> – Barnet and Cavanagh,
> *Global Dreams*, 1994

cultivation of specialized niche markets. In the 1960s, the first waves of national media consolidation began, escalating into the global media mergers of the 1980s and 1990s.

Deregulation Trumps Regulation

During the rise of industry in the nineteenth century, entrepreneurs such as John D. Rockefeller in oil, Cornelius Vanderbilt in shipping and railroads, and Andrew Carnegie in steel created giant companies that monopolized their respective industries. In 1890, Congress passed the Sherman Antitrust Act, outlawing the monopoly practices and corporate trusts that often fixed prices to force competitors out of business. In 1911, the government used the act to break up both the American Tobacco Company and Rockefeller's Standard Oil Company, which was divided into thirty smaller competing firms. In 1914, Congress passed the Clayton Antitrust Act, prohibiting manufacturers from selling only to dealers and contractors who agreed to reject the products of business rivals. The Celler-Kefauver Act of 1950 further strengthened antitrust rules by limiting any corporate mergers and joint ventures that reduced competition. Today, these laws are enforced by the Federal Trade Commission and the antitrust division of the Department of Justice.

In recent decades, government regulation has often been denounced as a barrier to the more flexible flow of capital. Although the Carter administration (1976–80) actually initiated deregulation, under President Reagan (1980–88) most controls on business were drastically weakened. Sometimes the deregulation and the decline in government oversight had severe consequences—such as the savings and loan industry scandal, which cost consumers billions of dollars—but many businesses flourished in this new pro-commerce climate. Deregulation also led to easier mergers, corporate diversification, and increased tendencies in some sectors (airlines, energy, communications, and financial services) toward oligopolies.[6]

In the broadcast industry, the Telecommunications Act of 1996 lifted most restrictions on how many radio and TV stations one corporation could own. The act further welcomed the seven powerful regional telephone companies, known as the Baby Bells, into the cable TV business. In addition, cable operators not only regained the right to raise cable rates with less oversight but also were authorized to compete in the local telephone business (although high costs kept cable out of the phone business). Economists thought the new competition would bring down consumer prices for a time but would also encourage more mergers and eventually an oligopoly controlling *both* the telephone and the cable industries. In fact, AT&T's 1999 purchase of cable giant TCI and the subsequent AT&T-Comcast merger in 2002 foreshadow a time when one megacorporation could control most of the wires entering a home and dictate both phone and cable TV pricing.

● This screen for high-definition digital television is inspected in Hong Kong. In order to help develop the new TV standard, beginning in the fall of 1998 broadcast networks were required by Congress to air programs using both the old analog and new digital signals.

Since the 1980s, a spirit of deregulation and special exemptions has guided communication legislation. For example, in 1995, despite complaints from NBC, Rupert Murdoch's Australian company News Corp. received a special dispensation from the FCC and Congress, allowing the firm to continue owning and operating the Fox network and a number of local TV stations. The Murdoch decision ran counter to the government decisions made right after World War I. At that time, the government feared outside owners and limited foreign investment in U.S. broadcast operations to 20 percent.

Deregulation has also returned media economics to nineteenth-century principles, which suggest that markets can take care of themselves with little government interference. In this context, one of the ironies in broadcast history is that more than seventy years ago commercial radio broadcasters demanded government regulation to control technical interference and amateur competition. By the mid-1990s, however, the original impetus for regulation had reversed course. With new cable channels and Internet sites, broadcasting was no longer regarded as a scarce resource—once a major rationale for regulation as well as government funding of noncommercial and educational stations. Roughly thirteen thousand U.S. commercial and educational AM and FM stations and seventeen hundred commercial and educational VHF and UHF television stations now operate in U.S. cities.

Consolidation and Mergermania

In spite of the strong antitrust laws of the twentieth century, this legislation has been unevenly and curiously applied, especially in terms of the media. When International Telephone & Telegraph (ITT) tried to acquire ABC in the 1960s, loud protests and government investigations sank the deal. But when General Electric purchased RCA/NBC in the 1980s, the FTC, the FCC, and the Justice Department found few problems. Other actions have been even more significant. Even though the Justice Department broke up AT&T's century-old monopoly in the mid-1980s—creating telephone competition—at the same time the government was also authorizing a number of mass media mergers that consolidated power in the hands of a few large companies.

Although the original Big Three TV networks—ABC, CBS, and NBC—constituted a prime-time oligopoly from the 1950s into the 1980s, competition from cable and VCRs changed the economic terrain. Eventually, the government allowed GE to buy back RCA for its NBC network in 1985. Then, in 1996, Microsoft joined with NBC to create a CNN alternative, MSNBC: a 24-hour interactive news channel available on both cable and the World Wide Web.

Among the world's biggest media deals, Disney acquired ABC in 1995 for $19 billion. To ensure its rank as the world's largest media conglomerate, Time Warner bought Turner Broadcasting in 1995 for $7.5 billion. In 2001, Time Warner merged with AOL in the largest media deal in history, worth over $160 billion. A year later, the federal government approved a $72 billion deal uniting AT&T's cable division with Comcast, creating a cable company twice the size of its nearest competitor.

Until the 1980s, antitrust rules had historically attempted to ensure diversity of ownership among competing businesses. Sometimes this happened, as in the breakup of AT&T, and sometimes it did not, as in the cases of local newspaper and cable monopolies. What has occurred consistently, though, is that media competition has been usurped by media consolidation. Today, the same anticompetitive spirit exists that once allowed a few utility and railroad companies to control their industries—in the days before antitrust laws.

Most media companies have skirted monopoly charges by purchasing diverse types of mass media rather than trying to control just one medium. For example, Disney, rather than trying to dominate one area, provides programming to a TV

> **"Big is bad if it stifles competition . . . but big is good if it produces quality programs."**
> —Michael Eisner, CEO, Disney, 1995

> **"It's a small world, after all."**
> —theme song, Disney theme parks

network, cable channels, and movie theaters. The company evades charges of monopoly by scattering products across many media ventures. In 1995, Disney CEO Michael Eisner defended the ABC takeover on a number of ABC News shows. According to Eisner, as long as large companies remain dedicated to quality—and as long as Disney did not try to buy the phone lines and TV cables running into homes—such mergers benefit America. But Eisner's position raises questions: If companies cannot make money on quality products, what happens? If ABC News cannot make a substantial profit, should Disney's managers lay off their national or international news staff? How should the government and citizens respond? (See "Examining Ethics: Two Views on Media Consolidation" on page 463.)

Flexible Markets

In addition to the trend toward consolidation, today's information culture is also characterized by flexibility. It emphasizes "the new, the fleeting . . . and the contingent in modern life, rather than the more solid values implanted" during Henry Ford's day, when relatively stable mass production drove mass consumption.[7] The new elastic economy features the expansion of the service sector (most notably in health care, banking, real estate, fast food, video rental, Internet dot-com ventures, and computer software) and the search for products to serve individual consumer preferences. This type of economy relies on cheap labor, often exploiting poor workers in sweatshop conditions, and on quick high-volume sales to offset the costs of making so many niche products for specialized markets.

Given that 80 to 90 percent of new consumer and media products typically fail (witness the failure of many dot-com companies), a flexible economy demands rapid product development and efficient market research. Companies need to score a few hits to offset investments in their failed products. For instance, during the peak summer movie season, studios premiere dozens of new feature films. A few are hits but many more miss, and studios hope to recoup their losses via video rentals. Similarly, TV networks introduce scores of new programs in the fall and then quickly replace those that fail to attract high numbers or the "right" kind of affluent viewers. At the same time, new music recordings are released daily on radio and in stores, while magazines vie for attention on supermarket shelves and through direct-mail solicitation. This flexible media system, of course, heavily favors large companies with greater access to capital over small businesses that cannot so easily absorb the losses incurred from failed products.

Global Markets and Specialization

Labor unions made strong gains on behalf of workers after World War II and throughout the 1950s. In response, manufacturers and other large industries began to look for ways to cut the rising cost of labor. With the shift to an information economy, many jobs, such as making CD players, TV sets, and VCRs, were exported to avoid the high price of U.S. unionized labor. As large companies bought up small companies across national boundaries, commerce developed rapidly at the international level.

More recently, as global firms sought greater profits, they looked to even less economically developed countries that were short on jobs and lacked national health and safety regulations for workers. But in many cases global expansion by U.S. companies ran counter to America's early-twentieth-century vision. Henry Ford, for example, followed his wife's suggestion to lower prices so workers could afford Ford cars. (In fact, with assembly-line production, Ford managed to drop the price of the average Model T from $850 in 1908 to $260 by 1925.) In many countries today, however, most workers cannot afford the stereo equipment and TV sets they are making primarily for U.S. and European markets.

EXAMINING ETHICS

Two Views on Media Consolidation

View 1: A Consumer's Paradise

When the D.C. Appeals court in 2002 struck down an FCC prohibition against owning a TV station and cable system in the same market, the ruling "set off shock waves in the journalism business," according to the current issue of the *Columbia Journalism Review*. The CJR analysis continues: "If you're a colossus like AOL Time Warner, Disney, GE, News Corporation, or Viacom, this trend is a ticket to even grander magnitude. Corporate chieftains prefer to expand their kingdoms unhampered by pesky government decrees, and that, unquestionably, is the way things have been going for years. But if you're an ordinary consumer, your news diet will be controlled by fewer and fewer owners . . . the media world is becoming more and more like a real-life Monopoly game."

They're right about the trend. GE owns NBC. Disney owns ABC. Westinghouse [now Viacom] owns CBS. AOL Time Warner is "synergizing" even as I write. And Gannett continues to swallow up small and mid-sized newspapers throughout the country. But has this "corporatization" of the media in fact produced less variety? Or resulted in poorer quality? Journalism academics have spent years researching these trends, and with near unanimity, conclude that the answer is "yes." But an hour on my sofa watching DirecTV last Saturday suggests that they're wrong.

I first came to this conclusion watching a show on handicapped Frisbee golfers competing in California's "Master's Cup" tournament. When I flipped to the Do-It-Yourself channel (yes, there is one), I learned to build a log cabin. Moments later, over on the Home and Garden Network, I was scribbling down decorating tips for my new abode from one Christopher Lowell, an interior decorator who might be the identical twin of the 1-800-FLOWERS guy. Later, on the Food Channel, I caught a thirty-minute analysis of the different uses of wheat in America and Europe.

When I had the sports itch, I chose from the Women's College World Series, surfing, a 1970s golf match between Sam Snead and Roberto diVicenzo, a Trans-Am series auto race, the WNBA, a handful of baseball games, and even "The Best of Backyard Wrestling." I considered the "variety" question settled. And I clicked on, in search of what the hand-wringers might call "quality" television. . . .

Late Saturday afternoon, I could have watched any one of 14 kids' channels, 7 religious channels, 17 Spanish channels, or 54 movies. There were—not including the networks or the news broadcasts in Italian and German—10 news channels.

And on and on it went. Is there any question that news consumers today have more options—and more high-quality options—today than ever before? Include news websites and, more recently, smart and informative weblogs, and the "media consolidation" arguments crumble.

The critics will likely dismiss my little argument. It's admittedly not a scientific look at the "problem" of consolidation. And, after all, *The Weekly Standard* is owned by Rupert Murdoch's News Corp., which also owns the *New York Post,* Fox News and Sports, Sky News . . .

Source: Stephen F. Hayes, "Beware, Corporate Domination: Concerned journalists think media consolidation is a tragedy. They couldn't be more wrong," *The Weekly Standard,* May 31, 2002.

View 2: A Danger to Democracy

The U.S. Court of Appeals in Washington is making media policy for the nation. It is throwing out old ownership rules designed to preserve competition by pressuring the Federal Communications Commission to dismantle the remaining barriers to the merging of broadcast, cable, and newspaper companies. The Court of Appeals, FCC Chairman Michael Powell, and media-company executives argue that digital cable, satellite television, and the Internet have sharply increased the diversity of news sources to the public, so consolidation is no threat. American citizens will get all the information they need to make democracy work. We question that supposition. Advocates of media deregulation are confusing the proliferation of channels with diversity of news and analysis. There's no denying that consumers can get hundreds of channels on cable and plug into thousands of Web sites, but most people get their news and views from a handful of trusted media outlets that survive by selling ads. On September 11, most Americans didn't turn to channel 642 or nuttyideas.com to learn what was happening and how it affected them.

The truth is that when big media conglomerates own most, if not all, the mass-market outlets in a community, diversity will probably suffer. Without restraints, media companies will naturally seek the largest audience and advertising base possible. Independent voices will be less able to sustain themselves financially. And conglomerates will tend to cut back on their own news programming because it's simply not as profitable as entertainment. Walt Disney Co., owner of ABC Inc., was being true to itself in trying to replace Ted Koppel's *Nightline* with David Letterman.

Proliferation of channels is not the same as diversity of information. The Court of Appeals and the FCC should look beyond their legal and ideological agendas to see what media consolidation will really cost the nation.

Source: Editorial, "The Cost of Media Consolidation," *Business Week,* April 29, 2002, p. 130.

The new globalism has coincided with the rise of specialization. The magazine, radio, and cable industries sought specialized markets both in the United States and overseas, in part to counter television's mass appeal at the national level. By the 1980s, however, even television—confronted with the growing popularity of home video and cable—began niche marketing, targeting eighteen- to thirty-four-year-old viewers, who controlled the bulk of consumer spending. Younger and older audiences were increasingly abandoned by the networks but were sought by other media outlets and advertisers. Magazines such as *Seventeen* and *Modern Maturity* flourished. Cable channels such as Nickelodeon and the Cartoon Network served the under-eighteen market, while A&E and Lifetime addressed viewers over age fifty and women.

Beyond specialization and national mergers, though, what really distinguishes current media economics is the extension of synergy to international levels. In Henry Ford's day, national companies competed against one another, and national pride was at stake. "Made in Japan," for instance, went from being a label of inferiority in the 1950s to a mark of superiority in the 1980s, especially in the automobile and electronics industries. Major foreign electronics firms began purchasing American popular culture by the boatload—to guarantee content for their audio and video technologies.

The global extension of America's vast popular media output occurred for a couple of key reasons. First, media technologies became cheaper and more portable, allowing proliferation both inside and outside national boundaries. Audiocassettes and CDs became compact enough to fit into a Sony Walkman, transportable to every room in the house and beyond. Thus, even when U.S. radio stations were not heard outside national borders, American music went everywhere. More recently, the swapping of audio and video files on the Internet (both legal and illegal instances) has expanded the global flow of popular culture. Furthermore, the transmission of visual images via satellite made North American and European TV available at the global level. Cable services such as CNN and MTV quickly took their national acts to the international stage, and by the twenty-first century, CNN and MTV were available in more than two hundred countries.

Second, as we have noted, American VCR, CD, DVD, and TV manufacturers lowered costs by moving production plants outside the country. In addition, global manufacturing permitted companies that lost money on products at home to profit in the international market. About 80 percent of American movies, for instance, do not earn back their costs in the United States and depend on foreign circulation as well as home-video formats to recoup early losses.

In the global television market, certain programs were not particularly successful in the United States but became hits internationally. Consider the 1990s phenomenon *Baywatch,* which went into first-run syndication in 1991 after being canceled by NBC. The program's producers claimed that by the late 1990s *Baywatch,* a show about the adventures of underdressed lifeguards who make beaches safer for everyone, was the most-watched program in the world, with more than a billion viewers. The dialogue in the series, like that of action movies, was limited and fairly simple, making it easy and inexpensive to translate into other languages.

Disney: A Postmodern Media Conglomerate

To understand the contemporary story of media economics, we need only examine the transformation of Disney from a struggling cartoon producer to one of the world's largest media conglomerates (see Table 13.2). Walt Disney's first cartoon company, Laugh-O-Gram, went bankrupt in 1922, when Disney himself was twenty-one years old. But when Disney moved to Hollywood, he found his niche. After

Table 13.2 The Top 10 Media Companies, 2001

Rank	Company	Country	2001 Media Revenues ($ billion) (North American revenues only)
1	AOL Time Warner	USA	$40.3
2	Viacom	USA	18.8
3	Disney	USA	15.7
4	Sony	Japan	9.3
5	Bertelsmann AG	Germany	7.8
6	Thomson	Canada	7.0
7	Omnicom Group	USA	6.9
8	Interpublic Group	USA	6.7
9	Reed Elsevier	UK	6.6
10	Gannett	USA	6.3

Source: Veronis Suhler Communications Industry Report, 20th Edition, October 2002.

inventing Mickey Mouse (originally named Mortimer) in the first sound cartoons in the late 1920s, Disney developed the first feature-length cartoon, *Snow White and the Seven Dwarfs,* completed in 1937.

The first economic period for Disney—roughly from the late 1920s to the late 1940s—set the standard for popular cartoons and children's culture for much of the twentieth century. The *Silly Symphonies* series (1929–39), which featured classic cartoon shorts like "The Three Little Pigs," established the studio's production reputation for quality cartoons. The series ran before feature movies throughout the Great Depression, providing escape, humor, and morality tales. Although the Disney Company remained a minor studio during this period, *Fantasia* and *Pinocchio*—the two top-grossing films of 1940—each made more than $40 million. Nonetheless, the studio barely broke even because cartoon projects took time and commanded the company's entire attention. *Snow White,* for example, took four years to produce.

The second Disney period, encompassing the 1950s and early 1960s, was marked by corporate diversification. With the demise of the cartoon film short, Disney expanded into other areas. In 1949, for example, the studio made its first nature documentary short, *Seal Island,* and in 1953 its first feature documentary, *The Living Desert.* In 1950, Disney also produced its first live-action feature, *Treasure Island.*

Disney was also among the first film studios to embrace television. In 1954, the company launched a long-running prime-time show, an even more popular venue than theaters for displaying its products. Then, in 1955, Disneyland opened in Southern California. Eventually, the theme parks would produce the bulk of the studio's revenues (Walt Disney World in Orlando, Florida, began operation in 1971).

❝ **In the States, going to Disneyland is a secular rite of passage, like visiting Mecca.** ❞

–Simon Hoggart, the *Guardian,* 1999

In 1953, Disney started Buena Vista, its own distribution company. This was the first step in making the studio into a major player. In addition, the company began fully exploiting the box-office power of its early cartoon features. *Snow White,* for example, was successfully rereleased in theaters to many new generations of children before finally going to videocassette.

In 1966, the death of Walt Disney triggered a period of decline for the studio. But in 1984 a new management team, led by Michael Eisner, initiated the third Disney period. Eisner inherited Disney's newly created Touchstone division. Touchstone's *Who Framed Roger Rabbit?* (1988) reinvented the live-action cartoon for adults as well as children. A string of animated hits followed, including *The Little Mermaid* (1989), *Beauty and the Beast* (1991), *The Lion King* (1994), *Mulan* (1998), *Fantasia 2000,* and *The Emperor's New Groove* (2001). Along with opening a chain of merchandise outlets, the studio began releasing its classic cartoons on video. Disney movies dominated videocassette sales from 1988 through the early 2000s.

Although some critics regard **synergy** as a monopolistic practice, Disney epitomizes the synergistic possibilities of media consolidation. Disney can produce an animated feature for both theatrical release and home-video distribution. With its ABC network, it can spin off a cartoon version of the movie and place it on ABC's Saturday-morning schedule. A book version can be released through Disney's publishing arm, Hyperion, and "the-making-of" versions can appear on cable's Disney Channel or ABC Family (formerly Fox Family), as well as in *Disney Adventures,* the company's popular children's magazine. Characters from the movie can eventually become attractions at Disney's theme parks or incentives for buying a kid's meal at a fast-food chain. In fact, some Disney films have had upwards of seventeen thousand licensed products, including clothing, dinnerware, CD-ROM games, toys, lampshades, and dog food bowls.

Throughout the 1990s, Disney continued to find new sources of revenue in both entertainment and distribution. Through its purchase of ABC, Disney also became the owner of the cable sports channels ESPN and ESPN2, and later expanded the brand with ESPNews and ESPN Classic channels, *ESPN The Magazine,* ESPN Radio, ESPN.com, and ESPN Zone, a sport-theme restaurant chain. Building on its sports interests, Disney bought the NHL's Mighty Ducks and major-league baseball's Angels, both located in Anaheim, near Disneyland. Across the country in New York, Disney renovated several theaters and launched theater versions of *Beauty and the Beast* and *The Lion King* as successful Broadway musicals. In cyberspace, Disney purchased Infoseek, a Web browser, and used it to create the Internet portal Go, a search engine that linked all the Disney properties together. In the instance of the Go portal at least, Disney discovered that corporate synergy strategies don't always work. After the company found its Web users didn't want to be channeled through a single Disney portal, it abandoned the Go site and let its popular Web sites such as ESPN.com and Disney Online stand alone.

Building on the international appeal of its cartoon features, in 1983 Disney extended its global reach by opening a successful theme park in Japan. In 1992, the studio also signed a ten-year deal with Russian television, which began showing six hours of Disney programming each week. In exchange, Disney received exclusive rights to sell ads during those programs. In 1986, the company started marketing cartoons to Chinese television, attracting an estimated 300 million viewers per week. This stopped in 1990 because of the rampant counterfeiting in China of popular Disney-trademark products, but the studio resumed the deal in 1992, eventually starting a Disney magazine in Chinese and opening several Disney merchandise stores.

In the early 1990s, EuroDisney (now called Disneyland Paris) opened outside Paris. The French, though, did not eagerly embrace the theme park. It lost millions each month, well into the mid-1990s, before finally making money. Many Europeans

News That Serves the Bottom Line?

Do the financial interests of the business side of the media organization affect the tone of the news division's coverage of certain topics? To investigate, we'll look at the example of the *New York Times'* coverage of the debate over the North American Free Trade Agreement.

Description. The North American Free Trade Agreement (NAFTA) was promoted in 1993 as a boon to the economies and workers of the United States, Mexico, and Canada. The White House, the Mexican government, and the United States' corporate elite led a multimillion-dollar public relations campaign to get Congress to adopt the accord. A coalition of labor unions, environmental organizers, and human rights groups opposed the proposed structure of NAFTA, but did not have the wealth of campaign resources their government and corporate counterparts had. Who were the sources? Note other differences in the news coverage.

Analysis. What patterns emerge in the coverage? One researcher, who studied more than three hundred *New York Times* articles on the NAFTA debate, found that the newspaper parroted the campaign for the trade deal, with dominant storylines claiming that NAFTA would bring greater prosperity and democracy to the working people of North America and prevent Mexico from falling into the economic sphere of Japan or Europe. The *Times* coverage also ignored labor sources to a large degree and (as did White House strategists) "deploy[ed] a personalization storyline and construct[ed] [H. Ross] Perot as the synecdoche for the NAFTA opposition."[1] The result is that the stories tended to be more about personal narratives and not substantial analysis.

Interpretation. One possible interpretation for the *Times'* approach to the coverage is that the *New York Times* has its own self-interest at stake in the debate. The *Times* is the flagship newspaper of the New York Times Company, one of the nation's top media corporations, which also owns more than a dozen other newspapers and television and radio stations and has stakes in two paper mills in the United States and Canada. Reducing trade and labor costs serves the bottom line of the corporation.

Evaluation. More even-handed coverage of the then-proposed North American Free Trade Agreement would have helped Americans understand the potential consequences of the trade policy. Since that time, the worst fears of NAFTA's critics have become true. Seven years after NAFTA's 1994 implementation, the Economic Policy Institute's review of the agreement concluded that "NAFTA has eliminated some 766,000 job opportunities—primarily for non-college-educated workers in manufacturing. Contrary to what the American promoters of NAFTA promised U.S. workers, the agreement did not result in an increased trade surplus with Mexico, but the reverse." The only parties to benefit by NAFTA were the "specific set of interests" who received "extraordinary government protections," according to the EPI's review: "investors and financiers in all three countries who search for cheaper labor and production costs."[2]

continued to criticize the company for pushing out and vulgarizing classical culture. On the home front, a proposed historical park in Virginia, Disney's America, suffered defeat at the hands of citizens who raised concerns about Disney misinterpreting or romanticizing American history. Meanwhile, in 1995, shortly after the company purchased ABC, Disney suffered criticism for running a flattering company profile one evening on ABC's evening news program. (See "Applied Critical Process: News That Serves the Bottom Line?" above.)

Despite criticism, little has slowed Disney's global expansion. Indeed, in 1997 Orbit—a Saudi-owned satellite relay station based in Rome—introduced Disney's 24-hour premium cable channel to twenty-three countries in the Middle East and North Africa. In the book *Global Dreams*, the authors set forth a formula for becoming

Building on the global reach and appeal of its ubiquitous cartoon characters— especially Mickey and Minnie Mouse— Disney opened a theme park in Japan *(shown here)* in the early 1980s and another outside Paris in the early 1990s. The original Disneyland theme park opened in California in 1955.

a "great media conglomerate," a formula that Disney exemplifies: "Companies able to use visuals to sell sound, movies to sell books, or software to sell hardware would become the winners in the new global commercial order."[8] In 2002, Disney was the world's third-largest media conglomerate.

Social Issues in Media Economics

In recent years, we have witnessed billion-dollar takeovers and mergers between Time Inc. and Warner Communication, Viacom and Paramount, MCA/Universal and PolyGram, Disney and ABC, Viacom and CBS, Time Warner and Turner, AT&T and TCI, Vivendi and Universal Studios, AOL and Time Warner, and AT&T's cable division and Comcast. This mergermania accompanied stripped-down regulation, which has virtually suspended most ownership limits on media industries. As a result, a number of consumer advocates and citizen groups have raised questions about deregulation and ownership consolidation.

One longtime critic of media mergers, Ben Bagdikian, author of *Media Monopoly*, worries that although there are abundant products in the market—"1,700 daily papers, more than 8,000 weeklies, 10,000 radio and television stations, 11,000 magazines, 2,500 book publishers"—only a limited number of companies are in charge of those products.[9] Bagdikian and others fear that this represents a dangerous antidemocratic tendency in which a handful of media moguls wield a disproportionate amount of economic control.

The Limits of Antitrust Laws

The current consolidation of media owners has limited the number of independent voices and owners. Although meant to ensure multiple voices and owners, American antitrust laws have been easily subverted since the 1980s. As we have noted, most media companies diversify among different product lines, never completely dominating a particular media industry. AOL Time Warner, for example, spreads its holdings among television programming, film, music, publishing, cable, and its Internet divisions.

Such diversification strategies, of course, promote oligopolies in which a few behemoth companies control media production and distribution. This kind of economic arrangement makes it difficult for many products—especially those offered outside an oligopoly—to compete in the marketplace. For instance, in broadcast

> 66 Time Warner is going to think twice about criticizing AOL if it is owned by Time Warner. 99
>
> –Ralph Nader, consumer advocate and presidential candidate, 2000

> 66 What they were really looking forward to was creating the biggest shopping mall in the world. 99
>
> –Ben Bagdikian, author of *Media Monopoly*, on the AOL Time Warner merger, 2000

programming, the few networks that control prime time—most of them now owned by film companies—offer several competing programs at any given time. These programs are selected from known production companies that the networks either contract with on a regular basis or own outright. Thus even with a very good program or series idea, an independent production company, especially one that operates outside Los Angeles or New York, has a very difficult time entering the national TV market.

Occasionally, independent voices raise issues that aid the Justice Department and the FTC in their antitrust cases. For example, when Echostar proposed to purchase DirecTV in 2001, a number of rural, consumer, and Latino organizations spoke out against the merger for a number of reasons. Latino organizations opposed the merger because in many U.S. markets Direct Broadcast Satellite (DBS) service offers the only available Spanish-language television programming. The merger would have left the United States with just one major direct satellite broadcasting company, a virtual DBS monopoly for Echostar, which historically had fewer Spanish-language offerings than DirecTV. In 2002, the FCC declined to approve the merger, saying it would not serve the public interest, convenience, and necessity.

Because antitrust laws aim to curb national monopolies, most media monopolies today operate locally. For instance, although Gannett owns more than ninety daily newspapers, it controls less than 10 percent of daily U.S. newspaper circulation. Nonetheless, almost all Gannett papers are monopolies: They are the only papers in their various towns. Virtually every cable company has been granted monopoly status in its local community; these firms alone often decide which channels are made available and what rates are charged. Furthermore, antitrust laws have no teeth globally. Although in late 1996 representatives from 160 countries met to discuss enforcing international copyright laws to protect the work of musicians and writers, no international antitrust rules exist to prohibit transnational companies from buying up as many media companies as they can afford.

Consumer Choice versus Consumer Control

During the wave of mergers in the 1980s and 1990s, a number of consumer critics pointed to the lack of public debate surrounding the tightening oligopoly structure of international media. This lack of public involvement dates from the 1920s and 1930s. In that era, commercial radio executives, many of whom befriended FCC members, succeeded in portraying themselves as operating in the public interest while labeling their noncommercial counterparts in education, labor, or religion as mere voices of propaganda. In these early debates, the political ideas of democracy became closely allied with the economic structures of capitalism.

Throughout the Cold War period in the 1950s and 1960s, it became increasingly difficult to even criticize capitalism, which had become a synonym for democracy in many circles. In this context, any criticism of capitalism became an attack on the free marketplace. This, in turn, appeared to be a criticism of free speech, because the business community often sees its right to operate in a free marketplace as an extension of its right to buy commercial speech. As longtime CBS chief William Paley told a group of educators in 1937: "He who attacks the fundamentals of the American system" of commercial broadcasting "attacks democracy itself."[10] Broadcast historian Robert McChesney, discussing the rise of commercial radio in the 1930s, has noted that leaders like Paley "equated capitalism with the free and equal marketplace, the free and equal marketplace with democracy, and democracy with 'Americanism.'"[11] The collapse of the former Soviet Union's communist economy in the 1990s is often portrayed as a triumph for democracy. As we know today, it was more accurately a victory for capitalism and free-market economies.

As many economists point out, capitalism is arranged vertically, with powerful corporate leaders at the top and hourly wage workers at the bottom. But democracy, in principle, represents a more horizontal model in which each individual has an opportunity to have his or her voice heard and vote counted. In discussing free markets, economists also distinguish between *consumer control* over marketplace goods and freedom of *consumer choice*: "The former requires that consumers participate in deciding what is to be offered; the latter is satisfied if [consumers are] free to select among the options chosen for them by producers."[12] Most Americans and the citizens of other economically developed nations clearly have options among a range of media products. Yet consumers and even employees have limited power in deciding what kinds of media get created and circulated.

Cultural Imperialism

The influence of American popular culture has created considerable debate in international circles. On the one hand, the notion of freedom that is associated with innovation and rebellion in American culture has been embraced internationally. The global spread of media software and electronic hardware has made it harder for political leaders to secretly repress dissident groups because so much police and state activity (such as the 1989 student uprising and massacre in China) can now be documented on video and dispatched by satellite around the world. On the other hand, American media are shaping the cultures and identities of other nations. American styles in fashion and food, as well as media fare, dominate the global market—what many critics have identified as **cultural imperialism**. Today, numerous international observers contend that the idea of consumer control or input is even more remote in countries inundated by American fashion, food, movies, music, and television. Even mainstream U.S. newspapers report with skepticism on the 470,000 Brazilian Avon "beauty consultants," many of whom travel the backwaters of the Amazon jungle selling American cosmetics to women who can barely afford shoes.

Although many indigenous forms of media culture—such as Brazil's *telenovela* (a TV soap opera), Jamaica's reggae, and Ireland's Riverdance—are extremely popular, U.S. dominance in producing and distributing mass media puts a severe burden on countries attempting to produce their own cultural products. For example, American TV producers have generally recouped the costs of production in national syndication by the time their TV shows are exported. This enables American distributors to offer these programs to other countries at bargain rates, thereby undercutting local production companies trying to create original programs in their own language.

Defenders of American popular culture argue that because some of our culture challenges authority, national boundaries, and outmoded traditions, this creates an arena in which citizens can raise questions. Supporters also argue that a universal popular culture creates a global village and fosters communication across national boundaries. Critics, however, believe that although American popular culture often contains protests against social wrongs, such protests "can be turned into consumer products and lose their bite. Protest itself becomes something to sell."[13] The harshest critics have labeled American culture in the international arena a kind of cultural imperialism that both hampers the development of native cultures and negatively influences teenagers, who abandon their own rituals to adopt the tastes of their American counterparts. The exportation of U.S. entertainment media is sometimes viewed as "cultural dumping," because it discourages the development of original local products.

The opening up of markets in Asia, Africa, and Eastern Europe, particularly after the failure of various totalitarian regimes in the 1980s, spurred the growth of global popular culture. At the same time, an economic form of piracy developed worldwide with the unlicensed pilfering and duplicating of cassettes, CDs, videos, DVDs, and software. Although heavy fines and jail sentences are on the books to stop pirating, many governments have been reluctant to act against their own bootleggers, especially because pirating remains a source of jobs.

Perhaps the greatest concern regarding a global economic village is elevating expectations among people whose standards of living are not routinely portrayed in contemporary media. By 2003, about two-thirds of the world's population could not afford most of the products advertised on American, Japanese, and European television. Yet more and more of the world's populations were able to glimpse consumer abundance and middle-class values through satellite technology and magazine distribution. Media managers as early as the 1950s feared political fallout—"the revolution of rising expectations"—in that ads and products would raise the hopes of poor people but not keep pace with their actual living conditions.[14] Furthermore, the conspicuousness of consumer culture makes it difficult for many of us to even imagine other ways of living that are not heavily dependent on the mass media and brand-name products.

The Media Marketplace and Democracy

We will continue to be involved in major global transformations of economies, cultures, and societies. The best way to monitor the impact of transnational economies is through vigorous news attention and lively public discussions on fundamental issues. Clearly, however, this process is hampered. In the 1990s, for example, news organizations, concerned about the bottom line, severely cut back the number of reporters assigned to cover international developments. This occurred—especially after 9/11—just as global news became critical to an informed citizenry. We live in a society in which consumer concerns, stock market quotes, and profit aspirations, rather than broader issues, increasingly dominate the media agenda. In response, critics have posed some key questions: As consumers, do we care who owns the media so long as most of us have a broad selection of products? Do we care who owns the media so long as multiple voices *appear* to exist in the market?

Merged and multinational media corporations will continue to control more aspects of production and distribution. Of pressing concern is the impact of mergers on news operations, particularly the influences of large corporations on their news subsidiaries. These companies have the capacity to use major news resources to promote their products and determine national coverage.

In spite of (and perhaps because of) the growth in channels of communication, it has become increasingly difficult to sustain a public debate on economic and own-

❝The top management of the networks, with a few notable exceptions, has been trained in advertising, research, or show business. But by the nature of the corporate structure, they also make the final and crucial decisions having to do with news and public affairs. Frequently they have neither the time nor the competence to do this.❞

—Edward R. Murrow, broadcast news pioneer, 1958

ership issues. During the 2000 presidential campaign, third-party candidates Pat Buchanan on the Right and Ralph Nader on the Left both attempted to raise as a major issue the dangers to democracy of increasingly centralized corporate power. Yet neither George W. Bush nor Al Gore, the major-party candidates—both of whom benefited from the multimillion corporate dollars that funded their campaigns—addressed this as a central or even marginal issue for the citizenry. And neither did the mainstream media representatives (employed by many of the corporations that supported the two mainstream candidates) who covered the campaign.

The promises of multichannel cable systems and the Internet, which would potentially give voices to the voiceless, may be in jeopardy because these systems are being bought or controlled at a rapid pace by large global conglomerates. Whether these multinational companies will open up their systems to alternative and regional points of view or offer opportunities to people who cannot afford access is yet to be determined.

One promising spot in the current economic atmosphere concerns the role of independent and alternative producers, artists, writers, and publishers. Despite the movement toward economic consolidation, the fringes of the media industry still offer a diversity of opinions and ideas. In fact, when independent views become even marginally popular, they are often pursued by large media companies that seek to make them subsidiaries or to capitalize on their innovations. Alternative voices in the mass media often tap into social concerns that are not normally discussed in corporate boardrooms. Moreover, business leaders "at the top" depend on independent ideas "from below" to generate new product lines. A number of transnational corporations encourage the development of local artists—talented individuals who might have the capacity to transcend the regional or national level and become the next global phenomenon.

One key paradox of the Information Age is that for economic discussions to be meaningful and democratic, they must be carried out in the popular media as well as in educational settings. Yet public debates about the structure and ownership of the media are often not in the best economic interests of media owners. Nonetheless, in some places, local groups and consumer movements are addressing media issues that affect individual and community life. Such movements—like the November-December 1999 Seattle protests against the World Trade Organization and subsequent protests at WTO and World Bank meetings around the globe—may be united by geographic ties, by common ethnic background, or by shared concerns about politics or technology. The Internet has made it possible for such groups to form globally, uniting around such issues as contesting censorship or monitoring the activities of multinational corporations.

Perhaps we are ready to question some of these hierarchical and undemocratic arrangements. Even in the face of so many media mergers, the public arena today seems open to such examinations, which might improve the global economy and also serve the public good. By understanding media economics, we can make a contribution to critiquing media organizations and evaluating their impact on democracy.

● During the 2000 presidential campaign, third-party candidates such as Pat Buchanan of the Reform Party and (pictured here) Ralph Nader of the Green Party attempted to raise the issue of increasing centralized power in the hands of a decreasing number of international corporations. But both candidates were excluded from the televised debates, and neither of the major-party candidates—whose campaigns greatly benefited from contributions from such international companies—focused on the issue.

REVIEW QUESTIONS

Analyzing the Media Economy

1. How are the three basic structures of mass-media organizations—monopoly, oligopoly, and limited competition—different from one another?

2. What are the differences between direct and indirect payments for media products?

3. What are some of society's key expectations of its media organizations?

The Transition to an Information Economy

4. Why has the federal government emphasized deregulation at a time when so many media companies are growing so large?

5. How have media mergers changed the economics of mass media?

6. How do global and specialized markets factor into the new media economy?

7. Using Disney as an example, what is the role of synergy in the current climate of media mergers?

Social Issues in Media Economics

8. What are the differences between freedom of consumer choice and consumer control?

9. What is cultural imperialism, and what does it have to do with the United States?

The Media Marketplace and Democracy

10. What do critics and activists fear most about the concentration of media ownership? How do media managers and executives respond to these fears?

11. What are some promising signs regarding the relationship between media economics and democracy?

QUESTIONING THE MEDIA

1. Are you exposed to popular culture from other countries? Why or why not? Give some examples.

2. Do you read international news? Why or why not?

3. What steps can reporters and editors take to cover media ownership issues in a better way?

4. How does the concentration of media ownership limit the number of voices in the marketplace? Do we need rules limiting media ownership?

5. Is there such a thing as a global village? What does this concept mean to you?

SEARCHING THE INTERNET

http://www.veronissuhler.com

Site for Veronis, Suhler & Associates Inc., a leading research and investment firm devoted to publishing, broadcasting, cable, and new media industries.

http://www.hoovers.com

Site for Hoover's Inc., a Texas-based company devoted to tracking the nation's largest industries, including media; features links to related sites.

http://www.mediainfo.com

Site for *Editor & Publisher,* the trade publication for the newspaper industry; provides statistics and links to other companies.

http://www.cjr.org/owners

The *Columbia Journalism Review*'s "Who Owns What" site,

which lists the holdings of more than forty major media corporations.

http://www.fortune.com

This site provides overviews and summaries of revenues, assets, and other data on Fortune 500 companies.

http://www.aflcio.org/paywatch/index.htm

Part of the AFL-CIO labor-union site, PayWatch keeps track of the top U.S. CEOs' salaries.

http://www.usdoj.gov/atr/

The Antitrust Division of the U.S. Department of Justice, which includes current antitrust case information and antitrust laws.

In Brief

Imagine that you are either a small independent record label or a book publisher. You have produced a high-quality product, but it has limited appeal. Without relying on signing distribution agreements with giant companies, how might you go about creating a market for your product and reaching the audience that might be interested in your product? Be specific.

In Depth

Split the class into three groups and stage a mock public forum on the issue of media mergers. Specifically, groups should examine whether it would be beneficial for yet another media corporation (for example, Sony, Gannett, or Bertelsmann) to buy a television network. Students may volunteer for one of the following groups:

- *Group 1*: the pro-business team, which supports the globalization of media and mergers as healthy steps for the American and world economy
- *Group 2*: the pro-consumer or citizens' activist group, which worries about the increasing concentration of media ownership
- *Group 3*: journalists who cover the forum and ask key questions

The class should check *Hoover's Handbook* <www.hoovers.com> or *Columbia Journalism Review* <www.cjr.org/owners> for a list of what the takeover company already owns. Then each group should meet and prepare for the forum. Groups 1 and 2 should appoint two or three spokespeople as "specialists" on various issues. Groups 1 and 2 should also anticipate the questions that reporters might ask and should prepare answers. Group 3 should brainstorm and devise a list of questions to be asked.

After the groups plan their strategies, the class should reconvene. Groups 1 and 2 should then briefly state their positions before opening up the forum to questions from reporters.

After the forum and toward the end of class, each group should gather and write the first two or three sentences of a news story that reports on the forum. The news reports should highlight the key moments or findings of the forum. The groups should then share their abbreviated news stories, tell why they chose their particular story openings, and comment on one another's story. How do the stories of Groups 1 and 2 differ from that of Group 3? What are the agendas of each group? Can compromises be achieved that satisfy the interests of both business and democracy?

KEY TERMS

monopoly, 456
oligopoly, 457
limited competition, 457

direct payment, 457
indirect payment, 457
economies of scale, 458

synergy, 466
cultural imperialism, 471

the culture of journalism

values, ethics, and democracy

In 1994, someone fired bullets into the Dublin home of an Irish investigative reporter as she put her five-year-old son to bed. In 1995, a man forced his way into the reporter's home, held a gun to her head, lowered his aim, and shot her in the thigh. For Veronica Guerin, journalism had become a dangerous business.

Guerin was the first reporter to cover Ireland's escalating organized-crime and drug problem. She worked for Dublin's *Sunday Independent.* A few days after the 1995 assault, she wrote about the incident, vowing to

continue her reporting despite her fears about safety. Later that year, she was punched in the face by the suspected head of Ireland's gang scene. He threatened to hurt Guerin's son and kill her if she wrote about him. She kept writing. In December 1995, she flew to New York to receive the International Press Freedom Award from the Committee to Protect Journalists.

When Guerin returned to Dublin, she continued her investigations, which went into greater and greater depth. She began naming names of gang members

14

suspected of masterminding drug-related crimes and a string of eleven unsolved contract murders. Then, in June 1996, while waiting in her car at a suburban Dublin intersection, she was shot five times by two hired killers on a motorcycle. Veronica Guerin had become contract murder victim number twelve. Ireland mourned Guerin's death for three days. After her funeral, which was held at the church where she had gone to Mass each Sunday, the government invoked her name and passed a series of laws. The legislation allowed judges to deny bail to dangerous suspects and created a special bureau to confiscate money and property from suspected drug criminals and gang members.

In an *Independent* article after a 1995 incident, Guerin had discussed the danger she faced: "I have already said, and I will continue to say it again now, that I have no intention of stopping my work. I shall continue as an investigative reporter, the job I believe I do best. My employers have offered alternatives—any area I wish to write about seems to be open to me—but somehow I cannot see myself reporting from the fashion catwalks or preparing a gardening column."[1]

In contrast to modern American journalism, there is something unusual about the openness and directness of Guerin's writing. After all, for much of the twentieth century U.S. journalism operated on the premise that reporters should detach from the turmoil they reported about. Guerin, however, became centrally involved in Ireland's crime and drug world. Her tough reports and tragic death connected her to her readers. Her powerful first-person stories were very different from the neutral third-person accounts that dominate most front-page coverage.

news-related issues receive special attention in this chapter because journalism is the only media enterprise that democracy absolutely requires—and it is the only media practice that is specifically protected by the U.S. Constitution. However, with the gradual decline in news audiences, the growing criticism of an elite corps of East Coast journalists, and the rise of 24-hour cable news talk, traditional journalists are searching for ways to reconnect with citizens. In this chapter, we will examine the changing news landscape and definitions of journalism. We will look at the implicit values underlying news practice and the ethical dilemmas confronting journalists. Next, we will study the legacy of print-news conventions and rituals. We will then turn to the impact of television and images on news. Finally, we will take up recent controversial developments in journalism and democracy, specifically examining the rise and the role of public journalism.

> **" A journalist is the lookout on the bridge of the ship of state. He peers through the fog and storm to give warnings of dangers ahead. . . . He Is there to watch over the safety and the welfare of the people who trust him. "**
>
> —Joseph Pulitzer, 1904

Modern Journalism in the Information Age

In modern America, serious journalism has sought to provide information that enables citizens to make intelligent decisions. Today, this guiding principle has been partially derailed. First, in a world engulfed in media outlets and computer highways, we may be producing too much information. According to social critic Neil Postman, as a result of developments in media technology, by the mid-1990s society had developed an "information glut," transforming news and information into "a form of garbage."[2] Postman believes that scientists, technicians, managers, and journalists have merely piled up mountains of new data, which add to the problems and anxieties of everyday life. As a result, too much unchecked data and too little thoughtful discussion emanate from too many channels of communication.

A second, related problem suggests that the amount of information the media now provide has made little impact on improving public and political life. In fact, many people feel cut off from our major institutions, including journalism. As a result, many citizens are looking for ways to take part in public conversations and civic debates—to renew a democracy in which many voices participate. In fact, one of the benefits of the contested and unpredictable 2000 presidential election vote was the way its legal and political complications engaged the citizenry at a much deeper level than the predictable, staged campaigns themselves did. We will look at these issues—particularly information overload and public alienation—as we explore the culture of news in this chapter.

What Is News?

In a 1963 staff memo, NBC news president Reuven Frank outlined the narrative strategies integral to all news: "Every news story should . . . display the attributes of fiction, of drama. It should have structure and conflict, problem and denouement, rising and falling action, a beginning, a middle, and an end."[3] Despite Frank's candid insights, most journalists today are not comfortable thinking of themselves as storytellers. Instead, they view themselves mainly as information-gatherers.

Over time, most journalists and journalism textbooks have come to define news by a set of criteria for determining **newsworthiness**—information most worthy of transformation into news stories. Although other elements could be added to the list, news criteria generally include the attributes of timeliness, proximity, conflict, prominence, human interest, consequence, usefulness, novelty, and deviance.[4] Journalists are socialized professionally to select and develop news stories based on different combinations of these criteria.

● Some media critics argue that one serious problem of the new millennium is "way too much information." One result is that citizens find it increasingly difficult to distinguish useful and meaningful information from the glut of data "garbage" that litters cyberspace and other media avenues.

Most issues and events that journalists select as news are *timely* or *new*. Reporters, for example, cover speeches, meetings, crimes, or court cases that have just happened. In order to rate as news, most of these events also have to occur close by, or in proximity to, readers and viewers. Although local papers usually offer some national and international news, readers and viewers expect to find the bulk of news devoted to their own towns and communities. In addition to being new and near, most news stories are narratives and thus contain a healthy dose of *conflict*—a key ingredient in narrative writing. In fact, in developing news narratives, reporters are encouraged to seek contentious quotes from those with opposing views. For example, stories on the 2000 presidential contest almost always featured dramatically opposing Republican and Democratic positions. And stories in the aftermath of the terrorist attacks of September 11, 2001, often pitted the values of the East against those of Western culture—for example, Islam versus Christianity or premodern traditional values versus contemporary consumerism (see "Case Study: Story Missed: How a Report on Terrorism Flew under the Radar," on page 482).

For newsworthiness, *prominence* and *human interest* play a role as well. Reader and viewer surveys indicate that most people identify more closely with an individual than with an abstract issue. Therefore, the news media tend to report stories on powerful or influential people. Because these individuals often play a role in shaping the rules and values of a community, journalists have traditionally been responsible for keeping a watchful eye on them. But reporters also look for the human interest story: extraordinary incidents that happen to "ordinary" people. In fact, good reporters can often relate a story about a complicated issue (such as unemployment, tax rates, or homelessness) by illustrating its impact on one "normal" person or family.

Two other criteria for newsworthiness, found less often in news stories, are *consequence* and *usefulness*. Stories about isolated or bizarre crimes, even though they might be new, near, or notorious, often have little impact on our daily lives. To balance these kinds of stories, many editors and reporters believe that some news must also be of consequence to a majority of readers or viewers. For example, stories about issues or events that affect a family's income or change a community's laws

66 The 'information' the modern media provide leaves people feeling useless not because it's so bleak but because it's so trivial. It doesn't inform at all; it only bombards with random data bits, faux trends and surveys that reinforce preconceptions. 99

—Susan Faludi, the *Nation*, 1996

have consequence. Likewise, many people look for stories with a practical use: hints on buying a used car or choosing a college, strategies for training a pet or removing a stain.

Finally, news is often about the *novel* and the *deviant*. When events happen that are outside the routine of daily life, such as a seven-year-old girl trying to pilot a plane across the country, the news media are there. Reporters also cover events that appear to deviate from social norms, including murders, rapes, fatal car crashes, fires, political scandals, and gang activities. In 2002, the highway snipers who randomly stalked and killed innocent drivers and mall shoppers in the Washington, D.C., area represented the kind of deviant behavior that qualifies as major news.

Although newsworthiness criteria are a useful way to define news, they do not reveal much about the cultural aspects of news. As culture, news is both a product and a process. It is both the morning paper or evening newscast and a set of subtle values and shifting rituals that have been adapted to historical and social circumstances, such as the partisan-press ideals of the 1700s and the informational standards of the 1900s. As culture, then, **news** in the twentieth century became the process of gathering information and making narrative reports—edited by individuals in a for-profit news organization—that offer selected frames of reference; within those frames, news helps the public make sense of prominent people, important events, and unusual happenings in everyday life.

Neutrality and Other Values in American Journalism

In 1841, Horace Greeley described the newly founded *New York Tribune* as "a journal removed alike from servile partisanship on the one hand and from gagged, mincing neutrality on the other."[5] Greeley feared that too much neutrality would make reporters look like wimps who stood for nothing. Yet the neutrality Greeley warned against is today a major value of conventional journalism. Such a value, ironically, is in the spirit of value-free science, with reporters assuming they are acting as detached and all-seeing observers of social experience. A news report, however, is seldom scientific; it remains essentially a literary or writing activity. As former

> **"** Real news is bad news—bad news about somebody, or bad news for somebody.**"**
>
> –Marshall McLuhan,
> *Understanding Media*, 1964

● The major symbol of twentieth-century investigative journalism, Carl Bernstein and Bob Woodward's coverage of the Watergate scandal for the *Washington Post* helped topple the Nixon White House. In *All the President's Men,* the newsmen's book about their investigation, Woodward and Bernstein portrayed reporters as tenacious individuals locked in a bitter battle with corrupt institutions.

Former senators Gary Hart
and Warren Rudman.

Story Missed:
How a Report on Terrorism
Flew under the Radar

By Harold Evans

We were warned. Some of the best minds in the United States attempted to alert the nation that, without a new emphasis on homeland security and attention to terrorism, "Americans will likely die on American soil, possibly in large numbers" as the result of terrorist attacks. The first warning came in September 1999, when former senators Gary Hart and Warren Rudman, co-chairs, used those words in the first of three documents from an entity called the United States Commission on National Security, created during a rare moment of agreement between President Clinton and House

speaker Newt Gingrich. Then, seven months before the attacks on the World Trade Center and the Pentagon, the commission reemphasized its warning, this time with a detailed agenda for action to make America safer from terrorism. The report was scary but it was also constructive and authoritative. And it is fair to say that most Americans never heard of it until after the attacks.

What happened?

On January 31, Hart and Rudman looked with satisfaction on the television cameras and print reporters assembled in the Mansfield Room of the United States Senate. They were there to present the commission's final report of 150 pages. It was called *Road Map for National Security: Imperative for Change* and was signed by their twelve fellow commissioners, who represented the kind of blue-ribbon braintrust Washington is so good at putting together. Over a three-year period, the wise men had visited twenty-five countries and consulted more than a hundred experts. Hart and Rudman had as their executive director the one-time fighter pilot Charles (Chuck) Boyd, the only graduate of the Hanoi Hilton to make four-star general. They and their staffs went to great lengths to alert the press in advance to the gravity of the commissioners' findings.

"Hell," says Rudman, "it was the first comprehensive rethinking of national security since Harry Truman in 1947." The conclusions were startling: "States, terrorists, and other disaffected groups will acquire weapons of mass destruction, and some will use them. Americans will likely die on American soil, possibly in large numbers." The commission also explored many of the underlying factors. Hart told me: "We got a terrific sense of the resentment building against the U.S. as a bully, which alarmed us."

The report was a devastating indictment of the "fragmented and inadequate" structures and strategies already in place to prevent, and then respond to, the attacks on U.S. cities, which the commissioners predicted. Hart specifically mentioned the lack of preparation for "a weapon of mass destruction in a high-rise building." But the report was not simply alarmist. It was unusually constructive, avoiding grandiose language for a step-by-step blueprint of what urgently needed to be done to create a National Homeland Security Agency, revive the frontline public services, and pull together the forty discrete official bodies with responsibility for national security.

A number of the commissioners visited the editorial boards of the *New York Times*, the *Wall Street Journal,* and the *Washington Post* before they released their report. They brought with them a press kit containing a crisp executive summary of the report.

Press conferences and private briefings were all to little avail.

Network television news ignored the report; so did the serious evening news on public television. Only CNN did it justice with a full discussion. The *New York Times* and the *Wall Street Journal* did not carry a line, either of the report or of the press conference. Boyd told me: "I won't ever forget that day in Senate Room 207." He watched in disbelief as the *Times* reporter left before the presentation was over, saying it was not much of a story. Coverage was excellent in the *Washington Post* and *Los Angeles Times,* with a smattering of good stories in *USA Today* and the smaller and regional newspapers using AP and Reuters. But what most astonished and then outraged the commissioners was that none of the major newspapers, except the *Los Angeles Times* briefly, offered any kind of follow-up or critical analysis in editorials or op-ed pieces. Nowhere did Hart-Rudman get the kind of discussion and amplification of the sort that tends to prompt the political machinery to operate. In short, the report passed under the radar.

The Hart-Rudman report is the kind that required elite opinion to engage in a sustained dialogue to probe, improve, explain, and then press for action. None of the network talk shows took it up. But the commissioners were particularly bewildered by the blackout at the *New York Times*; they pitched an op-ed article signed by Hart and Rudman in the hope that it would induce the *Times* to take a proper look at the commission's work. The article was rejected.

Newspapers, by their nature, are bound to miss stories from time to time; a good newspaper will then follow up, trying to recover. There was no attempt to repair the omission in the *Times* or the *Journal*. The performance of the *Times*, the country's leading newspaper, is curious since it has distinguished itself over the years by giving prominence to Saddam Hussein's mischiefs, and to notable front-page reports by Judith Miller, William Broad, and Stephen Engelberg on the threats of bioterrorism. Its editorials on state-sponsored terrorism have been robust. Inquiries to the *Times* failed to elicit a response.

The commissioners are variously "dumbfounded" (Hart), "surprised" (Schlesinger), "stunned" (Gelb), "appalled" (Rudman). "*The New York Times,*" says the agreeably forthright Rudman, "deserves its ass kicked." Gingrich is more rueful: "I was very saddened. I don't expect the networks, people who cover daily events, to be interested. But I thought, in particular, for the *New York Times* and the *Washington Post* and the *Wall Street Journal* not to give it really serious coverage was a significant failure in providing educated citizens with an important report. And frankly, other than [creating an office of] Homeland Security they still haven't gone back and contemplated the scale of change we're describing."

None of the commissioners suggests that headlines or informed comment about their report would have forestalled September 11. But national planning could have been six months ahead, sparing us much of the public health chaos over anthrax. If Hart-Rudman had got the national attention it deserved, the administration almost surely would have moved sooner. There is a keen sense of frustration among the fourteen commissioners that the marriage of the two inertias—one in the serious press, the other in the administration—delayed the taking of action. "We lost momentum," says Rudman.

The failure of the most respected, agenda-setting editorial and news pages to acknowledge such informed analyses of the complex, essentially life-and-death issues of national security is puzzling. The *New York Times* on October 9 even had the nerve to report: "Tom Ridge was sworn in today as the first director of homeland security, *a position the country's leaders never felt was needed before September 11*" (emphasis added). Finger pointing is uncomfortable in the light of the unique malevolence of the atrocity of September 11. But the print and electronic press, which have legitimately been criticizing gaps in the U.S. intelligence system, have so far failed to point the finger at themselves.

Source: Harold Evans, "Warning Given . . . Story Missed: How a Report on Terrorism Flew under the Radar," *Columbia Journalism Review,* November/December 2001, p. 12.

reporter and journalism professor David Eason notes: "Reporters . . . have no special method for determining the truth of a situation nor a special language for reporting their findings. They make sense of events by telling stories about them."[6]

Even though journalists transform events into stories, they generally believe that they are—or should be—neutral observers who present facts without passing judgment on them. Conventions such as the inverted-pyramid news lead, the careful attribution of sources, the minimal use of adverbs and adjectives, and a detached third-person point of view all help reporters perform their work in a supposedly neutral way.

Like lawyers, therapists, and other professionals, many modern journalists believe that their credibility derives from personal detachment. Yet the roots of this view reside in less noble territory. Jon Katz, *Wired* magazine media critic and former CBS News producer, discusses the history of the neutral pose:

> The idea of respectable detachment wasn't conceived as a moral principle so much as a marketing device. Once newspapers began to mass market themselves in the mid-1880s, after steam- and rotary-powered presses made it possible to print lots of papers and make lots of money, publishers ceased being working, opinionated journalists. They mutated instead into business-men eager to reach the broadest number of readers and antagonize the fewest. . . .
>
> Objectivity works well for publishers, protecting the status quo and keeping journalism's voice militantly moderate.[7]

To reach as many people as possible across a wide spectrum, publishers and editors realized as early as the 1840s that softening their partisanship might boost sales.

Neutral journalism remains a selective process. Reporters and editors turn some happenings into reports and discard many others. This process is governed by a deeper set of subjective beliefs that are not neutral. Sociologist Herbert Gans, who studied the newsroom cultures of CBS, NBC, *Newsweek,* and *Time* in the 1970s, has generalized that several basic "enduring values" are shared by most American reporters and editors. The most prominent of these values are ethnocentrism, responsible capitalism, small-town pastoralism, and individualism.[8] By **ethnocentrism** Gans means that in most news reporting, especially foreign coverage, reporters judge other countries and cultures on the basis of how "they live up to or imitate American practices and values." Critics outside the United States, for instance, point out that CNN's international news channels portray world events and cultures primarily from an American point of view rather than through a neutral global lens.

Gans also identified **responsible capitalism** as an underlying value, contending that journalists sometimes naively assume that businesspeople compete with one another not primarily to maximize profits but "to create increased prosperity for all." Gans points out that although most reporters and editors condemn monopolies, "there is little implicit or explicit criticism of the oligopolistic nature of much of

today's economy."[9] In fact, by 2002, most journalists worked in monopoly newspaper towns or for oligopoly parent companies. Thus writing about the limitations of such economic structures constituted biting the hand that fed you.

Another value that Gans found was the romanticization of **small-town pastoralism**: favoring the small over the large and the rural over the urban. Reporters and editors, like most Americans, tend to prefer natural settings to their metropolitan counterparts. Many journalists equate small-town life with innocence and harbor deep suspicions of cities, their governments, and daily urban experiences. Consequently, stories about rustic communities with drug or crime problems are usually framed as if the purity of country life had been contaminated by brutish city values.

Finally, **individualism**, according to Gans, remains the most prominent value underpinning daily journalism. Many idealistic reporters are attracted to this profession because it rewards the rugged tenacity needed to confront and expose corruption. Beyond this, individuals who overcome personal adversity are the subjects of many enterprising news stories. Often, however, journalism that focuses on personal triumphs fails to explain how large institutions work or fail. Many conventional reporters and editors are unwilling or unsure of how to tackle the problems raised by institutional decay. In addition, because they value their own individualism and are accustomed to working alone, many journalists dislike cooperating on team projects or participating in citizen forums in which community members discuss their own interests.[10]

Traditionally, reporters have aligned facts with an objective position and values with subjective feelings.[11] Within this context, news reports offer readers and viewers details, data, and description. It then becomes the citizen's responsibility to judge and take a stand about the social problems represented by the news. Given these assumptions, reporters are responsible only for adhering to the traditions of the trade—"getting the facts." As a result, many reporters view themselves as neutral "channels" of information rather than as citizens themselves, actively involved in public life. (See "Applied Critical Process: Telling Stories and Covering Crime" on page 486.)

● Journalism sometimes provides citizens with stories and reports that they use to mobilize and organize. Here, early in 2000, residents of the Bronx protest the "not guilty" verdict in the case of four police officers charged in the wrongful shooting of Amadou Diallo, an unarmed West African immigrant, who died trying to enter his own apartment. The acquitted officers, who fired more than 40 shots at Diallo, testified that the victim's wallet looked like a gun.

Ethics and the News Media

In late April 1992, a not-guilty verdict was returned in a suburban Simi Valley courtroom, acquitting four Los Angeles police officers who had been charged with using excessive force against Rodney King, an ex-con who had led police on a three-mile, high-speed chase through Los Angeles in 1991. According to police reports, King first

Telling Stories and Covering Crime

Here are four opening sentences—or leads—from news stories describing the capture of the Washington-area snipers in October 2002. Note both the similarities and the variety among these leads. Some are straightforward and some are very dramatic. Note the word choices used to symbolically represent this event.

> *New York Daily News* (10/25/02)—"The Beltway snipers' three week reign of terror and one of the nation's biggest manhunts ended yesterday with the peaceful arrest of a sleeping ex-soldier and a teenager he called his stepson."
>
> *Boston Globe* (10/25/02)—"One of the most extraordinary manhunts in American history came to a peaceful conclusion yesterday with the predawn arrest of a former U.S. Army soldier and a teenage companion as they slept in their car at a Maryland rest stop."
>
> ABC's *World News Tonight* (10/24/02)—Peter Jennings: "Good evening, everyone. The police in Maryland say tonight that the two men who have terrorized the Washington suburbs are behind bars."
>
> *CBS Evening News* (10/24/02)—Dan Rather: "It's over. They got them. After three weeks of murder, three weeks of terror in suburban Washington, police believe tonight they have cracked the case of the serial sniper."

Although modern journalists claim objectivity as a goal, it is unlikely that a profession in the story-telling business can approximate any sort of scientific objectivity. The best journalists can do is be fair, reporting and telling their stories in such a way that they best represent for their communities the complicated experiences that they are symbolically converting into print or pictures.

After discussing these October 2002 leads in class, try this exercise using your own examples from local crime coverage in your area:

Description. Find print and broadcast news versions of the *same* crime story from two different days of the week. Make copies of each story. For the broadcast stories, make notes on the pictures chosen to tell the story.

Analysis. Find patterns in the coverage. How are the stories treated differently in print and on television? Are there similarities in the words chosen or images used? What kinds of crime are depicted? Who are the sources the reporters use to verify their information?

Interpretation. What do these patterns suggest? Can you make any interpretations or arguments based on the kinds of crime covered, sources used, areas of community covered, or words/images chosen? How prominently are the stories played in relationship to their importance to the entire community being served? How complex are these stories? Do they relate the events to the larger social problem of crime, or are the stories treated as isolated or individual problems?

Evaluation. Which stories are the strongest? Why? Which are the weakest? Why? Make a judgment on how well these crime stories serve your interests as a citizen and the interests of the larger community.

refused to get out of his car and then resisted arrest; officers used batons and stun guns to subdue him. Without police knowledge, however, the incident was captured by a bystander on a home video. Played over and over on news programs, the video showed King on the ground offering little resistance as several officers kicked and beat him. The subsequent not-guilty verdict against the officers triggered fighting, looting, and arson in South Central Los Angeles. Fifty-eight people died. Officials estimated more than $1 billion in property damages. After the tragedy, the federal government filed a civil case against the four officers, charging them with deliberately depriving Rodney King of his civil rights. In 1993, two of the officers were found guilty and sentenced to thirty months in prison.

In the spring of 1992, between Rodney King's criminal and civil cases, Ted Koppel abandoned his command desk at ABC's *Nightline* and relocated to a church in South Central L.A. for a special edition of *Nightline*. Featuring interviews with gang members, church leaders, community activists, and neighbors, *Nightline* looked a lot like Oprah and her talk program when she has visited urban housing projects. On the program, one older minister challenged Koppel's authority by accusing *Nightline* of pitting gang members against religious leaders to generate conflict for a more dramatic news story. Koppel, used to the more detached stance of the contemporary news reporter, was visibly uncomfortable and quickly changed the subject.

Ethical Predicaments

Ted Koppel's dilemma raises an ethical question: What is the moral and social responsibility of journalists, not only for the stories they report but for the actual events or issues they are shaping for millions of people? Wrestling with such media ethics involves determining the moral response to a situation through critical reasoning. Koppel's ethical jam was more subtle than many situations faced by journalists on a daily basis. He "solved" it by avoiding it (that is, by changing the subject), but media professionals respond in other ways to a variety of ethical problems. The most frequent ethical dilemmas encountered in newsrooms across the United States involve intentional deception, privacy invasions, and conflicts of interest.

Deploying Deception

Ever since Nellie Bly faked insanity to get inside an asylum in the 1880s, investigative journalists have used deception to get stories. Today, journalists continue to use disguises and assume false identities to gather information on social transgressions. Beyond legal considerations, though, a key ethical question comes into play: Does the end justify the means? For example, can a newspaper or TV newsmagazine use deceptive ploys to go undercover and expose a suspected fraudulent clinic that promises miracle cures at a high cost? By posing as clients desperate for a cure, are news professionals justified in using deception?

In terms of ethics, there are at least two major positions and multiple variations. First, *absolutist ethics* suggest that a moral society has laws and codes, including honesty, that everyone must live by. This means citizens, including members of the news media, should tell the truth at all times and in all cases. In other words, the ends (exposing a phony clinic) never justify the means (using deception to get the story). At the other end of the spectrum are *situational ethics*, which promote ethical decisions on a case-by-case basis. If a greater public good was served by using deceit, many journalists would sanction deception as a practice. An editor who is an absolutist, however, would shun deceptive measures. Instead, he or she might cover this story by ordering a reporter to find victims who have been ripped off by the clinic, telling the story through their eyes.

Should a journalist withhold information about his or her professional identity to get a quote or a story from an interview subject? Many sources and witnesses are reluctant to talk with journalists, especially about a sensitive subject that might jeopardize a job or hurt another person's reputation. Journalists know they can sometimes obtain information by posing as someone other than a journalist, such as a curious student or a licensed therapist. Most newsrooms frown on such deception. In particular situations, though, such a practice might be condoned if reporters and their editors believed that the public needed the information. The ethics code adopted by the Society of Professional Journalists (SPJ) is fairly silent on issues of deception. The code "requires journalists to perform with intelligence, objectivity, accuracy, and fairness," but it also says that "truth is our ultimate goal."[12]

● On a Massachusetts beach, carved initials and a driftwood cross mark the anniversary of the July 1999 private plane crash that killed John F. Kennedy Jr., his wife, Carolyn Bessette Kennedy, and her sister, Lauren Bessette. The catastrophe led to the kind of intense news coverage that draws equally intense outrage at "pack" or "herd" journalists who stalk a story, often exploiting private tragedy for increased circulation and ratings.

Invading Privacy

To achieve the truth, journalists routinely straddle a line between the public's right to know and a person's right to privacy. For example, journalists may be sent to hospitals to gather quotes from victims or from relatives of individuals who have suffered some injury. In many of these cases, there is very little the public might gain from such a quote, but journalists worry that if they don't get the quote, a competitor might. In these instances, have the news media responsibly weighed the protection of individual privacy against the public's right to know? Although the latter is not constitutionally guaranteed, journalists invoke the public's right to know as justification for many types of stories.

Privacy issues also affect corporations and institutions. For example, in 1998 a *Cincinnati Enquirer* reporter got into trouble for illegally gaining access to the voice-mail system at Chiquita, a company best known for selling bananas. The reporter used information obtained from voice mail to report on the company's business practices. Although a few journalists applauded the reporter's resourcefulness, many critics said such a technique represented a violation of the company's privacy rights. At the very least, in our digital age, when reporters can gain access to private e-mail messages as well as voice mail, such reporting practices raise serious questions about how far a reporter can or should go to get information.

In regard to both individual and institutional privacy, do the news media always ask the ethical questions: What public good is being served here? What significant public knowledge will be gained through the exploitation of a tragic private moment? Although journalism's code of ethics says, "The news media must guard against invading a person's right to privacy," this clashes with another part of the code, "The public's right to know of events of public importance and interest is the overriding mission of the mass media."[13] When these two ethical standards collide, journalists usually err on the side of the public's right to know.

Conflict of Interest

Journalism's code of ethics also warns reporters and editors not to place themselves in positions that produce a **conflict of interest**—that is, any situation in which journalists may stand to benefit personally from stories they produce. "Gifts, favors, free travel, special treatment or privileges," the code states, "can compromise the integrity of journalists and their employers. Nothing of value should be accepted."[14] For instance, at large mainstream news media that subscribe to the code, newspapers or broadcast stations pay for the game tickets of their sportswriters and for the meals of their restaurant critics. Small newspapers, however, with limited resources and poorly paid reporters, might accept such "freebies" from a local business or interview subject. This practice may be an economic necessity, but it is one that increases the likelihood of conflict of interest that produces favorable or uncritical coverage.

On a broader level, ethical guidelines at many news outlets attempt to protect journalists from compromising positions. For instance, in most cities journalists do not actively participate in politics or support social causes. Some journalists will not reveal their political affiliations and occasionally will even refuse to vote. For these journalists, the rationale behind their decisions is straightforward: Journalists should not place themselves in a situation in which they might have to report on the misdeeds of an organization or political party to which they belong. If a journalist has a tie to any group, and that group is later discovered to be involved in shady practices or criminal activity, the reporter's ability to report on that group would be compromised—along with the credibility of the news outlet for which he or she works. Conversely, other journalists believe that not actively participating in politics or social causes is tantamount to abandoning one's civic obligations. They believe that fairness, not objectivity, is their primary obligation.

Resolving Ethical Problems

When a journalist is criticized for ethical indiscretions or questionable reporting tactics, a typical response might be "I'm just doing my job" or "I was just getting the facts." In retrospect, such explanations are troubling because in responding this way reporters are transferring personal responsibility for the story to a set of institutional rituals.

There are, of course, ethical alternatives to comments like "I'm just doing my job" that force journalists to think through complex issues. With the crush of deadlines and daily duties, most media professionals deal with ethical situations only on a case-by-case basis as dilemmas arise. However, examining major ethical models and theories provides a common strategy for addressing ethics on a general rather than a situational basis. Ethical and philosophical guidelines also offer universal measures for testing individual values and codes.

Although we cannot address all major moral codes here, a few key precepts can guide us. One principle entails the "categorical imperative," developed by German philosopher Immanuel Kant (1724–1804). A moral imperative or command maintains that a society must adhere to moral codes that are universal and unconditional, applicable in all situations at all times. For example, the Golden Rule—Do unto others as you would have them do unto you—operates as such an absolutist moral principle. The First Amendment, which prevents Congress from abridging free speech and other rights, has likewise served as a national unconditional law.

● For almost three months, security guard Richard Jewell was the FBI's main suspect in the July 1996 Olympic Park bombing that killed one person. When the FBI finally exonerated Jewell, he filed a libel suit against the *Atlanta Journal-Constitution*, CNN, and NBC.

Another ethical principle, derived from British philosophers Jeremy Bentham (1748–1832) and John Stuart Mill (1806–1873), promotes "the greatest good for the greatest number," directing us "to distribute a good consequence to more people rather than to fewer, whenever we have a choice."[15] The most well-known ethical standard, the Judeo-Christian command to "love your neighbor as yourself," also provides the basis for constructing ethical guidelines.

Arriving at ethical decisions involves several stages. These include laying out the case; pinpointing the key issues; identifying involved parties, their intent, and their competing values; studying ethical models; presenting strategies and options; and formulating a decision. In terms of privacy issues, for instance, the goal would be to develop an ethical policy that the news media might implement in covering the private lives of people who have become prominent in the news. (See Figure 14.1 for the SPJ Code of Ethics.)

Consider Richard Jewell, the Atlanta security guard who, for eighty-eight days, was the FBI's prime suspect in the park bombing at the 1996 Olympics. The FBI never charged Jewell with a crime, and he later successfully sued several news organizations for libel. Putting legal issues aside, the Jewell story involved a rivalry among various news media to report unusual or important developments before the competition could do so. The battle for newspaper circulation and broadcast ratings added a complex dimension. As has occurred in other instances, editors were reluctant to back away from the story once it had begun circulating in the major media.

Figure 14.1 Society of Professional Journalists Code of Ethics

Code Of Ethics

Preamble

Members of the Society of Professional Journalists believe that public enlightenment is the forerunner of justice and the foundation of democracy. The duty of the journalist is to further those ends by seeking truth and providing a fair and comprehensive account of events and issues. Conscientious journalists from all media and specialties strive to serve the public with thoroughness and honesty. Professional integrity is the cornerstone of a journalist's credibility.

Members of the Society share a dedication to ethical behavior and adopt this code to declare the Society's principles and standards of practice.

Seek Truth and Report It

Journalists should be honest, fair and courageous in gathering, reporting and interpreting information.

Journalists should:

- Test the accuracy of information from all sources and exercise care to avoid inadvertent error. Deliberate distortion is never permissible.
- Diligently seek out subjects of news stories to give them the opportunity to respond to allegations of wrongdoing.
- Identify sources whenever feasible. The public is entitled to as much information as possible on sources' reliability.
- Always question sources' motives before promising anonymity. Clarify conditions attached to any promise made in exchange for information. Keep promises.
- Make certain that headlines, news teases and promotional material, photos, video, audio, graphics, sound bites and quotations do not misrepresent. They should not oversimplify or highlight incidents out of context.
- Never distort the content of news photos or video. Image enhancement for technical clarity is always permissible. Label montages and photo illustrations.
- Avoid misleading re-enactments or staged news events. If re-enactment is necessary to tell a story, label it.
- Avoid undercover or other surreptitious methods of gathering information except when traditional open methods will not yield information vital to the public. Use of such methods should be explained as part of the story.
- Never plagiarize.
- Tell the story of the diversity and magnitude of the human experience boldly, even when it is unpopular to do so.
- Examine their own cultural values and avoid imposing those values on others.
- Avoid stereotyping by race, gender, age, religion, ethnicity, geography, sexual orientation, disability, physical appearance or social status.
- Support the open exchange of views, even views they find repugnant.
- Give voice to the voiceless; official and unofficial sources of information can be equally valid.
- Distinguish between advocacy and news reporting. Analysis and commentary should be labeled and not misrepresent fact or context.
- Distinguish news from advertising and shun hybrids that blur the lines between the two.
- Recognize a special obligation to ensure that the public's business is conducted in the open and that government records are open to inspection.

Minimize Harm

Ethical journalists treat sources, subjects and colleagues as human beings deserving of respect.

Journalists should:

- Show compassion for those who may be affected adversely by news coverage. Use special sensitivity when dealing with children and inexperienced sources or subjects.
- Be sensitive when seeking or using interviews or photographs of those affected by tragedy or grief.
- Recognize that gathering and reporting information may cause harm or discomfort. Pursuit of the news is not a license for arrogance.
- Recognize that private people have a greater right to control information about themselves than do public officials and others who seek power, influence or attention. Only an overriding public need can justify intrusion into anyone's privacy.
- Show good taste. Avoid pandering to lurid curiosity.
- Be cautious about identifying juvenile suspects or victims of sex crimes.
- Be judicious about naming criminal suspects before the formal filing of charges.
- Balance a criminal suspect's fair trial rights with the public's right to be informed.

Act Independently

Journalists should be free of obligation to any interest other than the public's right to know.

Journalists should:

- Avoid conflicts of interest, real or perceived.
- Remain free of associations and activities that may compromise integrity or damage credibility.
- Refuse gifts, favors, free travel and special treatment, and shun secondary employment, political involvement, public office and service in community organizations if they compromise journalistic integrity.
- Disclose unavoidable conflicts.
- Be vigilant and courageous about holding those with power accountable.
- Deny favored treatment to advertisers and special interests and resist their pressure to influence news coverage.
- Be wary of sources offering information for favors or money; avoid bidding for news.

Be Accountable

Journalists are accountable to their readers, listeners, viewers and each other.

Journalists should:

- Clarify and explain news coverage and invite dialogue with the public over journalistic conduct.
- Encourage the public to voice grievances against the news media.
- Admit mistakes and correct them promptly.
- Expose unethical practices of journalists and the news media.
- Abide by the same high standards to which they hold others.

Source: Society of Professional Journalists.

At least two key ethical questions emerged from the Jewell story: (1) Should the news media have named Jewell as a suspect even though he was never charged with a crime? (2) Should the media have camped out daily in front of his mother's house in an attempt to interview him and his mother? The incidents surrounding the Richard Jewell case pit the media's right to tell stories and earn profits against a citizen's right to be left alone.

Journalists' livelihoods partly depend on using stories that attract audiences and keep up with their competition. To defend their behavior toward the Jewells, for example, the news media might invoke their constitutional right to free expression or argue that their intent was to serve the public's right to know. Similar justifications were employed by the photographers who hounded Britain's Princess Diana in 1997, creating an atmosphere that contributed to events leading to her death. To criticize such media behavior, however, we might ask whether any significant public knowledge is gained by stalking a potential interview subject.

As journalists formally work through various ethical stages, they eventually formulate policies and ground them in an overarching moral principle, such as the commandment to "love your neighbor as yourself."[16] Would reporters, for instance, be willing to treat themselves, their families, or their friends the way they treated the Jewells? Ethical reporters could also invoke Aristotle's "golden mean": seeking moral virtue between extreme positions. In Richard Jewell's situation, this might have entailed developing guidelines that would attempt to balance the interests of the suspect and those of the news media. For example, during his eighty-eight-day ordeal, in reparation for using Jewell's name in early accounts, reporters might have called off their stakeout and allowed him to set interview times at a neutral site. At such a location, he might have talked with a small pool of journalists designated to relay information to other media outlets.

Reporting Rituals and the Legacy of Print Journalism

Unfamiliar with being questioned themselves, many reporters are uncomfortable discussing their personal values or their strategies for getting stories. Nevertheless, a stock of rituals, derived from basic American values, underlie the practice of reporting. These include focusing on the present, relying on experts, balancing story conflict, and acting as adversaries toward leaders and institutions.

Focusing on the Present

Historians mark the 1830s as the beginning of the transition between the partisan and modern press eras. Though American journalism began as a platform for partisan politics (encouraging debate over issues such as constitutional amendments, slavery, and states' rights), in the nineteenth century publishers figured out how to sell news more profitably as a product. They used modern technology to substantially cut their costs; they also began to change news content to appeal to emerging middle- and working-class people, who could now afford a paper and had some leisure time to read one. Publishers realized that they needed more practical or everyday content because many less affluent or educated readers were not particularly interested in the intricacies of partisan politics.

In the 1840s, when the telegraph first enabled news to instantly crisscross America, modern journalism was born. To complement the new technical advances, editors called for a dogged focus on the immediacy of the present. Modern print journalism de-emphasized political discussions and historical context, accenting instead the new and the now.

As members of an emerging modern profession, many journalists and newspapers ignored Joseph Pulitzer's call for news that maintained a continuity with the past. As a result, the profession began drawing criticism for failing to offer historical analyses of important phenomena. This is a pattern that continues today. In news stories about drugs, for example, individual characters—dealers, addicts, abusers, police, medical experts—pass through the frame of news, but only up to a point. Once these characters are no longer timely, they no longer meet the narrative requirements of daily news. For example, urban drug stories heavily dominated print and network news during the 1986 and 1988 election years. Such stories, however, virtually disappeared from the news by 1992, although the nation's serious drug and addiction problems had not diminished.[17] Drug stories simply became "yesterday's news."

Modern journalism tends to reject "old news" for whatever new event or idea disrupts today's routines. In the mid-1990s, when statistics revealed that drug use among middle-class high-school students was rising, reporters again latched on to new versions of the drug story during the 1996 elections, but their reports made only limited references to the 1980s. And although drug problems and addiction rates did not diminish in subsequent years, these topics were virtually ignored by journalists during the 2000 and 2002 national elections. Indeed, given the space and time constraints of current news practices, reporters seldom link stories to the past or to the ebb and flow of history.

Getting a Good Story

Early in the 1980s, the Janet Cooke–Pulitzer Prize hoax demonstrated the difference between a reporter merely telling a good story and her social responsibility for the actual experience.[18] The main criticism against the former *Washington Post* reporter focused on her fabrication of an investigative report (for which she won a Pulitzer that was later revoked). She had created a cast of characters featuring a mother who contributed to the heroin addiction of her eight-year-old son. At the time the hoax was exposed, Chicago columnist Mike Royko criticized conventional journalism for allowing narrative conventions—getting a good story—to trump journalism's responsibility to the daily lives it documents: "There's something more important than a story here. This eight-year-old kid is being murdered. The editors should have said forget the story, find the kid.... People in any other profession would have gone right to the police."[19] Had editors at the *Post* demanded such help, Cooke's hoax would never have gone as far as it did.

According to Don Hewitt, the creator and executive producer of *60 Minutes,* "There's a very simple formula if you're in Hollywood, Broadway, opera, publishing, broadcasting, newspapering. It's four very simple words—tell me a story."[20] For most journalists, the bottom line is getting a story—an edict that overrides most other concerns. Getting a timely story fills up a journalist's day and enables him or her to meet routine deadline demands. It is the standard against which reporters measure one another and their profession.

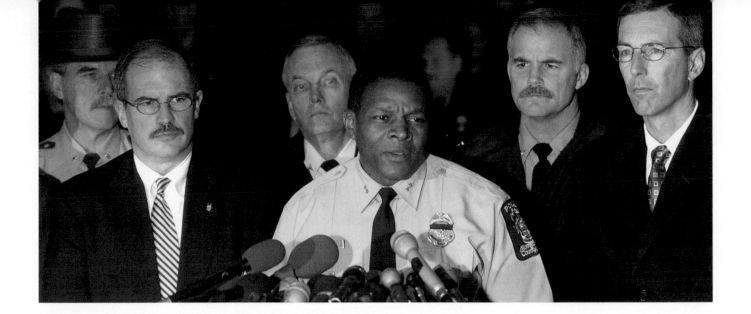

Getting a Story First

In a discussion on public television about the press coverage of a fatal airline crash in Milwaukee in the 1980s, a news photographer was asked to discuss his role in covering the tragedy. Rather than take up the poignant and heartbreaking aspects of witnessing the aftermath of such an event, the excited photographer launched into a dramatic recounting of how he had slipped behind police barricades to snap the first grim photos, which later appeared in the *Milwaukee Journal*. As part of their socialization into the profession, reporters often enjoy recounting how they evaded a PR flack or an authority figure to secure a story ahead of the competition.

The photojournalist's retelling points up the important role journalism plays in calling public attention to serious events and issues. Yet he also talked about the news-gathering process as a game that journalists play. Indeed, it has become routine for local television stations and newspapers today to run self-promotions about how they beat competitors to a story. In addition, during political elections local television stations and networks project winners in particular races and often hype their projections when they are able to forecast results before the competition does. Their race to do this led to the fiasco in November 2000 of all the major networks and cable news services badly flubbing their predictions regarding the outcome of voting in Florida in the presidential election.

Journalistic *scoops* and exclusive stories attempt to portray reporters in a heroic light: They have won a race for facts, which they have gathered and presented ahead of their rivals. It is not always clear, though, how the public is better served by a journalist's claim to have gotten a story first. Certainly, enterprising journalists can get a story started by calling attention to an important problem or issue. But on occasion, as with the July 1999 plane crash that killed John F. Kennedy Jr., his wife, and his sister-in-law, scoop behavior has led to **herd journalism**, which occurs when reporters stake out a house or follow a story in such large groups that the entire profession comes under attack for invading people's privacy and exploiting their personal tragedies. Although readers and viewers might value the tenacity of adventurous reporters, the earliest reports are not necessarily better or more significant than stories written days later with more context and perspective.

Relying on Experts

Another ritual of modern print journalism—relying on outside sources—has made reporters heavily dependent on experts. Reporters, though often experts themselves in certain areas by virtue of having covered them over time, are not typically allowed

● Montgomery County (Maryland) Police Chief Charles Moose deals with the media frenzy generated by the terrifying sniper murders in the Washington area in fall 2002. Early in 2003 Moose signed book and film deals, immediately raising two ethical issues: (1) police commanders are usually prohibited from profiting from their connections to major criminal investigations; and (2) lawyers for the leading suspects complained that the commercial interests of the publisher, Dutton Books, and its publication date for the book would coincide with the trial date, making it difficult to select an impartial jury.

to display their expertise. Instead, they must seek outside authorities to give credibility to their seemingly neutral reports. What daily reporters know is generally subordinate to knowing whom to consult.

During the early 1900s, progressive politicians and leaders of opinion such as Woodrow Wilson and Walter Lippmann believed in the cultivation of strong ties among national reporters, government officials, scientists, business managers, and researchers. They wanted journalists supplied with expertise across a variety of areas. Today, a widening gap exists between citizens with expertise and those without it, creating a need for public mediators. Reporters have assumed this role, becoming surrogate citizens who represent both leaders' and readers' interests. With their access to experts, reporters are able to act as agents for citizens, transforming specialized knowledge into the everyday commonsense language of news stories.

In the quest for facts, reporters frequently use experts to create narrative conflict by pitting a series of quotes against one another. On occasion, reporters also use experts to support a particular position (which, because of neutrality requirements, reporters are not allowed to state overtly). In addition, the use of experts enables journalists to distance themselves from daily experience; they are able to attribute the responsibility for the events or issues reported in a story to those who are quoted.

In the ritual use of experts, journalists are required to make direct contact with a source—by phone or e-mail or in person. Journalists do not, however, heavily cite the work of other writers; that would violate the reporters' obligation to not only get a story first but to get it on their own. Telephone calls and face-to-face interviews are the stuff of daily journalism. More carefully researched interpretation is often assumed to be a different kind of writing, more the province of academics or magazine writers.

Of expert sources in general, *Newsweek*'s Jonathan Alter once called them the "usual suspects." Alter contended that "the impression conveyed is of a world that contains only a handful of knowledgeable people. . . . Their public exposure is a result not only of their own abilities, but of deadlines and a failure of imagination on the part of the press."[21] In addition, expert sources have historically been predominantly white and male. For example, based on a forty-month analysis of guests on ABC's *Nightline* between 1985 and 1988, Fairness and Accuracy in Reporting (FAIR) found that "89 percent of the U.S. guests were men, 92 percent were white, and 80 percent were professionals, government officials, or corporate representatives."[22] Beginning in 1995, coverage of the O.J. Simpson trials helped change this profile somewhat. Legal sources, especially on CNN and CNBC, featured a far more diverse array of expert participants. Nevertheless, as journalists have increased their reliance on experts over the years, they have inadvertently alienated many readers, who feel they no longer have a stake in day-to-day social and political life. After all, authoritative experts and knowledgeable journalists seem to be handling things.

By the late 1990s, many journalists were being criticized for blurring the line between remaining neutral and being an expert. While shows like CNN's *Crossfire* have pitted opinionated columnists and reporters against one another since the 1980s, the boom in 24-hour cable news programs in the late 1990s led to a tremendous news vacuum that is now filled with talk shows and interviews with journalists willing to give their views on the hot stories of the day. During events with intense media coverage, such as the 2000 presidential election and the terrorist attacks of September 11, 2001, many print journalists appeared several times a day on various cable programs acting as experts on the story, sometimes providing factual information but mostly offering opinion and speculation. Some editors even encourage their reporters to go on these shows in the hope of selling more magazines and newspapers. Reporters and columnists from the *Washington Post,* for example, routinely appear in remote TV shots with the paper's logo prominently displayed in the background.

> **❝Cable news is full of spin doctors shouting at each other. . . . Jerry Springer without the hair pulling.❞**
>
> –Tom Rawlins, editor, *St. Petersburg Times,* 1998

Many critics contend that these practices erode the credibility of the profession by blending journalism with celebrity culture and commercialism.

Balancing Story Conflict

Embedded deep within journalism is a belief in the two-dimensionality of news. A reporter sent to cover property-tax increases might be given this editorial advice: "Interview Republican and Democratic leaders from the district and have them fight it out in the story." Such "balance" is a narrative device that helps generate story conflict. For most journalists, balance means presenting all sides of an issue without appearing to favor any one position. Unfortunately, because time and space constraints do not always permit representing all sides, in practice this value has often been reduced to "telling both sides of a story." In recounting news stories as two-sided dramas, however, reporting often misrepresents the multifaceted complexity of social issues. The abortion controversy, for example, is often treated as a story that pits two extreme positions (anti-abortion vs. pro-choice) against each other. Yet people whose views do not fall at either end of the spectrum are seldom represented; they are too far inside the outermost boundaries of a two-dimensional narrative conflict.

Although many journalists claim to be detached, they often stake out a moderate or middle-of-the-road position between the two sides represented in a story. In claiming neutrality and inviting readers to share in their detached point of view, journalists circumvent their own values. The authority of their distant, third-person, all-knowing point of view (a narrative device that many novelists use as well) enhances the impression of neutrality by making the reporter appear value-free (or valueless).

The claim for balanced stories, like the claim for neutrality, disguises journalism's narrative functions. After all, when reporters choose quotes for a story, these are usually the most dramatic or conflict-oriented words that emerge from an interview, press conference, or public meeting. Choosing quotes often has more to do with enhancing drama than with being fair or establishing neutrality. The balance claim is also in the financial interest of modern news organizations that stake out the middle ground. William Greider, a former *Washington Post* editor, makes the connection between good business and balanced journalism: "If you're going to be a mass circulation journal, that means you're going to be talking simultaneously to lots of groups that have opposing views. So you've got to modulate your voice and pretend to be talking to all of them."[23]

Acting as Adversaries

Complementing the search for conflict, the value that journalists take the most pride in is their adversarial relationship with the prominent leaders and major institutions they cover. The prime narrative frame for portraying this relationship is sometimes called a *gotcha story*, which refers to the moment when the reporter nabs "the bad guy" or wrongdoer. This narrative strategy—part of the *tough-questioning style* of many reporters—is frequently used in political reporting. Many journalists assume that leaders are hiding something and that the reporter's main job is to ferret out the truth through tenacious fact-gathering and "gotcha" questions. An extension of the search for balance, this stance locates the reporter in the middle, between "them" and "us," between political leaders and the people they represent.

Mike Wallace interviews the Devil

Critics of the tough-question style of reporting argue that it fosters a cynicism among journalists that actually harms the democratic process. Although journalists need to guard against becoming too cozy with their political sources, they sometimes go to opposite extremes. By constantly searching for what politicians may be hiding, some reporters may miss other issues.

News scholar Jay Rosen argues that "the essential problem is that the journalist's method of being critical is not disciplined by any political vision."[24] In other words, the bottom line for neutral or conventional journalists, who claim to have no political agenda, is maintaining an adversarial stance rather than improving the quality of political stories and discussions. When journalists employ the gotcha model to cover news, being tough often becomes an end in itself. Thus reporters believe they have done their job just by roughing up an interview subject or by answering the limited "What is going on here?" question. Yet the Pulitzer Prize, the highest award honoring journalism, often goes to the reporter who asks the ethically charged and open-ended questions, such as "Why is this going on?" and "What ought to be done about it?"

Journalism in the Age of Television

The rules and rituals governing American journalism began shifting in the 1950s. At the time, former radio reporter John Daly hosted the CBS game show *What's My Line?* When he began moonlighting as the evening TV news anchor on ABC, the fledgling network blurred the entertainment and information border, foreshadowing what by the 1990s had become a central criticism of journalism.

In those early days, the most influential and respected television news program was CBS's *See It Now*. Coproduced by Fred Friendly and Edward R. Murrow, *See It Now* practiced a kind of TV journalism lodged somewhere between the neutral and narrative traditions. Serving as the conscience of TV news in its early days, Murrow also worked as the program's anchor and main reporter, introducing the investigative model of journalism to television—a model that programs like *60 Minutes*, *20/20*, and *Dateline* would later imitate.

Generally regarded as "the first and definitive" news documentary on American television, *See It Now* sought "to report in depth—to tell and show the American audience what was happening in the world using film as a narrative tool."[25] In the early 1960s, *CBS Reports* carried on the traditions of *See It Now*, and as that decade unfolded, the literary model of reporting played a more significant role in the program. Friendly endorsed the importance of the narrative tradition to *CBS Reports*: "Though based on truth, the programs still have to have stories of their own, with the basic outline of beginning, middle and end."[26]

Differences between Print and Television News

Although TV news reporters share many values, beliefs, and conventions with their print counterparts, television has transformed journalism in a number of significant ways. First, broadcast news is often driven by its technology. If a camera crew and microwave-relay van (which bounces a broadcast signal back to the station) are dispatched to a remote location for a live broadcast, reporters are expected to justify the expense by developing a story, even though nothing significant is occurring. This happens, for instance, when a national political candidate does not arrive at the local airport in time for an interview on the evening news, leaving the reporter and crew to report live on a flight delay. Print reporters, however, slide their notebooks

or laptop computers back into their bags and report on a story when one actually occurs.

Second, although print editors must cut stories to fit a physical space around the slots allocated for ads, TV news directors have to time stories to fit news in between commercials. They are under pressure to condense the day's main events into a visual show. Despite the fact that a much higher percentage of space is devoted to print ads (more than 60 percent at most dailies), TV ads (which take up less than 25 percent of the time in a typical thirty-minute news program) generally seem more intrusive to viewers, perhaps because TV ads take up time rather than space.

Third, whereas modern print journalists are expected to be detached, TV news derives its credibility from live, on-the-spot reporting, believable imagery, and viewers' trust in the reporters and anchors who read the news. In fact, since the early 1970s, the annual Roper polls have indicated that the majority of viewers find television news a more credible resource than print news. Viewers tend to feel a personal regard for the local anchors who appear each evening on TV sets in their homes. Many print journalists have even come to resent operating in the relative anonymity of newspaper work while their TV counterparts become mini-celebrities.

By the mid-1970s, the public's fascination with the Watergate scandal, combined with the improved quality of TV journalism, helped local news departments realize profits. In an effort to retain high ratings, stations began hiring consultants, who advised news directors to invest in one of the national packaged formats, such as Action News or Eyewitness News (sometimes mocked as Eyewitless News). Traveling the country, viewers noticed similar theme music and opening visuals from market to market. Consultants also suggested that stations lead their newscasts with *crime blocks*: a group of TV stories that recount the worst criminal transgressions of the day. A cynical slogan soon developed in the industry: "If it bleeds, it leads."

A few stations around the country have responded to viewers and critics who complain about overemphasizing crime—especially given that FBI statistics show that crime and murder rates fell in most major urban areas during the 1990s. In 1996, the news director at KVUE-TV in Austin, Texas, concerned about crime coverage, launched a new set of criteria that had to be met for news reports to qualify as responsible crime stories. She asked that her reporters answer the following questions: Do citizens or officials need to take action? Is there an immediate threat to

● News media camp out in front of the governor's mansion in Austin, Texas, the day after the November 7, 2000, presidential election ended in a virtual dead heat between Texas governor George W. Bush and Vice President Al Gore. After the TV networks mistakenly projected the winner—twice—on election night, the outcome was in doubt for more than a month before the U.S. Supreme Court finally settled the matter.

safety? Is there a threat to children? Does the crime have significant community impact? Does the story lend itself to a crime-prevention effort? With KVUE's new standards, the station eliminated many routine crime stories. Instead, the station provided a context for understanding crime rather than a mindless running tally of what crimes were being committed each day.[27]

Sound Bitten

Beginning in the 1980s, the term **sound bite** became part of the public lexicon. The TV equivalent of a quote in print news, a sound bite is the part of a broadcast news report in which an expert, celebrity, victim, or person-on-the-street responds in an interview to some aspect of an event or issue. With the 1988 national elections, sound bites became the focus of intense criticism. Various studies revealed that during political campaigns the typical sound bite from candidates had shrunk from an average duration of forty seconds in the 1950s and 1960s to fewer than eight seconds by the late 1990s. With shorter comments from interview subjects, TV news sometimes seemed like dueling sound bites, with reporters creating dramatic tension by editing competing viewpoints together as if the individuals had actually been in the same location speaking to one another. Of course, print news also pits one quote against another in a story, even though the actual interview subjects may never have met. Once again, these reporting techniques are evidence of the profession's reliance on storytelling devices to replicate or create conflict.

Pretty-Face and Happy-Talk Culture

In the early 1970s, at a Milwaukee TV station, consultants advised the station's news director that the evening anchor looked too old. Showing a bit of gray, the anchor was replaced and went on to serve as the station's editorial director. He was thirty-two years old at the time. In the late 1970s, a woman reporter at the same station was fired because of a weight problem, although that was not given as the official reason. Earlier that year, she had given birth to her first child. In 1983, Christine Craft, formerly a Kansas City television news anchor, initially won $500,000 in damages in a sex-discrimination suit against station KMBC (she eventually lost the monetary award when the station appealed). She had been fired because consultants believed she was too old, too unattractive, and not deferential enough to men.

Such stories are rampant in the annals of TV news. They have helped create a stereotype of the half-witted but attractive news anchor, reinforced by popular-culture images (such as Ted Baxter on the *Mary Tyler Moore Show* and the character played by William Hurt in the 1987 movie *Broadcast News*). Although the situation has improved slightly, a generation of national news consultants sets the agenda for what local reporters should cover—lots of local crime—as well as how they should look—young, attractive, pleasant, and usually white, with no regional accent. Essentially, news consultants—also known as *news doctors*—tried to replicate in modern local TV news the predominant male and female advertising images of the 1960s and 1970s.

Another news strategy favored by news consultants has been *happy talk*: the ad-libbed or scripted banter that goes on among local news anchors, reporters, meteorologists, and sports reporters before and after news reports. During the 1970s, consultants often recommended such chatter to create a more relaxed feeling on the news set and to foster the illusion of conversational intimacy with viewers. Some news doctors also believed that happy talk would counter much of that era's "bad news," which included coverage of urban riots and the Vietnam War. A strategy still used today, happy talk often appears forced and may create awkward transitions, especially when anchors must report on events that are sad or tragic.

● Managers of television news departments have often overemphasized the visual nature of their medium, placing more weight on the physical attractiveness of anchors than on their skills as reporters. In the early 1980s, news anchor Christine Craft was fired because consultants believed she was no longer youthful and attractive enough to draw a large audience.

Visual Language and Critical Limits

The brevity of a televised report is often compared unfavorably with the length of print news. However, newspaper reviewers and other TV critics seldom discuss the visual language of TV news and the ways in which images may capture events more powerfully than words.

In contemporary America, the shift from a print-dominated culture to an electronic-digital culture requires thoughtful scrutiny. Instead, the complexity of this shift is often reduced to a two-dimensional debate about information versus entertainment. Yet over the past fifty years television news has dramatized America's key events and provided a clearinghouse for shared information. Civil rights activists, for instance, acknowledge that the movement benefited enormously from televised pictures that documented the plight of southern blacks in the 1960s. Other enduring TV images, unfurled as a part of history to each new generation, are embedded in our collective memory: the Kennedy and King assassinations in the 1960s; the turmoil of Watergate in the 1970s; the first space shuttle disaster and the Chinese student uprisings in the 1980s; the Persian Gulf War, the bombing of the Oklahoma City federal building, the Centennial Olympics, and the Clinton impeachment hearings in the 1990s; and in 2001 the airliner hijackings and the attacks on the Pentagon and New York's World Trade Center. During these critical events, TV news has been a cultural reference point marking the strengths and weaknesses of a nation.

In contrast, many print critics overlooked a disturbing TV news strategy that developed in the mid to late 1980s. In their coverage of crack cocaine, news operations formulated a visual shot in which news photographers, or *shooters* (using shaky, handheld cameras), leaped from the back of police vans and followed gun-wielding authorities as they broke down the doors of various crack houses. At the time, few critics mentioned that in such a shot TV news actually represented the police's or state's point of view. A profession that prides itself on neutrality and on watching over the police on society's behalf apparently did not question whether it was appropriate for reporters to implicitly tell these stories from the police viewpoint. Many critics, untrained in analyzing and interpreting visual language, failed to comment.

Conventional News, Public Journalism, and Democracy

In 1990, Poland was experiencing growing pains as it shifted from a state-controlled economic system to a more open market economy. The country's leading newspaper, *Gazeta Wyborcza*, the first noncommunist newspaper to appear in Eastern Europe since the 1940s, was also undergoing challenges. Based in Warsaw with a circulation of about 350,000 at the time, *Gazeta Wyborcza* had to report on and explain the new economy and the new crime wave that accompanied it. Especially troubling to the news staff and to Polish citizens were gangs that preyed on American and Western European tourists at railway stations. Apparently, an inner circle of thieves snatched purses, wallets, and luggage, sometimes assaulting tourists in the process. The stolen goods would then pass to an outer circle whose members transferred the goods to still another exterior ring of thieves. Even if the police caught the inner-circle members, the loot disappeared.

These developments triggered heated discussions in the newsroom. A small group of young reporters, some of whom had recently worked in the United States, argued that the best way to cover the story was to describe the new crime wave and relay the facts to readers in a neutral manner. Another group, many of whom were older and more experienced, felt that the paper should take an advocacy stance and condemn the criminals through interpretive columns on the front page. The older guard won this particular debate, and more interpretive pieces appeared.[28]

The Future of News

The Polish newsroom story illustrates the two competing models that have influenced American and European journalism since the early 1900s. The first—the *informational* or *modern model*—emphasizes describing events and issues from a neutral point of view. The second—a more *partisan* and *European model*—stresses analyzing occurrences and advocating remedies from an acknowledged point of view. In most American newspapers today, the informational model dominates the front page, whereas the partisan model remains confined to the editorial pages and an occasional front-page piece. Supplementing both models, photographs in newspapers and images on television tell parts of a story not easily captured in words. An alternative model—often labeled "public journalism"—emerged in the late 1980s to challenge modern journalistic ideals.

What Is Public Journalism?

Since the late 1980s, a number of newspapers have been experimenting with ways to more actively involve readers in the news process. These experiments have surfaced primarily at midsize daily papers, including the *Charlotte Observer,* the *Wichita Eagle,* the *Virginian-Pilot,* and the *Minneapolis Star Tribune.* Davis "Buzz" Merritt, editor and vice president of the *Wichita Eagle,* has defined key aspects of **public journalism**:

- It moves beyond the limited mission of "telling the news" to a broader mission of helping public life go well, and acts out that imperative. . . .
- It moves from detachment to being a fair-minded participant in public life. . . .
- It moves beyond only describing what is "going wrong" to also imagining what "going right" would be like. . . .
- It moves from seeing people as consumers—as readers or nonreaders, as bystanders to be informed—to seeing them as a public, as potential actors in arriving at democratic solutions to public problems.[29]

Public journalism might best be imagined as a conversational model for journalistic practice. Modern journalism draws a distinct line between reporter detachment and community involvement; public journalism—driven by citizen forums, community conversations, and even talk shows—redraws this line.

The stimulus behind public journalism was the realization that many citizens felt and still feel alienated from participating in public life in a meaningful way. This alienation arises, in part, from watching passively as the political process plays out in the news media. The process stars the politicians who run for office, the spin doctors who manage the campaigns, and the reporters who dig into every nook and cranny. Meanwhile, readers and viewers serve as spectators, watching a play that does not seem to involve them.

The public-journalism movement has drawn both criticism and praise. Though not a substitute for investigative reporting or the routine coverage of daily events, public journalism is a way to involve both the public and journalists more centrally in civic and political life. Editors and reporters interested in addressing citizen alienation—and reporter cynicism—began devising ways to engage people as conversational partners in determining the news. In an effort to draw the public into discussions about community priorities, these journalists began sponsoring reader and citizen forums, where readers were supposed to have a voice in shaping aspects of the news that directly affected them.

● A television image showing the point at which the House of Representatives vote reached 218 on the first article of impeachment, Saturday, December 19, 1998. 218 represented the simple majority required to approve the first article against President Clinton and send the matter to the Senate for trial.

Although isolated citizen projects and reader forums are sprinkled throughout the history of journalism, the current public-journalism movement began in earnest in 1987 and 1988, in Columbus, Georgia. The city was suffering from a depressed economy, an alienated citizenry, and unresponsive leadership. In response, a team of reporters from the *Columbus Ledger-Enquirer,* part of the Knight-Ridder chain, surveyed and talked with community leaders and other citizens about the future of the city. Based on the findings, the paper published an eight-part series.

When the provocative series evoked little public response, the paper's leadership realized there was no mechanism or forum for continuing the public discussions about the issues raised in the series. Consequently, the paper created such a forum by organizing a town meeting. Three hundred citizens showed up. The editor of the paper, Jack Swift, organized a follow-up cookout at his own home at which seventy-five concerned citizens created a new civic organization called United Beyond 2000, led by a steering committee with Swift as a leading member. Staffed by community volunteers, task forces formed around issues such as recreation, child care, racial tension, and teenage behavior. The committees spurred the city's managers and other political leaders into action. The Columbus project generated public discussion, involved more people in the news process, and eased race and class tensions by bringing various groups together in public conversations. In the newsroom, the *Ledger-Enquirer* reimagined the place of journalists in politics: "Instead of standing outside the political community and reporting on its pathologies, they took up residence within its borders."[30]

Another important public-journalism project began in Wichita, Kansas, after the 1988 elections. Editor Davis Merritt was so discouraged by the *Wichita Eagle*'s typical and conventional political coverage that he led a campaign to use public journalism as a catalyst for reinventing political news. The *Eagle*'s first voter project during the 1990 campaign for governor used reader surveys and public forums to refocus the paper around a citizens' agenda. This involved dropping the tired horse-race metaphor—who's winning, who's losing—that usually frames political coverage. Merritt argued that "public life cannot regain its vitality on a diet of information alone." He believed that a new direction for journalism must "re-engage citizens in public life" through two steps: "(1) Add to the definition of our job the additional objective of helping public life go well, and then (2) Develop the journalistic tools and reflexes necessary to reach that objective."[31] The *Eagle*'s project partially revitalized regional politics in Kansas in the early 1990s and into the new millennium. It influenced other papers as well, including the *Charlotte Observer,* which created a citizens' agenda to determine key issues for its election coverage throughout the 1990s.

A final example involves editors at Norfolk's *Virginian-Pilot,* which undertook a mission to change the culture of the newsroom in the 1990s (see Figure 14.2). Defying the

Figure 14.2 Changing the Culture of the Newsroom: Two Models at the *Virginian-Pilot*

In 1995, in the spirit of public journalism, the editors at the *Virginian-Pilot* attempted to transform the "belief system" of their newsroom, imagining themselves primarily as citizens helping to improve public life.

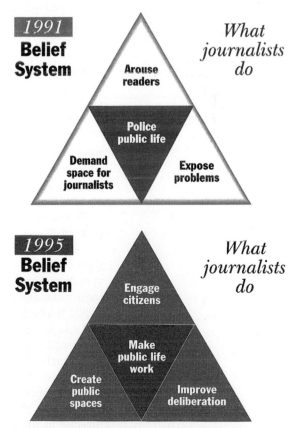

1991
Belief System

What journalists do

Arouse readers

Police public life

Demand space for journalists

Expose problems

1995
Belief System

What journalists do

Engage citizens

Make public life work

Create public spaces

Improve deliberation

Source: Used by permission of the *Virginian-Pilot.*

long-standing tradition of lone reporters covering beats and topics on their own, the paper reorganized reporters into teams. The editors also began using deliberative citizen forums, called *community conversations,* to discover not what people want to read but how "to name and frame issues" central to the community. These issues then became the driving force behind some of the paper's coverage. According to the leading theorist of public journalism, New York University's Jay Rosen, "The idea is to frame stories from the citizen's view, rather than inserting man-in-the-street quotes into a frame dominated by professionals."[32]

Criticizing Public Journalism

By 2000, more than a hundred newspapers, many teamed with local television and public radio stations, practiced some form of public journalism. Yet many critics and journalists remain skeptical of the experiment.[33] They are primarily concerned about civic journalism projects that undermine traditional styles of reporting and journalists' long-standing role as neutral watchdogs.

Critics of public journalism have raised a number of other issues. First, some editors and reporters argue that such journalism merely panders to what readers— and therefore corporate publishers—want and takes editorial control away from the newsrooms. They believe that very small focus-group samples and poll research— tools of the marketing department—blur the boundary between the editorial and business functions of a paper. Journalists have traditionally viewed their work as a public service and rarely think of the news as a product or a commodity. Some journalists fear that as they become more active in the community they may be perceived as community boosters rather than as community watchdogs. These journalists raise legitimate concerns that their work may be compromised if later they are required to report on the wrongdoings of other civic organizations.

Second, some critics worry that public journalism might compromise the profession's credibility, which today derives from detachment. They argue that public journalism turns reporters into participants rather than observers. However, as Merritt points out, professionals who have credibility are regarded as "honest, intelligent, well-intentioned, trustworthy" and "share some basic values about life, some common ground about common good." Yet conventional journalists insist they "don't share values, with anyone; that [they] are value-neutral."[34] Merritt argues that modern journalism, as a result, actually has little credibility with the public. This view is buoyed by polls that reveal the public's basic distrust of most major news media. Research studies in 1988, for instance, indicated that 50 percent of surveyed respondents had "a great deal of confidence in newspapers"; by 1993 and through 2000, similar polls showed that the confidence factor had dropped to less than 25 percent.[35]

Third, some reporters and editors argue that public-journalism projects remove their control over both stories and the writing process. They are concerned that conversational models of reporting may undermine their narrative voices as well as their independence, especially if they are placed in reporting teams. Defenders of public journalism, however, respond that its goal is merely to create more frames and narrative models—not to eliminate reporters' control over stories or to eradicate traditional investigative forms of journalism.

Fourth, critics contend that public journalism undermines the both-sides-of-a-story convention by constantly seeking common ground and community consensus. Public journalists counter that they are trying to set aside more room for centrist positions. Such positions are often representative of many in the community but are missing in the mainstream news, which is more interested in the extremist views that make for a gripping story. Many journalists who seek to portray conflict by means of extreme viewpoints worry that in seeking a middle ground, public journalism runs the risk of dulling the rough edges of democratic speech.

Fifth, considered by many traditional reporters as merely a tool of marketers and business managers, public journalism has not addressed the changing economic structure of the news business. With more newspapers (and broadcast stations) in the hands of fewer owners, both public journalists and traditional reporters need to raise tough questions about the disappearance of competing daily papers and the large profit margins generated by local monopoly newspapers. Facing little competition, will newspapers continue the 1990s trend of cutting reporting staffs or expensive investigative projects and reducing the space for news? Such a trend may increase profits and satisfy stockholders, but it also limits the voices and views in a community. (See "Examining Ethics: WTO Protesters, TV News, and Corporate Power" on page 504.)

Democracy and Reimagining Reporting's Role

Journalism is central to democracy — that is, freedom requires that both citizens and the media have access to the information that we all need to make important decisions. As this chapter illustrated, however, this is a complicated idea. For example, in the aftermath of September 11, 2001, some government officials claimed that whenever the news media raised questions about fighting terrorism or invading Iraq, somehow reporters or columnists were being unpatriotic. But the basic principles of democracy require citizens and the media to ask questions. In fact, a counter-argument could be made that patriotism demands that we question our leaders and our government. Isn't this, after all, what the American Revolution was originally all about?

Conventional journalists will fight ferociously for the overt principles that underpin reporting's basic tenets — questioning government, freedom of the press, the public's right to know, and two sides to every story. These are all worthy ideals, but they do have limitations. All of these tenets, for example, generally do not acknowledge any moral or ethical duty for journalists to improve the quality of daily life. Rather, journalism values its important news-gathering capabilities and the well-constructed news narrative, leaving the improvement of civic life to political groups, nonprofit organizations, business philanthropists, and individual citizens.

Social Responsibility

Although reporters have traditionally thought of themselves first and foremost as observers and recorders, some journalists have occasionally acknowledged social responsibility. Among them was James Agee in the 1930s. In his book *Let Us Now Praise Famous Men*, which was accompanied by the Depression-era photography of Walker Evans, Agee regarded conventional journalism as dishonest, partly because the act of observing intruded on people and turned them into story characters, whom newspapers and magazines exploited for profit.

Agee also worried that readers would retreat into the comfort of his writing — his narrative — instead of confronting what for many families was the horror of the Great Depression. For Agee, the question of responsibility extended not only to journalism and himself but to the readers of his stories as well: "The reader is no less centrally involved than the authors and those of whom they tell."[36] Agee's self-conscious analysis provides insights into journalism's hidden agendas and the responsibility of all citizens for making public life better.

EXAMINING ETHICS

WTO Protesters, TV News, and Corporate Power

In July 2001, thousands of demonstrators gathered in Genoa, Italy, to demand that the world's richest nations put an end to Third World debt. One protester died. The mostly peaceful demonstrations represented an ongoing struggle that had begun in December 1999, when 40,000 protesters gathered in Seattle to protest the global meeting of the World Trade Organization (WTO). Protest leaders called for the WTO's 135 members to reform their secretive style and capitalistic values and pay more attention to workers' rights and environmental destruction. Many predicted that the event would put global greed and multinational might on the news agenda in the

same way that Earth Day in 1970 shoved environmental issues onto the national media's radar screen.

The WTO protesters understood that a massive made-for-TV demonstration was the way to make headway in mainstream TV news. But how do you take a TV picture of globalization and its attendant problems and possibilities? This is not easy—unless you call attention to it via old-fashioned, 1960s-style chaos in the streets. This is something TV news seems to understand.

In the 1990s, a decade when crime declined, TV news reporting of crime escalated. A "cash cow" for news operations for decades, crime stories, after all, are easy to track (via police scanners), cheap to produce, and simple to report. They've got narrative conflict and they're easy to personalize, removing crime from the context of a complex social or community problem to the status of the individual pathology of demented criminals or misguided protesters.

The WTO protesters offered a rainbow coalition of political voices—from conservative Pat Buchanan to environmental activists to labor unionists to plain folks upset about the triumph of the multinational corporate ethos. Using the Internet to organize and spread the word about the planned protest demonstrations, they at least got TV news to focus on globalization for part of its short attention span. Unfortunately, the demonstrations also led to looting, fights, tear gas, and more than five hundred arrests.

For the most part, TV news did not take up the serious global issues of substandard wages or environmental disasters that the protesters were calling attention to. Overlooking the serious issues in favor of petty crime news, MSNBC's morning-after coverage didn't even mention the protesters' main points. Instead the cable network framed the story as if it were merely about a bunch of thoughtless college students and sports fans trashing their town after the Big Win. Cable guru Chris Matthews demanded at the top of MSNBC's *Hardball* that the on-the-scene street reporter "forget the issues" and regale him with details of her dramatic escape from looters who were not like her.

This situation raises an ethical dilemma. Mainstream national TV news did not go for the bigger story here—even though a 1999 Pew Research Center study showed that just 37 percent of American families earning less than $50,000 a year held "a positive view of global free trade," whereas 63 percent of families earning more than $75,000 had a positive view of global free trade.[1] Unfortunately, network news is implicated in globalization at the start of the 2000s in a way it was not implicated in ecology in the 1970s. Today the network news organizations are all owned by major global economic powers—ABC by Disney, NBC by General Electric, CBS by Viacom, Fox by News Corp., CNN by AOL Time Warner. Even though it is in the interests of citizens in a democracy to know the inner workings of global businesses, it is not in the corporate interest to have the news divisions of these behemoth companies look too closely at the impact of their own global expansion.

In this context it is instructive to see the 1999 movie *The Insider*—a Hollywood account of the CBS program *60 Minutes* buckling under business pressures for the first time in the program's three-decade history. The movie relates how our nation's most powerful symbol of investigative journalism caved in to big tobacco and its own corporate bosses at a time when CBS was being sold to Westinghouse. Late in 1995, the program killed an investigative story on tobacco industry cover-ups of nicotine and addiction studies after CBS was threatened with a lawsuit. As media critic Jon Katz foretold in *Rolling Stone* in March 1992, citizens and consumers are sometimes getting more truthful information from "New News" outlets—from "rock, rap, and the movies"—than they get from "Old News"—from Tom, Dan, Peter, and *60 Minutes*,

manning their powerful command and control centers at corporate news headquarters.[2]

The lesson from *The Insider* is this: Journalism, so central to American democracy that it's the only business enterprise the founders protected in the Constitution, spent the first part of the nineteenth century freeing itself from political partisanship only to find itself at the beginning of the twenty-first century under the thumb of corporate and global interests.

But there is hope. While mainstream national print journalism like the *New York Times* does a good job covering the complexity of issues related to the WTO and the entanglements of news media in the values of their corporate parents, the Internet has spawned a wealth of alternative resources. These include activists and journalists reporting for the Independent Media Center <www.indymedia.org>, Free Speech TV <www.freespeech.org>, CorpWatch <www.corpwatch.org>, and World Trade Observer <www.earthjustice.org/observer/ home.htm>. In addition, many 24-hour news channels occasionally turn to the big picture, trying to tell the story of our increasingly interconnected world on the small screen.

● In *Let Us Now Praise Famous Men,* which begins with haunting photos taken by Walker Evans, author James Agee questioned the basic honesty of daily journalism in the late 1930s. He thought that professional journalists could too easily exploit interview subjects simply as news stories that serve a business enterprise without actively engaging in changing the conditions of social life.

Deliberative Democracy

According to advocates of public journalism, when reporters are chiefly concerned with maintaining their antagonistic relationship to politics and are less willing to improve political discourse, news and democracy suffer. *Washington Post* columnist David Broder thinks that national journalists like him—through rising salaries, prestige, and formal education—have distanced themselves "from the people that we are writing for and have become much, much closer to people we are writing about."[37] Broder believes that journalists need to become activists, not for a particular party but for the political process and in the interest of re-energizing public life. For the news media, this might involve spearheading voter-registration drives or setting up pressrooms in public libraries or even in shopping malls, where people converge in large numbers.

By advocating a more active role for reporters and the news media, public journalism at its best promises to reinvigorate both reporting and politics. Most of all, it offers people models for how to deliberate in forums, and then it covers those deliberations. Public journalism aims to improve our standard *representative democracy,* in which most of us sit back and watch elected officials act on our behalf, by reinvigorating *deliberative democracy,* in which citizen groups, local government, and the news media together take a more active stand in shaping social, economic, and political agendas. In a more deliberative democracy, a large segment of the community discusses public life and social policy before advising or electing officials who represent the community's interests.

In 1989, the historian Christopher Lasch argued that "the job of the press is to encourage debate, not to supply the public with information."[38] Although he overstated his case—journalism does both and more—Lasch made a cogent point about how conventional journalism has lost its bearings. Adrift in data, mainstream journalism lost touch with its partisan roots. The early mission of journalism—to advocate opinions and encourage public debate—has been relegated to alternative magazines, the editorial pages, and cable news channels starring elite East Coast reporters. Ironically, Lasch connected the gradual decline in voter participation, which began in the 1920s, to more responsible conduct on the part of professional journalists. With a modern "objective" press, he contended, the public increasingly began to defer to the "more professional" news media to watch over civic life on its behalf.

As the advocates of public journalism acknowledge, people have grown used to letting their representatives think and act for them. Public journalism and other civic projects offer citizens an opportunity to deliberate and to influence their leaders. Public journalism asks the mainstream press to reconsider its role in deliberative democracy. For journalists, this may include broadening the story frames they use to recount experiences; paying more attention to the historical context of these stories; doing more investigative reports that analyze both news conventions and social issues; taking more responsibility for their news narratives; and participating more fully in the public life of their communities. Such a role should also include making investigations into the impact of economics on news media.

Arguing that for too long journalism has defined its role only in negative terms, news scholar Jay Rosen notes: "To be adversarial, critical, to ask tough questions, to expose scandal and wrongdoing . . . these are necessary tasks, even noble tasks, but they are negative tasks." In addition, he suggests, journalism should assert itself as a positive force, not merely as a watchdog or as a neutral information conduit to readers but as "a support system for public life."[39]

> **❝ Neither journalism nor public life will move forward until we actually rethink, redescribe, and reinterpret what journalism is; not the science of information of our culture but its poetry and conversation. ❞**
>
> –James Carey,
> *Kettering Review,* 1992

www.

To create an individualized study plan for Chapter 14, go to the interactive *Media and Culture* Online Study Guide at: bedfordstmartins.com/ mediaculture

REVIEW QUESTIONS

Modern Journalism in the Information Age

1. What are the drawbacks of the informational model of journalism?

2. What is news?

3. What are some of the key values that underlie modern journalism?

Ethics and the News Media

4. How do issues such as deception and privacy present ethical problems for journalists?

5. Why is getting a story first important to reporters?

6. What are the connections between so-called neutral journalism and economics?

Reporting Rituals and the Legacy of Print Journalism

7. Why have reporters become so dependent on experts?

8. Why do many conventional journalists (and citizens) believe firmly in the idea that there are two sides to every story?

Journalism in the Age of Television

9. How is credibility established in TV news as compared to print journalism?

10. With regard to TV news, what are sound bites and happy talk?

Conventional News, Public Journalism, and Democracy

11. What is public journalism? How does it propose to make journalism better?

12. What are the major criticisms of the public-journalism movement, and why do the mainstream national media have concerns about public journalism?

13. How do public and conventional journalists differ when it comes to maintaining credibility with their audience?

14. What is deliberative democracy, and what does it have to do with journalism?

QUESTIONING THE MEDIA

1. What are your main criticisms of the state of news today? In your opinion, what are the news media doing well?

2. If you were a reporter or editor, would you quit voting to demonstrate your ability to be neutral? Why or why not?

3. How would you go about formulating an ethical policy with regard to using deceptive means to get a story?

4. For a reporter, what are the dangers of both detachment from and involvement in public life?

5. What steps would you take to make journalism work better in a democracy?

SEARCHING THE INTERNET

http://www.journalism.org

The site for Project for Excellence in Journalism, initiated by journalists concerned about standards. The site offers research studies and critical essays on topics related to journalism.

http://www.cjr.org

The Web site for the *Columbia Journalism Review,* one of the nation's premier critics of contemporary journalism. Run by the Columbia Graduate School of Journalism, the site not only contains current CJR magazine articles on national and international news coverage but also offers a valuable updated list of "who owns what" in the media.

http://ajr.newslink.org

The site for the *American Journalism Review,* another top national magazine that takes a critical look at contemporary journalism. Run by the School of Journalism at the University of Maryland, the site features current articles from the magazine and a "joblink" service.

http://www.aim.org

The Web site for the conservative media watchdog group Accuracy in Media (AIM). Among other issues, the site showcases articles from its national newsletter and tracks what AIM regards as anti-business bias in national news reporting.

http://www.fair.org

The Web site for the progressive and left-leaning media watchdog group Fairness and Accuracy in Reporting (FAIR). The site contains articles from its national magazine EXTRA! and a feature called "economic reporting review" that examines news coverage of money-related issues.

In Brief

Make a short list of questionable or illegal methods that a reporter might use to get a story (e.g., withholding her identity as a reporter). Discuss the circumstances under which these methods might be justified.

In Depth

The purpose of this project is to extend your critical approach to the news. With a partner, choose for reading and viewing one local daily paper, the *New York Times,* and one network or CNN newscast—all from the same weekday.

Devise a series of charts and a descriptive scheme that will enable you to compare who gets quoted as expert sources in the stories for that particular day. For example, devise one chart that compares the occupations of the sources. Are they from academic, business, or government sectors? Or are they "ordinary" people? Throughout this project, limit your focus to local, national, or international news.

Description. Count the total number of sources used by each newspaper or network program. Look for quotes in news articles and for sound bites on television. Are all sources identified? How are they identified? Can you tell which area of the country these sources are from? What kinds of experts are quoted in the news? What jobs do they seem to hold? What gender are the news sources?

Analysis. After completing your charts, write one or two paragraphs discussing patterns that emerge. Who seems to get quoted most frequently? Among those quoted, what kinds of occupations generally appear? Do male or female sources dominate?

Interpretation. Write a one- or two-paragraph critical interpretation of your findings. How are the sources used? Why do you think certain sources appear in this day's news more frequently than others? Why do reporters seek out certain types of sources rather than others? Does the gender of sources mean anything?

Evaluation. Discuss the limitations of your study and whether you think print or television handles sources best. Did circumstances on the particular day you chose suggest why one type of expert appears more often than other types?

(Note: This assignment works either as an in-class presentation or as a written project. Either way, it should include charts that help organize the material.)

KEY TERMS

newsworthiness, 479
news, 481
ethnocentrism, 484
responsible capitalism, 484

small-town pastoralism, 485
individualism, 485
conflict of interest, 488

herd journalism, 493
sound bite, 498
public journalism, 500

media effects

and cultural approaches to research

In 1966, NBC showed the Rod Serling made-for-television thriller *The Doomsday Flight,* the first movie to depict an airplane hijacking. In the story, a man plants a bomb and tries to extract ransom money from an airline. In the days following the telecast, the nation's major airlines reported a dramatic rise in anonymous bomb threats, some of them classified as teenage pranks. The network agreed not to run the film again.

In 1985, the popular heavy-metal band Judas Priest made headlines when two Nevada teenagers shot themselves after listening to the group's allegedly subliminal suicidal message on their 1978 *Stained Class* album. One teen died instantly; the other lived for three more years, in constant pain from severe facial injuries. The teenagers' parents lost a civil product-liability suit against the British metal band and CBS Records.

In 1995, an eighteen-year-old woman and her boyfriend went on a killing spree in Louisiana after reportedly watching Oliver Stone's 1994 film *Natural Born Killers* more than twenty times.

15

The family of one of the victims filed a lawsuit against Stone and Time Warner, charging that the film—starring Juliette Lewis and Woody Harrelson as a demented, celebrity-craving young couple on a murderous rampage—irresponsibly incited real-life violence. Part of the family's case was based on a 1996 interview in which Stone said: "The most pacifist people in the world said they came out of this movie and wanted to kill somebody." Stone and Time Warner argued that the lawsuit should be dismissed on the grounds of free speech, and the case was finally thrown out in 2001. There was no evidence, according to the judge, that Stone had intended to incite violence.

In 1999, two heavily armed students wearing trench coats attacked Columbine High School in Littleton, Colorado. They planted as many as fifty bombs and murdered twelve fellow students and a teacher before killing themselves. In the wake of this tragedy many people blamed the mass media, speculating that the killers had immersed themselves in the dark lyrics of shock rocker Marilyn Manson and were desensitized to violence by "first-

● Woody Harrelson in *Natural Born Killers* (1994).

person shooter" video games such as *Doom.* Still others looked to the influence of films like *The Basketball Diaries,* in which a drug-using, trench-coated teenager (played by Leonardo DiCaprio) imagines shooting a teacher and his classmates.

Finally, since Fall 2000, a parade of fans of the MTV program and movie *Jackass* have been injured, sometimes severely, while imitating the dangerous stunts performed on the show by host Johnny Knoxville and others. In one incident, a trio of teenage boys in Kentucky decided to videotape a person getting hit by a car. One held the camera as the other drove at 30 to 40 miles per hour into the third one, sending him flipping over the car and ultimately sending him to the hospital with chest, leg, and neck injuries. In other incidents,

younger boys doused themselves with flammable liquid and lit themselves on fire. Another put himself on a barbecue grill. All of the injured cited *Jackass* as their inspiration. MTV runs disclaimers at the beginning of each episode and has denied responsibility for the incidents.

Each of these incidents has renewed long-standing cultural debates over the suggestive power of music, visual imagery, and screen violence. Since the emergence of popular music, movies, and television as influential mass media, the relationship between make-believe stories and real-life imitation has drawn a great deal of attention. Concerns have been raised not only by parents, teachers, and politicians but by several generations of mass-communication researchers as well.

When it comes to government- or university-sponsored mass-media research, no social groups have been pondered and probed more than children and teens. The dominant strain of this research—known in shorthand as **media effects** because of its focus on attempting to understand, explain, and predict the effects of mass media on individuals and society—has focused on one particular area: the connection between aggressive behavior and violent media stories. In the late 1960s, government leaders—reacting to the social upheavals of that decade—first set aside $1 million to examine this connection. Since that time, thousands of studies have told us what most kindergarten teachers have come to believe instinctively: Violent scenes on television and in movies stimulate aggressive behavior in children—especially young boys. Over the years, children have imitated physical fight scenes from *Zorro, Mighty Mouse Playhouse, Batman, Teenage Mutant Ninja Turtles,* and professional wrestling shows, leading generations of adults to suspect the effects of mass media.

In this chapter, we will examine the evolution of media research over time. After looking at some early research efforts, we will focus on two major directions in media research: effects research and cultural studies. We will investigate the strengths and limitations of these two approaches. Finally, we will consider how media research interacts with democratic ideals.

Early Developments in Media Research

In the early days of the United States, philosophical and historical writings tried to explain the nature of news and print media. For instance, Frenchman Alexis de Tocqueville, author of *Democracy in America,* noted differences between French and American newspapers in the early 1830s:

> In France the space allotted to commercial advertisements is very limited, and . . . the essential part of the journal is the discussion of the politics of the day. In America three quarters of the enormous sheet are filled with advertisements and the remainder is frequently occupied by political intelligence or trivial anecdotes; it is only from time to time that one finds a corner devoted to the passionate discussions like those which the journalists of France every day give to their readers.[1]

During the mid to late nineteenth century, the major models of media analysis were based on moral and political arguments, as suggested in de Tocqueville's writings.[2]

More scientific approaches to mass-media research did not begin to develop until the late 1920s and 1930s. It was in 1920 that Walter Lippmann, in his book *Liberty and the News,* called on journalists to operate more like scientific researchers in gathering and analyzing factual material. Lippmann's next book, *Public Opinion,* published in 1922, applied principles of psychology to journalism. It is considered by many academics to be "the founding book in American media studies."[3]

In America, the emphasis on applied research led to an expanded analysis of the effects of the media, emphasizing data collection and numerical measurement. According to media historian Daniel Czitrom, by the 1930s "an aggressively empirical spirit, stressing new and increasingly sophisticated research techniques, characterized the study of modern communication in America."[4] Czitrom traces four early trends between 1930 and 1960 that contributed to the rise of modern media research: propaganda analysis, public-opinion research, social psychology studies, and marketing research.

Propaganda Analysis

After World War I, some media researchers became interested in the ways in which propaganda had been used to advance the American war effort. They found that during the war, governments routinely relied on propaganda divisions as part of their "information" apparatus. Though propaganda was considered a positive force for mobilizing public opinion during the war, researchers after the war labeled propaganda as "partisan appeal based on half-truths and devious manipulation of communication channels."[5] Harold Lasswell's important 1927 study, *Propaganda Technique in the World War,* focused on media representations, defining propaganda as "the control of opinion by significant symbols, . . . by stories, rumors, reports, pictures and other forms of social communication."[6] *Propaganda analysis* became a major early focus of mass-media research.

Public-Opinion Research

Researchers soon extended the study of war propaganda to include general concerns about how the mass media filtered information and shaped public attitudes. In the face of growing media influence, Walter Lippmann distrusted the public's ability to function as knowledgeable citizens as well as journalism's ability to help the public separate truth from lies. In promoting the place of the expert in modern life, Lippmann celebrated the social scientist as part of a new expert class that could best make "unseen facts intelligible to those who have to make decisions."[7]

Today, Lippmann's expert class conducts citizen surveys in the form of *public-opinion research,* which has become especially influential during political elections. On the upside, research on diverse populations has provided insights into citizen behavior and social differences, especially during election periods or following major national events. For example, polls conducted about a week before the 2000 presidential election found that registered voters were more likely to think that Al Gore was more qualified to be president than George W. Bush, but also that they felt Bush was more personally likable than Gore. In another example, polls conducted after the first O.J. Simpson verdict convincingly documented a wide disparity among white and black citizens regarding their relative trust or suspicion of police officers. A number of research studies — informally copied by such network newsmagazines as ABC's *Primetime Live* (now *20/20*) — also demonstrated that a car with a group of young white males cruising a city's main thoroughfare was far less likely to be routinely stopped by police than was a similar car occupied by young black males driving along the same route.

On the downside, the journalism profession has become increasingly dependent on political polls. Some critics ask whether this heavy reliance on measured public opinion has begun to adversely affect active political involvement. For example, there are numerous stories and studies about citizens who do not vote because they have already seen poll projections on television and decided that their votes would not make a difference in the outcome. Furthermore, because the public does not design a CBS News or Gallup poll, it is just passively responding to surveys that mainly measure opinions on topics of interest to business, government, academics, and the mainstream news media.

● One of the earliest forms of U.S. mass communication research — propaganda analysis — was prominent during the twentieth century's two world wars. Researchers studied the impact of war posters and other government information campaigns to determine how audiences could be persuaded through stirring media messages about patriotism and duty.

● Concerns about film violence are not new. This 1930 movie, *Little Caesar,* follows the career of gangster Rico Bandello (played by Edward G. Robinson, shown), who kills his way to the top of the crime establishment, and gets the girl as well. The Motion Picture Production Code, which was established a few years after this movie's release, reined in sexual themes and profane language, set restrictions on film violence, and attempted to prevent audiences from sympathizing with bad guys like Rico.

Social Psychology Studies

Whereas opinion polls measure public attitudes, *social psychology studies* measure individual behavior and cognition. The most influential of these early investigations, the Payne Fund Studies, encompassed a series of thirteen research projects conducted by social psychologists between 1929 and 1932. Named after the private philanthropic organization that provided financial support for the research, the Payne Fund Studies emerged from a growing national concern about the effects of motion pictures, which had become a particularly popular pastime for young people in the 1920s. These beginning studies, which were later used by politicians to attack the movie industry, linked frequent movie attendance to juvenile delinquency, promiscuity, and other antisocial behaviors, arguing that movies took "emotional possession" of young filmgoers.[8]

In one of the Payne studies, for example, children were taken to a movie house and wired with electrodes to galvanometers, mechanisms that detect any heightened response via the subject's skin. The researchers interpreted any galvanic changes in the skin as evidence of emotional arousal. In retrospect, the findings hardly seem surprising: The youngest children in the group (nine-year-olds) had the strongest reaction to violent or tragic movie scenes, and the teenage subjects reacted most strongly to scenes with romantic and sexual content. The researchers concluded that films could be dangerous for young children and might foster sexual promiscuity among teenagers. The conclusions of this and other Payne Fund Studies contributed to the establishment of the film industry's production code, which tamed movie content from the 1930s through the 1950s. As forerunners of today's TV violence and aggression research, the Payne Fund Studies became the model for media research beginning in the late 1960s. (See Figure 15.1 for one example of a

The TV industry continues to study its self-imposed rating categories, promising to fine-tune them to ensure that the government keeps its distance. These standards are one example of a policy that was shaped in part by media research. Since the 1960s, accumulated evidence has pointed to links between violent TV images and increased levels of aggression among children and adolescents.

Figure 15.1 TV Parental Guidelines

The following categories apply to programs designed solely for children:

 All Children.
This program is designed to be appropriate for all children.

 Directed to Older Children.
This program is designed for children age 7 and above.

 Note: For those programs where fantasy violence may be more intense or more combative than other programs in this category, such programs will be designated **TV-Y7-FV.**

The following categories apply to programs designed for the entire audience:

 General Audience.
Most parents would find this program suitable for all ages.

 Parental Guidance Suggested.
This program contains material that parents may find unsuitable for younger children.

 Parents Strongly Cautioned.
This program contains some material that many parents would find unsuitable for children under 14 years of age.

 Mature Audiences Only.
This program is specifically designed to be viewed by adults and therefore may be unsuitable for children under 17.

 For programs rated **TV-PG, TV-14,** and **TV-MA,** labels are included to provide more information about contents, where appropriate:

D — **suggestive dialogue**
L — **coarse language**
S — **sexual situations**
V — **violence**

Source: National Cable Television Association, <http://www.tvguidelines.org>, 1/28/03.

contemporary policy that has developed from media research. Also see "Examining Ethics: TV's Changing Language and the 'Sopranos Effect,'" page 517, for the debate on network television standards and practices concerning adult language.)

Marketing Research

A fourth influential area of media research, primarily private, developed through the efforts of advertisers and product companies. They began conducting surveys on consumer buying habits, known as *marketing research*. Specialized researchers, using improved audience sampling and statistical techniques, began selling their services to advertisers and media firms in the 1920s. The emergence of commercial radio led to the first ratings systems that measured how many people were listening on a given night. By the 1930s, radio networks, advertisers, large stations, and advertising agencies all subscribed to ratings services. However, compared with print media, whose circulation departments kept careful track of customers' names and addresses, radio listeners were more difficult to trace. This problem precipitated the development of increasingly sophisticated direct-mail diaries, television meters, phone surveys, the telemarketing industry, and eventually Internet tracking in trying to determine consumer preferences and measure media use worldwide.

> **❝ Research is formalized curiosity. It is poking and prying with a purpose.❞**
>
> **– Zora Neale Hurston, writer**

EXAMINING ETHICS

TV's Changing Language and the "Sopranos Effect"

● James Gandolfini (right) as Tony Soprano, the anxiety-prone boss of the most powerful criminal organization in New Jersey. The gritty realism of *The Sopranos,* a critically acclaimed HBO series since 1999, is changing television drama

Even within the loosening restrictions of network television, the Fox series *24* is shaping up to be groundbreaking. So far it's featured heroin use, underage sex, rape, male prostitution, murder, kidnapping, and a bombed plane.

Cinematic in both quality and content, *24* probably couldn't have aired as recently as two years ago, says Virgil Williams, one of the show's writers. "Things have changed, absolutely," Williams says.

And it's all because of one show: *The Sopranos.*

"It's flat-out better. It's stealing our audiences," Williams says. "Networks have no choice but to react." That means pushing the boundaries of language, violence, and sexuality that are allowed on network television, to make programs more realistic. It isn't something executives announce, but Standards and Practices departments are less restrictive this season. And the American Federal Communications Commission, which only five years ago was embroiled in a debate over television ratings and the V-chip, has taken a more hands-off approach.

Insults and references once limited to a program like *NYPD Blue,* if they aired at all, have drifted across the dial. Recently, every program on NBC's Thursday night line-up, from *Friends* to *ER,* used "son of a b——" at least once. Viewers don't seem to mind; in fact, they demand it, says Jack Myers, the [Canadian] National Media Advisory Board chairman. "There is not a meaningful amount of controversy about the content of these programs," Myers says. "Audiences are responding positively to realism."

Myers says this season's looser rules were foreshadowed by NBC president Bob Wright, who wrote an open letter last April asking critics and producers their opinion about the boundary limits of prime-time programming. "I want you to help think about an issue that I believe is having a major impact on our business—the mature content in HBO's *The Sopranos,*" he wrote. Wright was perhaps over-defensive, Myers says, since ratings for *The Sopranos* are not as high as many NBC programs, and *The West Wing* ended up winning last year's best-drama Emmy.

But there is a feeling among network executives that the critical success of *The Sopranos* and *Sex and the City* is making their shows look silly, says Robert Thompson, professor of media at Syracuse University. "You're seeing The Sopranos'

effect because they don't want to suffer the Falcone effect," he says.

Falcone, a short-lived CBS program about an FBI agent working undercover in the mob, used tame language and implied violence. It was hard to imagine gangsters being so chaste, Thompson says. "You just wanted to laugh at them."

When the 2001–02 television season started, Aaron Sorkin lobbied for his fictional president to use the Lord's name in vain. Steven Bochco wanted "bull——" on his drama *Philly.* Sorkin won, Bochco lost, but other admissions were granted with little fanfare.

While the success of *The Sopranos* has encouraged producers to push for more adult content, the ratings system and V-chip have provided a defense, says Jeffrey Cole, director of the Center for Communication Policy at the University of California, Los Angeles. The V-chip, standard on new televisions since 2000, allows parents to "lock out" mature-rated programming.

The FCC does not have concrete rules on what is allowed, defining obscene content as something that is "generally objectionable" to the public. The low use of the V-chip may demonstrate how little is objectionable these days, Cole says. According to the Kaiser Family Foundation, only 17 percent of parents who own a V-chip use it to block programming.

But Mark Honig, executive director of the Parents Television Council, a group that campaigns for less profanity and violence on TV, says parents want to watch a show like *ER* without worrying about its content. Parents who would object most strongly have already tuned to cable channels geared to families, or home videos. He says others have been "desensitized."

Source: Stephen Lynch, "Son of a . . . : *The Sopranos* has changed what you see, and hear, on TV," *Calgary Herald,* February 5, 2002, p. B11.

Research on Media Effects

As concern about public opinion, propaganda, and the impact of the media merged with the growth of journalism and mass communication departments in colleges and universities, media researchers looked more and more to behavioral science as a model. Between 1930 and 1960, "who says what to whom with what effect" became the key question "defining the scope and problems of American communications research."[9] Addressing these issues activated a major push in media effects research, with questions such as this: If children watch a lot of TV cartoons (stimulus or cause), will this repeated act influence their behavior toward their peers (response or effect)?

For most of the twentieth century, both media researchers and news reporters used different methods to answer similar sets of questions—who, what, when, and where—about our daily experiences. In practicing their professions, researchers and reporters have typically remained suspicious of concepts such as interpretation, subjectivity, and personal values, seeing them as problems to be avoided or even as dangerous contaminators of their work. An important difference exists between the two fields, however. Whereas daily news reporters *describe* what happens when teenagers watch violent movies, media researchers not only describe but try to *explain* why it happens and attempt to predict whether it will happen again.

Media research generally comes from the private or public sector—each type with distinguishing features. *Private research,* sometimes called *proprietary research,* is generally conducted for a business, corporation, or even a political campaign. It is usually applied research in the sense that the information it uncovers typically addresses some real-life problem or need, such as determining consumer buying habits or market trends, trying to discover the hot-button issues for a political race, or measuring test-audience responses to variations of a movie ending. *Public research,* on the other hand, usually takes place in academic and government settings. It involves information that is often more *theoretical* than applied; it tries to clarify, explain, or predict the effects of mass media rather than to address a consumer problem. Most public research is subject to examination and refutation by other academics. In contrast, private research is seldom shared, although the results of some private opinion polls or broadcast ratings may be released to the public with the owners' permission.

● Researchers released the National Television Violence Study in 1996. After analyzing 2,693 television programs from twenty-three channels, they concluded that a majority of programs contain "harmful violence." For example, in 73 percent of the violent scenes studied, the offender went unpunished, leading the researchers to reason that children might learn that committing violent acts carries few negative consequences. The study's release corresponded with the introduction of the V-chip (shown here with its inventor, Tim Collings), a device that helps parents block programs rated too violent.

Key Phases in Research Approaches

A major goal of scientific research is to develop theories or laws that can consistently explain or predict human behavior. The varied impacts of the mass media and the diverse ways in which people make popular culture, however, tend to defy predictable rules. Historical, economic, and political factors influence media industries, making it difficult to develop systematic theories that explain communication. What has developed instead are a number of small theories, or models, that help explain individual behavior rather than the impact of the media on large populations. But before these small theories began to emerge in the 1970s, mass-media research followed several other models. Developing between the 1930s and the 1970s, these major approaches included the hypodermic-needle, minimal-effects, and uses and gratifications models.

Hypodermic-Needle Model

One of the earliest and least persuasive media theories attributed powerful effects to the mass media. A number of intellectuals and academics were particularly fearful of the popularity of film and radio, which became influential cultural forces in the 1920s and 1930s. Some of these observations were made by social psychologists and sociologists who arrived in this country after fleeing Hitler and Nazism in the 1930s. Having watched Hitler use radio, film, and print media as propaganda tools for Nazism, they worried that the popular media in America also had a strong hold over vulnerable audiences. This concept of powerful media affecting weak audiences has been labeled the **hypodermic-needle model**, sometimes also called the *magic-bullet theory* or the *direct-effects model*. It suggests that the media shoot their potent effects directly into unsuspecting victims.

● Early media researchers were concerned about Adolf Hitler's use of national radio to control information and indoctrinate the German people throughout the 1930s. Germany's wartime international broadcasts, however, were considered failures. Trying to undermine morale using broadcasts aimed at Allied soldiers and British citizens, Germany hired British defector William Joyce ("Lord Haw Haw") and Ohioan Mildred Gillars ("Axis Sally"). Because so many media messages competed with Nazi propaganda in democratic countries, these radio traitors had little impact.

One of the earliest challenges to the hypodermic-needle model of effects involved a study of Orson Welles' legendary October 30, 1938, broadcast of *The War of the Worlds,* which presented a fictional news report of Martian invaders (see Chapter 4, page 121). Welles' radio program frightened millions of listeners who didn't realize that the show was an adaptation of the H. G. Wells science-fiction novel. In a 1940 book-length study, *The Invasion from Mars: A Study in the Psychology of Panic,* radio researcher Hadley Cantril argued that contrary to expectations according to the hypodermic-needle model, not all listeners thought the radio program was a real news report. Instead, Cantril noted—after conducting personal interviews and a nationwide survey of listeners, and analyzing newspaper reports and listener mail to CBS Radio and the FCC—that some people were more likely than others to believe in the report about a Martian invasion. Factors like the listening situation were found to be important, especially for people who tuned in late and missed the initial disclaimers for the program. Personal characteristics, too, were linked to the gullibility of certain audience members. For example, listeners with strong fundamentalist religious beliefs were more likely to think the invasion was an act of God and that the end of the world had indeed arrived.

Cantril's research helped to lay the groundwork for the minimal-effects model, which would become more popular in the following decades. Although the hypodermic-needle model has been disregarded or disproved by social scientists, many people still attribute such direct effects to the mass media, particularly in the case of children.

Minimal-Effects Model

With the rise of empirical research techniques, social scientists began demonstrating that the media alone do not cause people to change their attitudes and behaviors. At this point, the limited or **minimal-effects model** emerged. Based on tightly controlled experiments and surveys, researchers generally argued that people engage in **selective exposure** and **selective retention** with regard to the media. That is, we selectively expose ourselves to media messages that are most familiar to us, and we retain messages that confirm values and attitudes we already hold. Minimal-effects researchers argued that in most cases the mass media reinforce existing behaviors and attitudes rather than change them.

The findings from the first comprehensive study of children and television, by Wilbur Schramm, Jack Lyle, and Edwin Parker in the late 1950s, best capture the minimal-effects tradition:

> For *some* children, under some conditions, some television is harmful. For *other* children under the same conditions, or for the same children under *other* conditions, it may be beneficial. For *most* children, under *most* conditions, *most* television is probably neither particularly harmful nor particularly beneficial.[10]

Joseph Klapper's important 1960 research review, *The Effects of Mass Communication,* found that the mass media influenced individuals who did not already hold strong views on an issue and that the media also had a greater impact on poor and uneducated heavy users. Solidifying the minimal-effects argument, Klapper concluded that strong media effects occur largely at an individual level and do not appear to have large-scale, measurable, and direct effects on society as a whole.[11]

Uses and Gratifications Model

Aside from difficulties in proving direct cause-effect relationships, the effects tradition usually assumed that audiences were passive and were acted upon by the media. As early as the late 1950s, Schramm, Lyle, and Parker suggested that there were problems with this position:

> In a sense the term "effect" is misleading because it suggests that television "does something" to children. The connotation is that television is the actor, the children are acted upon. Children are thus made to seem relatively inert; television, relatively active. Children are sitting victims; television bites them. Nothing can be further from the fact. It is the children who are most active in this relationship. It is they who use television, rather than television that uses them.[12]

Indeed, as the authors observed, numerous studies have concluded that viewers—especially young children—are often *actively* engaged in the media, using various forms to guide their play.

A response to the minimal-effects theory, the **uses and gratifications model** was proposed in the 1940s to contest the notion of audience passivity. Under this model, researchers—usually using in-depth interviews to supplement survey questionnaires—studied the ways in which people used the media to satisfy various emotional or intellectual needs. The uses and gratifications model represented a middle position between the hypodermic-needle and the minimal-effects models. Instead of asking "What effects do the media have on us?" researchers asked "Why do we use the media?"

Asking the *why* question enabled media researchers to develop inventories cataloguing how people employed the media. For example, individuals used the media to see authority figures elevated or toppled, to seek a sense of community and connectedness, to fulfill a need for drama and stories, and to confirm moral or spiritual values.[13] Though the uses and gratifications model addressed the *functions* of the mass media for individuals, it did not address the important questions related to the impact of the media on society. Once researchers had accumulated substantial lists of uses and functions, they often did not move in new directions. Consequently, the uses and gratifications model never became a dominant strain in media research.

Approaches to Media Effects

Most media research today, whether conducted in universities or in public-policy institutes, has focused on the effects of the media on such issues as learning, attitudes, aggression, and voting habits. This research employs the **scientific method**, a blueprint long used by scientists and scholars to study phenomena in systematic stages. These steps include:

1. identifying the research problem
2. reviewing existing research and theories related to the problem
3. developing working hypotheses or predictions about what the study might find
4. determining an appropriate method or research design
5. collecting information or relevant data
6. analyzing results to see if the hypotheses have been verified
7. interpreting the implications of the study to determine whether they explain or predict patterns in human behavior

The scientific method relies on *objectivity* (eliminating bias and judgments on the part of researchers); *reliability* (getting the same answers or outcomes from a study or measure during repeated testing); and *validity* (demonstrating that a study actually measures what it claims to measure).

In scientific studies, researchers pose one or more **hypotheses**: tentative general statements that predict a relationship between a *dependent variable* that is influenced by an *independent variable*. For example, a researcher might hypothesize that heavy levels of TV viewing among adolescents (independent variable) cause poor performance (dependent variable) in traditional school settings. Broadly speaking, the

● Two boys play a shooting game in a Colorado arcade. In recent years, researchers have looked at video games where the players actually become the violent character who destroys everyone. Although new studies suggest that violent video games make children violent, researchers have yet to respond to some national statistics: youth violence has fallen in recent years, even as access to violent video games and round-the-clock movie and TV entertainment has increased.

methods for studying media effects on audiences have taken two forms—experiments and survey research. To supplement these approaches, researchers also use content analysis as a technique for counting and documenting specific messages in mass media. We will look at all three.

Experiments

Like all studies that use the scientific method, **experiments** in media research isolate some aspect of content, suggest a hypothesis, and manipulate variables to discover a particular medium's impact on attitude, emotion, or behavior. To test whether a hypothesis is true, researchers expose an *experimental group*—the group under study—to a selected media program or text. To ensure valid results, researchers use a control group, which serves as a basis for comparison; this group is not exposed to the selected media content. Subjects are picked for each group through **random assignment**, which simply means that every subject has an equal chance of being placed in either group. Random assignment generally ensures that the variables researchers want to control are distributed to each group in the same way.

For instance, researchers might take a group of ten-year-old boys and randomly assign them to two groups. They expose the experimental group to a violent action movie that the control group does not see. Later, both groups are exposed to a staged fight between two other boys so that the researchers can observe how each group responds to an actual physical confrontation. Researchers then determine whether there is a statistically measurable difference between the two groups' responses to the fight. For example, perhaps the control subjects tried to break up the fight but the experimental subjects did not. Because the groups were randomly selected and the only measurable difference between them was the viewing of the movie, researchers may conclude that under these conditions the violent film caused a different behavior.

When experiments carefully account for variables through random assignment, they generally work well in substantiating direct cause-effect links. Such research takes place both in laboratory settings and in field settings, where people can be observed using the media in their everyday environments. In field experiments, however, it is more difficult for researchers to control variables. In lab settings, researchers have more control, but other problems may occur. For example, when subjects are removed from the environments in which they regularly use the media, they may act differently—often with fewer inhibitions—than they would in their everyday surroundings.

Experiments have other limitations as well. For instance, they are not generalizable to a larger population; they cannot tell us whether cause-effect results can be duplicated outside the laboratory. In addition, most academic experiments today are performed on college students, who are convenient subjects for research but are not representative of the general public. Although most experiments are fairly good at predicting short-term media effects under controlled conditions, they do not predict how subjects will behave months or years later in the real world.

Surveys

For long-term studies of the media, surveys usually work best. In its simplest terms, **survey research** is a method of collecting and measuring data taken from a group of respondents. Using random sampling techniques that give each potential subject an equal chance to be included in the survey, this research method draws on much larger populations than those used in experimental studies. Surveys are simply measuring instruments and do not control variables through randomly assigned groups. Survey investigators cannot account for all the variables that might affect media use; therefore, they cannot show cause-effect relationships. Survey research can, however, reveal *correlations*—or associations—between two variables. For example, a random questionnaire survey of ten-year-old boys might demonstrate that a correlation exists between aggressive behavior and watching violent TV programs, but it does not explain which causes which. Unlike experimental research, however, surveys are usually generalizable to the larger society.

Surveys are also useful measures for comparing voting behavior and levels of media use. To aid survey research, subjects are sometimes assigned to panel studies in which smaller groups of people are interviewed in depth on several occasions. In addition, surveys enable researchers to investigate various populations in long-term studies. For example, survey research might measure subjects when they are ten, twenty, and thirty years old to track changes in how frequently they watch television and what kinds of programs they prefer at different ages.

It is important to note, though, that surveys are only as good as the wording of their questions. The validity of survey questions—measuring the effect that the study claims to measure—is a chronic problem for survey practitioners. For example, in 1992 Americans were shocked to hear that a national survey had found that about 20 percent of Americans doubted the Holocaust ever happened. However, the results were later attributed to a confusing question, which asked, "Does it seem possible or does it seem impossible to you that the Nazi extermination of the Jews never happened?" A 1994 poll asked a more clearly stated version of the question: "Does it seem possible to you that the Nazi extermination of the Jews never happened, or do you feel certain that it happened?" In replying to the updated question, only 2 percent of the respondents consistently denied the Holocaust.

Using direct mail, personal interviews, telephone calls, e-mail, and Web sites, survey researchers can accumulate large amounts of information by surveying diverse cross sections of people. These data help to examine attitudes and demographic factors such as educational background, income levels, race, gender, age, lifestyle profiles, and political affiliations. Large government and academic survey databases are now widely available and contribute to the development of more long-range—or **longitudinal**—**studies**, which make it possible for social scientists to compare new studies with those conducted years earlier. In general, however, it is cheaper and easier to do short-term experimental and survey research, analyzing the effects of the media on particular individuals. Effects research focused on a large community or on societal responses to the media over time is much more difficult to conduct and sustain.

Content Analysis

Over the years, researchers recognized that traditional media-effects studies generally ignored specific media messages. As a corrective, researchers developed a method known as **content analysis** to study the messages of print and visual media. Such analysis is a systematic method of coding and measuring media content.

Although content analyses were first used during World War II, more recent studies have focused on television, tracking the number of male and female, black and white, and blue- and white-collar characters in daytime and prime-time programming. Probably the most influential content analyses have been conducted by George Gerbner and his colleagues at the University of Pennsylvania; since the late 1960s, they have coded and counted acts of violence on network television. Combined with survey methods, these annual "violence profiles" have shown that heavy watchers of television, including both children and retired Americans, tend to overestimate the amount of violence that exists in the actual world.[14]

The limits of content analysis have been well documented. This technique does not measure the effects of the media or explain why a particular media message

> **"** Writing survey questions and gathering data are easy; writing good questions and collecting useful data are not. **"**
>
> —Michael Singletary, *Mass Communication Research*, 1994

gets produced in the first place. Because content analysis is basically descriptive, it is often used in combination with other research techniques. This enables researchers to analyze and interpret the figures produced by content counts. For example, a content analysis by the Kaiser Family Foundation of more than 1,300 television shows found that 56 percent of television shows had sexual content. Content analysis alone, however, cannot tell us exactly what this means to viewers who regularly watch television.

Problems of definition also occur. For instance, researchers in the Kaiser Foundation study defined sexual content as flirting, kissing, talking about sex, intimate touching, depictions of sexual intercourse, or the strong suggestion of it.[15] But would most television viewers define sexual content in the same way? Or, in the case of coding and counting acts of violence, how do researchers distinguish slapstick cartoon aggression from the violent murders or rapes in an evening police drama? Critics point out that such varied depictions may have diverse and subtle effects on viewers that are difficult to measure or quantify.

As content analysis grew as a primary tool in media research, it sometimes pushed to the sidelines other ways of thinking about television and media content. Broad questions concerning the media as a popular art form, as a democratic influence, or as a force for social control are difficult to address through strict measurement techniques. Critics of content analysis, in fact, have objected to the kind of social science that reduces culture to acts of counting. Such criticism has addressed the tendency by some researchers to favor measurement accuracy over intellectual discipline and inquiry.[16]

Explaining Media Effects

By the 1960s, the first departments of mass communication began graduating Ph.D.-level researchers schooled in experimental or survey techniques and content analysis. These researchers began documenting consistent patterns that can be found in mass communication. Two of the most influential contemporary frameworks that help explain media effects have been agenda-setting and the cultivation effect.

Agenda-Setting

A key phenomenon posited by media-effects researchers has been **agenda-setting**: the idea that when the mass media pay attention to particular events or issues, they determine — that is, set the agenda for — the major topics of discussion for individuals and society. Like the uses and gratifications approach, agenda-setting research has tried to strike a balance between the views of the mass media as all-powerful and as barely powerful. Essentially, agenda-setting researchers have argued that the mass media do not so much tell us what to think as *what to think about*. Traceable to Walter Lippmann's notion in the early 1920s that the media "create pictures in our heads," the first social science investigations of agenda-setting began in the 1970s.[17]

Over the years, agenda-setting research has demonstrated that the more stories the news media do on a particular subject, the more importance audiences attach to that subject. For instance, when the media seriously began to cover ecology issues after the first Earth Day in 1970, a much higher percentage of the population began listing the environment as a primary social concern in surveys. When *Jaws* became the top box-office movie in 1975, the news media started featuring more shark-attack stories; even landlocked people in the Midwest began ranking sharks as a problem, despite the rarity of such incidents worldwide.

During the 1986 elections, local and national candidates often spoke about the problems of crime and illegal drugs. At the time, researchers documented a big leap

● On March 23, 2003, an estimated 200,000 people marched down Broadway in New York City to protest the war with Iraq.

in the media's attention to drugs, especially to crack cocaine; they found more than four hundred news stories dealing with cocaine over a forty-week period in America's major papers, newsmagazines, and newscasts.[18] Not surprisingly, the big jump in drug stories was accompanied by a parallel rise in concern over drugs as reflected in public-opinion polls. In April 1986, only 2 percent of the respondents to a *New York Times*/CBS News poll identified drugs as the nation's most important problem. By early September 1986, however, a survey found that drugs topped the list, with 13 percent of 1,210 adults interviewed identifying drugs as the nation's most serious problem. This shift occurred even though government statisticians showed that despite rises in the use of crack cocaine, illicit drug use had generally dipped and leveled off since peaking in 1979–80.[19] Although many people's attitudes toward drugs were not affected by the increased coverage in news stories, the marked shift in public opinion is a good example of the agenda-setting effect of the news media.

The Cultivation Effect

Another mass-media phenomenon—the **cultivation effect**—suggests that heavy viewing of television leads individuals to perceive reality in ways that are consistent with the portrayals they see on television. In essence, this area of effects research attempts to push researchers past the focus on individual behavior and toward larger ideas about the media's impact on society. The major research in this area grew from the TV-violence profiles of George Gerbner and his colleagues, who attempted to make broad generalizations about the impact of televised violence on real life. The basic idea suggests that the more time an audience spends viewing television and absorbing its viewpoints, the more likely it is that the audience's own views of social reality will be "cultivated" by the images and portrayals they see on television.[20] For example, although fewer than 1 percent of Americans are victims of violent crime in any single year, people who watch a lot of television tend to overestimate this percentage. Such exaggerated perceptions, Gerbner and his colleagues argue, are part of a "mean world" syndrome in which viewers with heavy, long-term exposure to television are more likely to believe that the external world is a mean and dangerous place.

According to the cultivation effect, media messages interact in complicated ways with personal, social, political, and cultural factors; they are one of a number of important factors in determining individual behavior and defining social values. Some critics have charged that cultivation research has provided limited evidence to support these findings. The cultivation framework, however, deserves close attention, especially with regard to findings about heavy television viewers who believe that the world is a meaner place than it actually is.

Evaluating Research on Media Effects

The mainstream models of media research have made valuable contributions to our understanding of the mass media, submitting content and audiences to rigorous testing. This wealth of research exists partly because funding for studies regarding the effects of the media on young people remains popular among politicians and has drawn ready government support since the 1960s. Media critic Richard Rhodes argues that media-effects research is inconsistent and often flawed but continues to resonate with politicians and parents because it generates an easy-to-blame social cause for real-world violence. "When violence among youths does erupt, as in the recent school shootings, parents look for a cause and blame the pale imitations of violence that their children watch on TV."[21]

Although the potential for government funding restricts the scope of some media research, other limits also exist, including the inability to address how the media affect communities and social institutions. Because most media research operates best in examining media and individual behavior, fewer research studies exist on media's impact on community and social life. Research has begun to address these limits and to turn more attention to the increasing impact of media technology on national life and international communication.

Cultural Approaches to Media Research

During the rise of modern media research, approaches with a stronger historical and interpretive edge developed as well, often in direct opposition to the scientific models. In the late 1930s, some social scientists began to warn about the limits of "gathering data and charting trends," particularly when research served advertisers and media organizations. Such private market research tended to be narrowly focused on individual behavior, ignoring questions like "Where are institutions taking us?" and "Where do we want them to take us?"[22]

It is important here to distinguish directions in American media studies from British-European traditions. In Europe, media studies have favored interpretive rather than scientific approaches; in other words, researchers there have approached media questions and problems as if they were literary or cultural critics rather than experimental or survey researchers. Such approaches built on the writings of political philosophers such as Karl Marx and Antonio Gramsci; these types of research investigated how the mass media have been used to maintain existing hierarchies in society. They examined, for example, the ways in which popular culture or sports distracted people from redressing social injustices. They also studied the subordinate status of some social groups in attempting to address some of the deficiencies of emerging social-science research.

In the United States, early criticism of modern media research came from the Frankfurt School, a group of European researchers who were transplanted from Germany to America after they fled Nazi persecution in the 1930s. Under the leadership of Max Horkheimer, T. W. Adorno, and Leo Lowenthal, this perspective pointed to at least three inadequacies of traditional scientific approaches, arguing that they (1) reduced large "cultural questions" to measurable and "verifiable categories"; (2) depended on "an atmosphere of rigidly enforced neutrality"; and (3) refused to place "the phenomena of modern life" in a "historical and moral context."[23] The researchers of the Frankfurt School did not reject outright the usefulness of measuring and counting data. They contended, however, that historical and cultural approaches would focus critical attention on the long-range processes of the mass media and their complex relations with audiences.

Cultural Studies

Since the time of the Frankfurt School, criticisms of the effects tradition and its methods have continued, with calls for more interpretive studies of the rituals of mass communication. Academics who have embraced a cultural approach try to understand how media and culture are tied to the actual patterns of communication in daily life. An important body of research—loosely labeled **cultural studies**—began challenging the mainstream media-effects models in the 1960s. These studies have generally focused on how people make meaning, apprehend reality, and order experience through their use of cultural symbols in print and visual media. This research has attempted to make everyday culture the centerpiece of media studies, focusing on the subtle ways in which mass communication shapes and is shaped by history, politics, and economics. For example, in the 1970s Stuart Hall and his colleagues studied the British print media and the police as forms of urban surveillance. In *Policing the Crisis*, the authors revealed how political, economic, and cultural constraints aided the news media's success in mobilizing public opinion about crime.[24]

Cultural research focuses on the investigation of daily experience, especially on issues of race, gender, class, and sexuality, and on the unequal arrangements of power and status in contemporary society. Such research highlights the nature of cultural differences, emphasizing how some social groups have been marginalized and ignored throughout history. Consequently, cultural studies have attempted to recover lost or silenced voices, particularly among African American, Native American, Asian and Asian American, Arabic, Latino, gay and lesbian, and women's cultures. The major analytical approaches to cultural research are textual analysis, audience studies, and political economy.

Textual Analysis

In cultural research, the equivalent to measurement methods and content analysis has been labeled **textual analysis**: the close reading and interpretation of the meanings of culture, including the study of books, movies, and TV programs. Whereas content analysis approaches media messages with the tools of modern social science—replicability, objectivity, and data—textual analysis looks at rituals, narratives, and meanings. (See "Applied Critical Process: A Cultural Approach to Studying the News," page 528.)

Although textual analysis has a long and rich history in film and literary studies, a significant shift occurred in 1974 with Horace Newcomb's *TV: The Most Popular Art*, considered the first serious academic analysis of television stories. Newcomb analyzed and interpreted why certain TV programs became predominant, especially

APPLIED CRITICAL PROCESS
A Cultural Approach to Studying the News

One method of textual analysis that is useful for studying the news involves analyzing the *frames* of news stories; that is, the consistent ways in which journalists interpret certain news events. For this exercise, we look at the ways in which the news media frame stories about a particular topic, specifically, labor unions. Labor union membership has dropped from a high of 34.7 percent of the workforce in 1954 to less than 13 percent by 2003. Could the way in which news stories frame labor unions have an impact on how people in the United States understand them?

Description. In a major study, we looked at hundreds of network television news (ABC, CBS, and NBC) and national newspaper (*New York Times* and *USA Today*) reports involving labor over a ten-year period to get a sense of how such stories are framed.[1]

Analysis. An interesting pattern emerges. Instead of reflecting a simple bias against labor, news stories seem to frame labor in a way that prioritizes the consumer perspective (as opposed to a citizen or worker perspective). That is, labor unions aren't represented as inherently bad, but any kind of collective action by workers, citizens, and communities that upsets the American consumer economy and the decisions of its business leaders and entrepreneurs is portrayed as a bad thing. This news media frame disapproves of collective action—including strikes, slowdowns, boycotts, and protests.

Interpretation. The news media view collective action as bad for a number of typical reasons: It is in-

flationary, un-American, protectionist and naïve; it causes bureaucratic red tape, disrupts consumer demand and behavior, stirs up fear and violence, and so on. The frame carries an interesting underlying assumption: that economic intervention by citizens should happen only at the individual level (e.g., tell your boss to "take this job and shove it" if you are dissatisfied, or "vote with your pocketbook" if you don't like something). Of course, individual action preempts collective action, which can be more democratic and potent. Indeed, the corporate news might frame labor stories in a way that is in harmony with the media corporations' own economic priorities but also make sense to their audience without the appearance of an obvious bias, which would undermine their credibility. The news media do so by framing stories in the common-sense context of the consumer-oriented media system.

Evaluation. With such framing, the news media's stories undercut a legal institution—labor unions—that might serve as a useful remedy to millions of U.S. workers who want independent representation in their workplace for collective bargaining and dispute resolution, as well as a voice in the economy. In fact, national surveys have shown that the majority of U.S. workers would like a stronger voice in their workplaces but have negative opinions about unions, so they aren't very likely to consider joining them.[2]

comedies, westerns, mysteries, soap operas, news, and sports. Newcomb took television programs seriously, examining patterns in the most popular programs, such as the *Beverly Hillbillies, Bewitched,* and *Dragnet,* which traditional researchers had usually snubbed or ignored. Trained as a literary scholar, Newcomb argued that content analysis and other social-science approaches often ignored artistic traditions and social context. For Newcomb, "the task for the student of the popular arts is to find a technique through which many different qualities of the work—aesthetic, social, psychological—may be explored" and to discover "why certain formulas . . . are popular in American television."[25]

Prior to Newcomb's work, textual analysis generally focused on "important" debates, films, poems, and books—either significant examples of democratic information or highly regarded works of art. But by the end of the 1970s a new generation of media-studies scholars, who had grown up on television and rock and roll, became interested in less elite forms of culture. They extended the notion of what a "text" is to architecture, fashion, tabloid magazines, pop icons like Madonna, rock music, soap operas, movies, cockfights, shopping malls, TV drug news, rap, Martha Stewart, and professional wrestling, trying to make sense of the most taken-for-granted aspects of everyday culture.

Often these seemingly minor elements of popular culture provide insight into broader meanings within our society. For example, a 1998 textual analysis examined the sexual etiquette endorsed for teenage women in popular magazines such as *YM*, *Teen*, *Seventeen*, *Glamour*, and *Mademoiselle*. The researchers looked at advice columns and features from a sample of magazines between 1974 and 1994. They concluded that the stories of sexual etiquette changed very little during those twenty years and that the magazines encouraged young women "to subordinate self for others and to be contained."[26]

Audience Studies

Cultural research that focuses on how people use and interpret cultural content is called *audience-* or *reader-response research*. For example, in *Reading the Romance: Women, Patriarchy and Popular Literature*, Janice Radway studied a group of midwestern women who were fans of the romance novel. Using her training in literary criticism but also employing interviews and questionnaires, Radway investigated the meaning of romance reading. She argued that this cultural activity functioned as personal time for some women, whose complex family and work lives provided very little time for themselves. The study also suggested that these particular romance-novel fans identified with the active, independent qualities of the romantic heroines they most admired. As a cultural study, Radway's work did not claim to be scientific, and her findings are not generalizable to a large group of women. Rather, Radway was interested in investigating and interpreting the relationship between reading popular fiction and ordinary life.[27]

As Radway's study demonstrated, cultural research uses a variety of interpretive methods and displays some common features. Most important, these studies define culture in broad terms, as being made up of both the *products* a society fashions and the *processes* that forge those products. As we discussed in Chapter 1, culture consists of the symbols of expression that individuals, groups, and societies use to make sense of daily life and articulate their values. Within this context, culture is viewed in part as a struggle over who controls symbols and meaning in society. (See "Case Study: Online Gaming Reveals Gender Stereotypes," page 530.) For example, the battles over the meaning of rock and roll in the 1950s or of hip-hop in the 1980s were important cultural battles that addressed issues of race, class, region, and religion as well as generational differences.

Political Economy

The focus on the production of popular culture and the forces behind it are the topic of *political-economy studies*. The greatest concern political-economy studies have about the media is the increasing conglomeration of ownership, as noted in Chapter 13. This concentration of ownership means that the production of media content is being controlled by fewer and fewer organizations, investing those companies with more power. Moreover, the domination of public discourse by for-profit corporations may mean that the bottom line for all public communication and popular culture is money, not democratic expression.

Political-economy studies work best when combined with the textual-analysis and audience-studies approaches, which provide a well-rounded context for under-

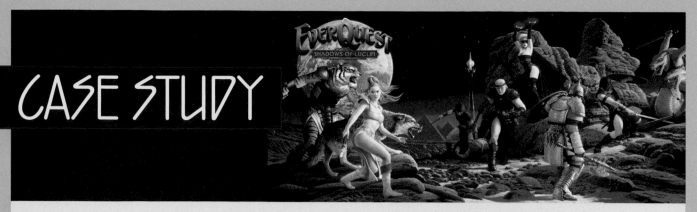

Online Gaming Reveals Gender Stereotypes

by Alex Pham

In her flowing crimson cape, thigh-high leather boots, and metal-studded red leather bustier, Cardinal is a bow-and-arrow-toting femme fatale.

But not only is Cardinal not real—she's a character in the popular computer game "Ultima Online"—she's not really female. Cardinal is the alter ego of Kenn Gold, a thirty-three-year-old former Army sergeant with thorny green-and-black tattoos covering both of his muscular arms.

As one of the thousands of online gamers who play characters of the opposite gender, Gold created Cardinal as a tactical move: Female characters generally get treated better in the male-dominated world of virtual adventuring. Yet he was unprepared for the shock of seeing the world through a woman's eyes. "I can't even begin to tell you how funny it is to watch guys trip all over themselves and be dumb," Gold said. "It's very amusing to see them try to be really sophisticated and cool, when they're turning out to be just the opposite."

Changing genders has long been a piece of online role-playing games—part juvenile mischievousness, part theatrical posing, and part psychological release. But as the genre explodes—online games now attract hundreds of thousands of players—it's prompted a blossoming of cross-gender experimentation and created sexually amorphous virtual worlds that some revel in and others curse. . . .

In "EverQuest," the most popular of the games with more than 360,000 subscribers, players spend an average of twenty hours a week online. Players call it "EverCrack" because it's so addictive. Much of the allure is the ability to put mundane daily life aside and pretend to be something they're not—an elf, a woodsman, a knight.

Encouraging the make-believe are online avatars—the graphic representation of a player's character. Scantily clad women are impossibly thin and full-bosomed. Men are muscular and rendered in heroic proportions. As a result, the contrast between avatar and player can be striking, even when gamers are playing their own gender.

In "EverQuest," only 20 percent of subscribers are women, but 40 percent of avatars are. Even accounting for the number of women who play male characters, that amounts to roughly half the female characters in "EverQuest" being played by men.

This might be fun and games, but as any serious player of such adventures will attest, online experiences—with their power to make people laugh, cry, or become angry—can have real-life consequences.

"It certainly makes you more aware of how men treat women," said Ralph Koster, age twenty-nine, who has played a female character for years in an early online text-based game, "LegendMUD." "You're more aware that there are a lot of gendered interactions that we don't recognize as such. It makes you think more about what you're saying and how you're sending subtle messages without being aware of it."

Players who wish to escape gender constraints online ironically find themselves in a medium that, if anything, reinforces sexual stereotypes.

"Females tend to get in groups faster, but we get harassed," said Aaron Harvey, a twenty-six-year-old freelance Web designer from Ventura who plays a female gnome in "EverQuest." "People are constantly trying to pick us up. I've been offered [more powerful weaponry] for cybersex, which I turn down rather quickly."

Often, players who gender-swap online are reluctant to talk about their reasons.

"It's not something you would talk about or be proud of," said Pavel Curtis, who developed a well-known text-based online community called LambdaMOO when he was a researcher at Xerox's Palo Alto Research Center. "Society doesn't see it as a healthy form of experimentation. At best, it's seen as duplicitous. At worst, it's sick and perverted."

Such strongly held views underscore how important gender identity is to people—even online, where physical appearances are not supposed to matter.

As a result, much effort goes into spotting fakes. The clues cited by players are telling indications of how people perceive gender. One player recalled a time when she tried to pass as a male character but was instantly pegged as an impostor. How? "It was just my style of speaking. I used long sentences with lots of adjectives, which is seen as stereotypic of females," she said.

"Everybody, it seems, needs to know," Koster said. "It's like a void that needs to be filled, and it's deeply ingrained in our culture. There's this notion that the Internet will give us this utopia where gender, age, and race don't matter. The idea that we'll all be disembodied floating lights just ain't gonna happen."

Source: Alex Pham, "Boy, You Fight Like a Girl," *Los Angeles Times,* May 17, 2001.

standing the cultural content, the production of the content, and the audience's reception of it. For example, a major media corporation may, for commercial reasons, create a film and market it relentlessly through a number of venues (political economy), but the film's meaning or popularity makes sense only within the historical and narrative contexts of the culture (textual analysis), and it may be interpreted by various audiences in ways both anticipated and unexpected (audience studies).

Evaluating Cultural Approaches

In opposition to media-effects research, cultural studies involve "reading" written texts and visual programs as a sequence of spoken or written symbols that contain interpretation. As James Carey has put it, a more cultural approach "does not seek to explain human behavior, but to understand it. . . . It does not attempt to predict human behavior, but to diagnose human meanings."[28] In other words, a cultural approach does not provide explanations for the laws that govern the mass media. Rather, it offers interpretations of the stories, messages, and meanings that circulate throughout our culture.

One of the main strengths of a cultural approach is the freedom it affords to broadly interpret the impact of the mass media. Because cultural work is not bound by the precise control of variables, researchers can more easily examine the ties between media messages and the broader social, economic, and political scene. For example, effects research on politics has generally concentrated on election polls and voting patterns, whereas cultural research has broadened the scope of politics to include class and income differences and the various uses of power by individuals and institutions in authority. Following Horace Newcomb, cultural investigators have also expanded the study of media content beyond "serious" works. They have studied many popular forms, including music, movies, and prime-time television.

Just as social-science measurement has limits, so do cultural studies. Sometimes such studies have focused too heavily on the meanings of media programs or "texts," ignoring their effect on audiences. More recent cultural studies, however, have tried to address this deficiency. For example, Elizabeth Bird's *For Enquiring Minds: A Cultural Study of Supermarket Tabloids* set up a three-part analysis that included (1) interviews with the writers and editors of popular tabloids, (2) in-depth discussions with tabloid readers, and (3) an analysis of the form and content of tabloids. Bird's research demonstrated how individuals derive their own diverse meanings from this one ordinary form of popular culture, and how a researcher can combine textual analysis, audience studies, and political-economy approaches.[29]

Both media-effects and cultural researchers today have begun to look at the limitations of their work more closely, borrowing ideas from each other to better assess the complexity of the media's impact. For instance, in *Democracy without Citizens*, political scientist Robert Entman employed both perspectives to examine journalism and politics. He used cultural theories about economics and politics to reveal how journalists slant the news and oversimplify complex issues. He supplemented his cultural inquiry with surveys that measured the impact of slanted reports on public opinion. By combining the two approaches, Entman strengthened his argument, which called for substantial journalistic reform.[30]

> **❝ I take culture . . . and the analysis of it to be therefore not an experimental science in search of law but an interpretive one in search of meaning. ❞**
>
> —Clifford Geertz, cultural anthropologist, 1973

● Cultural-studies researchers are interested in the production, meaning, and audience response to a wide range of elements within communication culture, including the pop singer Madonna (here dressed like the Hindu deity Shiva).

★ Media Research, Ivory Towers, and Democracy

One charge frequently leveled at academic studies is that they fail to address the everyday problems of life; they often seem to have little practical application. With the growth of mass media departments in colleges and universities has come an increase in special terminology and jargon, which tend to intimidate nonacademics. Although media research has built a growing knowledge base and dramatically advanced what we know about individuals and societies, the academic world has paid a price. That is, the larger public has often been excluded from access to the research process. Researchers themselves have even found it difficult to speak to one another across disciplines because of the obscure language used to analyze and report findings.

The acceleration of jargon occurred with the splintering of academic life into narrow areas of specialization in the 1970s. We understand why chemistry, physics, math, and engineering require special symbols and languages. It is not as clear, however, why this practice extends to so many social science and humanities disciplines. Although cultural research has affected academic scholars in English, history, sociology, anthropology, and communication, they do not talk easily to one another about their work. Most social science research is intended only for other social scientists with similar training and experience. For example, understanding the elaborate statistical analyses used to document media effects requires special training. This kind of research advances knowledge, but it does not generally engage a larger public.

Even in cultural research, the language used is often incomprehensible to students and to other audiences who use the mass media. Cultural research tends to identify with marginalized groups, yet this scholarship can be self-defeating if its complexity is too removed from the daily experience of the groups it addresses and the students it is designed to educate.

A now famous hoax in 1996 pointed out just how inaccessible some academic jargon can be. Alan Sokal, a New York University physics professor, submitted an impenetrable article, "Transgressing the Boundaries: Toward a Transformative Hermeneutics of Quantum Gravity," to a special issue of the academic journal *Social Text* devoted to science and postmodernism. As he had expected, the article—a hoax designed to point out how dense academic jargon can sometimes mask sloppy thinking—was published. According to the journal's editor, about six reviewers had read the article but didn't suspect that it was phony. A public debate ensued after Sokal revealed his hoax. Sokal said he worries that jargon and intellectual fads cause academics to lose contact with the real world and "undermine the prospect for progressive social critique."[31]

In addition to the issue of specialized language, other problems have arisen involving media research and democracy. In the 1990s, lawmakers and the public had become increasingly concerned about the emphasis on research over teaching at most major universities. Throughout the 1990s and into the 2000s, as the government slashed support for student loans and university research, universities escalated their campaigns to raise money and become affiliated with corporations. The late historian Christopher Lasch, however, warned of the dangers "of corporate control of the universities" and the potential for "corruption" in higher education: "It is corporate control that has diverted social resources from the humanities into military and technological research, fostered an obsession with quantification that has destroyed the social sciences, replaced the English language with bureaucratic jargon, and created a top-heavy administrative apparatus whose educational vision begins and ends with the bottom line."[32]

Especially with the substantial tuition hikes at most universities across the United States in the early 2000s, it was also becoming more difficult for middle- and

> " In quantum gravity, as we shall see, the space-time manifold ceases to exist as an objective reality; geometry becomes relational and contextual; and the foundational conceptual categories of prior science — among them, existence itself — become problematized and relativized. This conceptual revolution, I will argue, has profound implications for the content of a future postmodern and liberatory science. "
>
> – from Alan Sokal's published jargon-riddled hoax, 1996

working-class students to attend college. This seemed to contradict the democratic progress that had been going on in higher education since the 1950s and 1960s, which brought government GI loans to war veterans and wider access to the universities spurred on by the women's and Civil Rights movements. These democratic movements also ushered in the study of popular culture and the mass media. The news media's coverage of the Watergate scandal alone sparked heightened interest in journalism as an undergraduate major throughout the country.

Ironically, while campuses were becoming more democratic, increasing specialization in the 1970s began isolating many researchers from life outside the university. Academics were once again locked away in their ivory towers. Early in the twentieth century, it was common for academics to operate as public intellectuals. But the proliferation of specialized fields widened the gap between the public and the university.

Facing a number of critical problems in higher education, more academics began stepping forward to broaden their ideas of research and to become active in political and cultural life by the 1980s and 1990s. For example, literary scholar Henry Louis Gates Jr. began writing essays for *Time* and the *New Yorker* magazines. Cultural critic Mike Davis created heated discussions about the future of Los Angeles in his popular books *City of Quartz* and *Ecology of Fear*. Linguist Noam Chomsky, who tirelessly writes and speaks about excessive government and media power, was even the subject of an award-winning 1992 documentary, *Manufacturing Consent: Noam Chomsky and the Media*. And essayist and cultural critic Barbara Ehrenreich has written accessibly and potently about labor and economic issues in magazines such as *Time* and the *Nation*. The author of twelve books, she most recently completed *Nickel and Dimed: On (Not) Getting By in America*, a chronicle of her three months working at low-wage working-class jobs in various parts of the United States. Popular academic books ranging from conservative accounts (Allan Bloom's *The Closing of the American Mind*) to progressive accounts (Thomas Frank's *The Conquest of Cool*) extended academic ideas beyond the boundaries of the university.

In recent presidential election campaign seasons, Kathleen Hall Jamieson, dean of the communication college at the University of Pennsylvania, made regular appearances on PBS—and guest appearances on the *Tonight Show*—to analyze the presidential elections and perform textual analyses of political advertising. The TV coverage of the Persian Gulf War in the early 1990s and the U.S.-led invasion of Iraq in 2003 has included many political scientists, military historians, and religion professors, who interpreted the events in the larger context of historic Middle Eastern struggles.

In the wake of the O.J. Simpson trials from 1994 to 1997, many academics have made regular television appearances, trying to place current events in a historical and legal context. This trend has continued with a seemingly endless string of academics and pundits involved in the media blitzes surrounding the Clinton-Lewinsky scandal and the subsequent impeachment process, as well as the 2000 presidential election recount dispute and the September 11, 2001, terrorist attacks. Like public journalists, public intellectuals based on campuses help to carry on the conversations of society and culture, actively circulating the most important new ideas of the day and serving as models for how to participate in public life.

● As model contemporary intellectuals, Cornel West *(center)* and Henry Louis Gates Jr. *(right)* have dedicated much of their careers to communicating ideas to both the academic community and the larger public. Pictured here with Nobel Prize–winning Nigerian author Wole Soyinka *(left)*, West and Gates write academic texts and mass-market books, and also make appearances on radio and TV news and talk programs.

> ❝ In many ways the modern university has replaced its function as a creative/subversive institution with a fondness for structure and organization among its parts, and the rigid compartmentalization of knowledge within these structures. ❞
>
> –David Sholle and Stan Denski, *Media Education*, 1994

www.

To create an individualized study plan for Chapter 15, go to the interactive *Media and Culture* Online Study Guide at: bedfordstmartins.com/mediaculture

REVIEW QUESTIONS

Early Developments in Media Research

1. What were the earliest types of media studies, and why weren't they more scientific?

2. What were the major influences that led to scientific media research?

Research on Media Effects

3. What are the differences between experiments and surveys as media-research strategies?

4. What is content analysis, and why is it significant?

5. What are the differences between the hypodermic-needle model and the minimal-effects model in the history of media research?

6. What are agenda-setting and the cultivation effect?

7. What are some strengths and limitations of modern media research?

Cultural Approaches to Media Research

8. Why did cultural approaches to media studies develop in opposition to media-effects research?

9. What are the features of cultural studies?

10. How is textual analysis different from content analysis?

11. What are some of the strengths and limitations of cultural research?

Media Research, Ivory Towers, and Democracy

12. How has specialization in academic research influenced universities?

13. How can public intellectuals and academics improve the relationship between campuses and the general public?

QUESTIONING THE MEDIA

1. What are your main concerns or criticisms about the state of media studies at your college or university?

2. One charge that has been leveled against a lot of media research—both the effects and the cultural models—is that it has very little impact on changing our media institutions. Do you agree or disagree, and why?

3. Can you think of an issue that a media industry and academic researchers could study together? Explain.

4. In looking at media courses in a college curriculum, what do you think is the relationship between theory and practice? Do hands-on, practical skills courses such as news reporting, advertising copywriting, or TV production belong in a liberal arts college or in a separate mass-communication college? Explain your answer.

SEARCHING THE INTERNET

http://people-press.org/

The Pew Research Center for the People and the Press is an independent public opinion research group. The Center's surveys measure public attitudes about the media and also track how closely the public follows major news stories.

http://www.kff.org

The Kaiser Family Foundation has funded a number of media partnerships and studies in recent years, including national surveys on topics such as television and the Internet, with partners like National Public Radio, *The NewsHour with Jim Lehrer,* and the *Washington Post.*

http://www.scripps.ohiou.edu/wjmcr/index.htm

The *Web Journal of Mass Communication Research* was begun in 1997 to publish original mass-communication research on the Web.

http://www.imagesjournal.com

Images is an online journal of media criticism that publishes accessible articles about movies, television, videos, and other popular visual arts.

THE CRITICAL PROCESS

In Brief

Consider the incidents outlined in the chapter's preview story, as well as any other recent media stories about violence, and discuss the following questions in class: Does media-effects research support the charge that mass media should be responsible for the tragic instances of copycat behavior? How would you balance the First Amendment free-expression rights of the mass media with issues of social and moral responsibility?

In Depth

The purpose of this project is to extend your critical approach to media research and to the academic culture that has developed over the years. Here are three assignments that can work either as group projects in class or as individual writing assignments. For these assignments, it is up to you to determine the best methodological approach—either a more social scientific method, or the cultural approach using the critical process introduced in Chapter 1.

1. Create your own hypothesis with regard to the media, or test one of the following arguments:

   - College students are less informed about current news events than their parents are.
   - Watching late-night TV talk-show monologues makes us more cynical about issues in the news.

   Come up with two or three different plans for testing either your own hypothesis or one of the hypotheses listed above. What types of research would you use? Why?

2. Choose an issue from two contemporary media research journals—one devoted mostly to mainstream research (such as *Journalism & Mass Communication Quarterly*) and one devoted to cultural research (such as *Critical Studies in Mass Communication*). Make a list or chart of the topics that each particular issue covers. Pick one article from each issue, and write a paragraph critiquing how well you think the researchers made and supported their arguments. How accessible was the language in each article, and how important was the research? As a journalist, what would you report about these media-research projects?

3. Choose one well-established media-research journal—*Journalism & Mass Communication Quarterly, Public Opinion Quarterly,* or *Film Quarterly*—and read an issue of the journal for each decade from the 1930s or 1940s to the present. In your group or in an essay, document the subject matter and explain how the journal has changed over the years. Which issues did you find to be the best, and why?

KEY TERMS

media effects, 513
hypodermic-needle model, 519
minimal-effects model, 520
selective exposure, 520
selective retention, 520
uses and gratifications model, 520

scientific method, 521
hypotheses, 521
experiments, 522
random assignment, 522
survey research, 522
longitudinal studies, 523

content analysis, 523
agenda-setting, 524
cultivation effect, 525
cultural studies, 527
textual analysis, 527

legal controls

and freedom of expression

The days after the September 11, 2001, terrorist attacks brought not only the beginnings of the war on terrorism but also internal battles over free speech and press freedom. In his speech to the nation, President George W. Bush said that "freedom and fear are at war." That statement was true not only in world politics but within the United States' own mass media, where the normal conditions of freedom of speech and press became a casualty of chest-thumping patriotism.

At least three journalists — Tom Gutting of the *Texas City Sun*, Dan Guthrie of the *Daily Courier* in Grants Pass, Oregon, and Jackie Anderson of the *Sun Advocate* in Price, Utah — were fired for writing comments that were critical of the president's activities on September 11 or that questioned a response of war. Bill Maher of ABC's late-night talk show *Politically Incorrect* was criticized for being — of all things — politically incorrect. Several sponsors and at least three affiliates dropped the show after Maher said the hijacker terrorists willing to die for their cause were not cowards, but the United States was cowardly for

16

"lobbing cruise missiles from 2,000 miles away." White House spokesman Ari Fleischer chimed in with criticism of Maher (who in 2003 moved from ABC to HBO) by noting that "it's a terrible thing to say, and it's unfortunate. There are reminders to all Americans that they need to watch what they say, watch what they do."

The attacks on dissenting views led one journalist from the *San Antonio Express-News* to write, "Somebody pinch me. I'm beginning to think this is 1954 and that Sen. Joe McCarthy is alive and well and running roughshod over the Bill of Rights."[1] Indeed, the First Amendment's protections were designed to sustain the press's and people's right to freedom, especially when the government or partisans would attempt to crush opposing voices. Ironically, though, some attempted to suppress one of the things most distinctly American — the right of free speech and press — in the name of patriotism. But, as Lucy Dalglish, executive director of the Reporters Committee for the Freedom of the Press, reminded us in this war over words, blocking critical information and dissenting views doesn't make us any more secure: "No one has demonstrated that an ignorant society is a safe society."[2]

● On previous page: U.S. Attorney General John Ashcroft, who has restricted many civil liberties in response to the September 11 attacks.

t he cultural and social struggles over free speech and press freedom have defined the nature of American democracy. In 1989, when Supreme Court Justice William Brennan Jr. was asked to comment on his "favorite part of the Constitution," he replied, "The First Amendment, I expect. Its enforcement gives us this society. The other provisions of the Constitution really only embellish it." Of all the issues that involve the mass media and popular culture, none are more central, or explosive, than freedom of expression and the First Amendment. Our nation's fundamental development can often be traced to how much or how little speech was tolerated during particular historical periods.

The current era is a volatile time for free-speech issues. Our society has debated hate-speech codes on campuses, explicit lyrics in music, violent images in film, and the swapping of media files on the Internet. In this chapter, we will examine expression issues, focusing primarily on the implications of the First Amendment for a variety of mass media. We will investigate the origins of *free* expression and the standard models that underlie press freedoms. We will look at the definition of censorship and corresponding legal cases. Next, we will study the types of expression that are not always protected as speech. Focusing on the impact of cameras in the courtroom, we will examine some of the clashes between the First and Sixth Amendments. With regard to film, we will review the social and political pressures that gave rise to early censorship boards and the current film ratings system. We will turn to issues in broadcasting and examine why it has been treated differently from print media. Among other topics, we will inspect the idea of indecency in broadcasting and the demise of the Fairness Doctrine. Finally, we will explore the newest frontier in speech—expression in cyberspace and concerns about speech on the Internet.

> 66 Congress shall make no law respecting an establishment of religion, or prohibiting the free exercise thereof; or abridging the freedom of speech, or of the press; or the right of the people peaceably to assemble, and to petition the government for a redress of grievances. 99
>
> —First Amendment, U.S. Constitution, 1791

The Origins of Free Expression and a Free Press

When students from other cultures attend school in the United States, many are astounded by the number of books, news articles, editorials, cartoons, films, and TV shows that make fun of U.S. presidents. When writer-director Hugh Wilson toured Spain after his comedy film *Police Academy* (1984) appeared there, he was astonished to discover that many Spanish citizens regarded him as a hero for "criticizing" the police. Many countries' governments throughout history have jailed, even killed, their citizens for such speech "violations." In the past decade, nearly 400 journalists have been killed in the line of duty, often because someone disagrees with what they write or report.[3] In the United States, however, we have generally taken for granted our right to criticize and poke fun at elected officials, politicians, and the police. Many of us are unaware of the ideas that underpin the freedoms we have. Indeed, when reporters have surveyed unwitting Americans about the First Amendment to the U.S. Constitution, the majority of respondents, unfamiliar with the amendment's wording, have usually indicated that its freedoms are far too generous.

To understand the development of free expression in the United States, we must understand a key idea underlying the First Amendment. In Europe throughout the 1600s, in order to monitor—and punish, if necessary—the speech of editors and writers, governments controlled the circulation of ideas by requiring printers to obtain licenses. In 1644, English poet John Milton, author of *Paradise Lost*, published his essay *Areopagitica*, which opposed government licenses for printers and defended a free press. Milton argued that all sorts of ideas, even false ones, should circulate freely in a democratic society and that truth would eventually emerge. In

1695, England stopped licensing newspapers, and most of Europe followed. In many democracies today, publishing a newspaper, magazine, or newsletter remains one of the few public or service enterprises that require no license.

Models for Expression and Speech

In 2002, an international survey of the news media in 186 countries, conducted by the human rights organization Freedom House, reported that nearly 80 percent of the world's people lived in countries with a less than free press. The survey related that sixty-one nations had virtually no press freedom; those governments exercised tight control over the news media, and this included jailing, intimidating, and even executing journalists. Moreover, in the wake of the September 11, 2001 terrorist attacks, the Freedom House cited potentially negative consequences from increased surveillance and the tightening of freedom of information laws in many free press countries in Europe and the United States and Canada.[4]

Since the mid-1950s, four models for speech and journalism have been used to categorize the widely differing ideas underlying free expression.[5] These models include the authoritarian, communist, libertarian, and social-responsibility concepts. They are distinguished by the levels of freedom they allow and by the attitudes of the ruling and political classes toward the freedoms granted to the average citizen. Today, given the diversity among nations, the experimentation of journalists, and the collapse of many communist press systems, these categories are no longer as relevant as they were formerly. Nevertheless, they offer a good point of departure for discussing the press and democracy.

The **authoritarian model** developed about the time the printing press arrived in sixteenth-century England. Its advocates held that the general public, largely illiterate in those days, needed guidance from an elite and educated ruling class. Government criticism and public dissent were not tolerated, especially if such speech undermined "the common good"—an ideal that ruling elites and leaders defined and controlled. Censorship was frequent, and the government issued printing licenses primarily to publishers who were sympathetic to government and ruling-class agendas.

Today, many authoritarian systems operate in developing countries throughout Asia, Latin America, and Africa, where journalism often joins with government and business to foster economic growth, minimize political dissent, and promote social stability. The leaders in these systems generally believe that too much outspoken speech and press freedom would undermine the delicate stability of their social and political infrastructures. In these societies, criticizing government programs may be viewed as an obstacle to keeping the peace, and both reporters and citizens may be punished if they question leaders and the status quo too fiercely.

Under most authoritarian models, the news is still controlled by private enterprise. But under the **communist** or **state model**, press control rests in the lap of government. Speaking for ordinary citizens and workers, state leaders believe they are enlightened and that the press should serve the common goals of the state. Although some state systems encourage media and government cooperation, political and military leaders still dictate the agendas for newspapers and the broadcast media. Some government criticism is tolerated, but ideas that challenge the basic premises of state authority are not. Although state media systems were in decline throughout the 1990s, they were still operating in China, Cuba, Iran, Iraq, and North Korea, among other countries, at the outset of 2003.

The **libertarian model**, the flip side of state and authoritarian systems, encourages vigorous government criticism and supports the highest degree of freedom for individual speech and news operations. In a strict libertarian model, no restrictions are placed on the mass media or on individual speech. Libertarians tolerate the expression of everything, from publishing pornography to advocating anarchy. In North America and Europe, many political and alternative newspapers and magazines operate on such a model. Placing a great deal of trust in citizens' ability to distinguish truth from fabrication, libertarians maintain that the best way to fight outrageous lies or repulsive speech is not to suppress them but to speak out and write against them.

Along with the libertarian model, a **social-responsibility model** characterizes the main ideals of mainstream journalism in the United States. The concepts and assumptions behind this model coalesced in the controversial 1947 Hutchins Commission, which was formed to examine the increasing influence of the press. Henry Luce, then head of the Time-Life magazine empire, funded the commission with a large grant to his friend Robert Maynard Hutchins, chancellor of the University of Chicago. Hutchins used the grant to assemble a committee to study

> **"** Consider what would happen if — during this 200th anniversary of the Bill of Rights — the First Amendment were placed on the ballot in every town, city, and state. The choices: affirm, reject, or amend.
>
> I would bet there is no place in the United States where the First Amendment would survive intact. **"**
>
> –Nat Hentoff, writer, 1991

● Internet cafés, called "coffeenets" in Iran, became widely available in Iran in early 2000 and have skyrocketed in popularity. Charging about $2 an hour online, the cybercafés have provided an uncensored and private medium for communication in a nation ruled by a conservative Islamic government. Many of the country's top clerics have even decided to embrace the Internet, to offer their religious guidance and interpret official decrees. Here, a twenty-four-year-old university student researches a project at an Internet café in North Tehran.

the press. Luce hoped the commission would endorse free-press ideals and keep outsiders from watching over the press. But to Luce's dismay, the commission's report called for the development of press-watchdog groups. The report argued that the mass media had grown too powerful and needed to become more socially responsible. Key recommendations encouraged comprehensive news reports that put issues and events in context, more news forums for the exchange of ideas, better coverage of society's range of economic classes and social groups, and stronger overviews of our nation's social values, ideals, and goals.

A socially responsible press is usually privately owned (although the government technically operates the broadcast media in most European democracies). In this model, the press functions as a **Fourth Estate**—that is, as an unofficial branch of government that monitors the legislative, judicial, and executive branches for abuses of power. In theory, private ownership keeps the news media independent of government. Thus they are better able to watch over the system on behalf of citizens. Under this model, which is heavily influenced by the libertarian view, the press supplies information to citizens so they can make wise decisions regarding political and social issues; the press also operates without excessive government meddling in matters of content.

Censorship as Prior Restraint

In the United States, the First Amendment has theoretically prohibited censorship. Over time, Supreme Court decisions have defined censorship as **prior restraint**. This means that courts and governments cannot block any publication or speech before it actually occurs, on the principle that a law has not been broken until an illegal act has been committed. In 1931, for example, the Supreme Court determined in *Near v. Minnesota* that a Minneapolis newspaper could not be stopped from publishing "scandalous and defamatory" material about police and law officials who were negligent in arresting and punishing local gangsters.[6] However, the Court left open the idea that the news media could be ordered to halt publication in exceptional cases. During a declared war, for instance, if a U.S. court judged that the publication of an article threatened national security, such expression could be restrained prior to its printing. In fact, during World War I the U.S. Navy seized all wireless radio transmitters. This was done to ensure control over critical information about weather conditions and troop movements that might inadvertently aid the enemy. In the 1970s, though, the Pentagon Papers decision and the *Progressive* magazine case tested important concepts underlying prior restraint.

The Pentagon Papers Case

In 1971, with the Vietnam War still in progress, Daniel Ellsberg, a former Defense Department employee, stole a copy of a forty-seven-volume document, "History of U.S. Decision-Making Process on Vietnam Policy." A thorough study of U.S. involvement in Vietnam since World War II, the papers were classified by the government as top secret. Ellsberg and a friend leaked the study—nicknamed the Pentagon Papers—to the *New York Times* and the *Washington Post*. In June 1971, the *Times* began publishing articles based on the study. To block any further publication, the Nixon administration received a temporary restraining order to prepare its case, arguing that publishing the documents posed "a clear and present danger" to national security. The administration had five national security experts testify that publicizing the Pentagon Papers would impede the war effort.

A lower U.S. district court supported the newspaper's right to publish, but the government's appeal placed the case in the Supreme Court less than three weeks after the first articles were published. In a 6–3 vote, the Court sided with the news-

papers. Justice Hugo Black, speaking for the majority, attacked the government's attempt to suppress publication: "Both the history and language of the First Amendment support the view that the press must be left free to publish news, whatever the source, without censorship, injunctions, or prior restraints."[7] (See "Applied Critical Process: How Much Freedom of Information?" on page 544.)

The *Progressive* Magazine Case

The issue of prior restraint surfaced again in 1979, when an injunction was issued to block publication of the *Progressive,* a national left-wing magazine; the editors had announced that they were running an article entitled "The H-Bomb Secret: How We Got It, Why We're Telling It." The dispute began when the editor of the magazine sent a draft to the Department of Energy to verify technical portions of the article. Believing that the article contained sensitive data that might damage U.S. efforts to halt the proliferation of nuclear weapons, the Energy Department asked the magazine not to publish it. When the magazine said it would proceed anyway, the government sued the *Progressive* and asked a federal district court to block publication.

Judge Robert Warren sought to balance the *Progressive's* First Amendment rights against the government's claim that the article would spread dangerous information and undermine national security. In an unprecedented action, Warren sided with the government, deciding that "a mistake in ruling against the United States could pave the way for thermonuclear annihilation for us all. In that event, our right to life is extinguished and the right to publish becomes moot."[8] During appeals and further

● In 1971, Daniel Ellsberg surrendered to government prosecutors in Boston. Ellsberg was a former Pentagon researcher who turned against America's military policy in Vietnam and leaked information to the press. He was charged with unauthorized possession of top-secret federal documents. Later called the Pentagon Papers, the documents contained evidence on the military's bungled handling of the Vietnam War. In 1973, an exasperated federal judge dismissed the case when illegal government-sponsored wiretaps of Ellsberg's psychoanalyst came to light during the Watergate scandal.

How Much Freedom of Information?

A national Freedom of Information Act was passed in 1966 to give journalists and citizens access to government documents from federal agencies when they make a request in writing. All fifty states have various open-record laws as well. (See the National Freedom of Information Coalition's State & National Freedom of Information Resources, <http://www.nfoic.org/web/index.htm>.) Although these laws are on the books, are government documents open in practice? Journalists in many states periodically conduct statewide audits to determine this. Below is a critical investigation by a group of journalists in one state.

Description. In 2000, thirteen newspapers in Iowa conducted a cooperative investigation of the state's open-record law. Iowa's law permits journalists and citizens to inspect government records without having to identify themselves or how they will use the information. To gather data, journalists presented themselves as regular Iowa citizens at public offices in the state's ninety-nine counties and requested various types of legally public information.

Analysis. Certain patterns were clearly evident. According to a published report:

- 58 percent of the sheriff departments denied access to information about people who have received permits to carry concealed weapons.
- 42 percent of police departments in the largest city in each county denied access to reports of the most recent incidents with which officers dealt.
- 9 percent of city offices denied access to expense reports filed by the city manager, city administrator, or public works director.
- 2 percent of county auditor offices refused to make available records detailing expenses filed by county supervisors.
- 2 percent of cities denied access to building permit files.
- All county treasurers provided information about the sheriff's personal property-tax bills.[1]

Interpretation. Some public officials were simply unaware of the open-records law and didn't know their records should be public. Others were uncomfortable with the law's provisions, which do not require citizens to provide identification when making a request. In one county, a *Des Moines Register* reporter who made a request for gun permit records was threatened with arrest by a suspicious sheriff.

Evaluation. The Freedom of Information Act and state open-records laws help make the government more accountable. For example, citizens and journalists can investigate state records on child care facilities and nursing homes, workplace safety reports, or federal government spending. But what exceptions, if any, should be made to open-records rules to balance concerns for privacy, personal safety, identity theft, or terrorism?

litigation, several other publications, including the *Milwaukee Sentinel* and *Scientific American,* published articles related to the H-bomb, getting much of their information from publications already in circulation. None of these articles, including the one published in the *Progressive,* contained the precise technical details needed to actually design a nuclear weapon; nor did they provide information on where to obtain the sensitive ingredients. Although the government dropped the case, Warren's injunction stands as the first time in American history that a prior-restraint order imposed in the name of national security actually stopped the initial publication of a controversial news report.

Unprotected Forms of Expression

Early in our nation's history, the Federalist Party, which controlled Congress, enacted the Sedition Act to silence opposition to an anticipated war against France. The act tried to curb criticism by the opposition Democratic-Republican Party. Many anti-

Federalists supported France and America's newly arrived French immigrants. Led by President John Adams, the Federalists believed that defamatory articles might stir up discontent against the elected government and undermine its authority. Adams signed the act in 1798. Over the next three years, twenty-five individuals were arrested and ten were convicted under the act, which was also used to prosecute anti-Federalist newspapers. After failing to curb opposition, the Sedition Act expired in 1801 during Thomas Jefferson's presidency. Jefferson, a Democratic-Republican who had challenged the act's constitutionality, pardoned all defendants convicted under the Sedition Act.[9]

Despite the First Amendment's order that "Congress shall make no law" restricting speech and press freedoms, the federal government has made other laws like the Sedition Act, especially during times of war. For instance, the Espionage Acts of 1917 and 1918, which were enforced during World Wars I and II, made it a federal crime to disrupt the nation's war effort. These acts also authorized severe punishment for seditious statements. Beyond the federal government, state laws and local ordinances have on occasion curbed expression, and over the years the court system has determined that some kinds of expression do not merit protection as speech under the Constitution. Today, for example, false or misleading advertising is not protected by law; nor are expressions that intentionally threaten public safety.

In the landmark *Schenck v. United States* appeal case during World War I, the Supreme Court upheld the conviction of a Socialist Party leader, Charles T. Schenck, for distributing leaflets urging American men to protest the draft, a violation of the recently passed Espionage Act. In upholding the act, Justice Oliver Wendell Holmes wrote two of the more famous interpretations and phrases in the First Amendment's legal history:

> But the character of every act depends upon the circumstances in which it is done. The most stringent protection of free speech would not protect a man in falsely shouting fire in a theater and causing a panic.

> The question in every case is whether the words used are used in such circumstances and are of such a nature as to create a clear and present danger that they will bring about the substantive evils that Congress has a right to prevent.

In supporting Schenck's sentence—a ten-year prison term—Holmes noted that the Socialist leaflets were entitled to First Amendment protection, but only during times of peace. In establishing the "clear and present danger" criterion for expression, the Supreme Court demonstrated the limits of the First Amendment. Beyond this judicial standard, several other kinds of expression are exceptions to the First Amendment's guarantee of free speech and press. These include copyright, libel, invasion of privacy, and obscenity.

Copyright

Appropriating a writer's or artist's words or music without consent or payment is a form of expression that is not protected as speech. Hip-hop performers, in fact, have faced a number of court battles for copyright infringement; they have been accused of stealing other musicians' work by sampling their music, a technique fundamental to rap (see "Case Study: 'Pretty Woman,' Rap, and Copyright Law" on page 546). A **copyright** legally protects the rights of authors and producers to their published or unpublished writing, music and lyrics, TV programs and movies, or graphic art designs. As noted earlier, file-swapping on the Internet has raised an entirely new class of copyright concerns, not only in the music industry but in every media sector. Copyright protection was extended with the Digital Millennium Copyright Act of 1998, which goes beyond traditional copyright protection to outlaw technology or

© 2 Live Crew.

"Pretty Woman," Rap, and Copyright Law

by Michael M. Epstein

The protection of copyright has long helped writers, artists, and filmmakers control where, when, and how their creative works are used by others. Under U.S. copyright law, the original creators can sue people who imitate or adapt their works commercially without permission. In most cases, the rule is as follows: If you make money off someone else's creative material, that money belongs to the person who owns the copyright to the material unless you have obtained his or her prior approval. One exception to copyright protection, known as *fair use,* allows journalists, critics, scholars, and students to excerpt limited portions of other peoples' creations for a variety of purposes.

Until recently, parody was usually considered to be covered by copyright's fair-use exception, yet the Supreme Court did not rule on the issue until March 7, 1994. The Court unanimously found that the rap group 2 Live Crew did not violate U.S. copyright law when it released its 1989 song "Pretty Woman." A subversive, cynical, and controversial parody of Roy Orbison's 1964 anthem of hope and fulfillment, "Oh, Pretty Woman," the 2 Live Crew version developed a huge and profitable following among hip-hop audiences. Although the rap group had sought permission to use the song's signature first line for its parody, the owner of the song's copyright, Acuff-Rose Music, decided not to let the group use the famous ballad. When 2 Live Crew went ahead and used the song anyway, Acuff-Rose filed suit in federal court.

2 Live Crew members argued that their version of "Oh, Pretty Woman" was intended to be a parody of Orbison's song. As author Luther R. Campbell explained in a letter to Acuff-Rose, the group's purpose was "through comical lyrics, to satirize the original work." These lyrics, considered offensive and sexist by many, transformed Orbison's pretty woman into a "big hairy woman," "a bald-headed woman," and a "two-timin' woman." Although 2 Live Crew gave credit for "Oh, Pretty Woman" to Roy Orbison and his coauthor, William Dees, on their album *Clean as They Wanna Be,* Acuff-Rose argued that Campbell's creation was nothing more than a commercial rip-off that made money for the rap group at the copyright owner's expense. Lawyers for the rappers argued, however, that "Pretty Woman" was a legitimate parody and thus exempt from copyright claims.

Although the federal district court in Nashville decided in favor of 2 Live Crew, a U.S. court of appeals later reversed the lower court's ruling, causing a furor in the creative community. The appellate court concluded that by "taking the heart of the original and making it the heart of a new work," the band had borrowed too much of the original song. The court also ruled that "Pretty Woman" could not be protected as fair use under copyright law because the rappers had recorded their version for "blatantly commercial purposes."

Justice David Souter, writing for a unanimous Supreme Court, rejected the ruling of the appellate court. Souter suggested that the rap version could be understood "as a comment on the naiveté of the original of an earlier day, as a rejection of its sentiment that ignores the ugliness of street life and the debasement it signifies." Stating that parody's "art lies in the tension between a known original and its parodic twin," the Supreme Court ruled that works that adapt or transform an original creation "lie at the heart of the fair-use doctrine's guarantee of breathing space within the confines of copyright." Souter noted that Campbell's parody deserved credit for both "shedding light on an earlier work and . . . creating a new one."

In a media-saturated world that has seen the sampling by rap artists of previous recordings and the composite imaging of archival photos and films by computer, it is no wonder that the "Pretty Woman" case attracted wide attention. Satirists as diverse as *Mad Magazine* and political humorist Mark Russell filed friend-of-the-court briefs on behalf of 2 Live Crew. On the other hand, many songwriters and composers filed briefs in support of the music company.

It is still too early to tell whether the composers have lost the copyright-protection war. Indeed, since the ruling in *Campbell v. Acuff-Rose Music,* instances of copyright infringement are still decided on a case-by-case basis. Whether or not a parodist, or anyone else, is granted protection under copyright law is still subject to the general rules governing fair use. For example, if a parody is likely to damage the market for the original work, then the creator may be able to collect damages from the parodist. As the courts see it, imitation is still the sincerest form of flattery—but only up to a point.

Michael M. Epstein is a professor at Southwestern University School of Law in Los Angeles.

actions that circumvent copyright protection systems. In other words, it may be illegal to merely create or distribute technology that enables someone to make illegal copies of digital content, such as a music CD or a DVD movie.

Libel

The biggest single legal worry that haunts editors and publishers is the issue of libel, another form of expression that is not protected as speech under the First Amendment. Whereas **slander** constitutes spoken language that defames a person's character, **libel** refers to defamation of character in written or broadcast expression. Inherited from British common law, libel is generally defined as a false statement that holds a person up to public ridicule, contempt, or hatred or injures a person's business or occupation. Examples of potentially libelous statements include falsely accusing someone of professional dishonesty or incompetence (such as medical malpractice); falsely accusing a person of a crime (such as drug dealing); falsely charging a person with mental illness or unacceptable behavior (such as public drunkenness); or falsely accusing a person of associating with a disreputable organization or cause (such as the Mafia or a neo-Nazi military group).

To protect the news media's right to aggressively pursue wrongdoing and stories, courts since the mid-1960s have tried to make it more difficult for public officials to win libel suits. This has not, however, deterred some individuals and organizations from intimidating the news media by either threatening to file or actually filing libel suits. Such legal actions in civil law can prove costly, particularly to a small newspaper or magazine, even when the defendant wins the case. As a result, over the years many small news organizations have avoided tough, probing stories, and large organizations have hired lawyers to advise them on the libel implications of their more controversial investigative stories. In 2001, seventeen libel cases against the media went to trial, and of these, media defendants won about half of the cases. Libel awards are getting bigger, however. Prior to the 1960s, libel awards rarely exceeded $25,000; the median award in 2001 was $1 million (although the awards are sometimes reduced by higher courts on appeal).[10]

Since 1964, the *New York Times v. Sullivan* case has served as the standard for libel law. The case stems from a 1960 full-page advertisement placed in the *New York Times* by the Committee to Defend Martin Luther King Jr. and the Struggle for Freedom in the South. Without naming names, the ad criticized the general law-enforcement tactics of southern cities, including Montgomery, Alabama, for the methods used to break up civil rights demonstrations. The ad condemned "southern violators of the Constitution" bent on destroying King and the movement. Taking exception, the city commissioner of Montgomery, L. B. Sullivan, sued the *Times* for libel, claiming the ad defamed him indirectly. Although Alabama civil courts awarded Sullivan $500,000, the newspaper's lawyers appealed to the Supreme Court, which unanimously reversed the ruling, holding that Alabama libel law violated the *Times*'s First Amendment rights.[11]

In the *Sullivan* decision, the Supreme Court asked future civil courts to distinguish whether plaintiffs are public officials or private individuals. (In later cases, *public figures* such as entertainment or sports celebrities were added to this mix.) Within this framework, private individuals have to prove three things to successfully argue a libel case:

1. that the public statement about them was false;
2. that damages or actual injury occurred, such as the loss of a job, harm to reputation, public humiliation, or mental anguish;
3. that the publisher or broadcaster was negligent.

But if a court determines that a plaintiff is a *public official* or figure, that person has to prove falsehood, damages, negligence, and **actual malice** on the part of the

> " You cannot hold us to the same [libel] standards as a newscast or you kill talk radio. If we had to qualify everything we said, talk radio would cease to exist. "
>
> – Lionel, WABC talk radio morning host, 1999

● This is the 1960 *New York Times* advertisement that triggered one of the most influential and important libel cases in U.S. history.

news medium. The latter test means that the reporter or editor knew the statement was false and printed or broadcast it anyway, or acted with a reckless disregard for the truth. Again, because actual malice is hard to prove, it remains difficult for public figures to win libel suits. The Court's rationale for the principle of actual malice not only protects the First Amendment rights of the media but, in theory, allows news operations to aggressively pursue legitimate news stories without fear of continuous litigation. In practice, however, the mere threat of a libel suit still scares off many in the news media.

Under current libel law, civil courts determine, on a case-by-case basis, whether plaintiffs are public or private persons. In general, public officials must have substantial responsibilities in conducting government affairs; therefore presidents, senators, mayors, police detectives, and city managers count as examples of public officials. Citizens with more "ordinary" jobs, such as city sanitation employees, undercover police informants, nurses, or unknown actors, are normally classified as private individuals.

Judges often have a tough time deciding who is a public figure. Many vague categories exist, such as public high-school teachers, police officers, and court-appointed attorneys. Individuals from these professions have ended up in either category depending on a particular court's ruling. The Supreme Court has distinguished two categories of public figures: (1) public celebrities or people who "occupy positions of such pervasive power and influence that they are deemed public figures for all purposes," and (2) individuals who have thrown themselves—usually voluntarily but sometimes involuntarily—into the middle of "a significant public controversy," such as a lawyer defending a prominent client, an advocate for an antismoking ordinance, a labor-union activist, or a security guard like Richard Jewell.

Made famous by the news media, Jewell was initially suspected of setting off the pipe bomb that killed a woman at the 1996 Olympics in Atlanta, Georgia. After the FBI cleared Jewell, NBC News, ABC News, CNN, and the *New York Post* settled libel cases with him. His lawyers had charged that after news media reports named him as the only suspect, he could not find work even though he was never charged with the crime. But the *Atlanta Journal and Constitution* did not settle out of court with Jewell, and a bitter libel lawsuit between them ensued. A Georgia court ruled that because Jewell had consented to media interviews, he was a public figure—thus he had to prove the Atlanta newspaper used actual malice, and not just negligence. In late 2002, the U.S. Supreme Court declined to hear an appeal from Jewell, and the case—which started in 1997—returned to the Georgia state court.

Defenses Against Libel Charges

Since the 1730s, the best defense against libel in U.S. civil court has been the truth. In most cases, if libel defendants can demonstrate that they printed or broadcast statements that were essentially true, such evidence usually bars plaintiffs from recovering any damages—even if their reputations were harmed. To this end, the news media are particularly careful about using any direct quotes in which a source may have lied, employing legal staffs to check the veracity of controversial stories before publication. If a source, for instance, libels a private person in a news report, the paper may also be held accountable. Even if the reporter did not know the quote was false, he or she might be considered negligent for not checking the truthfulness of the statement more carefully.

Beyond the truth, there are other defenses against libel. Prosecutors, for example, receive *absolute privilege* in a court of law when they make potentially damaging statements about a defendant's reputation. When prosecutor Marcia Clark (who became an NBC cable news host after the trial) accused O.J. Simpson of being a murderer and he was later acquitted, she was protected from libel on the legal theory that in public courtrooms the interests of an individual are overridden by the larger common good of the legal process. The reporters who printed or broadcast her statement were also protected against libel. Entitled to conditional or **qualified privilege**, journalists are allowed to report judicial or legislative proceedings even though the public statements being reported may be libelous.

When police detectives, judges, or prosecutors make unsubstantiated claims about a defendant, or when legislators verbally attack each other during a session, reporters are allowed to report those incidents—even when potentially libelous statements are relayed secondhand by the reporter. As a condition for qualified privilege, the reporting of these public events must be fair and accurate. If a reporter, for instance, has prior knowledge that a public statement is untrue and still reports it as the truth, a judge may suspend qualified privilege and hold the reporter accountable for libel.

Another defense against libel concerns the area of *opinion and fair comment*. For example, after O.J. Simpson was acquitted of murder in October 1995, many legal commentators and talk-show hosts continued to suggest that in their *opinion* he was guilty of killing his former wife, Nicole Brown, and her friend Ron Goldman. Generally, however, libel applies only to misstatements of factual information rather than opinion, although the line between fact and opinion is often hazy. Some libel cases turn on a plaintiff's ability to persuade a judge or jury that a defendant's statement

● On Larry King's cable talk show in 1997, Moral Majority leader Rev. Jerry Falwell (*right*) discusses pornography and forgiveness with *Hustler* magazine publisher Larry Flynt (*center*)—their first face-to-face meeting since their 1984 libel trial.

was a factual error and not merely opinion or fair comment. For this reason, lawyers advise journalists to first set forth the facts on which a viewpoint is based and then to state their opinion based on those facts. In other words, journalists should make it clear that a statement is a criticism and not an allegation of fact. Libel laws protect satire, comedy, and opinions expressed in reviews of books, plays, movies, or restaurants. Such laws may not, however, protect malicious statements in which plaintiffs can prove that defendants used their free-speech rights to mount a damaging personal attack.

One of the most famous tests of opinion and fair comment occurred in a case pitting conservative minister and political activist Jerry Falwell against Larry Flynt, publisher of *Hustler* magazine. The case became the subject of a major Hollywood movie, *The People vs. Larry Flynt* (1996). The actual *Falwell v. Flynt* case developed after a November 1983 issue of *Hustler* made an outrageous reference to Falwell. In a spoof of a Campari aperitif ad, the magazine asked readers to recall the "first time" they drank Campari. The parody stated that Falwell needed to be drunk before he could preach; it also described his "first time" as an incestuous encounter with his own mother. In fine print at the bottom of the page, a disclaimer read: "Ad parody—not to be taken seriously."

Often a target of Flynt's irreverence and questionable taste, Falwell sued for libel, asking for $45 million in damages. In the verdict, the jury rejected the libel suit but found that Flynt had intentionally caused Falwell emotional distress, awarding him $200,000. It was an unprecedented verdict in American legal history. Flynt's lawyers appealed, and in 1988 the Supreme Court unanimously overturned the verdict. Although the Court did not condone the *Hustler* spoof, the justices did say that the magazine was entitled to constitutional protection. The case drew enormous media attention and raised concerns about the erosion of the media's right to free speech. In affirming *Hustler*'s speech rights, the Court suggested that even though parodies and insults of public figures might indeed cause emotional pain, denying the right to publish them would undermine a key democratic principle and violate the spirit of the First Amendment.[12]

The Right to Privacy

Whereas libel laws safeguard a person's character and reputation, the right to privacy protects an individual's peace of mind and personal feelings. Any public figure who has ever been subjected to intense scrutiny by the media has experienced an invasion of privacy. But, in general, the news media have been granted wide protections under the First Amendment to subject public figures to the spotlight. Local municipalities and states, however, have passed laws that protect most individuals from unwarranted surveillance. During her lifetime, for instance, Jacqueline Kennedy Onassis successfully sought court orders to keep photographers at a minimum distance, although the technology of powerful zoom lenses often overcame this obstacle.

Public figures have received some legal relief, but every year brings a few stories of a Hollywood actor or sports figure punching a tabloid photographer or TV cameraman who got too close. Similarly, actor Jennifer Aniston brought a privacy lawsuit against *Celebrity Skin* magazine in 2000 for printing photos of her sunbathing topless in her backyard. The suit claimed a photographer climbed a neighbor's fence to snap the photos. Such cases, as well as Princess Diana's death in 1997—partly attributed to harassment by paparazzi—have spawned a flurry of legislation attempting to protect celebrities and public figures from invasions of privacy. Such anti-paparazzi laws include prohibition of trespassing or using electronic devices (such as zoom lenses on cameras) that can capture audio or video images of a celebrity or crime victim engaged in personal or family activity on private property or outside public

● Actor Winona Ryder with an attorney. Although many Hollywood stars disdain excessive coverage of their personal lives, Ryder had no choice in being the subject of heavy media scrutiny, so much so that her arm was broken in a run-in with a group of reporters. Her arrest for shoplifting more than $5000 worth of clothing from a Saks Fifth Avenue store in Beverly Hills resulted in a trial that received sensational coverage in 2002. She was ultimately found guilty by a California court, fined, and sentenced to community service.

forums. In some states, the American Civil Liberties Union (ACLU) has challenged these laws as an infringement of the First Amendment rights of photographers and the news media. In 1999, the Supreme Court ruled that photographers and video news crews could not accompany police inside private property on authorized crime raids, such as a drug search, unless they received prior approval to enter the home or place of business from the occupants.

In the simplest terms, **invasion of privacy** addresses a person's right to be left alone, without his or her name, image, or daily activities becoming public property. Invasions of privacy occur in different situations, the most common of which are listed here:

1. intrusion, in which unauthorized tape recorders, wiretaps, microphones, or other surveillance equipment are used to secretly record a person's private affairs
2. the publication of private matters, such as the unauthorized disclosure of private statements about an individual's health, sexual activities, or economic status
3. the unauthorized appropriation of a person's name or image for advertising or other commercial benefit

As we have noted, the courts have generally given the news media a lot of lee-way under the First Amendment. For instance, the names and pictures of both private individuals and public figures can usually be used without their consent in most news stories. If private citizens become part of public controversies and subsequent news stories, the courts have usually allowed the news media to record their quotes and use their images without the individuals' permission. In regard to these situations, the courts have generally argued that the greater public good served by news coverage outweighs the individuals' right to privacy. The courts have even ruled that accurate reports of criminal and court records, including the identification of rape victims, do not normally constitute privacy invasions. Nevertheless, most newspapers and broadcast outlets use their own internal guidelines and ethical codes to protect the privacy of victims and defendants, especially in cases involving rape and abused children.

Obscenity

Privacy and libel issues are part of civil or private law: individuals filing personal lawsuits against another individual or a media organization. Obscenity issues, though, are often guided by federal law and can be prosecuted as criminal offenses: a prosecutor making a case against a purveyor of obscene material on behalf of "the people."

For most of this nation's history, it has generally been argued that obscenity does not constitute a legitimate form of expression. The problem, however, is that little agreement has existed on how to define an obscene work. In the 1860s, a court could judge an entire book obscene if it contained a single passage believed capable of corrupting a person. In fact, throughout the 1800s certain government authorities outside the courts—especially U.S. post office and customs officials—held the power to censor or destroy written material they deemed obscene.

This began to change in the 1930s during the trial involving the celebrated novel *Ulysses* by Irish writer James Joyce. Portions of *Ulysses* had been serialized in the early 1920s in an American magazine, which was later seized and burned by postal officials. The publishers of the magazine, *Little Review,* were fined $50 and nearly sent to prison. Because of the four-letter words contained in the novel and the book-burning incident, British and American publishing houses backed away from the book, which was eventually published in Paris in 1922. In 1928, the U.S. Customs Office officially banned *Ulysses* as an obscene work. Ultimately, Random House agreed to publish the work in America only if it was declared "legal." Finally, in 1933, a U.S. judge ruled that *Ulysses* was an important literary work and removed it from unprotected status.

Battles over obscenity continued. In a landmark case, *Roth v. United States,* the Supreme Court in 1957 offered this test of obscenity: whether to an "average person," applying "contemporary standards," the major thrust or theme of the material, "taken as a whole," appealed to "prurient interest" (in other words, was intended to "incite lust"). By the 1960s, based on *Roth,* expression no longer constituted obscenity if only a small part of the work lacked "redeeming social value." Refining *Roth,* the current legal definition of **obscenity** derives from the 1973 *Miller v. California* case, which involved sanctions for using the mail to promote or send pornographic materials. After a series of appeals, the Supreme Court argued that an obscene work had to meet three criteria:

1. The average person, applying contemporary community standards, would find that the material as a whole appeals to prurient interest.
2. The material depicts or describes sexual conduct in a patently offensive way.
3. The material, as a whole, lacks serious literary, artistic, political, or scientific value.

66 I shall not today attempt to define [obscenity]. . . . And perhaps I never could succeed in intelligibly doing so. But I know it when I see it. 99

–Supreme Court Justice Potter Stewart, 1964

Since this decision, courts have granted great latitude to printed and visual pornography. By the 1980s and 1990s, major cases prosecuting obscenity had become rare in the United States, as the legal system advanced the concept that a free and democratic society must tolerate even repulsive kinds of speech.

The *Miller* refinement of the *Roth* precedent contained two important ideas. First, it acknowledged that different communities and regions of the country have different values and standards; what is considered obscene in Fargo, North Dakota, for example, may not be judged obscene in Miami. The ruling sent various municipalities and states scrambling to develop lists of obscene acts and language that violated their communities' standards. (Some of these lists, when tested, were declared unconstitutional and had to undergo numerous revisions.) Second, the *Miller* decision also required that a work be judged *as a whole*. This removed a loophole in which some publishers would insert a political essay or literary poem to demonstrate in court that their publications contained redeeming features.

First Amendment versus Sixth Amendment

Over the years, First Amendment protections of speech and the press have often clashed with the Sixth Amendment, which guarantees an accused individual in "all criminal prosecutions . . . the right to a speedy and public trial, by an impartial jury." In 1954, for example, the Sam Sheppard case, loosely the inspiration for the TV series *The Fugitive* and the subsequent 1994 film of the same name, involved enormous publicity. Featuring lurid details about the murder of Sheppard's wife, the Cleveland press editorialized in favor of Sheppard's quick arrest; some papers even pronounced him guilty. A prominent and wealthy osteopath, Sheppard was convicted of the murder. Twelve years later, though, Sheppard's new lawyer, F. Lee Bailey, argued before the Supreme Court that his client had not received a fair trial because of prejudicial publicity. The Court overturned the conviction and freed Sheppard.

Gag Orders and Shield Laws

One of the major criticisms of the O.J. Simpson criminal case in 1994–95 concerned the ways in which defense lawyers used the news media to comment publicly on court matters outside the presence of a sequestered jury. After the Sheppard reversal in the 1960s, the Supreme Court had suggested safeguards—some used in the Simpson case—that judges could employ to ensure a fair trial in a heavily publicized case. These included sequestering juries (Sheppard's jury was not sequestered), moving cases to other jurisdictions, limiting the number of reporters, seating reporters in a particular place in courtrooms, and placing restrictions, or **gag orders**, on lawyers and witnesses. Historically, gag orders have been issued to prohibit the press from releasing preliminary information that might prejudice jury selection. In most instances, however, especially since a Supreme Court review in 1976, gag rules have been struck down as a prior-restraint violation of the First Amendment.

In opposition to gag rules, **shield laws** have favored the First Amendment rights of reporters, protecting them from having to reveal their sources for controversial information used in news stories. The news media have argued that protecting the confidentiality of key sources maintains a reporter's credibility, protects a source from possible retaliation, and serves the public interest in that a source gives readers or viewers information they might not otherwise receive. In the 1960s and early 1970s, when the First Amendment rights of reporters clashed with Sixth Amendment fair-trial concerns, judges usually favored the Sixth Amendment arguments. In 1972, a New Jersey journalist became the first reporter jailed for contempt of court for refusing to identify sources in an investigative probe of the Newark housing authority. After this case, a number of legal measures were developed to protect the news media. By 2003, thirty-one states had enacted some type of shield law, and many other states recognized the reporter's First Amendment rights not to divulge sources. In a few states, however, shield laws do not protect reporters who have been subpoenaed in grand-jury investigations. In 2000, for instance, a reporter from Artois, California, was jailed for contempt of court after he refused to reveal his news source in an article about a California Highway Patrol officer accused of stealing a gun.

Cameras in the Courtroom

When Sam Sheppard was originally convicted in the 1950s, television news was in its infancy and did not play a major role in the coverage of that trial. But by the mid-1990s, particularly during the Simpson criminal trial, TV cameras in the courtroom had become central to public discussions of our legal system. More and more judges and lawyers had come to believe that the presence of cameras made the judicial system more accountable and helped the public learn how U.S. law operated.

This view, however, took a long time to evolve. The debates over intrusive electronic broadcast equipment and photographers actually date to the sensationalized coverage of the Bruno Hauptmann trial in the mid-1930s. Hauptmann was convicted and executed for the kidnap-murder of the nineteen-month-old son of Anne and Charles Lindbergh (the aviation hero who made the first solo flight across the Atlantic Ocean in 1927). During the trial, Hauptmann and his attorney had complained that the circus atmosphere fueled by the presence of radio and flash cameras prejudiced the jury and turned the public against him.

After the trial, the American Bar Association amended a professional-ethics code, Canon 35, stating that electronic equipment in the courtroom detracted "from the essential dignity of the proceedings." Calling for a ban on photographers and radio equipment, the association believed that if such elements were not banned, lawyers would begin playing to audiences and negatively alter the judicial process. For years after the Hauptmann trial, almost every state banned photographic, radio, and TV equipment from courtrooms.

As broadcast equipment became more portable and less obtrusive, however, and as television became the major news source for most Americans, courts gradually reevaluated their bans on broadcast equipment. In fact, in the early 1980s the Supreme Court ruled that the presence of TV equipment did not make it impossible for a fair trial to occur, leaving it up to each state to implement its own system. In 2001, North Dakota became the last of the fifty states to end a complete ban on cameras in courtrooms. Most states still have certain restrictions on television coverage of courtrooms, though, often leaving it up to the discretion of the presiding judge. In 1991, U.S. federal courts began allowing limited coverage of trials. The Supreme Court still bans TV from its proceedings, but in 2000 the court broke its anti-radio rule by permitting delayed broadcasts of the hearings on the Florida vote recount case that determined the winner of the 2000 presidential election.

The judicial system got its very own national cable service when the Courtroom Television Network — Court TV — debuted in 1991. By 2002, the channel was available in nearly sixty-five million homes, carrying both live and taped coverage of trials from around the United States in the daytime, and court-related dramas and reality shows in the evenings. The Simpson criminal trial — the most publicized case in history — gave Court TV its greatest boost in 1994. The channel was selected to provide the one "pool" camera allowed at the trial, supplying all local news channels and the networks with the only footage from inside the courtroom. Before and during the criminal trial, a number of national discussions took place regarding the impact of the courtroom camera. Judge Lance Ito threatened to pull the plug on at least two oc-

● Photographers surround aviator Charles A. Lindbergh (without hat) as he leaves the courthouse in Flemington, N.J., during the trial of Bruno Hauptmann on charges of kidnapping and murdering the Lindbergh baby boy in 1935.

casions—once when the camera briefly panned across an alternate juror, and another time when he thought the camera had zoomed in too tightly on the defendant taking notes. (In Simpson's civil trial, which ended in 1997, the judge banned TV coverage.)

Critical analysis of the first Simpson trial continued long after the outcome. In retrospect, many legal analysts thought that the nine-month duration of the trial—the longest in California history—resulted from too many lawyers overacting for a national audience. Certainly, such intense focus on the case took attention away from other issues that the news media might have covered more fully had the trial not occurred. Still, televising the criminal trial contributed to the democratic process in at least two important ways. First, the Simpson criminal trial gave many people their first sustained glimpse into the strengths and weaknesses of the U.S. legal system. Second, the TV trial focused national attention on the problems of spousal abuse, racial tension, and the need for judicial reform, creating national debates on these issues that went on for months after the trial ended.

The Clinton impeachment hearings and subsequent trial again brought legal matters to the small screen. Covered round-the-clock by CNN, Court TV, MSNBC, CNBC, and Fox News, as well as by two C-Span channels, the Clinton affair gave many members of Congress, formerly unknown outside their own regions, a national platform. Throughout the hearings there just didn't seem to be enough legislators—or law professors—to fill all the talk time on these cable channels. During the 1999 Senate trial, U.S. senators often started their day with TV appearances, conducted their business in the Senate, then spent their evenings once more making the cable rounds to discuss Clinton and the trial. As critics noted, one advantage of extending the trial was the free national TV publicity it afforded senators. But a few senators rejected the spotlight. For example, presidential candidate John McCain, a Republican from Arizona, said that as a sitting impeachment juror during the Clinton trial, it was irresponsible for him to discuss the trial on television.

Curbing the Law's Chilling Effect

As libel law and the growing acceptance of courtroom cameras indicate, the legal process has generally, though not always, tried to ensure that print and other news media are able to cover public issues broadly without fear of reprisals. Since the 1960s especially, legislators have sculpted laws that would not have a chilling effect on the news media, that would not curb their ability to actively pursue and report stories that are in the public interest. In a democracy, we expect journalists to act as watchdogs on public issues of vital importance. Such an expectation necessitates broad speech and press freedom. Because of this First Amendment freedom, as a society we occasionally tolerate pornography, hate speech, and other forms of expression that we may not support personally. We can, however, exercise our own free-speech rights and speak out against—or even boycott—language and expression that we find offensive, demeaning, or hateful.

Film and the First Amendment

When the First Amendment was ratified in 1791, even the most enlightened leaders of our nation could not have predicted the coming of visual media such as film and television. Consequently, new communication technologies have not always received the same kinds of protection as those granted to speech, pamphlets, newspapers, magazines, and books. For example, movies, in existence since the late 1890s, earned speech protection under the law only after a 1952 Supreme Court decision. In addition, broadcast stations, unlike newspapers or magazines, are licensed by the federal government and are subject to legislation that does not affect print media.

Social and Political Pressure on the Movies

During the early part of the twentieth century, movies rose in popularity among European immigrants and others from modest socioeconomic groups. This, in turn, spurred the formation of censorship groups, which believed that the popular new medium would threaten children, incite violence, and undermine morality. The number of nickelodeon theaters—often housed in ramshackle buildings—surged in

● A native of Galveston, Texas, Jack Johnson (1878–1946) was the first black heavyweight boxing champion, from 1908 to 1914. His stunning victory over white champion Jim Jeffries (who had earlier refused to fight black boxers) in 1910 resulted in race riots across the country, and led to a ban on the interstate transportation of boxing films.

1905 and drew the attention of public-health inspectors and city social workers. During this time, according to media historian Douglas Gomery, criticism of movies converged on four areas: "the effects on children, the potential health problems, the negative influences on morals and manners, and the lack of a proper role for educational and religious institutions in the development of movies."[13]

Film-Review Boards

Public pressure on movies came both from conservatives, who saw them as a potential threat to the authority of traditional institutions, and from progressives, who worried that children and adults were more attracted to movie houses than to social organizations and urban education centers. Afraid that movies created an illusory dreamworld, civic leaders publicly escalated their pressure, organizing local review boards that screened movies for their communities. In 1907, the Chicago City Council created an ordinance that gave the police authority to issue permits for a movie's exhibition. By 1920, more than ninety cities in the United States had some type of movie-censorship board made up of vice-squad officers, politicians, or citizen groups. By 1923, twenty-two states had established such boards.

Pressure began to translate into law as politicians, wanting to please their constituencies, began to legislate against films. Support mounted for a federal censorship bill. When Jack Johnson won the heavyweight championship in 1908, boxing films became the target of the first federal law aimed at the motion-picture industry. In 1912, the government outlawed the transportation of boxing movies across state lines. The laws against boxing films, however, had more to do with Johnson's race than with concern over violence in movies. The first black heavyweight champion, he was perceived as a threat to the white community.

The first Supreme Court decision regarding film's protection under the First Amendment was handed down in 1915 and went against the movie industry. In *Mutual v. Ohio*, the Mutual Film Company of Detroit sued the state of Ohio, whose review board had censored a number of the Michigan distributor's films. On appeal, the case arrived at the Supreme Court, which unanimously ruled that film was not a form of speech but "a business pure and simple" and, like a circus, merely a "spectacle" for entertainment with "a special capacity for evil." This ruling would stand as a precedent for thirty-seven years. Although the U.S. movement to create a national censorship board failed, legislation to monitor and control movies, especially those from America, had passed in many other countries.

Industry Self-Regulation

As the film industry expanded after World War I, the impact of public pressure and review boards began to affect movie studios and executives who wanted to ensure control over their economic well-being. In the early 1920s, a series of scandals rocked Hollywood: actress Mary Pickford's divorce and quick marriage to actor

66 **No approval by the Production Code Administration shall be given to the use of . . . damn [or] hell (excepting when the use of said last two words shall be essential and required for portrayal, in proper historical context, of any scene or dialogue based upon historical fact or folklore, or for the presentation in proper literary context of a Biblical, or other religious quotation, or a quotation from a literary work provided that no such use shall be permitted which is intrinsically objectionable or offends good taste).** 99

—Motion Picture Production Code, 1934

Douglas Fairbanks; director William Desmond Taylor's unsolved murder; and actor Wallace Reid's death from a drug overdose. The most sensational scandal involved aspiring actress Virginia Rappe, who died a few days after a wild party in a San Francisco hotel hosted by popular silent-film comedian Fatty Arbuckle. After Rappe's death, the comedian was indicted for rape and manslaughter. After two hung juries, Arbuckle's career was ruined. Censorship boards across the country banned his films, even though he was acquitted at his third trial in 1922. Despite his exoneration, the movie industry tried to send a signal about the kind of values and lifestyles it would tolerate: Arbuckle was banned from acting in Hollywood. He later directed several films under the name Will B. Goode.

In response to the scandals, particularly the first Arbuckle trial, the movie industry formed the Motion Picture Producers and Distributors of America (MPPDA) and hired as its president Will Hays, former postmaster general and Republican National Committee chair. Hays was paid $100,000 annually to clean up "sin city." Known as the Hays Office, the MPPDA attempted to smooth out problems between the public and the industry. Hays blacklisted promising actors or movie extras with even minor police records. Later, he developed an MPPDA public-relations division, which successfully lobbied against a movie censorship rule in Massachusetts and stopped a national movement for a federal law censoring movies.

The Motion Picture Production Code

During the 1930s, the movie business faced a new round of challenges. First, various conservative and religious groups—including the influential Catholic Legion of Decency—increased their scrutiny of the industry. Second, deteriorating economic conditions during the Great Depression forced the industry to tighten self-regulation to keep harmful public pressure at bay. In 1927, the Hays Office had developed a list of "Don'ts and Be Carefuls" to steer producers and directors away from questionable sexual, moral, and social themes. Nevertheless, pressure for a more formal and sweeping code mounted. In the early 1930s, the Hays Office established the Motion Picture Production Code, whose overseers officially stamped almost every Hollywood film with a moral seal of approval.

The code laid out its mission in its first general principle: "No picture shall be produced which will lower the moral standards of those who see it. Hence the sympathy of the audience shall never be thrown to the side of crime, wrong-doing, evil or sin." The self-regulatory code dictated how producers and directors should handle "methods of crime," "repellent subjects," "illegal drug traffic," and "sex hygiene." A section on profanity outlawed a long list of phrases and topics, including "toilet gags" and "traveling salesmen and farmer's daughter jokes." In the late 1930s, the producers of *Gone with the Wind* had to seek a special dispensation so that actor Clark Gable could say "damn." Under "scenes of passion," the code dictated that "excessive and lustful kissing, lustful embraces, suggestive postures and gestures are not to be shown," and it required that "passion should be treated in such a manner as not to stimulate the lower and baser emotions." The section on religion revealed the influences of Jesuit priest Daniel Lord and Catholic publisher Martin Quigley, who helped write the code: "No film or episode may throw ridicule on any religious faith," and "ministers of religion . . . should not be used as comic characters or as villains."

Adopted by 95 percent of the industry, the code influenced nearly every commercial movie made between the mid-1930s and the early 1950s. It also gave the industry a relative degree of freedom, enabling the major studios to remain independent of outside regulation. When television arrived, however, competition from the new family medium forced movie producers to explore more adult subjects.

In 1952, the Supreme Court heard the *Miracle* case—officially *Burstyn v. Wilson*— named for the movie distributor who sued the head of the New York Film Licensing

Board for banning Roberto Rossellini's film *Il Miracolo* (*The Miracle*). A few New York City religious and political leaders considered the 1948 Italian film sacrilegious and pressured the film board for the ban. In the film, an unmarried peasant girl is impregnated by a scheming vagrant (played by Federico Fellini, who also wrote the story). In simple faith, she believes the tramp's story: He is St. Joseph and she has conceived the baby Jesus. The importers of the film argued that censoring it constituted illegal prior restraint; because such an action could not be imposed on a print version of the story, the same freedom should attach to the film. The Supreme Court eventually agreed, declaring movies "a significant medium for the communication of ideas." The decision granted films the same protections as those enjoyed by the print media and other forms of speech. Even more important, the decision rendered most activities of film-review boards unconstitutional, because they had generally been engaged in prior restraint. Although a few local boards survived into the 1990s to handle complaints about movies that were considered obscene, most of them disbanded by the 1970s.

Rating Movie Content

The current voluntary movie rating system—the model for the advisory labels the music business and television now use—developed in the late 1960s after another round of pressure over movie content. *The Pawnbroker* in 1965, for instance, contained brief female nudity, and in 1966 *Who's Afraid of Virginia Woolf?* featured a level of profanity that had not been heard before in a major studio film. In 1966, the movie industry hired Jack Valenti to run the MPAA (Motion Picture Association of America, formerly the MPPDA), and in 1968 he established an industry board to rate movies. Eventually, G, PG, R, and X ratings emerged as guideposts for the suitability of films for various age groups. Prompted by the releases of *Gremlins* and *Indiana Jones and the Temple of Doom,* in 1984 the MPAA added PG–13 and sandwiched it between PG and R to distinguish slightly higher levels of violence or adult themes in movies that might otherwise qualify as PG (see Figure 16.1).

The MPAA copyrighted all ratings designations as trademarks, except for the X rating, which was gradually appropriated as a promotional tool by the pornographic film industry. In fact, between 1972 and 1989 the MPAA stopped issuing the X rating. In 1990, however, based on protests from filmmakers over movies with adult sexual themes that they did not consider pornographic, the industry copyrighted the NC–17 rating —no children age seventeen or under—and awarded the first NC–17 to *Henry & June*. In 1995, *Showgirls* became the first movie to intentionally seek an NC–17 to demonstrate that the rating was commercially viable. However, many theater chains in the mid-1990s refused to carry NC–17 movies, fearing economic sanctions and boycotts by their customers, religious groups, and other concerned citizens. Many newspapers also refused to carry ads for NC–17 films. Panned by the critics, *Showgirls* flopped at the box office. Since then, the NC–17 rating has not proved commercially viable and distributors avoid releasing films with the rating. When films such as *Eyes Wide Shut* (1999) and *American Psycho* (2000) initially received an NC–17 rating, the directors agreed to alter or cut graphic sexual scenes from each of these films in order to secure an R rating.

Figure 16.1 The Voluntary Movie Rating System

Source: © 1996 Motion Picture Association of America, Inc.

Expression over the Airwaves

During the Cold War, a vigorous campaign led by Joseph McCarthy, an ultraconservative senator from Wisconsin, tried to rid both government and the media of so-called communist subversives who were allegedly challenging the American way of life. In 1950, a publication called *Red Channels: The Report of Communist Influence in Radio and Television* aimed "to show how the Communists have been able to carry out their plan of infiltration of the radio and television industry." *Red Channels*, inspired by McCarthy and produced by a group of former FBI agents, named 151 performers, writers, and musicians who were "sympathetic" to communist or "left-wing" causes. Among those named were Leonard Bernstein, Will Geer (who later played the grandfather on *The Waltons*), Dashiell Hammett, Lillian Hellman, Lena Horne, Burgess Meredith, Arthur Miller, Dorothy Parker, Pete Seeger (the labor folksinger who in 1994 received a Kennedy Center Honors Award from President Clinton), Irwin Shaw, and Orson Welles. For a time, all were banned from working in television and radio even though no one on the list was ever charged with a crime.[14]

Although the First Amendment protects an individual's right to hold controversial political views, network executives either sympathized with the anticommunist movement or feared losing ad revenue. At any rate, the networks did not stand up to the communist witch-hunters. In order to work, a blacklisted or "suspected" performer required the support of the program's sponsor. Though *I Love Lucy's* Lucille Ball, who in sympathy with her father once registered to vote as a communist in the 1930s, retained Philip Morris's sponsorship of her popular program, other performers were not as fortunate. Philip Loeb, who played the father on *The Goldbergs*, an early 1950s TV sitcom that came over from radio, found his name listed in *Red Channels*. Gertrude Berg, who owned and starred in the series, supported him. Nevertheless, boycott pressure on the program's sponsor, Sanka coffee, a General Foods brand, forced the company to abandon the program, which was dropped from CBS in 1951. After several months it resurfaced on NBC, but Loeb had been replaced. Four years later, depressed and unable to find work, he committed suicide. Although no evidence was ever introduced to show how entertainment programs circulated communist propaganda, by the early 1950s the TV networks were asking actors and other workers to sign loyalty oaths denouncing communism—a low point for the First Amendment.

● In 1950, the 215-page *Red Channels,* published by American Business Consultants (a group of former FBI agents), placed 151 prominent writers, directors, and performers from radio, movies, and television on a blacklist, many of them simply for sympathizing with left-wing democratic causes. Although no one on the list was ever charged with a crime, many of the talented individuals targeted by *Red Channels* did not work in their professions for years.

The communist witch-hunts demonstrated key differences between print and broadcast protection under the First Amendment—differences that are perhaps best illustrated in legal history. On the one hand, licenses for printers and publishers have been outlawed since the eighteenth century. On the other hand, in the late 1920s commercial broadcasters themselves asked the federal government to step in and regulate the airwaves. At that time, they wanted the government to clear up technical problems, channel noise, noncommercial competition, and amateur interference. Ever since, most broadcasters have been trying to free themselves from the government intrusion they once demanded.

FCC Rules, Broadcasting, and Indecency

Drawing on the scarcity argument (that limited broadcast signals constitute a scarce national resource), the Communications Act of 1934 mandated in Section 309 that broadcasters operate in "the public interest, convenience, or necessity." Since the 1980s, however, with cable increasing channel capacity, station managers have lobbied for "ownership" of their airwave assignments. Although the 1996 Telecommunications Act did not grant such ownership, stations continue to challenge the "public interest" statute. They argue that because the government is not allowed to dictate content in newspapers, it should not be allowed to control licenses or mandate any broadcast programming. (See "Examining Ethics—Media Mergers: Survival of the Biggest" on page 562.)

Print vs. Broadcast Rules

Two cases—*Red Lion Broadcasting Co. v. FCC* (1969) and the *Miami Herald Publishing Co. v. Tornillo* (1974)—demonstrate the historic legal differences between broadcast and print. In the *Red Lion* decision, the operators of the small-town station in Red Lion, Pennsylvania, refused to give airtime to Fred Cook, author of a book that criticized Barry Goldwater, the Republican Party's presidential candidate in 1964. Cook then was verbally attacked by a conservative radio preacher and Goldwater fan, the Reverend Billy James Hargis, and asked for response time from the two hundred stations that carried the Hargis attack. Most stations complied, granting Cook free reply time. But WGCB, the Red Lion station, offered only to sell Cook time. He appealed to the FCC, which ordered the station to give Cook free time. The station refused, claiming that its First Amendment rights granted it control over its program content. On appeal, the Supreme Court sided with the FCC, deciding that whenever a broadcaster's rights conflict with the public interest, it is the public interest that is paramount. In 1969, interpreting broadcasting as different from print, the Supreme Court upheld the constitutionality of the 1934 Communications Act by reaffirming that broadcasters' responsibilities to program in the public interest may outweigh their rights to program whatever they want.

In contrast, five years later, in *Miami Herald Publishing Co. v. Tornillo*, the Supreme Court sided with the newspaper in a case in which a political candidate, Pat Tornillo Jr., requested space to reply to an editorial opposing his candidacy. Previously, Florida had enacted a right-to-reply law, which permitted a candidate to respond, in print, to editorial criticisms from newspapers. Counter to the *Red Lion* decision, the Court in this case struck down the Florida state law as unconstitutional. The Court argued that mandating that a newspaper give a candidate space to reply violated the paper's First Amendment rights to publish what it chose to publish. The two decisions demonstrate that for most of the twentieth century the unlicensed print media received protections under the First Amendment that have not always been available to licensed broadcast media.

Dirty Words and Indecent Speech

Although considered tame in a culture that now includes "shock jock" Howard Stern's lurid sexual programming, *topless radio* in the 1960s featured deejays and callers discussing intimate sexual subjects in the middle of the afternoon. The gov-

June 9, 1969
❝ It is the right of the viewers and listeners, not the right of the broadcasters, which is paramount. . . . ❞

–Supreme Court decision in *Red Lion Broadcasting Co. v. FCC*, 395 U.S. 367

June 25, 1974
❝ A responsible press is an undoubtedly desirable goal, but press responsibility is not mandated by the Constitution and like many other virtues it cannot be legislated. ❞

–Supreme Court decision in *Miami Herald Publishing Co. v. Tornillo*, 418 U.S. 241

EXAMINING ETHICS

Media Mergers: Survival of the Biggest

by Brian Lowry and Sallie Hofmeister

Speculation has been ricocheting across Wall Street about a new round of media mergers, sending broadcast stocks soaring but leaving consumer advocates angry about the possibility of greater corporate concentration of information.

The widely conflicting emotions were triggered by a federal court ruling that has opened the door for entertainment conglomerates to capture larger chunks of the national TV audience.

In its February 2002 ruling, the court ordered the Federal Communications Commission to reconsider its rule preventing broadcast corporations from reaching more than 35% of households with televisions. The court also set aside a rule that prevented companies from owning a cable system and a TV station in the same market. Investors, knowing that FCC Chairman Michael K. Powell is a fan of deregulation, saw the court order as practically an invitation for major broadcasters to swallow smaller ones. Giant cable operators such as AOL Time Warner could create an even broader empire by buying companies that own TV stations.

The largest deals, however, might not materialize for some time because the strongest buyers are suffering from operating troubles, the recession, and retrenchments of their own.

"It's too premature to predict whether this is terrible or good, or just how things will play out," said Blair Levin, an analyst at brokerage firm Legg Mason. "This is like a chessboard with 64 potential spaces to move and everybody's moves have ripple effects."

Potential network buyers—such as NBC, CBS, ABC, and Fox—insist that further consolidation would only strengthen the broadcast industry.

Fox, for example, says the company has been able to bolster news operations and entertainment choices at the stations it has purchased.

That's why network executives say a relaxation—if not elimination—of FCC rules is in the public interest.

FCC's Powell agrees and sees another reason for softening the rules. He has called the media "more diverse in 2001 than at any time in their history" because of the Internet and the proliferation of cable channels.

But critics have a different view.

"Even if you live in a 500-channel universe, what you get from your [cable or satellite] box is delivered to you by four companies," said Marty Kaplan, associate dean of the USC Annenberg School for Communication and director of the Norman Lear Center. He called industry consolidation "a real threat to diversity."

Groups entrenched in the entertainment industry also have grown uneasy watching the growth of conglomerates, prompting the Writers Guild of America recently to call for hearings on the ramifications of media concentration.

In an FCC filing signed by some of the industry's most influential writers, the guild maintained that consolidation of television "has adversely affected the public interest, . . . resulted in the lack of diversity and has caused creativity to suffer, . . . [depriving] the American public of access to a great variety of opinions and sensibilities."

Consumer advocates are most concerned about the ramifications on news operations, particularly in small cities, where mergers have chipped away at the number of voices in the market.

Some media critics contend that the diminishing resources spent on news-gathering has left the public uninformed about important world events, including the international context of last fall's terrorist attacks.

"Especially after September 11, people recognize the media's role in shaping the public debate," said Jeff Chester, executive director of the nonprofit Center for Digital Democracy.

If wholesale TV station sales do take place, what has happened in radio could provide a template.

Clear Channel Communications Inc.—owner of nearly 1,200 stations—and CBS led the merger frenzy within the radio business, with one of the two companies controlling as much as 40% of the stations in many of the nation's largest markets.

Deregulation also has led to layoffs, along with fewer locally produced programs, including those for children.

Because fortunes in television rise and fall based on ratings, the public ultimately will have final say. Still, USC's Kaplan sees unfettered consolidation as making the industry less responsive.

"It's like the phone company was when Lily Tomlin was making fun of it," he said. "'We don't care. We're the phone company.' Well, in this case, 'We're the TV company.'"

Source: Abridged version of Brian Lowry and Sallie Hofmeister, "Ruling on FCC Turns Up the Volume on Media Mergers," *Los Angeles Times,* February 21, 2002.

ernment curbed the practice in 1973, when the chairman of the FCC denounced topless radio as "a new breed of air pollution . . . with the suggestive, coaxing, pearshaped tones of the smut-hustling host."[15] After an FCC investigation, a couple of stations lost their licenses, some were fined, and topless radio was checked temporarily. It reemerged in the 1980s, only with modern doctors and therapists—instead of deejays—offering intimate counsel over the airwaves.

In theory, communication law prevents the government from censoring broadcast content. Accordingly, the government may not interfere with programs or engage in prior restraint, although it may punish broadcasters after the fact. Over the years, a handful of radio stations have had their licenses suspended or denied after an unfavorable FCC review of past programming records. Concerns over indecent broadcast programming probably date from 1937. That year, NBC was scolded by the FCC after running a sketch featuring comedian-actress Mae West on ventriloquist Edgar Bergen's network program. West had the following conversation with Bergen's famous wooden dummy, Charlie McCarthy:

WEST:	That's all right. I like a man that takes his time. Why don't you come home with me? I'll let you play in my woodpile . . . you're all wood and a yard long. . . .
CHARLIE:	Oh, Mae, don't, don't . . . don't be so rough. To me love is peace and quiet.
WEST:	That ain't love—that's sleep.[16]

After the sketch, West did not appear on radio for years. Ever since, the FCC has periodically fined or reprimanded stations for indecent programming, especially during times when children might be listening.

The current precedent for regulating radio indecency stems from one complaint to the FCC in 1973. In the middle of the afternoon, Pacifica's WBAI in New York aired George Carlin's famous comedy album about the seven dirty words that could not be uttered by broadcasters. A father, riding in a car with his fifteen-year-old son, heard the program and complained to the FCC, which sent WBAI a simple letter of reprimand. Although no fine was involved, the station appealed on principle and won its case in court. The FCC persisted, however, appealing all the way to the Supreme Court. Although no court has legally defined indecency, the Supreme Court's unexpected ruling in 1978 sided with the FCC and upheld the agency's authority to require broadcasters to air adult programming at later times. The Court ruled that so-called indecent programming, though not in violation of federal obscenity laws, was a nuisance (like a pig in a parlor, the Court said) and could be restricted to late-evening hours to protect children. The commission intended to ban indecent programs from most stations between 6 A.M. and 10 P.M. In 1990, the FCC tried to ban such programs entirely. Although a federal court ruled this move unconstitutional, it still upheld the time restrictions intended to protect children. This ruling lies at the heart of the indecency fines—totaling more than $1 million—that the FCC has leveled over the last several years against Howard Stern's syndicated morning program. Still, penalties for indecency on the radio are not frequently enforced. David Tillotson, the attorney who defended WBAI in its case, recommends that stations delay paying fines, because doing so is an admission of culpability, and that "there is a reasonable chance" that the U.S. government will not take action to collect the fines.[17]

Political Broadcasts and Equal Opportunity

In addition to indecency rules, another law that the print media do not encounter is **Section 315** of the 1934 Communications Act, which mandates that during elections broadcast stations must provide equal opportunities and response time for qualified political candidates. In other words, if broadcasters give or sell time to one candidate, they must give or sell the same opportunity to others. Local broadcasters and networks have fought this law for years, complaining that it has required them to include poorly funded third-party candidates in political discussions. Broadcasters claim that because no Section 315–type rule applies to newspapers or magazines, the law violates their First Amendment right to control content. In fact, because of this rule, many stations have avoided all political programming. Ironically in these cases, a rule meant to serve the public interest by increasing communication backfired as stations decided to skirt the law.

The TV networks managed to get the law amended in 1959 to exempt newscasts, press conferences, and other events—such as political debates—that qualify as news. For instance, if a senator running for office appears in a news story, candidates running against him or her cannot invoke Section 315 and demand free time. Because of this provision, many stations from the late 1960s through the 1980s pulled

TV movies starring Ronald Reagan. Because his film appearances did not count as bona fide news stories, politicians opposing Reagan as a presidential candidate could demand free time in markets that ran old Reagan movies. Supporters of the equal-opportunity law argue that it has provided forums for lesser-known candidates representing views counter to those of the Democratic and Republican parties. They further note that one of the few ways for alternative candidates to circulate their messages widely is to buy political ads, thus limiting serious outside contenders to wealthy candidates, such as Ross Perot, Steve Forbes, or members of the Bush or Kennedy families.

The Demise of the Fairness Doctrine

Considered an important corollary to Section 315, the **Fairness Doctrine** was to controversial issues what Section 315 is to political speech. Initiated in 1949, this FCC rule required stations (1) to air and engage in controversial-issue programs that affected their communities, and (2) when offering such programming, to provide competing points of view. Antismoking activist John Banzhaf ingeniously invoked the Fairness Doctrine to force cigarette advertising off television in 1971. When the FCC mandated antismoking public-service announcements to counter "controversial" smoking commercials, tobacco companies decided to accept an outright ban rather than tolerate a flood of antismoking spots authorized by the Fairness Doctrine.

With little public debate, the Fairness Doctrine ended in 1987 after a federal court ruled that it was merely a regulation rather than an extension of Section 315 law. Over the years, broadcasters had argued that the doctrine forced many of them to play down controversial issues; they claimed that mandating opposing views every time a program covered a controversial issue was a burden not required of the print media. Since 1987, there has been periodic interest in reviving the Fairness Doctrine. Its supporters argue that broadcasting is fundamentally different from—and more pervasive than—the print media, requiring greater accountability to the public. Although many broadcasters disagree, supporters of fairness rules insist that as long as broadcasters are licensed as public trustees of the airwaves—unlike newspaper or magazine publishers—legal precedent permits the courts and the FCC to demand responsible content and behavior from radio and TV stations.

By the mid-1990s, broadcast and cable operators were increasingly demanding the same First Amendment rights as the print media. This pressure, combined with a suspect belief (until the stock market collapse in 2001–02) that a free market can solve most economic problems, allowed a relaxation of the rules governing broadcasting and cable. Still, public concerns about visual violence and children's programming kept regulatory issues prominent during the presidential campaigns of 1992, 1996, and 2000. But questions about the negative impact of concentrated media

> **"** There is no doubt about the unique impact of radio and television. But this fact alone does not justify government regulation. In fact, quite the contrary. We should recall that the printed press was the only medium of mass communication in the early days of the republic—and yet this did not deter our predecessors from passing the First Amendment to prohibit abridgement of its freedoms. **"**
>
> —Chief Judge David Bazelon, U.S. court of appeals, 1972

ownership rarely surfaced. In fact, when they did surface, they were raised most frequently by activist and Green Party candidate Ralph Nader.

Should deregulation accelerate, however, the remaining public and noncommercial broadcast outlets are at risk. For example, Jesse Ventura, the former Reform Party governor of Minnesota, made eliminating government funding of public radio and television a priority for his state in 1999. Public broadcasting already faced severe revenue cutbacks in the mid-1990s, so more deregulation of the communications industry might cause a recurrence of the problems of the late 1920s and early 1930s. As we noted in Chapter 4, the Great Depression crippled noncommercial broadcasters because many of them were forced to sell or transfer their licenses to commercial interests. Although Congress in 1996 mandated that the broadcast networks carry three hours of educational programs a week, public radio and television still offer the bulk of programming that is not commercially viable. Yet even public radio is doing less for free speech. A 1996 law required National Public Radio (NPR) affiliate stations to provide free airtime to political candidates. In 2000, after some candidates took notice of the law and asked for airtime in the election, NPR effectively lobbied Congress to be released from the requirement, before future candidates could make demands on public radio time. In addition, NPR, with the help of commercial radio's National Association of Broadcasters, successfully lobbied to have the FCC's plan for a new class of nonprofit, low-power FM stations severely curtailed before the first licenses were issued in 2001.[18]

★ Cyberspace, Expression, and Democracy

Since the beginnings of the United States more than two hundred years ago, there have been periods of war and heightened national security in which some in the government and some who consider themselves patriots attempt to suppress dissenting views. The time following the September 11, 2001, terrorist attacks and the 2003 invasion of Iraq mark two of those periods. Yet another concern for advocates of democratic expression has been the barriers to communicating in a commercialized mass-media system that has generally favored corporate interests and media industries. For example, it is far easier for large corporations and advertisers such as Disney or General Motors to buy commercial speech than it is for small grassroots organizations that have important messages but limited finances. As a result, messages that counter mainstream culture might appear only in alternative magazines or on cable-access channels, where entry is cheap but audience reach is limited.

Communication Policy in Cyberspace

Another arena that increases the voices—and noise—circulating in culture is the Internet. Its current global expansion is comparable to the early days of broadcasting, when economic and technological growth outstripped law and regulation. At that time, noncommercial experiments by amateurs and engineering students provided a testing ground that commercial interests later exploited for profit. Indeed, before the Radio Act of 1927, many noncommercial groups experimented extensively with the possibilities of the new broadcast medium.

In much the same way, "amateurs," students, and various interest groups have explored and extended the communication possibilities of the Internet. They have experimented so successfully that commercial vendors are now racing to buy up pieces of the information highway. As in radio in the 1920s, the Internet's noncommercial developers in the 1990s and early 2000s have been selling off services to commercial entrepreneurs. This is especially true of university consortiums, which

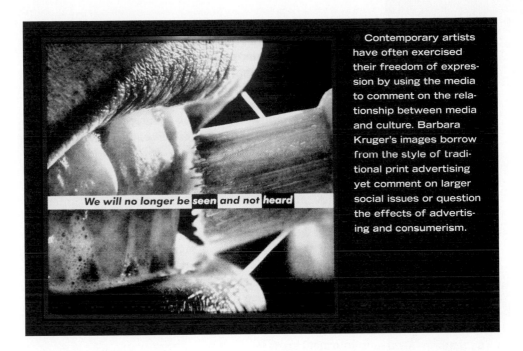

Contemporary artists have often exercised their freedom of expression by using the media to comment on the relationship between media and culture. Barbara Kruger's images borrow from the style of traditional print advertising yet comment on larger social issues or question the effects of advertising and consumerism.

We will no longer be seen and not heard

had been running most of the regional Internet services. As in radio, experimenting and risk-taking took place at the noncommercial level before commercial adventurers stepped in to explore and exploit the profit possibilities.

The last serious widespread public debate on mass-media ownership occurred in the early 1930s and ended with the passage of the 1934 Communications Act and the defeat of the Wagner-Hatfield Amendment (which would have reserved 25 percent of the broadcast spectrum for noncommercial radio). Public conversations about the Internet have not typically been about ownership questions. Instead, the debates—often triggered by the news media—have focused on First Amendment issues such as civility and pornography in cyberspace. Reporters, in fact, tend to view Internet issues as entrepreneurial business stories ("What company is marketing the next software breakthrough?") with free-speech implications ("Who is using the highway for pornographic purposes?"). Not unlike the public's concern over television's sexual and violent images, the scrutiny of the Internet is mainly about harmful images and information in cyberspace, not about who controls it and for what purposes.

For example, one of the issues largely ignored in public debates has been the increasing commercialization of search engines. In an effort to create more revenue beyond the sales of banner ads, most search engines and directories are imposing listing fees: They rank search results according to who has paid the most (pay-for-position); they charge sites to ensure them a place in their database (pay-for-inclusion); and they often rank sites according to popularity—a criterion that often prioritizes the commercial sites that advertise the most, and/or link to the most

66 One of the most striking paradoxes of Internet culture is that children are the most computer literate among us, but their vulnerability to on-line predators prevents their being able to enjoy or explore freely what is likely to be the defining medium of their lives.99 —Denise Caruso, *New York Times*, 1998

pages. Most search engine users assume that their search term queries generate an objective list of relevant sites, but that is becoming far from the case. As some of the most popular portals to the Web, search engines increasingly behave less like information libraries and more like paid infomercials.

As we watch the rapid expansion of the Internet worldwide, an important question confronts us: Will the Internet continue to develop democratically rather than hierarchically, evading government or corporate plans to contain it, change it, and closely monitor who has access? In the early days of broadcasting, commercial interests became dominant partly because the companies running radio (such as the Hearst Corporation, which also owned chains of newspapers and magazines) did not report on ownership questions as serious news stories. It was not in their economic interest to do so. Today, once again, it has not been in the news media's economic interest to organize or lead the ownership debate; the major print and broadcast owners, after all, are heavily invested in the Internet.

Critics and observers hope that a vigorous debate will develop on new communication technologies—a debate that will go beyond First Amendment issues. The promise of the Internet as a democratic forum—adding millions of new users each month—encourages the formation of all sorts of regional, national, and global interest groups. Whether such cyber communities could eventually help to frame and solve society-level problems remains at issue.

A positive sign is that global movements abound that use the Internet to fight political forms of censorship. The Digital Freedom Network, for example, has circulated material that has been banned or restricted in certain countries, including excerpts from dissident Chinese writer Wei Jingsheng and Indonesian novelist Pramoedya Ananta Toer, and it also conducts global online chats with people such as Myanmar's pro-democracy leader and Nobel Peace Prize winner Aung San Suu Kyi. The organization also sends e-mail notices to members and helps them easily send letters of protest to international officials. In this example, the digital highway works as a global freeway—a democratic communication "weapon," bypassing both government bans and political restrictions. Just as fax machines, satellites, and home videos helped to document and expedite the fall of totalitarian regimes in Eastern Europe in the late 1980s, Internet services help to spread the word and activate social change today.

● Thai singers Thai Thanawut (right) and Peter Kopdalendo jump on a pile of pirate disks during a destruction of counterfeit goods at a police compound in Bangkok in 2000. Thai police destroyed more than 3,500 fake designer watches and 136,000 video and music cassettes and CDs in advance of a major United Nations trade conference to show the government's commitment to respecting intellectual property rights.

Watchdog Citizens

For most of our nation's history, citizens have counted on journalism to monitor abuses in government and business. During the muckraking period in the early part of the twentieth century, writers like Ida Tarbell, Upton Sinclair, and Sinclair Lewis made strong contributions in reporting corporate expansion and social change. Unfortunately, however, stories on business issues today are usually reduced to consumer-affairs reporting. In other words, when a labor strike or a factory recall is covered, the reporter mainly tries to answer the question "How do these events affect consumers?" Although this is an important news angle, other questions remain:

"How does the strike affect the families and future of workers and managers?" and "What is the role of unions and manufacturing industries as we begin the twenty-first century?" At this point, citizen discussions about media ownership or labor-management ethics are not part of the news frame that journalists typically use. When companies announce mergers, reporters do not routinely question the economic wisdom or social impact of such changes. Instead, they tend to write stories about how individual consumers will be affected.

At one level, journalists have been compromised by the ongoing frenzy of media mergers involving newspapers, TV stations, radio stations, and Internet corporations. As Bill Kovach, former curator of Harvard's Nieman Foundation for Journalism, pointed out, "This rush to merge mainly entertainment organizations that have news operations with companies deeply involved in doing business with the government raises ominous questions about the future of watchdog journalism."[19] In other words, how can journalists adequately cover and lead discussions on issues of media ownership when the very companies they work for are the prime buyers and sellers of major news-media outlets?

With the news media increasingly compromised by their complex relations to their corporations, it is becoming increasingly important that the civic role of watchdog be shared by citizens as well as journalists. After all, the First Amendment protects not only the news media's free-speech rights but the rights of all of us to speak out. Mounting concerns over who can afford access to the media go to the heart of free expression.

As we struggle to determine the future of converging print, electronic, and digital media and to broaden the democratic spirit underlying media technology, we need to stay engaged in spirited public debates about media ownership and control, about the differences between commercial speech and free expression. As citizens, we need to pay attention to who is included and excluded from the opportunities not only to buy products but to speak out and shape the cultural landscape. To accomplish this, we need to challenge our journalists and our leaders. More important, we need to challenge ourselves to become watchdogs—critical consumers and engaged citizens—who learn from the past, care about the present, and map mass media's future.

www.

To create an individualized study plan for Chapter 16, go to the Interactive *Media and Culture* Online Study Guide at: bedfordstmartins.com/ mediaculture

REVIEW QUESTIONS

The Origins of Free Expression and a Free Press

1. What is the basic philosophical concept that underlies America's notion of free expression?

2. Explain the various models of the news media that exist under different political systems.

3. How has censorship been defined historically?

4. What is the significance of the Pentagon Papers and the *Progressive* magazine cases?

5. Why is the case of *New York Times v. Sullivan* so significant in First Amendment history?

6. What does a public figure have to do to win a libel case? What are the main defenses that a newspaper can use to thwart a charge of libel?

7. What is the legal significance of the *Falwell v. Flynt* case?

8. How does a court determine, in a legal sense, whether a magazine article constitutes obscenity?

Film and the First Amendment

9. Why were films not constitutionally protected as a form of speech until 1952?

10. Why did film-review boards develop, and why did they eventually disband?

11. How did both the Motion Picture Production Code and the current movie rating system come into being?

Expression over the Airwaves

12. The government and the courts view print and broadcasting as different forms of expression. What are the major differences?

13. What is the significance of Section 315 of the Communications Act of 1934?

14. Why didn't broadcasters like the Fairness Doctrine?

Cyberspace, Expression, and Democracy

15. What are the similarities and differences between the debates over broadcast ownership in the 1920s and Internet ownership today?

16. Why is the Internet a potentially more democratic form than broadcasting?

QUESTIONING THE MEDIA

1. Have you ever had an experience in which you thought personal or public expression went too far and should be curbed? Explain. How might you remedy this situation?

2. If you owned a community newspaper and had to formulate a policy for your editors about which letters from readers appear in a limited space on your editorial page, what kinds of letters would you eliminate, and why? Would you be acting as a censor in this situation? Why or why not?

3. The writer A. J. Liebling once said that freedom of the press belonged only to those who owned one. Explain why you agree or disagree.

4. What do you think of the movie rating system the industry now uses? Should it be changed? Why or why not?

5. Should the Fairness Doctrine be revived? Why or why not?

SEARCHING THE INTERNET

http://www.freedomforum.org

The Freedom Forum deals with all First Amendment issues, including religion, free press, free speech, assembly, and technology. It also includes original articles as well as stories from the Associated Press.

http://www.freeexpression.org

The Free Expression Network is a national coalition of organizations and individuals united in the belief that free expression is the indispensable precondition of liberty.

http://www.rcfp.org

The Reporters Committee for Freedom of the Press, started in 1970, serves as a clearinghouse for press freedom and freedom of speech issues, including up-to-date reports on libel, freedom of information, and shield law cases.

http://ericnuzum.com/banned

Eric Nuzum maintains this site, which documents banned and censored (or otherwise altered) music, beginning in the 1940s, and keeps track of current music censorship issues.

http://www.fcc.gov/eb/broadcast/obscind.html

This site posts the Federal Communications Commission's obscene and indecent broadcast enforcement policies, and lists of U.S. radio stations with recent violations of the regulations.

THE CRITICAL PROCESS

In Brief

If you were the owner of a community newspaper, what would be your policy on accepting advertising for pornographic movie theaters and movies rated NC–17? Justify whatever policy you develop.

In Depth

In small groups, investigate the age restriction policies of local retail outlets that carry media content for mature audiences.

Description. First, call or visit local movie theaters, video/DVD stores, music retailers, magazine shops, and outlets that carry video games. What are their respective policies for (1) selling tickets or selling/renting videos to the proper age groups for rated movies, especially those rated R and NC–17; (2) selling recordings with parental advisory labels; (3) displaying and selling adult magazines; and (4) selling video games rated "mature" or "adults only"? (You can review video game ratings from the Entertainment Software Rating Board at <http://www.esrb.org/>.) Second, you can also interview customers of these media outlets. Have their buying/renting experiences been restricted according to age, or do retailers ignore age guidelines?

Analysis. Look for patterns. Are there consistent policies across media outlets; for example, do all movie theaters have the same admissions policies? Are age policies consistent across all four types of outlets; for example, are magazine shops more or less strict on enforcement than music stores or video game retailers?

Interpretation. What are the meanings of the patterns? You might wish to consider the main clientele of each media outlet. For example, are movie theaters highly dependent on young audiences, even for R-rated films?

Evaluation. Are age restrictions for media content a good idea? Should enforcement be left up to retailers, or should some other entity become involved? Is censorship a concern? What responsibilities do marketers of media content have on this issue? What responsibilities do parents have? What responsibilities do underage customers have?

KEY TERMS

authoritarian model, 540
communist or state model, 541
libertarian model, 541
social-responsibility model, 541
Fourth Estate, 542
prior restraint, 542

copyright, 545
slander, 547
libel, 547
actual malice, 547
qualified privilege, 549
invasion of privacy, 551

obscenity, 552
gag orders, 553
shield laws, 553
Section 315, 564
Fairness Doctrine, 565

bibliography

Chapter 1

1. Neil Postman, *Amusing Ourselves to Death: Public Discourse in the Age of Show Business* (New York: Penguin Books, 1984), 19.
2. James W. Carey, *Communication as Culture: Essays on Media and Society* (Boston: Unwin Hyman, 1989), 203.
3. Postman, *Amusing Ourselves to Death*, 65. See also Elizabeth Eisenstein, *The Printing Press as an Agent of Change*, 2 vols. (Cambridge: Cambridge University Press, 1979).
4. See Plato, *The Republic*, Book II, 377B.
5. For a historical discussion of culture, see Lawrence Levine, *Highbrow/Lowbrow: The Emergence of Cultural Hierarchy in America* (Cambridge, Mass.: Harvard University Press, 1988).
6. For an example of this critical position, see Allan Bloom, *The Closing of the American Mind: How Higher Education Has Failed Democracy and Impoverished the Souls of Today's Students* (New York: Simon & Schuster, 1987).
7. For overviews of this position, see Postman, *Amusing Ourselves to Death;* and Stuart Ewen, *Captains of Consciousness: Advertising and the Social Roots of the Consumer Culture* (New York: McGraw-Hill, 1976).
8. See Carey, *Communication as Culture.*
9. For more on this idea, see Cecelia Tichi, *Electronic Hearth: Creating an American Television Culture* (New York: Oxford University Press, 1991), 187–188.
10. See Jon Katz, "Rock, Rap and Movies Bring You the News," *Rolling Stone*, March 5, 1992, p. 33.

Examining Ethics: Staging Stunts Takes TV to New Low, p. 14.

1. See Anna Mundow, "It's Like Total Excrement; Forget ABC!—The New Key Demographic Is the Young, Americanised Male," *The Irish Times*, August 3, 2002, magazine sec. p. 75 ff.
2. See Paul Gallager, "Springer Sued over 'Murderous' Show," *The Scotsman*, July 12, 2002, p. 5.
3. See Philip Kennicott, "Theater of the Odd Birds; With Jenny Jones, Reality Is Beside the Point," *Washington Post*, April 18, 2002, Style sec. p. C01.
4. For reference and guidance on media ethics, see Clifford Christians, Mark Fackler, and Kim Rotzoll, *Media Ethics: Cases & Moral Reasoning*, 4th ed. (White Plains, N.Y.: Longman, 1995); and Thomas H. Bivins, "A Worksheet for Ethics Instruction and Exercises in Reason," *Journalism Educator* (Summer 1993): 4–16.

The Global Village: Bedouins, Camels, Transistors, and Coke, p. 30

1. Václav Havel, "A Time for Transcendence," *Utne Reader* (January/February 1995): 53.
2. Dan Rather, "The Threat to Foreign News," *Newsweek* (July 17, 1989): 9.

CHAPTER 2

1. Daniel Burstein and David Kline, *Road Warriors: Dreams and Nightmares along the Information Highway* (New York: Dutton, 1995), 105.
2. Nielsen NetRatings, "Global Net Population at Least 459m," August 31, 2001, <http://www.nua.ie/surveys/>.
3. Burstein and Kline, *Road Warriors*, 101–130.
4. Charles C. Mann, "The End of Moore's Law," *Technology Review*, May/June 2000, <http://www.techreview.com/articles/may00/mann.htm>.
5. Nicholas Negroponte, *Being Digital* (New York: Alfred A. Knopf, 1995), 23.
6. Hobbes's Internet Timeline <http://www.zakon.org/robert/internet/timeline/>.
7. Noah Robinson, "Browser Beware," *Brill's Content* (July/August 1998): 40–44.
8. Burstein and Kline, *Road Warriors*, 104.
9. Amy Harmon, "'Hacktivists' of All Persuasions Take Their Struggle to the Web," *New York Times*, October 31, 1998, p. A1.
10. Steve Lawrence and Lee C. Giles, "Accessibility of Information on the Web," *Nature* 400 (July 8, 1999): 107–109.
11. Amy Harmon, "The Rebel Code," *New York Times Magazine*, February 21, 1999, pp. 34–37.
12. Florence Olsen, "Colleges Collaborate on Software That Would Allow Ad-Free 'Portal' Sites," *Chronicle of Higher Education*, June 9, 2000, <http://chronicle.com>.
13. See Lawrence and Giles, "Accessibility of Information." Also see <http://www.searchterms.com> for a listing of the most popular search terms.
14. See Federal Trade Commission, *Privacy Online: Fair Information Practices in the Electronic Marketplace*, May 2000, <http://www.ftc.gov/reports/privacy2000.pdf>.
15. Also see Robert Scheer, "Nowhere to Hide," *Yahoo! Internet Life* (October 2000): 100–102.
16. The Annie E. Casey Foundation, "Connecting Kids to Technology: Challenges and Opportunities," June 2002, p. 3, <http://www.aecf.org/publications.pdfs/snapshot_june2002.pdf>.

17. Kris Axtman, "Houston to Make Computing a Right, Not a Privilege," *Christian Science Monitor,* August 22, 2001, p. 2.
18. Mark Fineman, "Internet Arrives in Haiti, and Some Wonder about Priorities," *Boston Globe,* July 23, 2000, p. A14.
19. Marc Gunther, "What's Your Stake in It All: Information Highway Looks Like a Rough Road," *Detroit Free Press,* November 18, 1993, p. D1.
20. See About.com's "Urban Legends and Folklore," <http://urbanlegends.about.com/science/urbanlegends/>.
21. Douglas Gomery, "In Search of the Cybermarket," *Wilson Quarterly* (Summer 1994): 10.

CHAPTER 3

1. Thomas Edison, quoted in Marshall McLuhan, *Understanding Media* (New York: McGraw-Hill, 1964), 276.
2. See Bruce Tucker, " 'Tell Tchaikovsky the News': Postmodernism, Popular Culture and the Emergence of Rock 'n' Roll," *Black Music Research Journal* 9, no. 2 (Fall 1989): 280.
3. LeRoi Jones, *Blues People* (New York: Morrow Quill, 1963), 168.
4. Mick Jagger, quoted in Jann S. Wenner, "Jagger Remembers," *Rolling Stone,* December 14, 1995, p. 66.
5. See Mac Rebennack (Dr. John) with Jack Rummel, *Under a Hoodoo Moon* (New York: St. Martin's Press, 1994), 58.
6. Little Richard, quoted in Charles White, *The Life and Times of Little Richard: The Quasar of Rock* (New York: Harmony Books, 1984), 65–66.
7. Quoted in Dave Marsh and James Bernard, *The New Book of Rock Lists* (New York: Fireside, 1994), 15.
8. Tucker, " 'Tell Tchaikovsky the News,' " 287.
9. Ed Ward, quoted in Ward, Geoffrey Stokes, and Ken Tucker, *Rock of Ages: The Rolling Stone History of Rock & Roll* (New York: Rolling Stone Press, 1986), 89.
10. Stuart Goldman, "That Old Devil Music," *National Review,* February 24, 1989, p. 29.
11. See Gerri Hershey, *Nowhere to Run: The Story of Soul Music* (New York: Penguin Books, 1984).
12. See Karen Schoemer, "Rockers, Models and the New Allure of Heroin," *Newsweek,* August 26, 1996, 50–54.
13. K. Tucker, in Ward, Stokes, and Tucker, *Rock of Ages,* 521.
14. Ibid., 560.
15. Stephen Thomas Erlewine, "Nirvana," in *All Music Guide: The Best CDs, Albums, & Tapes,* 2nd ed., Michael Erlewine, ed. (San Francisco: Miller Freeman Books, 1994), 233.
16. See Mikal Gilmore, "Puff Daddy," *Rolling Stone,* August 7, 1997, pp. 50–56, 70–72.
17. Associated Press, "Music Industry Targets Net Swappers," *New York Times,* October 4, 2002, <http://www.nytimes.com>.
18. IFPI, "Fighting Piracy," <http://www.ifpi.org/antipiracy/piracy2001.html>.
19. Amy Harmon, "Unknown Musicians Finding Payoffs through the Internet Jukebox," *New York Times on the Web,* July 20, 2000, <http://www.nytimes.com/library/tech/yr/mo/biztech/articles/20tune.html>.
20. Nat Hentoff, "Many Dreams Fueled Long Development of U.S. Music," *Milwaukee Journal*/United Press International, February 26, 1978, p. 2.

Applied Critical Process: Music's Mooks and Midriffs: Does the Music Industry Sell Music or Sexual Stereotypes?, p. 98.

1. "Sheryl Crow Tells Caroline Sullivan about Britney, Beyoncé, and the State of Rock and Roll," *The Guardian,* March 29, 2002, p. 6.

2. See "A talk with the producers of 'The Merchants of Cool,'" <http://www.pbs.org/wgbh/pages/frontline/shows/cool/etc/producers.html>.

CHAPTER 4

1. Eric Boehlert, "Suit: Clear Channel Is an Illegal Monopoly," Salon.com, August 8, 2001, <http://www.salon.com/ent/clear_channel/2001/08/08/antitrust/>.
2. Tom Lewis, *Empire of the Air: The Men Who Made Radio* (New York: HarperCollins, 1991), 181.
3. Ibid., 32.
4. Ibid., 73.
5. For a full discussion of early broadcast history and the formation of RCA, see Eric Barnouw, *Tube of Plenty* (New York: Oxford University Press, 1982); Susan Douglas, *Inventing American Broadcasting 1899–1922* (Baltimore: Johns Hopkins University Press, 1987); and Christopher Sterling and John Kitross, *Stay Tuned: A Concise History of American Broadcasting* (Belmont, Calif.: Wadsworth, 1990).
6. Lowell Thomas, quoted in Lawrence Lichty and Malachi Topping, *American Broadcasting: A Source Book on the History of Radio and Television* (New York: Hastings House, 1975), 229.
7. Neil Strauss, "Pay-for-Play on the Air But This Rendition Is Legal," *New York Times,* March 31, 1998, pp. A1, A21.
8. Neil Strauss, "Birth and Rebirth on the Airwaves," *New York Times,* July 21, 1996, pp. 26–27.
9. See Ed Ward, Geoffrey Stokes, and Ken Tucker, *Rock of Ages: The Rolling Stone History of Rock & Roll* (New York: Rolling Stone Press, 1986), 484.
10. David Leonhardt, "Let a Thousand New Voices Bloom," *New York Times,* July 16, 2000, sec. 4, p. 4.
11. Ed Shane, "The State of the Industry: Radio's Shifting Paradigm," *Journal of Radio Studies* 5, no. 2 (1998): 1–7.
12. "Statement of FCC Chairman William E. Kennard on Low Power FM Radio Initiative," March 27, 2000, <www.fee.gov/Speeches/Kennard/Statements/2000/stwek024.html>.
13. Tony Sanders, Duncan's American Radio, June 22, 2001, <http://www.duncanradio.com/PR%20on%20Radio%20Ownership.htm>.

CHAPTER 5

1. See Elizabeth Kolbert, "Americans Despair of Popular Culture," *New York Times,* August 20, 1995, sec. 2, pp. 1, 23.
2. J. Fred MacDonald, *One Nation under Television: The Rise and Decline of Network TV* (Chicago: Nelson-Hall Publishers, 1994), 132.
3. Ibid., 70.
4. Edgar Bergen, quoted in MacDonald, *One Nation under Television,* 78.
5. See Horace Newcomb, *TV: The Most Popular Art* (Garden City, N.Y.: Anchor Books, 1974), 31, 39.
6. Ibid., 35.
7. Paddy Chayefsky, quoted in Eric Barnouw, *Tube of Plenty: The Evolution of American Television,* rev. ed. (New York: Oxford University Press, 1982), 163.
8. Barnouw, *Tube of Plenty,* 163.
9. Ibid., 163.
10. MacDonald, *One Nation under Television,* 181.

11. See Bill Carter, "Cadillac-Sized Hits by the VW of Producers," *New York Times*, January 22, 1996, p. C1.
12. See Richard Campbell, "Don Hewitt's Durable Hour," *Columbia Journalism Review* (September–October 1993): 25.
13. "Who Is Paper Tiger Anyway?," December 15, 2002, <www.papertiger.org>.
14. Quoted in B. J. Bullert, "Public Television: Safe Programming and Faustian Bargains," *Chronicle of Higher Education*, September 19, 1998, p. B7.

Tracking Technology: Digital TV and the End of Analog, p. 150

1. See Joel Brinkley, "F.C.C. Clears New Standard for Digital TV," *New York Times*, December 25, 1996, pp. C1, C15.
2. See Eric Traub, "The Big Picture on Digital TV: It's Still Fuzzy," *New York Times*, September 12, 2002, sec. G, p. 1; and Frank Ahrens, "FCC Moves to Speed Shift to Digital," *Washington Post*, August 9, 2002, sec. A, p. 1.

Applied Critical Process: TV and International Syndication, p. 171

1. Peter Crawford, "The Revolt on Planet Hollywood," *Australian Financial Review*, July 13, 2002, p. 45.

Case Study: Anatomy of a TV "Failure," p. 176

1. See Andrew Pulve, "Now You See It: ABC Pulls the Plug on David Lynch's TV Series, *Mulholland Drive*," *The Guardian*, May 11, 2001, p. 10; and Andy Klein, "David Lynch: Still the Wizard of Weird," *Hamilton Spectator*, November 17, 2001, p. M16.
2. All Tim Reid and Hugh Wilson quotes from Jimmie L. Reeves and Richard Campbell, "Misplacing *Frank's Place*: Do You Know What It Means to Miss New Orleans?" *Television Quarterly* 24 (1989): 45–57.

CHAPTER 6

1. *United States v. Midwest Video Corp.*, 440 U.S. 689 (1979).
2. National Cable & Telecommunications Association, "Industry Statistics," November 10, 2002, <www.ncta.com>.
3. Federal Communications Commission, *Report on Cable Industry Prices*, April 4, 2002, <http://hraunfoss.fcc.gov/edocs_public/attachmatch/FCC-02-107A1.txt>.
4. National Cable & Telecommunications Association, "Industry Statistics," November 10, 2002, <www.ncta.com>.
5. Ibid.
6. Pierre Brunel-Lantena, quoted in "Top of the News," *Economist* (May 9, 1992): 89.
7. T. Seideman, "Four Labels Ink Vidclip Deals with MTV," *Billboard* (June 23, 1984): 1, 67. See also other issues of *Billboard* and *Variety* through this period.
8. "Tom Freston: The Pied Piper of Television," *Broadcasting & Cable* (September 19, 1994): 40.
9. Satellite Broadcasting and Communications Association, "Satellite Television Industry Celebrates Its 25th Anniversary," August 2, 2001, <http://www.sbca.com/press/Aug026-01.htm>.
10. National Cable Television Association, June 2002, <www.ncta.com>.
11. Stephen Labaton, "AT&T's Acquisition of MediaOne Wins Approval by F.C.C.," *New York Times*, June 6, 2000, p. A1.
12. Federal Communications Commission, *Report on Cable Industry Prices*, April 4, 2002, <http://hraunfoss.fcc.gov/edocs_public/attachmatch/FCC-02-107A1.txt>.

13. William J. Ray, "Private Enterprise, Privileged Enterprise, or Free Enterprise," January 28, 2003, <www.glasgow-Ky.com/papers/#PrivateEnterprise>.
14. Ibid.

CHAPTER 7

1. John Cawelti, *Adventure, Mystery, and Romance: Formula Stories as Art and Popular Culture* (Chicago: University of Chicago Press, 1976), 35.
2. See Charles Musser, *The Emergence of Cinema: The American Screen to 1907* (New York: Scribner's, 1991).
3. Douglas Gomery, *Shared Pleasures: A History of Movie Presentation in the United States* (Madison: University of Wisconsin Press, 1992), 18.
4. Richard Schickel, *Movies: The History of an Art and an Institution* (New York: Basic Books, 1964), 44.
5. Douglas Gomery, *Movie History: A Survey* (Belmont, Calif.: Wadsworth, 1991), 53.
6. Ibid., 167.
7. See Cawelti, *Adventure, Mystery, and Romance*, 80–98.
8. See Barbara Koenig Quart, *Women Directors: The Emergence of a New Cinema* (New York: Praeger, 1988).
9. Ismail Merchant, "Kitschy as Ever, Hollywood Is Branching Out," *New York Times*, November 22, 1998, sec. 2, pp. 15, 30.
10. See Gomery, *Shared Pleasures*, 171–180.
11. See Eric Barnouw, *Tube of Plenty: The Evolution of American Television*, rev. ed. (New York: Oxford University Press, 1975, 1982), 108–109.
12. See Douglas Gomery, "Who Killed Hollywood?" *Wilson Quarterly* (Summer 1991): 106–112.
13. Mike Snider, "DVDs Conquer the Movie World," *USA Today*, October 18, 2002, p. 1E.
14. Gomery, *Movie History*, 429.
15. Motion Picture Association of America, "Valenti Reports Record-Breaking Box Office Results," March 5, 2002, <htpp://www.mpaa.org/jack/2002/2002_03_05a.htm>.
16. Jennifer Mann, "AMC Makes Surprise Bid for Rival Theater Chain," *Kansas City Star*, July 12, 2001, p. A1.
17. David Thorburn, "Television as an Aesthetic Medium," *Critical Studies in Mass Communication* (June 1987): 168.

Case Study: Breaking through Hollywood's Race Barrier, p. 233

1. Douglas Gomery, *Shared Pleasures: A History of Movie Presentation in the United States* (Madison: University of Wisconsin Press, 1992), 155–170.

CHAPTER 8

1. See Brooke Kroeger, *Nellie Bly: Daredevil, Reporter, Feminist* (New York: Times Books/Random House, 1994).
2. See Kay Mills, *A Place in the News: From the Women's Pages to the Front Page* (New York: Dodd, Mead, 1988).
3. Piers Brendon, *The Life and Death of the Press Barons* (New York: Atheneum, 1983), 136.
4. William Randolph Hearst, quoted in Brendon, *The Life and Death of the Press Barons*, 134.
5. Michael Schudson, *Discovering the News: A Social History of American Newspapers* (New York: Basic Books, 1978), 23.
6. See David T. Z. Mindich, "Edwin M. Stanton, the Inverted Pyramid, and Information Control," *Journalism Monographs*, no. 140 (August 1993).

7. John C. Merrill, "Objectivity: An Attitude," in Merrill and Ralph L. Lowenstein, eds., *Media, Messages and Men* (New York: David McKay, 1971), 240.

8. Roy Peter Clark, "A New Shape for the News," *Washington Journalism Review* (March 1984): 47.

9. Ibid., 143, 189.

10. See Edwin Emery, *The Press and America: An Interpretative History of the Mass Media*, 3rd ed. (Englewood Cliffs, N.J.: Prentice-Hall, 1972), 562.

11. Walter Lippmann, *Liberty and the News* (New York: Harcourt, Brace and Howe, 1920), 92.

12. American Society of Newspaper Editors, *Problems of Journalism* (Washington, D.C.: ASNE, 1933), 74.

13. Lippmann, *Liberty and the News*, 64.

14. Tom Wicker, *On Press* (New York: Viking, 1978), 3–5.

15. Jack Newfield, "The 'Truth' about Objectivity and the New Journalism," in Charles C. Flippen, ed., *Liberating the Media* (Washington, D.C.: Acropolis Books, 1973), 63–64.

16. Tom Wolfe, quoted in Leonard W. Robinson, "The New Journalism: A Panel Discussion . . . ," in Ronald Weber, ed., *The Reporter as Artist: A Look at the New Journalism Controversy* (New York: Hastings House, 1974), 67. See also Tom Wolfe and E. E. Johnson, eds., *The New Journalism* (New York: Harper & Row, 1973).

17. Jon Katz, "Online or Not, Newspapers Suck," *Wired* (September 1994): 5.

18. Newspaper Association of America, *Facts about Newspapers 2002*, <www.naa.org>.

19. See Sreenath Sreenivasan, "As Mainstream Papers Struggle, the Ethnic Press Is Thriving," *New York Times*, July 22, 1996, p. C7.

20. Wil Cruz, "The New New Yorker: Ethnic Media Fill the Void," *Newsday*, June 26, 2002, p. A25.

21. See Phyl Garland, "The Black Press: Down but Not Out," *Columbia Journalism Review* (September–October 1982): 43–50.

22. Gregory Stanford, "Media Have a Way to Go on the Road to Diversity," *Milwaukee Journal Sentinel*, July 28, 2002, Crossroads sec., p. 04J.

23. See Allen R. Myerson, "Newspapers Cut Spanish-Language Publications," *New York Times*, October 16, 1995, p. C7.

24. Maria Elena Salinas, "The Dismal State of Hispanics in the News Media," *San Diego Union-Tribune*, June 12, 2002, Opinion sec., p. B9.

25. Stanford, "Media Have a Way to Go," p. 04J.

26. Newspaper Association of America, *Facts about Newspapers 2002*, <www.naa.org>.

27. Michael Emery and Edwin Emery, *The Press and America: An Interpretative History of the Mass Media*, 7th ed. (Englewood Cliffs, N.J.: Prentice-Hall, 1992), 536.

28. Newspaper Association of America, *Facts about Newspapers 2002*, <www.naa.org>.

29. See Philip Meyer, "Learning to Love Lower Profits," *American Journalism Review* (December 1995): 40–44.

30. See Douglas Gomery, "In TV, the Big Get Bigger," *American Journalism Review* (October 1996): 64.

31. See William Glaberson, "Newspaper Owners Do the Shuffle," *New York Times*, February 19, 1996, pp. C1, C4.

32. Matt Wells, "*Big Issue* Faces Cash Crisis," *The Guardian*, May 15, 2002, Home sec., p. 5; Sally Jackson, "Tide Turns for 'Good Read, Good Deed' Mag," *The Australian*, July 18, 2002, p. M09.

33. Committee to Protect Journalists, "Journalists Killed in the Line of Duty, Statistics for 1992-2001," <www.cpj.org>.

Case Study: The Alternative Journalism of Dorothy Day and I. F. Stone, p. 286.

1. Stone, quoted in Jack Lule, "I. F. Stone: Professional Excellence in Raising Hell," *QS News* (Summer 1989): 3.

CHAPTER 9

1. John Tebbel and Mary Ellen Zuckerman, *The Magazine in America, 1741–1900* (New York: Oxford University Press, 1991), 68.

2. See Theodore Peterson, *Magazines in the Twentieth Century* (Urbana: University of Illinois Press, 1964), 5.

3. See Richard Ohmann, *Selling Culture: Magazines, Markets, and Class at the Turn of the Century* (New York: Verso, 1996).

4. See Peterson, *Magazines*, 5.

5. Lincoln Steffens, quoted in Justin Kaplan, *Lincoln Steffens: A Biography* (New York: Simon & Schuster, 1974), 106.

6. See discussion in Peterson, *Magazines*, 228; and Tebbel and Zuckerman, *The Magazine in America*, 223.

7. Alexander Graham Bell, quoted in William H. Taft, *American Magazines for the 1980s* (New York: Hastings House, 1982), 60.

8. Harold Ross, quoted in John Tebbel, *The American Magazine: A Compact History* (New York: Hawthorn Books, 1969), 234.

9. Generoso Pope, quoted in Taft, *American Magazines for the 1980s*, 226–227.

10. See S. Elizabeth Bird, *For Enquiring Minds: A Cultural Study of Supermarket Tabloids* (Knoxville: University of Tennessee Press, 1992), 24.

11. See Taft, *American Magazines*, 229.

12. See Iver Peterson, "Media: Supermarket Tabloids Lose Circulation," *New York Times*, September 9, 1996, p. C5.

13. Ibid.

14. See Deirdre Carmody, "Magazines Go Niche-Hunting with Custom-Made Sections," *New York Times*, June 26, 1995, p. C7.

15. See Robin Pogrebin, "The Number of Ad Pages Does Not Make the Magazine," *New York Times*, August 26, 1996, p. C1.

16. See Gloria Steinem, "Sex, Lies & Advertising," *Ms.* (July–August 1990): 18–28.

17. Robin Pogrebin, "Once a Renegade, Hachette Magazine Chief Gains Respect," *New York Times*, April 6, 1998, p. C1.

CHAPTER 10

1. Richard Corliss, "Why 'Harry Potter' Did a Harry Houdini," July 21, 2000, <http://www.cnn.com/2000/books/new/07/21/potter7_21.a.tm/>.

2. See Elizabeth Eisenstein, *The Printing Press as an Agent of Social Change*, 2 vols. (Cambridge: Cambridge University Press, 1980).

3. See Quentin Reynolds, *The Fiction Factory: From Pulp Row to Quality Street* (New York: Street & Smith/Random House, 1955), 72–74.

4. For a comprehensive historical overview of the publishing industry and the rise of publishing houses, see John A. Tebbel, *A History of Book Publishing in the United States,*

vol. 1, 1630–1865; vol. 2, 1865–1919; vol. 3, 1920–1940; vol. 4, 1940–1980 (New York: R. R. Bowker, 1972–1981).

5. Annual Survey of Colleges, The College Board, <http://www.collegboard.com/press/cost02/html/CBTrendsPricing02.pdf>.

6. Janet Kornblum, "Students Go Buy the Book—on the Net," *USA Today*, August 28, 2002, p. 8D.

7. For a historical overview of paperbacks, see Kenneth Davis, *Two-Bit Culture: The Paperbacking of America* (Boston: Houghton Mifflin, 1984).

8. See John P. Dessauer, *Book Publishing: What It Is, What It Does* (New York: R. R. Bowker, 1974), 48.

9. Patricia Nelson Limerick, "Dancing with Professors: The Trouble with Academic Prose," *New York Times Book Review*, October 31, 1993, p. 3.

10. David D. Kirkpatrick, "Report to the Authors Guild Midlist Books Study Committee," 2000, <http://www.authorsguild.org/prmidlist.html>.

11. See Doreen Carvajal, "Well-Known Book Clubs Agree to Form Partnership," *New York Times*, March 2, 2000, p. C2.

12. Veronis Suhler Stevenson, *15th Annual Communications Industry Forecast*, 2001, <www.veronissuhler.com/publications/forecast/highlights2001.html>.

13. Bibb Porter, "In Publishing, Bigger Is Better," *New York Times*, March 31, 1998, p. A27.

14. James Kaplan, "Inside the Club," *New York Times Magazine*, June 11, 1989, p. 62.

15. See Wilson Dizard Jr., *Old Media New Media: Mass Communication in the Information Age* (White Plains, N.Y.: Longman, 1994), 164.

16. Stephen King, quoted in Joseph Menn, "E-Book Publishing: Much Ado about Nothing Much," *Los Angeles Times*, July 24, 2000, <http://www.latimes.com>.

17. Thomas Rosenstiel, quoted in Doreen Carvajal, "Cross-Media Deals Mean Bonanza for Publishers," *New York Times on the Web*, January 25, 1999, <www.nytimes.com>.

18. International Children's Digital Library, January 27, 2003, <http://www.icdlbooks.org/frameadults.html>.

19. See Alvin Kernan, *The Death of Literature* (New Haven: Yale University Press, 1990).

CHAPTER 11

1. For a written and pictorial history of early advertising, see Charles Goodrum and Helen Dalrymple, *Advertising in America, the First 200 Years* (New York: Harry N. Abrams, 1990), 13–34.

2. Ibid.

3. Michael Schudson, *Advertising, the Uneasy Persuasion* (New York: Basic Books, 1984), 165. See also Arthur Marquette, *Brands, Trademarks, and Good Will* (New York: McGraw-Hill, 1967).

4. Goodrum and Dalrymple, *Advertising in America*, 31.

5. See Schudson, *Advertising*, 164.

6. Stuart Elliott, "Advertising's Big Four: It's Their World Now," *New York Times*, March 31, 2002, sec. 3 (Money and Business), p. 1.

7. Darren Rovell, "Bedazzling Ballhandlers Make Video a Stomping Success," ESPN.com, July 21, 2001, <http://espn.go.com/nba/s/2001/0614/1213974.html>.

8. American Association of Advertising Agencies, "AAAA's TV Commercial Production Survey Shows Largest Cost Increase in 13 Years," November 16, 2000, <http://www.aaaa.org/news/>.

9. Randall Rothenberg, *Where the Suckers Moon: An Advertising Story* (New York: Alfred A. Knopf, 1994), 20.

10. Leslie Savan, "Op Ad: Sneakers and Nothingness," *Village Voice*, April 2, 1991, p. 43.

11. Stephen Brook, "Coke Keeps Its Fizz as World's Biggest Brand," *The Australian*, August 1, 2002, p. M03.

12. See Mary Kuntz and Joseph Weber, "The New Hucksterism," *Business Week*, July 1, 1999, p. 79.

13. Ibid.

14. Schudson, *Advertising*, 210.

15. Vance Packard, *The Hidden Persuaders* (New York: Basic Books, 1957, 1978), 229.

16. See Eileen Dempsey, "Auld Lang Syne," *Columbus Dispatch*, December 28, 2000, p. 1G; and Stuart Elliott, "The Great Auto Ad Glut," *USA Today*, December 19, 1989, p. 1B.

17. See Schudson, *Advertising*, 36–43; and Andrew Robertson, *The Lessons of Failure* (London: MacDonald, 1974).

18. Kim Campbell and Kent Davis-Packard, "How Ads Get Kids to Say, I Want It!" *Christian Science Monitor*, September 18, 2000, p. 1.

19. Susan Linn and Diane Levin, "Stop Marketing 'Yummy Food' to Children," *Christian Science Monitor*, June 20, 2002, Opinion sec., p. 9.

20. See Jay Mathews, "Channel One: Classroom Coup or a 'Sham'?" *Washington Post*, December 26, 1994, p. A1+.

21. See Michael F. Jacobson and Laurie Ann Mazur, *Marketing Madness: A Survival Guide for a Consumer Society* (Boulder, Colo.: Westview Press, 1995), 29–31.

22. Phyllis Furman, "Diageo Seeks Booze Tube," *New York Daily News*, September 7, 2002, Business sec., p. 7.

23. Leonie Wood, "Battery Bunnies Still Beating the Drum," *The Age* (Melbourne), July 27, 2002, Business sec., p. 2.

24. For a discussion of deceptive ads, see Jacobson and Mazur, *Marketing Madness*, 143–148.

25. Sally Squires, "Diet Ads That Are Hard to Swallow," *Washington Post*, September 24, 2002, p. F02.

26. G. Pascal Zachary, "Many Journalists See a Growing Reluctance to Criticize Advertisers," *Wall Street Journal*, February 6, 1992, pp. A1, A6.

27. James McKinley Jr., "Car Dealers Settle with State," *New York Times*, August 10, 2001, sec. B, p. 4.

28. Ibid., p. A6.

29. Marion Just and Rosalind Levine, "Brought to You by . . . Sponsor Interference," *Columbia Journalism Review* (November/December 2000): 93.

30. Terry Lefton, "Super-Charging the Banner Ad," *The Industry Standard*, August 24, 2001, <http://www.thestandard.com/article/0,1902,28811,00.html>.

31. Robert Scheer, "Nowhere to Hide," *Yahoo! Internet Life* (October 2000): 100–102.

32. Kathleen Hall Jamieson, "Truth and Advertising," *New York Times*, January 27, 1996, p. 15.

33. See Stephen Ansolabehere and Shanto Iyengar, *Going Negative: How Attack Ads Shrink and Polarize the Electorate* (New York: Free Press, 1996).

34. Television Bureau of Advertising, "Political Advertising on Broadcast Television," December 10, 2000, <http://www.tvb.org/tvfacts/tvbasics/basics30.html>.

The Global Village: Smoking Up the Global Market, p. 408

1. Mark O'Neill, "Weeding Out the Profits," *South China Morning Post*, August 1, 2002, p. 1; and Rina Omar, "Light Up, Lights Out?" *New Strait Times* (Malaysia), May 31, 2002, p. 1.

CHAPTER 12

1. Matthew J. Culligan and Dolph Greene, *Getting Back to the Basics of Public Relations & Publicity* (New York: Crown Publishers, 1982), 90.
2. Ibid., 100.
3. See Stuart Ewen, *PR! A Social History of Spin* (New York: Basic Books, 1996).
4. Suzanne Heck, "Multimedia Sharpshooter Brought Buffalo Bill Fame," *Public Relations Journal* (October–November 1994): 12.
5. Marvin N. Olasky, "The Development of Corporate Public Relations, 1850–1930," *Journalism Monographs,* no. 102 (April 1987): 3.
6. Quoted in Alfred McClung Lee, *The Daily Newspaper in America* (New York: Macmillan, 1937), 436.
7. Olasky, "The Development of Corporate Public Relations," 14.
8. Ibid., 15.
9. See Ewen, *PR!*, 47.
10. See Scott M. Cutlip, *The Unseen Power: Public Relations — A History* (Hillsdale, N.J.: Lawrence Erlbaum, 1994).
11. Edward Bernays, *Crystallizing Public Opinion* (New York: Horace Liveright, 1923), 217.
12. Michael Schudson, *Discovering the News: A Social History of American Newspapers* (New York: Basic Books, 1978), 136.
13. Walter Lippmann, *Public Opinion* (New York: Free Press, 1922, 1949), 218.
14. See Daniel Boorstin, *The Image: A Guide to Pseudo-Events in America* (New York: Atheneum, 1961), 11–12, 205–210.
15. The author of this book, Richard Campbell, worked briefly as the assistant PR director for Milwaukee's Summerfest in the early 1980s.
16. PRSA, Welcome to 'Poverty USA.' Silver Anvil Awards '02 Category 05C Public Service, 2002, <http://www.prsa.org/_Awards/silver/html/6bw0205c16.html>.
17. See Ewen, *PR!*, 28–29; and John R. McArthur, *The Second Front: Censorship and Propaganda in the Gulf War* (New York: Hill & Wang, 1992), 58–59.
18. Philip Shenon, "3 Partners Quit Firm Handling Saudis' P.R.," *New York Times on the Web,* December 6, 2002, <http://www.nytimes.com/2002/12/06/international/middleeast/06SAUD.html?ex=1040199544&ei=1&en=c061b2d98376e7ba>.
19. Stanley Walker, "Playing the Deep Bassoons," *Harper's* (February 1932): 365.
20. Ibid., 370.
21. Ivy Lee, *Publicity* (New York: Industries Publishing, 1925), 21.
22. Luke Timmerman, "Are PR Firms Going Too Far? Survey Asks," *Seattle Times,* May 17, 2000, p. D2.
23. Schudson, *Discovering the News,* 136.
24. Ivy Lee, quoted in Ray Eldon Hiebert, *Courtier to the Crowd: The Story of Ivy Lee and the Development of Public Relations* (Ames: Iowa State University Press, 1966), 114.
25. See Lippmann, *Public Opinion,* 221.
26. See Jonathan Tasini, "Lost in the Margins: Labor and the Media," *Extra!* (Summer 1992): 2–11.
27. See J. David Pincus et al., "Newspaper Editors' Perceptions of Public Relations: How Business, News, and Sports Editors Differ," *Journal of Public Relations Research* 5, no. 1 (1993): 27–45.
28. John Stauber and Sheldon Rampton, "Flack Attack," *PR Watch* 4, no. 1 (1997), <http://www.prwatch.org/prw_issues/1997-Q1/index.html>.
29. John Stauber, "Corporate PR: A Threat to Journalism?" Radio National/Australian Broadcasting Association, March 30, 1997, <http://www.abc.net.au/rn/talks/bbing/stories/s10602.htm>.
30. William Small, quoted in Walker, "Playing the Deep Bassoons," 174–175.
31. See Alicia Mundy, "Is the Press Any Match for Powerhouse PR?" in Hiebert, ed., *Impact of Mass Media* (White Plains: Longman, 1995), 179–188.

Applied Critical Process: The Invisible Hand of PR, p. 444

1. John Stauber, "Corporate PR: A Threat to Journalism?" *Background Briefing: Radio International,* March 30, 1997, <http://www.abc.net.au/rn/talks/bbing/stories/s10602.htm>.

Examining Ethics: Levi Strauss and Anti-Sweatshop Public Relations, p. 446

1. Public Relations Society of America, PRSA *Silver Anvil Awards* (New York: PRSA, 1994), 9–10.
2. Ibid., 10.
3. See Levi Strauss & Co., "Social Responsibility/Sourcing Guidelines," January 28, 2003. <http://www.levistrauss.com/responsibility/conduct/>.
4. See National Labor Committee, <www.nlcnet.org>.

CHAPTER 13

1. Ronald Grover, "Moguls Who Shopped Till They Dropped," *Business Week,* August 5, 2002.
2. For this section I am indebted to the ideas and scholarship of my former teacher Douglas Gomery, a media economist and historian from the University of Maryland.
3. Douglas Gomery, "The Centrality of Media Economics," in *Defining Media Studies,* Mark R. Levy and Michael Gurevitch, eds. (New York: Oxford University Press, 1994), 202.
4. Ibid., 200.
5. Ibid., 203–204.
6. David Harvey, *The Condition of Postmodernity: An Enquiry into the Origins of Cultural Change* (Oxford: Basil Blackwell, 1989), 171.
7. Ibid., 158.
8. Richard J. Barnet and John Cavanagh, *Global Dreams: Imperial Corporations and the New World Order* (New York: Simon & Schuster, 1994), 131.
9. Ben Bagdikian, *The Media Monopoly,* 6th ed. (Boston: Beacon Press, 2000), 222.
10. William Paley, quoted in Robert W. McChesney, *Telecommunications, Mass Media, & Democracy: The Battle for Control of U.S. Broadcasting, 1928–1935* (New York: Oxford University Press, 1993), 251.
11. McChesney, *Telecommunications, Mass Media, & Democracy,* 264.
12. Edward Herman, "Democratic Media," *Z Papers* (January–March 1992): 23.
13. Barnet and Cavanagh, *Global Dreams,* 38.
14. Richard J. Barnet and Ronald E. Muller, *Global Reach: The Power of Multinational Corporations* (New York: Simon & Schuster, 1974), 175.

Applied Critical Process: News That Serves the Bottom Line?, p. 467

1. Brian Michael Goss, "'All Our Kids Get Better Jobs Tomorrow': The North American Free Trade Agreement in *The New York Times,*" *Journalism & Communication Monographs* 3, no. 1 (Spring 2001): 5–47.
2. Jeff Faux, *Briefing Paper: NAFTA at Seven—Its Impact on Workers in All Three Nations* (Washington, D.C.: Economic Policy Institute, April, 2001), <http://www.epinet.org/briefingpapers/nafta01/nafta-at-7.pdf>, p. 1.

CHAPTER 14

1. Veronica Guerin, quoted in Warren Hoge, "Reporter Roused Ireland's Conscience," *New York Times,* November 23, 1996, pp. 1, 4.
2. Neil Postman, "Currents," *Utne Reader* (July–August 1995): 35.
3. Reuven Frank, "Memorandum from a Television Newsman," reprinted as Appendix 2 in A. William Bluem, *Documentary in American Television* (New York: Hastings House, 1965), 276.
4. For another list and alternative analysis of news criteria, see Brian S. Brooks et al., *The Missouri Group: News Reporting and Writing* (New York: St. Martin's Press, 1996), 2–4.
5. Horace Greeley, quoted in Christopher Lasch, "Journalism, Publicity and the Lost Art of Argument," *Gannett Center Journal* 4, no. 2 (Spring 1990): 2.
6. David Eason, "Telling Stories and Making Sense," *Journal of Popular Culture* 15, no. 2 (Fall 1981): 125.
7. Jon Katz, "AIDS and the Media: Shifting out of Neutral," *Rolling Stone,* May 27, 1993, p. 32.
8. Herbert Gans, *Deciding What's News* (New York: Pantheon, 1979), 42–48.
9. Ibid.
10. Ibid., 48–51.
11. See Michael Schudson, *Discovering the News: A Social History of American Newspapers* (New York: Basic Books, 1978), 3–11.
12. Code of Ethics, reprinted in Melvin Mencher, *News Reporting and Writing,* 3rd ed. (Dubuque, Iowa: William C. Brown, 1984), 443–444.
13. Ibid.
14. Ibid., 443.
15. For reference and guidance on media ethics, see Clifford Christians, Mark Fackler, and Kim Rotzoll, *Media Ethics: Cases & Moral Reasoning,* 4th ed. (White Plains, N.Y.: Longman, 1995); and Thomas H. Bivins, "A Worksheet for Ethics Instruction and Exercises in Reason," *Journalism Educator* (Summer 1993): 4–16.
16. Christians, Fackler, and Rotzoll, *Media Ethics,* 15.
17. See Jimmie Reeves and Richard Campbell, *Cracked Coverage: Television News, the Anti-Cocaine Crusade, and the Reagan Legacy* (Durham, N.C.: Duke University Press, 1994).
18. See David Eason, "On Journalistic Authority: The Janet Cooke Scandal," *Critical Studies in Mass Communications* 3, no. 4 (December 1986): 429–447.
19. Mike Royko, quoted in "News Media: A Searching of Conscience," *Newsweek,* May 4, 1981, p. 53.
20. Don Hewitt, interview conducted at *60 Minutes,* CBS News, New York, February 21, 1989.
21. Jonathan Alter, "News Media: Round Up the Usual Suspects," *Newsweek,* March 25, 1985, p. 69.
22. William Hoynes and David Croteau, "All the Usual Suspects: MacNeil/Lehrer and Nightline," *Extra!* Special Issue 3, no. 4 (Winter 1990): 2. This article reports on the original *Nightline* study and offers a follow-up study on both *Nightline* and *MacNeil/Lehrer,* which reveals roughly the same gender patterns. See Hoynes and Croteau, "Are You on the Nightline Guest List?" *Extra!* 2, no. 4 (January–February 1989): 2–15.
23. William Greider, quoted in Mark Hertsgaard, *On Bended Knee: The Press and the Reagan Presidency* (New York: Farrar, Straus, and Giroux, 1988), 78.
24. Jay Rosen, "Politics, Vision, and the Press: Toward a Public Agenda for Journalism," in Jay Rosen and Paul Taylor, *The New News v. the Old News: The Press and Politics in the 1990s* (New York: Twentieth Century Fund, 1992), 6.
25. Bluem, *Documentary in American Television,* 94.
26. Fred Friendly, quoted in Joseph Michalak, "CBS Reports Covers Assortment of Topics," *New York Times,* December 13, 1959, sec. 2, p. 21.
27. See Joe Holley, "Should the Coverage Fit the Crime?" *Columbia Journalism Review* (May–June 1996), <www.cjr.org/year/96/coverage.asp>.
28. Based on notes made by the author's wife, Dianna Campbell, after a visit to Warsaw and discussions with a number of journalists working for *Gazeta Wyborcza* in 1990.
29. Davis "Buzz" Merritt, *Public Journalism & Public Life: Why Telling the News Is Not Enough* (Hillsdale, N.J.: Lawrence Erlbaum, 1995), 113–114.
30. Rosen, "Politics, Vision, and the Press," 14.
31. Davis Merritt and Jay Rosen, "Imagining Public Journalism: An Editor and a Scholar Reflect on the Birth of an Idea," *Roy W. Howard Public Lecture* (Bloomington: Indiana University), no. 5, April 13, 1995, p. 11.
32. Ibid., 15.
33. See Jonathan Cohn, "Should Journalists Do Community Service?" *American Prospect* (Summer 1995): 15.
34. Merritt and Rosen, "Imagining Public Journalism," 12.
35. Poll statistics cited in Merritt, *Public Journalism & Public Life,* xv–xvi; see Philip Meyer, "Raising Trust in Newspapers . . . ," *USA Today,* January 11, 1999, p. 15A; and Project for Excellence in Journalism, <www.journalism.org>, for current research data.
36. James Agee and Walker Evans, *Let Us Now Praise Famous Men* (Boston: Houghton Mifflin, 1960), xiv.
37. David Broder, quoted in "Squaring with the Reader: A Seminar on Journalism," *Kettering Review* (Winter 1992): 48.
38. Christopher Lasch, "Journalism, Publicity and the Lost Art of Argument," *Gannett Center Journal* 4, no. 2 (Spring 1990): 1.
39. Jay Rosen, "Forming and Informing the Public," *Kettering Review* (Winter 1992): 69–70.

Examining Ethics: WTO Protesters, TV News, and Corporate Power, p. 504

1. Thomas Egan, "Free Trade Takes on Free Speech," *New York Times,* December 5, 1999, <www.nytimes.com>.
2. Jon Katz, "Rock, Rap and Movies Bring You the News," *Rolling Stone,* March 5, 1992, pp. 33–40, 78.

CHAPTER 15

1. Alexis de Tocqueville, *Democracy in America* (New York: Modern Library, 1835, 1840, 1945, 1981), 96–97.
2. Steve Fore, "Lost in Translation: The Social Uses of Mass Communications Research," *AFTERIMAGE*, no. 20 (April 1993): 10.
3. James Carey, *Communication as Culture: Essays on Media and Society* (Boston: Unwin Hyman, 1989), 75.
4. Daniel Czitrom, *Media and the American Mind: From Morse to McLuhan* (Chapel Hill: University of North Carolina Press, 1982), 122–125.
5. Ibid., 123.
6. Harold Lasswell, *Propaganda Techniques in the World War* (New York: Alfred A. Knopf, 1927), 9.
7. Walter Lippmann, *Public Opinion* (New York: Macmillan, 1922), 18.
8. See W. W. Charters, *Motion Pictures and Youth: A Summary* (New York: Macmillan, 1934); and Garth Jowett, *Film: The Democratic Art* (Boston: Little, Brown, 1976), 220–229.
9. Czitrom, *Media and the American Mind,* 132. See also Harold Lasswell, "The Structure and Function of Communication in Society," in Lyman Bryson, ed., *The Communication of Ideas* (New York: Harper and Brothers, 1948), 37–51.
10. Wilbur Schramm, Jack Lyle, and Edwin Parker, *Television in the Lives of Our Children* (Stanford, Calif.: Stanford University Press, 1961), 1.
11. See Joseph Klapper, *The Effects of Mass Communication* (New York: Free Press, 1960).
12. Schramm, Lyle, and Parker, *Television,* 1.
13. For an early overview of uses and gratifications, see Jay Blumler and Elihu Katz, *The Uses of Mass Communication* (Beverly Hills, Calif.: Sage, 1974).
14. See George Gerbner et al., "The Demonstration of Power: Violence Profile No. 10," *Journal of Communication* 29, no. 3 (1979): 177–196.
15. *Sex on TV: A Biennial Report to the Kaiser Family Foundation, 1999* (Menlo Park, Calif.: Henry C. Kaiser Family Foundation).
16. Robert P. Snow, *Creating Media Culture* (Beverly Hills, Calif.: Sage, 1983), 47.
17. See Maxwell McCombs and Donald Shaw, "The Agenda-Setting Function of Mass Media," *Public Opinion Quarterly* 36, no. 2 (1972): 176–187.
18. See Stephen D. Reese and Lucig H. Danielton, "A Closer Look at Intermedia Influences on Agenda Setting: The Cocaine Issue of 1986," in Pamela J. Shoemaker, ed., *Communication Campaigns about Drugs: Government, Media, and the Public* (Hillsdale, N.J.: Lawrence Erlbaum, 1989), 47–66; and Peter Kerr, "Anatomy of the Drug Issue: How, after Years, It Erupted," *New York Times,* November 17, 1986, p. A12.
19. See Craig Reinarman and Harry G. Levine, "Crack in Context: Politics and Media in the Making of the Drug Scare," *Contemporary Drug Problems* (Winter 1989): 546; see also Adam Clymer, "Public Found Ready to Sacrifice in Drug Fight," *New York Times,* September 2, 1986, pp. A1, D16.
20. See Nancy Signorielli and Michael Morgan, *Cultivation Analysis: New Directions in Media Effects Research* (Newbury Park, Calif.: Sage, 1990).
21. Richard Rhodes, "The Media-Violence Myth," *Rolling Stone,* November 23, 2000, pp. 55–58.
22. Robert Lynd, *Knowledge for What? The Place of Social Science in American Culture* (Princeton, N.J.: Princeton University Press, 1939), 120.
23. Czitrom, *Media and the American Mind,* 143; and Leo Lowenthal, "Historical Perspectives of Popular Culture," in Bernard Rosenberg and David White, eds., *Mass Culture: The Popular Arts in America* (Glencoe, Ill.: Free Press, 1957), 52.
24. See Stuart Hall et al., *Policing the Crisis: Mugging, the State, and Law and Order* (London: Macmillan, 1978).
25. Horace Newcomb, *TV: The Most Popular Art* (Garden City, N.Y.: Anchor Books, 1974), 19, 23.
26. Ana Garner, Helen M. Sterk, and Shawn Adams, "Narrative Analysis of Sexual Etiquette in Teenage Magazines," *Journal of Communication* 48, no. 4 (Autumn 1998): 59–78.
27. See Janice Radway, *Reading the Romance: Women, Patriarchy and Popular Literature* (Chapel Hill: University of North Carolina Press, 1984).
28. James Carey, "Mass Communication Research and Cultural Studies: An American View," in James Curran, Michael Gurevitch, and Janet Woollacott, eds., *Mass Communication and Society* (London: Edward Arnold, 1977), 418, 421.
29. See S. Elizabeth Bird, *For Enquiring Minds: A Cultural Study of Supermarket Tabloids* (Knoxville: University of Tennessee Press, 1992).
30. Robert M. Entman, *Democracy without Citizens* (New York: Oxford University Press, 1989).
31. Scott Janny, "Postmodern Gravity Deconstructed, Slyly," *New York Times,* May 18, 1996, p. 1. See also The Editors of Lingua Franca, eds., *The Sokal Hoax: The Sham That Shook the Academy* (Lincoln, Nebr.: Bison Press, 2000).
32. Christopher Lasch, "Politics and Culture," *Salmagundi* (Winter–Spring 1990): 33.

Applied Critical Process: A Cultural Approach to Studying the News, p. 528

1. Christopher Martin, *Framed! Labor and the Corporate Media* (Ithaca, N.Y.: Cornell University Press, 2003).
2. Richard B. Freeman and Joel Rogers, *What Workers Want* (Ithaca, N.Y.: Cornell University Press, 1999).

CHAPTER 16

1. Jan Jarboe Russell, "It Is the Return of the Bad Old Days," *San Antonio Express-News,* December 27, 2001, p. 9C.
2. Lucy Dalglish, *Homefront Confidential,* 2nd ed., The Reporters Committee for the Freedom of the Press, <http://www.rcfp.org/news/documents/Homefront_Confidential2.pdf>.
3. See Committee to Protect Journalists, "Journalists Killed in the Line of Duty," <http://www.cpj.org/killed/Ten_Year_Killed/stats.html>, January 28, 2003.
4. See Freedom House, *The Annual Survey of Press Freedom 2002,* <http://www.freedomhouse.org/pfs2002/pfs2002.pdf>, January 28, 2003.
5. Fred Siebert, Theodore Peterson, and Wilbur Schramm, *Four Theories of the Press* (Urbana: University of Illinois, 1956).
6. See Douglas M. Fraleigh and Joseph S. Tuman, *Freedom of Speech in the Marketplace of Ideas* (New York: St. Martin's Press, 1997), 125.

7. Hugo Black, quoted in "New York Times Company v. U.S.: 1971," in Edward W. Knappman, ed., *Great American Trials: From Salem Witchcraft to Rodney King* (Detroit: Visible Ink Press, 1994), 609.

8. Robert Warren, quoted in "U.S. v. The Progressive: 1979," in Knappman, ed., *Great American Trials*, 684.

9. See Fraleigh and Tuman, *Freedom of Speech*, 71–73.

10. See the Libel Defense Resource Center, *Media Defendants' Win Rate Higher . . . But So Are Damage Awards,* <http://www.ldrc.com/Press_Releases/bull2002-1.html>.

11. See Knappman, ed., *Great American Trials*, 517–519.

12. Ibid., 741–743.

13. Douglas Gomery, *Movie History: A Survey* (Belmont, Calif.: Wadsworth, 1991), 57.

14. See Eric Barnouw, *Tube of Plenty: The Evolution of American Television*, rev. ed. (New York: Oxford University Press, 1982), 118–130.

15. Dean Burch, quoted in Peter Fornatale and Joshua Mills, *Radio in the Television Age* (Woodstock, N.Y.: Overlook Press, 1980), 85.

16. See "Dummy and Dame Arouse the Nation," *Broadcasting-Telecasting,* October 15, 1956, p. 258; and Lawrence Lichty and Malachi Topping, *American Broadcasting: A Source Book on the History of Radio and Television* (New York: Hastings House, 1975), 530.

17. David Tillotson, "Don't Be So Quick to Pay Fines," *Radio World,* December 20, 2000, p. 34.

18. Stephen Labaton, "Congress Severely Curtails Plan for Low-Power Radio Stations," *New York Times on the Web,* December 19, 2000, <http://www.nytimes.com/2000/12/19/business/19RADI.html>.

19. Bill Kovach, "Big Deals, with Journalism Thrown In," *New York Times,* August 3, 1995, p. A17.

Applied Critical Process: How Much Freedom of Information?, p. 544

1. Associated Press, "Survey: Iowa Residents Often Denied Access to Public Records," September 25, 2000, <http://www.freedomforum.org/templates/document.asp?documentID=3631>.

glossary

A&R agents short for artist & repertoire agents, these talent scouts of the music business discover, develop, and sometimes manage performers.

absolutist ethic the principle that in a moral society legal or ethical codes must be followed without exception; no one is above the law or above a society's fundamental moral principles.

access channels in cable television, a tier of nonbroadcast channels dedicated to local education, government, and the public.

account executives in advertising, client liaisons responsible for bringing in new business and managing the accounts of established clients.

account reviews in advertising, the process of evaluating or reinvigorating an ad campaign, which results in either renewing the contract with the original ad agency or hiring a new agency.

acquisitions editors in the book industry, editors who seek out and sign authors to contracts.

actual malice in libel law, a reckless disregard for the truth, such as when a reporter or an editor knows that a statement is false and prints or airs it anyway.

Adult Contemporary (AC) one of the oldest and most popular radio music formats, typically featuring a mix of news, talk, oldies, and soft rock.

advocacy journalism often associated with a journalistic trend in the 1960s but actually part of a tradition that dates to the early days of the partisan press, this approach to journalism features the reporter actively promoting a particular cause or viewpoint.

affiliate stations radio or TV stations that, though independently owned, sign a contract to be part of a network and receive money to carry the network's programs; in exchange, the network reserves time slots, which it sells to national advertisers.

agenda-setting a media-research argument that says when the mass media pay attention to particular events or issues, they determine—that is, set the agenda for—the major topics of discussion for individuals and society.

album-oriented rock (AOR) the radio music format that features album cuts from mainstream rock bands.

alternative rock nonmainstream rock music, which includes many types of experimental music and some forms of punk and grunge.

AM amplitude modulation; a type of radio and sound transmission that stresses the volume or height of radio waves.

analog recording a recording that is made by capturing the fluctuations of the original sound waves and storing those signals on records or cassettes as a continuous stream of magneticism—analogous to the actual sound.

analysis the second step in the critical process, it involves discovering significant patterns that emerge from the description stage.

anthology drama a popular form of early TV programming that brought live dramatic theater to television; influenced by stage plays, anthologies offered new teleplays, casts, directors, writers, and sets from week to week.

ARPAnet the original Internet, designed by the U.S. Defense Department's Advanced Research Projects Agency (ARPA).

association principle in advertising, a persuasive technique that associates a product with some cultural value or image that has a positive connotation but may have little connection to the actual product.

attack ad a type of political ad that uses repeated negative assaults on another candidate's character.

audiotape lightweight magnetized strands of ribbon that make possible sound editing and multiple-track mixing; instrumentals or vocals can be recorded at one location and later mixed onto a master recording in another studio.

authoritarian model a model for journalism and speech that tolerates little criticism of government or public dissent; it holds that the general public needs guidance from an elite and educated ruling class.

bandwagon effect an advertising strategy that incorporates exaggerated claims that everyone is using a particular product so you should, too.

barter deal in TV syndication, an arrangement in which no money changes hands between the local station and the syndicator; instead, a syndicator offers a new program to a local TV station in exchange for a portion of the advertising revenue.

basic cable in cable programming, a tier of channels composed of local broadcast signals, nonbroadcast access channels (for local government, education, and general public use), a few regional PBS stations, and a variety of popular channels downlinked from communication satellites.

Big Five/Little Three from the late 1920s through the late 1940s, the major movie studios that were vertically integrated and that dominated the industry. The Big Five were Paramount, MGM, Warner Brothers, Twentieth Century Fox, and RKO. The Little Three were those studios that did not own theaters: Columbia, Universal, and United Artists.

bits a computer term coined from BInary digiTS, which refers to information that represents two values, such as yes/no, on/off, or 0/1.

black-box technologies any of the newly emerging TV technologies—such as TiVo—that permits viewers to record and save TV programs by digital storage means rather than onto tape via older VCR formats.

block-booking an early tactic of movie studios to control exhibition involving pressuring theater operators to accept marginal films with no stars in order to get access to films with the most popular stars.

blockbuster the type of big-budget special effects films that typically have summer or holiday release dates, heavy promotion, and lucrative merchandising tie-ins.

block printing a printing technique developed by early Chinese printers, who hand-carved characters and illustrations into a block of wood, applied ink to the block, and then printed copies on multiple sheets of paper.

blues originally a kind of black folk music, this music emerged as a distinct category in the early 1900s; it was influenced by African American spirituals, ballads, and work songs in the rural South, and by urban guitar and vocal solos from the 1930s and 1940s.

books on tape audiotape books that generally feature actors or authors reading abridged versions of popular fiction and nonfiction trade books.

bootlegging the illegal counterfeiting or pirating of CDs, cassettes, and videos that are produced and/or sold without official permission from the original songwriter, performer, or copyright holder.

boutique agencies in advertising, small regional ad agencies that offer personalized services.

broadcasting the transmission of radio waves or TV signals to a broad public audience.

browsers information-search services, such as Netscape's Navigator and Microsoft's Explorer, that offer detailed organizational maps to the World Wide Web.

button fatigue in TV audience measurement, the phenomenon of weary viewers failing to log on and report their viewing.

cable franchise in cable television, a local monopoly business awarded by a community to the most attractive cable bidder, usually for a fifteen-year period.

cable music the commercial-free, format-music services offered via cable or DBS.

cash deal in TV syndication, an arrangement in which the distributor of a program offers a series to the highest bidder in a TV market or to a station trying to fill a particular time slot.

cash-plus deal in TV syndication, an arrangement in which the distributor of a program offers a series to the highest bidder in a TV market but retains some time to sell national commercial spots.

CATV (community antenna television) an early cable system that originated where mountains or tall buildings blocked TV signals; because of early technical and regulatory limits, CATV contained only twelve channels.

CD-ROM a computer term coined from Compact-Disc Read-Only Memory; a CD technology that permits the storage of vast amounts of computer software and information (one CD-ROM can store as much information as seven hundred conventional floppy disks).

CD-Rs recordable compact discs that can be recorded only once.

CD-RWs rewriteable compact discs that can be recorded over many times.

Celluloid a transparent and pliable film that can hold a coating of chemicals sensitive to light.

channel in mass communication, a medium that delivers messages from senders to receivers.

chapter shows in television production, any situation comedy or dramatic program whose narrative structure includes self-contained stories that feature a problem, a series of conflicts, and a resolution from week to week (for contrast, see **serial programs** and **episodic series**).

cinema verité French term for *truth film,* a documentary style that records fragments of everyday life unobtrusively; it often features a rough, grainy look and shaky, handheld camera work.

clearance rule established in the 1940s by the Justice Department and the FCC, this rule mandated that all local affiliates are ultimately responsible for the content of their channels and must clear, or approve, all network programming.

coaxial cable a system for transmitting TV signals via a solid core of copper-clad aluminum wire encircled by an outer axis of braided wires; these bundles of thin wire accommodate fifty or more separate channels running side by side with virtually no interference.

codex an early type of book in which paperlike sheets were cut and sewed together along the edge, then bound with thin pieces of wood and covered with leather.

commercial speech any print or broadcast expression for which a fee is charged to the organization or individual buying time or space in the mass media.

common carrier a communication or transportation business, such as a phone company or a taxi service, that is required by law to offer service on a first-come, first-served basis to whoever can pay the rate; such companies do not get involved in content.

communication the process of creating symbol systems that convey information and meaning (for example, language, Morse code, film, computer codes).

communist or state model a model for journalism and speech that places control in the hands of an enlightened government, which speaks for ordinary citizens and workers in order to serve the common goals of the state.

compact discs (CDs) playback-only storage discs for music that incorporate pure and very precise digital techniques, thus eliminating noise during recording and editing sessions.

complementary copy positive, upbeat articles—often about food, fashion, and cosmetics—that support the ads carried in various consumer magazines.

conflict of interest considered unethical, a compromising situation in which a journalist stands to benefit personally from the news report he or she produces.

conflict-oriented journalism found in metropolitan areas, newspapers that define news primarily as events, issues, or experiences that deviate from social norms; journalists see their role as observers who monitor their city's institutions and problems.

consensus-oriented papers found in small communities, newspapers that promote social and economic harmony by providing community calendars and meeting notices and carrying articles on local schools, social events, town government, property crimes, and zoning issues.

contemporary hits radio (CHR) originally called Top 40 radio, this radio format encompasses everything from hip-hop to children's songs; it remains the most popular format in radio for people age 18 to 24.

content analysis in social-science research, a method for studying and coding media texts and programs.

continuity editing an editing technique that makes space and time seem continuous and seamless; it is used in most traditional Hollywood films.

control group in social-science research, the group that serves as a basis for comparison to the experimental group; the control group has not been exposed to the particular phenomenon or media content being studied.

controlled circulation the process of earning magazine revenue from advertising or corporate sponsorship by targeting captive audiences, such as airline passengers or association members, who receive the publications free.

cookies information profiles about a user that are usually automatically accepted by the Web browser and stored on the user's own computer hard drive.

copy editors the people in magazine, newspaper, and book publishing who attend to specific problems in writing such as style, content, and length.

copyright the legal right of authors and producers to own and control the use of their published or unpublished writing, music, and lyrics; TV programs and movies; or graphic art designs.

Corporation for Public Broadcasting (CPB) a private, nonprofit corporation created by Congress in 1967 to funnel federal funds to nonprofit radio and public television.

country claiming the largest number of radio stations in the United States, this radio format includes such subdivisions as old-time, progressive, country-rock, western swing, and country-gospel.

cover music songs recorded or performed by musicians who did not originally write or perform the music; in the 1950s, cover music was an attempt by white producers and artists to capitalize on popular songs by blacks.

crisis management in public relations, the strategic response to uncontrolled negative publicity about an individual, client, or company; also known as *damage control*.

cultivation effect in media research, the idea that heavy television viewing leads individuals to perceive reality in ways that are consistent with the portrayals they see on television.

cultural imperialism the phenomenon of American media, fashion, and food dominating the global market and shaping the cultures and identities of other nations.

cultural studies in media research, the approaches that try to understand how the media and culture are tied to the actual patterns of communication used in daily life; these studies focus on how people make meanings, apprehend reality, and order experience through the use of stories and symbols.

culture the symbols of expression that individuals, groups, and societies use to make sense of daily life and to articulate their values; a process that delivers the values of a society through products or other meaning-making forms.

cyberspace the region to which the networks of computer communication transport their users—a territory that does not recognize conventional geographic boundaries or social hierarchies.

day parts in radio programming, the division of each day into time blocks—usually 6 to 10 A.M., 10 A.M. to 3 P.M., 3 to 7 P.M., and 7 to 12 midnight—in order to reach various listening audiences.

DBS (direct broadcast satellites) See **direct broadcast satellites**.

deficit financing in television, the process whereby a TV production company leases its programs to a network for a license fee that is actually less than the cost of production; the company hopes to recoup this loss later in rerun syndication.

deliberative democracy a political culture in which citizen groups, local governments, and the news media join together to actively shape social and political agendas.

demographic editions national magazines whose advertising is tailored to subscribers and readers according to occupation, class, and zip-code address.

demographics in market research, the study of audiences or consumers by age, gender, occupation, ethnicity, education, and income.

description the first step in the critical process, it involves paying close attention, taking notes, and researching the cultural product to be studied.

desktop publishing a computer technology that enables an aspiring publisher-editor to inexpensively write, design, lay out, and even print a small newsletter or magazine.

developmental editors in book publishing, the editors who provide authors with feedback, make suggestions for improvements, and obtain advice from knowledgeable members of the academic community.

digital communication images, texts, and sounds that use pulses of electric current or flashes of laser lights and are converted (or encoded) into electronic signals represented as varied combinations of binary numbers, usually ones and zeros; these signals are then reassembled (decoded) as a precise reproduction of a TV picture, a magazine article, or a telephone voice.

digital divide the socioeconomic disparity between those who do and do not have access to digital technology and media, such as the Internet.

digital recording music recorded and played back by laser beam rather than by needle or magnetic tape.

dime novels sometimes identified as pulp fiction, these cheaply produced and low-priced novels were popular in the United States beginning in the 1860s.

direct broadcast satellites (DBS) satellite-based services that for a monthly fee downlink hundreds of satellite channels and services and began distributing video programming directly to households in 1994.

directories review and cataloguing services that group Web sites under particular categories (e.g., Arts & Humanities, News & Media, Entertainment).

direct payment in media economics, the payment of money, primarily by consumers, for a book, a music CD, a movie, an online computer service, or a cable TV subscription.

disassociation corollary in advertising, a persuasive technique that tries to distance the consumer from a large product manufacturer or parent company.

distribution the network of individuals or companies in the mass-media business that deliver media products to various regional, national, and international markets.

documentary a movie or TV news genre that documents reality by recording actual characters and settings.

domain names extensions on Web addresses, such as ".edu," that indicate the origination of a Web site.

domestic comedy a TV hybrid of the sitcom in which characters and settings are usually more important than complicated situations; it generally features a domestic problem or work issue that characters have to solve.

dramedy in TV programming, a narrative that blurs serious and comic themes.

drive time in radio programming, the periods between 6 and 10 A.M. and 4 and 7 P.M., when people are commuting to and from work or school; these periods constitute the largest listening audiences of the day.

DVD digital video disc, a digital storage format that looks like a CD but has greater capacity, enabling it to handle feature-length films as well as graphics, video, multichannel audio, and interactivity.

e-commerce electronic commerce, or commercial activity, on the Web.

economies of scale the economic process of increasing production levels so as to reduce the overall cost per unit.

electromagnetic waves invisible electronic impulses similar to visible light; electricity, magnetism, light, broadcast signals, and heat are part of such waves, which radiate in space at the speed of light, about 186,000 miles per second.

Electronica often referred to as "techno," an underground music genre that developed in the 1990s; it features keyboards, drum machine beats, and music samples often sequenced with computers.

electronic publisher a communication business, such as a broadcaster or a cable TV company, that is entitled to choose what channels or content to carry.

episodic series a narrative form well suited to television because main characters appear every week, sets and locales remain the same, and technical crews stay with the program; episodic series feature new adventures each week, but a handful of characters emerge with whom viewers can regularly identify (for contrast, see **chapter shows**).

ethnocentrism an underlying value held by many U.S. journalists and citizens, it involves judging other countries and cultures according to how they live up to or imitate American practices and ideals.

evaluation the fourth step in the critical process, it involves arriving at a judgment about whether a cultural product is good, bad, or mediocre; this requires subordinating one's personal taste to the critical assessment resulting from the first three stages (description, analysis, and interpretation).

evergreens in TV syndication, popular and lucrative enduring network reruns such as the *Andy Griffith Show* or *I Love Lucy*.

exhibition the individuals or companies in the mass-media business who exhibit media products; the term usually refers to companies that control movie theaters.

experiment in regard to the mass media, research that isolates some aspect of content, suggests a hypothesis, and manipulates variables to discover a particular medium's impact on attitudes, emotions, or behavior.

experimental group in social-science research, the group under study that has been exposed to a particular phenomenon or media content.

Fairness Doctrine repealed in 1987, this FCC rule required broadcast stations to air and engage in controversial-issue programs that affected their communities and, when offering such programming, to provide competing points of view.

famous-person testimonial an advertising strategy that associates a product with the endorsement of a well-known person.

feature syndicates commercial outlets or brokers, such as United Features and King Features, that contract with newspapers to provide work from well-known political writers, editorial cartoonists, comic-strip artists, and self-help columnists.

Federal Communications Act of 1934 the far-reaching act that established the FCC and the federal regulatory structure for U.S. broadcasting.

Federal Communications Commission (FCC) an independent U.S. government agency charged with regulating interstate and international communications by radio, television, wire, satellite, and cable.

Federal Radio Commission (FRC) established in 1927 to oversee radio licenses and negotiate channel problems.

feedback responses from receivers to the senders of messages.

fiber-optic cable thin glass bundles of fiber capable of transmitting thousands of messages converted to shooting pulses of light along cable wires; these bundles of fiber can carry broadcast channels, telephone signals, and all sorts of digital codes.

film noir French for *black film*, this film genre is usually shot in black and white, uses low-lighting techniques, shows few daytime scenes, displays bleak urban settings, and explores the sinister side of human nature.

Financial Interest and Syndication Rules (fin-syn) FCC rules that prohibited the major networks from running their own syndication companies or from charging production companies additional fees after shows had completed their prime-time runs; most fin-syn rules were rescinded in the mid-1990s.

first-run syndication in television, the process whereby new programs are specifically produced for sale in syndication markets rather than for network television.

flack a derogatory term that journalists use to refer to a public relations agent.

FM frequency modulation; a type of radio and sound transmission that offers static-less reception and greater fidelity and clarity than AM radio by accentuating the pitch or distance between radio waves.

focus group a common research method in psychographic analysis in which a moderator leads a small-group discussion about a product or an issue, usually with six to twelve people.

folk music music performed by untrained musicians and passed down through oral traditions; it encompasses a wide range of music, from Appalachian fiddle tunes to the accordion-led zydeco of Louisiana.

folk-rock amplified folk music, often featuring politically overt lyrics; influenced by rock and roll.

format radio the concept of radio stations developing and playing specific styles (or formats) geared to listeners' age, race, or gender; in format radio, management, rather than deejays, controls programming choices.

Fourth Estate the notion that the press operates as an unofficial branch of government, monitoring the legislative, judicial, and executive branches for abuses of power.

franchise fees the money a cable company pays a city annually for the right to operate the local cable system; these fees are limited by law to no more than 5 percent of the company's gross annual revenue.

fringe time in television, the time slot either immediately before the evening's prime-time schedule (called *early fringe*) or immediately following the local evening news or the network's late-night talk shows (called *late fringe*).

gag orders legal restrictions prohibiting the press from releasing preliminary information that might prejudice jury selection.

gangsta rap a style of rap music that depicts the hardships of urban life and sometimes glorifies the violent style of street gangs.

gatekeepers editors, producers, and other media managers who function as message filters, making decisions about what types of messages actually get produced for particular audiences.

general-interest magazine a type of magazine that addresses a wide variety of topics and is aimed at a broad national audience.

gotcha stories news reports in which journalists nab evil-doers or interview subjects who were caught in an act of deception.

grunge rock music that takes the spirit of punk and infuses it with more attention to melody.

halo effect in TV audience measurement, the phenomenon of viewers reporting not what they actually watched but what they think they should have watched.

happy talk in TV journalism, the ad-libbed or scripted banter that goes on among local news anchors, reporters, meteorologists, and sportscasters before and after news reports.

headend a cable TV system's computerized nerve center, where TV signals from local broadcast stations and satellites are received, processed, and distributed to area homes.

herd journalism a situation in which reporters stake out a house or follow a story in such large groups that the entire profession comes under attack for invading people's privacy or exploiting their personal tragedies.

hidden-fear appeal an advertising strategy that plays on a sense of insecurity, trying to persuade consumers that only a specific product can offer relief.

high culture a symbolic expression that has come to mean "good taste"; often supported by wealthy patrons and corporate donors, it is associated with fine art (such as ballet, the symphony, painting, and classical literature), which is available primarily in theaters or museums.

high-definition television (HDTV) a new digital standard for U.S. television sets that has more than twice the resolution of the system that served as the standard from the 1940s through the 1990s.

hip-hop music that combines spoken street dialect with cuts (or samples) from older records and bears the influences of social politics, male boasting, and comic lyrics carried forward from blues, R&B, soul, and rock and roll.

Hollywood Ten the nine screenwriters and one film director subpoenaed by the House Un-American Activities Committee (HUAC) who were sent to prison in the late 1940s for refusing to discuss their memberships or to identify communist sympathizers.

HTML (HyperText Markup Language) the written code that creates Web pages and links; a language all computers can read.

human-interest stories news accounts that focus on the trials and tribulations of the human condition, often featuring ordinary individuals facing extraordinary challenges.

hypertext a data-linking feature of the World Wide Web, it enables a user to click on a highlighted word or phrase and skip directly to other files related to that subject in other computer systems.

hypodermic-needle model an early model in mass-communication research that attempted to explain media effects by arguing that the media shoot their powerful effects directly into unsuspecting or weak audiences; sometimes called the *bullet theory* or *direct effects model*.

hypotheses in social-science research, tentative general statements that predict a relationship between a dependent variable and an independent variable.

illuminated manuscripts books from the Middle Ages that featured decorative, colorful designs and illustrations on each page.

independent station a TV station, such as WGN in Chicago or WTBS in Atlanta, that finds its own original and syndicated programming and is not affiliated with any of the major networks.

indies independent music and film production houses that work outside industry oligopolies; they often produce less mainstream music and film.

indirect payment in media economics, the financial support of media products by advertisers, who pay for the quantity or quality of audience members that a particular medium attracts.

individualism an underlying value held by most U.S. journalists and citizens, it favors individual rights and responsibilities over group needs or institutional mandates.

infomercials thirty-minute late-night and daytime programs that usually feature fading TV and music celebrities, who advertise a product in a format that looks like a talk show.

information highway the circulation of both personal communication and mass media on personal computers and modems, high-speed telephone links, communication satellites, and television screens.

infotainment a type of television program that packages human-interest and celebrity stories in TV news style.

ink-jet imaging a computer technique that enables a magazine publisher or advertiser to print personalized messages to individual subscribers.

instant book in the book industry, a marketing strategy that involves publishing a topical book quickly after a major event occurs.

instant messaging services a Web feature that enables users to chat with buddies in real time via pop-up windows assigned to each conversation.

interactive channels two-way cable channels that enable users to connect to their local services, such as banks and the fire department, and also offer two-way entertainment, such as play-along versions of game shows and the ability to guess the next play during a football game.

interactivity a communication process that allows immediate two-way communication (as via telephones or e-mail) between senders and receivers of media messages.

Internet the vast central network of high-speed telephone lines designed to link and carry computer information worldwide.

Internet2 (I2) the next generation of online technology, deployed on an experimental basis in 1999, that is expected to be one thousand times faster than today's Internet.

Internet radio online radio stations that either "stream" simulcast versions of on-air radio broadcasts over the Web, or are created exclusively for the Internet.

Internet Service Provider (ISP) a company that provides Internet access to homes and businesses for a fee.

interpretation the third step in the critical process, it asks and answers the "What does that mean?" and "So what?" questions about one's findings.

interpretive journalism a type of journalism that involves analyzing and explaining key issues or events and placing them in a broader historical or social context.

invasion of privacy the violation of a person's right to be left alone, without his or her name, image, or daily activities becoming public property.

inverted-pyramid style a style of journalism in which news reports begin with the most dramatic or newsworthy information—answering *who, what, where,* and *when* (and less frequently *why* or *how*) questions at the top of the story—and then tail off with less significant details.

irritation advertising an advertising strategy that tries to create product-name recognition by being annoying or obnoxious.

jazz an improvisational and mostly instrumental musical form that absorbs and integrates a diverse body of musical styles, including African rhythms, blues, big band, and gospel.

joint operating agreement (JOA) in the newspaper industry, an economic arrangement, sanctioned by the government, that permits competing newspapers to operate separate editorial divisions while merging business and production operations.

kinescope before the days of videotape, a 1950s technique for preserving television broadcasts by using a film camera to record a live TV show off a studio monitor.

kinetograph an early movie camera developed by Thomas Edison's assistant in the 1890s.

kinetoscope an early film projection system that served as a kind of peep show in which viewers looked through a hole and saw images moving on a tiny plate.

leased channels in cable television, channels that allow citizens to buy time for producing programs or presenting their own viewpoints.

libel in media law, the defamation of character in written expression.

libertarian model a model for journalism and speech that encourages vigorous government criticism and supports the highest degree of freedom for individual speech and news operations.

limited competition in media economics, a market with many producers and sellers but only a few differentiable products within a particular category; sometimes called *monopolistic competition*.

linotype a technology introduced in the nineteenth century that enabled printers to set type mechanically using a typewriter-style keyboard.

literary journalism news reports that adapt fictional storytelling techniques to nonfictional material; sometimes called *new journalism*.

lobbying in government public relations, the process of attempting to influence the voting of lawmakers to support a client's or an organization's best interests.

longitudinal studies a term used for research studies that are conducted over long periods of time and often rely on large government and academic survey databases.

low culture a symbolic expression allegedly aligned with the questionable tastes of the "masses," who enjoy the commercial "junk" circulated by the mass media, such as soap operas, rock music, talk radio, comic books, and monster truck pulls.

magazine a nondaily periodical that comprises a collection of articles, stories, and ads.

manuscript culture a period during the Middle Ages when priests and monks advanced the art of bookmaking.

market research in advertising and public relations agencies, the department that uses social-science techniques to assess the behaviors and attitudes of consumers toward particular products before any ads are created.

mass communication the process of designing and delivering cultural messages and stories to diverse audiences through media channels as old as the book and as new as the Internet.

mass customization the process whereby product companies and content providers customize a Web page, print ad, or other media form for an individual consumer.

mass-market paperbacks low-priced paperback books sold mostly on racks in drugstores, supermarkets, and airports, as well as in bookstores.

mass media the cultural industries—the channels of communication—that produce and distribute songs, novels, news, movies, online computer services, and other cultural products to a large number of people.

mechanical royalty the copyright fee, usually about one-half cent for each CD or audiotape sold, received by songwriters and publishers when they allow their music to be recorded.

media buyers in advertising, the individuals who choose and purchase the types of media that are best suited to carry a client's ads and reach the targeted audience.

media convergence the process whereby old and new media are available via the integration of personal computers and high-speed satellite-based phone or cable links.

media-effects research the mainstream tradition in mass-communication research, it attempts to understand, explain, and predict the impact—or effects—of the mass media on individuals and society.

media literacy an understanding of the mass-communication process through the development of critical thinking tools—description, analysis, interpretation, evaluation—that enable a person to become more engaged as a citizen and more discerning as a consumer of mass-media products.

mega-agencies in advertising, large firms or holding companies that are formed by merging several individual agencies and that maintain worldwide regional offices; they provide both advertising and public relations services and operate in-house radio and TV production studios.

megaplexes movie theater facilities with fourteen or more screens.

messages the texts, images, and sounds transmitted from senders to receivers.

microchips/microprocessors miniature circuits that process and store electronic signals, integrating thousands of electronic components into thin strands of silicon along which binary codes travel.

minimal-effects model a mass-communication research model based on tightly controlled experiments and survey findings; it argues that the mass media have limited effects on audiences, reinforcing existing behaviors and attitudes rather than changing them.

miniseries a serial television program that runs over a two-day to two-week period, usually on consecutive nights.

modern period a historical era spanning the time from the rise of the Industrial Revolution in the eighteenth and nineteenth centuries to the present; its social values include celebrating the individual, believing in rational order, working efficiently, and rejecting tradition.

monopoly in media economics, an organizational structure that occurs when a single firm dominates production and distribution in a particular industry, either nationally or locally.

Morse Code a system of sending electrical impulses from a transmitter through a cable to a reception point; developed by the American inventor Samuel Morse.

movie palaces ornate, lavish single-screen movie theaters that emerged in the 1910s in the United States.

MP3 short for MPEG-1 Layer 3, an advanced type of audio compression that reduces file size, enabling audio to be easily distributed over the Internet and to be digitally transmitted in real time.

muckraking a style of early-twentieth-century investigative journalism that referred to reporters who were willing to crawl around in society's muck to uncover a story.

multiple-system operators (MSOs) large corporations that own numerous cable television systems.

multiplexes contemporary movie theaters that exhibit many movies at the same time on multiple screens.

must-carry rules rules established by the FCC requiring all cable operators to assign channels to and carry all local TV broadcasts on their systems, thereby ensuring that local network affiliates, independent stations (those not carrying network programs), and

public television channels would benefit from cable's clearer reception.

myth analysis a strategy for critiquing advertising that provides insights into how ads work on a cultural level; according to this strategy, ads are narratives with stories to tell and social conflicts to resolve.

narrative the structure underlying most media products, it includes two components: the story (what happens to whom) and the discourse (how the story is told).

narrative films movies that tell a story, with dramatic action and conflict emerging mainly from individual characters.

narrowcasting any specialized electronic programming or media channel aimed at a target audience.

National Public Radio (NPR) noncommercial radio established in 1967 by the U.S. Congress to provide an alternative to commercial radio.

network a broadcast process that links, through special phone lines or satellite transmissions, groups of radio or TV stations that share programming produced at a central location.

network era the period in television history, roughly from the mid-1950s to the late 1970s, that refers to the dominance of the Big Three networks—ABC, CBS, and NBC—over programming and prime-time viewing habits; the era began eroding with a decline in viewing and with the development of VCRs, cable, and new TV networks.

news the process of gathering information and making narrative reports—edited by individuals in a news organization—that create selected frames of reference and help the public make sense of prominent people, important events, and unusual happenings in everyday life.

newsgroups organized computer conferences consisting of bulletin boards and individual messages, or postings, that are circulated twenty-four hours a day via the Internet and cover a range of topics.

newshole the space left over in a newspaper for news content after all the ads are placed.

newspaper chains large companies that own several papers throughout the country.

newsreels weekly ten-minute magazine-style compilations of filmed news events from around the world organized in a sequence of short reports; prominent in movie theaters between the 1920s and the 1950s.

news/talk the fastest-growing radio format in the 1990s.

newsworthiness the often unstated criteria that journalists use to determine which events and issues should become news reports, including timeliness, proximity, conflict, prominence, human interest, consequence, usefulness, novelty, and deviance.

nickelodeons the first small makeshift movie theaters, which were often converted cigar stores, pawnshops, or restaurants redecorated to mimic vaudeville theaters.

O & Os TV stations "owned and operated" by networks.

objective journalism a modern style of journalism that distinguishes factual reports from opinion columns; reporters strive to remain neutral toward the issue or event they cover, searching out competing points of view among the sources for a story.

objectivity in social-science research, the elimination of bias and judgments on the part of researchers.

obscenity expression that is not protected as speech if these three legal tests are all met: (1) the average person, applying contemporary community standards, would find that the material as a whole appeals to prurient interest; (2) the material depicts or describes sexual conduct in a patently offensive way; (3) the material, as a whole, lacks serious literary, artistic, political, or scientific value.

off-network syndication in television, the process whereby older programs that no longer run during prime time are made available for reruns to local stations, cable operators, online services, and foreign markets.

offset lithography a technology that enabled books to be printed from photographic plates rather than metal casts, reducing the cost of color and illustrations and eventually permitting computers to perform typesetting.

oligopoly in media economics, an organizational structure in which a few firms control most of an industry's production and distribution resources.

open-source software noncommercial software shared freely and developed collectively on the Internet.

opt-in/opt-out policies controversial Web-site policies over personal data gathering: *opt in* means Web sites must gain explicit permission from online consumers before the site can collect their personal data; *opt out* means that Web sites can automatically collect personal data unless the consumer goes to the trouble of filling out a specific form to restrict the practice.

option time now considered illegal, a procedure whereby a radio network paid an affiliate station a set fee per hour for an option to control programming and advertising on that station.

paid circulation the process of earning magazine revenue from consumers who pay either for regular subscriptions or for individual copies at newsstands or supermarkets.

paperback books books made with cheap paper covers, introduced in the United States in the mid-1800s.

papyrus one of the first substances to hold written language and symbols; obtained from plant reeds found along the Nile River.

parchment treated animal skin that replaced papyrus as an early pre-paper substance on which to document written language.

partisan press an early dominant style of American journalism distinguished by opinion newspapers, which generally argued one political point of view or pushed the plan of the particular party that subsidized the paper.

pass-along readership the total number of people who come into contact with a single copy of a magazine.

pay-for-play up-front payments from record companies to radio stations to play a song a specific number of times.

payola the unethical (but not always illegal) practice of record promoters paying deejays or radio programmers to favor particular songs over others.

pay-per-view (PPV) a cable-television service that allows customers to select a particular movie for a fee, or to pay $25 to $40 for a special onetime event.

penny papers (also *penny press*) refers to newspapers that, because of technological innovations in printing, were able to drop their price to one cent beginning in the 1830s, thereby making papers affordable to working and emerging middle classes and enabling newspapers to become a genuine mass medium.

people meters in TV audience measurement, devices that are hooked up to a random sample of households to determine their viewing behavior.

performance royalty the copyright fee paid to songwriters and performers whenever their music is used on radio, television, or other media channels.

photojournalism the use of photos to document events and people's lives.

plain-folks pitch an advertising strategy that associates a product with simplicity and the common person.

pop music popular music that appeals either to a wide cross section of the public or to sizable subdivisions within the larger public based on age, region, or ethnic background; the word *pop* has also been used as a label to distinguish popular music from classical music.

portal an entry point to the Internet, such as a search engine.

postmodern period a contemporary historical era spanning the 1960s to the present; its social values include opposing hierarchy, diversifying and recycling culture, questioning scientific reasoning, and embracing paradox.

precision journalism a type of journalism that attempts to push news reporting in the direction of science, maintaining that by applying rigorous social-science methods, such as using poll surveys and questionnaires, journalism can better offer a valid portrait of social reality.

premium cable in cable programming, a tier of channels that subscribers can order at an additional monthly fee over their basic cable service; these may include movie channels and interactive services.

press agent the earliest type of public relations practitioner, who sought to advance a client's image through media exposure.

press release in public relations, an announcement—written in the style of a news report—that gives new information about an individual, a company, or an organization and pitches a story idea to the news media.

prime time in television programming, the hours between 8 and 11 P.M. (or 7 and 10 P.M. in the Midwest), when networks have traditionally drawn their largest audiences and charged their highest advertising rates.

Prime-Time Access Rule (PTAR) an FCC rule that in 1970 took the 7:30 to 8 P.M. time slot (6:30 to 7 P.M. central) away from the TV networks and gave it exclusively to local stations in the nation's fifty largest television markets.

printing press a fifteenth-century invention whose movable metallic type technology spawned modern mass communication by creating the first method for mass production; it reduced the size and cost of books, made them the first mass medium affordable to less affluent people, and provided the impetus for the Industrial Revolution, assembly-line production, modern capitalism, and the rise of consumer culture.

prior restraint the legal definition of censorship in the United States, which prohibits courts and governments from blocking any publication or speech before it actually occurs.

production the network of individuals or companies in the mass-media business in charge of creating movies, TV programs, music recordings, magazines, books, and other media products.

product placement the advertising tactic of buying space for a particular product so that it appears on a movie set or a program as a supporting prop.

professional books technical books that target various occupational groups and are not intended for the general consumer market.

program-length commercials thirty-minute cartoon programs developed for TV syndication primarily to promote a line of toys.

propaganda in advertising and public relations, a communication strategy that tries to manipulate public opinion to gain support for a special issue, program, or policy, such as a nation's war effort.

pseudo-event in public relations, any circumstance or event created solely for the purpose of obtaining coverage in the media.

psychographics in market research, the study of audience or consumer attitudes, beliefs, interests, and motivations.

Public Broadcasting Act of 1967 the act by the U.S. Congress that established the Corporation for Public Broadcasting, which oversees the Public Broadcasting Service (PBS) and National Public Radio (NPR).

Public Broadcasting Service (PBS) the noncommercial television network established in 1967 as an alternative to commercial television.

public journalism a type of journalism, driven by citizen forums, that goes beyond telling the news to embrace a broader mission of improving the quality of public life; also called *civic journalism*.

public relations the total communication strategy conducted by a person, a government, or an organization attempting to reach and persuade its audiences to adopt a point of view.

publicity in public relations, the positive and negative messages that spread controlled and uncontrolled information about a person, corporation, issue, or policy in various media.

public-service announcements (PSAs) reports or announcements, carried free by radio and TV stations, that promote government programs, educational projects, voluntary agencies, or social reform.

publishing houses companies that try to identify and produce the works of good writers.

puffery bordering on deception, advertisements that use hyperbole and exaggeration.

pulp fiction a term used to describe many late-nineteenth-century popular paperbacks and dime novels, which were constructed of cheap machine-made pulp material.

punk rock rock music that challenges the orthodoxy and commercialism of the recording business; it is characterized by loud, unpolished qualities, a jackhammer beat, primal vocal screams, crude aggression, and defiant or comic lyrics.

qualified privilege a legal right allowing journalists to report judicial or legislative proceedings even though the public statements being reported may be libelous.

rack jobbers sales agents in the music business who contract with general retailers such as Wal-Mart to stock their racks or shelves with the latest CDs, audiocassettes, and music videos.

Radio Act of 1912 the first radio legislation passed by Congress, it addressed the problem of amateur radio operators increasingly cramming the airwaves.

Radio Act of 1927 the second radio legislation passed by Congress; in an attempt to restore order to the airwaves, it stated that licensees did not own their channels but could license them as long as they operated in order to serve the "public interest, convenience, or necessity."

Radio Corporation of America (RCA) a company developed during World War I that was designed, with government approval, to pool radio patents; the formation of RCA gave the United States almost total control over the emerging mass medium of broadcasting.

radio waves a portion of the electromagnetic wave spectrum that was harnessed so that signals could be sent from a transmission point and obtained at a reception point.

random assignment a social-science research method for assigning research subjects; it ensures that every subject has an equal chance of being placed in either the experimental group or the control group.

rating in TV audience measurement, a statistical estimate expressed as a percentage of households tuned to a program in the local or national market being sampled.

receivers the target of messages crafted by a sender.

reference books dictionaries, encyclopedias, atlases, and other reference manuals related to particular professions or trades.

regional editions national magazines whose content is tailored to the interests of different geographic areas.

reliability in social-science research, getting the same answers or outcomes from a study or measure during repeated testing.

religious books Bibles, hymnals, and other materials related to religious observances.

rerun syndication in television, the process whereby programs that stay in a network's lineup long enough to build up a certain number of episodes (usually four seasons' worth) are sold, or syndicated, to hundreds of TV markets in the United States and abroad.

responsible capitalism an underlying value held by many U.S. journalists and citizens, it assumes that businesspeople compete with one another not primarily to maximize profits but to increase prosperity for all.

retransmission consent consent periodically given by commercial broadcast stations permitting cable companies to retransmit their signal on cable, usually in exchange for monetary compensation from the cable companies.

rhythm and blues (R&B) music that merged urban blues with big-band sounds.

rockabilly music that mixed bluegrass and country influences with those of black folk music and early amplified blues.

rock and roll music that mixed the vocal and instrumental traditions of popular music; it merged the black influences of urban blues, gospel, and R&B with the white influences of country, folk, and pop vocals.

rotation in format radio programming, the practice of playing the most popular or best-selling songs many times throughout the day.

satellite radio pay radio services that deliver various radio formats nationally via satellite.

saturation advertising the strategy of inundating a variety of print and visual media with ads aimed at target audiences.

scientific method a widely used research method that studies phenomena in systematic stages; it includes identifying the research problem, reviewing existing research, developing working hypotheses, determining an appropriate research design, collecting information, analyzing results to see if the hypotheses have been verified, and interpreting the implications of the study.

scoop an exclusive story obtained by a journalist, who publicly presents the story ahead of all rivals.

search engines computer programs that allow users to enter key words or queries to find related sites on the World Wide Web.

Section 315 part of the 1934 Communications Act; it mandates that during elections, broadcast stations must provide equal opportunities and response time for qualified political candidates.

seditious libel in law, the act of defaming a public official's character in print.

selective exposure the phenomenon whereby audiences seek messages and meanings that correspond to their preexisting beliefs and values.

selective retention the phenomenon whereby audiences remember or retain messages and meanings that correspond to their preexisting beliefs and values.

senders the authors, producers, agencies, and organizations that transmit messages to receivers.

serial programs radio or TV programs, such as soap operas, that feature continuing story lines from day to day or week to week (for contrast, see **chapter shows**).

servers individual "host" computer centers run (or hosted) by universities, corporations, and government agencies, all of which are connected to the Internet by special high-speed phone lines.

share in TV audience measurement, a statistical estimate of the percentage of homes tuned to a certain program, compared with those simply using their sets at the time of a sample.

shield laws laws protecting the confidentiality of key interview subjects and reporters' rights not to reveal the sources of controversial information used in news stories.

shortwave radio a type of radio transmission, used mostly by amateur—or ham—radio operators and governments, that can bounce a radio signal off the ionosphere to locations halfway around the world.

situational ethics the principle that in a moral society ethical decisions are arrived at on an individual or case-by-case basis.

situation comedy (sitcom) a type of comedy series that features a recurring cast and set as well as several narrative scenes; each episode establishes a situation, complicates it, develops increasing confusion among its characters, and then resolves the complications.

sketch comedies short television comedy skits that are usually segments of TV variety shows; sometimes known as *vaudeo,* the marriage of vaudeville and video.

slander in law, spoken language that defames a person's character.

slogan in advertising, a catchy phrase that attempts to promote or sell a product by capturing its essence in words.

small-town pastoralism an underlying value held by many U.S. journalists and citizens, it favors the small over the large and the rural over the urban.

snob appeal an advertising strategy that attempts to convince consumers that using a product will enable them to maintain or elevate their social station.

social-responsibility model a model for journalism and speech, influenced by the libertarian model, that encourages the free flow of information to citizens so they can make wise decisions regarding political and social issues.

soul music music that mixes gospel, blues, and urban and southern black styles with slower, more emotional, and melancholic lyrics.

sound bite in TV journalism, the equivalent of a quote in print; the part of a news report in which an expert, a celebrity, a victim, or a person on the street is interviewed about some aspect of an event or issue.

space brokers in the days before modern advertising, individuals who purchased space in newspapers and sold it to various merchants.

spam a computer term referring to unsolicited e-mail.

spin doctors political consultants who manage campaigns and attempt to favorably shape the news media's image of a candidate.

split-run editions editions of national magazines that tailor ads to different geographic areas.

spyware software with secretive codes that enable commercial firms to "spy" on users and gain access to their computers.

stereo the recording of two separate channels or tracks of sound.

stereotyping the process of assigning individuals to groups, whose members are falsely assumed to act as a single entity and to display certain characteristics, which are usually negative.

storyboard in advertising, a blueprint or roughly drawn comic-strip version of a proposed advertisement.

stripping in TV syndication, the showing of programs — either older network reruns or programs made for syndication — five days a week.

studio system an early film-production system that constituted a sort of assembly-line process for moviemaking; major film studios controlled not only actors but directors, editors, writers, and other employees, all of whom worked under exclusive contracts.

subliminal advertising a 1950s term that refers to hidden or disguised print and visual messages that allegedly register on the unconscious, creating false needs and seducing people into buying products.

subsidiary rights in the book industry, selling the rights to a book for use in other media forms, such as a mass-market paperback, a CD-ROM, or the basis for a movie screenplay.

supermarket tabloids newspapers that feature bizarre human-interest stories, gruesome murder tales, violent accident accounts, unexplained phenomena stories, and malicious celebrity gossip.

superstations local independent TV stations, such as WTBS in Atlanta or WGN in Chicago, that have uplinked their signals onto a communication satellite to make themselves available nationwide.

superstore a large retail business that sells books, recordings, and new media; this contemporary trend in bookselling adapts the large retail-store concept to the publishing industry.

survey research in social-science research, a method of collecting and measuring data taken from a group of respondents.

sweeps in TV ratings, month-long measurement periods — conducted four times a year (six times in larger markets) — that determine both local and national ad rates.

syndicated exclusivity (syndex) Repealed in 1980, FCC rules that gave local stations exclusive rights in their area to syndicate TV programs, such as off-network reruns, that they had purchased.

synergy in media economics, the promotion and sale of a product (and all its versions) throughout the various subsidiaries of a media conglomerate.

talkies movies with sound, beginning in 1927.

Telecommunications Act of 1996 the sweeping update of telecommunications law that led to a wave of media consolidation.

telegraph invented in the 1840s, it sent electical impulses through a cable from a transmitter to a reception point, transmitting Morse Code.

textbooks books made for the el-hi (elementary and high school) and college markets.

textual analysis in media research, a method for closely and critically examining and interpreting the meanings of culture, including architecture, fashion, books, movies, and TV programs.

timeshifting the process whereby television viewers tape shows and watch them later, when it is convenient for them.

Top 40 format the first radio format, in which stations played the forty most popular hits in a given week as measured by record sales.

trade books the most visible book industry segment, featuring hardbound and paperback books aimed at general readers and sold at bookstores and other retail outlets.

transistor invented by Bell Laboratories in 1947, this tiny technology, which receives and amplifies radio signals, made portable radios possible.

transponders the relay points on a communication satellite that receive and transmit telephone and TV signals.

TV newsmagazines a TV news program format, pioneered by CBS's *60 Minutes* in the late 1960s, that features multiple segments in an hour-long episode, usually ranging from a celebrity or political feature story to a hard-hitting investigative report.

UHF ultrahigh frequency; in broadcasting, the band in the electromagnetic spectrum that the FCC allocated for TV channels 14 through 69.

underground press radical newspapers, run on shoestring budgets, that question mainstream political policies and conventional values; the term usually refers to a journalism movement of the 1960s.

university press the segment of the book industry that publishes scholarly books in specialized areas.

urban one of radio's more popular formats, primarily targeting African American listeners in urban areas with dance, R&B, and hip-hop music.

uses and gratifications model a mass-communication research model, usually employing in-depth interviews and survey questionnaires, that argues that people use the media to satisfy various emotional desires or intellectual needs.

validity in social-science research, demonstrating that a study actually measures what it claims to measure.

VALS short for *values and lifestyles,* a market-research strategy that divides consumers into types and measures psychological factors, including how consumers think and feel about products and how they achieve (or do not achieve) the lifestyles to which they aspire.

vellum a handmade paper made from treated animal skin, used in the Gutenberg Bibles.

vertical integration in media economics, the phenomenon of controlling a mass-media industry at its three essential levels: production, distribution, and exhibition; the term is most frequently used in reference to the film industry.

VHF very high frequency; in broadcasting, the band in the electromagnetic spectrum that the FCC allocated for TV channels 2 through 13.

videocassette recorders (VCRs) recorders that use a half-inch video format known as VHS (video home system), which enables viewers to record and play back programs from television or to watch movies rented from video stores.

video news release (VNR) in public relations, the visual counterpart to a press release; it pitches a story idea to the TV news media by mimicking the style of a broadcast news report.

video-on-demand cable television technology that enables viewers to instantly order programming such as movies to be digitally delivered to their sets.

virtual communities groups of computer users who are separated geographically but connected nationally and globally by their shared interests or business and their access to an online service or the Internet.

vitascope a large-screen movie projection system developed by Thomas Edison.

Webzines magazines that publish on the World Wide Web.

weighting in TV audience measurement, assigning more weight to a particular respondent in an attempt to correct the underrepresented group in the original sample.

wire services commercial organizations, such as the Associated Press, that share news stories and information by relaying them around the country and the world, originally via telegraph and now via satellite transmission.

wireless telegraphy the forerunner of radio, a form of voiceless point-to-point communication; it preceded the voice and sound transmissions of one-to-many mass communication that became known as broadcasting.

wireless telephony early experiments in wireless voice and music transmissions, which later developed into modern radio.

world music sometimes called *international* or *ethnic songs,* this category includes the many different styles of popular regional and folk music from cultures throughout the world; it usually excludes classical music and the most popular forms of American or European music.

World Wide Web (WWW) a free and open data-linking system for organizing and standardizing information on the Internet; the WWW enables computer-accessed information to associate with—or link to—other information no matter where it is on the Internet.

yellow journalism a newspaper style or era that peaked in the 1890s, it emphasized high-interest stories, sensational crime news, large headlines, and serious reports that exposed corruption, particularly in business and government.

zapping using a VCR to edit out commercials during the videotaping process.

zines self-published magazines produced on personal computer programs or on the Internet.

zipping using a VCR to fast-forward a videotaped program through the ads during the recorded viewing.

credits

Text Credits

5, David Halberstam. Quote from "Why America Napped." From www.salon.com. October 1, 2001. Reprinted with permission of Salon.com. All rights reserved; **26–27**, Todd Purdum. "Mixed Messages Bombard Teens on Sex and Violence." From *The New York Times*, September 17, 2000, Section 4. P. 1. Copyright © 2000 by The New York Times Company. Reprinted with permission; **41**, Figure 2.1: "Distributed Networks." Excerpted data from p. 59 in *Where Wizards Stay Up Late* by Katie Hafner and Matthew Lyon. Copyright © 1996 by Katie Hafner and Matthew Lyon. Reprinted with permission of Simon & Schuster Adult Publishing Group; **50**, Amy Harmon. Brief quote from *The New York Times*, 1998. Copyright © 1998 by The New York Times Company. Reprinted with permission; **56**, Mike Himowitz. "Beware of Freeware set to buy your PC and you." From *The Baltimore Sun*, April 11, 2002, p. 1C. Reprinted by permission; **60**, "The Internet's Iranian Frontier." Original title: "Internet Reaches Another Technological Outpost . . . the Iranian Village." From the Associated Press, July 4, 2002. Reprinted with the permission of the Associated Press; **100**, Charlie Gillett. "The International Beat of World Music." Adapted from "Go Global: The idea of world music was invented here. So how come Britain is missing out on so much of it, asks Charlie Gillett." *The Guardian* (London), November 1, 2001, p. 11. Copyright © 2001 The Guardian Newspapers Unlimited. Reprinted by permission; **109**, Figure 4.1: "The Electromagnetic Spectrum." From *The World Book Encyclopedia* (Volume 6, p. 202). Copyright © 1988 World Book, Inc. Reprinted with permission; **129**, Figure 4.4: "Most Popular Radio Formats in the United States." From *Radio Marketing and Fact Book for Advertisers 2001–2002 Edition*, Radio Advertising Bureau. Reprinted with permission; **159**, Table 5.1: "Selected Situation and Domestic Comedies Rated in the Top 10." Adapted from data published in *The Complete Directory to Prime Time Network and Cable TV Shows* Seventh Edition edited by Tim Brooks and Earle Marsh. Copyright © 1999 by Tim Brooks and Earle Marsh. Reprinted by permission of Ballantine Books; *Times Almanac 1999*, published by Information Please, LLC. Copyright © 1998 Information Please, LLC. and A.C. Nielsen Media Research; **175**, Table 5.2: "The Top 10 Highest-Rated TV Series, Individual Programs (since 1960)." From *The World Almanac and Book of Facts 1997*; *World Almanac Books 1996* (296); *TV Facts* by Corbett Steinberg. Copyright © 1985 by Corbett Steinberg. Reprinted by permission of Facts on File, Inc. and A.C. Nielsen Media Research; **196**, Figure 6.3: "Market Share of Multichannel Video Program Distributors 2002." Adapted from data posted on www.ncta.com. Cable Television Industry Overview, mid-year 2002; **198**, Maureen Tkacik.

"ESPN's X Games Go to the Dogs." " 'Extreme' Sports Programming Goes to Dogs." *Wall Street Journal*, August 30, 2002, p. B1. Copyright © 2002 Dow Jones & Company, Inc. Republished by permission of Dow Jones, Inc. via Copyright Clearance Center, Inc. All Rights Reserved Worldwide; **199**, Figure 6.4: "The Top 21 Cable Networks, 2001 (Ranked by Number of Subscribers)." From data posted on www.ncta.com. June 2002. National Cable Television Association; **209**, Susan Katlin. "Video-on-Demand on the Cusp of Broad Release." Originally titled, "How It Works: Video-on-Demand is Ready, But the Market is Not." From *The New York Times*, October 10, 2002, p. G8. Copyright © 2002 by The New York Times Company. Reprinted by permission; **212**, Table 6.1: "Top 10 U.S. Cable Operators, 2002." Adapted from data posted on www.ncta.com. June 30, 2002. National Cable Television Association; **223**, Table 7.1: "The Top 10 American Box Office Champions, 2003." Adapted from "The 50 All Time Highest Grossing Movies." From www.movieweb.com. Copyright © 2003 Movieweb. All Rights Reserved; **251**, Figure 7.1: "Gross Revenues from Box-Office Sales, 1984–2002." Adapted from data posted on www.mpaa.com *U.S. Economic Reviews, 2001*; "A Big Fat Box Office Increase." Rick Lyman, *The New York Times*, December 30, 2002. www.nytimes.com; **254**, Table 7.3: "Top 10 Movie Theater Chains in North America." Adapted from data presented on www.nationline.org. "Top 10 Circuits (as of June 1, 2002)." National Theater Chains in North America; **255**, Figure 7.2: "Indoor Theater Screens in the United States, 1977–2001." Adapted from data posted on www.mpaa.com. *U.S. Economic Reviews, 2001*, Motion Picture Association of America; **256**, Table 7.4: "The Major Players in the Movie Business." Adapted from data posted on www.boxoffice.com. BOXOFFICE Magazine Special Report, Giants of Exhibition 2001; **273**, Table 8.1: "The Nation's Largest Daily Newspapers." *The New York Times*, November 6, 2002, section C. p. 3. Copyright © 2002 by The New York Times Company. Reprinted by permission; **291**, Figure 8.2: "Newspapers' Slice of the U.S. Advertising Pie, 2001." Adapted from data posted on www.naa.org. 2002. Newspaper Association of America; **293**, Todd Lappin. "Web Offers a Balanced Worldview." Originally titled "Turning the Page to a Fresh Worldview." From *The New York Times*, October 4, 2001, p. G9. Copyright © 2001 by The New York Times Company. Reprinted by permission; **309**, Table 9.1: "The Top 10 Magazines (ranked by paid U.S. circulation 1972 vs. 2002)." Adapted from data posted on www.magazine.org. Magazine Publishers of America; **319**, Table 9.2: "Number of New Consumer Magazine Launches by Interest Categories 2002." Adapted from data posted on www.magazine.org. Magazine Publishers of America; **329**, Dan Frost. "Is a Magazine without Ads Possible? *Ms.* Thinks So." Originally titled "*Ms.* Ready for Latest Makeover." From the *San Francisco Chronicle,* July 17, 2002, p. B1. Reprinted by permission; **330,** Figure 9.1: "The Changing Balance of Magazine Circulation: Subscription vs. Single-Copy Sales." Adapted from data provided by Magazine Publishers of America, 2002; **332–3,** Table 9.3: Major Magazine Chains (selected holdings as of 2003). Adapted from data posted on www.hoovers.com. Hoover's Online, *Advertising Age,* Ad Age DataCenter. www.adage.com; **341,** Table 10.1: "Annual Numbers of New Book Titles Published, Selected Years." Adapted from data (figures through 1945) published in *A History of Book Publishing,* by John Tebbel, 4 vols (1978); figures after 1945 from various editions of *The Bowker Annual Library* and *Trade Book Almanac.* Reprinted by permission; **348,** Figure 10.1: "2001 Publishers' Net Sales." Adapted from data posted on www.publishers.org. American Association of Publishers; **352,** Figure 10.2: "Where the New Textbook Dollar Goes." Adapted from data posted on www.nacs.org. Copyright © 2002 by the National Association of College Stores; **353,** Figure 10.3: "Consumer Adult Book Purchasing, by Outlet." Adapted from data posted on www.bookweb.org. 2002 American Booksellers Association; **361,** Table 10.3: "Bookstores in the United States, 2001." Adapted from data published in *The Bowker Annual Library* and *Trade Book Almanac 2002;* **364,** Table 10.4: "New York Times Bestseller Scorecard: Hardcover Nonfiction Bestsellers, 2001." From analysis (via SIMBA Information Inc.) of the 2001 New York Times best seller lists through Sunday November 18, 2001. Copyright © 2001 by The New York Times Company. Reprinted by permission; **371,** "The Top 15 Most Frequently Challenged Books of the 1990s." Courtesy of the American Library Association; **384,** Table 11.1: "The Top Ten National Advertisers." Adapted from data posted on www.adage.com. "100 Leading National Advertisers, November 17, 2002. Advertising Age Datacenter; **389,** Table 11.2: "The World's Largest Advertising Agencies, 2001." Adapted from data posted on www.adage.com. "World's Top 100 Advertising Organizations, November 17, 2002." Advertising Age, Ad Age Datacenter; **392,** Figure 11.1: "VALS Types and Characteristics." Copyright © by SRI Consulting Business Intelligence, 2002. www.futuresri.com. Reprinted by permission. All rights reserved; **428,** Table 12.1: "The Top 15 Public Relations Firms, 2001." Adapted from data posted on www.adage.com; **432–3,** Melanie Shortman and Jonah Bloom. "The Top PR Campaigns Ever?" Originally titled, "The Greatest Campaigns Ever?" from *PR Week,* July 15, 2002, p. 14. Copyright © 2002 PR Week, Inc. Reprinted by permission; **443,** Table 12.2: "Public Relations Society of America Ethics Code." Full text is available at www.prsa.org. Courtesy of the Public Relations Society of America; **458,** Table 13.1: "Consumer Spending per Person per Year on Selected Media." From Veronis Suhler Communications Industry Forcast, Fifteenth Edition, July 2001; **463,** "Two Views on Media Consolidation." View 1: Stephen F. Hayes, "A Consumer's Paradise." Originally titled "Beware, Corporate Domination: Concerned journalists think media consolidation is a tragedy. They couldn't be more wrong." From *The Daily Standard,* May 31, 2002. Reprinted by permission. View 2: Originally titled, "The Cost of Media Consolidation." Editorial from *Business Week,* April 29, 2002, p. 130; **485,** Table 13.2: "The Top Media Companies, 2001." From Veronis Suhler Communications Industry Report, Twentieth Edition, Oct. 2002; **482–3,** Harold Evans. "Story Missed: How a Report on Terrorism Flew Under the Radar." Originally titled, "Warning Given . . . Story Missed: How a Report on Terrorism Flew Under the Radar." *Columbia Journalism Review,* November/December 2001, p. 12. Copyright © 2001 by Harold Evans. Reprinted by permission; **490,**

Figure 14.1: Society of Professional Journalists Code of Ethics. Courtesy of the SPJ; **538,** Alex Pham. "Online Gaming Reveals Gender Stereotypes." Originally titled, "Boy, You Fight Like a Girl." From the *Los Angeles Times,* May 17, 2001. Copyright © 2001 Los Angeles Times. Reprinted by permission of Tribune Media Services; **540,** Stephen Lynch. "TV's Changing Language and the 'Sopranos Effect.'" Originally titled, "Son of a . . . *The Sopranos* has changed what you see, and hear, on TV," from the *Calgary Herald,* February 5, 2002, p. 11. Copyright 2002 Calgary Herald. Reprinted by permission; **559,** Figure 16.1: "The Voluntary Movie Rating System." Copyright © 1996 Motion Picture Association of America, Inc. Reprinted by permission; **562,** Brian Lowry and Sallie Hofmeister. "Media Mergers: Survival of the Biggest." Abridged version of Brian Lowry and Sallie Hofmeister, "Ruling on FCC Turns Up the Volume on Media Mergers." From the *Los Angeles Times,* February 21, 2002. Copyright © 2002 Tribune Media Services. Reprinted by permission.

Photo Credits

Key: A-G = Archive Photos—gettyimages; AP-WW = Associated Press/WideWorld Photos; BA-CO = Bettmann Archive—CORBIS Pictures; CO = CORBIS Pictures; CO-Sa = CORBIS-Saba; CO-SM = CORBIS-Stock Market; CO-Sy = CORBIS-Sygma; G = gettyimages; TIW = The Image Works; KC = The Kobal Collection/thepicturedesk; L-G = Liaison—gettyimages; NYPL = The New York Public Library; PF = Photofest; TEC = The Everett Collection

Cover images, from left to right: J. R. Eyerman/TIMEPIX/G; Jon Feingerish/CO-SM; Marvel Entertainment, Inc. All rights reserved; Katsumi Kasahara/AP Photo; Roger Ball/CO-SM. From top to bottom: BA-CO; © Reuters NewMedia Inc.; BA-CO, Culver Pictures; TEC; xvi (top) Katsumi Kasahara/AP Photo; xvi (bot.) Bibliotheque Nationale, Paris/Art Resource, NY; **xvii** (top) Don Heupel/AP Photo; **xvii** (cent.) AP-WW; **xvii** (bot.) CO; **xviii** (top) Roger Violett-L-G; **xviii** (cent.) TEC; **xviii** (bot.) © 1999 John Hughes/Photopresse; **xix** (top) Al Bello/G; **xix** (cent.) Paul Schutzer/TIMEPIX/G; **xix** (bot.) TEC; **xx** (top) © Christopher Martin; **xx** (cent.) TEC; **xx** (bot.) Lucien Aigner/CO; **xxi** (top) Ken Lambert/AP-WW; **xxi** (cent.) *Rolling Stone* Cover photo of Justin Timberlake by Herb Ritts; **xxi** (bot.) Alan Schein/CO-SM; **xxii** (top); **xxii** (cent.) © 2003 Rich Pilling/MLB Photos; **xxii** (bot.) AP-WW; **xxiii** (top) B. Nation/CO-Sy; **xxiii** (cent.) Ron Edmons/AP-WW; **xxiii** (bot.) Don Mason/CO-SM; **xxiv** (top) KC/thepicturedesk; **xxiv** (cent.) Bryan Snyder/A-G; **xxiv** (bot.) Peter Blakely/CO-Sa; **xxv** (top) BA-CO; **xxv** (cent.) Fred Prouser/AP-WW; **xxv** (bot.) AP-WW; **3,** © Reuters New-Media Inc.CO; **5,** AP-WW; Bibliotheque Nationale, Paris/Art Resource, NY; **10,** Sondra Dawes/IW; **13,** BA-CO; **14,** Ralf-Finn Hestoft/CO-Sa; **18** (both), PF; **20,** Krista Niles/AP Photo; **21,** © Zoran Milich/Masterfile; **26,** courtesy EIDOS Interactive; **30,** CO; **35,** PHOTODISC; **36,** Katsumi Kasahara/AP Photo; **43** (l.), Jeremy Burgess/Science Photo Library/Photo Researchers; **43** (r.), Chuck Nacke/Woodfin Camp & Associates; **44–45,** Davidson/Photo Researchers; **44,** Jon Feingerish/CO-SM; **46,** courtesy, Duke University; **48** (both), Lou Brooks; **52** (l.), courtesy, Larry Ewing; **52** (r.), Paul Sakuma/AP/WW; **54,** art by Dave Black; courtesy U.S. NEWS & WORLD REPORT; **56,** Don Heupel/AP Photo; **57,** James Wilson/Woodfin Camp & Associates; **59,** courtesy Shahkooh; **60,** courtesy Samsung Corp.; **65,** CO; **67,** BA-CO; **71,** courtesy Harman Multimedia; **74** (top), Frank Driggs/A-G; **74** (cent.-l.), NYPL-Theatre Collection;

index

about the authors

Richard Campbell teaches in the School of Journalism at Middle Tennessee State University and is the author of *60 Minutes and the News: A Mythology for Middle America* (1991) and co-author of *Cracked Coverage: Television News, the Anti-Cocaine Crusade and the Reagan Legacy* (1994). He has written articles and essays on mass media for publications including *Columbia Journalism Review, Critical Studies in Mass Communication, Journal of Communication, Media Studies Journal,* and *Television Quarterly,* where he is on the editorial board. As a writer and media critic, he is a frequent speaker on public radio and television.

Bettina Fabos, an award-winning video maker and former print reporter, teaches in the Department of Communication Studies at the University of Northern Iowa. As an Iowa Fellow at the University of Iowa, she focused on analyzing the role of the Internet in education, and she has written extensively about media representations of popular culture. Fabos is the recipient of a Spencer Fellowship.

Christopher R. Martin is an associate professor in the Department of Communication Studies at the University of Northern Iowa. He has written articles and reviews on journalism, televised sports, the Internet, and labor for publications including *Communication Research, Journal of Communication, Journal of Communication Inquiry, Labor Studies Journal,* and *Culture, Sport, and Society.*